Abating Treatment
with Critically Ill Patients

Abating Treatment with Critically Ill Patients

*Ethical and Legal Limits
to the Medical Prolongation of Life*

ROBERT F. WEIR

University of Iowa
College of Medicine

New York   Oxford
OXFORD UNIVERSITY PRESS
1989

Oxford University Press

Oxford   New York   Toronto
Delhi   Bombay   Calcutta   Madras   Karachi
Petaling Jaya   Singapore   Hong Kong   Tokyo
Nairobi   Dar es Salaam   Cape Town
Melbourne   Auckland

and associated companies in
Berlin   Ibadan

Library of Congress Cataloging-in-Publication Data
Weir, Robert F., 1943–
Abating treatment with critically ill patients :
ethical and legal limits to the medical
prolongation of life / Robert F. Weir.
p.   cm.   Includes bibliographies and index.
ISBN 0-19-504528-9
1. Euthanasia—Moral and ethical aspects.
2. Terminal care—Moral and ethical aspects.
3. Life support systems (Critical care)—Moral and ethical aspects.
4. Critical care medicine—Moral and ethical aspects.
I. Title.   [DNLM   1. Critical Care.
2. Ethics, Medical.   3. Life Support Care—legislation.
4. Right to Die—legislation.
W 32.6 W425a]   R726.W39   1989   174 .24—dc19
DNLM/DLC   for Library of Congress   89-2881   CIP

9 8 7 6 5 4 3 2 1

Printed in the United States of America
on acid-free paper

For Melinda and Randall Weir

Preface

I

This book is about one of the most important and controversial issues of our time. Sometimes called "passive euthanasia," "negotiated death," "allowing to die," or "death with dignity," the issue of abating life-sustaining treatment confronts many of us with genuine life-and-death choices. Whether we are health care consumers or health care professionals, patients or physicians, decision makers regarding our own medical treatment or decision makers on the behalf of others, we must work to establish reasonable ethical and legal limits to the technological prolongation of life lest we become unthinking and uncaring slaves to that technology.

The issue of abating life-sustaining treatment has now moved beyond the surreptitious practices previously carried out in some hospitals. Rather than using "slow codes," "show codes," or secretive symbol systems (such as the practice in one New York hospital of posting purple dots on the medical charts of dying patients who were not to be resuscitated) to camouflage the connection between some medical decisions and the deaths of some patients, we are now confronting these important decisions in the light provided by public debate. No longer content to leave such decisions to physicians and patients in the quasi-privacy of hospital rooms, we are wrestling with the issue of abating treatment in several public settings: legislative chambers, courtrooms, and the printed and electronic media.

One indication of the public attention being given to this issue is the political activism of numerous groups at the state and national levels. Every time a court takes on a treatment-abatement case, and every time a state legislature considers natural-death-act legislation, the judges and legislators are confronted with *amici curiae* briefs and lobbying efforts from both sides of the political and philosophical spectrum. From one side there are pro-life groups attempting to restrict the right of patients to refuse life-sustaining treatment, while on the other side are right-to-die groups trying to expand the circumstances in which autonomous patients (or the surrogates of nonautonomous patients) can refuse life-sustaining treatment regarded as more burdensome than beneficial to the patient.

The U.S. Supreme Court has yet to address the issue of abating life-sustaining treatment. Activists on both sides of the issue, however, expect the nation's highest court to take up this issue in the near future, most likely by answering the question whether the constitutionally based right to privacy encompasses the right to refuse recommended medical treatment. Should the court decide such a case, it might choose to expand on the statement emphasized in the 1973 case of *Doe v. Bolton:* that *"the freedom to care for one's health and person"* is constitutionally protected.

As the debate over the morality and legality of treatment abatement has developed, each phase of the debate has seemed to generate more heat and less light. As the debate continues, especially in regard to the morality of abating technological feeding and hydration, it is my hope that this book will reverse this trend by providing light as well as heat.

Iowa City, Iowa   R.F.W.
November 1988

Acknowledgments

Many persons and organizations have helped me during the writing of this book. Without this help, the ideas and proposals put forward in the book would probably still remain buried in the piles of paper in my cluttered office.

My research was greatly aided by funding secured from several organizations. The W.K. Kellogg Foundation paid for several weeks of research in Great Britain as part of my Kellogg national fellowship. The National Endowment for the Humanities helped me once again by granting me a summer stipend to complete the manuscript. The Oklahoma Foundation for the Humanities and the research office in the College of Arts and Sciences at Oklahoma State University also contributed research grants along the way.

Two organizations discussed in the book helped my research efforts considerably. A.J. Levinson granted me complete access to the resources and files at Concern for Dying, and Giles Scofield supplied me with texts of legal cases whenever I requested such of him. At the Society for the Right to Die, Fenella Rouse helped me in numerous ways: by sending me copies of legal cases, answering my questions regarding the law, and periodically sending me updated fact sheets on new cases.

A number of persons helped me in a variety of ways. Cicely Saunders, Robert Twycross, George Adams, and Grimley Evans helped me learn about the British hospice system and the practice of geriatric medicine in Great Britain. Joanne Lynn suggested some resource materials on geriatric care in the United States. Robert Barry, Edward Grant, and Robert Veatch supplied unpublished materials that aided my research. Richard Eggerman, Edward Lawry, and Walter Scott (three of my former colleagues) were helpful to my writing in ways that they probably do not even realize.

I am indebted to several individuals who spent considerable time reading chapters and providing me with criticisms and suggestions for improvement. The chapters pertaining to the law were read and critiqued by Frances Miller and William McNichols. The chapters dealing with medical matters were read and critiqued by Ronald Cranford, Bernard Lo, Peter Jebson, and Steve Hata. James Childress and Robert Radford read the remaining chapters and provided numerous suggestions to me regarding the ethics of abating treatment. At Oxford

University Press, Jeff House once again made editorial suggestions at several points that undoubtedly improved the final product. To all of these readers, my sincere thanks.

Three persons combined their efforts in doing the final wordprocessing of the manuscript. Marilyn Verhalen, Melissa Macomb, and Anita Milner worked long and hard, showed great patience with me, and actually seemed to be interested in the subject matter they were turning into a final manuscript. To these secretaries and wordprocessing experts, my thanks.

Finally, my thanks go to the members of my family. My father has often inquired about the progress of the book, my mother has sent me newspaper and magazine items in her role of "unpaid research assistant," and my mother-in-law, Edwina Bonnell, has contributed her share of newspaper clippings as well. My wife, Jerry, has been supportive of my efforts in ways too numerous to count. The book is dedicated to my daughter and son.

Contents

Abating Treatment
with Critically Ill Patients

1

From Death Observed to Death Forestalled: Changes in Perspective toward Life-Threatening Illness

The life-sustaining capability of modern medicine, coupled with its difficult ethical choices, has become the physician's most challenging moral dilemma. . . . Caring for critically ill and dying patients is a difficult task that often vacillates between the rational and the absurd, the uplifting and the morbid.

WILLIAM WINDENWERDER, JR., M.D.[1]

You don't have to do everything for everybody. The question is, where do you stop? At what point do you say, what are you doing? Do we care what we are doing?

DAVID FINLEY, M.D.[2]

Johnny Gunther was 16 when he and his parents discovered, in 1946, that he had a brain tumor. A student at Deerfield Academy at the time, Johnny struggled valiantly for 15 months against hopeless odds—to finish Deerfield, to be admitted to Harvard, to continue living. As told by his father, Johnny's story is one of personal courage and achievement, 15 months of aggressive cancer treatment, dedicated physicians, unpreventable suffering, and death. In reflecting on the inability of physicians to prevent his son's death, John Gunther comments: "All the doctors!—helpless flies now, climbing across the granite face of death."[3]

Cornelius Ryan, an internationally known author of military histories, found out in 1970 that he had prostate cancer. He immediately embarked on what he described as "a private battle" with his cancer, a battle that ended 4 years later with his death. From the beginning the battle involved doing "everything possible": treatment by the best physicians in the United States, trips to see European specialists, access to "the best and most complete medical information available," sophisticated surgery and therapy programs, and little thought given to the financial costs as long as "one gets to the right place and into the hands of the right people."[4]

Dax Cowart's world exploded in a flash of burning gas on a country road in Texas in 1973. Twenty-six at the time, Cowart had loved action and excitement: high school athletics, military service as a jet pilot, outdoor sports, rodeo competition. A car explosion caused by a leaking propane gas line killed his father

3

and left him with second- and third-degree burns over 65 percent of his body. Both of his eyes were blinded, his ears were mostly destroyed, and his hands were melted into virtually useless, unsightly stubs. After months of treatment in three Texas hospitals—repeated skin grafting, enucleation of one eye, amputation of parts of his fingers, and excruciatingly painful daily baths in a Hubbard tank—he insisted on stopping further treatment and being allowed to return home, where he would surely die from overwhelming infection. Although a psychiatrist concluded that Cowart was mentally competent, the burn specialists (supported by Cowart's mother and family attorney) continued to treat his burns. The months of treatment improved his physical condition to the point that he was subsequently able to return home, manage a real estate business, marry, get a law degree, and discuss the needs and rights of critically ill patients with numerous groups throughout the country. Nevertheless, in spite of his remarkable recovery and his physicians' continuing belief that not treating him would have been tantamount to killing him, Cowart to this day maintains that he should have been allowed to refuse treatment.[5]

Emily Bauer (a fictitious name) discovered in 1977 that she had amyotrophic lateral sclerosis (ALS), a fatal illness also known as Lou Gehrig's disease. A psychologist and college professor, a wife and mother, pregnant for the second time, Bauer vowed to be the first person with ALS not to succumb to the progressive deterioration caused by the disease. Yet, over a 2-year period ALS brought about the virtually complete paralysis of her body while leaving her mind unaffected. She went from a cane to crutches to a walker to a wheelchair to a motorized wheelchair to a bedridden existence in which she could not talk, could not swallow, could not breathe spontaneously, and could not control her own body functions. She could communicate only by blinking her eyes in response to questions, and by laboriously forming messages on a printer activated by her slight head movements. At one point she tapped out the message: "I want to die." For 5 months after that day, her husband refused to kill her but negotiated unsuccessfully with uncooperative physicians and hospital administrators to get them to stop the mechanical ventilation that was keeping his wife alive against her will. Finally, with the help of Concern for Dying (a leading right-to-die organization), a cooperative attorney, and two cooperative physicians not employed by the hospital in which she was a patient, Bauer got her wish. Having returned home for one day, she said goodbye to friends and family, was given an injection of chlorpromazine (Thorazine, for sleep) by the first physician, formed the words "thank you" with her lips, was removed from the portable ventilator, and was declared dead by the second physician.[6]

Scott Rose was a talented young teenager who loved poetry, music, writing, and acting. Unfortunately, he had a rare condition known as Nezelof's syndrome, an immune-deficiency disease similar to the condition of the famous "Bubble Boy" in Houston. Scott refused to remain in a similar enclosure, preferring to live as normal a life as his condition permitted. At the age of 14, with his lungs deteriorating and his suffering increasing, Scott decided in 1982 that he could accept no more life-sustaining treatment. Against his physician's wishes but with tacit approval from his family, Scott died by disconnecting himself from the ventilator that was keeping him alive.[7]

Brenda Hewitt, a poet and editor, was 54 when she died in a New York hospital in 1984. A diabetic since her youth, she had received her first emergency dialysis in 1976. Since that time she had been supported in a state of constant severe anemia by a dialysis machine at home, had become blind in one eye, was unable to walk, and had multiple other medical problems. Concerned about the efforts that might be made to keep her alive in an emergency situation, she wrote a personalized advance directive in which she said she had reached "the logical end" of her life, did not want life-sustaining treatment, and did not want to be resuscitated. She gave her common-law husband of 16 years written authorization to make health care decisions on her behalf and specifically told him to refuse artificial life-support measures and any resuscitative measures. Soon thereafter she had a cardiac arrest while hospitalized for treatment of a possible infection, and the "heroic" lifesaving measures she had wanted to avoid were used in spite of her husband's protests. She was given cardiopulmonary resuscitation (CPR) and, even though she had experienced extensive brain damage, was placed on a ventilator. After 2 days of conflict with the physicians in the case, her husband finally got them to remove the ventilator.[8]

Larry Brown's cancer of the brain was diagnosed in late 1984. Aged 42, a former worker on offshore oil rigs, Brown was devastated by the news. By the time cobalt treatment was begun, the cancer had metastasized to both kidneys and his ribs. After 3 months of treatment with a variety of drugs for relief of pain, anxiety, depression, and the side effects of the cancer, Brown became a hospice patient. With the more flexible hospice guidelines regarding medication and with the aid of a Hickman catheter for the administration of morphine and diazepam (Valium), he lived out his last days in relative comfort.[9]

Megan O'Rourke, aged 77, lived in a nursing home. She was sometimes confused and disoriented, but seemed aware of herself, the people around her, and much of what was happening to her. She had severe emphysema, arteriosclerotic heart disease, symptomatic congestive heart failure, and both receptive and expressive aphasia. Recently she was taken to the emergency room of a local hospital, where she was diagnosed as having chronic obstructive pulmonary disease, congestive heart failure, and lung cancer with pneumonia. The house staff wanted to perform a bronchoscopy to help make a more definitive diagnosis of the type of cancer. Given Mrs. O'Rourke's mental condition, the physicians asked her daughter for consent. Her daughter refused the bronchoscopy for her mother and rejected the possibility of chemotherapy, but insisted that "everything else be done" for her—including prolonged intubation, placement in the intensive care unit (ICU), full resuscitative efforts, and use of vasopressors if necessary.[10]

Jim Adams was a patient in the AIDS unit at City General Hospital. The staff in the unit was aware that many patients with human immunodeficiency virus (HIV) infection refuse certain forms of life-sustaining treatment as their conditions worsen. As a consequence, the staff initiated a policy whereby each patient admitted to the unit was asked about preferences regarding life-sustaining treatments, including resuscitation. Unfortunately, Adams was admitted prior to the establishment of the policy and could not later give his views, because he had AIDS-related dementia as well as Kaposi's sarcoma, *Pneumocystis carinii* pneumonia, extensive candidiasis, cryptosporidiosis, and severe diarrhea. He had already been resuscitated twice and was now comatose and on a ventilator. Severe renal failure had supervened, and his physician was planning to start dialysis. When asked by a nurse why Adams was going to be dialyzed, the physician said that he had no choice, since Adams had not refused to be resuscitated earlier.[11]

Joseph Davies, aged 75, had begun having serious mental and physical problems 5 years previously while living with his brother and sister-in-law. One day Joseph choked on his food and went into respiratory distress. He was rushed to a hospital, treated for aspiration pneumonia, and fed for 5 days with a nasogastric (NG) tube that he seemed to despise. He was then placed in a nursing home, where he continued to have difficulty in swallowing and showed no interest in eating. His brother reluctantly consented to have a NG tube inserted again to provide Joseph with adequate nourishment. Joseph's condition continued deteriorating until he was diagnosed to be in a severe state of senile dementia. Joseph's brother asked 4 months later that the tube be removed, saying that he and his wife had concluded that the tube feeding was an "extraordinary" means of prolonging life and that Joseph had reached "a time to die" mentioned in the biblical book of Ecclesiastes. Joseph's physician agreed, removed the feeding tube, and ordered that he be given "supportive care only." The patient was sedated, kept comfortable, and offered food and water by spoon and cup. He died a few weeks later.[12]

These 10 cases all involve critically ill patients and the need to make decisions about life-sustaining treatment. They are similar in several ways: they concern real people (some of the names having been changed), reveal some of the dynamics of trying to combat life-threatening diseases, and do not involve court action by any of the parties. The cases are also very different in that they involve patients with significant age differences, significant differences in mental capacity, a variety of life-threatening medical conditions, a variety of life-sustaining technologies, a variety of treatment settings, and variable approaches to decisions about abating life-sustaining treatment.

As indicated by these brief case histories, modern medical technology confronts all of us with an issue of major importance: how to determine the appropriate moral and legal limits to the medical prolongation of life. Of course, as the stories of Johnny Gunther, Cornelius Ryan, Emily Bauer, and Jim Adams illustrate, there are natural limits beyond which medicine cannot go in prolonging the lives of some critically ill patients. Regardless of a patient's will to live, financial resources, age, or submission to the most advanced technological and pharmacological treatment, there are numerous medical conditions that lead inevitably to death.

By contrast, as illustrated by the story of Dax Cowart, there are numerous other medical conditions that cause critically ill patients to undergo expensive treatment, prolonged suffering, and anguished thought about the alternative of death—only to submit to continued medical treatment. Because of their medical treatment, these patients have health restored or at least have health and physical well-being sufficiently improved that they can lead reasonably normal lives.

Still other medical situations, including those mentioned in the cases of Scott Rose, Brenda Hewitt, Larry Brown, Megan O'Rourke, and Joseph Davies, necessitate decisions by the patient or by a surrogate of the patient regarding the extent to which life-sustaining treatment is to be used. Is there to be aggressive treatment in an effort to restore health and prolong life? Is there to be only supportive or palliative treatment to meet a terminally ill patient's needs for pain relief, symptom management, nutrition, and hydration? Is there to be a termination of treatment so that a patient may die rather quickly in the absence of life-support systems?

These questions indicate some of the terrain to be covered in this book. The terrain will be rugged, because the multiple issues involved in discussing the subject of treatment abatement are medically, legally, and philosophically complex. The terrain will be demanding, because doing justice to these issues requires prolonged, serious thinking. At times the terrain will impose emotional costs, because our companions on this journey toward understanding will be real people who will live, suffer, make excruciating decisions, and sometimes die.

This chapter will introduce the rest of the book in three ways: by explaining some of the terminology to be used in the remaining chapters, by providing some historical background on the changes in perspective toward life-threatening illness over the past 150 years or so, and by laying out three developmental phases in the debate over abating treatment that has taken place (and is taking place) during the second half of the twentieth century.

On the Matter of Terminology

The media loosely and often inaccurately refers to treatment termination issues with disparate slogans such as "the right to life," "the right to die," "death with dignity," "negotiated death," "euthanasia," and "mercy killing." These terms have widely differing meanings, and their continued usage by the print and electronic media often oversimplifies and confuses the subject this book addresses. Greater clarity is gained through the distinctions and terminology commonly found in the medical, legal, and ethical literature on the care of critically ill and terminally ill patients. For example, much of the scholarly literature draws the distinction between withholding and withdrawing life-sustaining treatment, which is intended to indicate the difference between (1) not starting a certain mode of treatment and (2) stopping a certain mode of treatment after it has been used for a period of time. The psychological, ethical, and legal aspects of this distinction will be discussed later.

Likewise, much of the scholarly literature draws the distinction between allowing critically ill patients to die (especially those believed to be dying) and killing them, although both the exact meaning of the distinction and its moral significance, if any, are seriously debated in the philosophical literature. The meaning and significance of this distinction will be discussed at several points in subsequent chapters.

Even the scholarly literature, however, lacks sufficiently clear terminology to describe the subject of this book. Several individuals who believe that intentionally killing patients is wrong have tried over the years to coin words that can be used to distinguish acts of euthanasia (in the sense of intentionally killing patients) from morally acceptable acts of allowing some terminally ill patients to die apart from life-support systems. For example, Paul Ramsey once suggested that "agathanasia" might be wording to adopt.[13] Instead of going to the Greek for adequate terminology, Arthur Dyck chose the Latin alternative and discussed the merits of an "ethic of benemortasia."[14]

Interdisciplinary groups of scholars in medicine, law, ethics, and other professional fields have had similar problems in arriving at correct terminology. A leading example is the President's Commission for the Study of Ethical Problems in Medicine and Biomedical and Behavioral Research (hereafter referred to as the President's Commission), which met in 1980–1983. The members of the commission chose to call their report on this subject the "foregoing of life-sustaining treatment," intending thereby to include "both the noninitiation of a treatment and the discontinuation of an ongoing treatment."[15] This choice of language is unsatisfactory for a couple of reasons. The term *forego* is problematic on grammatical grounds in that, while some dictionaries indicate that "forego" and "forgo" are variants of each other, other dictionaries and style manuals insist that only the latter word means "to abstain from." More significantly, when applied to clinical contexts involving critically ill patients, the commission's language of "foregoing of life-sustaining treatment" unfortunately connotes an abstaining from or renouncing of *all* treatment.

Another group of physicians, attorneys, ethicists, and members of several health care fields also had problems coming up with an acceptable title for their project. Organized by the Hastings Center, this project was initially described as an effort to develop guidelines for the termination of treatment. But members of the project, who met periodically in 1985–1987, eventually decided to call it by a dual name: guidelines on the termination of life-sustaining treatment *and* the care of the dying.[16] The language was intended to indicate that care of dying patients should continue even when the patients or their surrogates have refused further life-sustaining efforts.

I was a participant in some of the Hastings Center project's meetings. I have also been privileged to speak at a number of conferences dealing with decisions at the end of life, and have had an opportunity to discuss end-of-life treatment decisions with a working party at the Ian Ramsey Center at Oxford University. In all of these contexts, the issue of terminology has come up for serious discussion and debate. Various suggestions have been advanced for improving on the President's Commission's language, with the most common suggestion being "treatment termination." However, as members of the Hastings Center project recognized, this language shares the second problem that "foregoing" has: it suggests that decisions to withhold or to withdraw certain forms of life-sustaining treatment from critically ill patients entail *doing nothing further to care* for these patients. Understandably, many health care professionals (especially hospice physicians and nurses) reject this possible misinterpretation of their professional roles in providing alternative treatments for patients in the terminal phase of life.

My concern about appropriate terminology was sharpened by a comment from Cicely Saunders, the executive director of St. Christopher's Hospice in suburban London. During a visit to this internationally known hospice, I mentioned to Dr. Saunders that I was working on this book, referring to its working title as "treatment termination with critically ill patients." She physically recoiled, and emphatically urged me not to use that language because it would suggest that, once life-sustaining treatment was stopped, "nothing more could be done" for patients. She pointed out that her professional career had been devoted to providing better pain control and symptom management for patients who could not be cured, and that St. Christopher's was founded on the idea that patients in the terminal phase of life should be given palliative care to enhance their living. She told me to "find a better title" for the book.

I have tried to follow her advice and come up with language that avoids two common problems: (1) the unfortunate implications of the termination-of-treatment language, and (2) easy confusion with the language of euthanasia. Consequently, I have decided not to refer to the subject of this book as "foregoing treatment" or "treatment termination," nor to use the language of "allowing to die" or "passive euthanasia."

I prefer to call the subject under discussion *treatment abatement*. Although some of the other terms will be used from time to time in subsequent chapters, *abatement* has three meanings that help clarify the subject at hand. First, it means "deduction," "omission," or "subtraction." Used in this sense, abatement includes decisions to withhold—or not to initiate—a form of treatment. The treatment is deducted, omitted, or subtracted from the range of treatment options available for a particular patient. Second, abatement means "a reduction in degree or intensity" or a "progressive diminishing." Used in this sense, it describes the clinical consequences of decisions made by patients or their surrogates to pull back from aggressive treatment, or to withdraw one or more treatment modalities from a wider range of alternative treatments, or to lessen a particular form of treatment in some manner, and thereby to acknowledge that life-sustaining treatments usually need to be replaced by palliative treatments when patients are diagnosed as being terminally ill. Third, abatement means "nullification" or "termination." Used in this sense, abatement encompasses decisions by autonomous, critically ill or terminally ill patients (or the surrogates of nonautonomous patients) to refuse all forms of life-sustaining treatment. Moreover, this third meaning of "abatement" includes decisions by autonomous patients or by surrogates acting on the behalf of nonautonomous patients to refuse the one specific treatment (e.g., mechanical ventilation, or technological nutrition and hydration) that is keeping the patients alive.

All three of these meanings of treatment abatement will be used in this book. In addition, decisions regarding treatment abatement will be distinguished in a subsequent chapter from decisions regarding other end-of-life issues with which treatment abatement is often confused: the determination of death, suicide, assisted suicide, and euthanasia. Now, however, we will turn to a discussion of the changes in perspective toward life-threatening illness that have led to the current debate over the morality and legality of abating life-sustaining treatment.

The Changing Features of Critical Illness

How have developments in medicine during this century pushed treatment abatement, basically a nonissue before this century, to the fore as one of the major issues of our time? How, and why, have we moved from the general perspective of gently watching critically ill persons die to the widely held perspective that the deaths of critically ill persons should be forestalled whenever such interventions are medically possible? To gain some historical perspective on these questions, we will look at five interrelated changes in the approach medicine has taken toward critical illness over the past century.

Change in types of illness

First, it is important to point out that the types of critical illness have changed significantly during this century. A number of influences have led to a clearly

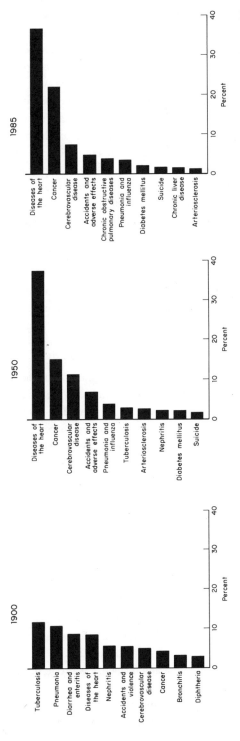

FIGURE 1.1 The 10 leading causes of death as a percentage of all deaths: 1900, 1950, 1985. *Source:* Reproduced from the National Center for Health Statistics, *Health, United States, 1987* (Washington, D.C.: U.S. Government Printing Office, 1988), pp. 10–11.

discernible trend in the multiple forms that critical illness takes. That epidemi-ological trend, especially when considering critical illnesses that lead to death, is usually described as moving from the predominance of *communicable diseases* at the beginning of the century to the predominance of *chronic* or *degenerative diseases* as we move toward the end of the century. Described in other ways, the trend is sometimes said to be moving from the diseases of childhood to the diseases of aging, or from the diseases of poverty to the diseases of affluence.[17]

At the turn of the twentieth century, to be more specific, many of the major life-threatening medical conditions were diseases such as tuberculosis, pneumo-nia, influenza, nephritis, gastritis, duodenitis, enteritis, measles, diphtheria, scarlet fever, typhoid fever, rheumatic fever, syphilis, typhus, streptococcal sore throat, and whooping cough. The prevalence of some of these diseases as causes of death is evident from Figure 1.1, based on data put together by the National Center for Health Statistics. The first part of the figure indicates that the leading causes of death in 1900 were tuberculosis and pneumonia (including influenza), with tuberculosis accounting for 11 percent of all deaths and pneumonia–influenza responsible for 10 percent of all deaths. By contrast, cardiovascular disease represented only 8 percent, cerebrovascular disease only 5 percent, and various forms of cancer only 4 percent of the total deaths in the United States at the beginning of the century.

By 1950 tuberculosis had dropped to sixth place in the ranking of causes of death, accounting for only 2 percent of total deaths. Pneumonia and influenza had dropped to fifth place, accounting for 4 percent of all deaths. In their places as the leading causes of death were "the big three": cardiovascular disease, cancer, and cerebrovascular disease. With heart disease causing 38 percent of deaths and cancer causing another 16 percent of deaths, these two diseases alone were responsible for over one-half of the total deaths in the United States. With an additional 12 percent of deaths resulting from cerebrovascular disease, these three diseases accounted for two-thirds of the total deaths.

By 1985 the previous three leading causes of death had become, for all practical purposes, "the big two." With heart disease still causing approxi-mately 38 percent of all deaths and with cancer becoming the cause of death in approximately 22 percent of all deaths, these two types of medical conditions accounted for approximately 60 percent of total deaths in the United States. By contrast, tuberculosis (accounting for only 1,700 of the 2 million U.S. deaths), diarrhea and enteritis, nephritis, bronchitis, and diphtheria were no longer listed among the 10 leading causes of death. The only type of infectious disease remaining as a leading cause of death was pneumonia–influenza, and the per-centage of deaths in 1985 attributed to pneumonia and influenza was one-third of the percentage in 1900.[18]

When these statistics are adjusted for age, an important step because of the dramatically changing age distribution in this century, the trend from commu-

TABLE 1.1   Trends in Selected Causes of Mortality, United States*

	Age-adjusted death rate/100,000				Crude death rate 1983
Causes of mortality	1 1900–1904	2 1940–1944	3 1980–1983	% Change (1–3)	
Selected communicable diseases					
Tuberculosis	188.5	43.0	0.4	−99	0.8
Syphilis	16.6	12.3	—		0.0
Typhoid fever	26.8	0.7	—		—
Whooping cough	8.0	2.0	—		—
Measles	8.1	1.1	—		—
Influenza and pneumonia	190.9	60.3	11.9	−94	21.2
Gastritis and enteritis	91.6	8.9	—		—
Diphtheria	27.3	0.9	—		—
Scarlet fever	9.6	0.3	—		—
Selected chronic diseases					
Major cardiovascular	437.2	469.1	243.7	−44	416.3
Malignant neoplasms	83.9	118.4	132.5	+58	188.6
Diabetes	14.6	25.1	9.8	−44	15.2
Violence					
Accidents	83.1	71.6	38.6	−54	38.5
(Motor vehicle)	(—)†	(22.6)	(20.6)		18.2
(All other)	(83.1)	(49.0)	(18.3)	−78	20.3
Suicide	12.1	11.7	11.5	−5	11.9
Homicide	1.2	5.7	9.8	+817	8.2
All other	508.2		145.4	−71	

*Data from National Center for Health Statistics and U.S. Bureau of the Census. Rates per 100,000 population.
†Indicates a rate of <0.1.
Source: Reproduced from Myron E. Wegman, "Annual Summary of Vital Statistics—1983," Pediatrics 74 (December 1984): 986.

nicable to chronic causes (and violent causes) of death is particularly clear. One such study of the changes in mortality figures was done by Myron Wegman, and is reproduced in Table 1.1.

Perhaps the most remarkable feature of Table 1.1 is the virtual disappearance of communicable diseases as causes of death. Regarding the chronic conditions presented in the table, several changes can be seen. Major cardiovascular diseases, though now the leading cause of death by a wide margin, have actually declined since the beginning of the century when the statistics are adjusted for age. A similar decline has occurred with diabetes when the deaths from diabetes are placed on an age-adjusted scale. By contrast, deaths caused by various forms of cancer have increased at a dramatic rate, with a 58 percent jump in deaths on an age-adjusted scale compared with the 1900–1904 period. Also troubling is the dramatic increase in deaths from homicide, with the present rate being more than eight times higher than the rate at the turn of the century.

The trend toward hospitalization

Second, the location in which critically ill patients are normally found has
changed over the past 150 years or so. Throughout the nineteenth century and
during the first part of the twentieth century, the majority of people contracting
some form of critical illness remained in their homes for the duration of the
illness. People living in cities at the turn of the century were sometimes taken to
small neighborhood hospitals when they "came down" with a communicable
disease, but in most instances people with a communicable disease or other
life-threatening condition remained at home until they regained their health or,
more likely, died from the illness. Even those city dwellers who were admitted
to hospitals with some form of critical illness were frequently discharged to the
care of their families and sent home to die when their conditions proved incurable.

The home, therefore, was the traditional location in which critically ill patients
struggled, against great odds, to continue living. Most families could depict
several "deathbed" scenes that had occurred in the home, ranging from the
deaths of infants and young children to the deaths of women as a consequence of
childbirth to the deaths of other adult family members who had succumbed to
influenza and/or pneumonia.

Hospitals, at least until the turn of the century, did not offer an effective
alternative to the home as a place for critically ill patients. Having been started
years earlier as charitable or religious institutions for the care of strangers (e.g.,
seamen and other travelers away from home) or indigent individuals, hospitals
were widely regarded with dread as places where one was more likely to become
more ill than to become well. Even the discovery of anesthesia in the 1840s, the
beginning of professional nursing in the 1870s, and the employment of antiseptic
surgical techniques in the 1880s did not substantially change the public view of
hospitals as dangerous places. As Paul Starr observes:

Before 1900 the hospital had no special advantages over the home, and the infections that
periodically swept through hospital wards made physicians cautious about sending patients there. Even after the danger of cross-infection had been reduced, the lingering
image of the hospital as a house of death and its status as a charity interfered with its
growth.[19]

Of course the public view of hospitals has changed dramatically during the
present century. Although most people, when asked about their preferences for
a place to die, consistently indicate that they would prefer to die at home rather
than at a hospital, the trend toward placing critically and terminally ill patients
in institutional settings has steadily increased over the decades. By 1949, hospitals and other institutions (typically, nursing homes) were the sites for 50
percent of all deaths in the United States. By 1958, that proportion had increased
to 61 percent.[20] By 1976, the figure had grown to 70 percent.[21] The President's

Commission observed in 1983 that "perhaps 80 percent of the deaths in the United States now occur in hospitals and long-term care institutions, such as nursing homes."[22]

With approximately 2 million people dying in the United States each year, hospitals and related institutions now account for around 1.6 million deaths a year. Given these figures, the location of the "deathbed" for the majority of the readers of this book (and most other persons) will most likely be a hospital. Should that happen, the location of death will be an institution poorly equipped to handle patient deaths because the major resources of the institution go toward restoring acutely ill, "salvageable" patients to health. Whether the hospice movement will have a significant impact on this trend toward hospitalization, even during the terminal phase of critically ill patients' lives, remains to be seen.

Changes in community

A third change has accompanied the trend toward hospitalization. With an increasing percentage of critically and terminally ill patients being located in hospitals rather than in their own homes, the community surrounding critically ill persons has also changed in important ways during the past 150 years or so. As an example of former practices, consider the following account taken from the diary of a nineteenth-century daughter.

Case 1.1

Mother Drinkwater was critically ill, but none of her family realized the seriousness of her condition. Never having been to a hospital and without recent contact with a physician, she remained in bed while the rest of the family carried out their regular activities. They took turns caring for her as best they could.

One night while Mary was sitting up with her, Mother Drinkwater "seemed to die in her sleep." Her husband, sons, and daughter [the diarist] were asleep in other parts of the house.

The next day her son-in-law and grandsons arrived, and the "poor boys were much upset" when they "saw their dear Grandmama." Within a matter of hours, the family members carried out several tasks brought on by the death:

> My dear brothers all assisted to put her in her coffin and carried it into the sitting room where we all kissed her for the last time. My brothers screwed the coffin down, Mary had cut out a cross and covered it with artificial flowers and put it on top of the coffin. My dear boys went with their uncles as mourners. My poor Father read the service, a fearful trial. John and the boys returned to "Northbrook" after the funeral, I shall remain with my dear Father for some time.[23]

As illustrated by this account, Mother Drinkwater went through the terminal phase of life surrounded by her family in the privacy of her own home. Although details of her dying are sketchy, it is reasonable to think that her dying followed the general pattern of the time: she was probably ill with influenza and/or pneumonia, hoped to recover on her own, to some degree orchestrated the activities of her family members as they took care of her, used alcohol and opiates for the relief of pain and suffering (drugs were available without prescription until the Harrison Act of 1914), and prepared for death.[24] The presence of family members throughout the process was standard practice:

> Everyone knew about death at first hand; there was nothing unfamiliar or even queer about the phenomenon. People seem to have known a lot more about the process itself than is the case today. The "deathbed" was a real place, and the dying person usually knew where he was and when it was time to assemble the family and call for the priest.[25]

However long her illness was, Mother Drinkwater was in all likelihood rarely without the companionship, concern, and care of her family. Her autonomy as a person was probably never questioned (at least in her presence), and her wishes were carried out whenever it was possible to do so. Of course, one side effect of this close personal contact by her family may well have been the transmission of her disease to one or more of them. Other side effects, in some families, could also have been the "exposure" of the dying person to family dissension, emotional appeals for the "spoils" remaining after death, and so on.

The contrast with the "community" now available to critically and terminally ill patients in hospitals is obvious. In far too many instances such patients never benefit from the support of a community that cares for them as individual persons, for at least two reasons. The community that was traditionally available to critically ill persons, the family, is now often severely hampered by limited hospital visiting hours, the isolation of patients in ICUs and other critical care units in medical centers, the refusal of many hospitals to allow visits to patients by minors under a certain age, and medical concern over the emotional and physical impact of lengthy visits with patients. Given these restraints, many critically ill patients undergo multiple forms of medical treatment and in numerous instances approach death isolated from the love and nonmedical care best provided by family members. In addition, the medical personnel who have replaced the family at the bedside of critically ill patients are frequently not known personally by individual patients, sometimes display greater interest in efficiency than in compassion, and often rely more heavily on electronic monitors and computer printouts of biochemical data than on personal conversations with patients. In such circumstances, any semblance of community disappears whenever medical personnel "strip" critically and terminally ill patients of their personal identities by referring to them only by room number, ICU bed number, or disease category.

Change in physicians' perspective

Fourth, the perspective of physicians toward critical illness has substantially changed over the past century. In the latter half of the nineteenth century, physicians were still functioning to some extent under the indictment made by Jacob Bigelow in 1835, namely that "the unbiased opinion of most medical men of sound judgment and long experience" was that "the amount of death and disaster in the world would be less, if all disease were left to itself."[26] Even during the last two decades of that century, physicians often had little choice but to "leave diseases to themselves" because of the proud self-sufficiency of many American families (especially in rural areas), the time required to travel by horse to a largely rural population, the limited number of patients (fewer than 10) who could be seen in a day, the limited number of hospitals (only a few hundred hospitals existed in 1880, but more than 4,000 were available by 1910), the frequent necessity of adapting the use of ether and antisepsis to "kitchen surgery" performed in patients' homes, and the therapeutic poverty of medicine in the face of critical illness (some physicians still offered disastrous "heroic therapy," such as bleeding, purging, and large doses of mercury).[27]

By the beginning of the twentieth century, however, the role of physicians and the perspective they had on critical illness began to change. Having in earlier years consoled patients more often than they cured them, and having witnessed death more often than they prevented it, they began to take a more combative role against critical illness. The increased availability of telephones (having first become available in the late 1870s), the increased availability and reliability of automobiles (physicians were often the first persons in a town to purchase cars), and the increased number of hard-surface roads combined to make physicians easier to contact in times of critical illness and to reduce their travel time when going to see patients. The general acceptance of the germ theory of disease, the widespread use of antiseptic and aseptic techniques to control infection, and the increased availability of improved diagnostic instruments (stethoscope, ophthalmoscope, X-ray machines, etc.) combined to help physicians diagnose disease more easily and to offer patients more effective treatments (especially in terms of surgery) than had ever been possible. The upshot of these changes was that "the physician, previously an unimportant, often uninvited, and usually reluctant attendant to the terminally ill patient, had moved into a position of centrality" in the fight against disease and death.[28] Or, as Paul Starr puts it, "one came to expect the doctor's intervention."[29]

The unprecedented achievements of medical science and technology in the twentieth century—along with numerous other improvements in housing, sanitation, transportation, and transmission of information—have accelerated the trend from consolation to cure. Modern physicians, armed with biochemical and technological weapons that earlier physicians could not have imagined, sally forth to do battle against recalcitrant forms of critical illness not yet conquered by medicine. Having already won major battles against previously "incurable" diseases (e.g., tuberculosis, pneumonia, and polio), physicians and biomedical researchers now pursue other cures—for heart disease, various cancers, the acquired immune deficiency syndrome (AIDS), and all other major life-threatening conditions. Of course, we hope they succeed. But the price we pay is a frequently unbridled approach to medicine in which critically ill patients are more interesting to work with if they present an unusual and "challenging" medical condition, and terminally ill patients are often viewed as professional failures by physicians and other health care personnel. The extremes to which this "medicine-as-war" approach to critical illness can go are illustrated by the following case, written by Irwin Nash, M.D.

Case 1.2

"Recently, I visited my 73-year-old uncle, who was widowed and childless, in the intensive care unit of a major medical center. A man with chronic moderate compromise of renal and pulmonary function, he had undergone a Whipple procedure for carcinoma of the head of the pancreas. One node revealed metastases on final pathological examination— a sign of an invariably terminal prognosis. Hooked up to a respirator, with numerous abdominal drains communicating with postoperative abscesses, and invaded by multiple intravenous lines and a Swan–Ganz catheter, he was an all too familiar hospital figure but was almost unrecognizable as the thoughtful and gentle brother-in-law of my father.

Despite the fact that he was reasonably alert, communicating with him was extremely difficult. The endotracheal tube precluded his speaking. Multiple lines, wrist restraints, and his obvious discomfort prevented him from feeling the warmth of efforts to touch him. What constrained him were not just the lines of his "life support" but the interweaving strands of medical dilemma. One such strand was his endotracheal tube, a major source of his discomfort. He wanted it out and would have pulled it out but for the wrist restraints. His physicians were hoping to extubate him, but before they could proceed, his blood gases had to be right. It was necessary for them to know that his respiratory system could compensate for his metabolic acidosis on its own. Thus, he could not be sedated and made more comfortable, because if he had been, they could not have determined whether or not he could "tolerate" being off the respirator. Despite a grim prognosis (a few months), he had to suffer to win, perhaps, a short-term reprieve.

He was fixed to his bed and his suffering as if by a Gordian knot. What he needed was an Alexander, or at least a physician-general who could put the problem in a new perspective, cut through the knot, change the therapeutic direction from cure to palliation, and order adequate analgesia for a dying man. Unfortunately, though there were a few kind and harried nurse-foot soldiers around, the general and his lieutenants were on another field, fighting another battle. My uncle died four days later."[30]

Increasing costs of critical illness

Another physician, Roscoe Dean, discussed the changes in perspective toward life-threatening diseases by comparing two cases. The first case involved his Aunt Jennie, who lived with her brother years ago on a South Dakota farm. At the age of 82, she became ill with carcinoma of the colon. One day the rest of the family was informed by Uncle Bill that "Jennie took to bed." Although the family physician advised Jennie to go to the Mayo Clinic, she refused, saying, "No, my family will look after me." They did, by bringing food and words of comfort. The physician left medication for rest and pain, and later admitted Jennie as a patient in a small country hospital. She died there, leaving a total cost for her terminal care of a few hundred dollars.

Recently, according to Dean, a 72-year-old woman "of like temperament with a similar problem" was admitted to the hospital where he works. Chemotherapy had removed her hair. She was bedridden with multiple tubes and surgical scars. Her slightest movement caused her to cringe and often scream with pain. Her medical bills were about $50,000, and she had nothing to look forward to "other than pain and institutional care." Having known the woman for years and having greatly admired her, Dean gently asked her why she had consented to the continued, obviously losing battle. She answered, "The doctors at the university said there was a chance." She died a few weeks later.[31]

These cases reflect a fifth change that has taken place concerning critical illness, namely the steadily increasing costs of being critically or terminally ill. When Mother Drinkwater became critically ill in the late nineteenth century, the financial costs of her illness were negligible: her family paid no hospital bills, no physicians' fees, and probably very little for medicine. Even the disposal of her dead body involved only minor expenses, since most if not all of the work connected with her funeral and burial was done by her survivors. When Jennie "took to bed" earlier this century, the costs of her critical illness were minimal. By contrast, Irwin Nash's uncle undoubtedly left medical bills and hospital bills running to five or six figures when he died. Those bills for his critical illness, probably handled by a third-party payer, included charges for direct ICU costs (labor, equipment, etc.), indirect ICU costs (e.g., housekeeping, hospital overhead), physicians' fees, laboratory fees, and an array of other charges on a computer printout probably several pages long. In a hospital version of adding insult to injury, some of the charges to be paid by his insurance and/or by Medicare were for types of life-sustaining treatment he apparently did not want.

Roscoe Dean's friend consented to her treatment, but still left substantial medical and hospital bills for someone to pay.

The expenses involved in critical illness can be seen in recent figures for three categories of patients having—or likely to have—critical illness: patients in adult ICUs, patients over the age of 65, and terminally ill patients. According to a study by the Office of Technology Assessment (OTA), the average charge for an intensive care bed had increased to $408 a day by 1982, a figure 2.5 times as high as the cost of a private bed in a regular hospital room. The same study places the national cost for adult intensive care at $15 billion a year.[32]

As helpful as the OTA study is, the figures cited by the OTA fail to give an accurate picture of how expensive intensive care has become. The OTA figures are too general in that they fail to reflect the variability in ICU expenses for patients with differing medical conditions. To mention the obvious: when patients are compared in terms of acute/chronic conditions, simple/complicated conditions, younger/older patient, and survivor/nonsurvivor of the ICU, patients falling into the second of the contrasting categories generally have substantially higher ICU expenses than do the other patients. Moreover, the OTA figures are much too low for individual patients because the figures do not include all intensive care-related expenses: laboratory work, pharmacy charges, physician services, and so forth. When these expenses are included in a calculation of the basic daily ICU cost, that figure easily tops $1,000 a day and may be three times the figure provided by the OTA.[33] Leigh Thompson puts these figures into perspective when he comments that a day of intensive care "costs about $1,000, a heart attack may be worth a Mercedes Benz, a burn may equal a house, and the lifetime care of a totally disabled child is worth $1 million."[34]

Costs for older adult patients are also rising steadily, for a number of reasons. The progressively larger percentage of older adults in our society, the increase in chronic medical conditions, the decline of family support systems, and the greater use of health services by older adults combine with generally rising health care costs to create much higher health expenditures (only partially paid by Medicare) for older adults than for the younger population. For persons over the age of 65, per capita health care expenses are now 3.5 times greater than for persons under 65 years of age. Even when health care costs are restricted to hospital-related expenses (excluding nursing home care, hospice care, outpatient expenses, drugs, and other health care costs), the charges for patients over 65 remain 3.5 times higher than for younger patients. Particularly expensive medical conditions for older adults include circulatory diseases, digestive diseases, and mental disorders (for females and males), diseases of the musculoskeletal system and connective tissue (for females especially), and various types of cancer (particularly for males). The difference that age makes in expenditures for these conditions is evident in Table 1.2.

TABLE 1.2 Per capita personal health care expenditures and rank for leading medical conditions, according to age and sex: United States, 1980

Medical condition*	Persons under 65 years of age		Persons 65 years of age and over	
	Male	Female	Male	Female
	Per capita amount			
Circulatory diseases	$ 67	$ 61	$674	$848
Digestive diseases	110	143	213	223
Mental disorders	73	69	181	246
Injury and poisoning	86	61	105	203
Respiratory diseases	60	68	192	137
Neoplasms	30	50	244	178
Musculoskeletal system and connective tissue diseases	40	55	91	187
Genitourinary system diseases	21	82	128	70
Nervous system and sense organ diseases	57	69	168	176
Endocrine, nutritional, metabolic diseases	15	31	82	138
	Rank			
Circulatory diseases	4	7	1	1
Digestive diseases	1	1	3	3
Mental disorders	3	4	5	2
Injury and poisoning	2	6	8	4
Respiratory diseases	5	5	4	9
Neoplasms	8	9	2	6
Musculoskeletal system and connective tissue diseases	7	8	9	5
Genitourinary system diseases	9	2	7	10
Nervous system and sense organ diseases	6	3	6	7
Endocrine, nutritional, metabolic diseases	10	10	10	8

*Conditions are based on the *International Classification of Diseases,* 9th Revision, *Clinical Modification.*
Source: Reproduced from Thomas A. Hodgson and Andrea N. Kopstein, "Health Care Expenditures for Major Diseases," in *Health—United States 1983* (Washington, D.C.: Department of Health and Human Services, 1983), p. 82.

The escalation of costs for terminally ill patients (such as Irwin Nash's uncle) is particularly troubling, especially since these costs increase even more dramatically as death nears. The rapid increase in these costs is demonstrated by a recent government study of Medicare payments for services on behalf of enrollees in their last and next-to-last years of life. Using data from 1976–1978, when 1.3 million of the 1.9 million persons whe died in 1978 were Medicare enrollees, the study shows that the Medicare program spent an average of $4,527 per enrollee who died in 1978—a figure 6.2 times greater than the average payments to Medicare enrollees who did not die in 1978. Even more indicative of the

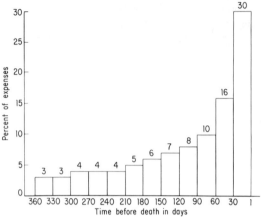

SOURCE: Health Care Financing Administration:
Data from the Medicare Statistical System.

FIGURE 1.2 Percentage of Medicare expenses in the last year of life, according to selected time intervals before death: United States, 1976. *Source:* Reproduced from James Lubitz and Ronald Prihoda, "Use and Costs of Medicare Services in the Last Years of Life," in *Health—United States, 1983* (Washington, D.C.: Department of Health and Human Services, 1983), p. 74.

escalation of health care costs in the last year of life is the finding that 30 percent of all medical expenses during the last year of life occur in the last 30 days of life, 46 percent of these expenses happen during the last 60 days of life, and 77 percent of these expenses take place in the last 6 months of life. The dramatic rise in expenses as death approaches is portrayed in Figure 1.2.

Do these figures mean that current expenditures on dying patients are disproportionate, unreasonable, or unjust?[35] For many terminally ill patients, this question has to be answered in the negative. Anne Scitovsky, in an important study on the "high cost of dying," argues that the available data do not suggest disproportionate expenditures for dying patients. Rather, she says that "today, as in previous periods, most sick people who die are given the kind of medical care generally given the sick—and such care is expensive, especially for patients who are sicker than the average."[36] Nevertheless, in an increasing number of cases, serious questions need to be raised (by patients, relatives, physicians, and hospital administrators) regarding the amount of money being spent to forestall a patient's death, especially when the patient's condition seems to be terminal and the treatment offered is, at best, marginally useful. One study, for example, indicated that the average expense by several hundred patients for medical care in a California hospital in the last 12 months of life was $22,597.[37] Given such cost figures, many patients and their relatives (and the health care professionals entrusted with the patients' care) find that treatment abatement is an inescapable issue to be addressed, that decelerating or stopping expensive treatments is sometimes in a patient's best interests, and that hospice care is (among other things) an attractive cost-saving alternative to the institutional care of dying patients in hospitals and nursing homes.

Development of Treatment Abatement as an Issue

The five features just outlined have unquestionably played major roles in bringing about a changed perspective toward life-threatening illness in the United States as this century has moved on. The first four—that is, the changing types of critical illness, the changing locations for care of critically ill persons, the changing community surrounding critically ill patients, and the changing views of physicians toward critical illness—had already occurred to a great extent by 1950. In addition, developments in pharmacology, medical technology, and intensive care medicine took place in the 1940s and 1950s that contributed to an unprecedented concern—at least among knowledgeable persons—regarding the extent to which physicians and other health care professionals *should* try to forestall the deaths of critically ill and terminally ill patients. One sign of that concern was an increased interest on the part of some people in the United Kingdom (e.g., Glanville Williams) and the United States (e.g., Joseph Fletcher) in the legalization of voluntary euthanasia. Another sign of that concern was the initiation of a debate regarding the moral permissibility of abating life-sustaining treatment in some cases of critical illness.

The first phase of the debate over abating treatment can be dated from 1957, when an anesthesiologist submitted several questions to Pope Pius XII regarding the morality of resuscitation. Bruno Haid, chief of anesthesia at the surgical clinic of the University of Innsbruck, was the physician whose questions prompted the Pope to address the subject of "the prolongation of life" at an international medical conference in Rome that year. The morality of resuscitation concerned Haid because of the increasing ability of anesthesiologists to intervene in life-threatening episodes involving asphyxia, whether such episodes occurred in operating rooms or during hospital emergencies such as strangulation, open chest wounds, poliomyelitis, accidental poisoning by sedatives, or brain trauma.[38] For Haid, the unprecedented ability of anesthesiologists to prolong the lives of some patients incapable of spontaneous breathing was the cause of serious moral doubt, which he put in the form of three questions. Does an anesthesiologist have the right or obligation to use "modern artificial respiration apparatus" on all patients, even those whose prognosis is completely hopeless to the physician? Does an anesthesiologist sometimes have the right or possibly an obligation to remove ventilation equipment from a comatose patient, knowing that the patient will probably die in the absence of such equipment? Should an artificially maintained, comatose patient ever be considered dead, especially when such a patient fails to improve over a significant period of time?[39] These questions and the responses they elicited from the Pope, especially in the importance that Pius XII placed on the distinction between ordinary and extraordinary means of prolonging life, will be discussed in a subsequent chapter.

The second phase of the development of treatment abatement as an important subject began in 1976. Three events in the United States that year had major impact on the thinking of informed persons—especially professionals in medicine, law, and ethics—concerning the placing of ethical and legal limits on the medical prolongation of life. First, one type of life-sustaining treatment given to Karen Ann Quinlan was challenged in the courts of New Jersey. At the age of 21, Quinlan had collapsed at a party in April 1975, had been rushed to a hospital and placed on a ventilator, and had remained on the ventilator as she became the focal point of a legal battle that continued until March 1976. The point at issue in the legal controversy was the subject of abating treatment: did Karen's parents, who had decided that their brain-damaged, comatose daughter was no longer being helped by the ventilator, have the moral and legal right to have the ventilator removed? The Supreme Court of New Jersey ruled that the ''right of privacy'' permits ''termination of treatment in the circumstances of this case,'' thereby allowing the patient to be removed from the ventilator.

Second, the Massachusetts General Hospital and Beth Israel Hospital in Boston took the lead among hospitals by publishing guidelines for certain aspects of treatment abatement. The clinical care committee at the first of these hospitals published guidelines for dividing critically ill patients into four treatment groups, ranging from class A patients, who are to be given ''maximal therapeutic effort without reservation,'' to class D patients, for whom ''all therapy can be discontinued . . . though maximum comfort to the patient may be continued.''[40] The Beth Israel guidelines concerned decisions not to resuscitate some patients who had experienced cardiac or respiratory arrest.[41]

Third, California became the first state to pass a Natural Death Act. Californians, who like all American citizens have at least a common-law right to refuse life-sustaining treatment, were given a specific legal mechanism in September 1976, to facilitate the carrying out of that legal right.[42] Thus events in three states in the same year demonstrated that the use of life-sustaining technology is sometimes limited by the medical conditions of critically ill patients and by the moral and legal right of patients (or their surrogates) to refuse treatment.

In 1985, the debate over abating treatment moved into a third, even more politically oriented phase. During the previous 2 years, the discussion of treatment abatement in professional journals had begun to focus on the abatement of life-sustaining nutrition and hydration, and at least one interdisciplinary conference had been held on this topic. In 1985, three developments in a single year again took on national and possibly international significance as courts, legislatures, and activist groups in the United States addressed the rights of critically ill and terminally ill patients (or their surrogates) to decelerate or stop life-sustaining treatment, including the technological provision of nutrition and hydration.

The first of the developments in 1985 was a widely publicized decision handed down by the Supreme Court of New Jersey as the year began. The case concerned Claire Conroy, an 84-year-old nursing home patient with serious, irreversible physical and mental impairments and a limited life expectancy. The point at issue in the case was whether technological nutrition and hydration (in this instance, by means of an NG tube) could be removed from a nonautonomous patient at the request of the patient's surrogate. The court's decision was to allow the removal of the feeding tube because the continued use of the tube was judged contrary to Conroy's best interests (we will return to this case and the Quinlan case in subsequent chapters).

The second development in that year was a dramatic increase in legislation having to do with advance directives related to the administration of medical care toward the end of one's life. After a decade of a gradual, rather spasmodic increase in the number of states passing natural death acts, 13 states passed such legislation in 1985. All of these statutes contained specific statements on technological nutrition and hydration. The addition of these states represented more than a 50 percent increase in the number of states having natural death acts, bringing the total of these statutes at the end of that year to 36 (35 states plus the District of Columbia).

The third development in 1985 was closely linked to the increased activity in the state legislatures regarding natural-death-act legislation. As more legislatures signaled their willingness to give serious attention to the merits of natural death acts, and as the publicity of the legislative debates over proposed statutes increased, activist groups supporting and opposing this kind of legislation intensified their efforts to influence both legislative and public opinion. Illustrative of this heightened activity on both sides of the debate was the publication and distribution of *The Physician and the Hopelessly Ill Patient*, a book prepared by the Society for the Right to Die—immediately countered by the distribution of a packet of readings, prepared by the American Life League, to legislators in various states indicating why they should oppose natural-death-act legislation.[43]

In the remaining chapters I will analyze the issue of abating treatment. We will discuss several of the clinical contexts in which treatment abatement takes place, the multiple legal aspects of this issue, the political importance of the issue, and the appropriate ethical context for decisions to abate life-sustaining treatment. The terminology, historical background, and developmental framework discussed in this chapter will represent a general context for the rest of the book.

Notes

1. William Winkenwerder, Jr., "Ethical Dilemmas for House Staff Physicians," *Journal of the American Medical Association* 254 (December 27, 1985): 3454.
2. Quoted by Dena Kleiman, "Doctors Ask, Who Lives? When to Die?" *New York Times,* January 16, 1985.
3. John Gunther, *Death Be Not Proud* (New York: Harper & Row, 1949), p. 89.
4. Cornelius Ryan and Kathryn Morgan Ryan, *A Private Battle* (New York: Simon & Schuster, 1979), p. 244.
5. Some of this account is taken from Robert B. White and H. Tristram Engelhardt, Jr., "Case Studies in Bioethics: A Demand to Die," *Hastings Center Report* 5 (June 1975): 9. The rest of the account is based on two films made about the case: "Please Let Me Die," a videotape made by Robert B. White, M.D.; and "Dax's Case," a film made by the Concern for Dying organization in 1984.
6. See Andrew H. Malcolm, "To Suffer a Prolonged Illness or Elect to Die: A Case Study," *New York Times,* December 16, 1984; and the book by Malcolm, *This Far and No More: A True Story* (New York: Times Books, 1987). An NBC movie about the case, entitled "Right to Die," was shown October 12, 1987.
7. Much of this account is taken from an article in *The Daily Oklahoman,* March 4, 1982.
8. Engelbert L. Schucking, "Death at a New York Hospital," *Law, Medicine, and Health Care* 13 (December 1985): 261–68.
9. Larry Brown was a patient in the Judith Karman Hospice in Stillwater, Oklahoma.
10. This case appears in Cynthia B. Cohen, ed., *Casebook on the Termination of Life-Sustaining Treatment and the Care of the Dying* (Bloomington, Ind.: Indiana University Press; and Briarcliff Manor, N.Y.: The Hastings Center, 1988), pp. 8–9.
11. Ibid., p. 34.
12. Ibid., pp. 55–56.
13. Paul Ramsey, *The Patient as Person* (New Haven, Conn.: Yale University Press, 1970), p. 149.
14. Arthur J. Dyck, "An Alternative to the Ethic of Euthanasia," in Robert H. Williams, ed., *To Live and to Die* (New York: Springer-Verlag, 1974), p. 102.
15. President's Commission for the Study of Ethical Problems in Medicine and Biomedical and Behavioral Research, *Deciding to Forego Life-Sustaining Treatment* (Washington, D.C.: U.S. Government Printing Office, 1983), p. 2n.
16. The Hastings Center project, *Guidelines on the Termination of Life-Sustaining Treatment and the Care of the Dying* (Briarcliff Manor, N.Y.: The Hastings Center, 1987).
17. An interesting interpretation is advanced by S. Jay Olshansky and A. Brian Ault in their article "The Fourth Stage of the Epidemiologic Transition: The Age of Delayed Degenerative Diseases," *Milbank Memorial Fund Quarterly* 64 (1986): 355–91.
18. Ibid. Also using statistics from the National Center for Health Statistics, Myron Wegman arrives at a significantly different percentage of deaths caused by cardiovascular disease. See his "Annual Summary of Vital Statistics—1986," *Pediatrics* 80 (December 1987): 824, where he says that major cardiovascular diseases cause 46.1 percent of all deaths in the United States.
19. Paul Starr, *The Social Transformation of American Medicine* (New York: Basic Books, 1983), p. 157.
20. Monroe Lerner, "When, Why, and Where People Die," in Orville G. Brim et al., eds., *The Dying Patient* (New York: Russell Sage Foundation, 1970), p. 22.

21. John C. Fletcher, "Ethics and the Costs of Dying," in Aubrey Milunsky and George J. Annas, eds., *Genetics and the Law II* (New York and London: Plenum Press, 1980), p. 192.
22. President's Commission, *Deciding to Forego,* pp. 17–18.
23. Paul C. Rosenblatt, *Bitter, Bitter Tears* (Minneapolis: University of Minnesota Press, 1983), p. 66.
24. The Harrison Act is discussed by the President's Commission in *Deciding to Forego,* p. 17.
25. Lewis Thomas, "Dying as Failure," *Annals of the American Academy of Political and Social Science* 447 (1980): 1, 3.
26. Starr, *Social Transformation,* p. 55.
27. Ibid., pp. 73, 95.
28. Charles W. Bodemer, "Physicians and the Dying: A Historical Sketch," *The Journal of Family Practice* 9 (1979): 831.
29. Starr, *Social Transformation,* p. 71.
30. Irwin Nash, "An ICU Death: A Gordian Knot in Search of Alexander" (Letter to the Editor), *The New England Journal of Medicine* 311 (December 27, 1984): 1705. Also see David Hilfiker, "Allowing the Debilitated to Die: Facing our Ethical Choices," *The New England Journal of Medicine* 308 (March 24, 1983): 716–19.
31. Roscoe E. Dean, "When Jennie Took to Bed," *Journal of the American Medical Association* 255 (February 7, 1986): 650.
32. Office of Technology Assessment (OTA), *Case Study #28: Intensive Care Units (ICUs): Clinical Outcomes, Costs, and Decisionmaking* (Washington, D.C.: U.S. Government Printing Office, 1984), pp. 22–23.
33. See, for example, George A. Gregory, "Who Should Receive Intensive Care?" *Critical Care Medicine* 11 (November 1983): 767. For discussions of the cost of intensive care, see George E. Thibault et al., "Medical Intensive Care: Indications, Interventions, and Outcomes," *The New England Journal of Medicine* 302 (April 24, 1980): 938–42; Jeffrey R. Parno et al., "Hospital Charges and Long-Term Survival of ICU versus non-ICU Patients," *Critical Care Medicine* 10 (October 1982): 569–74; David J. Cullen et al., "Results, Charges, and Benefits of Intensive Care for Critically Ill Patients: Update 1983," *Critical Care Medicine* 12 (December 1984): 102–6; and H. Tristram Englehardt, Jr. and Michael A. Rie, "Intensive Care Units, Scarce Resources, and Conflicting Principles of Justice," *Journal of the American Medical Association* 255 (March 7, 1986): 1159–64.
34. Leigh Thompson, "Structure of Critical Care: An Overview," in Joseph E. Parrillo and Steven M. Ayres, eds., *Major Issues in Critical Care Medicine* (Baltimore: Williams & Wilkins, 1984), p. 227.
35. Ronald Bayer et al., "The Care of the Terminally Ill: Morality and Economics," *The New England Journal of Medicine* 309 (December 15, 1983): 1490–94.
36. Anne A. Scitovsky, " 'The High Cost of Dying': What Do the Data Show?" *Milbank Memorial Fund Quarterly* 62 (1984): 604.
37. Anne A. Scitovsky, "Medical Care Expenditures in the Last Twelve Months of Life," final report to the John A. Hartford Foundation, March 1986. Cited in a discussion in the OTA report, *Life-Sustaining Technologies and the Elderly* (Washington, D.C.: U.S. Government Printing Office, 1987), pp. 65–72.
38. Stanley Joel Reiser, "Therapeutic Choice and Moral Doubt in a Technological Age," in John H. Knowles, ed., *Doing Better and Feeling Worse: Health in the United States* (New York: W.W. Norton, 1977), p. 47.

39. See Pope Pius XII, "The Prolongation of Life," *The Pope Speaks* 4 (1958): 393–98. Reprinted in Stanley Reiser, Arthur Dyck, and William Curran, eds., *Ethics in Medicine* (Cambridge, Mass.: MIT Press, 1977), pp. 501–4.

40. The Clinical Care Committee of the Massachusetts General Hospital, "Optimum Care for Hopelessly Ill Patients," *The New England Journal of Medicine* 295 (August 12, 1976): 362–64.

41. Mitchell T. Rabkin, Gerald Gillerman, and Nancy R. Rice, "Orders Not to Resuscitate," *The New England Journal of Medicine* 295 (August 12, 1976): 364–66. Also see the commentary in the same issue of the journal by Charles Fried, "Terminating Life Support: Out of the Closet!" pp. 390–91.

42. California Natural Death Act, Calif. Health & Safety Code §§ 7185–95 (1976).

43. Society for the Right to Die (SRD), *The Physician and the Hopelessly Ill Patient* (New York: SRD, 1985).

2

Clinical Settings for Decisions to Abate Treatment

From the beginning of their introduction in the mid-nineteenth century, automated machines that generated results in objective formats such as graphs and numbers were thought capable of purging from health care the distortions of subjective human opinion. . . . Machines can seem so accurate, so right. They can make us forget who made them, and who designed into them—with all the possibilities of human frailty and error—the programs that dictate their function. They can make us forget the hands and minds behind their creation; they can make us forget ourselves.

Stanley Joel Reiser, M.D.[1]

It is not medically appropriate to devote limited ICU resources to patients who do not have a reasonable chance of significant recovery, particularly when patients who might profit from ICU care are being turned away for lack of beds. Thus, it is inappropriate to continue ICU care of a patient who has deteriorated to a persistent vegetative state, or to otherwise employ ICU resources when no purpose will be served but a prolongation of the natural process of death.

NIH Consensus Development Conference on Critical Care Medicine[2]

Medical technology is the common denominator for the changing features of critical illness discussed in Chapter 1. Communicable diseases are no longer major causes of death because medical technology in the form of sulfa drugs (in the late 1930s), penicillin and other antibiotics (1940s), and polio and rubella vaccines (1950s and 1960s) produced "miracle drugs" to combat infectious diseases. Hospitals are now the location of choice for most critically ill patients and their physicians, because medical technology in a myriad of forms (emergency rooms, surgical facilities, ICUs, sophisticated diagnostic and monitoring equipment, etc.) has made hospitals the place in which critical illness can most successfully be combated. The community surrounding critically ill patients is now less personal than it was earlier this century because, to give one reason, some highly technical medical specialties dealing with critical illness involve virtually no direct contact with patients as persons; also, many physicians who do have contact with patients rely more on objective laboratory reports than on subjective judgments (including those made through conversations with patients) in making diagnostic and prognostic decisions. The perspective of physicians toward critical illness has changed dramatically because medical technology has been able to provide physicians with a seemingly endless array of sophisticated

29

preventive, diagnostic, and therapeutic "tools" to use against critical illness. In addition, the costs of being critically ill are steadily increasing, in spite of cost containment efforts (e.g., the use of diagnostic related groups, or DRGs), because the complex equipment of the widely publicized "prestige technologies" (cobalt therapy, open-heart surgery, renal dialysis, etc.) is expensive for hospitals to buy, and specialized critical care units are expensive for hospitals to maintain.[3]

The purpose of this chapter is to show how the impact of medical technology varies from one clinical setting to another, and why decisions are sometimes made to limit technological intervention in the treatment of critically and terminally ill patients. The chapter will have two distinct but related parts. We will begin with a brief discussion of the "technological imperative" in contemporary medicine and follow that with a longer discussion of three of the clinical settings in which treatment-abatement decisions are made: the specific hospital settings of various ICUs, the multifaceted settings of geriatric medicine, and the alternative hospital-based and residential-based settings of hospice care.

Lure of the "Technological Imperative"

With the advent of high technology, many of the technologies available in medicine are not only complex and expensive, but are also restricted in availability and necessitate specialized skills on the part of physicians and other caregivers. These technologies, regularly used in the diagnosis and treatment of critical illness, now play a central role in carrying out five functions that have long characterized the practice of medicine.[4]

1. *The visualization of physiological functions* has traditionally been carried out by a physician's trained eye, supplemented by X-ray films since Wilhelm Roentgen discovered in 1895 that cathode rays could reveal the skeleton within its covering of flesh. Now, the process of visualization includes the technologies of contrast radiology (e.g., angiography), ultrasound imaging, computerized tomography (CT) scanners, positron emission tomography (PET), and magnetic resonance imaging (MRI).

2. *The measurement of physiological functions* has been done by traditional technologies such as blood pressure machines, first demonstrated by Nikolai Korotkoff (1905) and popularized in this country by Harvey Cushing. Now, physiological functions are measured by a variety of technologies, including electroencephalograms (EEGs), electrocardiograms (ECGs), and other electrical monitoring devices for heart rate and respiration rate in ICU patients.

3. *The collecting and collating of information on the medical conditions* of patients has been done by physicians over the past two centuries through face-to-face dialogue with patients and physician-colleagues (when geo-

graphic proximity permitted such medical exchanges), and by letters, tele-graph (after 1843), and telephone (after 1876) when substantial distance separated physicians. Now, computers are routinely used to collect informa-tion for medical records, organize randomized clinical trials, report labora-tory results, record vital signs and drugs administered to patients, locate potential organ donors, transmit medical data around the world, and monitor (with integral microcomputers in ICU instruments) the cardiopulmonary ac-tivity of critically ill patients.

4. *The substitution of lost function* has traditionally been carried out by wooden legs, spectacles, and hearing aids. Now, high technology provides much more complicated substitutes such as pacemakers, dialysis machines, venti-lators, computerized prostheses, and artificial hearts.

5. *The correction of aberrant function* has been performed by surgeons with knives, saws, clamps, and needles for at least three centuries. Now, the correction of aberrant function includes not only sophisticated surgical equip-ment and techniques (heart–lung machines, coronary-bypass surgery, trans-plant surgery, microsurgery, and laser surgery), but also a plethora of drugs and other technological efforts (including chemotherapy and radiation ther-apy) to combat cancer and other life-threatening conditions.

In many ways these technological advances provide medicine with a "winning tradition" similar to the traditions of successful athletic teams. Like successful athletic teams, the era of high technology in medicine involves coordinated teamwork in which specialized "players" must carry out their designated roles to maximize the chances of victory. Having recorded a number of victories (in the case of medicine, the victories over disease and death this century), the "players" and their fans (hospital administrators, many patients, the media, etc.) now have a heightened expectation of continued success and a noticeable lack of tolerance for criticism, doubt, and failure (the "agony of defeat"). In order to continue winning, the authoritative decision makers (coaches, physi-cians) are frequently inclined to take unusual risks—and are sometimes moti-vated to continue a competitive struggle long after objective observers have judged that victory is no longer possible (at least in this particular game, or with this patient's condition).

The "technological imperative" in medicine—the belief that if we can, we must—is to be understood in this context. Against a historical background of major victories in the prevention, diagnosis, and treatment of previously uncon-trolled diseases, many contemporary physicians are convinced that technological medicine has virtually no limits that cannot be transcended with a game-winning technological "play" (medicine's version of a successful pass, a grand-slam home run, or a winning basketball shot from midcourt). Given a medical edu-cation that has trained them to combat disease and to cure sick patients (but often not to provide supportive care for patients who are beyond cure), many physicians are inclined to "do everything possible" to prevent or at least postpone the deaths of critically ill and terminally ill patients. Whether patients' illnesses call for ventilator support or chemotherapy or kidney dialysis or medical feeding or any number of other technological possiblities, physicians subscribing to the if-we-can-we-must philosophy of medical care feel obligated to continue life-sustaining treatment until some external power (God, or a court order) effectively takes the cases out of their hands.

Predictably, physicians carrying out the technological imperative produce mixed results. Many critically ill patients benefit from aggressive medical treatment to the point that some of them are unexpectedly restored to health and productive lives; others fail to benefit from similar treatment, are sometimes harmed by ineffective and possibly unwanted treatment, and have the terminal phase of their lives needlessly prolonged by misguided treatment efforts. The contrasting results produced by following the technological imperative are illustrated by the following cases.

Case 2.1

Week after week, Mary watched her youngest daughter and worried. In May 1983, 13-year-old Sandra complained of a stiff neck. Sandra's physician referred her to an orthopedic surgeon, who concluded from X-ray examinations that a strained muscle was the problem. However, Sandra soon could not turn her head from side to side. Another surgeon diagnosed a pinched nerve and recommended steam packs and traction. That therapy provided little relief, and Sandra grew progressively weaker, listless, and withdrawn.

On July 26, Mary took Sandra to neurosurgeon Harold Rekate at Cleveland's University Hospitals. Noting Sandra's atrophied neck muscles, facial numbness, and spastic lower limbs, Dr. Rekate immediately suspected a congenital malformation or tumor at the cervicomedullary juncture. A CT scan was inconclusive. Fortunately, Dr. Rekate had an alternative: MRI, an imaging technique that University Hospitals' physicians had used since 1981 even though this technology did not receive tentative Food and Drug Administration (FDA) approval until the summer of 1983. The MRI scan revealed a huge tumor pressing on Sandra's brain stem and spinal cord.

"Two years ago I wouldn't have known what to do next," Dr. Rekate says of the inconclusive CT scan. "Because of the location of the tumor, a lumbar puncture for a myelogram probably would have killed Sandra."

Guided by sagittal and cross-sectional views, Dr. Rekate emulsified the neurofibroma with an ultrasound aspirator. The surgery took 9 hours, and Sandra woke up in the recovery room asking to go home, her neurological functioning normal once again.

"The wonderful thing is that she's a cure," says Dr. Rekate. "Her case is unbelievable testimony to the marvels of high technology in medicine."[5]

Case 2.2

Thomas Creighton, a 33-year-old Tucson auto mechanic, made medical history during his last 4 days: he had his life sustained by four different hearts. The 4 days included Creighton's near-fatal cardiac arrest (3 years and 6 months after his first heart attack) and the maintenance of his body for more than 7 hours on a heart–lung machine; there followed three separate operations to replace his heart, including two human-heart transplants within 48 hours, a frantic search for an artificial heart that ended with the airlift of an experimental device built to be tested in a calf, and the opening of yet another chapter in the national debate over how fast to proceed in this brave new world of medical technology.

Suffering from cardiomyopathy, Creighton received his first heart transplant on Tuesday, March 12, 1985. The new heart, which had been damaged in a motorcycle crash, failed to function properly. Creighton's surgeon, Dr. Jack Copeland of the University of Arizona Medical Center, decided to let nothing—including the technical illegality of implanting an artificial heart without FDA approval—stand in the way of his trying to save his patient's life.

Copeland put Creighton on a heart–lung machine and began searching for another heart donor. When none could be found, he made arrangements to secure the "Phoenix heart" that its developer, Dr. Kevin Kuo-Tsai Cheng, had built for a calf. The experimental heart was placed in Creighton's body on Wednesday, where it remained for 11 hours; after this, a second human-heart transplant was performed. After another 36 hours, on Friday afternoon, with his lungs filling with fluid and his blood pressure falling, Creighton died.

The implant of the untested heart left the FDA with the choice of acquiescing in a serious breach of its regulations or punishing a physician who tried to save a patient from certain death. Copeland's response was to indicate that he would be tempted to do it all over again if he were faced with the same situation.[6]

Three Clinical Settings for Decisions to Abate Treatment

The cases of Sandra and of Thomas Creighton are paradigmatic for the debate over the use and abuse of life-sustaining technology. Motivated by the success stories of Sandra and other critically ill patients restored to health by technological medicine, many physicians and patients are convinced that morally responsible medicine can do nothing less than "go all out" in the effort to prolong lives. Many other physicians and patients, disturbed by the extremes to which life-sustaining treatment can go (whether or not an artificial heart is involved), are equally convinced that morally responsible medicine must set and heed limits for such treatment. Three specialized areas of medicine, while obviously not the only clinical settings for decisions about limiting technological intervention, represent regularly occurring contexts in which such decisions frequently have to be made: critical care medicine, geriatric medicine, and hospice care.

Critical Care Medicine

The practice of intensive care in the second half of the twentieth century is, in some ways, only an extension of the constant vigil or "death watch" carried out by relatives of critically and terminally ill patients during the nineteenth century (see Chapter 1). In many other ways, of course, the practice of intensive care is an unprecedented effort of technological medicine to support and prolong the lives of critically ill patients, and to correct the conditions that have caused them to be critically ill.

The modern version of intensive care began in the 1950s, with the management of poliomyelitis patients serving as a precursor to the later development of multiple critical care units. At that time patients with polio were isolated from other patients, placed in "iron lungs" (negative-pressure whole-body ventilators), and rehabilitated if possible with what Lewis Thomas describes as "halfway technology," until the advent of polio immunization made such treatment unnecessary.[7]

Anesthesiologists were in charge of these early respiratory units. Because of their specialized training, and because they were regularly available in hospitals during the day, anesthesiologists were also in charge of postoperative recovery rooms. The combination of their specialized skills, the concentration of patients with critical care needs in common areas, the continuous visual monitoring of these patients by nurses, and the improvement in life-sustaining procedures such as endotracheal intubation and cardiac defibrillation brought about improved patient care and the prolongation of patients' lives.

The success of these early special care areas led to the development of coronary care units (CCUs) in the 1960s. Subsequently, several other critical care units were developed for patients with similar medical problems requiring continuous organ system monitoring, organ system support and evaluation, and advanced life support. Now, depending on the size and type of hospital involved, a variety of critical care units are available for patients who need monitoring and/or treatment.

Listed here are the most common types of critical care units. Many hospitals do not have these multiple units, but offer critically ill patients a combined medical-surgical ICU. Other hospitals offer patients several ICUs (medical

ICUs, CCUs, and surgical ICUs being the most common), but not all of the specialized ICUs. And even hospitals offering a variety of specialized ICUs do not always agree about the titles of the units, whether the units are to be located in separate areas of a hospital or are to be combined in a multipurpose ICU complex of a hospital, and how the units are to be administered. Nevertheless, it is important to provide a brief description of some of the units currently available to portray the specialized treatment possible within critical care medicine. A few units, such as obstetrical ICUs and neonatal ICUs, will not be discussed here because they lie outside the purview of this book.[8]

Medical intensive care units provide monitoring and treatment for patients with medical emergencies. Sometimes called MICUs but more commonly only ICUs, such units have a heterogeneous patient population. A high percentage of ICU patients (more than 90 percent in one study) are transfers from emergency rooms, and at least half of ICU patients are admitted for monitoring purposes (because of injury, acute diseases, or acute deterioration of a chronic condition) rather than treatment. The more common diagnoses of ICU patients are myocardial infarction (MI), coronary insufficiency, arrhythmias, acute respiratory failure, congestive heart failure (CHF), chest pain, drug overdose, gastrointestinal (GI) bleeding, acute neurological disease, sepsis, and renal failure. The diagnosis, coupled with a patient's age, is a frequent determinant of how long patients remain in the ICU (the mean length of stay ranges from 3 days upward, depending on patients' conditions) and whether they are likely to survive this setting or die in the ICU (approximately 20 percent of ICU patients die there). Monitoring in ICUs includes not only cardiac activity (with ECGs) and other vital signs, but the results of comprehensive laboratory services as well (blood gas studies, electrolyte determinations, hemograms, renal function studies, etc.). Patients requiring major therapeutic interventions can be given endotracheal intubation, mechanical ventilation, technological nutrition and hydration, pulmonary artery catheter placement, multiple blood transfusions, hemodialysis, systemic arterial line placement, temporary pacemaker placement, and/or cardiopulmonary resuscitation (CPR).[9]

Coronary care units (CCUs), having been developed to monitor and treat early arrhythmias after acute MI, now accept all patients displaying cardiovascular instability and the need for monitoring and/or aggressive treatment. Although some CCUs still offer patients a protective environment focusing on rehabilitation and patient education, many CCUs now function basically as coronary ICUs. Such units provide intensive care for patients with MI, malignant arrhythmias, CHF of diverse etiology, pulmonary edema, cor pulmonale, cardiogenic shock, acute valvular dysfunction, unstable angina, and unstable pericardial syndromes. Candidates for open-heart surgery are also admitted to these units for monitoring and life support. Treatment options in CCUs include the use of defibrillators, respirators, inotropic agents (digoxin, dopamine, dobutamine, and others), vasodilators, bedside coronary angiography, intraaortic balloon pump insertion and maintenance, cardiac surgery, pacemakers, and a range of elaborate resuscitation equipment. Decisions to abate treatment depend primarily on the prognosis of individual patients, with such decisions for MI patients also taking into consideration patient age, as well as infarct type, size, and location, ventricular function, and past clinical history.[10]

Surgical intensive care units (SICUs) are the successors to the postanesthetic recovery rooms that developed earlier this century in military hospitals (during the world wars) and in civilian hospitals (during the 1950s). In some hospitals the SICU is now subdivided into a neurosurgical unit, a trauma or burn unit, and/or a cardiac postoperative unit. The postoperative patients in SICUs are ideal patients for the context of intensive care: they need sophisticated monitoring and treatment for a short period of time, have a good chance of survival, and may be restored to a satisfactory quality of life for a period of several months to many years. The surgical procedures performed on these patients prior to their admission to the SICU are quite varied, including elective and emergency major vascular operations, neurosurgery and head trauma operations, cancer operations, GI operations, thoracic operations, and cardiac operations. Treatment in an SICU involves ventilatory support and monitoring for most patients, coupled with multifaceted efforts to prevent and treat the common problems of atelectasis, pneumonia, and sepsis (with peritonitis being the most frequent and most serious infection encountered in these units). In contrast to other ICUs, SICUs are, in fact, rarely the setting for decisions to abate treatment because surgeons, having contracted to pull a patient through an operation, are most reluctant "to let a postoperative patient die until every possible effort has been exhausted" to combat whatever postoperative problems may develop.[11]

Respiratory intensive care units (RICUs) are available in some hospitals to meet the needs of patients requiring ventilator support. These units, usually directed by a pulmonologist or an anesthesiologist, are dedicated to the monitoring and treatment of respiratory failure and its related disorders; the units are staffed by a team of physicians, nurses, physical therapists, respiratory therapists, and supporting laboratory technicians. Patients admitted to RICUs may have chronic conditions such as asthma, bronchitis, emphysema, or chronic obstructive pulmonary disease (COPD); or they may have acute respiratory failure brought about by chest injury, drug intoxication, neurological disease, pneumonia, or postoperative complications. By approaching respiration as an integration of pulmonary, cardiac, and cellular function, the personnel in RICUs provide monitoring of multiple organ systems, prevention of disease complications, and treatment by means of mechanical and pharmacological interventions. Treatment options include oxygen therapy, endotracheal intubation, humidifiers, pulmonary physiotherapy, and mechanical ventilation by means of intermittent mandatory ventilation (IMV), continuous positive airway pressure (CPAP), and positive end-expiratory pressure (PEEP). Decisions to abate treatment in these units typically involve the withdrawal of ventilator support in order either to wean a patient from a ventilator no longer needed, or to permit a patient to die apart from a ventilator no longer wanted or no longer regarded as being in the patient's best interests.[12]

Neurological intensive care units have a variety of titles and acronyms, depending on the hospitals in which they are located (the most obvious acronym, NICU, is used by many hospitals to designate the neonatal intensive care unit). The neurologists or neurosurgeons who head these units work with patients who have head injuries, seizures, trauma, spinal cord injuries, and other cerebral or central nervous system (CNS) dysfunction. With comatose patients, the staff of the neurological unit provides emergency and ongoing support, attempts to isolate the cause of the coma (whether from drugs, cardiac arrest, stroke, trauma, subarachnoid hemorrhage, hepatic encephalopathy, or some metabolic disturbance), determines the level of patient consciousness, makes a prognosis regarding survival (approximately 60 percent of comatose patients die without recovery from coma, and another 12 percent never improve beyond a vegetative state), and determines when death has occurred. Diagnosis in the unit is accomplished by bedside observations of physical signs, aided by a number of technological tools: echoencephalography, EEGs, cerebral angiography, CT scanning, MRI, and lumbar puncture (in the absence of an intracranial mass). Treatment options include prolonged intubation, tracheostomy, mechanical ventilation, technological nutrition and hydration, intravenous medications, surgical intervention (e.g., in some cases of cerebral hemorrhage), and frequent changes in patient body position. Decisions to abate treatment often consist of withholding or withdrawing antibiotics, ventilatory support, and (less often) technological nutrition and hydration from patients in a persistent vegetative state.[13]

Burn centers offer intensive care to patients as the initial stage of a three-stage program of burn care. The intensive care stage for acute burn patients (30 percent of them having scald burns, 60 percent having flame burns) is followed by an intermediate care stage for patients in a chronic state (the area of full-thickness skin loss for such patients having been reduced to less than 20 percent), and then a convalescent care stage that provides therapy while autografting procedures are completed. The burn care team working with acute burn patients differs from the medical personnel in other ICUs in at least one important respect: they can make a prognosis for critically ill burn patients much more easily than intensivists in other ICUs can do with their patients. Because the depth and extent of a burn can be easily determined and quantified, and because mortality statistics for burn victims are readily available, the burn care team and their patients (if conscious and autonomous) can make decisions about treatment or treatment abatement with a degree of certitude not often experienced in other units. Consequently, if survival is unprecedented for a patient (in the case of a combination of massive

burns, severe smoke inhalation, and/or advanced age), the decision may be made
to forgo many of the treatment options available in the unit: intubation, ventilatory support, fluid replacement, antibiotics, skin grafting and surgical procedures, and so forth.[14]

In terms of their sophistication and hospital setting, all of these ICUs can be
ranked according to a stratified system. A National Institutes of Health (NIH)
Consensus Development Conference on Critical Care Medicine, which met in
1983, suggested the following classification system for all ICUs, whether multispecialty or single-purpose units. A level I unit is a comprehensive and multispecialty critical care unit (such as a university hospital research ICU), having
a physician-director (or qualified designee) immediately available at all times, a
nurse/patient ratio of 1 : 1 or greater, and all necessary invasive and noninvasive
monitoring systems in place. A level II unit may be a multipurpose or specific-
purpose unit (e.g., an RICU, CCU, NICU, or combined medical-surgical unit in
a teaching hospital or large community hospital), having a physician-director (or
designee) available in the hospital, a nurse/patient ratio of 1 : 1–1 : 3, and the
necessary invasive and noninvasive monitoring systems. A level III unit is characteristic of a community hospital; this type of unit has a physician-director (or
designee) readily available, provides in-hospital coverage by a physician cre-
dentialed by the hospital in life support and ventilator management, and has a
nurse/patient ratio of 1 : 2–1 : 4. A level IV specialty-care unit, usually found in
a small community or rural hospital, does not actually qualify as an ICU; this
type of unit provides basic CPR skills, noninvasive arrhythmia monitoring, and
a nurse/patient ratio of 1 : 4–1 : 5.[15]

All of the special types of ICUs just discussed, and others, are now firmly
established, even if inconsistently available and somewhat vaguely ranked, in the
arena of technological medicine. With the increasing importance of these units,
many of the physicians working in them have become convinced that the practice
of medicine required in the units is significantly different from the conventional
approach of modern medicine. Whereas mainstream medicine has steadily become more specialized, with patients "divided" according to organ systems for
each specialty and subspecialty, most critically ill patients have multiple vital
organ failure. And in most of these patients, but not all, organ systems fail in a
sequential pattern:

Respiratory failure usually occurs first, followed in order by cardiac, renal, hepatic,
hematologic, and gastrointestinal failure. This pattern results from the frequency of occurrence of causative factors that result in failure of specific organs; organ susceptibility
to the common factors of low flow, hypoxia, malnutrition, and sepsis; preexisting organ
disease; and the effect of failure of one organ on others.[16]

Increased awareness of the multiple organ failure syndrome—and the limitations of organ-specific specialists in dealing with the syndrome—led to the
founding of the Society of Critical Care Medicine. From its founding in 1970,

the society has grown to more than 2,200 members and now publishes its own journal, sponsors research symposia on critical care topics, and actively participates in major conferences such as the NIH conference mentioned earlier. In September 1980, the American Board of Medical Specialties approved critical care medicine as a subspecialty of internal medicine, anesthesiology, pediatrics, and surgery. Five years later, in March 1985, the same board—responding to an ongoing debate between organ-specific specialists (optimal care for critically ill patients requires specialized medical knowledge of an underlying disease pathophysiology) and critical care specialists (optimal care for critically ill patients often requires medical knowledge and technical skills that are multidisciplinary in nature)—decreed that physicians wishing to become certified in critical care medicine must first meet the training requirements of one of the four specialty areas and then also pass a subspecialty examination in critical care medicine.[17]

Aside from the intramural politics of medicine, including the excessive claims of virtue by critical care specialists and the excessive criticisms by their traditionally oriented colleagues, it seems unquestionable that critical care medicine is here to stay. Changes in the society will undoubtedly occur, as will changes in the various ICUs, but the multidisciplinary practice of critical care medicine will surely remain in some form to apply technological advances to the needs of critically ill patients who have experienced multiple organ failure. Working with all critically ill patients, regardless of age or disease process, the personnel in critical care medicine will surely also continue to be forced to wrestle with the dilemmas posed by desperately ill patients whose conditions are beyond the capacities of technological medicine.

Three questions regarding critical care medicine have bearing on decisions to abate treatment. Which patients are most likely to benefit from intensive care? According to the NIH Consensus Development Conference, ICU effectiveness for different patients can best be understood in terms of three typical patient categories. In the first category are patients "for whom the probability of survival without ICU intervention is low, but the survival probability with such intervention is high." Common clinical examples include patients with acute reversible respiratory failure due to drug overdose, and patients with cardiac conduction disturbances resulting in cardiovascular collapse but amenable to pacemaker therapy. For these patients, the benefits of ICU care are clear. The second category consists of patients "with a low probability of survival without intensive care, whose probability of survival with intensive care may be higher." Clinical examples include patients with septic or cardiogenic shock. For these patients, the benefits of ICU care seem to outweigh the risks, but this potential benefit "is not as clear" as with the first class of patients. The third category is composed of patients admitted to an ICU because they are at risk of becoming critically ill and need the monitoring and specialized personnel available in the ICU. For these patients, the effectiveness of ICU care "varies directly with the probability of a complication and with the difference in expected outcome inside and outside the ICU."[18]

Because of this variability in ICU benefit, and because critically ill patients cannot and should not simply be randomly assigned to an ICU, critical care specialists have devised predictive scoring systems in an effort to determine the relationship between severity of illness, intensive care, and the prospect of patient survival. The two most common systems are the Therapeutic Intervention Scoring System (TISS) and the Acute Physiology and Chronic Health Evaluation (APACHE). The TISS, developed initially by David Cullen and colleagues for postoperative patients, disregards the disease process causing illness by looking instead at the technology required to treat the illness and sustain life. Introduced in 1974 and revised in 1983, the TISS now consists of 76 items of technological intervention that are graded on the basis of a four-point-scale (ECG monitoring gets one point, peritoneal dialysis gets four); the accumulated points are then used to group patients into four classes (class I patients have fewer than 10 points, class IV patients more than 40) depending on the technology and nursing care required to sustain life.[19] The APACHE, developed by William Knaus and associates, adapts the TISS scoring system so that patients can be classified according to the severity of illness rather than by therapy alone. First proposed in 1981 and revised in 1985, the APACHE system (now known as APACHE II) divides ICU patients into three categories: (1) those needing only standard care, (2) those needing ICU monitoring (by personnel or technology), and (3) those requiring active treatment. Although the majority of patients in these groups benefit from ICU care, only patients falling into the third category require "direct therapy using techniques unique to or best performed in an ICU."[20]

We will return to the ethical implications of these scoring systems later. For the moment, it should suffice to make three observations. If one of these systems (or a better one, yet to be devised) comes to have wide acceptance among intensive care specialists, such a system may prove increasingly beneficial to clinicians trying to distinguish between critically ill patients who will survive the ICU and critically ill patients whose conditions are terminal. A second and closely related point is that if a scoring system such as these can accurately measure the severity of disease, with an increase in points over a period of time indicating a deteriorating medical condition, physicians and patients (or surrogates of patients) may be greatly aided in deciding when life-sustaining treatment is no longer beneficial for an individual patient. Third, if scoring systems such as these continue to be revised and updated, one needed improvement is that of addressing the concept of benefit being used. Thus far, the proponents of these systems seem to equate "beneficial" with "survival of the ICU," without sufficient attention being given to those patients who survive the ICU experience but continue to have severely debilitated lives (and, often, death within a matter of months after leaving the ICU).

How do physicians determine the appropriate level of technology to be used with critically ill patients? There are, according to James Hassett, three levels of technology available in ICUs: a *minimally invasive* or "watchful expectance" level characterized by intermittent blood sampling, monitoring of vital signs (including cardiac rhythm), and basic nutritional and respiratory support; a *moderately invasive* or "active-intervention" level characterized by all of the first-level procedures, plus continuous indwelling monitors, initial support of a single-organ failure (the respiratory system being the organ most commonly supported), and pharmacological support (usually with inotropic agents) of monitored function; and a *maximally invasive* or "full-court press" level characterized by all of the first- and second-level procedures, plus progressive support of individual organs involved in the multiple organ failure syndrome (e.g., hemodialysis) and pharmacological intervention for advanced disease or iatrogenic complications (such as sepsis).[21]

When there is no great uncertainty about diagnosis, the level of technology selected for individual cases of critical illness depends on patient variables (prognosis apart from intervention, patient preferences, effects of preexisting concurrent conditions, availability of an ICU bed), physician variables (prior experience, prejudices, hospital protocol), and variables related to the technology itself (relative ease of intervention, cost, possible side effects). In cases of medical uncertainty regarding diagnosis or the etiology of an illness, the level of technology selected may be inappropriate. If inappropriate, the level will usually be too high for the simple reason that an uncertain clinician normally chooses an initial level of technology that is higher than may be necessary.[22]

Two additional observations are in order. In relation to decisions to abate treatment, cases to be presented later will demonstrate a recurring problem with physicians and ICU technology: the greater the certainty a physician has that the technology being used in a given case is in the patient's best interests (i.e., the level of technology as well as particular technologies within the level), the more likely he or she is to resist requests to abate treatment by a patient or family that go counter to that medical certainty. To extend Hassett's basketball metaphor, a physician convinced that a "full-court press" is in order to combat disease and death is not likely to be receptive to requests to institute a fairly passive "zone" defense. Patients under the care of a physician who is uncertain about how much technology to use can be in an equally difficult position: the physician may engage in "technological overkill," resist patient or surrogate requests to withdraw some of the technological intervention, and refuse to admit (for reasons of professional pride, or perceptions of legal culpability) that the level of technology being used is inappropriate.

What other problems sometimes accompany the use of ICU technology? First, the ICU environment can have deleterious psychological effects on patients in the unit. Although the term *ICU psychosis* is much too general to describe adverse patient responses, there can be little doubt that patients often find the ICU to be a terrifying environment characterized by machines, tubes, strangers, lack of privacy, and severely limited visiting by loved ones; they may consequently respond with some combination of anxiety, fear, denial, despondency, depression, acute delirium, hostility, and refusal to obey rules.[23] Second, the use of technology can have harmful effects on the medical conditions of patients. Rather than experiencing improved health and being dismissed from the critical care unit, some patients experience iatrogenic complications (e.g., from ventilators, pulmonary artery catheters, hospital-acquired infections), prolonged suffering (e.g., the adult respiratory distress syndrome), and unnecessary treatment.[24] Third, the ICU environment affects the medical personnel who work in it. For physicians, there can be preoccupation with technical details, sensory overload, stress due to the constant exposure to crises and death, lack of regular hours and regular shifts, indecision when confronted with a discrepancy between technical data (whether monitored or computer-processed data) and information gained from physical examination of a patient, psychological changes brought about by an unbridled desire for victories over disease and death, and seeming indifference to the nontechnical needs of patients and families and nurses. Nurses in critical care are specifically subject to stress due to interpersonal conflicts with a supervisor or a physician, uncooperative patients, repeated emergency situations, unnecessary prolongation of patients' lives, and emotional reactions to patient suffering and patient deaths. Finally, ICU technology and the accompanying philosophy of care can have counterproductive results unintended by anyone. One such result occurs within the ICU whenever patients become completely dependent on the technology in the unit for their survival (the best example being respirator-dependent patients). Two other unintended results occur outside the ICU whenever patients or medical personnel become so enamored with the notion of "intensive care" that they downgrade the significance of "regular" care given on general medical-surgical floors, and whenever former ICU patients remain so disabled by their diseases and the complications resulting from ICU treatment that they can no longer have productive lives.

In terms of decisions to abate treatment, some of the psychological problems just mentioned can mean that a conscious ICU patient may be indecisive or inconsistent regarding the continuation/discontinuation of certain modes of treatment because of considerations not directly related to the failure of organ systems (e.g., medications administered to counter these psychological states). In addition, the unusual environment of the ICU occasionally prevents a treatment-abatement decision from being carried out. For example, some respirator patients experience anxiety when the weaning process begins, become more anxious during a psychiatric consultation, and are thus rendered physically incapable, at least transiently, of further weaning because of the increased metabolic demands and cardiac work brought on by the anxiety.[25]

Geriatric Medicine

Geriatric medicine, having developed rather slowly in the United States and the United Kingdom over the past four decades, differs in several ways from the newer subspecialty of critical care medicine. The image of critical care medicine, carefully cultivated by intensivists and hospital administrators, is one of glamour, action, high technology, excitement, heroism, novelty, and "the thrill of victory" against disease and death; the image of geriatric medicine, largely attributable to stereotypes used by persons outside the field, tends to be one of routine, passivity, age-imposed limitations, physical and/or mental debilitation, oldness, and "the agony of defeat" by chronic diseases and death. The patients in critical care medicine are located in highly specialized, geographically limited areas of hospitals; the patients in geriatric medicine are spread over large portions of the medical map—ICUs, oncology wards, geriatric wards, outpatient clinics or departments, nursing homes, and hospice units—with some patients having limited contact with any institutional setting for health care. The medical needs of critically ill patients (with age as only one of several variables) are understood by intensivists to be usually correctable by technological procedures, through organ system monitoring, advanced life support, and therapeutic interventions; the medical needs of patients in geriatric medicine, while often met by technological procedures, are understood in a broader sense by geriatricians, who view life-sustaining technological intervention as only one of several avenues of medical care. Furthermore, critical care medicine, having enjoyed impressive growth and unparalleled funding in recent years, now confronts a future made problematic by more limited budgets, an ongoing intramural debate with organ-specific specialists, and critical questions regarding the benefits of intensive care; geriatric medicine, having struggled for years for appropriate recognition, faces a future in which increasing numbers of persons (inside and outside medicine) recognize the rapidly aging nature of the population, understand advanced age as an important medical variable in patients, and forecast an unprecedented need for specialists in geriatric medicine over the next several decades.

In one respect, the historical development of geriatric medicine can be dated from 1914: that was the year the first American textbook on the subject was published by I. L. Nascher, who also is credited with having coined the term "geriatrics."[26] The textbook must not have sold very well, because a quarter of a century passed before the professional development of geriatric medicine began in earnest. The American Geriatrics Society (AGS) was established in 1942, with two categories of membership: voting membership was restricted to physicians, while membership without voting rights was offered to interested lay persons.[27] The American Gerontological Society was founded in 1945, with the expressed purpose of having a broadly based constituency interested in the multiple needs, problems, and contributions of elderly persons in the United States.

In Great Britain, the Medical Society for the Care of the Elderly (MSCE) was established in 1945. However, a more generally recognized starting point for geriatric medicine in Great Britain occurred the following year with the inauguration of the National Health Service (NHS). Two types of health care institutions had previously dominated the scene: the traditional "charity hospitals" had offered medical care only to patients having acute, treatable conditions, whereas the old "workhouses" had tended to have a patient population largely characterized by elderly, impoverished patients with chronic conditions. Under the NHS, the former institutions evolved into district general hospitals. The latter institutions became geriatric hospitals, with increased government funding for specialists in geriatric medicine willing to help clean up the old workhouses, correct the abuses in them, and provide quality medical care for a constituency primarily composed of elderly patients.[28] In 1959 the MSCE became known officially as the British Geriatric Society.

After four decades, geriatric medicine in both countries has yet to reach the position of acceptance and recognition long coveted by its practitioners. In the United States, the current situation is mixed. The AGS shows sustained growth in membership, publishes a widely respected journal, and increasingly raises the possibility of geriatric medicine as an officially recognized medical specialty. In addition, a growing number of medical schools (72 of 127 schools) require geriatric education as part of the medical curriculum, medical school faculties now include approximately 200 clinicians in geriatrics, and the first certification examination for special competence in geriatric medicine was offered in 1988.[29] Yet a survey by the American Medical Association (A.M.A.) indicated that only 0.2 percent of all responding physicians listed geriatric care as one of three possible areas of emphasis in their practice. In other words, the survey suggested that of 363,000 physicians, only 715 regarded geriatric medicine as an area of specialization.[30] These figures are problematic enough as indicators of a current need for additional specialists in geriatric medicine. When projected as far into the future as the year 2010, figures from the A.M.A.—and other studies by the Institute of Medicine and the Rand Corporation—indicate that future medical needs of elderly patients will require redirecting a substantial number of physicians from overcrowded specialties into geriatrics, training approximately 900 additional academic specialists to teach geriatric medicine, and securing another 1,700–2,500 researchers in geriatrics.[31]

Geriatricians in Great Britain seem to have made greater advances in terms of professional recognition, and geriatric medicine as a field there seems better prepared to meet the future needs of elderly patients. Yet how that future is to be shaped is currently a matter of considerable internal debate. Some British geriatricians want the future to be shaped by the past, with geriatric medicine being limited to rehabilitation and long-term care of patients with chronic conditions; other geriatricians opt for a future shaped by age-defined categories, with geriatric medicine serving only patients over 65 and rationing health services (such as coronary care and dialysis) on the basis of patient age. Still other geriatricians prefer a future shaped by an integrationist model of health care, with geriatric medicine serving all older patients without regard to specific age, whether the patient has an acute or chronic condition, or whether the patient is in a geriatric hospital or one of the district general hospitals.[32]

At the present time geriatric medicine is characterized by four features that have bearing on decisions made about life-sustaining treatment and/or treatment abatement. First, specialists in geriatric medicine recognize that *advanced age is a significant influence* in medical care. In fact, the advancing age of individual patients affects their conditions of physical health, as well as decisions made in regard to those conditions of health, in several ways:

1. There is a *general, predictable decline in physiological function* as the years accumulate in a person's life. Although there are other factors related to this physical decline (e.g., smoking, diet, exercise habits, life-style), the independent variable of age unquestionably contributes to the deterioration of physical health: the decrease in muscle tissue mass, the decrease in the number of nerve cells, the reduction of cardiac output, the decline in kidney function, the slowing of reflexes, the diminished sense of smell and taste, the degeneration of the air sacs, the loss of weight, the diminution of sight and hearing, the increased possibility of hypertension, the lowered immunity to infection, the lessening of memory, and so forth.[33]

2. *Specific medical conditions* are statistically more common to (and sometimes limited to) persons who have lived six decades or longer. For example, CHF is 10 times more common in persons older than 75 than in persons 45–64 years of age. The risk of having coronary artery disease increases 10-fold for "low-risk" patients when they reach 70 years of age, compared to when they were 40.[34] Likewise, acute oliguric renal failure is five times more common in elderly patients than in patients aged 40.[35] The numerous other medical conditions influenced by the longevity of patients include emphysema, lung cancer, prostate cancer, amyloidosis, valvular disease, and stroke.

3. Certain *age-related limitations are imposed on therapeutic options.* Examples from pharmacology will illustrate the point. Drug therapy with older patients is complicated in several ways. The smaller body size and reduced intracellular water and lean body mass in an elderly patient means that a smaller volume of a drug (e.g., digoxin) has to be administered; the reduced renal and hepatic flow results in a prolongation of the half-life of drugs eliminated by these routes. The presence of common chronic conditions (glaucoma, glucose intolerance) increases the risk of adverse drug reactions, and the multi-drug regimens of older patients also contributes to the risk of undesirable drug interactions.[36]

4. There is an *increased risk of suicide* among older adults. For a variety of reasons (e.g., poor health, economic problems, the loss of meaningful work, the deaths of spouses and close friends, the feelings of rejection and uselessness), the suicide rate for persons over 65 is 50 percent higher than the suicide rate for the general U.S. population. Within this older population, white males over 65 are at the highest risk of any group to commit suicide.[37]

Second, the *issue of patient autonomy* has an importance in geriatric medicine unmatched by other medical fields, with the exception of psychiatry. For many elderly patients, of course, there is no question about their capacity to make decisions about their health care, or their autonomous status in deciding to refuse one or more life-sustaining treatments. The normal process of aging does not include significant intellectual impairment: simply because a person is beyond the age of 65 or 75 (or whatever age standard may be used) does not automatically mean that he or she experiences undue confusion, depression, hallucinations, or delusions, and certainly does not mean that he or she experiences dementia or delirium.

Yet, the brain is particularly vulnerable to changes in the body's internal environment. Any number of disorders, including "cardiac, pulmonary, renal, or hepatic failure; endocrine disorders; water and electrolyte disturbances; anoxia; anemia; infections; nutritional deficiencies; and hypothermia or hyperthermia," can lead to the impairment of intellectual functions (dementia) or an abnormal mental state (delirium).[38] In terms of the number of elderly persons actually affected by clinically important intellectual impairment, a task force sponsored by the National Institute on Aging estimates that 10 percent of persons over 65 are affected and 50–75 percent of residents in nursing homes are affected.[39]

Intellectual impairment in elderly persons varies according to causation, severity, and reversibility with treatment. At one end of the spectrum are cases of reversible impaired intellectual function caused by adverse effects of medication, depression, infection, and metabolic disorders. At the other end of the spectrum are a few disorders (Alzheimer's disease, multiinfarct disease, Huntington's disease, and Creutzfeldt–Jakob disease), not currently subject to effective medical treatment, that result in irreversible dementia and other neurological abnormalities.[40]

In many of these cases, at one or more points along the way, the issue of decision-making capacity arises. Has the patient demonstrated, prior to the current medical circumstances, a patterned history of decision making? Does the patient now possess the ability to understand and deliberate? Does the patient have the capacity to communicate? If so, are the communicated preferences consistent with the patient's previously demonstrated value system? Is the patient capable of understanding the available medical and moral options? Does the patient understand the predictable outcomes of these options? Is the patient aware of the seriousness of the situation?

We will discuss the matter of patient autonomy in the next chapter. We will also discuss a number of cases in subsequent chapters in which such decision-making capacity, or the lack of it, is of fundamental importance. For the moment, it should suffice simply to emphasize the centrality of the issue of patient autonomy in decisions elderly (and other) patients make about abating treatment. How should such decisions be handled by a geriatrician, especially when the patient's decision is to refuse treatment needed to sustain life? Under what circumstances should an elderly patient's decision to forgo life-sustaining treatment be overridden by the physician, the patient's family, or the courts?

Third, the *location of patients* is a more important variable in geriatric medicine than in most medical fields. As previously mentioned, the location may be a hospital (ICU, oncology ward, geriatric ward, outpatient clinic), a nursing home, a physician's office, a patient's own home, or possibly a hospice. The location in any particular case significantly influences the physician–patient relationship, the patient's psychological status, the medical technologies available, treatment protocols, a patient's adherence to recommended treatment, and decisions to abate treatment.

Nursing homes and other long-term geriatric centers provide a ready example of the importance of location in decisions about treatment or treatment abatement. Residents in nursing homes tend to be among the "oldest old" persons in society, with an average age of 82 years. The drastically reduced autonomy of residents of nursing homes often means that such persons are under the care of a geriatrician, a specialist in internal medicine, or some other randomly selected physician (selected by the nursing home staff) who does not know them or their families personally and has, at best, a limited grasp of their preferences regarding treatment modalities. Because of the prevalence of significant intellectual impairment among residents in nursing homes, many residents are simply unable to participate in decisions about their own care and require surrogates to make such decisions on their behalf. Moreover, nursing homes, while almost always having some resuscitation equipment, may or may not have ventilators for residents who need them; they certainly do not have the elaborate life-sustaining armamentarium available in hospitals.

In addition, the context of a nursing home or geriatric center often changes the *nature* of decisions to abate treatment, whether such decisions are made by a geriatrician or someone else. Three types of such decisions are worth noting. One type of decision to abate treatment in nursing homes is also commonly made in hospitals: a DNR (do not resuscitate) decision on the part of a patient or patient's surrogate, or on the part of the attending physician. However, the nursing home context gives a DNR decision a somewhat different meaning, in that the detection of cardiac or respiratory arrest in a nursing home resident is predictably much slower than with hospitalized patients, resuscitation equipment is more limited and less sophisticated, and the resident's advanced age and multiple chronic conditions tend to make resuscitation efforts a less urgent option than with acute care patients in a hospital.

A second type of treatment-abatement decision in nursing homes is limited to nonhospital settings: the DNH (do not hospitalize) decision, normally made by the attending physician. Although a geriatrician or any other physician working in a nursing home realizes that many acute illnesses require the resources of a hospital, the physician may judge in a given case that "the experience of hospitalization would be more confusing and painful than the therapeutic gain would warrant."[41] The option of hospitalization poses risks for nursing home residents in two different ways: falls, nosocomial infections, and adverse drug reactions are hazards for an elderly patient in a hospital; in addition, that patient, upon return to the nursing home, may transmit a nosocomial infection to other nursing home residents.

A third type of decision to abate treatment is more easily made in nursing homes than in hospitals: the DNT (do not treat) decision, which in practice tends to be a decision to limit treatment rather than to terminate treatment entirely. Because of a resident's advanced age, possible mental impairment, and multiple chronic conditions, all parties involved in a case—patient (if possible), physician, family (if available), nursing home staff—frequently judge that the appropriate course of action in a particular case is to provide comfort for the resident rather than to attempt to prolong the patient's life.[42]

In some instances, decisions to abate treatment in nursing homes and geriatric centers become a matter of institutional policy. In Minnesota, for example, a recent study found that 66 percent of the surveyed long-term care facilities accept DNR orders, 73 percent of the institutions accept limited-treatment care plans, and 16 percent have limited-treatment protocols as a part of administrative policy. The study discovered that institutions with denominational connections and/or ethics committees are more likely to have limited-treatment policies.[43]

A specific institutional example of treatment-abatement policies is the Levindale Hebrew Geriatric Center and Hospital in Baltimore. For years, the policy at Levindale had been to divide critically ill patients into two groups: one group of patients was to be resuscitated in the event of cardiac or respiratory arrest, and one group of patients was not to be resuscitated. However, no one seemed confident regarding the criteria used to make this distinction among critically ill patients. A few years ago geriatricians and other staff members, having studied the limited-treatment policy of Massachusetts General Hospital, devised a classification system for the patients at Levindale in the dual hope of increasing patient autonomy and establishing clearer medical and moral grounds for limiting treatment in individual cases. Levindale thus adopted a classification system for critically ill and terminally ill patients (with class A patients receiving "maximum therapeutic effort'' and class D patients receiving "no therapeutic effort''), a separate classification system concerning resuscitation (class 1 calling for "maximum resuscitative effort," class 2 for "limited effort," and class 3 for "no resuscitative effort''), and institutional policies regarding how these guidelines are to be used. To maximize patient autonomy, long-term patients, if autonomous, are asked a question at an appropriate time such as the following: "While you are here, there may come a time when you become too ill to communicate with us about your medical care. Are there any specific instructions you might want us to follow at such a time?''[44]

Fourth, the *role of the physician is different* in geriatric medicine than in most medical fields. Because of the advanced age of geriatric patients, a specialist in geriatric medicine regularly works with patients having long-term medical problems. Even when geriatric patients have acute illnesses, those illnesses may be complicated by underlying chronic conditions. Even when a patient's condition is diagnosed as terminal, the patient may require medical care for at least 6 months; in some instances he or she may require medical care for 2 years or more. Because of the increased percentage of geriatric patients having intellectual impairment, compared with younger patients, geriatricians have a greater appreciation of patient autonomy than many physicians do. Likewise, geriatricians are more cognizant of the difficulties posed by patients having diminished capacity to make decisions, patients never having had such decision-making capacity, and other legally incompetent patients. Furthermore, because of the multiple locations for geriatric patients, geriatricians seem to have unusual flexibility in adapting treatment options to different circumstances, unusual openness to the views expressed by the families and trusted friends of patients, and unusual sensitivity to the importance of home and familiar territory for elderly patients.

With regard to life-sustaining treatment, specialists in geriatric medicine differ from many of their medical colleagues in two important respects. First, geriatricians are aware that life-sustaining efforts with elderly persons extend beyond the use of dramatic and complex technology in hospital settings. Of course, geriatricians use technological interventions (respirators, antibiotics, nasogastric feeding, intravenous hydration, surgery) when the medical and moral circumstances call for these interventions with elderly patients. However, they point out that life-sustaining interventions with elderly persons often involve measures not usually connected with technological medicine, yet possibly crucial to the sustaining of individual lives: adequate housing, Meals-on-Wheels, visiting nurses, home health aides, occupational and physical therapy, day care centers, foster-grandparent programs, and so on.[45]

A second difference concerns the limitations of medical technology. In contrast to many physicians, specialists in geriatric medicine realize that the "technological imperative" perceived by such physicians simply does not apply to many cases involving elderly patients. Stated another way, geriatricians recognize that "appropriate medical practice does not always mean employing the guns of medical technology."[46] The issue is not whether technological intervention is possible, or whether a particular technological intervention once started can morally be stopped, but "whether any of various courses of action and inaction that might be available to a patient would be more beneficial to that patient than his or her current status."[47]

What does all of this do to the role of the geriatrician? It changes the role of the physician from combatant against disease and death to companion and comforter in the presence of debilitating illness, suffering, and limited life span. In this role the physician uses various technological interventions when appropriate, but also engages in perhaps the more humane art of medicine by making sure elderly patients receive appropriate skin care, turning in bed, bowel and bladder management, mouth and eye hygiene, nutrition, and hydration. As stated by Christine Cassel, the geriatrician's role thus combines "competent familiarity with the capabilities of the latest in medical technology, a discerning sense of judgment about when and when not to use such interventions, and the courage and energy to take seriously the social role of advocate for a patient."[48] Such a role may not be "gratifying to those who want to heal and cure, but there are other satisfactions in performing tasks that ease the path to death" for elderly patients in need of such care.[49]

Hospice Care

Recognition of the limitations of medical technology to meet the needs of critically ill and, in particular, terminally ill patients is also a distinguishing feature of hospice care as it is practiced in the United Kingdom and the United States. As explained by Samuel Stoddard, the origin of the term *hospice* centuries ago designated a philosophy of care quite different from the philosophy of care one often encounters in modern hospitals:

[The hospice] offered an open door of welcome not only to the sick and dying, but to the hungry wayfarer, the woman in labor, the needy poor, the orphan, or the leper with his bell. The common base or denominator of the offering was "hospitality" in its original sense of protection, refreshment, "cherysshing," and fellowship, rather than the demand of a patient for a cure.[50]

In its current usage, the term hospice represents a combination of theory and practice. At the level of theory, hospice is a philosophy of care that differs in significant ways from the conventional philosophy of care held by many intensive care specialists, oncologists, and other medical specialists who work with patients having terminal conditions. At the level of practice, hospice comprises a system of terminal care that has had a significant impact on the practice of medicine in approximately two dozen countries around the world.

The philosophy of hospice care can be expressed through a series of eight evaluative statements.

1. *It is better to go through the terminal phase of one's life in knowledge than in ignorance about one's conditon.* Like the majority of adults in the United Kingdom and the United States, persons who become hospice patients are probably going to die from chronic conditions. However, in contrast to most adults who become terminally ill with chronic conditions, hospice patients are more likely to know that they are dying. The reason for this difference is simple. Depending on the value systems of their physicians, nonhospice patients may be victimized by a conspiracy of silence that keeps important information from them because they are considered unable to handle such devastating information. By contrast, persons entering a hospice program have almost always been told that they are dying, that further efforts at curative treatment are not recommended, and that they should embark on "the process of adjustment whereby one comes to terms with death."[51] Of course hospice patients vary in their willingness to accept this unwelcome news, and some hospice patients deny for a period of time that they are not going to recover. Sooner or later, however, hospice patients begin to confront the personal reality of dying, and they are helped by hospice personnel who regard death as an inevitable, natural event about which one can ask honest questions and express honest doubts and fears.

2. *It is better to maximize the quality of one's remaining days, weeks, or months than to prolong life without regard to quality.* One of the philosophical strands running through contemporary medicine is a vitalist perspective on life, according to which the prolongation of a patient's life is the ultimate good of responsible medical care. By contrast, the hospice philosophy recognizes that the prolongation of a patient's life is sometimes not possible without inflicting an enormous amount of suffering on that patient. Simply put, two of the goals of medicine—prolongation of life and relief of suffering—are sometimes mutually exclusive. Moreover, the hospice philosophy recognizes that the prolongation of life is not an ultimate good to be sought at all costs, so that even when the prolongation of life is technically possible without undue suffering, other considerations having to do with a patient's continuing ability to function may still rule out certain life-prolonging procedures. The purpose of medical treatment with terminally ill patients is thus not the addition of days to one's already limited life span, but the prolongation of a patient's ability to "make today count" during the terminal phase of life.

3. *It is better to adapt medical technology to terminal care than to place terminal care beyond the boundary of medical technology.* Hospice physicians often remark about their medical colleagues' overly narrow understanding of medical technology. They make this observation because it often seems that physicians working outside a hospice context understand medical technology

only in a curative mode: the purpose of technology is limited to the restoration of health, the prolongation of life, and the "salvaging" of patients who would otherwise die. When physicians with this perspective on technology encounter patients who cannot be salvaged—no matter how much medical technology is used—they seem to reach a conceptual cul-de-sac. Not able to cure or to prolong life, they simply say out of resignation, "there's nothing more I can do." For hospice physicians, such a statement is shortsighted and misplaced. Rather than placing terminally ill patients outside the boundary of technology, the hospice physician's task becomes that of discovering the appropriate application of technology in a caring mode. As stated by Robert Twycross and Sylvia Lack, the question is not " 'to treat or not to treat?' but 'what is appropriate treatment?' given the patient's biological prospects in the context of personal and social circumstances."[52]

4. *It is better to have coordinated terminal care than to have fragmented terminal care.* Terminally ill patients outside hospice programs often experience a disconcerting fragmentation of medical care, for a number of reasons. They may be under the care of several medical specialists. They may have to go to several clinics or hospitals to receive their medical advice and treatment. The health care professionals who work with them may be on "different wavelengths" (e.g., concerning truthtelling with terminally ill patients). The professionals working with them may conceptualize their needs and problems in terms of separable categories (e.g., medical, emotional, religious). Also, the various professionals involved in their cases may give them differing "signals" regarding prognosis, treatment possibilities, and the expected trajectory of their medical conditions. By contrast, the hospice approach to terminal care involves coordinated teamwork. Under the leadership of a medical director, an interdisciplinary team typically composed of a nurse (in the role of patient care coordinator), a psychologist, a social worker, and a director of volunteers devises an appropriate plan of care for the patient and family, meets regularly to discuss and revise the plan of care as needed, coordinates visits with the patient (especially if the patient is in a home care hospice), and deals with the variable problems and needs that can be experienced by a patient while under hospice care. Because of this teamwork, a hospice patient receives coordinated, consistent, dependable terminal care not often found in hospitals or nursing homes.

5. *It is better to live out one's remaining time in the midst of family and friends than in the midst of strangers.* The physical and social setting one inhabits while terminally ill has a significant impact on the manner in which one approaches death. In this regard, a hospital can be a terrible place to be terminally ill, because in many hospitals a dying patient is physically isolated from other patients, under the care of strangers, regarded as a failure by physicians and nurses bent on curative procedures, surrounded by unfamiliar equipment, subject

to innumerable invasions of privacy, and limited in contacts with visitors. Hospice patients, by contrast, are in more familiar, personal settings: if part of a home care hospice, they spend most of their time in the familiar surroundings of their own homes; and if part of a freestanding hospice or hospital-based hospice, they experience considerable freedom in terms of decorating their rooms, having visitors, and moving about in a facility (or portion thereof) specifically designed for terminally ill patients. Any of these hospice settings increases the likelihood that one will die in the midst of a caring community, not in the midst of strangers.

6. *It is better to include the family in terminal care than to care for a dying patient in isolation.* In contrast to the practices of many hospitals, which tend to isolate terminally ill patients from family members through age- and time-limited visiting policies, the hospice philosophy of care builds terminal care around the family. In fact, the family (or close friends, in some cases) is crucial to hospice care in two ways. First, home care hospices usually require a family member (or friend) to take on the role of primary careperson (PCP). Although nurses and volunteers assume some of the responsibilities of patient care and home management, the PCP has the greatest responsibility of providing ongoing care whenever and however that care may be needed. Second, the family is regarded not only as a provider of care but also as a recipient of hospice care. To that end, volunteers help meet not only the patient's needs but the needs of family members as well (by providing respite care, counseling, shopping, childcare, cooking, cleaning, etc.). In most hospice programs, family members continue to receive hospice care after the patient's death through a variety of bereavement services.

7. *It is better to relieve a patient's pain through effective medical management than either to be overly concerned about drug addiction or to relieve the patient's pain through intentional killing.* Not all terminally ill patients have problems with pain. In fact, studies of patients with advanced cancer indicate that one-third to one-half of such patients remain pain-free or have negligible pain.[53] Nevertheless, approximately 40 percent of patients with advanced cancer experience "severe, usually constant, pain," with the proportion of patients with severe pain increasing dramatically within the last week of life, and patients with prostate cancer and bone metastases reporting the greatest difficulty with pain.[54] Much of the medical management of hospice patients is therefore aimed at effective pain control, whenever that can be achieved, along with maintaining patient alertness. To attain the dual goal of effective pain control and patient alertness, the hallmark of hospice care involves (1) innovative administration (2) on a regular, preventive schedule of (3) the most effective drugs available. Given the frequent, if not complete, success of this approach to pain management, hospice physicians and nurses are convinced that concerns over patient drug addiction are misplaced and relatively unimportant. Likewise, especially in Brit-

ain where hospice care is often presented as an alternative to euthanasia, hospice physicians believe that effective pain control with terminally ill patients makes euthanasia a relatively unimportant if not bogus issue.[55]

8. *It is better to go through the terminal phase of life without worry over medical costs than to be concerned that one's medical expenses will bankrupt the family.* Terminal care is expensive, in whatever setting it occurs. In the United States, the National Hospice Study arrived at the following comparative figures: cancer patients receiving conventional oncology care in the last year of life average $14,799 in medical costs, patients in hospital-based hospice programs average $12,698, and patients in home care hospice programs average $10,798.[56] Many of these patients have insurance and Medicare coverage, but these financial resources do not always cover all of the expenses in terminal care; also, some terminally ill patients have no financial coverage at all. Unfortunately, that means that in an era of increasing numbers of for-profit hospitals, DRGs and other cost-containment practices, and the dismissal from hospitals of older patients "quicker and sicker" than ever before, terminally ill patients in need of prolonged inpatient care may be denied that care if they or their family cannot foot the bill. By contrast, the hospice philosophy calls for optimal terminal care regardless of a patient's ability to pay. This care, for hospices managing to survive financially, is generally covered through donations, fund-raising efforts, and, for some hospices, Medicare payments.[57]

In addition to this philosophy of care, hospice is also a system of terminal care that, especially since the early 1970s, has become an alternative within mainstream medicine in Britain, Canada, and the United States. The "roots" of the modern system of hospice care go back to Ireland in the middle of the nineteenth century. Concerned that persons dying with tuberculosis, cancer, and other chronic conditions often had no place to end their lives other than "workhouses" (or "poor law" institutions), the Irish Sisters of Charity established Our Lady's Hospice in Dublin in 1846 for the purpose of providing shelter and care for such persons. They subsequently established a similar institution in London: St. Joseph's Hospice, founded in 1905, offered long-term care for patients with chronic conditions as well as terminal care for patients with limited life expectations.[58]

More than four decades later Cicely Saunders, the pioneer of the modern hospice system, began to do research on pain control in advanced-cancer patients at St. Joseph's, as well as at St. Thomas' and St. Luke's Hospitals. In 1947 she worked with a terminally ill patient, a Jew from Warsaw, at St. Thomas's Hospital: before he died David Tasma became the "founding patient" of St. Christopher's Hospice (which would not be constructed until 1967) by giving Saunders a financial gift "to be a window in your home."[59]

St. Christopher's Hospice, built in Syndenham (a suburb of London), became the original model of a modern hospice. Constructed as a residential center for alternative medical care, St. Christopher's differed from earlier hospices in two important respects: it was the first hospice planned to care for a mixed group of patients (most of them with terminal conditions, but some requiring long-term chronic care), and it was the first hospice planned as a center for research and teaching on the management of terminal disease. As Saunders explains the purpose of her institution, St. Christopher's "offers an alternative form of treatment to the acute care of the general hospital, not in opposition but as a further resource for those for whom that is no longer appropriate."[60]

More than 20 years later, the personnel at St. Christopher's carry out several functions. Some of them are responsible for meeting the multiple needs (medical, emotional, and religious) of the patients who occupy the 62 beds in the facility. With an average patient stay of 3 weeks, an average of 15 patient deaths per week, and a mixed patient population (usually 54 cancer patients and 8 patients with ALS) described as "a community of the unlike," the residential staff has plenty of work to do. Other personnel, primarily nurses, are responsible for St. Christopher's home care program for terminally ill persons living within a 6-mile radius of the hospice. Since 2 million people live within that radius, the home care team also has plenty to do. Still other personnel are responsible for ongoing research projects, educational programs, and working with the 5,000 visitors from all parts of the world who visit St. Christopher's each year. When asked for a concise statement of the approach to terminal care at St. Christopher's, the staff members repeat the statement they make to new patients: "We can't cure your illness, but we can keep you comfortable."[61]

The hospice movement in Britain has gone through many changes over the past two decades, and several variations on the hospice theme can now be found throughout the country. In fact, at least five distinct models of hospice care are now available, with some of them completely outside the NHS, others receiving funds entirely through the NHS, and others operating on a combination of NHS and nongovernmental funding (St. Christopher's, for example, gets 45 percent of its annual budget from the NHS and the rest from donations). The British models of hospice care take the following forms:[62]

free standing residential units, such as St. Christopher's, geographically separate from all hospitals, partially or completely independent from the NHS, with a multidisciplinary clinical team, control over all beds in the facility, and freedom from bureaucratic entanglements at the NHS

hospital-based units, such as the Sir Michael Sobell House connected with Churchill Hospital in Oxford, partially funded by both the National Society for Cancer Relief (NSCR) and the NHS, offering both inpatient and outpatient services for terminally ill patients, sharing some operational expenses (house-keeping, laundry) with the adjoining hospital, benefiting from the financial security provided by NHS funding, and having ready access to the laboratory facilities and medical consultants in the hospital

home care teams, frequently called Macmillan nurses because of the origin of their funding, supported by NSCR, functioning either as an organizational alternative to residential hospices or as a supplement to residential care (both St. Christopher's and Sobell House have home care teams), and offering domiciliary services to dying patients because such services are less expensive than a residential hospice and are preferred by patients wishing to remain at home (30 percent of cancer patients in Britain die at home)

symptom control teams in hospitals, also known as support teams or Macmillan teams, are advisory palliative care teams initiated at St. Thomas's Hospital, now funded by the NSCR for hospitals throughout the country in order to provide hospice care for the majority of cancer patients (65 percent) who die in hospitals

a hospice for children, the first of its kind in the world, known as Helen House (because of a terminally ill girl who inspired its creation), opened in Oxford in 1982 under the direction of Mother Frances Dominica, described as "a home away from home for chronically ill children," operated by a multidis-ciplinary staff, offering residential care for 3–4 weeks a year (three to four visits of several days each) per child, meeting the multiple needs of a mixed population of up to eight children (the most common conditions being vari-ations of the mucopolysaccharidoses, multiple sclerosis, and cancer), and receiving its funding from the NHS and donations.

The hospice movement came to North America in the early 1970s. In Canada, the first hospice to open was the Palliative Care Unit at the Royal Victoria Hospital in Montreal. This hospital-based hospice was established in 1975 with Balfour Mount, sometimes referred to as "Mr. Hospice in Canada," as its medical director. In the United States, the first hospice went through several stages of development. Under the leadership of several persons in New Haven, the Connecticut Hospice was incorporated in 1971 and had several temporary administrative offices in its early years. A home care program began there in 1973 under the medical direction of Sylvia Lack. The hospice received $1.5 million from the Connecticut legislature and $1 million from Congress in 1977 to fund an inpatient facility, moved into the facility at Branford (outside New Haven) in 1979, and since that time has provided inpatient care, home care, training and research opportunities for professionals, and educational programs for an audience extending far beyond the state of Connecticut.

The growth of hospices in the United States has been dramatic, especially during the 1980s. In 1977, when the National Hospice Organization (NHO) was incorporated in Washington, D.C., there were fewer than 50 hospices under development. Two years later, when the Connecticut Hospice moved into its permanent facility, there were approximately 200 hospices in various stages of development throughout the country. By 1982, when Congress passed legislation providing for hospice reimbursement under Medicare, there were approximately 900 hospices; an unknown number of hospice programs had already failed because of inadequate funding. By 1986, figures provided by the NHO indicated that there were approximately 1,400 hospices, 8,000 hospice caregivers, and 100,000 hospice patients nationwide.

Of these hospices, approximately 200 are Medicare-certified and approximately 100 are accredited by the Joint Commission on the Accreditation of Healthcare Organizations. In addition to this classification, U.S. hospices can be classified according to organizational model, with the following five types represented: (1) a few freestanding units, such as the Connecticut Hospice, (2) hospital-based units, which account for approximately half of the U.S. hospices, (3) independent home care units, (4) home care units affiliated with home healthcare agencies, and (5) a few hospices for children, such as St. Mary's in New York and Casa de Niños in Houston. The National Hospice Study, in a simplification that may not have been necessary, placed all of these hospices in two categories: hospices with control over beds were classified as hospital-based units, and hospices without beds were classified as home care units.[63]

Given that all these hospices offer dying patients an alternative to the medical treatment they would receive in hospitals (e.g., in conventional oncology units), how does the treatment given hospice patients in the United Kingdom and the United States actually differ from conventional treatment? First, as already indicated, the *philosophy of treatment* in hospice programs differs from that in conventional medicine. Working with patients who have been diagnosed as being terminally ill, hospice physicians and nurses do not function in a curative mode, are not motivated by the "technological imperative," and thus do not administer treatments in an effort to prolong life. Rather, they administer treatments that are *appropriate* to a patient's biological condition, personal preferences, social circumstances, and need for pain relief and symptom management, with the aim of enabling the patient to live as fully as possible during the time he or she has remaining. Applying this philosophy to the treatment of advanced-cancer patients, Twycross and Lack state:

In far-advanced cancer the primary aim of treatment is no longer to prolong life but to make the life that remains as comfortable and as meaningful as possible. Thus, what may be appropriate treatment in an acutely ill patient may be inappropriate in the dying. Nasogastric tubes, intravenous infusions, antibiotics, cardiac resuscitation, and artificial respiration are all primarily supportive measures for use in acute or acute-on-chronic illnesses to assist a patient through the initial period towards recovery of health. To use such measures in patients who are close to death and have no expectancy of a return to health is generally inappropriate, and therefore bad medicine. Doctors have no right or duty, legal or ethical, to prescribe a lingering death.[64]

Second, hospice physicians and nurses recognize that "medical care is a continuum, ranging from complete cure at one end to symptom control at the other."[65] When cure is not possible, appropriate treatment may consist of anticancer palliation, or palliative treatment of ALS, CHF, AIDS, or whatever condition a patient has. In cases where palliative treatment is no longer effective, appropriate treatment consists of symptom control "as an end in itself." Moreover, when even symptom control cannot be managed, it is appropriate to "give death a chance": "The art of medicine, in this respect, is to decide when life sustenance is essentially futile and when to allow death to occur without further impediment."[66]

Third, the medical conditions of terminally ill patients usually mean that some kinds of treatment are inappropriate. Hospice patients, compared with hospital patients, are significantly less likely to receive diagnostic blood tests or X-ray examinations, or therapeutic interventions such as chemotherapy, radiotherapy, artificial ventilation, surgery, transfusions, or intravenous therapy.[67] Yet, Twycross and Lack emphasize that "it is important not to pigeon-hole a particular type of treatment into a specific category, but to keep the therapeutic aim clearly in mind when employing treatment of any kind."[68] Joanne Lynn observes that "relatively aggressive therapies" are occasionally justifiable, partially because of the ambiguities of prognosis, to control current symptoms and to "forestall likely future symptoms."[69] Thus appropriate treatment may, in a relatively few cases, call for palliative radiotherapy or chemotherapy for tumors, a diverting colostomy, or even antibiotic therapy for pneumonia in a patient having advanced cancer. In such instances, a "2-day rule" is sometimes recommended: if an advanced-cancer patient is "holding his own" after 2 days of straightforward symptom management, then a more aggressive therapy (such as antibiotics for pneumonia) may be prescribed; if the patient's condition has deteriorated over the 2 days, such treatment should not be prescribed, except on symptom control grounds alone.[70]

Finally, the management of terminal disease in hospice patients calls for innovative efforts in pain control and symptom management. For pain control, especially in advanced-cancer patients, hospice physicians and nurses often find the conventional "prn" (*pro re nata,* "as required") administration of drugs to be the cause of much unrelieved distress in patients. In fact, some hospice physicians indicate that for advanced cancer patients, "prn" means "physical relief negligible."[71] A preferable alternative is a regular, anticipatory, or preventive administration of the most effective narcotics (in Britain and Canada, morphine or heroin; in the United States, morphine, hydromorphone, methadone, or levorphanol) and other drugs available for the dual purpose of preventing the recurrence of pain and avoiding undue sedation.[72]

Symptom management requires preventive, flexible, and often novel efforts by the hospice team. Given the multiple symptoms other than pain that accompany advanced cancer, hospice personnel are continually on the lookout for better ways of caring for patients having anorexia, dyspnea, constipation, nausea, vomiting, decubitus ulcers, and other alimentary symptoms. Consequently, hospices are always ready to try special mattresses (e.g., egg crate mattresses, special airflow mattresses), improved wheelchairs, novel therapeutic equipment (e.g., "port-a-caths"), and other forms of caring for patients who need comfort even though they cannot be cured.

In sum, critically ill patients present physicians and other health care personnel with a variety of medical challenges, and with a variety of circumstances in which abating treatment sometimes becomes an alternative to a medical "full-court press." Of course, whether treatment abatement actually occurs, and the precise forms it takes when it occurs, depend on numerous variables, such as the clinical setting, the preferences of patients regarding treatment and treatment abatement, the capacity of critically ill patients actually to make decisions concerning treatment abatement, the views of family members, the views of attending physicians, and the involvement of institutional ethics committees in such decisions. For these reasons, the clinical settings discussed in this chapter represent the primary arena—the "front line," so to speak—in the debate over setting ethical and legal limits to the medical prolongation of life.

Notes

1. Stanley Joel Reiser, "The Machine at the Bedside: Technological Transformations of Practices and Values," in Stanley Joel Reiser and Michael Anbar, eds., *The Machine at the Bedside* (Cambridge and New York: Cambridge University Press, 1984), p. 18.
2. "NIH Consensus Development Conference on Critical Care Medicine," *Critical Care Medicine* 11 (June 1983): 467.
3. The "prestige technologies" are discussed in Louise B. Russell, *Technology in Hospitals* (Washington, D.C.: The Brookings Institution, 1979), pp. 99–131.
4. This schema is a revised version of the outline used by Bryan Jennett, "High Technology Medicine: How Defined and How Regarded," *Milbank Memorial Fund Quarterly* 63 (1985): 141–173. Also see the revised edition of his *High Technology Medicine* (Oxford and New York: Oxford University Press, 1986). Some of the historical data are from Stanley Joel Reiser, *Medicine and the Reign of Technology* (Cambridge and New York: Cambridge University Press, 1978).
5. Dianne Hales, "High-Tech Medicine: A Space-Age Arsenal," *Medical World News,* January 9, 1984, p. 63.
6. Jerry Adler et al., "When Life Is on the Line," *Newsweek,* March 18, 1985, pp. 50–51.
7. Lewis Thomas, *The Lives of a Cell: Notes of a Biology Watcher* (New York: Viking Press, 1974), p. 36; also see his "Notes of a Biology Watcher: The Technology of

Medicine," *The New England Journal of Medicine* 285 (December 9, 1971): 1366–68.

8. For an analysis of the moral dilemmas in neonatal ICUs, see my *Selective Nontreatment of Handicapped Newborns* (New York and Oxford: Oxford University Press, 1984).

9. See George E. Thibault, "The Medical Intensive Care Unit: A Five-Year Perspective," in Joseph E. Parillo and Stephen M. Ayres, eds., *Major Issues in Critical Care Medicine* (Baltimore: Williams & Wilkins, 1984), pp. 9–15; George E. Thibault, A.G. Mulley, G.O. Barnett et al., "Medical Intensive Care: Patients, Interventions and Costs, and Outcomes," *The New England Journal of Medicine* 302 (April 24, 1980): 938–42; John M. Kinney, "Design of the Intensive Care Unit," in James L. Berk and James E. Sampliner, eds., *Handbook of Critical Care*, 2nd ed. (Boston: Little, Brown, 1982), pp. 17–36; and James E. Sampliner, "General Care of the Critically Ill Patient," in Berk and Sampliner, *Handbook of Critical Care*, pp. 37–51.

10. See Bernadine Healy Bulkley, "The Coronary Care Unit," in Parillo and Ayres, *Major Issues in Critical Care Medicine*, pp. 3–8; Kanu Chatterjee, "Acute Heart Failure," in Berk and Sampliner, *Handbook of Critical Care*, pp. 203–26; and Hiltrud S. Mueller, "Treatment of Acute Myocardial Infarction," in William C. Shoemaker, W. Leigh Thompson, and Peter R. Holbrook, eds., *Textbook of Critical Care* (Philadelphia: W.B. Saunders, 1984), pp. 403–15.

11. Robert F. Wilson, "Surgical Intensive Care Units," in Parillo and Ayres, *Major Issues in Critical Care Medicine*, p. 29.

12. See John G. Weg, "The Respiratory Intensive Care Unit," in Parillo and Ayres, *Major Issues in Critical Care Medicine*, pp. 61–69; Hillary F. Don, "Ventilatory Management of the Critically Ill Patient," in Berk and Sampliner, *Handbook of Critical Care*, pp. 147–77; and Michael E. Douglas and John B. Downs, "Respiratory Therapy for Ventilatory Failure," in Shoemaker, Thompson, and Holbrook, *Textbook of Critical Care*, pp. 301–10.

13. See John J. Coronna, "The Neurological Intensive Care Unit," in Parillo and Ayres, *Major Issues in Critical Care Medicine*, pp. 199–205; Martin H. Weiss, "Critical Care of the Neurosurgical Patient," in Berk and Sampliner, *Handbook of Critical Care*, pp. 477–500; David L. Jackson, "Critical Care Neurology," in Shoemaker, Thompson, and Holbrook, *Textbook of Critical Care*, pp. 943–54; and several of the articles in Mark C. Rogers and Richard J. Traystman, eds., "Symposium on Neurologic Intensive Care," *Critical Care Clinics* 1/2 (July 1985): 195–425.

14. See Douglas R. Zusman, "Care of the Acute Burn Patient," in James M. Rippe and Marie E. Csete, eds., *Manual of Intensive Care Medicine* (Boston: Little, Brown, 1983), pp. 418–21; Sharon H. Imbus and Bruce E. Zawacki, "Autonomy for Burned Patients When Survival Is Unprecedented," *The New England Journal of Medicine* 297 (August 11, 1977): 309–11; Hal G. Bingham, H. Hollis Caffee, and Mary Powell, "Does an Intensive Care Burn Unit Really Make a Difference?" *Journal of the Florida Medical Association* 69 (October 1982): 858–59; and several of the articles in Thomas L. Wachtel, ed., "Symposium on Burns," *Critical Care Clinics* 1/1 (March 1985): 3–187.

15. "NIH Consensus Development Conference," pp. 468–69. Unfortunately, this ranking system reverses the numerical order of the current I–III ranking system for neonatal ICUs, which gives the *lowest* number to the *least* sophisticated units. See

Peter Budetti et al., *Case Study #10: The Costs and Effectiveness of Neonatal Intensive Care* (Washington, D.C.: Office of Technology Assessment, August 1981).

16. James L. Berk, "Multiple Organ Failure," in Berk and Sampliner, *Handbook of Critical Care*, p. 13.

17. William C. Shoemaker, W. Leigh Thompson, and Peter Holbrook, "Preface," in their edited *Textbook of Critical Care*, pp. xv–xvi; and Joseph E. Parrillo, "Critical Care Medicine," *Journal of the American Medical Association* 254 (October 25, 1985): 2228–90. Also see Ake Grenvik et al., "Critical Care Medicine: Certification as a Multidisciplinary Subspecialty," *Critical Care Medicine* 9 (February 1981): 117–25; Max Harry Weil and William C. Shoemaker, "Multispecialty Critical Care Medicine," *Critical Care Medicine* 12 (August 1984): 691; and Mark A. Kelley, "Critical Care Medicine—A New Specialty," *The New England Journal of Medicine* 318 (June 16, 1988): 1613–17.

18. "NIH Consensus Development Conference," p. 466.

19. See David J. Cullen et al., "Therapeutic Intervention Scoring System: A Method for Quantitative Comparison of Patient Care," *Critical Care Medicine* 2 (1974): 57–60; idem, "Indicators of Intensive Care in Critically Ill Patients," *Critical Care Medicine* 5 (1977): 173–79; and idem, "Therapeutic Intervention Scoring System: Update 1983," *Critical Care Medicine* 11 (January 1983): 1–3.

20. See William A. Knaus et al., "APACHE—Acute Physiology and Chronic Health Evaluation: A Physiologically Based Classification System," *Critical Care Medicine* 9 (1981): 591–97; William A. Knaus et al., "The Range of Intensive Care Services Today," *Journal of the American Medical Association* 246 (December 11, 1981): 2711–16; idem, "APACHE II: A Severity of Disease-Classification System," *Critical Care Medicine* 13 (1985): 819–29; and idem, "Prognosis in Acute Organ-System Failure," *Annals of Surgery* 202 (1985): 685–93. Also see Daniel Teres, Richard B. Brown, and Stanley Lemeshow, "Predicting Mortality of Intensive Care Unit Patients: The Importance of Coma," *Critical Care Medicine* 10 (February 1982): 86–95; and James V. Snyder et al., "Outcome of Intensive Care: An Application of a Predictive Model," *Critical Care Medicine* 9 (September 1981): 598–603.

21. James J. Hassett, "Technology's Front Line: The Intensive Care Unit," in Reiser and Anbar, *Machine at the Bedside*, p. 98.

22. Ibid., pp. 98–100.

23. Ned H. Cassem, "Critical Care Psychiatry," in Shoemaker, Thompson, and Holbrook, *Textbook of Critical Care*, pp. 981–89.

24. Roger C. Bone, "Critical Care Medicine: The Past and Changes in the Future," *Journal of the American Medical Association* 252 (October 19, 1984): 2060–61.

25. Cassem, "Critical Care Psychiatry," p. 987. Two collections of articles are especially helpful in regard to some of the ethical issues in critical care medicine. See John C. Moskop and Loretta Kopelman, eds., *Ethics and Critical Care Medicine* (Dordrecht and Boston: D. Reidel, 1985); and James P. Orlowski and George A. Kanoti, eds., *Critical Care Clinics: Ethical Moments in Critical Care Medicine* (Philadelphia: W.B. Saunders, 1986).

26. John C. Beck and Susan Vivell, "Development of Geriatrics in the United States," in Christine K. Cassel and John R. Walsh, eds., *Geriatric Medicine*, vol. 2 (New York: Springer-Verlag, 1984), p. 59.

27. Malford W. Thewlis, "History of the American Geriatrics Society," *Journal of the American Geriatrics Society* 1 (January 1953): 3–5.
28. Interviews with George Adams and Grimley Evans in Oxford, England, in July 1985. See G.F. Adams, "Eld Health," *British Medical Journal* (September 28, 1974): 789–91.
29. Patricia P. Barry and Richard J. Ham, "Geriatric Education: What the Medical Schools Are Doing Now," *Journal of the American Geriatrics Society* 33 (February 1985): 133–35; and Christine K. Cassel, "Certification: Another Step for Geriatric Medicine," *Journal of the American Medical Association* 258 (September 18, 1987): 1518–19.
30. Beck and Vivell, "Development of Geriatrics," p. 60.
31. Ibid., pp. 62–69. Also see John W. Rowe, et al., "Academic Geriatrics for the Year 2000: An Institute of Medicine Report," *The New England Journal of Medicine* 316 (May 28, 1987): 1425–28.
32. Interview with Grimley Evans in July 1985.
33. See Morris Rockstein and Marvin Sussman, *Biology of Aging* (Belmont, Calif.: Wadsworth, 1979); and Nicholas Coni, William Davison, and Stephen Webster, *Ageing: The Facts* (Oxford and New York: Oxford University Press, 1984).
34. Edward S. Murphy and Henry DeMots, "Cardiology," in Cassel and Walsh, *Geriatric Medicine,* vol. 1, pp. 155–56.
35. Stanley A. Hoffman, "Burn Injuries," in Laura B. Wilson, Sharon P. Simson, and Charles R. Baxter, eds., *Handbook of Geriatric Emergency Care* (Baltimore: University Park Press, 1984), p. 141.
36. Jerome L. Fleg, "Cardiovascular Emergencies," in Wilson, Simson, and Baxter, *Handbook of Geriatric Emergency Care,* pp. 38–39.
37. Michael Schwartz, Clark Hudak, and H.L.P. Resnik, "Suicide," in Wilson, Simson, and Baxter, *Handbook of Geriatric Emergency Care,* pp. 207–10.
38. Task Force of the National Institute on Aging, "Senility Reconsidered: Treatment Possibilities for Mental Impairment in the Elderly," *Journal of the American Medical Association* 244 (July 18, 1980): 259–60.
39. Ibid., p. 259. Also see Ruth Macklin, "The Geriatric Patient: Ethical Issues in Care and Treatment," in Bart Gruzalski and Carl Nelson, eds., *Value Conflicts in Health Care* (Cambridge, Mass.: Ballinger, 1982), pp. 121–30.
40. Task Force, "Senility Reconsidered," p. 260.
41. Richard W. Besdine, "Decisions to Withhold Treatment from Nursing Home Residents," *Journal of the American Geriatrics Society* 31 (October 1983): 604.
42. Ibid., pp. 602–6.
43. Steven H. Miles and Muriel B. Ryden, "Limited-Treatment Policies in Long-Term Care Facilities," *Journal of the American Geriatrics Society* 33 (October 1985): 707–11.
44. Steven A. Levenson, Noel D. List, and Bo Zaw-win, "Ethical Considerations in Critical and Terminal Illness in the Elderly," *Journal of the American Geriatrics Society* 29 (December 1981): 565.
45. D. Joanne Lynn, "Deciding about Life-Sustaining Therapy," in Cassel and Walsh, *Geriatric Medicine,* vol. 2, pp. 325–26.
46. Levenson, List, and Zaw-win, "Ethical Considerations," p. 566.
47. Lynn, "Deciding," p. 330.
48. Quoted by Donald E. Riesenberg, "Cassel: Physician Advocate for the Elderly," *Journal of the American Medical Association* 255 (February 21, 1986): 872–73.

49. Melvin Hershkowitz, "To Die at Home: Rejection of Medical Intervention by Geriatric Patients Who Had Serious Organic Disease," *Journal of the American Geriatrics Society* 32 (June 1984): 459.
50. Samuel Stoddard, *The Hospice Movement* (New York: Random House, 1978), p. 7.
51. Stewart Alsop, *Stay of Execution* (Philadelphia: J.B. Lippincott, 1973), p. 299.
52. Robert G. Twycross and Sylvia A. Lack, *Symptom Control in Far-Advanced Cancer: Alimentary Symptoms* (London: Pitman Publishing, 1986), p. 7.
53. Robert G. Twycross and Sylvia A. Lack, *Symptom Control in Far-Advanced Cancer: Pain Relief* (London: Pitman Publishing, 1983), p. 6; and John N. Morris et al., "The Effect of Treatment Setting and Patient Characteristics on Pain in Terminal Cancer Patients: A Report from the National Hospice Study," *Journal of Chronic Diseases* 39 (January 1986): 27–35.
54. Morris et al., "Effect of Treatment," pp. 27, 31–32.
55. See Cicely M. Saunders, ed., *The Management of Terminal Disease* (London: Edward Arnold, 1978); and Cicely Saunders, Dorothy H. Summers, and Neville Teller, eds., *Hospice: The Living Idea* (London: Edward Arnold, 1981).
56. Vincent Mor and David Kidder, "Cost Savings in Hospice: Final Results of the National Hospice Study," *HSR: Health Services Research* 20 (October 1985): 413.
57. For additional information on the hospice philosophy, see Saunders, *Management of Terminal Disease;* Stoddard, *Hospice Movement;* Robert G. Twycross, "Hospice Care—Redressing the Balance of Medicine," *Journal of the Royal Society of Medicine* 73 (1980): 475–81; Jack M. Zimmerman, *Hospice: Complete Care for the Terminally Ill* (Baltimore and Munich: Urban & Schwarzenberg, 1981); Margaret Gold, *Life Support: What Families Say about Hospital, Hospice and Home Care for the Fatally Ill* (Mount Vernon, N.Y.: Consumers Union Foundation, 1983); David S. Greer et al., "An Alternative in Terminal Care: Results of the National Hospice Study," *Journal of Chronic Diseases* 39 (January 1986): 9–26; and Wilma Bulkin and Herbert Lukashok, "Rx for Dying: The Case for Hospice," *The New England Journal of Medicine* 318 (February 11, 1988): 376–78.
58. Barbara Greenall, *Development of the United Kingdom Hospice Movement, 1976–1981* (London: The Polytechnic of North London, 1982), p. 21.
59. Saunders, Summers, and Teller, *Hospice,* p. 4.
60. Cicely Saunders, "Hospices," in A.S. Duncan, G.R. Dunstan, and R.B. Welbourn, eds., *The Dictionary of Medical Ethics,* 2nd ed. (New York: Crossroad, 1981), p. 219.
61. I was one of the those 5,000 visitors in 1985.
62. For additional information on the first four hospice models, see Greenall, *United Kingdom Hospice Movement,* pp. 21–25. Also see C. Murray Parkes and Jenny Parkes, " 'Hospice' Versus 'Hospital' Care—Re-evaluation after 10 Years as Seen by Surviving Spouses," *Postgraduate Medical Journal* 60 (1984): 120–24; and John Hinton, "Comparison of Places and Policies for Terminal Care," *The Lancet* 1 (January 6, 1979): 29–32.
63. David S. Greer and Vincent Mor, "An Overview of National Hospice Study Findings," *Journal of Chronic Diseases* 39 (January 1986): 5.
64. Twycross and Lack, *Symptom Control in Far-Advanced Cancer: Alimentary Symptoms,* p. 7.
65. Ibid., p. 8.
66. Ibid., p. 9.

67. Greer and Mor, "Overview," p. 6; and Greer et al., "Alternative in Terminal Care," p.16.
68. Twycross and Lack, *Symptom Control in Far-Advanced Cancer: Alimentary Symptoms*, p. 8.
69. D. Joanne Lynn, "Care Near the End of Life," in Cassel and Walsh, *Geriatric Medicine*, vol. 2, p. 333.
70. Twycross and Lack, *Symptom Control in Far-Advanced Cancer: Alimentary Symptoms*, p. 9.
71. Ibid., p. 18.
72. Robert G. Twycross, "Ethical and Clinical Aspects of Pain Treatment in Cancer Patients," *Acta Anaesthesiologica Scandinavica Supplementum* 74 (1982): 83–90; Cicely Saunders and Mary Baines, *Living with Dying: The Management of Terminal Disease* (Oxford and New York: Oxford University Press, 1983), pp. 12–42; D. Joanne Lynn, "Supportive Care for Dying Patients: An Introduction for Health Professionals," in the President's Commission, *Deciding to Forego Life-Sustaining Treatment* (Washington, D.C.: U.S. Government Printing Office, 1983), pp. 284–97; and Lynn, "Care Near the End of Life," pp. 333–37.

3

Autonomous Patients and the Legal Right to Refuse Life-Sustaining Treatment

> We find no requirement in the law that a competent, but otherwise mortally sick, patient undergo the surgery or treatment which constitutes the only hope for temporary prolongation of his life. This being so, we see little difference between a cancer-ridden patient who declines surgery, or chemotherapy, necessary for his temporary survival and the hopeless predicament which tragically afflicts Abe Perlmutter. It is true that the latter appears more drastic because affirmatively, a mechanical device must be disconnected, as distinct from mere inaction. Notwithstanding, the principle is the same, for in both instances the hapless, but mentally competent, victim is choosing not to avail himself of one of the expensive marvels of modern medical science.
>
> *Satz v. Perlmutter*[1]

> Here Elizabeth Bouvia's decision to forego medical treatment or life support through a mechanical means belongs to her. It is not a medical decision for her physicians to make. Neither is it a legal question whose soundness is to be resolved by lawyers or judges. It is not a conditional right subject to approval by ethics committees or courts of law. It is a moral and philosophical decision that, being a competent adult, is hers alone.
>
> *Bouvia v. Superior Court of the State of California*[2]

At first glance, the legal aspects of abating treatment look reasonably simple, especially for autonomous patients. The common-law right of self-determination has a long tradition in Great Britain and the United States. The U.S. Supreme Court affirmed the importance of this right in an often-quoted statement dating back to an 1891 decision: "No right is held more sacred or is more carefully guarded by the common law than the right of every individual to the possession and control of his own person, free from all restraints or interference by others, unless by clear and unquestionable authority of law."[3]

This common-law right of self-determination has numerous applications. In a medical context, this right has led to the development of the legal doctrine of informed consent whereby a physician has a duty to disclose sufficient information to a patient regarding recommended treatment, including its likely benefits and possible risks, that the patient can make an informed decision concerning that proposed treatment. The legal risk of administering treatment apart from patient consent, with the exception of emergency situations where consent is generally implied, was set forth in a 1914 decision, when Judge Cardozo wrote:

"Every human being of adult years and sound mind has a right to determine what shall be done with his own body; and a surgeon who performs an operation without his patient's consent commits an assault for which he is liable in damages."[4]

The right of self-determination cuts two ways in medical contexts. If a patient—at least an autonomous, adult patient—has the right to consent to recommended treatment before that treatment is administered, that same patient, or any other patient similarly situated, also has the right to refuse the treatment proposed by the physician. The law thus recognizes and affirms the right of autonomous patients to refuse treatment as the necessary corollary to the right to consent to the treatment. One of the clearest declarations of the right of treatment refusal appears in a 1960 malpractice decision in Kansas:

Anglo-American law starts with the premise of thoroughgoing self-determination. It follows that each man is considered to be master of his own body, and he may, if he be of sound mind, expressly prohibit the performance of lifesaving surgery or other medical treatment. A doctor may well believe that an operation or form of treatment is desirable or necessary, but the law does not permit him to substitute his own judgment for that of the patient by any form of artifice or deception.[5]

Thus by 1960, which was 3 years after Bruno Haid initiated the debate over abating treatment by urging Pope Pius XII to address the morality of resuscitation, the legal status of treatment refusal by patients in the United States was clear up to a point: any adult patient could refuse medical treatment, particularly treatment that was not regarded as life-sustaining in nature, on the common-law grounds of self-determination. The extent to which the common-law tradition at the time might have permitted an autonomous patient to refuse life-sustaining treatment is debatable, in spite of the quotations that opened this chapter, especially in cases involving (1) critically ill patients who could be restored to normal health through treatment, or (2) critically ill patients whose disabling conditions could arguably represent lives "not worth living," or (3) terminally ill patients whose deaths could not reasonably be said to be imminent. Such cases were yet to be decided in court, but at least patients falling into the "easy case" category—unquestioned autonomy, no dependent children, and "imminently" dying—could claim the right to refuse treatment and expect physicians and hospital administrators to honor the claim.

However, even during the first phase of the debate over abating treatment, and certainly during the second and third phases (see Chapter 1), the legal aspects of the debate moved far beyond the easy cases. Uncharted legal territory was explored as scores of cases, sometimes seeming to increase at an exponential rate, raised difficult and unavoidable questions. What should be done when the adult patient refusing treatment is the parent of dependent children? What about cases in which conventional lifesaving treatment is refused on the basis of a set of religious beliefs not widely accepted in society? What bearing does the emerging constitutional "right of privacy" have on treatment refusal cases? Does a prisoner retain the right to refuse lifesaving treatment and, if so, on what legal grounds (self-determination? religious belief? constitutionally protected privacy?)? How important are the claims made by some health care personnel that they have an overriding duty to preserve life, and that the termination of medical treatment represents an illegal killing of a patient? If an autonomous patient on life-sustaining equipment refuses treatment, does it matter legally if the patient's condition is or is not terminal? What should be done when an autonomous, terminally ill patient with a third-trimester pregnancy refuses life-sustaining treatment? Under what circumstances can parents refuse medical treatment recommended for their critically ill children? What should be done with nonautonomous, critically ill patients whose relatives or guardians want one or more modes of treatment stopped? Does it matter if the patient now lacking autonomy was previously capable of making decisions relating to medical treatment? What weight should be placed on the verbal or written preferences regarding treatment abatement previously expressed by a now-nonautonomous patient?

These questions regarding the law and abating treatment have been raised for numerous reasons: the unprecedented advances of medical technology over the past several decades, the increased recognition of patients' rights, the refusal by some physicians and hospital administrators to pull back from efforts at the technological prolongation of life, public awareness of the enormous costs (financial and otherwise) of keeping critically ill and terminally ill patients alive for indeterminate periods of time, the heightened profile and increased court involvement (often through *amici curiae* briefs) by pro-life groups and right-to-die groups, concern by physicians over possible civil or criminal actions against them, and so forth. As patients, guardians, physicians, attorneys, and others have wrestled with these questions—and often disagreed about the appropriate answers—the final arbiters have frequently turned out to be judges at the trial, appellate, and state supreme court levels.

With the U.S. Supreme Court not yet ruling on a treatment-abatement case (with the exception of the Reagan administration's unsuccessful appeal of the "Baby Jane Doe" case in 1986), and with state legislatures thus far failing to do much of a statutory nature concerning treatment-abatement cases (except on natural death acts, to be discussed in Chapter 5), the lower courts have been left to develop law by addressing the legal issues on a case-by-case basis. Consequently, over the past several decades courts in a number of jurisdictions have been forced to examine and reexamine the right of treatment refusal. In so doing, the courts have had to articulate legal grounds for refusing treatment in accordance with the common-law right of self-determination, balance the constitutional rights of autonomous patients against a variety of state interests, wrestle with the circumstances in which treatment abatement is permissible when patients (adults and children) lack the capacity to make decisions about their medical care, handle civil and/or criminal actions brought against physicians caring for critically ill patients, attempt to draw a line between "right-to-die" cases and cases calling for judicially mandated lifesaving treatment, and attempt to distinguish between cases involving the justifiable discontinuation of medical treatment and any cases involving the intentional killing of patients.

Unfortunately, the numerous decisions addressing various legal aspects of abating treatment have not been as consistent or as helpful as one could want. Nevertheless, it is important to examine case law on treatment abatement to identify points of judicial agreement, sort out areas of judicial disagreement, and indicate areas in the law where there are still important, unresolved issues. This chapter and Chapter 4 will therefore contain descriptions of the more significant judicial decisions concerning treatment abatement, and interpret the current legal status of various types of cases.

We will first turn to a terminological and conceptual problem that has bearing on such cases, then discuss cases involving patients with the capacity to make decisions to begin, continue, or abate treatment. In the next chapter we will discuss cases involving legally incompetent and other nonautonomous patients. Although there are significant differences from case to case—and obvious differences among categories of cases—all of the decisions contain the central legal question in treatment abatement: under what circumstances can critically ill patients or their surrogates exercise the right to discontinue medical treatment? The circumstances in most of the cases involve death as the probable outcome of discontinuing treatment, not necessarily because the patients want to die (they may simply choose to avoid or to stop treatment that is unwanted, futile, or repulsive), but because treatment-abatement cases not having death as the probable outcome are commonplace in many hospitals and rarely involve court procedures.

On another matter of terminology (and concept)

Before turning to the discussion of case law, it is necessary to address a problem that is often confusing in the handling of individual clinical cases. The problem is both terminological and conceptual, and it comes about in part because of differences in language in different professional fields. Stated as a question, the problem is: with what terminology should we describe patients who are able to make decisions about their health care, and what is the concept that underlies the terminology we use? In regard to the brief case histories presented in Chapter 1, how should we refer to patients such as Cornelius Ryan, Dax Cowart, and Emily Bauer?

Professionals trained in medicine or in law usually use the language of "competency" to refer to such patients, and refer to patients who are unable to make decisions about their health care as being "incompetent" or "mentally incompetent.'' Moreover, psychiatrists, other physicians, and attorneys have brought about fairly general usage of the competency/incompetency language, even though psychiatrists and attorneys themselves often have significantly different concepts underlying their common terminology.

Professionals trained in philosophy and other persons interested in clarity of language often use different terminology in reference to the Cornelius Ryans, Dax Cowarts, and Emily Bauers of the world. Rather than using the competency/incompetency language, they frequently refer to such patients as being "autonomous" or having "autonomy.'' Patients who are unable to make decisions about their health care are correspondingly referred to as being "nonautonomous.''

Because the concept of competence is task-specific (one is competent *to do something* under specified conditions), and because the legal determination of incompetency requires a judicial hearing that arrives at that conclusion about an individual, the commonplace comments made by health care professionals regarding "competent patients" and "incompetent patients" are problematic—especially when there have been no judicial decisions concerning the mental status of individual patients in the second category. Consequently, an increasing number of thoughtful persons in medicine, nursing, law, ethics, and other appropriate fields have in recent years wrestled with this terminological and conceptual problem. The goal has been to come up with replacement language that applies to the realities of clinical cases without suggesting the legal implications of the conventional competency/incompetency language.

Three interdisciplinary groups have made suggestions for alternative language. Members of the President's Commission, correctly pointing out "the sometimes confounding legal overtones associated with the terms competence and incompetence,'' used the terms *decision-making capacity* and *incapacity* in reference to patients who are able to make informed health care decisions for themselves and patients who are unable to do so.[6] The advisory panel and project staff for the Office of Technology Assessment (OTA) study of life-sustaining technologies and the elderly chose to refer to *decisionally capable* and *decisionally incapable* patients, thereby emphasizing the importance of any individual patient's mental capacity to make health care decisions—and the importance of assessing such capacity (or the lack of it) without the involvement of a court.[7] Members of the Hastings Center project on termination-of-treatment guidelines stated that "competence" and "incompetence" should be understood as "legal terms of art" and argued that the functional ability of patients in clinical settings should be assessed in terms of their capacity (or lack of same) to make informed, specific health care decisions "in accordance with personal values.''[8]

In my view, the autonomy/nonautonomy language is preferable to the conventional language in that (1) the terminology of "autonomous patients" and "nonautonomous patients" does not connote anything about a judicial determination of competency or incompetency, and (2) the concept of autonomy underlying the terminology is different from the concept of competence. Correctly understood, the concept of autonomy also conveys the core idea of an individual's decision-making capacity without requiring some of the linguistic gymnastics connected with some of the proposed replacement language mentioned earlier.

A related conceptual problem has to do with the personhood of patients. It is commonplace to refer to patients as persons, but are all critically ill and terminally ill patients *actually* persons? This question need not arise when the patient receiving care is a Cornelius Ryan, a Dax Cowart, or an Emily Bauer, because any patient capable of making decisions about his or her own health care meets any set of criteria for personhood seriously put forward by anyone. Consequently, the legal decisions that will be discussed in this chapter never raise the question of personhood in regard to any of the patients. The autonomous status of some of the patients will occasionally be questioned, but not their personhood.

In other kinds of cases, however, the personhood of patients is sometimes implicitly if not directly questioned. The cases of Megan O'Rourke, Jim Adams, and Joseph Davies presented in Chapter 1 provide illustrative examples. Some individuals involved in their cases could have wondered not only about the autonomy of these patients (because of O'Rourke's inability to express herself verbally or to understand spoken language, Adams's comatose condition, and Davies's severe dementia), but their personhood as well. The unfortunate, insensitive, but colloquial manner of referring to a wide variety of patients as "vegetables" is a simple way of intimating that such patients not only lack autonomy but also do not count (as the speaker counts) as persons. A number of the cases to be discussed in the next chapter have to do with such patients.

The concepts of personhood and autonomy are related to but distinguishable from the concept of competence. In fact, the concepts of personhood and autonomy provide the philosophical and psychological foundation on which the more conventional psychiatric-legal notions of competency and incompetency rest. Accordingly, the cases to be discussed in this chapter will be described as involving autonomous patients, and the cases in Chapter 4 will pertain to questionably autonomous or clearly nonautonomous patients. We will return in Chapter 9 to the question of personhood in the context of patients diagnosed as being in a persistent vegetative state (PVS). Throughout the remainder of the book patients will be described as "incompetent" only when there has been a judicial decision to that effect.

The legal cases in this chapter have to do with patients who refuse life-sustaining treatment, but who are unquestionably both (1) persons and (2) autonomous agents (with the possible exception of Delores Heston, whose autonomous status was questionable). But what does it mean to say that a patient is a *person* and is *autonomous?* Are such labels to be dismissed as a matter of semantics, or as philosophical mumbo jumbo? I hope not. The question of who should count as a person, or what the proper criteria for personhood are, is a profound philosophical question. Likewise, the question of who possesses (1) the general capacity of self-governance and (2) the specific capacity of making personal health care decisions is a crucial philosophical and psychological question related to the cases to be discussed in this and subsequent chapters. Both questions have obviously important implications for the handling of clinical cases and legal cases involving decisions to initiate, continue, or abate life-sustaining treatment.

A number of philosophers have discussed the properties of personhood.[9] The proposed lists of these properties vary somewhat from one philosopher to another, as do the thought experiments used to test the proposed lists of properties and expand their usage beyond human beings. Yet most philosophers agree on at least the core properties or traits of personhood, if not on all of their applications. Joel Feinberg, in his discussion of "commonsense personhood," puts forth the consensus view of personhood as being the possession of three necessary and jointly sufficient properties: (1) consciousness, (2) self-awareness, and (3) minimal rationality. In his words, these properties are "person-making characteristics."[10]

Personhood thus has to do with neurological development and, at least among human beings, the absence of profound neurological dysfunction or impairment. Personhood also is a necessary condition for autonomy in that no being lacking the properties of consciousness, self-awareness, and minimal rationality could possibly have the capacity of self-governance or be able to make decisions about anything.

What, then, is the concept of autonomy that underlies the terminology of "autonomous patients" and plays a crucial role in the assessment of which critically ill patients have the capacity to make their own decisions about life-sustaining treatment? At this point it is important to distinguish between the *general* concept of autonomy and the characteristic features of that concept, and the more *specific* meaning of autonomy that relates directly to the capacity an individual has to make a decision in regard to life-sustaining treatment.

The general concept of autonomy has to do with self-governance: the capacity most human beings have to make their own decisions about time management and resource management, to develop their own life plans, to choose their own friends, to control their own affairs apart from internal or external constraints, and so forth. This concept of autonomy has three cognitive and decisional components. First, to be an autonomous agent requires that one have the capacity for *understanding*. This feature of the concept of autonomy does not necessarily pertain to the possession of wisdom, an advanced education, the ability for abstract and quantitative thought, philosophical insights, or a certain intelligence level. Rather, it has to do with certain minimum cognitive and conceptual abilities that enable most of us to be aware of certain things going on about us, grasp basic pieces of information, figure out fundamental cause-and-effect relationships, and comprehend the consequences that will probably follow from certain actions we do or that might be done to us. Second, to be an autonomous agent requires that one have the capacity for *deliberation*. This aspect of autonomy means that one is able to perceive options, consider alternative actions and alternative outcomes of differing decisions, and make choices among the alternatives available at a given place and time. Third, to be an autonomous agent requires that one have the capacity for voluntary decisions and actions. For *voluntariness* to be present, one must be able to decide and act in the absence of internal constraints (such as fear, depression, anxiety, or the perception of severe pain) and external constraints (peer pressure, the influence of authority figures, dependence on others in fundamentally important ways) that can limit, reduce, or control an individual's decisions and actions.

All autonomous persons, whether patients or not, have these general capacities of understanding, deliberation, and voluntariness in decision and action. However, the capacities differ in degree from one person to another, and some persons have reduced autonomy that significantly affects their ability to make decisions about health care and other important matters.

A person possessing the decision-making capacity required to make a choice about initating, continuing, or abating life-sustaining treatment has three additional, more specific capacities that relate to such a decision. The first of these specific decision-making capacities is often called *authenticity*. This somewhat misleading label has to do with an individual patient's ability to make a decision to consent to or refuse life-sustaining treatment in a way that reflects his or her personal value system. In this sense, an autonomous decision specific to the realities of a given life-threatening medical condition and the possibilities of treating that condition is a decision that is consistent with the patient's earlier preferences, choices, and actions before becoming critically ill. The second of the specific decision-making capacities is *communication*. This aspect of deciding to initiate, continue, or abate life-sustaining treatment does not mean that a critically ill patient has to communicate verbally. Obviously a number of critically ill patients cannot engage in verbal communication because of their medical conditions or modes of treatment. However, an autonomous patient must be able to communicate his or her decision about treatment or the abatement of treatment in some manner, whether verbally, through body language, or through electronic communication devices. The third of the specific decision-making capacities is usually called *appreciation*. This misleading label has nothing to do, in the context of a life-threatening illness, with personal enjoyment, admiration, approval, or gratitude. Rather, for an autonomous patient to have the capacity of appreciation means that he or she realizes the intensely personal significance of refusing life-sustaining treatment. To appreciate the personal implications of such a decision is, simply put, to realize that *my* life will almost certainly end in a few hours, days, or weeks apart from the treatment.[11]

The cases to which we now turn are best interpreted in a framework other than that provided by the concept of *competence*. To go that way entails working with a task-specific concept that has to do with a delimited context, the abilities required to perform a particular task in that context, an all-or-nothing classification of persons according to their abilities to perform specific tasks, and the unavoidable legal implications of the concept. A preferable alternative is to interpret the following cases in the framework provided by the concept of *autonomy*. By using this concept, we will be able to understand how some patients are capable of making decisions about continuing or abating life-sustaining treatment; how physicians, nurses, and other individuals involved with particular clinical cases can determine if certain critically ill patients are capable of making such decisions; and how some critically ill patients can lack the capacity or have a reduced capacity to make decisions that pertain to their own continued living and their own deaths.

Cases of treatment refusal by autonomous adults

During the first period of the debate over treatment abatement, the "easy case" mentioned earlier was complicated by constitutional considerations of unusual religious beliefs and practices (the early religion-based refusal cases had Jehovah's Witnesses refusing blood transfusions; subsequent cases have had Christian Scientists and patients with other sectarian beliefs refusing other modalities of treatment). These religion-based refusal cases, in turn, were complicated by consideration of the state's interest in protecting dependent children who would be left without a parent should the autonomous patient's refusal to have treatment be honored. In subsequent cases involving the issue of treatment abatement, judges have wrestled with other complicating factors and have turned to balancing an autonomous patient's right to refuse treatment against several state interests: the preservation of life per se, the protection of third parties (surviving children, surviving adults, and other patients), the prevention of suicide, the maintenance of the ethical standards of medical practice, and the protection of hospitals from being "involuntary hosts" to nonconsenting patients. The fundamental question in such cases is when, if at all, one or more of these state interests becomes sufficiently compelling that it overrides the refusal of treatment by an autonomous patient. We now consider 12 such cases; additional cases are cited in the notes.

Case 3.1

In 1964, Bernice Brooks was a patient in McNeal General Hospital, Chicago, suffering from a peptic ulcer. Gilbert Demange, her physician, had been informed repeatedly over a 2-year period that Mrs. Brooks had religious convictions that precluded her from receiving blood transfusions.

Mrs. Brooks, her husband, and their two adult children were Jehovah's Witnesses. To indicate the religious basis for her refusal of a blood transfusion, Mrs. Brooks had given Dr. Demange a copy of "Blood, Medicine and the Law of God," a publication of the Jehovah's Witnesses that uses biblical passages (Leviticus 17:10, Acts 15:28–29, and others) and commentary to explain the organization's belief that blood transfusions violate God's law against "eating blood." According to this publication, anyone violating the "law on blood" stands to be condemned by God.

In addition, Mrs. Brooks and her husband had signed a document releasing Dr. Demange and the hospital from all civil liability that might result from the failure to administer a blood transfusion. In return, the patient had been assured that there would be no further attempt to persuade her to accept blood.

Nevertheless, without informing the Brooks family, Dr. Demange and several attorneys went before the probate division of the circuit court to have a conservator of the person of Bernice Brooks appointed. A conservator was appointed, consent for the transfusion was given, and the transfusion was done.

Convinced that their constitutional rights had been violated, the Brookses took the case to court. By the time the case reached the Illinois Supreme Court in 1965, the issues were clear. The Brookses argued that the transfusion should never have been administered and that the physician and hospital, in so doing, had violated the First Amendment's protection of Mrs. Brooks' religious freedom. The defendants responded by arguing that society has an overriding interest in protecting the lives of its citizens, that several legal cases (on compulsory vaccination, polygamous marriage, and the handling of snakes during religious rituals) provide precedent for overriding religious beliefs in some circumstances, and that a 1964 case (*Application of the President and Directors of Georgetown College*) offers a specific precedent for administering a blood transfusion to a nonconsenting, adult Jehovah's Witness.

The justices were not convinced by the defendants' appeal to precedent and specifically stated that the Georgetown College case was "an altogether unique proceeding," because the patient in that case, along with her husband, had agreed to court involvement. Regarding the plantiffs' appeal to religious freedom, the justices said:

> It seems to be clearly established that the First Amendment of the United States Constitution . . . protects the absolute right of every individual to freedom in his religious belief and the exercise thereof, subject only to the qualification that the exercise thereof may properly be limited by governmental action where such exercise endangers, clearly and presently, the public health, welfare or morals.

The justices found that Mrs. Brooks's refusal of the transfusion represented no "clear and present danger to society." They concluded:

> Even though we may consider appellant's beliefs unwise, foolish or ridiculous, in the absence of an overriding danger to society we may not permit interference therewith in the form of a conservatorship established in the waning hours of her life for the sole purpose of compelling her to accept medical treatment forbidden by her religious principles, and previously refused by her with full knowledge of the probable consequences.[12]

Case 3.2

Delores Heston, aged 22, unmarried, and a Jehovah's Witness, had a ruptured spleen as a result of an automobile accident. Taken to John F. Kennedy Memorial Hospital, she apparently refused to accept a blood transfusion before losing consciousness. Personnel at the plantiff hospital were convinced that Miss Heston would die without an operation, and that she would also die with an operation unless whole blood was administered. Nevertheless, her mother, also a Jehovah's Witness, refused to consent to the transfusion and signed a release of liability for the hospital and medical personnel.

With the patient's death imminent, the plaintiff, having notified Heston's mother, applied at 1:30 A.M. to a judge of the superior court for the appointment of a guardian who would consent to the transfusion needed to save Heston's life. A guardian was appointed, blood was administered as part of a 4:00 A.M. operation, and the patient survived.

The defendants then moved to vacate the order. The trial court refused, an appeal followed, and the case ended up at the New Jersey Supreme Court in 1971. That court, recognizing that the particular controversy was moot, accepted the case to resolve an issue the justices first addressed in *Raleigh Fitkin-Paul Morgan Memorial Hospital v. Anderson,* a case involving a pregnant Jehovah's Witness who refused a blood transfusion even though she was hemorrhaging.

The court, declaring that "it seems correct to say there is no constitutional right to choose to die," understood the case to involve two fundamental issues: whether there is a "compelling State interest" in life per se that permits the state to prevent death by overriding a patient's expressed views, and whether a hospital and staff have any legal alternative to accepting the burden imposed by the dictates of a patient's religious beliefs.

On the first issue, the court noted that only two religion-based treatment refusal cases (both involving Jehovah's Witnesses) had reached an appellate level. In *Georgetown College,* a justice of the court of appeals had ordered the transfusion, in large part because the patient was the mother of a 7-month-old child. In *In re Brooks' Estate,* the Supreme Court of Illinois, using the "clear and present danger'' test, had found interference with the patient's religious beliefs to be unwarranted. For the Supreme Court of New Jersey, the "compelling State interest" test was preferable to the test used in Illinois. And for them, the state's interest in life per se was the first of two compelling reasons to warrant the transfusion of blood in the Heston case.

On the second issue, the court argued that the interest of a hospital and staff in correctly handling a patient "thrust upon them" was a second reason for the transfusion of blood under the circumstances of this case. The justices stated:

> Hospitals exist to aid the sick and the injured. The medical and nursing professions are consecrated to preserving life. That is their professional creed. To them, a failure to use a simple, established procedure in the circumstances of this case would be malpractice, however the law may characterize that failure because of the patient's private convictions. A surgeon should not be asked to operate under the strain of knowing that a transfusion may not be administered even though medically required to save his patient. The hospital and its staff should not be required to decide whether the patient is or continues to be competent to make a judgment upon the subject, or whether the release tendered by the patient or a member of his family will protect them from civil responsibility. The hospital could hardly avoid the problem by compelling the removal of a dying patient, and Miss Heston's family made no effort to take her elsewhere. When the hospital and staff are thus involuntary hosts and their interests are pitted against the belief of the patient, we think it reasonable to resolve the problem by permitting the hospital and its staff to pursue their functions according to their professional standards.[13]

Case 3.3

Charles Osborne, aged 34 and the father of two young children, was admitted to a hospital in 1972 with injuries and internal bleeding caused by a tree falling on him. When the need for whole blood became apparent, the patient refused to give consent.

Osborne, his wife, his mother, and his grandparents were all Jehovah's Witnesses. The patient's father had died a few months earlier, with the family supporting his decision to refuse blood. Regarding Osborne's refusal of blood, his grandfather said that the patient "wants to live very much . . . He wants to live in the Bible's promised new world where life will never end. A few hours here would nowhere compare to everlasting life."

The District of Columbia Court of Appeals upheld Osborne's right to refuse the transfusion, for several reasons. First, the patient was unquestionably competent: he "knew what the doctor was saying," "understood the consequences of his decision," and "with full understanding" refused the recommended transfusion. Second, the patient's religious beliefs were strong, and in contrast to some Jehovah's Witness cases, did not allow for court intervention: he "viewed himself as deprived of life everlasting even if he involuntarily received the transfusion." Third, the patient released the hospital from liability. Fourth, the patient's two young children "would be well cared for" by the extended Osborne family. And finally, the court did not find any compelling state interest that justified overriding Osborne's decision.[14]

Case 3.4

Rosaria Candura, a 77-year-old widow, was hospitalized in 1978 with gangrene in her right foot and lower leg. After some vacillation, she refused to consent to have the leg amputated. Her daughter, Grace Lane, filed a petition in the probate court to have herself appointed as temporary guardian for the purpose of consenting to the operation on behalf of her mother. Lane's request was granted, and the guardian *ad litem* for Candura appealed the decision.

For the Appeals Court of Massachusetts, the central issue in the case was the question of the patient's competency. In reviewing the case, the justices found that the patient had "some indications of a degree of senility and confusion on some subjects," that she twice agreed to the amputation and then twice withdrew her consent, that she was "lucid on some matters and confused on others," that she did "not believe that the operation will cure her," that she did not wish "to live as an invalid or in a nursing home," that her relationship with her children was "marked by a considerable degree of conflict," and that she did "not fear death but welcomes it." Moreover, the justices found that the patient's competency was not questioned by anyone "until she changed her original decision and withdrew her consent to the amputation."

In citing a precedent for their decision, the justices referred to a New Jersey decision earlier in 1978 (*In the Matter of Quackenbush*). Like Candura, Robert Quackenbush had demonstrated "fluctuations in mental lucidity" but had been judged competent to reject a proposed amputation of gangrenous legs. The Massachusetts justices agreed with the New Jersey decision, stating:

> We hold that Mrs. Candura has the right under the law to refuse to submit either to medical treatment or a surgical operation, that on the evidence and findings in this case the decision is one that she may determine for herself, and that therefore her leg may not be amputated unless she consents to that course of action.[15]

Case 3.5

Kenneth Myers, aged 24 and unmarried, was a prisoner in a medium-security institution in Massachusetts. While in prison, Myers developed a kidney condition diagnosed as chronic glomerulonephritis and uremia. When the kidney condition worsened, he began receiving hemodialysis and also Kayexalate (sodium polystyrene sulfonate), a medication that lowers the blood's potassium level. The treatment continued for a year with no significant problems.

In late 1978, Myers refused to continue the treatment. In response, the commissioner of correction initiated proceedings against Myers in the superior court. Myers then resumed treatment, but threatened to refuse treatment at any time. The court concluded that Myers' refusal of treatment was unrelated to any religious objection to the treatment, was not an effort to die, and also had "little to do with his disease, the nature or effects of the dialysis treatment, or the personal ramifications of continuing such treatment for the remainder of his life." Rather, the court found that Myers' refusal of treatment was simply "a form of protest against his placement in a medium, as opposed to a minimum, security prison."

Subsequent to the superior court's order compelling treatment of this unconsenting, competent prisoner, the defendant was transferred to a minimum-security facility. There he received a kidney transplant. However, the commissioner was concerned that the kidney might be rejected, that Myers might refuse to take two daily medications related to retaining the kidney, and, should the kidney be rejected, that Myers might again refuse dialysis apart from judicial authorization of continued treatment.

Consequently, the case was heard by the Supreme Judicial Court of Massachusetts, because "the question of the right of prisoners to refuse lifesaving treatment in what amounts to an emergency situation is one of public importance." The justices interpreted the case in the light of their earlier *Saikewicz* decision (*Superintendent of Belchertown State School v. Saikewicz*). In that earlier case (see Case 4.2), the justices had identified two sources of judicial support for treatment refusal: the common-law right of self-determination and the constitutional right of privacy. They had also isolated four countervailing state interests: the preservation of life, the protection of third parties, the prevention of suicide, and the maintenance of the ethical integrity of the medical profession.

The second and third of these state interests were not involved in Myers' case. By contrast, the state's interest in the preservation of life "is directly implicated here" and is "the most significant of the asserted State interests." However, this state interest is not always controlling, as indicated by *Lane v. Candura*. The fourth state interest, maintaining the ethical integrity of the medical profession and permitting hospitals to care fully for patients under their control, also has bearing in this case, especially since the traumatic cost of the lifesaving treatment "is not inordinate and the prognosis is good."

Beyond these considerations, another reason that calls for authorizing treatment without consent "is a consideration not directly involved in *Saikewicz* and *Lane*—namely, the State's interest in upholding orderly prison administration.'' Although ''the fact of the defendant's incarceration does not per se divest him of his right of privacy and interest in bodily integrity, . . . it does impose limitations on these constitutional rights in terms of the State interests unique to the prison context.'' Because of the importance of maintaining internal order and discipline in a prison, providing institutional security, and rehabilitating prisoners, state interests ''override the defendant's refusal of lifesaving treatment.''[16]

Case 3.6

Abe Perlmutter was hospitalized with amyotrophic lateral sclerosis (ALS), a terminal condition offering a life expectancy of no more than 2 years from the time of diagnosis. Aged 73, Perlmutter was virtually incapable of movement, dependent on a respirator, and able to speak only with extreme effort. Nevertheless, he was ''in command of his mental faculties and legally competent.''

Perlmutter's hospitalization was seriously complicated by a conflict with the medical and nursing staff. His physician believed, based upon medical probability, that Perlmutter would have ''a reasonable life expectancy of less than 1 hour'' apart from the respirator. Yet Perlmutter, at great effort, had attempted to remove the respirator—only to have the hospital personnel, warned by an alarm, reconnect it.

Perlmutter then petitioned a trial court for the removal of the respirator. He was supported in his request by all of the members of his adult family, who had heard him repeatedly say, ''I'm miserable, take it out.'' At a bedside hearing, he told the trial judge that whatever might happen to him if the respirator were removed, ''it can't be worse than what I'm going through now.''

The trial judge's final judgement stated that ''Abe Perlmutter, in the exercise of his right of privacy, may remain in defendant hospital or leave said hospital, free of the mechanical respirator now attached to his body and all defendants and their staffs are restrained from interfering with Plaintiff's decision.''

The defendants, supported by the state attorney general, took the case to the district court of appeal. There the state argued that (1) it ''has an overriding duty to preserve life,'' and that (2) ''termination of supportive care, whether it be by the patient, his family or medical personnel, is an unlawful killing of a human being under the Florida Murder Statute.'' In addition, the state indicated that the fears of hospital administrators and physicians regarding the possibility of civil and criminal liability, should they aid in removal of the respirator, could not be discounted.

The district court of appeal interpreted the case in the context of the state interests put forth in *Saikewicz* and declared that "none of these four considerations surmount the individual wishes of Abe Perlmutter." Against the state's claim that "a patient has *no right* to refuse treatment," the court affirmed the trial court's decision by saying:

> It is our conclusion . . . that when these several public policy interests are weighed against the rights of Mr. Perlmutter, the latter must and should prevail. Abe Perlmutter should be allowed to make his choice to die with dignity, notwithstanding over a dozen legislative failures in this state to adopt suitable legislation in this field. It is all very convenient to insist on continuing Mr. Perlmutter's life so that there can be no question of foul play, no resulting civil liability and no possible trespass on medical ethics. However, it is quite another matter to do so at the patient's sole expense and against his competent will, thus inflicting never ending physical torture on his body until the inevitable, but artificially suspended, moment of death. Such a course of conduct invades the patient's constitutional right of privacy, removes his freedom of choice and invades his right to self-determination.

The day after the district court decision, Perlmutter summoned his family to his bedside. The respirator was then removed, and he died within an hour.

Fifteen months later, in 1980, the Supreme Court of Florida was asked to review the case. For the supreme court justices, the legal issue was "whether a competent adult patient, with no minor dependents, suffering from a terminal illness has the constitutional right to refuse or discontinue extraordinary medical treatment where all affected family members consent." They affirmed the district court of appeal's decision—and then criticized the Florida legislature. Saying that "the question of 'death with dignity' is a matter so complex that it should be left to the legislature," the justices nevertheless declared that they would "proceed on a case by case method" because "legislative inaction cannot serve to close the doors of the courtrooms of this state to its citizens who assert cognizable constitutional rights."[17]

Case 3.7

William Bartling, aged 70, had a history of medical problems. In April 1984, when he entered Glendale (California) Adventist Medical Center for the treatment of depression, he was also suffering from emphysema, arteriosclerosis, an abdominal aneurysm, and alcoholism. A routine examination revealed a malignant lung tumor. The lung collapsed during a biopsy of the tumor. Because of his emphysema, the hole made by the biopsy needle did not heal properly and the lung did not reinflate. A tracheotomy was performed, and Bartling was placed on a ventilator.

Bartling tried to remove the ventilator tubes several times—only to have his wrists placed in "soft restraints" to prevent him from disconnecting the ventilator. Despite requests from Bartling and his wife, the treating physicians and the hospital personnel refused to remove the ventilator and restraints.

Two months later Bartling and his wife sought an injunction to prohibit the hospital and physicians from administering any further treatment. They also filed a complaint seeking damages for battery (for unconsented medical treatment), violation of state and federal constitutional rights, breach of fiduciary duty, and intentional infliction of emotional distress.

Attached to the complaint were several documents: (1) a signed copy of the "Living Will" distributed by Concern for Dying, (2) a declaration of his wishes, (3) a California durable-power-of-attorney-for-health-care form, designating his wife as his proxy should he be judged incompetent, and (4) a document releasing the hospital and physicians from liability for compliance with his wishes. Bartling's personal declaration stated:

> While I have no wish to die, I find intolerable the living conditions forced upon me by my deteriorating lungs, heart, and blood vessel systems, and find intolerable my being continuously connected to this ventilator. . . . Therefore, I wish this Court to order that the sustaining of my respiration by this mechanical device violates my constitutional right, is contrary to my every wish, and constitutes a battery upon my person. I fully understand that my request to have the ventilator removed and discontinued . . . will very likely cause respiratory failure and ultimately lead to my death. I am willing to accept that risk rather than to continue the burden of this artificial existence which I find unbearable, degrading, and dehumanizing.

Bartling confirmed these views in a videotaped deposition a day before the superior court hearing. The views were challenged in court by the hospital and physicians, who claimed that Bartling had vacillated in his position, that "Glendale Adventist is a Christian hospital devoted to the preservation of life," that disconnecting life-support systems from "cognitive, sapient" patients would be unethical, and that they feared civil and criminal liability should they accede to Bartling's wishes.

The superior court ruled that Bartling could not legally be removed from the respirator, because the justices claimed that the right to refuse life-prolonging treatment was limited to comatose, terminally ill patients, or representatives acting on their behalf. Bartling appealed the decision, but died on November 6—one day before the court of appeal heard the case.

The court of appeal reversed the trial court. Citing *Candura, Saikewicz,* and especially *Barber (Barber v. Superior Court),* the court pointed out that "a clearly recognized legal right to control one's own medical treatment *predated* the [California] Natural Death Act [and] that a competent adult patient has the legal right to refuse medical treatment." This right "has its origins in the constitutional right of privacy" and, in this case, outweighs any state interest.

Glendale Adventist had argued that it is "a Christian, pro-life oriented hospital" in which the majority of physicians regard disconnecting life-support systems in a case such as this one as "inconsistent with the healing orientation of physicians." In response, the court declared:

> We do not doubt the sincerity of [the hospital and physicians'] moral and ethical beliefs, or their sincere belief in the position they have taken in this case. However, if the right of the patient to self-determination as to his own medical treatment is to have any meaning at all, it must be paramount to the interests of the patient's hospital and doctors. The right of a competent adult patient to refuse medical treatment is a constitutionally guaranteed right which must not be abridged.[18]

Case 3.8

Martha Tune, the widow of an Army officer, was admitted to Walter Reed Army Hospital in 1985. Checking out her complaints of chest discomfort and shortness of breath, physicians discovered a malignancy of the pericardium. While undergoing treatment for this condition, Tune suddenly experienced severe respiratory difficulty and was placed on a ventilator. Subsequent examinations discovered lung cancer. Tune's physicians judged her condition to be terminal.

Tune was aware of her medical condition and, as a clearly competent patient, requested to be removed from the ventilator. Her physicians, even though sympathetic to her wishes, declined her request. They admitted that had they known the severity of her lung cancer, they would not have placed her on the ventilator. Nevertheless, they felt obligated to continue the mechanical ventilation because they believed Army policy gave them no other choice once they had initiated the artificial means of sustaining her life.

The U.S. District Court for the District of Columbia ruled in Tune's favor, and clarified the physicians' understanding of the law. Declaring that patients in federal hospitals—including military hospitals—have the same rights as patients in other hospitals, the court held that Tune was entitled to refuse the life support provided by the ventilator. The court noted that a competent patient's legal right to make decisions about medical treatment is "as binding upon the government as it is upon the medical profession at large."[19]

Case 3.9

Elizabeth Bouvia, having had cerebral palsy since birth, entered the Riverside (California) General Hospital in 1983. She subsequently applied to the Riverside Superior Court for a permanent injunction to prevent the physicians and hospital personnel from administering any medical care to her beyond pain medication and hygienic care. In particular, she sought to enjoin them from giving her any fluid, food, or other nutrients. She was, simply put, attempting to compel the physicians and nurses at Riverside General to assist her in committing suicide by starvation.

The superior court was convinced that Bouvia was competent, "sincere in her desire to terminate her life," and in "a fairly constant degree of pain." Nevertheless, the court maintained that the state's interests in the preservation of life, protection of third parties, prevention of suicide, and maintenance of the ethical standards of the medical profession outweighed Bouvia's desire to end her life with the assistance of society. Consequently, the court ruled (in what has become known as *Bouvia I*) that forced feeding was permissible to save the life of a "nonterminal patient."[20]

Three years later, having been outside hospital settings and courtrooms for the intervening time, Bouvia again sought legal assistance in refusing medical treatment. This time the hospital was High Desert Hospital, a public hospital in Los Angeles County. This time the trial court was the superior court. This time Bouvia's multiple medical problems were considerably worse: she was quadriplegic, she weighed only 65–70 pounds, she was in continual pain from degenerative crippling arthritis, she was largely immobile, she was wholly unable to care for herself, she was dependent on spoon-feeding for nourishment, and she was dependent on morphine administered through a chest catheter for pain relief. Also, this time the issue involved in refusing treatment was different: rather than refusing food that she was physically able to eat (as in 1983), she was seeking a court order prohibiting the hospital from using a nasogastric (NG) feeding tube to supplement her oral intake of food. The feeding tube had been inserted against her will and contrary to her express instructions.

The trial court denied Bouvia's request for immediate relief, and her attorneys appealed the decision. The court of appeal ruled (in *Bouvia II*) in her favor, saying:

> [The] petitioner's ability to tolerate physical discomfort does not diminish her right to immediate relief. Her mental and emotional feelings are equally entitled to respect. . . . To petitioner it is a dismal prospect to live with this hated and unwanted device attached to her, through perhaps years of the law's slow process. She has the right to have it removed immediately. . . . Petitioner sought to enforce only a right which was exclusively hers and over which neither the medical profession nor the judiciary have any veto power.

The court of appeal found Bouvia, now 28 years old, to be "intelligent, very mentally competent." As a competent patient, she "has the right to refuse any medical treatment or medical service, even when such treatment is labeled 'furnishing nourishment and hydration.' This right exists even if its exercise creates a 'life-threatening condition.'"

Citing a previous California Supreme Court case (*Cobbs v. Grant*) and two previous court of appeal cases (*Barber, Bartling*), the court ruled that a patient's right to refuse "even life-continuing treatment" does not depend on the patient's being terminally ill or "imminently" dying. The court declared:

> We do not believe it is the policy of this State that all and every life must be preserved against the will of the sufferer. It is incongruous, if not monstrous, for medical practitioners to assert their right to preserve a life that someone else must live, or, more accurately, endure, for "15 to 20 years" [Bouvia's estimated life span on tubal feeding]. We cannot conceive it to be the policy of this State to inflict such an ordeal upon anyone.

In addition, the court addressed the question of Bouvia's motives in refusing the NG tube. Not believing her to be suicidal, the court nevertheless stated, "We find nothing in the law to suggest the right to refuse medical treatment may be exercised only if the patient's motives meet someone else's approval."[21]

Case 3.10

Beverly Requena, aged 55 and "fully competent," was terminally ill with ALS. She had been a patient at St. Clare's–Riverside Medical Center in Boonton, New Jersey, since April 1985. By September 1986 she had become respirator-dependent, paralyzed from the neck down, and significantly bothered by persistent pain. She had lost the ability to communicate verbally, but she could understand speech, read, watch television, and communicate with eye-blink responses to questions and also with an alphabet board and computer.

She could not be fed normally, but could suck fluids through a straw. Realizing that her ability to swallow would soon be entirely gone, she informed the physicians and nurses that she would not accept feeding through an NG tube or through any other technological means. Her physicians and the members of her family accepted her decision. However, the administration, emphasizing that the hospital was a Catholic-affiliated institution and was "pro-life" in its philosophy, responded to her decision by adopting an official policy that declared "food and water" to be basic human needs and stated that no personnel at the hospital would participate in abating "artificial feeding and/or fluids." When Requena refused to be transferred to another hospital 17 miles away, the hospital initiated court action to compel her to leave.

Judge Reginald Stanton, in his trial court decision, pointed out that Requena had been a patient in that hospital for 17 months and would be "emotionally and psychologically" harmed if she were forced to leave against her will. Simply because she was "not accepting the full range of treatment available" was not a sufficient reason to force her to leave. Acknowledging that allowing the patient to remain in the hospital would impose "a real burden on its nurses and technicians," he maintained that "it is fairer to ask them to give than it is to ask Beverly Requena to give."

Consequently, the judge ruled that the patient "may not be removed from the Hospital without her consent." She may "remain in the Hospital until her death," and her decision not to accept artificial feeding "must be honored by the Hospital." For Judge Stanton, the "key moral and legal value involved in this case is the personal worth, dignity, and integrity of the individual human being who happens to be a patient." A crucial part of that personal worth, dignity, and integrity is "the right to make informed, autonomous decisions about one's own treatment" without being coerced.

The court's decision was upheld at the appellate level, with the appellate court concluding that an important part of the circumstances of the case was the fact that Requena had no notice of the hospital's policy until she had been a patient there for 15 months. Requena died at St. Clare's—Riverside Medical Center in November 1986.[22]

Case 3.11

Hector Rodas, a 34-year-old father of two young children, suffered brain damage from drug abuse in February 1986. He was left in a permanently "locked-in" condition: mentally normal, but paralyzed below the neck, in constant pain, and unable to speak. He could move his head and blink his eyes, but he could not swallow. Nutrients and fluids were administered through a gastrostomy tube.

Rodas was a patient at the Hilltop Rehabilitation Center in Grand Junction, Colorado. In the summer of 1986 he informed his physician and his attorneys (using eye signals and an alphabet board) that he wanted to stop the tube feeding and all other treatment that was keeping him alive. The Hilltop administration (and the physician responsible for Rodas) refused to comply with his request, claiming that he was mentally incapable of making such a decision and that they did not want to be guilty of assisting a suicide. In August, the administration and physician petitioned a district court to address the issues raised by the case.

In January 1987, the trial court judge issued an opinion ordering Hilltop to remove the feeding tube, and granting the participants in the case civil and criminal immunity for abating the treatment keeping Rodas alive. Even though Rodas was said by psychiatrists to be paranoid and depressed, the judge found Rodas's decision to forgo treatment "rational and reasonable."

Judge Charles Buss stated that the tube feeding keeping Rodas alive was "an unnatural process . . . done only through medical intervention and invasion of his body." Buss maintained that the right of Rodas as an autonomous patient to refuse life-sustaining treatment outweighed all of the competing state interests, including the state interests in preserving life, protecting innocent third parties, and preserving the ethical integrity of the medical profession. In regard to the petitioners' argument that it was in Rodas's best interests to remain alive, the judge stated: "To allow others to decide what is in [Rodas's] best interests would be to disregard the clearly established legal and medical ethic that a competent adult is allowed to refuse medical treatment."

In conclusion, the judge said that "to permit Hilltop to continue this unwanted treatment of Mr. Rodas would be to permit an ongoing battery to be imposed upon him." Hilltop was thus ordered (since Rodas could not be cared for at home, and no other institution within a 250-mile radius was willing to accept him unconditionally) to terminate "medicinal, feeding and hydration treatment" and to provide Rodas with necessary nursing care through its hospice program.[23]

Case 3.12

In 1982, when she was a 33-year-old wife and mother, Kathleen Farrell first experienced symptoms of ALS. Later, she was admitted to a Philadelphia hospital where she underwent a tracheotomy and was connected to a respirator. In the fall of 1983, she was released from the hospital and returned home to New Jersey to live with her husband and two teenage sons. She was paralyzed, and required around-the-clock nursing care.

Two years later she told Francis Farrell, her husband, that she wanted to be disconnected from the respirator. She also discussed her decision with her sons, parents, and sister.

In June 1986, her husband sought court appointment as her special medical guardian—with specific authorization to disconnect her from the respirator. He also sought a declaratory judgment that he and anyone assisting him in disconnecting the respirator would not incur civil or criminal liability. The trial court appointed a guardian *ad litem* for the sons.

Part of the court hearing was held at the Farrells' home to enable the judge to communicate directly with the patient. The court record at the time indicated that Farrell weighed less than 100 pounds (she had weighed 161 pounds in 1982), had no control over her limbs, had difficulty in swallowing, could take no solid food by mouth, and could communicate only by saying "yes" and "no" and using an alphabet board. When asked why she had decided to disconnect the respirator and let nature take its course, she responded, "I'm tired of suffering." Two psychologists testified that Farrell was competent to make the decision to abate treatment.

The trial court granted the relief that the Farrells had requested, but stayed its order pending appellate review. Francis Farrell then petitioned the New

Jersey Supreme Court for direct certification, and the guardian *ad litem* also filed an appeal. Less than a week later, on June 29, 1986, Kathleen Farrell died while still connected to the respirator.

Nevertheless, the supreme court agreed to render a decision in the case. The court's unanimous decision, issued June 24, 1987, became the cornerstone for the "trilogy" of decisions announced that day (the other cases being *Jobes* and *Peter,* to be discussed in the next chapter). In the decision, written by Justice Garibaldi, the court reaffirmed that a patient's right to refuse treatment is protected both by the common-law right of self-determination and the federal and state constitutional right of privacy. None of the state interests in the case was held to outweigh the right of an autonomous patient to refuse medical treatment no longer wanted.

The court then set forth procedures for other cases involving competent patients who decide to discontinue life-sustaining treatment while living at home. The first procedural step is a determination of the patient's competency by two nonattending physicians. The second, related procedural step is a determination by the same physicians that the patient has made the decision to abate treatment voluntarily, without coercion, and with sufficient information regarding prognosis, medical alternatives, the risks involved, and the likely outcome if the life-sustaining treatment is discontinued. These procedural steps are sufficient, unless there is conflict among interested parties to the case, to preclude the need for any court action.

In affirming the right of competent patients to make a treatment-abatement decision at home, including a decision likely to result in the patient's death, the court emphasized that the right to refuse treatment "does not vary depending on whether the patient is in a medical institution or at home." In addition, the court emphasized that any other person acting "in good faith" to abate life-sustaining treatment at the request of a competent patient at home need not fear civil or criminal action, as long as the court's procedural steps are followed.[24]

Significance and limitations of these cases

These cases of treatment refusal by autonomous patients clearly indicate that the legal aspects of abating treatment, in any of the three ways it can be carried out, have been dealt with at some length by a variety of courts. The Brooks, Heston, and Osborne cases, all involving Jehovah's Witnesses trying to refuse blood transfusions, show that treatment-refusal cases sometimes take the form of a patient's choosing to *omit* life-sustaining treatment by having physicians *withhold available treatment* from the patient. The Candura and Quackenbush cases fall into this same category, because both cases concerned the right of autonomous patients to refuse medically recommended amputations. By contrast, the

Bouvia case (at least the 1986 court of appeal case) illustrates the second way that treatment abatement can be done: a patient's choosing to *reduce the level of treatment* by having physicians *withdraw* a *modality of treatment already begun.* The legal issue confronting the court of appeal was neither the withholding of one or more modes of treatment not yet initiated, nor the termination of all treatment so that death would ensue (Bouvia wanted oral feeding and pain medication continued), but the selective withdrawal or diminishing of treatment (in this case, an NG tube). The third way of abating life-sustaining treatment is illustrated by the Perlmutter, Bartling, Tune, Requena, Rodas, and Farrell cases: a patient's choosing to *discontinue life-sustaining efforts* by having physicians *terminate the modality of treatment* (mechanical ventilation or technological feeding, in each of these cases) *that is keeping the patient alive.*

There can be little doubt that these cases represent a significant development in American jurisprudence. Just how significant the decisions are, and why they are significant, depends on who is interpreting the cases. For the members of some pro-life groups, this series of judicial opinions is significant—and regrettable—because they believe the cases have opened the legal door to suicide and the intentional killing of critically ill patients. This claim is not true, as will be demonstrated in the discussion that follows. By contrast, some of the more idealistic and optimistic members of the right-to-die movement regard the decisions as significant because they think the cases—especially the later ones in the series—demonstrate that autonomous patients have a legally guaranteed, basically unqualified right to die. This view is also not true, although it is considerably closer to the truth than the pro-life claims about suicide and euthanasia.

What is the significance of these individual decisions? In summary form, the cases stack up in the following manner:

Brooks (Illinois Supreme Court, 1964): the second religion-based treatment-refusal case to reach the appellate level, the first case of this type to reach a state supreme court, the first ruling to allow for refusal of life-prolonging treatment on the grounds of religious freedom, and the case that called for the balancing of a patient's rights and state interests on the basis of the "clear and present danger to society" test.

Heston (New Jersey Supreme Court, 1971): found the "compelling state interest" test preferable to the test used in *Brooks,* regarded the professional standards of hospitals as a sufficient reason for overriding the views of a nonconsenting patient, and ruled that judicial and medical intervention was justifiable even in a case without minor children.

Osborne (District of Columbia Court of Appeals, 1972): demonstrated (like most Jehovah's Witness cases) that treatment refusal does not entail a desire to die, distinguished among religion-based treatment refusal cases on the basis of the sincerity of a patient's religious beliefs, and allowed for treatment refusal even when minor children would lose their biological father.[25]

Candura (Massachusetts Appeals Court, 1978): emphasized that neither irrationality nor vacillation in one's views is tantamount to incompetence, that an autonomous patient does not need family consent to refuse treatment, and that "the magnitude of the invasion proposed" is important in balancing refusal of treatment against various state interests.

Myers (Massachusetts Supreme Judicial Court, 1979): showed that refusals of treatment by prisoners are usually related to the prison confinement, and used the state's interest in upholding an orderly prison administration as a compelling reason for judicially compelled treatment.[26]

Perlmutter (Florida Supreme Court, 1980): the first clear right-to-die case involving an autonomous patient with nonreligious reasons, and the first such case to reach a state supreme court; the district court of appeal ruled that no state interests outweighed Perlmutter's right to choose to "die with dignity," that termination of life-sustaining treatment in this case did not represent unlawful killing, and that treatment refusal in this case was based on both the constitutional right of privacy and the common-law right to self-determination; the state supreme court affirmed the decision, but limited the ruling to the facts of the Perlmutter case: a competent patient, a terminal illness, refusal of "extraordinary" medical treatment, and consent of the family members.

Bartling (California Court of Appeal, 1984): affirmed that the right to refuse medical treatment is encompassed within the "constitutionally guaranteed right" of privacy (in both the federal and California constitutions), emphasized that a competent patient wanting to refuse treatment need not have signed a directive under the California Natural Death Act, and ruled that periodic wavering or vacillation in a patient's views is not tantamount to incompetence and does not justify an effort by physicians to ignore a patient's expressed wishes.

Tune (U.S. District Court, 1985): the first opinion containing a final federal court ruling on a patient's right to refuse life-sustaining treatment, and the first decision specifically stating that patients in federal hospitals have the same rights as patients in other hospitals.

Bouvia (California Court of Appeal, 1986): ruled that the right to refuse medical treatment is not limited to terminal patients, that this right does not depend on a patient's motives, that the right includes "any medical treatment" (such as artificial feeding), and that this right can be vetoed by neither the medical profession nor the judiciary.

Requena (Appellate Division of the Superior Court of New Jersey, 1986): the first judicial decision to hold that an autonomous patient's right to refuse life-sustaining treatment outweighs an opposing institutional policy and the offense and harm such a decision brings to the health care professionals who disagree with it.

Rodas (trial court in Colorado, 1987): ruled that some limited mental impairment did not sufficiently affect the patient's autonomous status, that the patient could appoint a proxy (under a general durable-power-of-attorney statute) to refuse treatment on his behalf should he become incapable of doing so himself, that technological feeding is to be regarded as a form of medical treatment, and that continuing life-sustaining treatment against a patient's wishes is a battery.[27]

Farrell (New Jersey Supreme Court, 1987): addressed the right to refuse treatment in a case having a different fact pattern from *Quinlan, Conroy, Jobes,* and *Peter;* set forth procedures for New Jersey cases involving autonomous patients living at home; stated that persons helping to carry out treatment abatement according to these procedures need not fear civil or criminal action as long as they act in good faith; and emphasized that courts usually need not get involved in such cases.[28]

In addition to their significance as individual cases, these decisions as a group represent an important trend in recent law. That trend, which consists of extending and clarifying the common-law tradition on the right of autonomous patients to refuse treatment, has several features that are worth noting. First, the common-law right of self-determination (as seen in the 1891, 1914, and 1960 decisions quoted earlier) has been supplemented by the constitutional right of religious freedom. As we have seen, cases involving autonomous patients refusing life-sustaining treatment on the grounds of religious freedom go back to the mid-1960s. The different rulings in *Georgetown College* and *Brooks* not only reflected different facts in the two cases, but also foreshadowed the mixed judicial record that cases pitting religious freedom versus state interests would have in several jurisdictions during succeeding years. The majority of these opinions upheld the right of autonomous patients to refuse medical treatment, with at least seven cases specifically affirming the right of autonomous patients to refuse life-sustaining treatment for reasons of religious belief: *Brooks, Osborne, Holmes v. Silver Cross Hospital, In re Phelps, In re Melideo, Mercy Hospital v. Jackson,* and *Randolph v. City of New York.*[29] Two additional cases were easier to decide, since the treatment being refused for reasons of religious belief was not regarded as life-sustaining: *Winters v. Miller,* and *In re Boyd.*[30] By contrast, seven other cases have had courts deciding to override a patient's religion-based refusal of treatment: *Georgetown College* (to protect a dependent child), *Raleigh Fitkin-Paul Morgan Memorial Hospital v. Anderson* (to preserve the life of a viable fetus), *Heston* (to preserve life per se, and to protect the professional standards of hospitals), *Powell v. Columbia Presbyterian Medical Center* (to protect six dependent children), *United States v. George* (to protect the ethical integrity of physicians), *Hamilton v. McAuliffe* (to protect a dependent child), and *Crouse Irving Memorial Hospital v. Paddock* (to preserve the life of a fetus).[31]

In spite of this mixed judicial record, the constitutional right of religious freedom clearly supplements the common-law tradition on self-determination in providing legal grounds for patients to refuse medical treatment. Although the right to refuse treatment for reasons of religious freedom is far from absolute, the First Amendment basis for refusing medical treatment is now an acceptable, if still problematic, feature of American jurisprudence. The change that has taken place from the cases in the 1960s is evident in three ways:

1. The right of an autonomous patient to refuse treatment for religious reasons is now regarded as paramount to virtually any state interest in cases in which the treatment is not regarded as life-sustaining.

2. Even in cases involving life-sustaining treatment, half of the courts, including two at the appellate level, have upheld the patient's refusal even though the courts knew these patients did not want to die.

3. The countervailing state interest that is most likely to bring about judicially compelled life-sustaining treatment, with the courts acting on the basis of the *parens patriae* doctrine, is the presence of one or more dependent children (or possibly, a late-term fetus).

In sum, treatment refusal by an autonomous patient on the basis of religious freedom is likely to be upheld should such a case go to court—unless the patient is a parent of one or more dependent children, and these children lack another parent who could care for their material needs.

Second, the common-law right of self-determination has been supplemented to an even greater extent by the constitutionally derived right of privacy. Although the right of privacy is not explicitly mentioned in the Constitution, the concept of such a right—and its application to physical integrity—can be traced back as far as the 1891 case quoted earlier.[32] The constitutional derivation of this right was first enunciated by Justice Douglas in *Griswold v. Connecticut,* when he stated that "specific guarantees in the Bill of Rights have penumbras" that create, among other things, "zones of privacy."[33] These zones of privacy permit individuals to use contraceptives (the legal issue in *Griswold*), to marry, to procreate, and to decide (as put forth in *Roe v. Wade*) to terminate an unwanted pregnancy.[34]

Since the landmark *Roe v. Wade* decision, several courts have used the right of privacy as the legal basis for upholding a patient's refusal of medical treatment. For example, a Pennsylvania court in *In re Yetter* upheld a schizophrenic patient's earlier refusal of recommended surgery for breast cancer by declaring that

[the] constitutional right of privacy includes the right of a mature competent adult to refuse to accept medical recommendations that may prolong one's life . . . in short, the right of privacy includes a right to die with which the State should not interfere where there are no minor or unborn children and no clear and present danger to public health, welfare or morals.[35]

Two landmark cases dealing with *nonautonomous* patients (we will discuss the cases at greater length in the next chapter) have placed substantial weight on the right of privacy. In 1976, the New Jersey Supreme Court decided in its famous *Quinlan* decision that state interests such as the preservation of life per se and the protection of the ethical integrity of medical decision making must be balanced against a patient's right of privacy:

We think that the State's interest *contra* weakens and the individual's right to privacy grows as the degree of bodily invasion increases and the prognosis dims. Ultimately there comes a point at which the individual's right overcomes the State's interest. It is for that reason that we believe Karen's choice, if she were competent to make it, would be vindicated by the law.[36]

In 1977, the Supreme Judicial Court of Massachusetts agreed with that aspect of the *Quinlan* decision by indicating in its *Saikewicz* opinion that various state interests could be overridden by a patient's right of privacy:

The constitutional right of privacy, as we conceive it, is an expression of the sanctity of individual free choice and self-determination as fundamental constituents of life. The value of life as so perceived is lessened not by a decision to refuse treatment, but by the failure to allow a competent human being the right of choice.[37]

With these legal precedents, it is hardly surprising that cases of treatment refusal by autonomous patients have in recent years been decided by judicial usage of the emergent right of privacy. The Myers, Perlmutter, Bartling, Bouvia, and Farrell cases specifically involve discussions of the right of privacy, and four of the five decisions agree that a patient's right of privacy can, depending on the factors in a case, outweigh competing state interests. Only the *Myers* court, with its concern over an orderly prison administration, overrrides a patient's right of privacy in refusing life-sustaining treatment. And that court, which 2 years earlier provided the *Saikewicz* decision, points out that even incarceration "does not per se divest" a patient of the right of privacy.

Thus a growing number of courts acknowledge that autonomous patients may refuse medical treatment on the legal grounds of privacy, even when the refusal (as in the Perlmutter case) will almost certainly result in the patient's death. The right of privacy in such cases is not absolute, and the U.S. Supreme Court has not yet addressed the application of this right to treatment refusal, but its importance is evident in that *no appellate court in the past decade has overridden an autonomous patient's refusal of life-sustaining treatment* when the patient has laid claim to this very personal right outside the context of a prison. However, there are limits to the right, depending on factors in cases and the jurisdiction in which a case is decided. Just how the right applies to prisoners is somewhat uncertain (the highest courts in Massachusetts, Georgia, and West Virginia disagree), and the breadth of the right's applicability in other treatment-refusal cases is also unclear: the Florida Supreme Court thus far limits the right to terminally ill patients with no minor dependents, whose affected adult family members agree with the decision to stop "extraordinary" treatment, whereas the California Court of Appeal deciding the Bartling and Bouvia cases extends the right of treatment refusal to cases in which an autonomous patient is neither terminally ill nor "imminently" dying.

Third, decisions by the New Jersey Supreme Court (in *Heston* and *Quinlan*) and the Supreme Judicial Court of Massachusetts (in *Saikewicz* and *Myers*) established a method for adjudication in treatment-refusal cases that has become normative for similar cases in other jurisdictions. That method consists of balancing an autonomous patient's right to refuse treatment (on the legal basis of self-determination, religious freedom, and/or privacy) against competing state interests to determine if one or more of the state interests is "compelling" and thus sufficient to override the patient's right.

In *Heston* and *Quinlan*, the New Jersey Supreme Court weighed the patient's right of religious freedom (Heston) or privacy (Quinlan) against two state interests: the preservation of human life, and the maintenance of the integrity of medical decision making. In *Saikewicz*, the Supreme Judicial Court of Massachusetts expanded the list of state interests to four: the preservation of human life, the protection of the interests of innocent third parties, the prevention of suicide, and the maintenance of the ethical integrity of the medical profession. And in *Myers*, as we have noted, the same court ruled that in the abnormal circumstance of a prisoner's refusing life-sustaining treatment, the maintenance of an orderly prison administration is a specific instance of the state interest in protecting innocent third parties.

Six particularly important cases of treatment refusal by autonomous patients (Myers, Perlmutter, Bartling, Bouvia, Requena, and Farrell) have reached appellate courts since the *Saikewicz* court articulated the four state interests possibly involved in such cases. Since the courts in the first four cases addressed the relative importance of these state interests to the case at bar, their collective efforts at balancing the patient's right to refuse treatment against the state's interests provide significant evidence about the relative "weight" of each of the state's interests. Moreover, these first four decisions—two of them made by the same court—provide important clues regarding the circumstances in which one or more of these interests might in the future be regarded as overriding the patient's right of treatment refusal.

The four courts agree that the preservation of life is the most important of the state's interests, but only the *Myers* court regarded this interest along with two other state interests (the second and fourth) as sufficiently compelling to override the patient's refusal of life-sustaining treatment. In terms of this state interest, the court reasoned that the recommended treatment offered Myers the opportunity of living a "normal" (although incarcerated) and "healthy" life. Significantly, however, the court cited *Lane v. Candura* and specifically stated that "the State's interest in the preservation of life does not invariably control the right to refuse treatment in cases of positive prognosis."[38]

For the other three courts, the state's interest in the preservation of life was decidedly less important because the medical treatment offered (mechanical ventilation for Perlmutter and Bartling, technological feeding for Bouvia) was not curative but only an artificial means of prolonging life for an indeterminate period of time. The *Perlmutter* court saw no point in prolonging a terminally ill patient's "wretched" situation and thus rejected the state's claim that it had an overriding duty to preserve life.[39] The *Bartling* court, dealing with a hospital intent on prolonging the patient's life indefinitely, declared that the patient's right to refuse treatment "must be paramount to the interests of the patient's hospital and doctors."[40] The same court, in its *Bouvia* decision, rejected the argument that the artificial prolongation of the patient's life for "an additional 15 to 20 years" outweighed her right to refuse the NG tube. Rather, the court of appeal decided that the trial court had erred by considering the prolongation of the patient's life in quantitative rather than qualitative terms. Given a patient whose quality of life "has been diminished to the point of hopelessness, uselessness, unenjoyability, and frustration," the court asked:

Who shall say what the minimum amount of available life must be? Does it matter if it be 15 to 20 years, 15 to 20 months, or 15 to 20 days, if such life has been physically destroyed and its quality, dignity, and purpose [are] gone? As in all matters lines must be drawn at some point, somewhere, but that decision must ultimately belong to the one whose life is in issue.[41]

The second state interest, the protection of the interests of innocent third parties, was not a concern in these four cases: Myers and Bouvia were single and had no children, Perlmutter was 73 and his family agreed with his decision, and Bartling was 70 and his wife joined him in the suit against Glendale Adventist Medical Center. However, as we have noted, several courts dealing with treatment refusal cases have regarded the protection of minor children and late-term fetuses as a compelling reason for overriding competent patients' religious freedom. The leading case of this sort is *Georgetown College,* while *Osborne* suggests that the presence of minor children does not always result in the patient's refusal of treatment being overridden.

In terms of the state's interest in preventing suicide, the four courts unanimously reject the claim that these autonomous patients, in refusing life-sustaining treatment, are actually committing suicide. For the *Myers* court, the issue of suicide was handled by quoting from the earlier *Saikewicz* decision: should

Myers die as a consequence of refusing treatment, his death would be from "'natural causes' since he would not have 'set the death-producing agent in motion' with the 'specific intent' of causing his own death."[42] For the *Perlmutter* court, Perlmutter's impending death in the absence of mechanical ventilation could not be considered a suicide for two reasons: his "basic wish to live, plus the fact that he did not seif-induce his horrible affliction, precludes his further refusal of treatment being classed as attempted suicide."[43]

The California Court of Appeal discussed the suicide issue at some length in both of its decisions. In *Bartling,* the court used three arguments to show that Bartling was not trying to commit suicide: (1) he had no "specific intent to die," (2) he was not causing his death since he did not "set the death-producing agent in motion," and (3) he was not engaged in "irrational self-destruction." Thus "there is no connection between the conduct here in issue and any State concern to prevent suicide."[44] In *Bouvia,* the suicide issue was especially important because her first trial court hearing 3 years earlier had centered on her request to be aided in committing suicide. By 1986, however, the court pointed out that Bouvia's medical condition had changed, as had her intention to commit suicide. Now the court said, "her decision to allow nature to take its course is not equivalent to an election to commit suicide." The court went on to add a statement not found in the other three cases: namely, that even if Bouvia did have suicidal motivation in refusing the tube feedings (which the court did not believe to be true), that motivation would not automatically preclude the exercise of her right to refuse treatment. In the court's words: "It certainly is not illegal or immoral to prefer a natural, albeit sooner, death than a drugged life attached to a mechanical device."[45]

The state's interest in maintaining the ethical integrity of medical decision making has changed somewhat over the years. Once this state interest clearly focused on the possibility that a patient's refusal of life-sustaining treatment might force physicians (as articulated in *U.S. v. George*) and/or hospitals (as argued in *Heston*) to acquiesce to decisions contrary to their professional standards (*George:* "ignore the mandates of their own conscience") regarding the restoration of patients' health and the prolongation of patients' lives. This problem still was an important part of the Requena and Rodas cases. However, in several recent treatment-refusal cases, the focal point has moved from consideration of physicians' (and nurses') professional ethical standards as such to questions of whether departure from these ethical standards may bring about legal liability, with the courts exploring the issue of whether medical cooperation and assistance with an autonomous patient's refusal of treatment constitute legal grounds for either civil or criminal liability. Simply put, the issue is whether physicians who carry out patients' wishes regarding treatment abatement (by stopping dialysis, disconnecting a ventilator, or discontinuing technological feeding) are liable to malpractice claims (for failing to carry out a customary practice), charges of aiding and abetting a suicide, or a variety of criminal homicide charges.

The judicial response in the four appellate-level cases we have been discussing is resoundingly clear. Contrary to the claims sometimes put forth by some pro-life representatives, all of these courts agree with the earlier *Saikewicz* court that a patient's refusal of medical treatment ''in appropriate circumstances'' should not be regarded as threatening the ethical standards of physicians or hospitals.[46] The *Myers* court, dealing with the unusual case of a prisoner, compelled treatment because the justices believed Myers's refusal of treatment to be inappropriate for the circumstances and contrary to medical ethics: ''the traumatic cost to the patient is not inordinate and the prognosis is good.''[47] In a very different and seemingly clear-cut case of treatment refusal by a terminally ill patient, the *Perlmutter* court specifically addressed the state's dual claim that ''termination of supportive treatment . . . is an unlawful killing of a human being'' under Florida law, and that any physicians assisting Perlmutter in removing the ventilator might be subject to civil or criminal charges. The court's response, as noted in the earlier case presentation, was to declare that Perlmutter's rights were superior to any physician or hospital administrator's convenience in insisting ''on continuing Mr. Perlmutter's life [merely] so that there can be no question of foul play, no resulting civil liability, and no possible trespass on medical ethics.''[48]

The California Court of Appeal, because of the murder charges brought against physicians in the earlier *Barber* case (see Case 4.12), addressed this issue even more explicitly. In *Bartling,* the physicians and administrators at Glendale Adventist Medical Center claimed that they might face civil and criminal charges if they complied with Bartling's wishes. Citing their earlier *Barber* decision, the justices made the following response:

[W]e are now satisfied the law as outlined is clear and if Mr. Bartling had lived real parties could not have been criminally or civilly liable for carrying out his instructions. Furthermore in future similar situations, parties facing the problems confronting real parties here should be free to act according to the patient's instruction without fear of liability and without advance court approval.[49]

Then, in the *Bouvia* decision, the court dismissed the claim that the removal of Bouvia's NG tube constituted the criminal act of aiding in suicide. The justices noted that aiding another person in committing suicide normally involves ''affirmative, assertive, proximate, direct conduct such as furnishing a gun, poison, knife, or other instrumentality or usable means by which another [can] physically and immediately inflict some death-producing injury upon himself.'' Such situations ''are far different than the mere presence of a doctor during the exercise of his patient's constitutional rights.'' The court concluded with a simple, far-reaching declaration: ''No criminal or civil liability attaches to honoring a competent, informed patient's refusal of medical service.''[50]

What do these court decisions suggest regarding future cases involving conflicts between an autonomous patient's right to refuse treatment and these four state interests? The decisions suggest that, despite the erroneous opinions of some trial judges, *all cases arriving at the appellate level are likely to have an autonomous patient's refusal of life-sustaining treatment upheld*—unless the recommended treatment (1) is minimally invasive and offers a good prognosis, or (2) third-party interests are overriding. In such cases, the first and fourth state interests might become compelling and override the patient's decision, but the court would surely be obligated to show *why even these two criteria* override an autonomous patient's privacy rights and what, precisely, "minimally invasive" and "good prognosis" mean in the case at bar. In addition, it is surely possible that the state's interests in protecting the interests of innocent third parties—a state interest recently addressed only in *Rodas*—could be regarded as a compelling reason to override a patient's refusal of life-sustaining treatment, but only in the circumstances of (1) one or more minor children (or possibly late-term fetuses) who (2) would be materially harmed in the event of the parent's death. In fact, given the state's traditional role according to the *parens patriae* doctrine, this second state interest could easily be regarded as the most important of the state's interests in treatment refusal cases involving parents of minor children. Even at that, however, it is not at all clear that this state interest, as important as it is, should be regarded as having more weight than a terminally ill patient's decision to refuse one or more modes of treatment. Finally, these cases suggest that a physician's civil and criminal liability for carrying out an autonomous patient's treatment refusal is no more significant—and possibly less significant— than the same physician's civil and criminal liability for refusing to comply with the patient's refusal of life-sustaining treatment. As indicated by *Bartling, Rodas,* and several other cases (including *Leach v. Shapiro,* which we will discuss in the next chapter), physicians are also liable to charges of battery, malpractice, and civil rights violations when they persist in administering unwanted and unconsented medical treatment to an autonomous patient.[51]

A legal right, or a conditional privilege?

What kinds of conclusions can we draw about the right of autonomous patients to refuse medical treatment? First, the preceding analysis demonstrates (at a minimum!) that *anyone denying that the right to refuse treatment exists is clearly wrong,* on both common-law and constitutional grounds. Anyone claiming that "a patient has *no right* to refuse treatment" (as a Florida state attorney asserted in the Perlmutter case) or that such a right does not exist in "a Christian, pro-life oriented hospital" (as the Glendale Adventist Medical Center claimed in the Bartling case) does not understand the law. Moreover, anyone now asserting that there "is no constitutional right to choose to die" (as, surprisingly, the New

Jersey Supreme Court claimed in the Heston case) does not have a correct interpretation of the law. If such views were ever true (before 1960? 1976?), they have been nullified by the case law of the past two decades. For example, even if the *Heston* statement were true in New Jersey in 1971, that interpretation of the law was abrogated by the *Quinlan* court 5 years later.

Second, even with the inevitable variation among jurisdictions, there is sufficient case law to allow us to identify *a number of features of the right to refuse medical treatment*. When an autonomous adult patient exercises the right to refuse treatment, including life-sustaining and dying-prolonging treatment, that decision

is not conditioned by the patient's age,

is not invalidated by periods of vacillation or wavering by the patient,

is not conditioned by the presence or absence of terminal illness,

does not depend on the patient's motives,

does not depend on the patient's having signed a natural death act in the state of residence,

does not require the consent of adult family members,

does not require medical approval,

does not require hospital approval,

does not require prior judicial approval,

is valid whether the person is in a medical institution or at home,

is valid in any hospital (private, state, or federal),

does not involve civil or criminal liability for a physician carrying out the decision,

does not implicate a cooperating physician or hospital in actions that might be judged criminal (assisting a suicide or intentionally killing a patient),

is rarely limited by any of the state's interests—

but also is not absolute.

Third, several policy statements and recommendations by authoritative groups indicate that the right of an autonomous patient to refuse treatment has in recent years gained *widespread acceptance in American society*. In 1983, the President's Commission arrived at the following conclusions regarding competent patients and life-sustaining treatment:

(1) The voluntary choice of a competent and informed patient should determine whether or not life-sustaining therapy will be undertaken, just as such choices provide the basis for other decisions about medical treatment. Health care institutions and professionals should try to enhance patients' abilities to make decisions on their own behalf and to promote understanding of the available treatment options.

(2) Health care professionals serve patients best by maintaining a presumption in favor of sustaining life, while recognizing that competent patients are entitled to choose to forego any treatments, including those that sustain life.[52]

In 1985, the American Hospital Association approved a policy statement regarding patients' choices of treatment options. The relevant part of the statement declared: "Whenever possible . . . the authority to determine the course of treatment, if any, should rest with the patient . . . the right to choose treatment includes the right to refuse a specific treatment *or all treatment.* . . ."[53] In early 1986, a joint committee of the Los Angeles County Bar Association and the Los Angeles County Medical Association published guidelines regarding life-sustaining treatment. The first guideline affirmed that it is "the right of an adult person capable of giving informed consent to make his or her own decision regarding medical care after having been fully informed about the benefits, risks, and consequences of treatment alternatives, even when such a decision might result in shortening the individual's life."[54] Later in 1986, the judicial council of the A.M.A. published guidelines on treatment abatement. The pertinent part of the statement declared: "The social commitment of the physician is to sustain life and relieve suffering. Where the performance of one duty conflicts with the other, the choice of the patient, or his family or legal representative if the patient is incompetent to act in his own behalf, should prevail."[55]

Nevertheless, there are, in spite of the legal backing and popular support for the right, *remaining problems in implementing the right to refuse medical treatment.* Decisions by appellate courts in California, Florida, Massachusetts, and New Jersey may or may not have bearing on the actual decisions about medical treatment made by patients and physicians in other states. Policy statements by prestigious national organizations may or may not filter down to the state and local level to influence—and change—the views of physicians, hospital administrators, hospital attorneys, and trial court judges. Judicial decisions clearly stating that physicians have no civil or criminal liability for honoring an autonomous patient's refusal of treatment may or may not be confirmed by state and county medical associations. The practical consequence of all this, unfortunately, can be that the legal right to refuse treatment degenerates—out of misinformation and ignorance of the law—into a "right" to do no more than to agree with one's physician regarding the merits of treatment.[56]

Alternatively, physicians, hospital administrators, and hospital attorneys in some locales may intentionally give "mere lip service to [what they regard as] a fictitious right."[57] For reasons of defensive medical practice, outdated hospital policy, adherence to the "technological imperative," disregard of patients' wishes, personal ethical convictions, refusal to discuss treatment options and likely outcomes with patients, financial gain, and sheer obstinacy, some physicians and their associates may (as Perlmutter, Bartling, and Bouvia found out) go to great lengths to thwart autonomous patients' efforts to implement their legal right to refuse treatment.

Three examples involving terminally ill cancer patients will help make the point. In one case, the patient became a pawn in a daily power play between two physicians who disagreed about the moral and legal permissibility of DNR (do not resuscitate) orders. Each morning the attending physician, an oncologist, would write a "no-code" directive on the patient's chart only to have a surgeon, unduly concerned about liability, cancel the directive each afternoon during his rounds.[58] In a second case, the patient was racked with intractable pain and pleaded with his physicians to let him die. Instead, the physicians in the case resuscitated the patient 52 times against his will! The patient died only when a compassionate nurse finally intervened by deciding not to call yet another "code blue."[59] In the third case, the patient was 26 weeks pregnant, imminently dying with metastatic cancer, and had indicated to her husband, her mother, and her physicians that she only wanted to be kept comfortable while she died. She specifically refused to consent to surgery to remove the fetus from her body. Nevertheless, attorneys for the George Washington University Medical Center contacted a judge, arranged for an emergency hearing at the hospital, then arranged for an extraordinary conference call with an appeals court justice, and then had a surgeon perform a cesarean delivery. The baby died soon afterwards, and the woman died 2 days later.[60]

The implications of all this for autonomous patients are threefold. Such patients should become informed about the legal right to refuse medical treatment, including modalities of treatment that are capable of sustaining life for indeterminate periods of time. They should seek the cooperation of a physician willing to adhere to their informed preferences about medical treatment, and they should sign a waiver or release form if the physician or hospital administrator thinks such a form is necessary for legal protection. Moreover, such patients should, in those rare instances when an uncooperative physician tries to turn this legal right into an ungranted "privilege," be prepared to change physicians or (should that not be a practical alternative) initiate legal action against the physician, with charges of malpractice, battery, and violation of the common-law and constitutionally based right to refuse medical treatment.

NOTES

1. Satz v. Perlmutter, 362 So.2d 160, 163 (Fla. Dist. Ct. App. 1978), aff'd, 379 So. 2d 359 (Fla. 1980).
2. Bouvia v. Superior Court, 179 Cal. App. 3d 1127, 225 Cal.Rptr. 297, 305 (Cal. App.2d Dist. 1986), review denied (Cal. June 5, 1986).
3. Union Pacific Railway Co. v. Botsford, 141 U.S. 250, 251, 11 S.Ct. 1000 (1891).
4. Schloendorff v. New York Hospital, 211 N.Y. 125, 129, 105 N.E. 92, 93 (1914).
5. Natanson v. Kline, 186 Kan. 393, 406–7, 350 P.2d 1093, 1104 (1960). This quotation is often used in the extensive legal literature on the right to refuse treatment. Among the more helpful articles in that literature are Beverly A. Gazza, "Compulsory Medical Treatment and Constitutional Guarantees: A Conflict?" University of Pittsburg Law Review 33 (1972): 628–37; Edward J. Gurney, "Is There a Right

to Die? A Study of the Law of Euthanasia,'' *Cumberland-Samford Law Review* 3 (1972): 235–61; Norman L. Cantor, "A Patient's Decision to Decline Life-Saving Medical Treatment," *Rutgers Law Review* 26 (Winter 1973): 228–64; Michael T. Sullivan, "The Dying Person—His Plight and His Right," *New England Law Review* 8 (1973): 197–216; Robert M. Byrn, "Compulsory Lifesaving Treatment for the Competent Adult," *Fordham Law Review* 44 (1975): 1–36; Thomas A. Rutledge, "Informed Consent for the Terminal Patient," *Baylor Law Review* 27 (Winter 1975): 11–21; Sonya Meyers Davis, "The Refusal of Life-Saving Medical Treatment vs. The State's Interest in the Preservation of Life: A Clarification of the Interests at Stake," *Washington University Law Quarterly* 58 (Winter 1980): 85–116; Andrew B. Roth and Robert Andrew Wild, "When the Patient Refuses Treatment: Some Observations and Proposals for Handling the Difficult Case," *Saint Louis University Law Journal* 23 (1979): 429–45; Henry Zee Shaub, "The Right to Refuse Medical Treatment: Under What Circumstances Does It Exist?" *Duquesne Law Review* 18 (1980): 607–28; Allison Newell, "A Right to Choose Death," *Cumberland Law Review* 13 (1982–1983): 117–42; Legal Advisers Committee of Concern for Dying, "The Right to Refuse Treatment: A Model Act," *American Journal of Public Health* 73 (1983): 918–21; George J. Annas and Joan E. Densberger, "Competence to Refuse Medical Treatment: Autonomy vs. Paternalism," *Toledo Law Review* 15 (Winter 1984): 561–96; Marigene Dessaint, "The Physician's Duty to Ascertain and Comply with a Competent Patient's Preferences Regarding Resuscitation," *Arizona State Law Journal* 1984 (1984): 305–33; Martha Swartz, "The Patient Who Refuses Medical Treatment: A Dilemma for Hospitals and Physicians," *American Journal of Law and Medicine* 11 (1985): 147–94; and Martha Alys Matthews, "Suicidal Competence and the Patient's Right to Refuse Lifesaving Treatment," *California Law Review* 75 (March 1987): 707–58.

6. President's Commission, *Making Health Care Decisions: Report* (Washington, D.C.: U.S. Government Printing Office, 1982), p. 56n.

7. Office of Technology Assessment (OTA), *Life-Sustaining Technologies and the Elderly* (Washington, D.C.: U.S. Government Printing Office, 1987), p. 443.

8. The Hastings Center Project, *Guidelines on the Termination of Life-Sustaining Treatment and the Care of the Dying* (Briarcliff Manor, N.Y.: The Hastings Center, 1987), pp. 131–32.

9. See Michael Tooley, "Abortion and Infanticide," *Philosophy and Public Affairs* 2 (Fall 1972): 37–65; idem, "Decisions to Terminate Life and the Concept of Person," in John Ladd, ed., *Ethical Issues Relating to Life and Death* (New York: Oxford University Press, 1979), pp. 62–93; idem, *Abortion and Infanticide* (Oxford and New York: Oxford University Press, 1983); Mary Anne Warren, "On the Moral and Legal Status of Abortion," *The Monist* 57 (January 1973): 43–61; Peter Singer, *Practical Ethics* (Cambridge and New York: Cambridge University Press, 1979); H. Tristram Engelhardt, Jr., *The Foundations of Bioethics* (New York: Oxford University Press, 1986); and Joel Feinberg, "Abortion," in Tom Regan, ed., *Matters of Life and Death* (New York: Random House, 1986), pp. 256–93.

10. Feinberg, "Abortion," p. 263.

11. My thinking about the concepts of competence and autonomy was greatly helped by Tom L. Beauchamp and James F. Childress, *Principles of Biomedical Ethics*, 2nd ed. (New York: Oxford University Press, 1983), pp. 59–105; Charles M. Culver and Bernard Gert, *Philosophy in Medicine* (New York: Oxford University Press, 1982), pp. 42–63; Tom L. Beauchamp and Laurence B. McCullough, *Medical Ethics: The*

Moral Responsibilities of Physicians (Englewood Cliffs, N.J.: Prentice-Hall, 1984), pp. 105–32; Allen Buchanan and Dan W. Brock, "Deciding for Others," *Milbank Memorial Fund Quarterly* 64 (Suppl. 2, 1986): 22–28; and Paul S. Appelbaum, Charles W. Lidz, and Alan Meisel, *Informed Consent: Legal Theory and Clinical Practice* (New York: Oxford University Press, 1987), pp. 81–111.

12. In re Brooks' Estate, 32 Ill.2d 361, 205 N.E.2d 435, 441–42 (1965). For the Georgetown College case, see Application of the President and Directors of Georgetown College, Inc., 331 F.2d 1000, *reh. denied,* 331 F.2d 1010 (D.C. Cir. 1964), *cert. denied,* 377 U.S. 978 (1964).

13. John F. Kennedy Memorial Hospital v. Heston, 58 N.J. 576, 279 A.2d 670, 673 (1971). *Heston* is sometimes interpreted as a case involving an autonomous patient, other times as a case with a nonautonomous patient. I place it in this chapter rather than Chapter 4, since the New Jersey Supreme Court stated in *Quinlan* that they had earlier acted "as if" Delores Heston were competent. For the earlier New Jersey case, see Raleigh Fitkin-Paul Morgan Memorial Hospital v. Anderson, 42 N.J. 421, 201 A.2d 537 (1964).

14. In re Osborne, 294 A.2d 372 (D.C. App. 1972).

15. Lane v. Candura, 6 Mass.App.Ct. 377, 376 N.E.2d 1232, 1233 (1978). In *Quackenbush,* the court held that the patient's right of privacy outweighed the state's interest in preserving life, largely because the recommended double amputation entailed extensive physical invasion. See In re Quackenbush, 156 N.J.Super. 282, 383 A.2d 785 (1978).

16. Commissioner of Corrections v. Myers, 399 N.E.2d 452, 457–58 (Mass. 1979). For the Saikewicz decision, see Superintendent of Belchertown State School v. Saikewicz, 373 Mass. 728, 370 N.E.2d 417 (1977).

17. Satz, *supra,* 362 So.2d 160, 164, 379 So.2d 359, 360.

18. Bartling v. Superior Court, 163 Cal.App.3d 186, 209 Cal.Rptr. 220 (1984). For the Barber case, see Barber v. Superior Court, 147 Cal.App.3d 1006, 195 Cal.Rptr. 484 (1983).

19. Tune v. Walter Reed Army Medical Hospital, 602 F.Supp. 1452 (1985). For another federal case on treatment abatement, see Foster v. Tourtellotte, 704 F.2d 1109 (1983). In *Foster,* a federal district court in California granted an injunction that required a physician at the Wadsworth Veterans Administration National Center to remove the ventilator on which William Foster was dependent for life. The order was stayed, pending an appeal, and Foster died before the stay expired.

20. Bouvia v. County of Riverside, No. 159780 (December 16, 1983). For a similar case in New York, see the Ross Henniger case: In the Matter of the Application of Plaza Health and Rehabilitation Center (Supreme Court, Onondaga County, February 2, 1984).

21. Bouvia v. Superior Court, *supra,* 225 Cal.Rptr. 297, 306. Bouvia subsequently sought and was granted payment for some of her legal fees in this case. See Bouvia v. Glenchur, 241 Cal.Rptr. 239 (Cal. App. 2d Dist. 1987).

22. In re Requena, 213 N.J. Super. 475, 517 A.2d 886 (N.J. Super. Ct. Ch. Div.), *aff'd,* 213 N.J. Super. 443, 517 A.2d 869 (Super. Ct. App. Div. 1986).

23. In re Rodas, No. 86PR139 (Colo. Dist. Ct. Mesa County, January 22, 1987). See Society for the Right to Die (SRD), "Right to Die Court Decisions" (New York: SRD, 1987), pp. CO-1 to CO-3 (update of SRD fact sheets).

24. In re Farrell, 108 N.J. 335, 529 A.2d 404 (N.J. 1987).

25. For additional Jehovah's Witness cases not previously cited, see United States v. George, 239 F.Supp. 752 (1965); Powell v. Columbia Presbyterian Medical Center, 49 Misc.2d 215, 267 N.Y.S.2d 450 (1965); In re Phelps, No. 459-207 (Milwaukee County Court, July 11, 1972); Holmes v. Silver Cross Hospital, 340 F.Supp. 125 (1972); and In re Melideo, 88 Misc.2d 974, 390 N.Y.S.2d 523 (1976).

26. For earlier prisoner cases of treatment refusal, see Petition of Baptista, 206 F.Supp. 288 (Mo. 1962); Haynes v. Harris, 344 F.2d 462 (8th Cir. 1965); Peek v. Ciccone, 288 F.Supp. 329 (Mo. 1968); Veale v. Ciccone, 281 F.Supp. 1017 (Mo. 1968); Smith v. Baker, 326 F.Supp. 787 (Mo. 1970). None of these prisoners was allowed to continue refusing treatment. Two recent cases have been decided by the highest courts in Georgia and West Virginia. In Georgia, the Supreme Court became the only appellate court to recognize a prisoner's right to refuse treatment. The decision differed from the *Myers* decision in part because the likely outcome for the prisoner (Prevatte) was death—with or without treatment (if he lived with treatment, he expected to be killed in prison by another inmate carrying out a "racial contract"). See Zant v. Prevatte, 286 S.E.2d 715 (Ga. 1982). By contrast, the Supreme Court of Appeals in West Virginia strongly criticized the *Prevatte* decision in their ruling later the same year. They declared that "West Virginia's interest in preserving life is superior to White's personal privacy . . . and freedom of expression right." See State ex rel White v. Narick, 292 S.E.2d 54, 58 (1982).

27. SRD, "Right-to-Die Court Decisions," pp. CO-2 to CO-3.

28. My interpretation of these cases has been aided by several helpful resources: Robert M. Veatch, *Death, Dying, and the Biological Revolution* (New Haven, Conn.: Yale University Press, 1976); David W. Meyers, *Medico-Legal Implications of Death and Dying* (Rochester, N.Y., and San Francisco: The Lawyers Co-Operative Publishing Co. and Bancroft-Whitney Co., 1981); John A. Robertson, *The Rights of the Critically Ill* (Cambridge, Mass.: Ballinger, 1983); SRD, "Right-to-Die Court Decisions"; and Swartz, "The Patient Who Refuses," *supra*, note 5.

29. Brooks, *supra*, 205 N.E.2d 435 (1965); Osborne, *supra*, 294 A.2d 372 (1972); Holmes, *supra*, 340 F.Supp. 125 (1972); Phelps, *supra*, Milwaukee County Court (1972); Melideo, *supra*, 390 N.Y.S.2d 523 (1976); Mercy Hospital v. Jackson, 62 Md.App. 409, 489 A.2d 1130 (1985); and Randolph v. City of New York, No. 17598-75 (N.Y. County Super. Ct., October 1, 1984). The earliest reported case upholding the right of a competent patient to refuse a blood transfusion was Erickson v. Dilgard, 44 Misc.2d 27, 252 N.Y.S.2d 705 (1962). This case is sometimes included in the list of religion-based refusal cases, even though the case contains no explicit appeal to the patient's religious beliefs or religious freedom.

30. Winters v. Miller, 446 F.2d 65 (1971); and In re Boyd, 403 A.2d 744 (1979).

31. Georgetown College, *supra*, 331 F.2d 1000 (1964); Anderson, *supra*, 201 A.2d 537 (1964); Heston, *supra*, 279 A.2d 670 (1971); Powell, *supra*, 267 N.Y.S.2d 450 (1965); George, *supra*, 239 F.Supp. 752 (1965); Hamilton v. McAuliffe, 277 Md. 336, 353 A.2d 634 (1976); and Crouse Irving Memorial Hospital v. Paddock, 127 Misc.2d 101 (1985).

32. Union Pacific Railway Co., *supra*, 141 U.S. 250 (1891). For the tracing of the concept of the right of privacy to this case, see Roe v. Wade, 410 U.S. 113, 93 S.Ct. 705 (1973).

33. Griswold v. State of Connecticut, 381 U.S. 479, 85 S.Ct. 1678 (1965).

34. Roe v. Wade, *supra*, 410 U.S. 113.

35. In re Yetter, 62 Pa.D. & C.2d 619 (1973). Quoted and discussed by Meyers, *Medico-Legal Implications*, p. 221.

36. In re Quinlan, 70 N.J. 10, 355 A.2d 647, 664 (1976).

37. Saikewicz, *supra*, 370 N.E.2d 417, 426 (1977).

38. Myers, *supra*, 399 N.E.2d 452, 456–57. The same reasoning appears in *Quackenbush*, where Judge Muir declares: "Under the circumstances of this case, I hold that the extensive bodily invasion involved here—the amputation of both legs above the knee and possibly the amputation of both legs entirely—is sufficient to make the state's interest in the preservation of life give way to Robert Quackenbush's right to privacy to decide his own future regardless of the absence of a dim prognosis." Quackenbush, *supra*, 383 A.2d 785, 789 (1978).

39. Satz, *supra*, 362 So.2d 160, 162.

40. Bartling, *supra*, 209 Cal.Rptr. 220, 225.

41. Bouvia v. Superior Court, *supra*, 225 Cal.Rptr. 297, 305.

42. Myers, *supra*, 399 N.E.2d 452, 456.

43. Satz, *supra*, 362 So.2d 160, 163.

44. Bartling, *supra*, 209 Cal.Rptr. 220, 226.

45. Bouvia v. Superior Court, *supra*, 225 Cal.Rptr. 297, 306.

46. Saikewicz, *supra*, 370 N.E.2d 417, 426–27. For a case with similar reasoning, see the earlier Palm Springs General Hospital, Inc. v. Martinez, No. 71-12687 (Dade County Cir. Ct., 1971), where the court concluded that "a conscious adult patient who is mentally competent has the right to refuse medical treatment, even when the best medical opinion deems it essential to save her life." Quoted and discussed by Meyers, *Medico-Legal Implications*, p. 234.

47. Myers, *supra*, 399 N.E.2d 452, 458.

48. Satz, *supra*, 362 So.2d 160, 164.

49. Bartling, *supra*, 209 Cal.Rptr. 220, 226.

50. Bouvia v. Superior Court, *supra*, 225 Cal.Rptr. 297, 306.

51. See Swartz, "The Patient Who Refuses," pp. 147–63.

52. President's Commission, *Deciding to Forego Life-Sustaining Treatment* (Washington, D.C.: U.S. Government Printing Office, 1983), p. 3.

53. Special Committee on Biomedical Ethics of the American Hospital Association, *Values in Conflict* (Chicago: American Hospital Association, 1985), p. 14.

54. Committee on Biomedical Ethics of the Los Angeles County Bar Association and the Los Angeles County Medical Association, "Principles and Guidelines Concerning the Foregoing of Life-Sustaining Treatment for Adult Patients," *LACMA Physician* (February 3, 1986): 21.

55. Council on Ethical and Judicial Affairs, *Current Opinion of the Council on Ethical and Judicial Affairs of the American Medical Association—1986* (Chicago: American Medical Association, 1986), p. 12.

56. Legal Advisers Committee of Concern for Dying, "Right to Refuse Treatment," p. 918.

57. Bouvia v. Superior Court, *supra*, 225 Cal.Rptr. 297, 304.

58. Michael Van Scoy-Mosher, "An Oncologist's Case for No-Code Orders," in A. Edward Doudera and J. Douglas Peters, eds., *Legal and Ethical Aspects of Treating Critically and Terminally Ill Patients* (Ann Arbor, Mich.: Health Administration Press, 1982), p. 16. Also see Susanna E. Bedell and Thomas L. Delbanco, "Choices about Cardiopulmonary Resuscitation in the Hospital," *The New England Journal of Medicine* 310 (April 26, 1984): 1089–93, where the authors point out that almost

one-third (8 of 25) of the survivors of CPR they interviewed later stated unequivocally that they had not wanted resuscitation.

59. Brenda Huttmann, "A Crime of Compassion," *Newsweek,* August 8, 1983, p. 15.
60. In re A.C., 533 A.2d 611 (D.C. App. 1987). For commentary on the case, see
George J. Annas, "Trying to Live Forever," *Law, Medicine, and Health Care* 15
(Winter 1987/88): 243.

4

Abating Treatment on the Behalf of Nonautonomous Patients

The problem before this court is not life or death. That question has already been decided. Edna Marie Leach is going to die. She is on the threshold of death, and man has, through a new medical technology, devised a way of holding her on that threshold. The basic question is how long will society require Mrs. Leach and others similarly situated to remain on the threshold of certain death suspended and sustained there by artificial life supports. Since man, through his ingenuity, has created a new state of human existence—minimal human life sustained by man-made life supports—society must now devise and fashion rules and parameters for that existence. That is the business this court is faced with. It is not an easy question to answer.

Leach v. Akron General Medical Center[1]

Prevailing medical ethical practice does not, without exception, demand that all efforts toward life prolongation be made in all circumstances. Rather as indicated in *Quinlan*, the prevailing ethical practice seems to be to recognize that the dying are more often in need of comfort than treatment. Recognition of the right to refuse necessary treatment in appropriate circumstances is consistent with existing medical mores; such a doctrine does not threaten either the integrity of the medical profession, the proper role of hospitals in caring for such patients or the State's interest in protecting the same.

Superintendent of Belchertown State School v. Saikewicz[2]

The legal right of autonomous patients to refuse medical treatment is undeniable, as demonstrated by the previous chapter, and has been affirmed by appellate courts in a number of jurisdictions in the United States since 1960. In many instances physicians and other health care personnel are cognizant of this legal right, and cooperate with the expressed preferences of their adult patients who make a decision for treatment abatement. In such cases various technologies and procedures—ventilators, hemodialysis, chemotherapy, surgery, NG tubes, CPR—are withheld or withdrawn as the patient has requested.

Such cooperation on the part of the attending physician may be due to respect for the patient's autonomy, an understanding of the patient's reasons for wanting treatment abatement, an agreement that the burdens outweigh the benefits of the available treatment, or an affirmation of the patient's constitutionally based rights of religious freedom and privacy. Alternatively, the cooperation by the physician may be given grudgingly only after he or she has failed to change the patient's mind about the merits of treatment, has found relatives of the patient unwilling or unable to dissuade the patient from treatment abatement, and has been informed by the hospital legal counsel that refusing to carry out the patient's request could lead to undesirable legal action against the physician and hospital.

The upshot of all this is that refusal of medical treatment, including life-sustaining treatment, by adult patients capable of such decisions is a regular feature of medical practice in most hospitals. In rare instances when a physician persists in refusing to cooperate with a patient's decision to abate treatment, and also refuses to withdraw from the case by transferring the care of the patient to another physician, court action will undoubtedly confirm that neither a physician nor anyone else connected with a case (other physicians, relatives of the patient, etc.) has veto power over the patient's right to refuse treatment. Whatever reasons a physician in such cases has for trying to thwart the patient's decision—a pro-life or vitalist philosophy that calls for the indefinite prolongation of all patients' lives, adherence to the "technological imperative," undue anxiety about civil or criminal prosecution, or some misunderstanding of the law—the preferences of an autonomous patient are going to carry the day. Unless one or more of the state's interests can be demonstrated to be compelling in such a case, the patient's legal right to refuse treatment will be affirmed by the court.

But what if a critically ill and possibly terminally ill patient is unable to make such a decision? What if—because of physical injury, trauma, unconsciousness, prolonged depression, previous drug use, vacillation in point of view, apparent irrationality, age, or immaturity—such a patient simply cannot make a reasonable choice between recommended medical treatment and treatment abatement? Such questions are obviously not new, as indicated by *Brooks* (1965), *Heston* (1971), and similar cases decided in the 1960s and early 1970s (see Chapter 3). Beginning in 1976, however, when the second phase of the debate over abating treatment began, numerous courts have wrestled at great length with a steadily increasing number of substantive and procedural questions inherent to cases in which the very person whose life and health is at issue is lacking in the capacity to make a decision appropriate to the clinical situation.

Among the questions addressed by the courts are the following ones. Is there an important difference between diminished "capacity" and a judicial determination of "incompetence"? What criteria or tests should be used to establish either incapacity or incompetency? How can one determine if a patient's incapacity is irreversible or temporary? Does a critically ill, nonautonomous patient have the same right to medical treatment as a mentally normal patient? Is it permissible on moral and legal grounds to abate treatment on a nonautonomous patient who is senile? Is it permissible to abate treatment on a nonautonomous patient who is permanently unconscious? Is it permissible to abate treatment on a nonautonomous patient who is terminally ill? Is it permissible to discontinue technological feeding with a nonautonomous patient? Is abating treatment with a nonautonomous patient equivalent to intentionally killing the patient? Is a physician who discontinues treatment on a nonautonomous patient liable for civil and/or criminal charges? Is the judicial sanctioning of treatment abatement with critically ill, nonautonomous patients the first step on the "slippery slope" toward societal acceptance of nonvoluntary euthanasia? Do critically ill minors have a right to refuse recommended medical treatment? Who should make decisions about prolonging or abating treatment on behalf of nonautonomous or legally incompetent patients? How can one best determine what a critically ill, nonautonomous patient wants or should have in terms of medical care? Do relatives have the right to stop treatment on a nonautonomous or legally incompetent patient? What should be done when relatives disagree among themselves regarding the merits of continuing or abating treatment on a nonautonomous patient? Is judicial approval necessary before treatment abatement can be carried out? Do institutional ethics committees (IECs) have an appropriate role in problematic treatment-abatement cases?[3]

Cases of treatment abatement with nonautonomous patients

Many, but not all, of these questions have been addressed by a number of courts since 1976, as will be evident in this section of the chapter. In subsequent sections we will discuss points of judicial consensus, issues lacking judicial agreement, and remaining questions in case law regarding the abatement of treatment on the behalf of patients who lack the capacity to make such decisions for themselves.

Not all of these questions can be answered decisively at this time, for several reasons: courts in only 25 jurisdictions have decided treatment-abatement cases involving nonautonomous patients, the courts in these jurisdictions have displayed considerable variability on some of the issues before them, and the U.S. Supreme Court has yet to rule on such a case. Simply put, the law on abating treatment with nonautonomous patients is, as seen in the following cases, still in the process of development.[4]

The cases will be presented in chronological order to depict the development of the law in a number of jurisdictions. The cases selected for presentation represent the variety that exists in such court cases, including patients with diminished or fluctuating capacity to make decisions (who may or may not be judged incompetent), patients with substantial incapacity to make decisions, patients with permanent loss of consciousness, and patients who lack the autonomy necessary for medical decision making because of young age and immaturity. We will begin with the landmark *Quinlan* and *Saikewicz* cases.

Case 4.1

Karen Ann Quinlan, aged 21, collapsed and ceased breathing for at least two 15-minute periods during a party in April 1975. She was rushed to a hospital and immediately placed on a respirator to maintain her breathing. Several days later she was transferred to another hospital, where she remained for weeks in a condition diagnosed as "chronic persistent vegetative state (PVS)."

After an early change in her unconscious condition—she went from sleep-like unresponsiveness to an "awake" unresponsiveness—Karen's neurological status remained basically static: her brain stem maintained certain physiological functions, but she was "totally unaware of anyone or anything around her." Her physical condition deteriorated as she became emaciated, lost approximately 40 pounds, had increasingly inflexible limbs, and assumed a "fetallike" physical position.

Karen's medical treatment included the use of a respirator, antibiotics, a catheter, feedings through an NG tube, and continual intensive nursing care. When her family, "finally reconciled to the certainty" of her impending death, requested the withdrawal of the respirator, her attending physician refused.

Karen's father consulted his parish priest regarding the morality of treatment abatement and then sought judicial authority to withdraw the respirator, by asking that he be appointed her guardian. His request was opposed by Karen's physicians, the hospital, a county prosecutor, Karen's guardian *ad litem,* and the state of New Jersey. A trial court judge, in denying the father's request to stop mechanical ventilation, stated: "The single most important temporal quality Karen Ann Quinlan has is life. This Court will not authorize that life to be taken from her."

When the case was appealed to the New Jersey Supreme Court, an *amicus curiae* brief was filed by the New Jersey Catholic Conference. In part, that brief referred to Pope Pius XII's comments in 1957 regarding "extraordinary means of treatment" and argued that the treatments involved in the Quinlan case "constitute extraordinary means of preserving life and so there is no obligation to use them nor to give the doctor permission to use them." The brief concluded that Joseph Quinlan's request to discontinue the respirator was, according to the teachings of the Catholic church, a "morally correct decision."

For the New Jersey Supreme Court, the central legal issue in the Quinlan case was not religious freedom. Rather, the main issue was the constitutionally based right of privacy:

> Here a living parent, *qua* parent and raising the rights of his incompetent and profoundly damaged daughter . . . seeks authorization to abandon specialized technological procedures which can only maintain for a time a body having no potential for resumption or continuance of other than a "vegetative" existence.
>
> We have no doubt . . . that if Karen were herself miraculously lucid for an interval . . . and perceptive of her irreversible condition, she could effectively

decide upon discontinuance of the life-support apparatus, even if it meant the prospect of natural death.

The court considered two state interests in continuing Karen's respirator care: the preservation of life and the professional integrity of physicians. But the court agreed with the plaintiff's claims that "Karen's present treatment serves only a maintenance function," that the respirator "at best can only prolong her inevitable slow deterioration and death," and that Karen's interests (as interpreted by her surrogate) were "predominant" to the interests of the attending physicians.

Given Karen's extremely poor prognosis ("She will never resume cognitive life") and the "very great" physical invasion entailed by her medical treatment, the court ruled that "the State's interest *contra* weakens and the individual's right to privacy grows as the degree of bodily invasion increases and the prognosis dims. Ultimately there comes a point at which the individual's rights overcome the State interest."

The court's opinion addressed several substantive and procedural issues related to the discontinuation of the respirator from a permanently unconscious patient. First, the court dismissed testimony regarding Karen's previous conversations with friends on the subject of technologically prolonged life, because "such testimony is without sufficient probative weight." Second, it stated that abating treatment in the circumstances of this case did not constitute criminal liability on the part of the physicians: "There is a real and in this case determinative distinction between the unlawful taking of the life of another and the ending of artificial life-support systems as a matter of self-determination." Third, it adopted the ordinary/extraordinary distinction put forth in the Catholic brief: "one would have to think that the use of the same respirator or like support could be considered 'ordinary' in the context of the possibly curable patient but 'extraordinary' in the context of the forced sustaining by cardiorespiratory processes of an irreversibly doomed patient." Finally, the court focused on an appropriate procedure to protect the interests of the permanently unconscious patient. That procedure required the concurrence of four parties—family, guardian, attending physicians (who could be chosen by Joseph Quinlan, the guardian), and a hospital "ethics committee"—before the respirator could be removed.[5]

Case 4.2

Joseph Saikewicz, aged 67, was profoundly mentally retarded. With an IQ of 10 and a mental age of approximately 2 years and 8 months, Saikewicz had been a mental patient at the Belchertown State School in Massachusetts for 48 years. He was basically without relatives, because his two sisters (the remaining members of his family) chose not to have any contact with him or be involved in his case in any way.

In April 1976 Saikewicz was diagnosed as having acute myeloblastic monocytic leukemia. William Jones, the superintendent of the Belchertown school, and Paul Rogers, a staff attorney at the school, then petitioned the probate court for the appointment of a guardian for Saikewicz and also a guardian *ad litem* who would have the authority to make decisions for Saikewicz regarding treatment for the leukemia. The guardian *ad litem,* initially convinced that the incompetent patient should be given chemotherapy for his cancer, changed his mind when he discovered that the physicians he consulted were against treating Saikewicz. Among their reasons were the serious side effects of the treatment (including severe anemia and increased susceptibility to infection), the limited possibilities of remission, the patient's advanced age, the necessity of having patient cooperation with treatment, the limited life span of the patient even if remission should occur, and the invariably fatal nature of the disease.

The guardian *ad litem* concluded that these factors outweighed the possible benefits of the treatment. He therefore recommended in the May court hearing that "not treating Mr. Saikewicz would be in his best interests." After the probate judge agreed with the recommendation, the case was appealed directly to the Supreme Judicial Court of Massachusetts. The highest court in the state affirmed the lower court's decision in July, but did not issue its written opinion until November 1977. Meanwhile, Saikewicz died from bronchial pneumonia (a complication of the leukemia) on September 4, 1976.

Like the *Quinlan* court, the *Saikewicz* court affirmed that persons do not lose their legal rights when they are judged incompetent. Rather, the court stated that "the substantive rights of the competent and the incompetent person are the same in regard to the right to decline potentially life-prolonging treatment."

Counterposed to the right to refuse medical treatment are four state interests that may, in some circumstances, override the patient's right: "(1) the preservation of life; (2) the protection of the interests of innocent third parties; (3) the prevention of suicide; and (4) maintaining the ethical integrity of the medical profession [see Chapter 3]."

Of these four possible state interests, the second and third interests did not apply to the Saikewicz case. The first state interest—called "the most significant of the asserted State interests"—obviously did apply, but was limited by the fact that Saikewicz's condition was terminal. In the court's words: "There is a substantial distinction in the State's insistence that human life be saved where the affliction is curable, as opposed to the State interest where, as here, the issue is not whether but when, for how long, and at what cost to the individual that life may be briefly extended." As to the fourth state interest, the court pointed out (in the statement used at the beginning of this chapter) that "in appropriate circumstances" the refusal of medical treatment need not be regarded as contrary to morally responsible medical practice.

Having established that Saikewicz and other terminally ill, incompetent patients *can* (through their surrogates) decline life-sustaining treatment, the court then turned to the substantive issue of how surrogates in such cases can most appropriately determine whether they *should* decline treatment on the behalf of the incompetent patient. Of the two standard "tests" that can be used in these cases, the court argued that the "substituted-judgment" test was preferable to the "best-interests" test. Acknowledging that the Saikewicz case was different from the Quinlan case in that Saikewicz had never been capable of making decisions, the court nevertheless followed the *Quinlan* court in applying the substituted-judgment test: this standard "commends itself simply because of its straightforward respect for the integrity and autonomy of the individual." To use the "statistical-factors" and "reasonable-person" thinking that tend to make the best-interests test more objective can also lead a surrogate to overlook "the complexities of the singular situation." Consequently, the primary test should be "subjective in nature—that is, the goal is to determine . . . the wants and needs of the individual involved." In short, the decision in cases such as this "should be that which would be made by the incompetent person, if that person were competent, but taking into account the present and future incompetency of the individual as one of the factors which would necessarily enter into the decision-making process of the competent person."

In terms of procedure, the court disagreed with the *Quinlan* court by stating that the New Jersey court wrongly attempted "to shift the ultimate decision-making responsibility away from the duly established courts of proper jurisdiction" to the patient's guardian, family, physicians, and a hospital "ethics committee." Rejecting the New Jersey court's view that judicial review of treatment-abatement cases involving incapacitated patients would be "a gratuitous encroachment upon the medical profession's field of competence," the Massachusetts court argued that "such questions of life and death seem to us to require the process of detached but passionate investigation and decision that forms the ideal on which the judicial branch of government was created."[6]

Case 4.3

Mary Northern was 72-years old when she entered Nashville General Hospital in 1978. She had gangrene of both feet, probably secondary to frostbite and then thermal burning of her feet. She had "a good memory" and was "coherent and intelligent in her conversation."

However, her capacity to make a decision regarding medical treatment became questionable when she was presented with the option of amputation. When it became apparent that she lacked decision-making capacity, the Tennessee Department of Human Services filed suit under a law entitled "Protective Services for Elderly Persons." A guardian *ad litem* was appointed for Northern, and she appealed the case.

The court of appeals, after hearing medical testimony, considering evidence presented by the guardian *ad litem,* and visiting Northern in the ICU, upheld the trial court decision regarding the patient's incompetence. The appeals court ruled that Northern

> is an intelligent, lucid, communicative and articulate individual who does not accept the fact of the serious condition of her feet and is unwilling to discuss the seriousness of such condition or its fatal potentiality . . . because of her inability or unwillingness to recognize the actual condition of her feet . . . she is incompetent to make a rational decision as to the amputation of her feet.

In making this decision, the court emphasized that the Northern case was not a "right-to-die" case. Rather than expressing a desire to die, Northern had displayed a strong desire to live *and* keep her gangrenous feet. Because she was unable to understand that she was holding on to mutually exclusive alternatives, she was found to lack "capacity to consent." Such capacity, in the court's words, means

> mental ability to make a rational decision, which includes the ability to perceive, appreciate all relevant facts and to reach a rational judgment upon such facts.
>
> Capacity is not necessarily synonymous with sanity. A blind person may be perfectly capable of observing the shape of small articles by handling them, but not capable of observing the shape of a cloud in the sky.
>
> A person may have "capacity" as to some matters and may lack "capacity" as to others.

The court found Northern to be "apparently of sound mind generally." However, on the specific subjects of death and amputation, "her comprehension is blocked, blinded or dimmed to the extent that she is incapable of recognizing facts which would be obvious to a person of normal perception." Simply put, she needs a guardian *ad litem* to make the decision for amputation because "she cannot or will not comprehend the facts."[7]

Case 4.4

Shirley Dinnerstein, aged 67, suffered from Alzheimer's disease. She had been in a nursing home for two years when a massive stroke left her left side totally paralyzed. By June 1978, she was hospitalized with multiple severe problems: deteriorating mental and physical abilities due to Alzheimer's, paralysis, high blood pressure, and a life-threatening coronary artery disease due to arteriosclerosis. Her medical condition was hopeless; her life expectancy was less than a year, and her attending physician thought she might go into cardiac or respiratory arrest at any time.

The physician had recommended that resuscitation efforts not be undertaken if and when cardiac or respiratory arrest occurred. The patient's family—a son (who was a physician) and a daughter (with whom the patient had lived for many years before entering the nursing home)—agreed with the physician's recommendation.

However, the *Saikewicz* decision had been interpreted by some legal and medical experts in Massachusetts as requiring judicial authorization before any treatment-abatement decision—including an order not to attempt resuscitation of an incompetent, terminally ill patient—could legally be carried out. For that reason, the physician, family, and hospital contacted a probate court judge: they wanted either to be told that a "no-code" order did not require judicial authorization, or, if it did, to be given that authorization. In response, the judge appointed a guardian *ad litem* who then opposed the request.

The case, never having an actual decision from the probate court, was reported to the Appeals Court of Massachusetts. For that court, the legal issue was whether, in the light of *Saikewicz,* a physician attending an incompetent, terminally ill patient, could legally withhold resuscitation measures without prior judicial approval. The court's answer was affirmative. If physicians could not legally withhold such measures from terminally ill patients, the court pointed out, the resultant attempts to resuscitate dying patients could "aptly be characterized as a pointless, even cruel, prolongation of the act of dying." Moreover, they argued that when the *Saikewicz* decision spoke of lifesaving or life-prolonging treatments, the court had never intended that statement to apply to terminally ill patients: " 'Prolongation of life,' as used in the *Saikewicz* case, does not mean a mere suspension of the act of dying, but contemplates, at the very least, a remission of symptoms enabling a return towards a normal, functioning, integrated existence." The *Saikewicz* requirement of judicial authorization was thus intended to apply only to cases where available treatment offers "hope of restoration" to a normal, functioning existence. The Dinnerstein case, by contrast, does not

> offer a lifesaving or life-prolonging treatment alternative within the meaning of the *Saikewicz* case. It presents a question peculiarly within the competence of the medical profession of what measures are appropriate to ease the imminent passing of an irreversibly, terminally ill patient in light of the patient's history and condition and the wishes of her family. That question is not one for judicial decision.[8]

Case 4.5

Chad Green, at the age of 20 months, was diagnosed in 1977 as having acute lymphocytic leukemia (ALL). He was treated with chemotherapy for a month, and the leukemia went into a state of remission. The treatment, the first phase of a 3-year treatment program, was administered at the University Medical Center in Omaha, Nebraska.

Chad's parents, disturbed by the use of cranial irradiation in the child's treatment program, apparently decided that the child's well-being would be better served if they returned to Massachusetts. There they placed Chad under the care of John Truman, a pediatric hematologist at Massachusetts General Hospital. Truman indicated that cranial irradiation would not be necessary. At the parents' request, he agreed to administer chemotherapy in conjunction with a diet of distilled water, vegetarian foods, and high dosages of vitamins. However, he emphasized to the parents that such a diet would have "absolutely no value" if used alone in the treatment of leukemia.

By February 1978 Truman was convinced that Chad, now 2 years old, was not receiving enough medication. Diagnostic tests indicated that the leukemia had recurred. Chad's parents, upon questioning by the doctor, admitted that out of concern for the treatment's side effects (cramps and constipation) and a "hope" that Chad's condition could be cured without the chemotherapy, they had stopped the chemotherapy tablets 3 months previously.

Dr. Truman petitioned a probate court for a guardian *ad litem* for Chad. When Chad's parents protested, Truman petitioned a district court to have the child's legal custody turned over to the Department of Public Welfare. The case was appealed to the superior court, which found that "denial of the recommended medical treatment means certain death for the minor, whereas continuation of such treatment offers him substantial hope for life." The court concluded that the child's "right to live" and the "state's duty to enforce that right" outweighed the family's interests in privacy and autonomy. Chad was committed to the legal custody of the welfare department for the purpose of receiving chemotherapy; his physical custody remained with his parents as long as they obeyed the court's ruling regarding treatment.

The case was appealed to the Supreme Judicial Court of Massachusetts. That court upheld the superior court's ruling and addressed several substantive issues in the case. First, they stated (citing *Prince v. Massachusetts)* that parental rights "do not clothe parents with life and death authority over their children." Second, they stated, on the basis of medical testimony, that Chad's medical condition was fatal if left untreated, and that chemotherapy offered him at least a 50% chance of long-term survival. Third, they said that in this case, "involving a child who is incompetent by reason of his tender years," the substituted-judgment test is consistent with the best-interests test. In the judgment of the court, the recommended treatment offered Chad the only possibility available "to engage in the activities of children of his age," the side effects of the treatment were reversible, and even his inability to understand "the temporary pain of chemotherapy" and "the significance of the treatment" could not overcome his long-term interest in leading a normal, healthy life. Finally, the court appealed to three state interests to support the judicially mandated treatment: the state's interest in preserving the welfare of children, preserving life, and protecting the ethical integrity of the medical profession.[9]

Case 4.6

Earle Spring was 77-years old, had been married for 55 years, and had an adult son. When the legal aspects of his case began in 1978, he was suffering from end-stage kidney disease and senility (or "chronic organic brain syndrome"). Because of his kidney disease, he was receiving hemodialysis treatment 3 days a week, 5 hours a day. Because of his senility, he was completely confused and disoriented. Both conditions were regarded as being permanent and irreversible.

The dialysis treatment simply kept him alive, with no prospect of bringing about a remission or restoring him to anything resembling a normal, functional existence. He experienced dizziness, leg cramps, and headaches as side effects of the treatment. More than once he resisted transportation for dialysis and pulled the dialysis needles out of his arm.

Spring's wife and son requested that the treatment be stopped. Spring's physicians refused. His son then began court action that would subsequently consume nearly 15 months of hearings, appeals, reversals, and stays until the Supreme Judicial Court of Massachusetts issued its opinion in May 1980. Meanwhile, Spring died in April 1980.

In spite of its interminableness, the Spring case is important for both substantive and procedural reasons. In terms of its substantive issues, the case involves a previously capable adult patient who was unquestionably incompetent as the court hearings were being held. Because he was "entirely and irreversibly incompetent," he was represented in court by his son, who had been appointed his temporary guardian. A guardian *ad litem* was also present throughout the proceedings.

Spring's son and wife acknowledged that while Spring was apparently competent, he had acquiesced in hemodialysis treatment, and had received such treatment for several months before losing his capacity to make decisions. Nevertheless, possessing no evidence that Spring while competent "had expressed any wish or desire as to the continuation or withdrawal of treatment in such circumstances," they were of the opinion that Spring "would, if competent, choose not to receive the life-prolonging treatment." All of the courts hearing the case agreed with them, because they were a close-knit family, "had only the best interests of the ward at heart," and were the persons best informed "as to his likely attitude."

The Massachusetts high court, following the pattern set in *Saikewicz, Dinnerstein,* and *Custody of a Minor,* stated that in cases involving incompetent patients, the right to refuse medical treatment has to be exercised for the patient through a "substituted judgment" in his or her behalf. This approach, according to the court, necessitates that a surrogate make the decision that "would be made by the incompetent person, if he were competent, taking into account his actual interests and preferences and also his present and future incompetency."

From the perspective of Spring's physicians, his case involved court-motivated questions regarding possible civil or criminal liability if they should terminate the dialysis treatment apart from judicial authorization. The high court dismissed concerns about criminal liability by indicating that the "precious little precedent" available suggested that a physician "will be protected if he acts on a good faith judgment that is not grievously unreasonable by medical standards." In a similar way, a physician is not likely to risk civil action whenever the physician "in good faith decides that a particular treatment is not called for." However, the court pointed out that even judicial authorization for treatment abatement does not guarantee total immunity, because there is always a modicum of risk "that in some subsequent litigation the omission will be found to have been negligent."

As to procedural matters, the court addressed the question (brought on by its *Saikewicz* decision) whether prior judicial approval was necessary before withholding treatment from an incompetent patient. The court's response was ambiguous. Stating that "our opinions should not be taken to establish any requirement of prior judicial approval," the court then listed a variety of factors that should be taken into account by decision makers in determining whether a court order might be needed before withholding treatment from such a patient:

> the extent of impairment of the patient's mental faculties, whether the patient is in the custody of a State institution, the prognosis without the proposed treatment, the prognosis with the proposed treatment, the complexity, risk and novelty of the proposed treatment, its possible side effects, the patient's level of understanding and probable reaction, the urgency of decision, the consent of the patient, spouse, or guardian, the good faith of those who participate in the decision, the clarity of professional opinion as to what is good medical practice, the interests of third persons, and the administrative requirements of any institution involved.[10]

Case 4.7

Mary Severns, aged 55, suffered irreversible brain damage in an automobile accident in late 1979. She remained in a coma at the Wilmington Medical Center throughout the 13 months the Delaware judicial system considered her case.

Having been an active member of the Euthanasia Educational Council of Delaware, and having made verbal statements clearly indicating that she never wanted to become a "vegetable" prolonged by "extraordinary means," she nevertheless became the focal point of a long legal battle between her husband and family (all of whom wanted her life-support systems removed), her attending physician (who would not remove the systems unless he had a court order), and the attorney general (who thought the removal of the systems would constitute murder under Delaware law).

The legal battle began when her husband, joined by her adult children and her siblings, petitioned the chancery court to be appointed her guardian for the purpose of requesting the termination of her life-prolonging treatment. The chancery court referred the petition to the state supreme court to see if the lower court had the authority to grant the relief sought by the Severns family.

Five months later the supreme court issued its opinion. According to the court, most of the facts in the case were not in dispute: a tracheotomy had been performed on Severns soon after her arrival at the hospital, she had been connected to a respirator, she had been given intravenous feedings then feedings through an NG tube, a catheter had been inserted, various drugs had been administered, her higher brain functions had suffered extensive damage in the accident, she had virtually no chance to be restored to a "sapient and sentient adult existence," her brain stem would probably heal sufficiently to be able to sustain her "primitive body functions," and she would be susceptible to pneumonia and respiratory infections if she were permanently removed from the respirator.

With that knowledge, William Severns had requested that the lower court appoint him as his wife's guardian and that the court give approval for (1) the discontinuance of the respirator, (2) the discontinuance of the tracheotomy, (3) the discontinuance of medications, (4) the ongoing withholding of these treatments once discontinued, and (5) an ongoing "no-code-blue" order so that no resuscitative steps would be taken. Moreover, he had requested the lower court to make clear that any physician cooperating with these requests would not be liable for civil or criminal charges.

Citing *Quinlan* and *Spring,* the supreme court held that the chancery court could appoint Severns as the guardian of the "person" of his wife and that the lower court should hold a full "evidentiary hearing" to determine if the facts of the case warranted the request to abate treatment. The court stated that the relief sought by William Severns was "extraordinary, . . . novel to Delaware and, relatively speaking, . . . new in our civilization." Further, the court said:

> Now . . . we are on the threshold of new terrain—the penumbra where death begins but life, in some form, continues. We have been led to it by the medical miracles which now compel us to distinguish between "death," as we have known it, and death in which the body lives in some fashion but the brain (or a significant part of it) does not.

After several more months, the chancery court issued its opinion. On the basis of its evidentiary hearing, the court appointed William Severns as his wife's guardian and approved his request regarding the abatement of life-support measures. Specifically, the court authorized that the comatose patient (1) not be returned to a respirator in the event of an emergency (the respirator had been used only intermittently), (2) not be fed through a tube in her trachea (the guardian's request did not seek removal of NG tube feeding), (3) not be given antibiotic drugs in the event of infection (but medications for constipation and diarrhea would continue), and (4) not be resuscitated in the event of cardiac or respiratory arrest.

Of these treatment measures, the attorney general had protested only the denial of antibiotics because antibiotics represent an "ordinary means of preserving life." The court's response in allowing the abatement of antibiotics was to state that "the patient's wish expressed through her guardian is clear. If the use of the medical process in question will not return her to a cognitive, sapient condition, she does not want it administered."

The court's reasoning depended in large part on the views Mary Severns had expressed prior to her accident. Specifically, the court noted that the previously competent patient had proposed to her husband in 1975 that each of them sign a living will. The only apparent reason that "her plan was not consummated" was her husband's reluctance to sign a document containing a request for treatment abatement.[11]

Case 4.8

Brother Joseph Fox, aged 83, had been a member of the Society of Mary, a Catholic religious order, for 66 years. In 1970 he had retired, but continued to do limited work at the order's Chaminade High School in Mineola, New York.

In 1979 he had an operation to repair a hernia. During the operation he suffered cardiac arrest, and had substantial brain damage due to loss of oxygen to the brain. He was placed on a respirator. Physicians informed Father

Philip Eichner, the director of the society at the school, that Brother Fox was in a PVS from which he would not recover. Two neurosurgeons confirmed the diagnosis.

Father Eichner requested that Brother Fox be removed from the respirator. The hospital refused to do so without a court authorization. Eichner, supported by the incompetent patient's living relatives, applied to become Fox's "committee of the person and property" under New York law, thereby having the authority to direct removal of the respirator. A guardian *ad litem* and the district attorney opposed the application.

The resulting litigation involved three state courts, lasted more than 1 year, and continued long after Brother Fox died in January 1980. All three courts agreed that Father Eichner was entitled to the relief sought and that the termination of respirator treatment was consistent with Brother Fox's previously expressed views, but the treatment was continued while the case was being appealed.

The trial court hearing clearly demonstrated that Brother Fox, while competent, had made his views on abating treatment known. In 1976 in the context of discussing the Karen Ann Quinlan case, he had stated that he would not want any of this "extraordinary business" done for him under similar circumstances. Later, only a couple of months before his surgery, he again stated that he "would not want his life prolonged by such measures if his condition were hopeless."

The supreme court (the trial court in New York) approved Eichner's request, noting that Brother Fox's opposition to using a respirator to maintain organ function in a permanently vegetative patient was "unchallenged at every turn and unimpeachable in its sincerity." The appellate division of the supreme court agreed. In a long opinion the court argued that, if Brother Fox or some other similarly situated incompetent patient had not indicated a preference regarding life-sustaining treatment before becoming incompetent, the appropriate judicial course would be to use the "substituted-judgment" test. Then the court put forth an elaborate, if not cumbersome set of procedures that should be followed before abating life-sustaining treatment.

In its March 1981 opinion, the court of appeals affirmed the other courts' decision regarding the respirator, rejected the district attorney's claims that (1) the right to refuse treatment is lost once a patient becomes incompetent and (2) any withdrawal of the respirator would constitute homicide, and refused to establish procedures that would have to be followed in future treatment-abatement cases in New York. The court established a standard of proof for future cases—the proof of "clear and convincing evidence"—that would prohibit relief for incompetent, hopelessly ill patients whenever the evidence regarding the patient's prior views on treatment abatement "is loose, equivocal or contradictory."[12]

Case 4.9

John Storar was 52 years old, but profoundly retarded. He had a mental age of about 18 months and had been a resident at a state mental facility since he was 5. He was an only child, and his 77-year-old mother lived near the institution and visited him daily.

Storar was diagnosed as having cancer of the bladder in 1979. When a Rochester hospital refused to treat him without the consent of a legal guardian, Mrs. Storar was appointed his guardian and consented for him to have radiation therapy. The cancer soon went into remission, but several months later Storar began losing blood because of the cancerous lesions in his bladder. He thus had two life-threatening conditions: bladder cancer and the more immediate threat of continuous blood loss.

Physicians at the institution requested permission to administer blood transfusions. Mrs. Storar consented but withdrew her consent after several weeks of transfusions (as much as two units of blood every 2 weeks), on the grounds that the transfusions were prolonging her son's suffering.

As with *Eichner,* Storar's case was taken to a trial court, subsequently involved an intermediate appellate court and the state's highest court, and was not finally decided until after his death. The trial court hearing of the case produced several points of agreement: Storar's cancer was terminal and had metastasized to his lungs, his life expectancy was 3–6 months, he was continuously losing blood, he found the transfusions disagreeable, and his mental state prevented him from comprehending his predicament or making a reasoned decision regarding treatment. The court decided that Mrs. Storar was the appropriate person to make a "substituted judgment" in her son's behalf. When she stated that she wanted "his suffering to stop and believes that he would want this also," the court ruled that the transfusions could be discontinued. The appellate division of the supreme court affirmed the lower court's decision with a brief memorandum. However, the transfusions were continued as the case was appealed to the court of appeals.

While admitting that this case was dissimilar in several ways from the Brother Fox case, New York's highest court reviewed them simultaneously. The results of that review were mixed: the court affirmed (with modifications) the earlier court decisions regarding Brother Fox, but reversed the lower court's handling of the Storar case.

The opinion by the New York court, in striking contrast to the decisions by the highest courts in other jurisdictions having considered treatment abatement with incompetent patients, was that medical treatment may not be withheld or withdrawn from such a patient unless the patient has specifically expressed a preference regarding life-sustaining treatment. The court reasoned that Storar, in contrast to Brother Fox, had never been competent "at any time in his life.'' Because Storar was mentally an infant, the court said ''it is unrealistic to attempt to determine whether he would want to continue potentially life-prolonging treatment if he were competent. . . . that would be similar to asking whether 'if it snowed all summer would it then be winter?' ''

Citing several cases involving minors (including *Custody of a Minor*), the court argued that parents and other surrogates may not simply allow a child to bleed to death. Rather, blood transfusions are analogous to food: they will not cure an underlying life-threatening condition, but they will at least ''eliminate the risk of death from another treatable cause.'' With the transfusions, Storar would thus be ''essentially the same as he was before except of course he had a fatal illness which would ultimately claim his life.''

For the court, the case was rather straightforward: the patient was a mental ''infant,'' he had never been able to express a preference regarding the transfusions, no one could make a ''substituted judgment'' for him, and the transfusions would prevent a short-term death from bleeding. The court concluded:

> Although we understand and respect his mother's despair, as we respect the beliefs of those who oppose transfusions on religious grounds, a court should not in the circumstances of this case allow an incompetent patient to bleed to death because someone, even someone as close as a parent or sibling, feels that this is best for one with an incurable disease.[13]

Case 4.10

Bertha Colyer, aged 69, sustained a cardiopulmonary arrest in March 1982. Although she was resuscitated by paramedics, her body had been without oxygen for approximately 10 minutes. As a result, she suffered massive brain damage. After admission to a hospital, she was placed on a respirator. There she remained in a PVS.

Colyer's husband was appointed her guardian, and a guardian *ad litem* was appointed to represent her interests. Mr. Colyer petitioned the superior court for authorization to remove his wife from the respirator. After a hearing, which included supporting testimony from two physicians and Bertha Colyer's sisters, the court ruled that the ''life-support systems presently in place and sustaining Bertha Colyer shall be withdrawn and terminated forthwith.'' The trial court stayed its order, however, pending review by the Supreme Court.

The Supreme Court of Washington affirmed the trial court's decision. The court then addressed the substantive and procedural issues involved in the case, because Colyer, never having signed a directive under the state's Natural Death Act, presented a situation not governed by that 1979 legislative act.

As to substantive issues, the court stated that Colyer's case involved the common-law right of self-determination and the constitutionally derived right to privacy. The court declared that "an adult who is incurably and terminally ill has a constitutional right of privacy that encompasses the right to refuse treatment that serves only to prolong the dying process, given the absence of countervailing state interests." An examination of the state interests put forth in *Saikewicz* convinced the court that none of the four possible state interests outweighed Colyer's right to refuse treatment.

The court then addressed procedural matters by asking, "who may exercise an incompetent's right to refuse life-sustaining treatment if no directive exists and the incompetent is unable to do so?" Comparing Colyer's case to that of Karen Quinlan, the court agreed with the *Quinlan* court that cases involving decisions to terminate life-sustaining treatment need not require judicial approval. The court disagreed with the *Quinlan* court on two issues: the probative value of prior statements made by a now-incompetent patient, and the requirement that a hospital "ethics committee" be a party in decisions to abate life-sustaining treatment.

Prior statements by a now-incompetent patient can be important, especially when the previously competent person (such as Brother Fox) was not merely making casual comments in a conversation. In fact, prior statements "may be probative" in determining the views of an incompetent patient, depending on "the age and maturity of the patient, the context of the statements, and the connection of the statements to the debilitating event." Even when an incompetent patient (such as Bertha Colyer) never "explicitly expressed her desire to refuse life-sustaining treatments," the patient's views may be inferred from other statements and actions prior to the period of incompetency. Thus the court believed that Mr. Colyer's request was consistent with his wife's views because he and her sisters unanimously agreed that Bertha Colyer, "if able to express her views . . . would have requested the treatment be withdrawn."

Even with this "substituted judgment," procedural guidelines are necessary to protect the rights of a permanently unconscious, terminally ill patient. The court issued four guidelines: (1) a unanimous concurrence of a "prognosis board" (the attending physician, plus two other disinterested physicians) that the patient's condition is incurable, (2) court appointment of a guardian and a guardian *ad litem*, (3) the guardian's best judgment that the patient, if competent, would refuse the life-sustaining treatment, and (4) if necessary (as an alternative to the third guideline), a court determination of the rights and wishes of the patient by using the guardian *ad litem* instead of the guardian.[14]

Case 4.11

Pamela Hamilton was 12 and suffering from Ewing's sarcoma when her father refused chemotherapy and radiation therapy on her behalf. He also refused to give permission for physicians to administer medication to combat the pain connected with the tumor.

When the Tennessee Department of Human Services was informed of the case, the department initiated a trial court hearing that resulted in Pamela's being declared "a dependent and neglected child" under Tennessee law. The trial court judge also appointed the director of human services as Pamela's guardian for the purpose of giving consent to the recommended medical treatment.

Pamela's father appealed the case to the court of appeals. That court affirmed, with one modification regarding the cancer's metastasization, the trial court's decision. The medical facts in the case were reasonably clear, according to the court: without treatment Pamela would die within 6–9 months, with treatment her chance of short-term improvement was at least 80 percent, and with treatment her chance of long-term remission was approximately 25 percent. The court pointed out that several medical centers have established "long-term remission of tumors in a significant number of patients suffering from Ewing's sarcoma."

Pamela's father objected to the proposed treatment on the grounds of religious freedom. He was a lay minister and the rest of the family were members of the Church of God of the Union Assembly, a Protestant sect in several southern states. A major tenet of the church states that "all members of the church are forbidden to use medicine, vaccinations or shots of any kind but are taught by the church to live by faith." When questioned as to his reasons for refusing treatment for Pamela, her father said, "If they can't guarantee it to heal you, why do it, because if a doctor were to tell me he had a medicine that would heal me I'd go right there in just a minute, but there ain't none."

Citing four other cases (including *Custody of a Minor*), the appeals court used the *parens patriae* doctrine to override the claim regarding religious freedom. In the court's words:

> there are times when the freedom of the individual must yield. Where a child is dying with cancer and experiencing pain which will surely become more excruciating as the disease progresses, as in Pamela's circumstance, . . . human considerations and lifesaving attempts outweigh unlimited practices of religious beliefs.[15]

Case 4.12

Clarence Herbert, a 55-year-old cancer patient, underwent a normally routine operation in 1983 for closure of an ileostomy. The surgery was performed by Robert Nejdl, the chief of surgery at Kaiser-Permanente's Harbor City Hospital in Los Angeles. However, Herbert, who had a history of cardiac problems, suffered a cardiac arrest in the recovery room. By the time he was resuscitated, he had experienced massive brain damage.

Herbert was immediately placed on a life-support system consisting of a ventilator, intravenous (IV) feedings, and antibiotics. For 3 days he remained in a deeply comatose state. A neurologist diagnosed Herbert as having irreversible brain damage, with the likelihood that his vegetative state would be permanent.

When Neil Barber, the attending physician, informed Herbert's family of the poor prognosis, they asked that all heroic measures be stopped. Barber asked the family to put their request in writing. Herbert's wife and eight children then drafted and signed a statement stating that they wanted "all machines taken off that are sustaining life."

Barber removed the respirator and was surprised when Herbert began to breathe spontaneously. Like Karen Quinlan, Herbert was nonresponsive, irreversibly brain-damaged, being maintained through IV feedings and antibiotics, but nevertheless breathing on his own. Two days later, Barber acceded to the family's request that the IV feedings also be discontinued. Barber died that same day, but only after Nejdl and the ICU supervising nurse had a serious disagreement over Nejdl's order that Herbert not be provided a misting machine after the removal of the respirator. The nurse, Sandra Bardenilla, believed that not misting Herbert violated standard ICU procedures.

Three days later Bardenilla contacted the district attorney, claiming that the physicians had dehydrated Herbert. After investigating the case, the district attorney charged Barber and Nejdl with two felonies: conspiracy to commit murder and murder, defined as "the deliberate, intentional taking of the life of another." The resulting legal case was the first time in U.S. history that physicians who had withdrawn life-sustaining procedures from an adult patient were brought to trial as defendants in a criminal prosecution.

The first step in this unprecedented legal case was a lengthy preliminary hearing before a municipal court judge in Los Angeles. That hearing resulted in a ruling that there was no evidence of unlawful conduct or malice aforethought: Barber and Nejdl acted in good faith, made sound medical and ethical judgments, and did not "kill" Herbert since their conduct was not the proximate cause of death. The judge concluded that "in severely terminal cases, the community understanding is clear; that is, termination of all life-support systems is indicated at some point during the dying process."[16]

The district attorney appealed, and the second step of this legal case took place in a superior court in May 1983. The superior court judge ruled that under California law, the intentional taking of the life of another constitutes murder. He stated that since Herbert had not been brain dead and also had not signed a directive under the California Natural Death Act—the two statutory exceptions to the homicide law as it applies to physicians—the physicians' actions in withdrawing treatment were potentially criminal. The original charges against the physicians were thus reinstated.

The third and last step in the case took place when the California Court of Appeal, in a writ of prohibition, overturned the superior court's ruling and stated that the felony charges could not be brought against Barber and Nejdl. The appellate opinion pointed out that the legal basis for treatment abatement was not limited to patients who had executed the Natural Death Act. In fact, the court noted that the right to refuse medical treatment in California had legal standing years before the Natural Death Act was enacted.

As to the charge of "unlawful killing," the court stated that the cessation of "heroic" life-support measures "is not an affirmative act but rather a withdrawal or omission of further treatment." Moreover, the court said:

> Even though these life-support devices are, to a degree, "self-propelled," each pulsation of the respirator or each drop of fluid introduced into the patient's body by intravenous feeding devices is comparable to a manually administered injection or item of medication. Hence "disconnecting" of the mechanical devices is comparable to withholding the manually administered injection or medication.

Furthermore, the court argued that, in terms of ethics and the law, the removal of the respirator and the discontinuation of artificial feeding can be the same. The question with these or any other life-prolonging technology is, "once undertaken, at what point does it cease to perform its intended function"? To state it another way, the issue of appropriate treatment abatement involves "the determination of whether the proposed treatment is proportionate or disproportionate in terms of the benefits to be gained versus the burdens caused."

The court thus concluded that "a physician has no duty to continue treatment, once it has proved to be ineffective." Also, when that ineffective treatment is being used to prolong the life of a permanently unconscious patient for whom no formal guardianship proceedings have been instituted, the patient's wife and family may be regarded as appropriate surrogate decision makers.

In deciding to abate treatment on the patient's behalf, these surrogates should first be guided by knowledge of the patient's views and, "if it is not possible to ascertain the choice the patient would have made," then by a determination of the patient's best interests. In the Herbert case, the first alternative was possible for his family, since he had previously indicated that he did not want "to be kept alive by machines or 'become another Karen Ann Quinlan.'"[17]

Case 4.13

Edna Marie Leach, aged 70 and the mother of two adult children, had amyotrophic lateral sclerosis (ALS). Her life expectancy had been estimated to be 3–5 years.

She was admitted to the Akron General Medical Center in July 1980; she was in a stuporous condition and had difficulty in breathing. There she had a cardiac arrest, was resuscitated, and was placed on a life-support system consisting of a respirator, an NG tube, and a catheter for bladder elimination. She remained on that life-support system for 4 months, with no evidence of improvement in her condition. In fact, her condition deteriorated during that time from "semicomatose" to a "chronic vegetative" state.

In October Mr. Leach requested that his wife be removed from the respirator. Howard Shapiro, the attending physician, refused. Acknowledging in a letter that the patient's medical condition was "hopeless" and that "her ultimate demise is only a matter of time," he stated that the life-support system could be removed only by court order.

Mr. Leach was appointed as his wife's legal guardian. With the support of the Leach children, he petitioned a trial court for an order to terminate the treatment that was merely prolonging his wife's dying. The court appointed a guardian *ad litem* to represent Mrs. Leach's interests.

At an evidentiary hearing in December, several of the 17 witnesses testified to having had conversations with Mrs. Leach regarding life-support systems. In each of the conversations, Mrs. Leach expressed a desire, if the circumstances should arise, not to be placed on a life-support system. In the words of one witness, Mrs. Leach had stated, "I don't want to live if I have to be a vegetable."

The court granted the petition to abate treatment. The respirator was disconnected in early January—18 days after the court decision—and Mrs. Leach died. The delay in abating treatment was due to a lack of cooperation by physicians: Shapiro withdrew from the case, and over 30 physicians were contacted before one was found who would comply with the court order.[18]

In July 1982, Mr. Leach and his children filed an action for damages against Shapiro and the hospital for the futile and unwanted effort at prolonging Mrs. Leach's life. The trial court dismissed the action, claiming that there was no legal basis for such an action. However, the court of appeals reversed the trial court and ruled that, as a matter of law, the unconsented, nonemergency treatment given Mrs. Leach represented a battery, for which the physicians and hospital could be liable in damages.

The plaintiffs made several charges: that Mrs. Leach, while having the capacity to make decisions, had "expressly advised defendants that she did not wish to be kept alive by machines"; that Mrs. Leach, after being resuscitated, was placed on a life-support system without the consent of the family; that the family had not been informed of Mrs. Leach's condition or prognosis for 2 months; and that the defendant physicians had administered experimental drugs to Mrs. Leach for 2 months without family consent "for the purpose of observing the effects of these drugs on a person in Mrs. Leach's condition.''

The court of appeals emphasized the importance of informed consent by patients and the corollary right of patients to refuse treatment. Even though emergency situations have brought about the theory of "implied consent" to medical treatment, a patient's right to refuse treatment "may not be overcome by the doctrine of implied consent." In addition, the court emphasized the importance of truthtelling with patients. In the court's opinion, the failure of a physician to disclose pertinent information to a patient, or to the representative of an incompetent patient, may "give rise to an action in fraud independent of malpractice." In sum, the court held that if the relatives of Mrs. Leach could show that treatment was administered without proper consent, they could recover for "pain, suffering, and mental anguish"—and possibly recover punitive damages as well.[19]

Case 4.14

Mary Hier, aged 92, had a history of mental illness. She had been a psychiatric patient in New York for 57 years before being transferred to a nursing home in Massachusetts in 1983. She had been given chlorpromazine (Thorazine) in both institutions to relieve her delusions and extreme agitation, and had suffered no adverse side effects.

Her major medical problem was nutritional. Because of her advanced age and disabilities (a hiatal hernia and a large cervical diverticulum, or sac, in her esophagus), ingestion of food and drink by mouth was "a practical impossibility." As a result, she had received a gastrostomy in 1974—but had repeatedly pulled out the gastric feeding tube (G-tube) in her stomach. Her abdomen showed "multiple scars from her old gastrostomy tube sites."

In 1984 Hier was transferred to a hospital after pulling the G-tube from her abdomen on several occasions. There she "adamantly refused to have any surgery performed." She also resisted chlorpromazine treatment, apparently because of an aversion to being injected by needles.

The administrator of the nursing home and a nurse filed a petition with the probate court for the appointment of a guardian who would consent on Hier's behalf to the administration of chlorpromazine and surgery to enable adequate nutritional support. Later, following the advice of two (out of three) physicians, they revised their request: they stated that the chlorpromazine, but not the surgery, was in Hier's best interests. By contrast, a guardian *ad litem* and an attorney appointed to represent Hier's interests argued that both forms of treatment were needed.

The probate judge, using the substituted-judgment approach put forth in *Saikewicz*, ruled that Hier, if competent, would opt for chlorpromazine treatment but would refuse the proposed surgery. The case was appealed, and the Appeals Court of Massachusetts upheld the decision.

The appeals court addressed the medical, legal, and ethical aspects of the case. The court observed that there were six theoretical alternatives for providing nutritional support: by mouth, by normal IV feeding (short-term, primarily for hydration), by NG tube (long-term nutritional support), by central hyperalimentation, by gastrostomy, and by surgical repair of the esophagus. For various reasons, the only realistic alternative was gastrostomy. In terms of the law, the guardian *ad litem* cited the *Storar* case (and the middle appellate decision in *Conroy*), and argued that a failure to provide nutrition for a patient who was not comatose, vegetative, or brain dead could not be permitted on any legal grounds.

The court dismissed the reference to *Storar,* because the New York court had rejected the substituted-judgment test but provided no other legal mechanism for deciding cases of treatment abatement on the behalf of never-competent patients or other nonautonomous patients who had never expressed their views on life-prolonging medical treatment. The court also stated that this case differed from *Conroy* (and *Barber*) in that the issue was not whether to terminate ongoing nutritional support, but whether "to put an unwilling patient" through the intrusiveness of a "major surgical procedure." On ethical grounds, the court argued that nutritional support was not different from other forms of treatment, and that the burdens of the proposed surgery in this case (complications from earlier operations, relatively high risk because of Hier's age, the need for physical restraints for a week following surgery, etc.) made it "more onerous" for Hier than it would be for other, younger, healthier persons.[20]

Case 4.15

Francis Landy was admitted to John F. Kennedy Memorial Hospital in West Palm Beach in April 1981. Within 2 days he stopped breathing and was placed on a mechanical ventilator. He was diagnosed as having permanent brain damage, acute respiratory failure, chronic interstitial fibrosis, and GI bleeding. The attending physician judged Landy's medical condition to be terminal.

Landy's wife gave the physician a document entitled "Mercy Will and Last Testament." Landy had signed the document in the presence of two witnesses in April 1975. Only 2 months prior to his hospitalization, Landy had received his wife's promise that she would make the document a part of his hospital record if he were ever hospitalized.

Landy was declared incompetent by a probate court, and his wife was appointed guardian of his person. She requested that "all extraordinary life-support systems'' be discontinued. The hospital's response, given the possibility of civil and criminal liability, was to seek a declaratory relief action from the trial court regarding the hospital's rights and responsibilities in the case. Landy died before the hearing, but the trial court decided that the case should proceed because of its importance.

In the view of the trial court, the Landy case and all other factually similar cases in Florida call for judicial approval of treatment abatement on a case-by-case basis. The hospital appealed the case to the district court of appeal. The court affirmed the trial court decision, then certified the central legal question in the case to the Florida Supreme Court:

> In the case of a comatose and terminally ill individual who has executed a so-called living or mercy will, is it necessary that a court-appointed guardian of his person obtain the approval of a court of competent jurisdiction before terminating extraordinary life-support systems in order for consenting family members, the attending physicians, and the hospital and its administrators to be relieved of civil and criminal liability?

The state's highest court made several points in answering the certified question. First, the court pointed out that terminally ill, incompetent patients have the same right of treatment refusal as terminally ill, competent patients. For both types of patients, modern technological procedures sometimes simply hold dying patients "on the threshold of death." Consequently, the technological procedures "can be accurately described as a means of prolonging the dying process rather than a means of continuing life."

Citing *Quinlan, Perlmutter,* and *Colyer,* the court stated that an incompetent patient's refusal of treatment may be exercised by (1) close family members or (2) a guardian of the person appointed by a court, if close family members are not available. Specifically disagreeing with the *Quinlan* and *Colyer* courts, the Florida court said that neither "ethics committees" nor guardians are required in all such cases.

However, before either a family member or a guardian may exercise the patient's right, the attending physician must certify—with two other physicians concurring—that the patient is in "a permanent vegetative state," that there is "no reasonable prospect that the patient will regain cognitive brain function," and that the patient's existence is being sustained "only through the use of extraordinary life-sustaining measures." At that point, the relative or guardian may use "substituted judgment" to indicate what he or she believes the patient, if competent, would have done under the circumstances.

For the court, the accuracy of such a substituted judgment would be considerably enhanced by the possession of a "living" or "mercy" will previously signed by the now-incompetent patient. Such a document, like the one signed by Landy, would be "persuasive evidence of that [now] incompetent person's intention and . . . should be given great weight by the person or persons'' making a decision regarding treatment abatement on the behalf of the patient.

Thus the court answered the certified question by saying that in cases of permanent loss of consciousness, with the dying process being prolonged through technical means, and with agreement regarding the merits of treatment abatement, physicians and hospital administrators need not seek judicial approval prior to abating treatment. To be relieved of potential civil and criminal liability, the parties to the decision need only act "in good faith." Prior judicial approval would be necessary only in cases involving disagreement among physicians or family members, or where there is a question of wrongful motives or malpractice.[21]

Case 4.16

In 1979 Claire Conroy, aged 78 and suffering from an organic brain syndrome, was adjudicated an incompetent. Thomas Whittemore, her nephew and only surviving blood relative, was appointed her guardian. He had his aunt placed in the Parkview Nursing Home, where she came under the medical care of Dr. Ahmed Kazemi, a family practitioner, and Catherine Rittel, who was a registered nurse and the nursing home administrator.

Three years later, when Conroy was hospitalized because of an elevated temperature and dehydration, Dr. Kazemi inserted an NG tube to facilitate her eating. The tube remained in place after she returned to the nursing home, because attempts to feed her by mouth were ineffective.

By January 1983, Whittemore had become convinced that the NG tube was contrary to his aunt's wishes, that she would refuse such treatment if she were competent, and that she should be allowed to die without this prolonged medical intervention. Now 82, his aunt was bedridden, severely demented, unable to move from a semifetal position, afflicted with several medical conditions (arteriosclerotic heart disease, hypertension, diabetes mellitus, a gangrenous left leg below the knee, and bed sores), incontinent, unable to swallow sufficient nutrients and water, and unable to speak. With these serious mental and physical impairments, she nevertheless was clearly not comatose, in a PVS, or brain dead.

When Whittemore requested that the feeding tube be removed, Dr. Kazemi refused and stated that the removal of the tube would be ''a violation of medical ethics.'' The nursing home supported the physician's refusal, but Rittel indicated that a court order to remove the tube would be followed.

Whittemore's subsequent request for a court order to permit treatment abatement initiated a judicial process in New Jersey that involved a trial court's decision to have the feeding tube removed, an appellate court's reversal of that decision, and the state supreme court's reversal of the appellate court (in January 1985). The judicial process took 23 months. Like the earlier Quinlan case, this landmark New Jersey case gained nationwide attention because of the substantive issues involved. Unlike the Quinlan case, the patient in *Conroy* died—with NG tube intact—while the initial appeal was pending.

For the justices of the New Jersey Supreme Court, a preliminary substantive issue in the case was one already addressed by several courts: the right of a competent patient to refuse medical treatment. Citing *Perlmutter* and other cases involving competent patients, the court concluded that "the right to self-determination ordinarily outweighs any countervailing state interests, and competent persons generally are permitted to refuse medical treatment, even at the risk of death."

With patients adjudicated incompetent, however, substitute decision makers bear the responsibility of determining when medical treatment should be continued and when it should be abated. In carrying out this task, the decision makers must "seek to respect simultaneously both aspects of the patient's right to self-determination—the right to live, and the right, in some cases, to die of natural causes without medical intervention."

How should such a decision be made on behalf of a patient who is elderly, awake and conscious, formerly competent but now with severely and permanently diminished capacity to make decisions, expected to die within a year, and a resident of a nursing home? The court addressed several substantive issues that apply to this type of case. The first such issue—described by the court as "a necessary prerequisite to surrogate decision making"—is that of the patient's incapacity to make a decision regarding medical treatment. The determination by a court that a patient is incompetent to make such a decision requires "clear and convincing" medical evidence provided by at least two physicians, followed by the court's designation of a guardian to make decisions on behalf of the incompetent patient.

For the guardian, the goal of deciding about treatment abatement "should be to determine and effectuate, insofar as possible, the decision that the patient would have made if competent." To achieve that goal, the guardian should follow one of three standards put forth by the *Conroy* court. The *subjective test* should be followed when it is clear—from an earlier oral directive by the patient, a written document, or a reasonable deduction from the patient's beliefs—that this patient "would have refused the treatment under the circumstances involved." Alternate standards are available for guardians who are responsible for patients who never clearly expressed their desires about life-sustaining treatment. The *limited-objective test* is a version of the "best-interests" test that should be followed when (1) there is some trustworthy, but not unequivocal evidence that the patient would have refused the treatment, and (2) the guardian is convinced that the burdens of the treatment outweigh the benefits of the treatment for the patient. The *pure-objective test* is another version of the "best-interests" test that should be followed when (1) there is no evidence that the patient would have refused treatment, but (2) the "net burdens" of the patient's life with the treatment "clearly and markedly outweigh the benefits that the patient derives from life."

Another substantive issue addressed by the court is the validity of four distinctions sometimes used in decisions to abate treatment: the active/passive distinction, the withholding/withdrawing distinction, the ordinary/extra-ordinary distinction, and the distinction between artificial feedings and other forms of life-sustaining medical treatment. The court rejected all of the distinctions, arguing in regard to artificial feedings that the use of NG tubes, gastrostomies, and IV infusions to compensate for a patient's impaired eating function is "analytically . . . equivalent to artificial breathing by means of a respirator" for a patient's impaired breathing function.

Finally, the court put forth an involved procedure that should be followed to protect the interests of incompetent patients in Conroy-type cases. That procedure, geared to the organizational structure of the state government in New Jersey, requires that the "Office of the Ombudsman" be notified whenever treatment abatement is considered for a Conroy-type patient, that the ombudsman investigate the case, and that the ombudsman (along with the patient's family and attending physician) concur with the guardian's decision to abate treatment. Under this procedure, no participant in the decision-making process is liable for civil or criminal charges.[22]

Case 4.17

Nancy Ellen Jobes had an automobile accident in 1980. She was 25-years old, married, and 4 months pregnant. The fetus died as a consequence of the car accident. During an operation to remove the fetus, Jobes sustained an acute cardiopulmonary collapse that resulted in massive, irreversible brain damage.

Jobes remained in a PVS for 5 years. Although she could breathe without artificial aid, she required artificial feeding: first by NG tube, subsequently by gastrostomy and jejunostomy tubes. The feedings were administered by the nursing staff at the Lincoln Park Nursing Home, where Jobes remained for the 5-year period.

In March 1986, her husband, who had been appointed her guardian 2 years earlier, petitioned a New Jersey trial court to have the feeding tube removed. He was supported in this action by her parents. A court-appointed guardian *ad litem,* whose judicial function was that of determining his client's best interests, agreed that in this case the patient's best interests called for the removal of the feeding tube.

The petition was opposed by the nursing home and the Office of the Public Advocate. In fact, the nursing home had a pretrial motion seeking the appointment of a "life advocate" who would "urge the continuation of all available means of medical treatment, regardless of [Jobes'] physical and mental condition." The motion was denied by the court.

The court approved the removal of the feeding tube. In arriving at that decision, the court stated that "clear and convincing evidence" was the necessary standard of proof in treatment-abatement cases involving life-sustaining treatment, that such evidence demonstrated that Jobes was in a PVS, and that such evidence indicated that Jobes had expressed her intention while autonomous never to have her life prolonged by artificial means if she were to become helpless and insensate. The court found Jobes' views on life-prolonging treatment to be clear and convincing in two ways: her comments in several conversations prior to the car accident, and her membership in the Presbyterian Church (U.S.A.), a denomination supporting the withdrawal of life-support systems in the circumstances of a PVS.

Citing *Quinlan* and *Conroy*, the court held that these two cases together provided authority for the removal of the feeding tube. Specifically, the court stated that the facts of the case satisfied the "limited-objective" test set forth in *Conroy*. In addition, the court pointed out that the removal of the feeding tube was consistent with the recent (March 15, 1986) policy statement on abating treatment made by the A.M.A.[23]

The case was appealed, and the New Jersey Supreme Court delivered the final opinion in the case in June 1987. Written by Justice Garibaldi, the opinion was one of the "trilogy" of cases decided at the same time (along with *Farrell* and *Peter*). The 6–1 decision reversed the lower court on two points. The trial court had found Jobes' earlier views to be "clear and convincing," and had said that the nursing home could refuse to participate in the abatement of tube feeding. The Supreme Court found the patient's earlier views (as reported by her husband and her friends) to be "remote, general, spontaneous and made in casual circumstances." The court also ruled that the nursing home had to honor the patient's refusal of treatment (as decided by her surrogate), saying that to allow the institution to discharge the patient "would essentially frustrate Mrs. Jobes' right of self-determination."

In addition, the court reiterated its position in *Conroy* that technological nutrition and hydration was a form of medical treatment. The court then supplemented *Quinlan* and *Conroy* by providing procedures to be followed by a surrogate who decided to have life-sustaining treatment abated in the care of a patient under the age of 60 (this age is significant, because of procedures having to do with the state ombudsman), diagnosed as having a persistent vegetative condition, and living in a nursing home. In such a case, a family member or designated friend or guardian is required to have "two indepen-

dent physicians knowledgeable in neurology'' confirm that the patient is in a
PVS and has no reasonable possibility of recovering to a ''cognitive, sapient
state.'' A decision to abate treatment made in this manner need not require
judicial review.[24]

Case 4.18

Helen Corbett, aged 75, had been in a PVS for 33 months following a massive
stroke in 1982. Married, but with no other living family, she had not indicated
her views on life-sustaining treatment in a written document prior to the stroke
and had never designated a proxy to make decisions on her behalf.

Corbett's neurological condition was diagnosed by three physicians, who
agreed that her life was being sustained only by artificial feedings administered through an NG tube. The physicians also agreed with the request by
Corbett's husband that the NG feedings be discontinued. However, they were
concerned about the legality of abating treatment in this situation because
Florida's ''Life-Prolonging Procedures Act'' seemed to indicate that the
abatement of artificial feeding was not a legal option.

To settle the legal issue, Mr. Corbett requested a declaratory judgment from
a trial court. State Attorney General Joseph D'Alessandro opposed Corbett's
request to have the NG tube removed. The trial court, in spite of agreeing with
Mr. Corbett that his wife of 45 years would have rejected the treatment and
that artificial feeding was to be interpreted as an ''extraordinary life-sustaining medical procedure,'' rejected the petition to have the feeding tube
removed. Helen Corbett died—NG tube still intact—after the trial court hearing but before the trial judge's decision.

Mr. Corbett appealed the case to the district court of appeal, to clarify the
law regarding similar cases in the future. That court overruled the trial court
by holding that artificial feeding is a medical procedure similar to other
life-sustaining medical procedures, and that all patients regardless of their
competency status have a constitutional right of privacy (a ''penumbral'' right
at the federal level, and ''express right of privacy'' in the Florida Constitution) that entails the right to refuse life-sustaining medical treatment. This
right, according to the court, cannot be abridged or limited by a state statute.[25]

Case 4.19

Paul Brophy, aged 46, was a firefighter and emergency medical technician in
Easton, Massachusetts. He was an active man, an outdoors sportsman, a
husband for 24 years, and the father of five children aged 15–23.

During the night of March 22, 1983, he complained to his wife, Patricia,
of a severe, ''splitting'' headache. He rolled over in bed and became uncon-

scious. He was transported by ambulance to Goddard Hospital in Stoughton, where an angiogram revealed the aneurysm located at the apex of the basilar artery. The rupture of the aneurysm had apparently produced his unconscious condition.

On April 6, Brophy underwent a right frontotemporal craniotomy. On June 28, he was transferred to the New England Sinai Hospital. On July 7, he was diagnosed as being in a "semivegetative or vegetative state." In August he contracted pneumonia. When the hospital requested Patricia Brophy's instructions regarding a DNR notation on Brophy's chart, she requested such a notation and the hospital complied. On December 22, he underwent a surgical procedure in which a G-tube was placed in his abdominal wall to facilitate the provision of nutrition and hydration.

In April 1984, Brophy was diagnosed as being in a continued vegetative state. Almost a year later, in February and March 1985, two neurological examinations confirmed that he was in an unusual form of a PVS. The form of PVS was unusual in that Brophy's cortex was largely undamaged; instead, the thalamus and portions of the midbrain were damaged, thus disconnecting the pathways to the cortex and leaving him without cognitive functioning ability.

Given this medical evidence regarding Brophy's condition, Patricia Brophy, acting as her husband's guardian, requested that the G-tube be removed or clamped. Brophy's physicians refused the request. After consultation with her family and her family priest, Mrs. Brophy sought a court order granting her the authority to have her husband's artificial feeding terminated. A judge of the probate and family court, following 7 months of motions, countermotions, and evidentiary hearings, ordered the continued use of the G-tube— even though he agreed that the patient, if competent, would decline to receive nutrition and hydration through the G-tube. The hospital and the guardian were enjoined from removing or clamping the tube.

Patricia Brophy appealed the decision, and the Supreme Judicial Court of Massachusetts took the case on its own motion. That court's landmark decision, announced September 11, 1986, was the first time that any state supreme court had ruled on the legality of withdrawing artificial feeding from a person who, though permanently unconscious, was still alive. In a 4–3 decision, with each of the dissenting justices writing strongly worded dissenting opinions, the majority of the court ruled that the trial court had erred in refusing the request to remove or clamp the feeding tube. However, the majority agreed with the trial court that the hospital and its staff should not be forced to participate in removing or clamping Brophy's G-tube, since the medical staff in the case regarded the removal of the feeding tube as being contrary to the moral integrity of the medical profession. Thus the court ordered the hospital only "to assist the guardian in transferring the ward to a

suitable facility, or to his home, where his wishes [in refusing the technological feeding] may be effectuated.''

For the court, the central issue in the case was whether ''the substituted
judgment of a person in a persistent vegetative state that the artificial maintenance of his nutrition and hydration be discontinued shall be honored.'' The
court's conclusion regarding the patient's views—based on his previously
expressed preferences and his religious convictions as a Roman Catholic—was
the availability of ''ample evidence which no one disputes, that Brophy's
judgment would be to decline the provision of food and water and to terminate
his life.'' Brophy's wife and family agreed with this inferred decision, and no
one connected with the case ever questioned their moral integrity.

However, Lajos Koncz, Brophy's attending physician, resisted the request
from the family for treatment abatement because he believed ''he would
willfully be causing Brophy's death.'' He was supported in this view by
Richard Field, the physician-in-chief at New England Sinai Hospital, even
though substantial evidence was given (including an official position taken by
the Massachusetts Medical Society on July 17, 1985) to show that ''a significant portion of the medical community . . . considers it appropriate to
withhold hydration and nutrition from individuals like Brophy when that is the
wish of the patient and his family.''

In ruling against the hospital's position, the court quoted John Stuart Mill's
views on liberty, cited numerous cases (especially *Bouvia, Conroy,* and *Corbett*) on the issue of treatment refusal, and held that three countervailing state
interests relevant to the case (the preservation of life, the prevention of suicide, and the maintenance of the medical profession's moral integrity) were
insufficient reasons to subject Brophy to the continued use of artificial feeding
for ''several years.'' In regard to the first state interest, the court stated that
this interest ''encompasses a broader interest than mere corporeal existence.''
Regarding the second possible interest, the court held that the discontinuation
of the G-tube feedings would not be the ''death-producing agent'' and that
death would be ''the result, primarily, of the underlying disease, and not the
result of a self-inflicted injury.'' As to the medical profession and the removal
of the feeding tube from a permanently unconscious patient who could not
chew or swallow, the court reasoned that ''so long as we decline to force the
hospital to participate in removing or clamping Brophy's G-tube, there is no
violation of the integrity of the medical profession.''[26]

Case 4.20

Hilda Peter, aged 65 and permanently unconscious, was a patient in a New
Jersey nursing home in 1987. Three years earlier, in 1984, Eberhard Johanning, her living companion, had found Peter collapsed on their kitchen floor.

She had been resuscitated by paramedics, but remained unconscious in a PVS. Sustained by feedings through an NG tube, she could have remained unconscious but alive, according to two physicians, for "many years, possibly decades."

In 1983, Peter had executed a "power-of-attorney" statement in which she authorized Johanning "to be given full and complete authority to manage and direct [her] medical care." In 1985, a year after Peter had permanently lost consciousness, Johanning sought to be appointed as her guardian. A trial court adjudicated Peter as an incompetent, appointed Johanning as her guardian, but required him to attain the approval of the state ombudsman before having the feeding tube removed (as mandated by *Conroy* for such cases). The ombudsman refused to agree, claiming that Hilda Peter, unlike Claire Conroy, did not meet the 1-year life-expectancy test put forth in *Conroy*.

Johanning appealed the ombudsman's decision directly to the New Jersey Supreme Court. In June 1987, the court announced its decision in the case (along with *Farrell* and *Jobes*). In the decision, the court pointed out that the fact pattern of the case was more similar to *Quinlan* than to *Conroy*. Consequently, the 1-year life-expectancy test (as well as the "limited-objective" and "objective" tests) did not apply to the case being considered. Instead, the *Conroy* "subjective" test was used to determine the patient's preferences regarding life-sustaining treatment.

In applying the subjective test, the court found that there was "clear and convincing evidence" that Peter would have wanted the technological feeding stopped. Although she had not signed an advance directive, she had directed Johanning to refuse life-sustaining treatment on her behalf in such a situation. In addition, the court considered "nine reliable hearsay accounts" of Peter's disinclination to have her life prolonged through technological means.

The court reiterated its earlier view that technological feeding is to be regarded as a form of medical treatment, and that the abatement of life-sustaining technological nutrition and hydration is not to be regarded as the cause of the patient's death. In the words of Justice Garibaldi: "Hilda Peter will not die from the withdrawal of the nasogastric tube, but because of her underlying medical problem, i.e., an inability to swallow."

The court then set forth several procedural steps for the handling of cases involving elderly nursing home patients with permanent unconsciousness. Such cases should center on the patient's previously expressed views, if possible. In this regard, even a durable-power-of-attorney statute not specifically authorizing health care decisions should be interpreted in that way. In addition, the court required the ombudsman's oversight in such cases, two independent medical opinions regarding the patient's permanently unconscious condition, and the appointment of a guardian in the absence of a family member or other surrogate.[27]

Case 4.21

Daniel Delio, aged 33, suffered cardiac arrest in 1986 during routine surgery to repair an anorectal fistula. The brain damage he suffered was so severe that he was diagnosed as being in a PVS (or "neocortically dead," according to the court record). The next day he was transferred to Westchester County Medical Center.

Three months later Julianne Delio, with the support of Daniel's mother, requested that a New York trial court appoint her as conservator of Daniel's personal and financial affairs—with the authority to order the removal of the G-tube and jejunostomy tube that were being used to keep her husband alive. The medical center opposed her application, saying that the removal of the feeding tubes would constitute "a deliberate act which would cause Daniel's death." The trial court judge, though acknowledging that "clear and convincing" evidence indicated that Daniel would have opposed the technological prolongation of his life, denied Julianne's request.

The appellate division granted Delio's request for expedited review of the trial court decision. The Society for the Right to Die filed an *amicus curiae* brief in the case. In June 1987, which was 6 months after the lower-court decision, the appellate court reversed that decision. In so doing, the appellate court joined the courts in several other jurisdictions in saying that nonautonomous patients have the right (through their surrogates) to refuse the prolongation of their lives by means of technological nutrition and hydration.

Three features of the decision are important. First, the evidence before the court left no doubt that Delio would have refused the technological feeding had he been able to do so. He was a marathon runner and exercise physiologist who had been "a markedly opinionated individual with clearly expressed ideas and strong views" on the subject of treatment abatement with nonautonomous patients. Delio's views on the subject "had been expressed repeatedly to his relatives and professional colleagues over the years."

Second, the appellate court rejected the medical center's argument regarding the causation of death. Even though the patient was relatively young and had a "nonterminal" medical condition, his death subsequent to removal of the feeding tubes could not be regarded as suicide or assisted suicide. In the court's words: "Daniel's death, when it occurs, will be the end result of his inability to chew and swallow spontaneously and not the result of a self-inflicted injury."

Third, the court chose not to require the medical center to terminate the technological feeding. Instead, the hospital was given an alternative: either "assist in the discontinuance of treatment," or "take whatever steps are reasonably necessary to assist" in the transfer of the patient to another facility or to his home, "where his wishes may be effectuated." A few days later,

Delio was transferred to Beth Israel Medical Center, where he was given palliative care for the remaining 9 days of his life.[28]

Case 4.22

Mildred Rasmussen was admitted to the Posada Del Sol Nursing Home in Tucson in 1979 at the age of 64. After her admission, she had three strokes, suffered from organic brain syndrome, was diagnosed as being in a PVS (in 1983), and remained in a fetal position on her bed. Her nutritional and fluid needs were met by means of NG-tube feedings. Her only relatives were three siblings living in Iowa.

In 1985, the Pima County public fiduciary requested to be appointed as Rasmussen's guardian for the purpose of consenting to the removal of the NG tube. The lower court handling the request appointed a guardian *ad litem* for Rasmussen, a physician to examine her, and an official "visitor" (according to state law) to see her. Rasmussen's relatives were informed of the court proceedings.

The trial court appointed the public fiduciary as Rasmussen's guardian without restriction, the guardian *ad litem* appealed the decision, and Rasmussen died from pneumonia during the appeals process. Nevertheless, the Arizona Supreme Court took the case on appeal because the issues in the case were regarded as important for persons facing "similar situations on a daily basis."

The court decided that the state Medical Treatment Decision Act was inapplicable to the case, that the right to refuse medical treatment was based on the right of privacy implicit or explicit to the federal and state constitutions, that no state interests outweighed Rasmussen's right of privacy, that either a family member or guardian could exercise the patient's right to refuse treatment, and that similar cases in the future should be handled according to the "best-interests" standard. Court involvement in such a case is not necessary, once it has handled the matters of incompetency and guardianship.[29]

Case 4.23

Joseph Gardner, aged 22, suffered "severe, permanent, and totally disabling" injuries to his head in 1985 when he fell from the back of a moving pickup. In spite of medical, surgical, and rehabilitative efforts, he remained in a PVS following the accident. A patient at Central Maine Medical Center in Lewiston, he was unable to chew or swallow and was kept alive by feedings through an NG tube.

When a trial court held hearings on the case, the court found out that prior to the accident Gardner had declared his "intent and desire that he not be maintained on the nasogastric tube.'' All of Gardner's family, his close friends, the Maine Department of Human Services, and his court-appointed guardian *ad litem* urged the court to respect his ''preaccident decision not to be kept alive artificially in a persistent vegetative state.'' The superior court agreed, but the district attorney opposed the decision and appealed it to the Supreme Judicial Court of Maine.

Maine's highest court received four *amici curiae* briefs on the case, including briefs from Americans United for Life Legal Defense Fund and the Society for the Right to Die. The court itself was seriously divided on the case, as indicated by its 4–3 vote to affirm the lower-court decision and approve the abatement of technological feeding.

The 1987 decision by the supreme judicial court centered on one major question, namely whether a patient diagnosed as persistently vegetative ''may compel the discontinuation of life-sustaining procedures by means of the decision that he declared before he lost competency.'' After considering the evidence regarding Gardner's repeated and specific statements that he ''would definitely want to die if he was ever in a vegetative state,'' the court observed that what really seemed to bother Gardner about the possibility of being kept alive in such a state was ''the utter helplessness of the permanently comatose person, the wasting of a once strong body, and the submission of the most private bodily functions to the attention of others.'' Pointing out that Gardner's earlier statements applied ''specifically to the circumstances in which he now exists,'' the court—or at least the majority of its members—decided to respect his earlier decision and permit the discontinuation of life-sustaining treatment.

In arriving at this decision, the court rejected any distinction between technological feeding and other forms of life-sustaining technology. It also rejected any suggestion that the abatement of life-sustaining treatment in the case was tantamount to suicide or assisted suicide. In the court's words: ''He in no sense has decided to kill himself. . . . Accident has brought him to that state. . . . [He] is simply exercising his right to control the course of his medical care.'' The cause of his death subsequent to treatment abatement ''will be not his refusal of care but rather his accident and his resulting medical condition, including his inability to ingest food and water.''[30]

Case 4.24

William Drabick, aged 39 at the time, received a severe head injury in an automobile accident in California in 1983. During emergency care, physicians introduced NG feeding but were not able to restore consciousness.

In 1985, David Drabick, the brother of William, was appointed as his conservator. Later that year, he petitioned the superior court to authorize the removal of the feeding tube from William's body. William's three other adult brothers supported the petition, as did the county public defender and Jeannine Gonzalez, with whom William had lived for approximately 12 years. Ms. Gonzalez told the court that when William had earlier seen his terminally ill father being maintained through technological means, he had said: "I would never want to be kept alive like that. . . . You've got to promise me. . . ."

The superior court denied the request, saying that "continued feeding is in the best interest of a patient who is not brain dead" and that it could not permit "the conservatee to starve and dehydrate to death." David Drabick appealed the decision, and the California Court of Appeal, Sixth District, made the final decision in the case in April 1988.

The court of appeal reversed the superior court's decision and directed the lower court to reconsider the petition in the light of several principles applicable to the case. Among those principles are the following: "human beings are not passive subjects of medical technology"; incompetent patients retain the right to have "appropriate medical decisions made on their behalf," based on their best interests; physicians have no legal obligation "to continue to forestall an inevitable death," particularly when the burdens of treatment are disproportionate to the benefits of the treatment; the patient's prior statements about treatment abatement may "inform the decision" of the conservator, but the conservator must "vicariously exercise the conservatee's rights" in terms of the conservatee's best interests; and judicial approval is not required for the abatement of life-sustaining treatment with PVS patients, unless the interested parties in a case disagree about the appropriate course of action.[31]

Significance of these cases

The cases just described, as well as the other cases cited in the end-of-chapter notes, are significant for several reasons. First, these brief case histories indicate the extent to which the courts have increasingly become involved in the debate over abating treatment. During the second phase of the debate, and especially during the post-1985 phase of the debate, the courts have addressed the questions of civil and criminal liability that sometimes arise with treatment-abatement cases in various clinical settings, grappled with unprecedented legal issues not yet covered by legislation, and helped shape public opinion regarding the merits of treatment abatement.

The cases are also significant because of the substantive issues inherent in any effort at abating treatment on the behalf of patients lacking such decision-making capacity themselves. The cases presented in this chapter are thus much more complex—and much more controversial—than the cases presented in the previous chapter. Although the Perlmutter, Bartling, and Bouvia cases drew nationwide attention, the debate over discontinuing treatment in those cases pales in comparison with the debate over discontinuing similar modalities of treatment in several of the cases just presented.

The reasons for this difference are obvious. When a decision about treatment abatement is made by a patient who possesses the capacity to make such a decision, only a relatively small number of vitalist physicians, anxious hospital administrators, and/or pro-life activists may try to thwart that decision. But when (1) a critically ill patient lacks the capacity to make a decision about medical treatment, (2) the decision about continuing or abating treatment is the responsibility of a proxy or surrogate, (3) information regarding the patient's views on medical treatment may or may not be available, (4) the possibility of an error in judgment is present, (5) the patient may die as a consequence of the decision, and (6) there are other parties in the case who may disagree with the decision and/or question the motives of the surrogate, the decision to abate treatment is made considerably more difficult.

Moreover, precisely because of third-party involvement, the possibility of error, and the irreversibility of some decisions to abate treatment, the stakes in such cases dramatically increase. As stated by the *Conroy* court, the responsibility that falls on the decision makers (surrogates and courts, whenever a court is involved) is that of avoiding an error in either of two ways: by keeping "a person alive under circumstances under which he would rather have been allowed to die," or by allowing "that person to die when he would have chosen to cling to life."[32]

The high stakes, in turn, add to the significance of these cases. Because of the vulnerability of these patients—brought about by diminished or fluctuating capacity, substantial incapacity, permanent loss of consciousness, or the immaturity of young age—decisions to abate treatment on their behalf are usually made with great caution, sometimes elicit court participation by activist groups advocating or challenging such decisions, and occasionally bring forth extraordinary interpretive claims regarding the long-term significance of the decisions. The unusual caution by participants in such cases is sometimes exhibited by a medical and legal version of "hot potato": physicians (unduly anxious about liability) refuse to comply with a surrogate's request to abate treatment, hospital administrators seek a declaratory relief judgment from a trial court, the trial court appoints a guardian *ad litem,* the guardian *ad litem* often opposes treatment abatement—and the case is finally resolved by means of a complicated procedure that must be followed before treatment abatement can be carried out. As to the participation by activist and professional groups, one need only note the increasing number of *amici curiae* briefs filed in court cases in recent years (e.g., *Conroy* had *amici curiae* briefs filed by nine different organizations). And surely a strong candidate for the most excessive interpretive comment on these cases is the statement by Peter Gubellini, the guardian *ad litem* in the Brophy case, who said after the decision by the Massachusetts Supreme Judicial Court:

It is a dark day for the citizens of the Commonwealth, especially those at the edges of life, such as the aged, the infirm, the handicapped, profoundly retarded, and even the unborn. This decision appears to be the first step in the selective killing of unproductive citizens.[33]

Emerging trends in these cases

As indicated by the previous quotation, the long-term significance of the cases presented in this chapter depends, at least in part, on the person or group doing the interpreting. For many individuals and groups in the right-to-die movement, this series of cases since 1976 represents only a logical extension to nonautonomous patients of the common-law and constitutional rights of self-determination, religious freedom, and privacy that autonomous patients have—including the derivative right to refuse life-sustaining medical treatment. For persons adhering to a vitalistic philosophy, physicians subscribing to the "technological imperative," and members of pro-life groups, this series of cases represents a disastrous, judicially approved move toward a societal acceptance of terminating the lives of patients who could—and should—continue to live with the aid of medical technology. In addition, to many practicing physicians (especially those who do not keep up with recent developments in health law and biomedical ethics), the same cases represent an inadequately known, widely misunderstood, and unquestionably anxiety-causing development in the law that complicates physician–patient relationships by further increasing the legal vulnerability of physicians who work with critically ill patients.

In my view, these cases represent fundamentally important developments in the law. It is true that many jurisdictions have still not developed case law regarding treatment abatement—especially involving nonautonomous patients. Nevertheless, it is also true that a steadily increasing number of jurisdictions are in the process of developing case law, often at the appellate and state supreme court levels, regarding the right of nonautonomous patients to have treatment abated that they (through their surrogates) regard as unwanted or contrary to their best interests. Many, but not all, of these decisions are right-to-die cases (*Northern, Hier,* and *Ingram* are cases in which the patient's death was not the focal point of abating treatment).

Since these cases still represent only a minority of jurisdictions, and since there are serious disagreements among the courts on certain questions inherent to the cases, it is difficult to say as much about judicial consensus here as could be said about judicial consensus regarding autonomous patients (see Chapter 3). Moreover, with the exceptions of the 13 jurisdictions that have decisions at the state supreme court level (New Jersey, Massachusetts, Delaware, New York, New Mexico, Washington, Florida, Georgia, Minnesota, Arizona, Missouri, Connecticut and Maine), it is difficult to be sure about the persuasiveness of these opinions as legal precedent.

What can be said with some certainty, however, is that these cases demonstrate a number of emerging trends that undoubtedly will affect the development of law in other jurisdictions. Several of these trends are important for the families and surrogates of nonautonomous patients, for physicians who work with nonautonomous patients (in ICUs, medical and surgical wards, nursing homes, and hospices), and for the rest of us who might for any number of reasons in the future become unable to make decisions about our medical treatment.

The first of the trends is the recognition that *an adult patient's right to accept or refuse medical treatment continues even though he or she loses the capacity to make such a decision personally.* After discussing the right of autonomous patients to accept or refuse medical treatment, all courts handling cases involving nonautonomous patients have uniformly held that the right to make decisions relative to medical treatment survives even a judicial determination of incompetency. The first court handling such a case decided that Karen Quinlan's right to refuse the life-sustaining treatment provided by a ventilator "should not be discarded solely on the basis that her condition prevents her conscious exercise of the choice."[34] A year later the *Saikewicz* court, faced with the plight of a conscious but profoundly retarded patient who had never had the capacity to make decisions about medical treatment, affirmed "a general right in all persons to refuse medical treatment in appropriate circumstances . . . recognition of that right must extend to the case of an incompetent, as well as a competent, patient because the value of human dignity extends to both."[35] Six years later the *Colyer* court agreed that the right to refuse life-sustaining treatment "inures equally" to competent and incompetent patients: "In harmony with other jurisdictions, we now hold that an adult who is incurably and terminally ill has a constitutional right of privacy that encompasses the right to refuse treatment that serves only to prolong the dying process."[36] The following year the Supreme Court of Florida, in its decision in the Landy case, joined the other jurisdictions by declaring that "terminally ill incompetent persons . . . have the same right to refuse to be held on the threshold of death as terminally ill competent persons."[37] And in 1985 the *Conroy* court reiterated the unanimous trend that started in New Jersey a decade earlier: "The right of an adult who, like Claire Conroy, was once competent, to determine the course of her medical treatment remains intact even when she is no longer able to assert that right or to appreciate its effectuation."[38]

A patient's incapacity to make a specific decision about medical treatment can differ from a judicial determination of a person's general incompetence. A number of courts have dealt with the related questions of decision-making incapacity and incompetency on the part of critically ill patients whose cases end up in court. In some instances, these patients are unquestionably incapacitated *and* legally incompetent because they are infants *(Barry),* young children *(Custody of a Minor),* profoundly retarded *(Saikewicz, Storar),* or permanently unconscious (at least 20 such cases from *Quinlan* to *Drabick).* In other instances, serious questions are sometimes raised about an otherwise autonomous patient's capacity to make a specific decision about medical treatment because of the patient's mental illness *(Winters, Yetter)*, diminished or fluctuating capacity *(Quackenbush, Northern)*, or refusal to make the decision that an attending physician thinks appropriate to the circumstances *(Candura)*. The trend that emerges from these cases has several features:

A patient is presumed to have decision-making capacity and to be competent unless demonstrated otherwise.

Incapacity to make a decision regarding proposed medical treatment is not to be equated with mental illness, objective status (in terms of age or diagnosis), vacillation or fluctuation in point of view, disagreement with a physician's recommendation, or legal incompetence.

The determination of incapacity depends on a specific patient's inability to understand the medical condition and the attendant risks of having or forgoing treatment.

The determination of incapacity or nonautonomy (as opposed to incompetency) requires neither psychiatric examination nor a judicial hearing.

For example, in a widely quoted opinion, the *Schiller* court put forth the following test to determine a patient's decision-making capacity: "Does the patient have sufficient mind to reasonably understand the condition, the nature and effect of the proposed treatment, attendant risks in pursuing the treatment, and not pursuing the treatment?"[39] And the *Ingram* court observed:

In this case Ingram, though legally incapable of managing her affairs or caring for herself, can nevertheless communicate with others and, at least to some extent, understand her plight. The weight to be accorded the ward's preferences should therefore be influenced by the extent to which the ward understands her problem and the possible treatment methods.[40]

A nonautonomous patient's surrogate has the legal authority to accept or refuse medical treatment on the behalf of the patient. Agreeing that all patients have the right to accept or refuse medical treatment, but acknowledging that nonautonomous patients cannot exercise that right personally, all the courts in this series of cases (with the exception of *Storar*) have affirmed the indispensable role to be carried out by the patient's surrogate.[41] Without a surrogate, a nonautonomous patient's right to accept or refuse medical treatment becomes meaningless. With a surrogate, a nonautonomous patient may exercise the right to choose between alternative treatments *(Ingram)*, refuse a specific modality of treatment (most of the cases in this series, from *Quinlan* to *Drabick)*, or refuse several forms of life-sustaining treatment *(Severns, Hamlin)*. Although the courts disagree about the appropriate standard to be used by the surrogate (we will discuss the courts' views on "substituted judgment" and "best interests" in the next section), they agree that an appropriate surrogate has the authority to decide for or against medical treatment on behalf of the patient whose life hangs in the balance. And although a few courts require that the surrogate be a court-appointed guardian, most of the recent court decisions allow for alternative surrogate decision makers depending on the facts in particular cases: a family member or other informally selected surrogate (apart from legal guardianship proceedings) in reasonably straightforward cases, or a court-appointed guardian where there are complicating problems (such as a critically ill patient without a family). The Supreme Court of Washington illustrates this recent change, since the acceptance of a more flexible surrogate arrangement in *Hamlin* was one of the reasons the court partially overrode the *Colyer* decision made a year earlier.[42]

The patient's surrogate has the legal authority to refuse all forms of life-sustaining treatment on the behalf of the patient. Some of the courts handling treatment-abatement cases with nonautonomous patients have dealt only with the request to abate the specific modality of treatment at issue in the case. Other courts have addressed the multiple forms of medical treatment that can be used to sustain a patient's life. No court making the final decision in any of these cases—not even the *Storar* court—has held that there are significant moral or legal distinctions among the various forms of treatment. Instead, the courts have declared that *any* life-sustaining treatment can be abated at the surrogate's request, as long as the surrogate's decision reflects the patient's own views on life-sustaining treatment or is based on a determination of the patient's best interests. For example, the *Conroy* court stated: "A competent patient has the right to decline *any* medical treatment, including artificial feeding, and should retain that right when and if he becomes incompetent" (emphasis added).[43] The most extended statement on this matter was made by the Court of Chancery of Delaware when, acting in response to a decision in the Severns case by the Supreme Court of Delaware, Chancellor Marvel declared:

I conclude that the prospective guardian's request for authorization to discontinue all medical supportive measures designed to keep Mrs. Severns alive in a comatose state . . . should be granted. In other words, those having the care of Mrs. Severns are not to return her to a respirator in order to sustain her breathing, are not to administer antibiotic drugs in the event of a pulmonary infection or the like, and a feeding tube is not to be inserted in her trachea. Furthermore, a no-code-blue order is to be posted on her medical chart, and finally no drugs or medicines are to be administered to Mrs. Severns other than those normally used to preserve bodily hygiene, particularly for the prevention or cure of constipation or diarrhea.[44]

There is no moral or legal difference between withholding treatment and withdrawing treatment already initiated. Courts addressing the alleged distinction between withholding and withdrawing treatment have acknowledged that many physicians find the distinction psychologically helpful, and that the distinction is often interpreted by physicians in terms of possible differences between omissions and actions. A reasonably common view among physicians is that withholding treatment is permissible, whereas withdrawing treatment (especially life-sustaining treatment) is morally questionable and may lead to legal problems should anyone interpret the withdrawal of treatment as having been a causative factor in a patient's death. With a unanimous voice, the courts have rejected this kind of reasoning. For them, the most important question is not whether the discontinuation of life-prolonging treatment is an "omission" or an "act," although some of the courts discuss this question. Instead, the important questions concern whether the treatment is proving beneficial to the patient, whether the treatment would have been wanted by the patient, and whether holding on to the false withholding/withdrawing distinction sometimes prevents physicians from trying modalities of treatment that could prove beneficial if given a chance. Thus the *Barber* court emphasized effectiveness as the appropriate test for continuing or discontinuing treatment already initiated: "A physician has no duty to continue treatment, once it has proved to be ineffective."[45] The *Torres* court emphasized patients' rights: "The individual's right to refuse treatment also includes the right to order the disconnection of extraordinary life-support systems."[46] And the *Conroy* court observed:

Whether necessary treatment is withheld at the outset or withdrawn later on, the consequence—the patient's death—is the same. Moreover, from a policy standpoint, it might well be unwise to forbid persons from discontinuing a treatment under circumstances in which the treatment could permissibly be withheld. Such a rule could discourage families and doctors from even attempting certain types of care and could thereby force them into hasty and premature decisions to allow a patient to die.[47]

The abatement of technological feeding and hydration is not morally or legally different from abating other forms of life-sustaining treatment. By 1983, many critically ill patients were having their lives prolonged through the use of various forms of technological feeding and hydration. That year intermediate appeals courts in New Jersey and California wrestled with two of the questions related to "artificial" feeding and hydration—Is artificial feeding and hydration to be regarded as medical treatment? Is it permissible to allow nonautonomous patients to die from lack of nourishment?—and came up with very different answers. For the appeals court in *Conroy,* which was later overruled by the New Jersey Supreme Court, the use of an NG tube is a part of "routine nursing care," and the removal of an NG tube in a nonautonomous patient is an illegal "act of euthanasia."[48] For the appeals court in *Barber,* which was the final court in this criminal case, the use of an IV tube for nutrition and hydration is "the same" as the use of respirators and other life-sustaining medical procedures, and the removal of an IV tube in a nonautonomous patient can be justifiable not as "an affirmative act but rather a withdrawal or omission of further treatment."[49] With the overturning of the *Conroy* decision, all appellate-level courts that have made final decisions in cases involving the abatement of technological feeding and hydration have been in agreement: technological feeding and hydration are to be regarded as a form of life-sustaining medical treatment, and this medical treatment, like other forms of medical treatment, can be stopped under appropriate circumstances.[50]

The previous views toward medical treatment held by now-nonautonomous patients have probative value, with that value increasing with the reliability and specificity of the views expressed. In the Quinlan case, the Supreme Court of New Jersey sustained the lower court's refusal to accept as admissible evidence the alleged comments Karen Quinlan had made to friends regarding life-sustaining treatment. In the words of the court: "the testimony of her previous conversations with friends . . . is without sufficient probative weight."[51] In the years since *Quinlan*, most other courts making final decisions in treatment-abatement cases with previously autonomous patients have rejected the position of the *Quinlan* court. Some courts have been willing to accept the inferred views of now-nonautonomous patients *(Spring, Colyer, Torres)*, other courts have admitted as evidence the quoted comments of such patients *(Eichner, Brophy, Peter, Delio, Gardner, Drabick)*, and other courts have placed substantial weight on advance directives that a patient had signed *(Landy)* or even planned to sign *(Severns)* before losing personal autonomy.

The trend in all of these cases indicates that the preferences toward life-sustaining treatment expressed by a now-nonautonomous patient can be presented in a variety of ways to a court, that different probative weight will likely be placed on the various types of evidence presented to a court, and that the greatest probative weight will be given to evidence demonstrating thoughtful and specific preferences previously made by the patient. For example, the *Eichner* court found Brother Fox's previously expressed opposition to the use of a respirator to prolong life in a vegetative state to be "unchallenged at every turn and unimpeachable in its sincerity," and concluded that "Brother Fox made the decision [to remove the respirator] for himself before he came incompetent."[52] The *Colyer* court observed that "prior statements may be probative in determining the wishes of an incompetent patient, with the age and maturity of the patient, the context of the statements, and the connection of the statements to the debilitating event being factors to be weighed by the guardian"[53] The *Bludworth* court accepted the fact that Landy had signed a "Mercy Will and Last Testament" as important evidence, and later said that whenever a now-nonautonomous individual had, while autonomous, executed "a so-called 'living' or 'mercy' will, that will would be persuasive evidence of that incompetent person's intention and it should be given great weight by the person or persons who substitute their judgment on behalf of the terminally ill incompetent."[54]

The Supreme Court of New Jersey, in its *Conroy* decision, admitted its earlier error: "we now believe that we were in error in *Quinlan* . . . to disregard evidence of statements that Ms. Quinlan made to friends." In fact, the court enumerated several forms of evidence it was now (in 1985) willing to accept: a written document or "living will," an oral directive to a family member, friend, or health care provider, the selection of a proxy to make health-related decisions (e.g., by means of a durable-power-of-attorney statute), reactions voiced by the patient regarding medical treatment administered to others, the patient's religious beliefs, and the patient's previously consistent pattern of behavior in regard to decisions about his or her own medical care. The court then concluded:

The probative value of such evidence may vary depending on the remoteness, consistency, and thoughtfulness of the prior statements or actions and the maturity of the person at the time. . . . Thus, for example, an offhand remark about not wanting to live under certain circumstances made by a person when young and in the peak of health would not in itself constitute clear proof twenty years later. . . . In contrast, a carefully considered position, especially if written, that a person had maintained over a number of years or that he had acted upon in comparable circumstances might be clear evidence of his intent.[55]

An adult, nonautonomous patient's right to refuse medical treatment, even when the patient's death is the likely result of that refusal, increasingly outweighs the state's countervailing interests as the physical invasion by the treatment becomes greater and the prognosis for the patient dims. The four state interests commonly discussed in treatment-abatement cases involving autonomous patients also regularly appear in the arguments put forth by physicians, hospital attorneys, guardians *ad litem,* state attorneys, and pro-life groups whenever one or more of these parties attempts to block decisions for treatment abatement made by nonautonomous patients through surrogates. In fact, the ordering and description of these four state interests—the preservation of life, the protection of innocent third parties, the prevention of suicide, and the maintenance of the ethical integrity of the medical profession—first appeared in the *Saikewicz* decision.[56] Since *Saikewicz* (and the earlier decision by the *Quinlan* court), the trend in adjudicating the conflict between an adult, critically ill, and nonautonomous patient's presumed personal interests (in self-determination, privacy, relief of pain, relief of psychological suffering, and dignified dying, among others) and the state's countervailing interests has been consistent in all courts of final decision. Although courts handling cases with nondying children *(Custody of a Minor, Hamilton)* have used state interests to override parental interests in autonomy, privacy, and/or religious freedom, virtually all final courts ruling on cases with adult, nonautonomous patients have decided that a critically ill patient's interests outweigh the countervailing interests of the state. This trend is best illustrated by the decisions of two state supreme courts when they ruled against the first and most significant state interest in two cases involving permanently unconscious patients. In *In re L.H.R.,* a case involving a 5-month-old, terminally ill infant, the Supreme Court of Georgia extended its reasoning to include adult, permanently unconscious, terminally ill patients who have not previously expressed preferences regarding medical treatment. The court's conclusion applies to both situations: "While the state has an interest in the prolongation of life, the state has no interest in the prolongation of dying."[57] And in *Brophy,* the Supreme Judicial Court of Massachusetts observed:

We must recognize that the State's interest in life encompasses a broader interest than mere corporeal existence. In certain, thankfully rare, circumstances the burden of maintaining the corporeal existence degrades the very humanity it was meant to serve. The law recognizes the individual's right to preserve his humanity, even if to preserve his humanity means to allow the natural processes of a disease or affliction to bring about a death with dignity.[58]

A decision to terminate life-sustaining treatment on the behalf of a permanently unconscious patient is not to be equated with assisting suicide. Some permanently unconscious patients do not appear to have "imminent" deaths (within a matter of days), nor do they seem to be "terminally ill" (expected to die within 6 months). Instead, some permanently unconscious patients continue to live with life-sustaining medical treatment for an indeterminate length of time. Consequently, in cases of PVS or other forms of permanent unconsciousness, opponents of abating treatment sometimes claim that a patient's death following the removal of a modality of life-sustaining treatment (ventilator, NG tube, antibiotics, etc.) would actually be suicide—and that the state's interest in preventing suicide precludes third parties from assisting in a suicide attempt. Judicial response in various jurisdictions has been consistent. From *Quinlan* to *Gardner,* a number of courts have rejected any necessary connection between treatment abatement on the behalf of nonautonomous patients and suicide. For the *Colyer* court, a death that occurs "after the removal of life-sustaining systems is from natural causes, neither set in motion nor intended by the patient."[59] For the *Conroy* court, the removal of the NG tube on the behalf of the patient "would not constitute attempted suicide, as the decision would probably be based on a wish to be free of medical intervention rather than a specific intent to die, and her death would result, if at all, from her underlying medical condition, which included her inability to swallow."[60]

The abatement of life-sustaining treatment on the behalf of an adult, nonautonomous patient is quite unlikely to result in civil or criminal liability for the attending physician. Moral disagreement with a surrogate's decision is one reason for some physicians to refuse to terminate life-sustaining treatment on a nonautonomous patient. Courts dealing with such cases, where treatment abatement is claimed to threaten the ethical integrity of the medical profession, consistently overrule this professional argument or (as in *Brophy*) circumvent the argument by means of a procedural maneuver. A more common (and often more weighty) reason for physicians to refuse to terminate life-sustaining treatment on a nonautonomous patient has to do with legal liability rather than ethical integrity. The majority of cases discussed in this chapter ended up in court because the physicians were anxious about what the *Quinlan* court called "the brooding presence of such possible liability.''[61] The judicial response could not have been clearer, unless physicians were to be granted legal immunity for abating treatment with critically ill patients. *Every court of final decision in every jurisdiction*—including the *Barber* court—has found physicians participating in the cases to be *free from civil or criminal sanctions.* Of course, the consistency of this judicial trend does not preclude legal action against a physician in a future case, particularly in a jurisdiction not yet having had such a case. However, since this trend will undoubtedly influence judicial decisions in future cases, the courts that have handled such cases thus far provide a number of reasons for thinking that physicians who carry out a surrogate's reasonable request to abate treatment on the behalf of a nonautonomous patient are not likely to have legal problems when the patient dies:

The patient's death is caused by the underlying medical condition, not the removal of life-sustaining treatment, and thus is not an act of homicide *(Quinlan, Colyer).*

The termination of artificial life-support systems is an effort to carry out the constitutional right of privacy on the part of a nonautonomous patient, and is thus protected from criminal prosecution *(Quinlan, Colyer).*

A good-faith decision by a physician that a particular treatment has a disproportionate balance of burden to benefit for a patient cannot be a battery, and is thus protected from civil liability *(Spring, Bludworth, Drabick).*

The removal of life-sustaining treatment, when that removal is judged in good faith either to be wanted by the patient or to be in the patient's best interests, is consistent with the ethics of responsible medical practice *(Saikewicz, Spring, Bludworth, Brophy, Jobes, Delio, Gardner).*

Prudent, well-established procedures (e.g., requiring agreement between family members and the attending physician, or possibly between those two parties and a prognosis committee) make any judicial action unlikely *(Quinlan, Colyer, Hamlin, Bludworth, Conroy).*[62]

Points of judicial disagreement

In the years since the Quinlan case was decided by the New Jersey Supreme Court, case law involving nonautonomous patients has become increasingly clear. As indicated by the discussion in the previous section, numerous trends in case law point to judicial agreement on many of the aspects of cases involving nonautonomous patients. The courts, however, do still disagree about the answers to several important questions germane to such cases.

Should the courts be involved in the decision-making process in treatment abatement cases to protect the interests of patients unable to make such decisions for themselves? For that matter, should the courts decide if treatment abatement is appropriate in these cases to protect physicians from civil or criminal prosecution? Among the courts that have specifically addressed the question of judicial intervention in these cases, three quite different positions have emerged. The first position (most consistently held by the New Jersey Supreme Court) calls for *judicial overview* of the decision-making process, primarily to protect the interests of the patient, but requires no direct court involvement in the decision to continue or to abate treatment. Initially articulated by the *Quinlan* court and subsequently reaffirmed by the *Colyer, Hamlin* (with modifications regarding guardianship), *Conroy,* and *Rasmussen* courts, this position holds that protection of the patient's interests can be accomplished through minimal court intrusion—and certainly without requiring the courts to be the final decision makers in such cases. Eschewing the role of ultimate decision maker, the courts holding this view are convinced that appropriate court involvement is limited to determining a patient's incompetency, appointing a guardian, and establishing procedural safeguards. To do more than this oversight role would be to do too much, as stated by the *Quinlan* court: "We consider that a practice of applying to a court to confirm such decisions would generally be inappropriate, not only because that would be a gratuitous encroachment upon the medical profession's field of competence, but because it would be impossibly cumbersome."[63] The *Colyer* court agreed, at least in part:

While we do not accept the *Quinlan* court's view that judicial intervention is an encroachment upon the medical profession, we do perceive the judicial process as an unresponsive and cumbersome mechanism for decisions of this nature. This fact is borne out by a number of the leading cases in which arguments were heard and opinions written long after the patient had died.[64]

The second position (often identified with the early decisions by the Supreme Judicial Court of Massachusetts) calls for considerable judicial involvement in any decision regarding treatment abatement that might result in a patient's death. Initially developed by the *Saikewicz* court in its response to *Quinlan,* this view of treatment-abatement decisions recommends *prior court approval* before unprecedented decisions can legally be carried out. Subsequently followed by the *Severns* court and modified in a rather ambiguous manner by the *Spring* court (see Case 4.6), this position states that any decision involving the dual possibility of a patient's death and a physician's liability to civil or criminal charges is not to be entrusted to a nonautonomous patient's family, the attending physicians, a guardian, an ethics committee, or any other decision maker outside the courts. For such an ultimate, life-and-death decision, judicial involvement is necessary:

We take a dim view of any attempt to shift the ultimate decision-making responsibility away from the duly established courts of proper jurisdiction to any committee, panel or group, ad hoc or permanent. . . . We do not view the judicial resolution of this most difficult and awesome question—whether potentially life-prolonging treatment should be withheld from a person incapable of making his own decision—as constituting a "gratuitous encroachment'' on the domain of medical expertise. Rather, such questions of life and death seem to us to require the process of detached but passionate investigation and decision that forms the ideal on which the judicial branch of government was created. Achieving this ideal is our responsibility and that of the lower court, and is not to be entrusted to any other group purporting to represent the ''morality and conscience of our society,'' no matter how highly motivated or impressively constituted.[65]

By contrast, the third position (most clearly articulated by the Supreme Court of Florida) calls for even less judicial intervention than the supreme courts of New Jersey, Washington, and Arizona deem necessary. This third view was initially put forward by the *Barber* court, later expanded by the *Bludworth* court, and affirmed shortly thereafter in the portion of the *L.H.R.* decision that addressed nonautonomous adults. For these courts in California, Florida, and Georgia, whenever a nonautonomous, adult patient has family members able and willing to make a treatment-abatement decision on the behalf of the patient—and the physicians central to the case concur with that decision—*no court intervention or oversight is necessary.* In such a case, there is no need for prior judicial approval, a judicial appointment of a guardian, or the establishment of procedural safeguards outside the immediate parties to the case. To require prior court approval, in the words of the *Bludworth* court, is ''too burdensome, is not necessary to protect the state's interests or the interests of the patient, and could render the right of the incompetent a nullity.'' Instead, the decision ''to terminate artificial life supports is a decision that normally should be made in the patient–doctor–family relationship.''[66] According to this view, judicial involvement in treatment-abatement cases with nonautonomous patients is necessary only when unusual problems arise: a critically ill patient without a family, disagreements among family members and/or physicians, or ''evidence of wrongful motives'' on the part of family members or physicians.

In jurisdictions not requiring judicial intervention in the substantive decision of treatment abatement, is the court appointment of a guardian necessary? On this particular question, the Supreme Court of Washington joins the courts of California, Florida, and Georgia. In *Hamlin,* the court distinguishes between ''*Colyer*-type situations'' (in which the patient had a family, and all parties in the case agreed that abating treatment was in the patient's best interests) and ''*Hamlin*-like situations'' (in which the patient had no available family). For the Washington court, a surrogate decision maker is necessary in the latter type of case to ensure that the patient's interests are represented and that decisions in such cases ''remain individualized.'' Consequently, a guardian must be appointed by a court. However, in the former type of case, family members should be permitted to make a decision to abate treatment ''free of the cumbersomeness and costs of legal guardianship proceedings.'' Thus ''a guardian is not necessary'' whenever the family, the treating physicians, and a prognosis committee agree that abating treatment is in the patient's best interests.[67]

The Supreme Court of New Jersey disagreed in its earlier decisions, possibly because of unusual factors in *Quinlan* (the unprecedented nature of the case) and *Conroy* (the "special vulnerability of mentally and physically impaired, elderly persons in nursing homes and the potential for abuse . . . in such homes"). The court placed significant weight on the role of the guardian in these two landmark cases. In *Quinlan,* the court discussed at some length the virtues of Mr. Quinlan and his suitability to be his daughter's guardian.[68] In *Conroy,* the court argued that the patient's nursing home situation meant that "life-sustaining treatment should not be withdrawn or withheld . . . in the absence of a guardian's decision."[69] However, the court moved away from this position in *Jobes* and *Peter,* saying that nursing home patients (young or old) do not need a guardian for treatment-abatement decisions if they have a family member or close friend designated to make such a decision on their behalf.[70]

Are procedural safeguards (other than the possible appointment of a guardian) necessary to protect nonautonomous patients from harmful actions by other parties in these cases? For two courts, dealing with a specific type of critically ill patient, the only procedural safeguard necessary is the concurrence of three physicians that a critically ill patient is in a PVS. Addressing only cases of patients having permanently lost consciousness, the *Bludworth* court and the *L.H.R.* court state that the legal protection of such adult patients requires merely that two physicians "with specialties relevant to the patient's condition" *(Bludworth)* and "with no interest in the outcome of the case" *(L.H.R.)* concur with the attending physician that the patient in question has no reasonable possibility of regaining cognitive function.[71]

In three other cases, however, courts have required procedural safeguards that go beyond the concurrence of consulting physicians. The *Quinlan* court, also addressing the case of a patient in a PVS, required the concurrence of what it incorrectly called a hospital "ethics committee" to ensure that the patient in question had no reasonable possibility of regaining cognitive function.[72] The *Colyer* court, dealing with the case of another PVS patient, required the concurrence of a medical "prognosis committee" to protect the patient "against erroneous diagnosis as well as questionable motives."[73] Furthermore, the *Conroy* court, addressing a different type of situation in which an elderly nursing home patient was conscious but incapable of making decisions, issued an opinion requiring several procedural safeguards in such cases in addition to the appointment of a guardian. For this court, the legal protection of patients such as Claire Conroy necessitates (1) investigation of the case by a state ombudsman, (2) a report of the ombudsman's findings to the appropriate governmental agency (usually the commissioner of human services), (3) confirmation of the patient's diagnosis and prognosis by two physicians "unaffiliated with the nursing home and with the attending physician," and (4) concurrence with the guardian's treatment-abatement decision by the attending physician.[74]

What standard should be used by a surrogate in making a decision regarding treatment abatement on the behalf of a nonautonomous patient? Again, three positions have been developed by the courts. The *Quinlan* court opted to follow the "substituted-judgment" standard, and most courts since *Quinlan* have also favored this standard to the alternative standard, usually referred to as the "best-interests" test. One court in particular, the Supreme Judicial Court of Massachusetts, has consistently argued that the substituted-judgment standard is preferable because it places patient "autonomy," "free choice," and "moral dignity" above the "paternalism" and "statistical determinations" of the best-interests standard. The court has therefore used "substituted judgment" in deciding several significantly different cases: *Saikewicz, Custody of a Minor* (here arguing, in the case of a child, that "the substituted-judgment doctrine is consistent with the 'best interests of the child' test"), *Spring,* and *Brophy.*

The substituted-judgment standard is a "subjective" test according to which a court (or other surrogate in states not emphasizing the role of the courts) attempts to "don the mental mantle of the incompetent" and thereby make the decision that the patient would have made had he or she been capable of making the decision. In the words of the influential *Saikewicz* decision: the decision "in cases such as this should be that which would be made by the incompetent person, if that person were competent, but taking into account the present and future incompetency of the individual as one of the factors which would necessarily enter into the decision-making process of the competent person." The goal of this subjective approach is "to determine with as much accuracy as possible the wants and needs of the individual involved." Consequently, the "problems of arriving at an accurate substituted judgment in matters of life and death vary greatly in degree, if not in kind, in different circumstances."[75]

In sum, the Massachusetts court is convinced that the decision on the behalf of a nonautonomous patient should reflect that individual patient's choice among several treatment alternatives, that patient's judgment regarding the merits of life-sustaining treatment, and that patient's evaluation of a life probably shortened by treatment abatement—not whether the same choices would be made by a "reasonable person," objective observers in the case, or most people in the same situation. Courts in New York (the *Eichner* decision), Delaware, Minnesota, Washington (in *Colyer* and *Ingram*), and Florida have followed the Massachusetts court in using the substituted-judgment standard. For example, the *Ingram* court interpreted the standard in this manner: "The goal is not to do what most people would do, or what the court believes is the wise thing to do, but rather what this particular individual would do if she were competent and understood all the circumstances, including her present and future competency." Given this goal, the *Ingram* court observed that a court (or other surrogate) should consider numerous factors that might influence an individual patient's decisions regarding treatment or treatment abatement:

the ward's prognosis if she chose no treatment; the prognosis if she chose one treatment over another; the risk of adverse side effects from the proposed treatments; the intrusiveness or severity of the proposed treatments; the ability of the ward to cooperate and assist with posttreatment therapy; the ward's religious or moral views regarding medical care of the dying process; and the wishes of family and friends, if those wishes would influence the ward's decision.[76]

In contrast to this majority position, a few courts have used the best-interests standard in making treatment-abatement decisions for patients unable to make such decisions for themselves. Because of differences in cases (e.g., patients who are no longer capable of making treatment decisions for themselves versus patients who have never had the capacity to make these decisions), and possibly because of philosophical differences among courts, some jurisdictions have chosen not to go with the subjective standard. Instead, they have opted for the more "objective" standard of trying to determine the probable benefits of available modalities of treatment to a patient, the possible burdens of that treatment, and the relative balance of those benefits and burdens. The goal of the best-interests standard is thus not to make the decision the patient would have made, because that information is often unknown and unknowable by a court or other surrogate. Rather, the goal is to determine two interrelated things: whether the available treatment is likely to be beneficial to the patient, and whether the modality of treatment in question would usually be chosen in similar medical circumstances by patients capable of understanding the alternatives available to them and making a decision on that basis.

The best-interests standard has been used in at least four important court cases. In *Storar* (see Case 4.9), the New York Court of Appeals held that because the patient was profoundly retarded and had never been capable of expressing his views regarding life-sustaining treatment, neither his mother nor anyone else was able to make a "substituted judgment" for him. Reasoning that Storar's mental capacity was analogous to the mental capacity of an 18-month-old infant, the court held that the substituted-judgment standard was inapplicable to the case: "It is unrealistic to attempt to determine whether he would want to continue potentially life-prolonging treatment if he were competent."[77] In *Hamlin,* the Supreme Court of Washington agreed that the substituted-judgment standard failed to meet the circumstances of a case involving a profoundly retarded patient with the mental age of approximately 1 year. Joseph Hamlin, aged 42, having experienced massive brain damage following a cardiopulmonary arrest, was diagnosed by "at least 20 physicians" as being in a vegetative state, unable to breathe without a respirator, and with "virtually no prospect of recovery." Having used substituted judgment in the two cases mentioned earlier (the *Ingram* decision was issued the same day as *Hamlin*), the Washington court emphasized that decisions in cases similar to that of Hamlin should be made "on a case-by-case basis with *particularized consideration of the best interests and rights of the specific individual.''*[78] In *Foody v. Manchester Memorial Hospital,* the Supreme Court for the Judicial District of Hartford, in the first such case in Connecticut, applied the best-interests standard to a patient who, also at the age of 42, had suffered from multiple sclerosis for 24 years, had recently experienced respiratory arrest and been resuscitated, and was being maintained in a semicomatose state on a ventilator. Since Sandra Foody had never expressed any preferences regarding life-sustaining treatment, the court observed that the best-interests standard was the appropriate standard for the case. Although subsequently combining aspects of both standards in its decision permitting treatment abatement, the court noted the importance of the more objective standard in such cases: "If the exercise of the right [to refuse medical treatment] is to be maintained where no expression has been made by an incompetent patient as to treatment, it must take place within the context of an analysis which seeks to implement what is in that person's best interests by reference to objective societally shared criteria."[79] And in *Drabick,* the Court of Appeal in California (Sixth District) emphasized that "an appropriate medical decision" made on the behalf of a nonautonomous patient is "one that is made in the patient's best interests."[80]

The Supreme Court of New Jersey established a third position in *Conroy* (Case 4.16). Having originated the legal debate over the appropriate standard to use in surrogate decisions to abate treatment, and having observed the subsequent judicial interpretations and applications of the substituted-judgment standard and the best-interests standard, the New Jersey court articulated *three alternative standards* that could be used in carrying out a nonautonomous patient's "right to consent to medical intervention" and correlative "right to refuse" such intervention. Since no surrogate decision maker can "ascertain definitively" the present desires of a nonautonomous patient regarding life-sustaining treatment, the court argued that a surrogate should, depending on the circumstances of a case, use the standard most applicable to a particular case.

If a patient's previous views regarding life-sustaining treatment are known (through earlier oral directives, written documents, or a reasonable deduction from the patient's beliefs and conduct), a "subjective standard" should be used to carry out "what the particular patient would have done if able to choose for himself." By contrast, if a now-nonautonomous patient never clearly expressed his or her views regarding life-sustaining treatment, either (1) a "limited-objective" test or (2) a "pure-objective" test should be used. The former version of the best-interests standard applies to cases in which there is a limited amount of evidence that the patient would refuse that treatment if able to do so, and a guardian (or, presumably, another surrogate in states not requiring the appointment of a guardian) agrees that the burdens of the treatment outweigh its possible benefits. The latter version of the best-interests standard applies to cases in which a guardian (or other surrogate) concludes in the absence of any evidence regarding the patient's previous views that the burdens of treatment "clearly and markedly outweigh" the benefits to the patient.[81] By setting out these three alternatives, the New Jersey court emphasized, in a way no other court had done, the importance of using a legal standard that fits the circumstances of a case, instead of forcing any and all cases to conform to a predetermined "correct" standard.

Is the ordinary/extraordinary distinction helpful in making treatment-abatement decisions on the behalf of incapable patients? The distinction between ordinary and extraordinary means of prolonging life was originally developed by Roman Catholic moral theologians trying to determine, prior to the discovery of antisepsis and anesthesia, whether the refusal of surgery by an autonomous patient was tantamount to suicide. The legal basis for the distinction is derived from the scope of the duty reasonably owed by a person (e.g., a physician, or the guardian of an incompetent patient) who undertakes the responsibility of care for another person.

The *Quinlan* court—dealing with a Catholic patient and devout Catholic parents, accepting an *amicus curiae* brief from the New Jersey Catholic Conference, discussing the 1957 address by Pope Pius XII, and quoting at length from a position paper by a Catholic bishop—found the ordinary/extraordinary distinction helpful in its decision regarding the removal of Karen Quinlan's respirator. With some reservation, the court observed:

[I]n light of the situation in the present case (while the record here is somewhat hazy in distinguishing between "ordinary" and "extraordinary" measures), one would have to think that the use of the same respirator or like support could be considered "ordinary" in the context of the possibly curable patient but "extraordinary" in the context of the forced sustaining by cardio-respiratory processes of an irreversibly doomed patient."[82]

Several other courts of final decision have followed the *Quinlan* court in using the ordinary/extraordinary distinction in treatment-abatement cases. Some courts (in *Saikewicz, Dinnerstein,* and *Severns*) have placed minimal importance on the distinction, using it simply to suggest a difference between curative and noncurative treatment.[83] By contrast, the Supreme Court of Florida based much of its decision in *Bludworth* on terminology taken from the ordinary/extraordinary distinction. In a manner similar to its handling of the Perlmutter case (see Case 3.6), the court consistently referred to treatments that merely prolong the dying process as being "extraordinary life-support systems," and ruled that such treatments can be discontinued.[84]

Three courts, however, have either challenged the validity of the distinction or at least limited its applicability in treatment-abatement cases. The *Barber* court, assessing the merits of the decisions to discontinue the use of a ventilator and IV feeding tubes with Clarence Herbert, charged that the use of the terms ordinary and extraordinary "begs the question." The court argued that "a more rational approach" would be a determination of the proportionality of a particular treatment in terms of its benefits and burdens: in this manner an "extremely painful or intrusive" treatment would still be "proportionate treatment if the prognosis was for complete cure or significant improvement in the patient's condition," and a "minimally painful or intrusive" treatment would be regarded as "disproportionate to the potential benefits if the prognosis is virtually hopeless for any significant improvement in condition."[85]

For the *Conroy* court, examining the merits of discontinuing artificial feeding for nursing home patients like Claire Conroy, the distinction that had been helpful 9 years earlier in *Quinlan* was now found to be "unpersuasive." Pointing out several problems with the distinction—the variable meanings given the terms, the linkage of the terminology to a constantly shifting continuum of medical treatments, and the court's recognition that the legal right to refuse treatment encompasses "even ordinary treatment"—the court concluded: "To draw a line on this basis for determining whether treatment should be given leads to a semantical milieu that does not advance the analysis."[86]

The *Brophy* court, in permitting the withdrawal of Paul Brophy's G-tube, also noted a change in its view of the distinction. The court pointedly refused to follow the *Conroy* court's rejection of the distinction, both in theory ("we believe that the distinction between extraordinary and ordinary care is a factor to be considered") and in relation to the facts of the case ("to be maintained by such artificial means over an extended period," with 37 years being the longest recorded survival with a G-tube, "is not only intrusive but extraordinary"). Nevertheless, the court noted severe limitations in the applicability of the distinction to cases such as *Brophy*. The variable meanings of the terms ("insertion of the G-tube might be considered extraordinary care, while its maintenance might be ordinary care"), the linkage of the distinction to technological developments in medicine ("what was viewed as extraordinary care ten years ago might be considered ordinary care today"), and any overemphasis on the distinction ("the use of such a distinction as the sole, or major, factor of decision tends, in a case such as this, to create a distinction without meaning") were all regarded as problematic.[87]

Toward greater clarity and consistency in the law

The two preceding sections describe the current state of the law regarding treatment abatement with nonautonomous patients. The agreement of many courts on many of the substantive features of such cases illustrates an important legal trend that will influence the handling of similar cases in other jurisdictions in the future. However, important differences remain. The unfortunate result of this variability among jurisdictions, much of it pertaining to procedures, is that similar cases (in terms of medicine and ethics) have been and may continue to be handled differently in different jurisdictions.

This situation of judicial variability needs to be changed, even though the courts that have already issued opinions will understandably be reluctant to revise their views. Nevertheless, given judicial agreement on most of the substantive aspects, the remaining points of disagreement need to be resolved—for the benefits of patients, families and other surrogates, physicians and other health care providers, and the courts themselves.

To aid in moving toward the goal of greater clarity and consistency, I have three suggestions regarding the law and treatment-abatement cases with nonautonomous patients. The suggestions are put forth in fairly general terms in the hope that persons trained in the law will develop and revise the recommendations as we move through the third stage of the debate over treatment abatement.[88]

First, the health care professionals commonly involved in the decision-making process in cases with nonautonomous patients can help the courts by developing a clearer and more consistent *classification scheme* for such patients. The classification scheme, in my view, needs to have three parts that can sort out important variables in these cases. The initial classification should address the *reason* for the patient's incapacity and/or the *type of incapacity* the patient has. As suggested earlier in this chapter, such a classification should distinguish among patients in the following categories:

1. Adult patients who have diminished or fluctuating capacity to make decisions, because of mental illness, senility, or shock (e.g., Mary Northern in Case 4.3, Earle Spring in Case 4.6, and Mary Hier in Case 4.14)
2. Patients with substantial incapacity to make decisions, because of mental retardation, brain damage, or the complications of multiple-organ failure (e.g., Joseph Saikewicz in Case 4.2, John Storar in Case 4.9, Edna Marie Leach in Case 4.13, Francis Landy in Case 4.15, and Claire Conroy in Case 4.16)
3. Patients with permanent loss of consciousness, with distinctions among patients in this group being made in terms of the different types of permanent unconsciousness now recognized by neurologists (e.g., Karen Quinlan in Case 4.1, Mary Severns in Case 4.7, Brother Fox in Case 4.8, Bertha Colyer in Case 4.10, Helen Corbett in Case 4.18, and Paul Brophy in Case 4.19)
4. Patients who are or may be nonautonomous in relation to important medical decisions because of young age and immaturity (such as Chad Green in Case 4.5 and Pamela Hamilton in Case 4.11).[89]

The next part of the classification scheme should distinguish among nonautonomous patients, as did the *Conroy* court, in terms of each patient's *expressed views* on treatment abatement. This type of classification could, as Richard O'Neil has pointed out, helpfully differentiate among several types of nonautonomous patients: (1) patients who previously, while autonomous, expressed written preferences on the subject of abating treatment; (2) patients who previously expressed reasonably specific verbal preferences; (3) patients whose previous views on treatment abatement can reasonably be inferred from their other beliefs and conduct; (4) patients whose previous views remain unknown because of insufficient evidence; (5) patients who have never had views on the prolongation or abatement of treatment because of severe mental retardation; and (6) patients who, because of their young age and immaturity, do not yet have thoughtful preferences regarding the prolongation or abatement of treatment.[90]

The last part of the classification scheme should distinguish, as the *Hamlin* court noted, between (1) nonautonomous patients who have family members available as surrogate decision makers and (2) nonautonomous patients who have no family members available, because an individual patient has outlived relatives, lost all contact with relatives, or (as in *Saikewicz*) has relatives who simply choose not to become involved in the case.[91] Such a differentiation between nonautonomous patients is important for at least two reasons. For one thing, this distinction between patients may influence the choice of the standard to be used in making a decision to prolong or abate treatment. Although the substituted-judgment standard can possibly apply to cases in which a patient is without a family, this subjective standard is more likely to be used when family members are available who may be able to produce documents written by the patient, remember conversations with the patient on treatment abatement, or provide insight regarding the patient's previous beliefs and conduct. In addition, this distinction can and should lead to different procedural safeguards in different cases. As the Supreme Court of Washington correctly observed, nonautonomous patients with one or more family members available do not generally need the protection provided by a court-appointed guardian—unless the family members disagree among themselves regarding treatment abatement, or other parties to a case become suspicious about the motive of the relatives.

Second, the surrogate decision makers in such cases need to be more consistent in *selecting the appropriate standard* for such decisions, with the selection being based on the particular circumstances of incapacity of individual patients and a determination of whether (and how) these patients had expressed preferences regarding treatment abatement. When treatment-abatement cases end up in court, jurisdictions that do not yet have case law on treatment abatement should follow the lead of the *Conroy* court in applying whatever standard most appropriately fits the circumstances of a particular case. Even better, courts should adopt the *patient's-best-interests (PBI) standard* and use it in *all* cases involving nonautonomous patients, as I will argue later (see Chapters 8 and 9). By so doing, courts will avoid the mistake of the Supreme Judicial Court of Massachusetts: that court, as we have noted, initially decided that the substituted-judgment standard is the applicable standard for most treatment-abatement cases involving nonautonomous patients, and has gone to remarkable lengths to make that subjective standard fit several quite different cases of nonautonomous patients (Joseph Saikewicz, Chad Green, and Earle Spring) who either had not or could not express preferences regarding the possibility of abating treatment. Another mistake to be avoided is the one made by the *Storar* court. Having rejected the applicability of the substituted-judgment test to the case, the court failed to use the best-interests test and thus left John Storar (and any other nonautonomous patients in New York who never expressed their views on treatment abatement) without a legal option regarding treatment abatement.

Finally, the courts, legislatures, and health care institutions that develop procedural guidelines for treatment-abatement cases need to devise *procedures that protect nonautonomous patients without thwarting their common-law and constitutional right to refuse medical treatment.* As we have observed in this chapter, the courts have differed widely in their views on the procedural safeguards necessary in such cases, with court involvement being advised in unprecedented cases in Massachusetts, prognosis committees being required in Washington, and the concurrence of multiple parties (guardian, attending physician, state ombudsman) being required in New Jersey.

My suggestion is to rely on institutional ethics committees (IECs) as the major procedural safeguard in the majority of cases, with the courts becoming involved only in especially problematic cases. In most instances, an IEC—organized as an interdisciplinary body, with appropriate medical specialties represented—is capable of gaining a confirmation of a patient's prognosis from appropriate medical experts, gathering the nonmedical facts pertinent to a case, determining the patient's preferences (if ever expressed) regarding treatment abatement, discussing the case with the patient's family and physicians, and concurring with (or disagreeing with) the surrogates in a given case that abating treatment would be the patient's preference or is in the patient's best interests in the existing clinical circumstances.[92]

Of course, the precise mandate of an IEC varies somewhat from institution to institution. My suggestion is to have an IEC (1) convene to consider any treatment-abatement case at the request of family members or physicians, when these parties are in disagreement over life-sustaining treatment; (2) always deliberate the merits of a case in which the treatment being abated is medical nutrition and hydration; and (3) always meet when a decision about abating life-sustaining treatment is necessary in a case involving a nonautonomous patient without a surrogate. In this manner, the rights of nonautonomous, critically ill patients can be carried out with adequate safeguards within an appropriate institutional setting. If the IEC's assessment of a case differs significantly from the recommendation of a patient's surrogate, the courts remain as an avenue of last resort for any of the parties to the case in question.

Notes

1. Leach v. Akron General Medical Center, 68 Ohio Misc. 1, 22 Ohio Ops.3d 49, 52, 426 N.E.2d 809 (Com. Pl. 1980).
2. Superintendent of Belchertown State School v. Saikewicz, 373 Mass. 728, 370 N.E.2d 417, 426–27 (1977).
3. Several of these questions are discussed in John A. Robertson, *The Rights of the Critically Ill* (Cambridge, Mass.: Ballinger, 1983) pp. 49–69. Also see Society for the Right to Die (SRD), *The Physician and the Hopelessly Ill Patient* (New York: SRD, 1985), pp. 19–33.
4. David W. Meyers, in his 1981 *Medico-Legal Implications of Death and Dying* (Rochester, N.Y. and San Francisco: The Lawyers Co-Operative Publishing Co. and Bancroft-Whitney Co.), comments about "the somewhat confusing patchwork of judicial authority in this area" (p. 380). John A. Robertson, in his 1983 *Rights of the Critically Ill,* observes: "Since the courts are just now grappling with the task of defining the rules that apply to the continuation of treatment on incompetent persons, the law here is particularly uncertain" (p. 49). Of course, substantial developments in case law have taken place since these comments were made, but greater clarity in the law is still needed.
5. In re Quinlan, 137 N.J. Sup. 227, 348 A.2d 801, *modified and remanded,* 70 N.J. 10, 355 A.2d 647, 662–63, 664 *cert. denied,* 429 U.S. 922 (1976). Karen Quinlan, having been weaned from her ventilator, was transferred to a nursing home in New Jersey in May 1976. There she remained for 9 years in a persistent vegetative state, sustained by NG feedings and antibiotics. She died in June 1985.
6. Saikewicz, *supra,* 370 N.E.2d 417, 425, 430, 435. Another case concerning patient competency and the right to refuse treatment was decided the same year. In New Jersey, *In re Schiller* centered on the patient's lack of capacity to make a decision regarding lifesaving amputation. See 148 N.J. Super. 168, 372 A.2d 360 (1977).
7. State Department of Human Services v. Northern, 563 S.W.2d 197, 205, 209 (1978).
8. In re Dinnerstein, 6 Mass. App. 466, 380 N.E.2d 134, 138–39 (1978).
9. Custody of a Minor, 375 Mass. 733, 379 N.E.2d 1053 (1978). For the earlier case, see Prince v. Massachusetts, 321 U.S. 158 (1944). Chad Green's parents soon left Massachusetts, traveled to Mexico, and continued to "treat" Chad with large doses of vitamins and laetrile. Chad died in Mexico. The parents were charged with contempt of court upon return to Massachusetts, but were not punished further.
10. In re Spring, 380 Mass. 629, 405 N.E.2d 115, 121 (1980). Three treatment-abatement cases with nonautonomous patients occurred in 1979, but are not presented in the text. See In re Boyd, 403 A.2d 744 (1979), a case involving a Christian Scientist patient who was in a mental hospital and adjudicated incompetent, but whose refusal of treatment had occurred prior to her mental illness and incompetency; In re V. Young, No. A100863 (Cal. Super. Ct. 1979), a case involving an 18-year-old boy who was comatose following an auto accident; and In re Hofbauer, 47 N.Y.2d 648, 393 N.E.2d 1009, 419 N.Y.S.2d 936 (1979), a case involving the use of laetrile as a treatment for an 8-year-old boy's Hodgkin's disease.
11. Severns v. Wilmington Medical Center, Inc., 421 A.2d 1334, 1344 (Del. 1980); and In re Severns, 425 A.2d 156, 160 (Del. Ch. 1980). For a helpful interpretation of the case, see SRD, "Right-to-Die Court Decisions" (New York: SRD, 1987), pp. DE-1 to DE-2.

12. In re Eichner, 102 Misc.2d 184, 423 N.Y.S.2d 580 (Sup. Ct. 1979), *modified sub nom,* Eichner v. Dillon, 73 A.D.2d 431, 426 N.Y.S.2d 517 (App. Div. 1980), *modified,* 52 N.Y.2d 363, 438 N.Y.S.2d 266, 420 N.E.2d 64 (1981). For an important 1982 case (the Peter Cinque case) that is not presented in the text, see In re Lydia E. Hall Hospital, 116 Misc.2d 477, 455 N.Y.S.2d 706 (Sup. Ct. 1982).

13. In re Storar, 106 Misc.2d 880,433 N.Y.S.2d 388 (Sup. Ct.), *aff'd,* 78 A.D.2d 1013, 434 N.Y.S.2d 46 (App. Div. 1980), *rev'd,* 52 N.Y.2d 363, 438 N.Y.S.2d 266, 275, 420 N.E.2d 64, *cert. denied,* 454 U.S. 858 (1981). See New Mexico ex rel. Smith v. Fort, No. 14,768 (N.M. 1983), for another case involving the denial of treatment abatement to a nonautonomous patient. At the time of this ruling, New Mexico did not have a statute permitting a guardian to request or authorize the discontinuation of treatment (hemodialysis in this case) from a nonautonomous patient. In 1984, the New Mexico Right to Die Act was amended to take care of such cases.

14. In re Colyer, 99 Wash.2d 114, 660 P.2d 738, 748 (1983), *overruled in part,* In re Guardianship of Hamlin, 102 Wash.2d 810, 689 P.2d 1372 (1984).

15. In re Hamilton, 657 S.W.2d 425, 429 (Tenn. 1983). Pamela Hamilton was finally given chemotherapy and went through a period of remission. However, the remission did not last, and she died in June 1985. For Custody of a Minor, see Case 4.5.

16. John J. Paris, ''The Decision to Withdraw Life-Sustaining Treatment and the Potential Role of an IEC: The Case of *People v. Barber and Nejdl,*'' in Ronald E. Cranford and A. Edward Doudera, eds., *Institutional Ethics Committees and Health Care Decision Making* (Ann Arbor, Mich.: Health Administration Press, 1984), p. 205.

17. Barber v. Superior Court, 147 Cal. App.2d 1006, 195 Cal.Rptr. 484, 490 (1983). Criminal charges had earlier been filed in Illinois against the parents and attending physician in a case of selective nontreatment with conjoined twin babies. However, that criminal case did not, for lack of evidence, get beyond a preliminary hearing. See my *Selective Nontreatment of Handicapped Newborns* (New York: Oxford University Press, 1984), pp. 95–97.

18. SRD, ''Right-to-Die Court Decisions,'' p. OH-1.

19. Leach, *supra,* 426 N.E.2d 809; and Estate of Leach v. Shapiro, 13 Ohio App.3d 393, 469 N.E.2d 1047 (1984). The court of appeals remanded the case to the trial court. The hospital, as defendant, settled with the plaintiffs prior to trial. The trial court subsequently ruled that there was insufficient evidence against Shapiro and dismissed the case.

20. In re Hier, 18 Mass. 200, 464 N.E.2d 959, *appeal denied,* 392 Mass. 1102, 465 N.E.2d 261 (1984). The Conroy case was subsequently reversed by the New Jersey Supreme Court (see Case 4.16). A month after the appellate decision, the trial court (using new medical evidence) authorized a gastrostomy operation on Mary Hier.

21. John F. Kennedy Memorial Hospital, Inc. v. Bludworth, 452 So.2d 921, 922, 926 (Fla. 1984). See Lurie v. Samaritan Health Service, No. C510198 (Ariz. Super. Ct. 1984), for another 1984 case (the case of Harriet Shulan) in which a previously signed living will played a significant role in bringing about court-mandated treatment abatement for an incapable, critically ill patient. Other treatment-abatement cases with nonautonomous patients occurred in 1984, but are not presented in the text. See Foody v. Manchester Memorial Hospital, 40 Conn. Supp. 127, 482 A.2d 713 (1984); In re Guardianship of Barry, 445 So.2d 365 (Fla. 1984); In re L.H.R., 253 Ga. 439, 321 S.E.2d 716 (1984); In re Guardianship of Ingram, 689 P.2d 1363

(Wash. 1984); In re Torres, 357 N.W.2d 332 (Minn. 1984); In re Moschella, No. 5806/84 (N.Y. Sup. Ct. 1984); and Hamlin, *supra*, 689 P.2d 1372 (1984). *Barry* and *L.H.R.*, although cases involving infants, are included in this list because they subsequently influenced judicial opinions in adult treatment-abatement cases.

22. In re Conroy, 98 N.J. 321, 486 A.2d 1209, 1236 (1985). For several articles on the Conroy case, see Joanne Lynn, ed., *By No Extraordinary Means: The Choice to Forego Life-Sustaining Food and Water* (Bloomington, Ind.: Indiana University Press, 1986), pp. 227–66.
23. In re Jobes, No. C-4971-85E (N.J. Super. Ct. Ch. Div. Morris Cty., April 23, 1986).
24. In re Jobes, 108 N.J. 394, 529 A.2d 434 (1987).
25. Corbett v. D'Alessandro, 487 So.2d 368 (Fla. Dist. Ct. App.), *review denied*, 492 So.2d 1331 (Fla. 1986). For helpful information on this case, see SRD, "Right-to-Die Court Decisions," pp. FL-5 to FL-7.
26. Brophy v. New England Sinai Hospital, Inc., 398 Mass. 417, 497 N.E.2d 626 (1986).
27. In re Peter 108 N.J. 365, 529 A.2d 419 (1987).
28. Delio v. Westchester County Medical Center, 129 A.D.2d 1, 516 N.Y.S.2d 677 (App. Div. 2d Dep't 1987). For helpful information on this case, see SRD, "Right-to-Die Court Decisions," pp. NY-10 to NY-12
29. Rasmussen v. Fleming, 741 P.2d 674 (Ariz. 1987).
30. In re Gardner, 534 A.2d 947 (Maine 1987).
31. In re Drabick, 200 Cal.App.3d 185, 245 Cal.Rptr. 840 (1988).
32. Conroy, *supra*, 486 A.2d 1209, 1220 (1985).
33. Matthew L. Wald, "Court Says Feeding May Stop for Man in a Vegetative State," *New York Times*, September 12, 1986.
34. Quinlan, *supra*, 355 A.2d 647, 664.
35. Saikewicz, *supra*, 370 N.E.2d 417, 427.
36. Colyer, *supra*, 660 P.2d 738, 742, 746.
37. Bludworth, *supra*, 452 So.2d 921, 923.
38. Conroy, *supra*, 486 A.2d 1209, 1229. Also see Severns, *supra*, 421 A.2d 1334, 1348; Spring, *supra*, 405 N.E.2d 115, 119; Hamlin, *supra*, 689 P.2d 1372, 1376; L.H.R., *supra*, 321 S.E.2d 716, 722; Ingram, *supra*, 689 P.2d 1363, 1372; and Torres, *supra*, 357 N.W.2d 332, 339.
39. Schiller, *supra*, 372 A.2d 360, 367.
40. Ingram, *supra*, 689 P.2d 1363, 1371. Also see Northern, *supra*, 563 S.W.2d 197, 209–10. For a helpful discussion of decision-making incapacity, see two of the President's Commission reports: *Making Health Care Decisions*, vol. 1, *Report* (Washington, D.C.: U.S. Government Printing Office, 1982), pp. 56–68, 169–88; and *Deciding to Forego Life-Sustaining Treatment* (Washington, D.C.: U.S. Government Printing Office, 1983), pp. 121–70.
41. See Storar, *supra*, 420 N.E.2d 64; and Smith, *supra*, No. 14,768 (N.M. 1983). With the updating of the New Mexico Right to Die Act (see n. 13), a similar case in New Mexico would now presumably be handled in a manner consistent with the other cases in this series. Thus *Storar* stands out as the only remaining exception to this series of cases.
42. Hamlin, *supra*, 689 P.2d 1372, 1377–78.
43. Conroy, *supra*, 486 A.2d 1209, 1236.
44. Severns, *supra*, 425 A.2d 156, 160 (Del. Ch. 1980).

45. Barber, *supra*, 195 Cal.Rptr. 484, 491.
46. Torres, *supra*, 357 N.W.2d 332, 339.
47. Conroy, *supra*, 486 A.2d 1209, 1234. The same point is made in Brophy, *supra*, 497 N.E.2d 626, 638.
48. In re Conroy, 464 A.2d 303, 315 (N.J. Super. A.D. 1983).
49. Barber, *supra*, 195 Cal.Rptr. 484, 490.
50. See Hier, *supra*, 464 N.E.2d 959, 964; Conroy, *supra*, 486 A.2d 1209, 1236; Jobes *supra*, No. C-4971-85E at pp. 13–14; Corbett, *supra*, 487 So.2d 368; Brophy, *supra*, 497 N.E.2d 626, 637; Peter, *supra*, 529 A.2d 419, 427–28; Delio, *supra*, 516 N.Y.S.2d 677, 687–89; Gardner, *supra*, 534 A.2d 947, 954–55; Gray v. Romeo, 697 F. Supp. 580 (D.R.I. 1988); and McConnell v. Beverly Enterprises, 209 Conn. 692 (1989). There is only one exception to this judicial view of technological feeding. The Missouri Supreme Court, in a 4–3 decision, reversed a trial court's decision and ruled that feeding tubes are not a form of medical treatment. The court took an aberrant position by stating that neither common law nor constitutional law provides a legal basis for the termination of technological feeding and hydration in the care of a permanently unconscious patient. See Cruzan v. Harmon, No. 70813 (Mo. Sup. Ct. Nov. 16, 1988).
51. Quinlan, *supra*, 355 A.2d 647, 664.
52. Eichner, *supra*, 438 N.Y.S.2d 266, 270, 274.
53. Colyer, *supra*, 660 P.2d 738, 748.
54. Bludworth, *supra*, 452 So.2d 921, 926.
55. Conroy, *supra*, 486 A.2d 1209, 1230. The only exception to this trend is the New York Court of Appeals. In *Storar* and in the more recent *O'Connor* decision, this court has used the "clear and convincing evidence" standard as a reason to refuse to permit treatment abatement with two nonautonomous patients. In *O'Connor* the court decided that Mary O'Connor's earlier statements (to her daughters and a long-time friend) about not wanting "artificial means" to be used to prolong her life were too general and had not been made with technological feeding in mind. Lacking sufficient proof of O'Connor's views on tube feeding (such as an advanced directive or some other written statement), the court reversed the opinion of the appellate division and granted the petition of Westchester County Medical Center to insert an NG tube to provide the 77-year-old patient with nutrients and fluids. See In re Westchester County Medical Center (O'Connor), 139 A.D.2d 344, 532 N.Y.S.2d 133, *reversed*, No. 312 (N.Y. Ct. App. Oct. 14, 1988).
56. Saikewicz, *supra*, 370 N.E.2d 417, 425–26.
57. L.H.R., *supra*, 321 S.E.2d 716, 723.
58. Brophy, *supra*, 497 N.E.2d 626, 635.
59. Colyer, *supra*, 660 P.2d 738, 743.
60. Conroy, *supra*, 486 A.2d 1209, 1226.
61. Quinlan, *supra*, 355 A.2d 647, 666.
62. See Quinlan, *supra*, 355 A.2d 647, 669–70; Saikewicz, *supra*, 370 N.E.2d 417, 426; Spring, *supra*, 405 N.E.2d 115, 121–22; Colyer, *supra*, 660 P.2d 738, 751; Bludworth, *supra*, 452 So.2d 921, 926; Conroy, *supra*, 486 A.2d 1209, 1242; Brophy, *supra*, 497 N.E.2d 626, 638–39; Drabick, *supra*, 245 Cal.Rptr. 840, 846–47; Jobes, *supra*, 529 A.2d 434, 448; Delio, *supra*, 516 N.Y.S. 2d 667, 693; and Gardner, *supra*, 534 A.2d 947, 956. Also see Leonard H. Glantz, "Withholding and Withdrawing Treatment: The Role of the Criminal Law," *Law, Medicine, and Health Care* 15 (Winter 1987/88): 232, where he lists four problems that

confront a prosecutor who might consider prosecuting a physician who has abated life-sustaining treatment.

63. Quinlan, *supra,* 355 A.2d 647, 669.
64. Colyer, *supra,* 660 P.2d 738, 746. Also see Conroy, *supra,* 486 A.2d 1209, 1240, 1242.
65. Saikewicz, *supra,* 370 N.E.2d 417, 434–35. Also see Spring, *supra,* 405 N.E.2d 115, 122.
66. Bludworth, *supra,* 452 So.2d 921, 925–26. Also see Barber, *supra,* 195 Cal.Rptr. 484, 493; and L.H.R., *supra,* 321 S.E.2d 716, 723.
67. Hamlin, *supra,,* 689 P.2d 1372, 1377.
68. Quinlan, *supra,* 355 A.2d 647, 657–58.
69. Conroy, *supra,* 486 A.2d 1209, 1240. Also see Torres, *supra,* 357 N.W.2d 332, 337.
70. Jobes, *supra,* 529 A.2d 434, 444–47; and Peter, *supra,* 529 A.2d 419, 429.
71. Bludworth, *supra,* 452 So.2d 921, 926; and L.H.R., *supra,* 321 S.E.2d 716, 723.
72. Quinlan, *supra,* 355 A.2d 647, 671. As the court has subsequently acknowledged, the "ethics committee' was actually set up as a prognosis committee similar to the committee later required by the Washington court in *Colyer.*
73. Colyer, *supra,* 660 P.2d 738, 749.
74. Conroy, *supra,* 486 A.2d 1209, 1241–42.
75. Saikewicz, *supra,* 370 N.E.2d 417, 430–31.
76. Ingram, *supra,* 689 P.2d 1363, 1369–70.
77. Storar, *supra,* 438 N.Y.S.2d 266, 275. This part of the *Storar* decision was later affirmed in a 1984 case: People v. Eulo, 63 N.Y.2d 341, 482 N.Y.S.2d 436, 472 N.E.2d 286.
78. Hamlin, *supra,* 689 P.2d 1372, 1375. The words emphasized by the court come from the language of the Washington guardianship statute, which was fundamentally important to the case, and need not be taken to mean that the court was placing unusual importance on the best-interests test.
79. Foody, *supra,* 482 A.2d 713, 721.
80. Drabick, *supra,* 245 Cal.Rptr. 840, 852.
81. Conroy, *supra,* 486 A.2d 1209, 1229–30.
82. Quinlan, *supra,* 355 A.2d 647, 667–68.
83. See Saikewicz, *supra,* 370 N.E.2d 417, 424; Dinnerstein, *supra,* 380 N.E.2d 134, 138; and Severns, *supra,* 421 A.2d 1334, 1349.
84. Bludworth, *supra,* 452 So.2d 921, 924, 926.
85. Barber, *supra,* 195 Cal.Rptr. 484, 491.
86. Conroy, *supra,* 486 A.2d 1209, 1234–35.
87. Brophy, *supra,* 497 N.E.2d 626, 637.
88. See Meyers, *Medico-Legal Implications,* pp. 380–85, for additional suggestions regarding what the law should be in the kinds of cases discussed in this chapter.
89. For a helpful discussion of patients lacking capacity and patients with permanent loss of consciousness, see the President's Commission, *Deciding to Forego,* pp. 121–96.
90. Richard O'Neil, "Determining Proxy Consent," *The Journal of Medicine and Philosophy* 8 (1983): 389–403.
91. See Robert M. Veatch, "An Ethical Framework for Terminal Care Decisions: A New Classification of Patients," *Journal of the American Geriatrics Society* 32 (September 1984): 665–69, for a discussion of the relevance of this distinction.

92. See several of the articles in Cranford and Doudera, *Institutional Ethics Committees*. Also see Beth L. Rubin, "Refusal of Life-Sustaining Treatment for Terminally Ill Incompetent Patients: Court Orders and an Alternative," *Columbia Journal of Law and Social Problems* 19 (1985): 47–68; and Bernard Lo, "Behind Closed Doors: Promises and Pitfalls of Ethics Committees," *The New England Journal of Medicine* 317 (July 2, 1987): 46–49.

5

Planning for the Possibility of Treatment Abatement

If . . . the situation should arise in which there is no reasonable expectation of my recovery from extreme physical or mental disability, I direct that I be allowed to die and not be kept alive by medications, artificial means or heroic measures. I do, however, ask that medication be mercifully administered to me to alleviate suffering even though this may shorten my remaining life.

Concern for Dying's "Living Will"[1]

If I should have an incurable or irreversible condition that will cause my death within a relatively short time, and I am no longer able to make decisions regarding my medical treatment, I direct my attending physician, pursuant to the Uniform Rights of the Terminally Ill act of this State, to withhold or withdraw treatment that only prolongs the process of dying and is not necessary to my comfort or to alleviate pain.

The "Declaration" portion of the "Uniform Rights of the Terminally Ill Act," drafted by the National Conference of Commissioners on Uniform State Laws[2]

The Karen Ann Quinlan case (Case 4.1) represents a watershed in the debate over abating treatment with critically ill patients. Prior to the New Jersey Supreme Court's decision in her case in 1976, the right-to-die movement had experienced only moderate success. The Euthanasia Educational Council (now known as Concern for Dying) had distributed approximately 750,000 copies of its "Living Will," 25 state legislatures had considered and rejected "right-to-die" bills, and an unknown number of thoughtful persons had verbalized preferences to relatives and friends regarding the limitation of life-prolonging treatment should they ever become critically ill.

With the Quinlan case, however, a new era began. The widespread publicity given the case turned the permanently unconscious patient, her parents, and her physicians into participants in a paradigm case that dramatically illustrated the need to place ethical and legal limits on the life-prolonging technologies of modern medicine. For many people, the case came to symbolize the nonvoluntary confinement of a hopelessly ill patient by "the system," a physician-dominated system of health care that seemed impervious to Quinlan's reported objections to the technological prolongation of life prior to her loss of consciousness, the request by her parents to remove the ventilator sustaining her biological existence, and the confirmation by officials of the Catholic church that the

170

Quinlans' request to remove the "extraordinary means of treatment" was the "morally correct decision" in this case. Quinlan herself, described in the media as emaciated and lying in a fetal position, became a symbol of the proverbial "vegetable" maintained artifically for an indeterminate period of time.

To the surprise of most observers, Quinlan continued to live in a PVS for 9 years following the removal of her ventilator. During that time the Quinlan case, in both its clinical and legal forms, brought about profound changes in perspective toward critical and terminal illness. One of those changes has to do with the development of case law concerning treatment abatement with permanently unconscious patients and other nonautonomous patients, as we discussed in Chapter 4. Building on the foundation laid by the New Jersey Supreme Court, courts in other jurisdictions subsequently agreed that an adult patient's right to refuse medical treatment continues even when the patient loses the capacity to make such decisions personally, that the views toward the medical prolongation of life held previously by a now-nonautonomous patient are valuable in determining whether life-sustaining treatment is to be administered to the patient, and that a nonautonomous patient's surrogate has the legal authority to refuse all forms of life-sustaining treatment on the behalf of the patient.

Another change began to take place within months of the *Quinlan* decision, as some health care institutions initiated new policies regarding the medical treatment of critically ill patients. As mentioned in Chapter 1, Massachusetts General Hospital was the first institution to announce publicly that not all critically ill patients admitted to the hospital in the future would receive maximal treatment. Instead, critically ill patients would be grouped according to the severity of their illnesses, and life-sustaining treatment would be abated in some cases in relation to the hopelessness of the patients' conditions.[3]

A third change occurred at the organizational level within the right-to-die movement. The Euthanasia Educational Council, established in 1967, had been divided almost from its inception in terms of organizational purpose: some of its members wanted to concentrate on the educational aspects of the right to die, whereas other members wanted to be more politically active in promoting right-to-die legislation. The aftermath of the *Quinlan* decision exacerbated this tension within the organization, with the educationally oriented group finding an upsurge of public interest in the council's advance directive (1.25 million copies of the "Living Will" were distributed during the 18 months the Quinlan case was in the news, almost double the total number distributed in the 7 years before the case). At the same time, the politically oriented group found increased public interest in limiting the futile prolongation of dying by means of legislative statute (the California Natural Death Act became law 7 months after *Quinlan*). In 1979, the two branches of the council officially separated, with the education group becoming known as Concern for Dying and the political group becoming the Society for the Right to Die.

Two additional changes in the post-*Quinlan* era are the subjects of this chapter: both concern efforts to avoid becoming ''another Quinlan'' through the advance communication of personal preferences regarding the technological prolongation of dying and the possibility of abating treatment. The first part of the chapter will deal with personal planning for the probable circumstances of dying through the use of nonstatutory advance directives and other measures that primarily address medical and moral concerns in the event of life-threatening illness. The second part of the chapter will focus on personal planning for the circumstances of dying by means of legislative statutes enacted for this purpose.

Planning apart from legislative statute

The impact of the Quinlan case is clearly evident in several of the cases presented in the two previous chapters. Mary Severns, having joined the Delaware Euthanasia Educational Council in 1973, frequently expressed a wish never to be kept alive in a vegetative state ''in the event she were to become unable to reason and care for herself as a result of an accident or illness.'' In 1975, at the height of the publicity surrounding the Quinlan case, Severns tried unsuccessfully to get her husband to join her in signing the council's ''Living Will.'' He declined, she failed to execute the document herself—and 4 years later had an automobile accident that left her with irreversible brain damage. Life-sustaining treatment was finally abated in her case after 13 months of judicial proceedings, at least partially because of the opposition she had voiced to such treatment years earlier while she was antonomous.[4]

Edna Marie Leach's opposition to the technological prolongation of dying was supported by six witnesses in a 1980 Ohio probate court hearing. All of them testified that Leach, terminally ill with ALS and in a chronic vegetative state at the time of the court hearing, had in numerous conversations expressed her desire never to be placed on a life-support system. The witnesses confirmed that Leach had held this position before becoming ill, and that she had affirmed the position as recently as 12 days before entering the hospital where she was placed on the type of life-support system she had wanted to avoid. In deciding for treatment abatement, the court quoted an earlier conversation in which Leach reportedly said: ''That's the one thing that terrifies me. I don't want to be put on life-support systems. I don't want to live if I have to be a vegetable.''[5]

Brother Joseph Fox also voiced opposition to the technological prolongation of dying. In 1976, while participating in a discussion of the Quinlan case at Chaminade High School (Mineola, New York), he expressed agreement with the explication of Catholic teaching in the New Jersey case. In particular, he expressed approval of the church's position that extraordinary means of prolonging life are optional, and stated that he would not want any of this ''extraordinary business'' done for him under circumstances similar to the

Quinlan case. Five years later the New York Court of Appeals, responding to the use of a ventilator to maintain Brother Fox in a PVS, ruled that the ventilator could be discontinued, largely because the court was convinced that the patient's previous opposition to this type of treatment was "unimpeachable in its sincerity."[6]

Clarence Herbert, a cancer patient with a history of cardiac problems, was also influenced by the Quinlan case to think about the probable circumstances of his dying. At some point prior to the surgical closing of his ileostomy in 1983— followed by his cardiac arrest in the recovery room, brain damage following resuscitation, and subsequent death after the removal of a ventilator and IV feedings—Herbert told his wife that he did not want "to be kept alive by machines or 'become another Karen Ann Quinlan.'" That reported statement apparently persuaded the California Court of Appeal that Herbert's family had carried out his wishes in requesting the discontinuation of mechanical ventilation and artificial feeding.[7]

When the Supreme Judicial Court of Massachusetts issued its *Brophy* decision in 1986, a major factor in that decision was Paul Brophy's frequently stated opposition to the technological prolongation of dying prior to his becoming permanently unconscious in 1983. Years before, when the Quinlan case was being publicized, he had reportedly told his wife: "I don't ever want to be on a life-support system. No way do I want to live like that; that is not living." One of his favorite sayings had been, "When your ticket is punched, it is punched." When he received a commendation for bravery in the early 1980s for rescuing an extensively burned man from a burning truck, he thought about the ordeal the man had gone through before dying a few months later, tossed the commendation in the trash, and said: "I should have been 5 minutes later. It would have been all over for him." Regarding that incident, he told his brother, "If I'm ever like that, just shoot me, pull the plug." And a week before losing consciousness, he commented about a local teenager being maintained on a life-support system: "No way, don't ever let that happen to me, no way."[8]

In contrast to these patients, William Bartling was still conscious and autonomous when he was hospitalized in 1984 for multiple medical problems, including lung cancer and emphysema. For 2 months his physicians refused requests from Bartling and his wife to disconnect his respirator, because they questioned his competency and believed that granting his request would be unethical. In response, Bartling filed a legal complaint against the physicians, and he tried to communicate his opposition to the technological prolongation of his life by means of a signed copy of Concern for Dying's "Living Will," a signed copy of the California durable-power-of-attorney-for-health-care form, a written declaration of his preference to die rather than continue his "degrading" and "intolerable" condition, a form releasing the physicians and hospital from liability if they carried out his wishes, and a videotaped disposition for a court hearing.

All of these efforts failed to persuade his physicians to discontinue the respirator.[9]

These cases, occurring in five states over a period of several years, suggest that numerous persons were influenced by the Quinlan case to the point of thinking seriously about the likely circumstances of their own dying in a way they may never have done before. When they did think about those hypothetical circumstances, most of these persons, like several of the individuals in these cases, probably used mental images drawn from the Quinlan case: a permanently unconscious patient, the prolongation of the patient's life with mechanical ventilation (the continued use of artificial feedings and antibiotics was not publicized as much as the ventilator), supportive parents at the bedside, uncooperative physicians, and a lengthy legal proceeding featuring courts that might or might not finally permit treatment abatement.

The most common responses elicited by these Quinlan-like images were those of repulsion and avoidance. Like Severns, Leach, Fox, Herbert, and Brophy, many persons seem to have been repulsed by the thought that they, too, might end up permanently uncounsious or for some other medical reason lost their capacity to make decisions about their medical care; that they, too, might end up with physicians unwilling to abate treatment, even at a knowledgeable surrogate's request; and that they, too, might be left at the mercy of the judicial system. Also like these five individuals prior to their critical illnesses, the challenge confronting persons repulsed by these undesirable possibilities was how to avoid repeating Quinlan's experience.

Thus numerous persons have in recent years undoubtedly made comments to relatives and friends indicating that they never want to become "a vegetable," or have "extraordinary procedures" used to prolong their lives, or be kept alive "artificially," or be permanently dependent on "life-support systems." Moreover, a large number of individuals have gone beyond verbal comments to give written expression to their opposition to the technological prolongation of dying. Some of these written advance directives have been original documents drawn up by reflective individuals, but most of the documents have probably been signed versions of Living Wills distributed by Concern for Dying and several other organizations. Whether oral or written, the intended purpose of these advance directives has been to use *moral persuasion* with relatives, friends, and health care professionals to set limits on the use of life-prolonging medical technology in the event that in the future one becomes critically ill but lacks the capacity at that time to communicate preferences regarding treatment abatement.

The Bartling case created a different set of problems for individuals wanting to plan for the possible circumstances of their dying, and to exercise some control over the manner of that dying should they ever be hopelessly ill in a health care institution. This case, in a way similar to the cases of Abe Perlmutter and Elizabeth Bouvia, illustrated that the preferences regarding treatment abatement expressed by autonomous, critically ill patients are sometimes disregarded by physicians in some hospitals. Unquestionably confirming that uncooperative physicians occasionally try to thwart a competent patient's moral and legal right to refuse life-prolonging treatment, especially when the patient is disabled or has difficulty communicating verbally, the case demonstrated that the courts are indispensable as a last-resort means of enforcing one's common-law and constitutional rights.

At the same time, the Bartling case reinforced the importance of planning for the possibility of treatment abatement in advance of critical illness. Of course, uncooperative physicians can reject the validity of statements made prior to the onsent of critical illness by a patient who retains autonomy—just as the *Quinlan* court did with the prior statements of a nonautonomous patient. However, if an autonomous patient can demonstrate, by means of a written advance directive or reported earlier comments to trustworthy relatives and friends, that he or she held a position on treatment abatement prior to the onset of critical illness that is consistent with the position now being expressed under the conditions imposed by a life-threatening illness, uncooperative physicians will at least have greater difficulty questioning the patient's competency, or resisting the patient's transfer to another physician.

Planning for the possibility of treatment abatement is therefore helpful, even if one retains the capacity to make decisions about medical treatment during critical or terminal illness. Such planning is especially helpful, however, for all persons who will, for whatever medical reason, subsequently lose the capacity to make such decisions. Critically ill patients who lack sufficient maturity because of young age or who were never autonomous because of severe mental retardation can obviously not benefit from this kind of planning, but all other critically ill patients who are nonautonomous—because of diminished or fluctuating capacity, substantial incapacity, or a permanent loss of consciousness—may retain the ability to influence the course of their medical treatment by means of a morally persuasive expression of preferences formulated months or years in advance. Moreover, the possibility of being morally persuasive in setting limits to the medical prolongation of one's life exists for all autonomous individuals apart from legislative statute, if they live in a state that has not passed a natural death act or if they simply prefer to communicate their preferences about treatment abatement apart from a statutory document.

For all persons wanting to plan for the possible circumstances of critical or terminal illness, such planning has several possible benefits. This kind of prospective planning (1) maximizes the possibilities that one's own perspective and value system will govern the decisions made regarding the use or the abatement of life-sustaining procedures; (2) enables an individual, especially when a personalized advance directive is formulated, to address the most likely circumstances of critical or terminal illness in light of the particularities of his or her own life situation (family diseases, personal life-style, personal health condition, most likely accidents or injuries, designated proxy, etc.); (3) provides information and guidance for one's proxy or surrogate in the event of personal incapacity to make decisions about treatment or treatment abatement; (4) creates the possibility of persuading physicians and other health care professionals to carry out one's preferences regarding the technological prolongation of life, or to transfer the responsibility for one's care to physicians who will be receptive to the preferences of a patient communicated prior to the onset of critical illness; (5) helps to allay concern that might arise later regarding any connection between the financial burden of prolonged medical care on the patient's family and a surrogate's request for treatment abatement; and (6) increases the possibilities of avoiding the time, effort, expense, and emotional trauma of having to go to court to have one's rights affirmed.

Nonstatutory alternatives

Planning for the possibility of treatment abatement can be done in a number of ways, with none of the alternative methods of prospective planning presented in this section requiring recourse to legislative statute. All of the alternatives to be discussed here go beyond the kinds of occasional comments that Severns, Leach, Fox, Herbert, and Brophy reportedly made before losing their capacity to participate personally in decisions about their medical care. In this respect, the alternatives presented in this section have a better chance of actually influencing the decisions that will need to be made in the event that one becomes critically ill. Also, in the unfortunate circumstance that a court hearing becomes necessary to determine the appropriate course of medical treatment in a case involving a nonautonomous patient, most of these alternatives will provide more reliable evidence regarding the patient's preferences than the hearsay evidence provided in the legal cases discussed earlier.

A written treatment plan

With the diagnosis of an illness that predictably will have a critical (and possibly a terminal) phase, a patient may choose to work with the primary physician in a case to formulate a written treatment plan for the illness. Drawn up while the patient has the capacity to project long-term goals of treatment and consider alternative courses of treatment that may achieve those goals, a treatment plan enables a patient to communicate personal preferences concerning medical treatment and the possibility of abating that treatment—before possibly experiencing a diminution or fluctuation in decision-making capacity, a substantial incapacity to make decisions about medical treatment, or a permanent loss of consciousness. Moreover, the formulation of such a plan with a cooperative physician maximizes the possiblity that the treatment administered to a patient will be consistent with the patient's personal value system, coherent even when the patient is under the care of multiple health care professionals in several institutional settings, and yet adaptable to the uncertainties that often arise during the course of an illness.

Ideally, a treatment plan devised by a patient and the primary physician is an evolving plan done in two basic phases. In the first phase, drawn up prior to the onset of critical illness, the treatment plan can address several kinds of decisions that are necessary early in an illness or will be required as the illness progresses: the long-range goals toward which treatment is to be directed, the more immediate goals toward which treatment is to be directed, the specific modalities of treatment that may be medically required at certain stages of the illness (mechanical ventilation, cardiac resuscitation, antibiotics, surgery, technological feeding, etc.), the preferred health care setting in which the patient can receive treatment, any personal particulars (such as age, religious beliefs, emotional problems, or financial limitations) that might influence subsequent decisions about continuing or abating treatment, and the identification of a proxy decision maker in the event of the patient's subsequent incapacity to continue communicating perferences about treatment.

In the second phase, drawn up when the patient's medical condition has become critical, the treatment plan can address the more limited range of treatment options still available. In addition to revising the long-range goals of treatment, the primary physician and patient (or proxy) can reformulate the more immediate goals of treatment, reconsider the specific technological interventions that may be appropriate as the illness continues, specifically discuss the possibility (as well as the timing and manner) of abating treatment, and reconsider the health care setting that would be most appropriate for the patient should life-sustaining treatment become futile.[10]

Such treatment plans are not without problems. One inherent problem with treatment plans is the changing and often unpredictable nature of an illness, which sometimes suggests therapeutic alternatives to a physician that had not previously been discussed with the patient. Treatment plans therefore need periodic modification as changes take place in the course of an illness, in the appropriate forms of treatment, in the physicians and other health care personnel taking care of the patient, and in the patient's own views regarding treatment. A second, related problem is the possibility of serious disagreements between the primary physician and the patient (or the patient's proxy) subsequent to the formulation of the treatment plan. Especially when unexpected changes take place in the patient's medical condition or when one of the participants in the development of a treatment plan (physician, patient, or proxy) begins to make recommendations or requests that seem unreasonable to the other person, the disagreement may need to be resolved by an institutional ethics committee (IEC) or some other institutional dispute-resolution mechanism.

A hospice plan of care

With the diagnosis of an illness that is terminal, a patient may choose to be admitted to a hospice program. Such a program—whether a freestanding hospice, a hospital-based hospice, a home care hospice, or a hospice program affiliated with a home health care agency—is committed to providing appropriate treatment to patients during the terminal phase of their lives. Not functioning in a curative mode and not motivated by the "technological imperative," hospice physicians and nurses offer their patients coordinated and dependable terminal care that often varies dramatically from the fragmented medical care the patients received before entering the hospice program.

In most hospices, the specific nature of the treatment to be administered to a patient is determined by a medical director working in conjunction with an interdisciplinary committee of health care professionals. The committee, meeting on a regular basis, works out a detailed plan that will provide terminal care that is appropriate for an individual patient, and updates the plan as the patient's medical condition or circumstances change.

By its very nature, a plan of appropriate care for terminally ill patients necessitates planning for treatment abatement. Whatever the nature of the terminal illness (advanced cancer, AIDS, ALS, etc.), the task in drawing up a plan of appropriate care is that of determining what kinds of treatment will help to combat a patient's pain, what kinds of treatment will be effective in ameliorating the symptoms connected with the illness, and what kinds of treatment will avoid leaving the patient sedated for long periods of time. Likewise, a plan of appropriate care frequently stipulates that certain modalities of treatment such as mechanical ventilation, surgery, chemotherapy, radiation therapy, antibiotics, and cardiac resuscitation are inappropriate in the management of a particular patient's terminal illness.

In determining what counts as appropriate care in a specific case, the medical director and interdisciplinary team place significant weight on the beliefs, values, and preferences of the patient whose terminal care is being planned. Moreover, given the importance placed on the family unit in hospice care and the necessary role of a family member as the primary careperson (PCP) in home care hospices, members of the patient's family can often influence the planning of treatment and treatment abatement. In fact, in many hospices the PCP in a case is welcome to attend the interdisciplinary committee's conferences and participate in the discussions regarding the appropriate care of a patient who needs comfort and compassion even when cure is no longer possible.

Written advance directives

As already indicated, many persons in the post-*Quinlan* era have used written documents to plan for the possibility of treatment abatement should they later become permanently unconscious or terminally ill. Waiting for neither the onset of critical illness nor a diagnosis of terminal illness, numerous individuals have chosen to try—often while still reasonably young and healthy—to communicate their preferences regarding life-sustaining treatment apart from statutory directives. Depending on the state of residence and the year in which they signed their advance directives, tens of thousands of persons have opted to exercise moral persuasion through nonstatutory forms at least partially because they had no legally enforceable alternative: their state legislatures, for reasons of inertia or successful pro-life lobbying, had not yet passed a natural death act.

Individuals executing written advance directives can choose among three forms that such directives take. Most advance directives are *treatment directives* intended to accomplish two tasks: provide information about a person's preferences regarding the use of medical treatment in the event of critical illness and especially in the event of terminal illness, and provide a rationale for these preferences in the event the signer of the document subsequently loses the capacity to communicate the preferences in person. Although treatment directives exist in great variety, this kind of planning document usually contains several of the following features:

a declaration that the signer of the document is competent at the time of executing the document, and is not signing the document under coercion or duress

a statement of personal preferences, which may be couched in fairly general terminology or be quite specific, regarding the use of life-sustaining treatment

a statement of personal preferences regarding the abatement of certain modalities of life-sustaining treatment

a request for pain relief and comfort measures in the event of critical or terminal illness

an indication of the preferred setting (hospital, nursing home, hospice, or home) for medical care during the terminal phase of life

the signatures of at least two witnesses who are unrelated to the principal signer of the document.

Other advance directives are *proxy directives* intended to designate another person (or persons) to make health care decisions on the behalf of the document's signer should that individual later become nonautonomous or legally incompetent. As a nonstatutory alternative to signing a durable-power-of-attorney form or designating a Committee of the Person, this kind of planning document enables the signer to specify (by name, relationship, or role) the person or persons to be entrusted with decisions that quite probably will be life-or-death decisions made years later in an ICU. Depending on its specificity, a proxy directive may delegate responsibility to the proxy in a fairly broad manner or specify that the proxy will have the right and the responsibility on the behalf of the document's signer to consent to medical treatment, refuse medical treatment (including life-sustaining treatment), expend or withhold funds for medical treatment and services provided by physicians and other health care personnel, change physicians, and/or change institutional settings.

Many persons choose to sign a *composite directive* intended to accomplish the goals of the other two documents. By combining the features of a treatment directive and a proxy directive in one form, signers of this kind of document follow a dual strategy in trying to influence decisions made about their medical care in any future circumstances of critical or terminal illness involving personal incapacity on their part. By providing written information and instructions regarding medical treatment to relatives, physicians, and any other concerned persons who may be present at that future time of illness, the signer can possibly influence decisions made at that time about medical treatment even if (as in an emergency situation) the designated surrogate is unavoidably absent. By designating a trusted relative or friend who should be capable of interpreting and implementing the signer's preferences at that future time of illness, the signer can possibly influence the decisions to treat or to abate treatment even if the exact wording of the written instructions is open to criticism or conflicting interpretations.

Three distinctive types of advance directives are currently in use: formalized documents distributed by organizations within the right-to-die movement, specialized documents provided by health care organizations and institutions, and personalized documents drawn up by individuals. The specific directives within each type or category often have significant differences, with some of the documents being treatment directives only, others being primarily proxy directives, and several of the more recent directives being composite documents. In addition to their being discussed here, representative examples of these documents are printed in the Appendix.

FORMALIZED REFUSAL-OF-TREATMENT DOCUMENTS. Without doubt, the best-known and most widely used advance directive is the "Living Will" distributed by Concern for Dying (CFD). This organization, headquartered in New York with James Sheffield as its executive director, is the largest of the organizations within the right-to-die movement. With its focus on educating the public about the right to refuse life-prolonging medical treatment and the difficulties that sometimes arise in trying to exercise that right, CFD publicizes and distributes the "Living Will," holds seminars for medical students and law students, publishes a newsletter received by 80,000 readers, responds to over 1,000 requests a year from attorneys who want additional information about the legal status of nonstatutory advance directives, distributes the CFD-produced film called *Dax's Case* (the film portrays the case of Dax Cowart, which is described in Chapter 1), and occasionally becomes involved in court cases through attorneys on its legal advisers committee (CFD participated in the Brother Fox, Bartling, Conroy, and Brophy cases) and the attorney added to its staff in 1987. In recent years the CFD professional seminars, called Interdisciplinary Collaboration on Death and Dying, have provided opportunities in death education for 2,000 students in medical and law schools.[11]

The "Living Will" was originally developed by Luis Kutner, a Chicago attorney. He drafted the first version of the document in the early 1930s in response to the "barbaric" medical treatment administered against the protests of a dying friend, and called it a "living will" because it sets forth an individual's choices and decisions that are to take effect prior to death should the individual become terminally ill. Bishop Fulton Sheen was the first person officially to sign Kutner's document (around 1940), and Errol Flynn was the second person to do so. Later, in the 1960s, Kutner shared his document with the founding members of the Euthanasia Educational Council, who revised the document and began distributing it in 1968.[12]

Now, some 20 years later, CFD has distributed more than 7 million copies of the "Living Will." The document has gone through four revisions, with updated versions being published in 1973, 1978, 1983, and 1984. The last two versions have contained updated suggestions regarding implementation that are intended to make the document more legally enforceable if court action should become necessary in a particular case. Concern for Dying has also established a Living Will Registry designed for signers of the document who may not have relatives or close friends to help implement their wishes or who simply want to ensure that their advance directive is always readily available upon request.

The formalized wording of the body of the "Living Will" has remained constant over the years. Consisting of three paragraphs, the document uses very general language to declare the signer's present competence and acceptance of death as "the one certainty of life," the signer's wish to have treatment abated in the event of "no reasonable expectation of my recovery from extreme physical or mental disability," and the signer's hope that other responsible persons "will regard themselves as morally bound by these provisions" if the signer subsequently loses the capacity to affirm the contents of the document personally. In addition to this treatment directive, which comprised the totality of the "Living Will" in its early versions, the current version of the document contains four optional features: (1) space for a more specific, personalized statement of preferences regarding unwanted modalities of life-sustaining treatment; (2) the designation of an attorney-in-fact who will have durable power of attorney for making medical treatment decisions, should the need arise; (3) a place for notarization of the document; and (4) an indication that the document is in CFD's registry.

An alternative refusal-of-treatment document is distributed by the Society for the Right to Die (SRD). While working under the auspices of the Euthanasia Educational Council in the 1970s, the SRD promoted legislation that would recognize an individual's right to refuse medical treatment and die with dignity. In 1975, the SRD published its first *Legislative Manual,* which contained a survey of legislative bills under consideration in a number of states at that time as well as a suggested model bill for the termination of unwanted medical treatment.

Since the 1979 split between CFD and the SRD, the SRD has been headquartered in New York with Alice Mehling as it executive director. The SRD has continued its original mission of promoting constructive legislation and judicial decisions that affirm the right of terminally ill patients to oppose the futile prolongation of their dying. As a part of that organizational task, the SRD has published the *Handbook of Living Will Laws 1981–1984,* the *Handbook of 1985 Living Will Laws,* the *Handbook of Living Will Laws* (1987 edition), and the regularly updated "Fact Sheets on Right-to-Die Court Decisions." The SRD has also increasingly been involved in right-to-die court cases. With the work of three staff attorneys, the SRD has filed *amicus* briefs in a number of the more recent cases: *Corbett, Jobes, Brophy, Peter, Palermo, Rasmussen, Requena, Gardner, Delio, Farrell,* and *Drabick).*[13] In addition, the SRD has sponsored conferences for physicians, aided in the publication of a major multiauthored article on hopelessly ill patients in *The New England Journal of Medicine,* published *The Physician and the Hopelessly Ill Patient,* and distributed its own advance directive entitled "Living Will Declaration."

In contrast to CFD, which has tended to prefer its nonstatutory advance directive to the natural death acts now available in most states, the SRD's "Living Will Declaration" is a form devised and distributed primarily to fill the remaining gaps in natural death act legislation: for persons living in states that have not yet enacted such legislation, or as a backup mechanism for communicating personal wishes regarding treatment abatement in case one is traveling and becomes hsopitalized in a state lacking such legislation. Promoted as "the best protection available to you" apart from natural death act legislation, the "Living Will Declaration" differs from the CFD form in several ways: it does not refer to artificial or "heroic" measures, but simply directs the attending physician "to withhold or withdraw treatment that merely prolongs my dying"; it declares that the directions are an expression of "my legal right to refuse treatment," it calls on relatives and physicians to regard themselves as *legally* as well as morally "bound to act in accord with my wishes," and it removes such persons from "any legal liability for having followed my directions." In the current version of the form (revised in 1986), the SRD composite directive includes three options that may be exercised at one's discretion: a personalized listing of specific treatment one does not want (such as cardiac resuscitation, mechanical respiration, or artificial feeding or fluid by tube), a personal statement concerning the type of care one *does want* in the event of critical or terminal illness (e.g., pain medication, or one's home as the preferred location of dying), and the designation of a proxy (and an alternate, should the first person be unavailable at the time needed).

A third refusal-of-treatment document is distributed by the Hemlock Society. This organization, founded by Derek Humphry and headquartered first in Los Angeles and now in Eugene, Oregon, differs from CFD and the SRD in that its fundamental organizational mission is "supporting the option of active voluntary euthanasia for the terminally ill." Established in 1980, the Hemlock Society now has 15,000 members; it publishes the *Hemlock Quarterly* and a number of books on suicide, assisted suicide, and euthanasia (*Jean's Way, Commonsense Suicide, Let Me Die Before I Wake,* etc.). The society also sponsors an annual conference on voluntary euthanasia and related issues, sponsors a journal entitled *The Euthanasia Review,* and actively cooperates with similar organizations in other countries (especially the British Voluntary Euthanasia Society, the Voluntary Euthanasia Society of Scotland, and the Netherlands Society for Voluntary Euthanasia). In 1986, Humphry and his second wife, Ann Wickett, authored a significant book entitled *The Right to Die.*[14]

The Hemlock Society's advance directive has changed in title and content over the years. Originally entitled "Directive to Withhold Treatment," the revised and copyrighted document is now called "A Living Will: A Directive to Withhold Treatment and for the Administration of Pain-killing Drugs." In contrast to the advance directives of CFD and the SRD, the Hemlock Society advance directive is modeled after the California Natural Death Act. Consisting of seven numbered paragraphs, a signed version of "A Living Will" states that the signer is competent and executing the document voluntarily; directs that in the event of terminal illness diagnosed by two physicians, with "imminent" death being forestalled "artificially" with life-sustaining procedures, such technological procedures shall be withheld or withdrawn to permit death to occur; directs that "whatever drugs may be required" to relieve pain shall be administered; names a proxy to make decisions relating to health care; and calls on relatives and physicians to honor the directive as "the final expression of my legal right to refuse or accept medical and surgical treatment." In addition, the document contains several California-specific provisions, which citizens of other states are advised to omit: a disclaimer regarding pregnancy, a statement that the signer has already been diagnosed as having a terminal condition, and a time limit of 5 years for the document's validity.

However, the Hemlock Society's agenda concerning advance directives is not limited to "A Living Will." Two other advance directives are available through the society. The first of these documents is called "Request for Help in Dying," which is an advance directive calling for the "acceleration" of one's dying in the event of a terminal illness diagnosed by two physicians. The second document is called "Request for Help in Dying by Proxy," which is a written directive signed by a terminally ill patient's proxy for the purpose of securing a physician's help in intentionally killing the patient. In both documents, the signer directs that the termination of life be "as quick and painless as possible."

SPECIALIZED ORGANIZATIONAL DIRECTIVES. With the exception of the Hemlock Society's advance directive to withhold treatment, which is problematic for non-California residents, the planning documents just discussed are intended for widespread usage. The universal nature of the language used in the documents, with signers of the CFD or SRD forms possibly supplementing the generic language with personalized comments, is one of the reasons for the popularity of the documents. The language enables all kinds of persons to communicate a preference for treatment abatement—or for euthanasia, for individuals signing one of the Hemlock Society's acceleration-of-death documents. Because none of these right-to-die organizations is oriented toward profit-making, partisan politics, or any particular religious perspective, their advance directives are distributed to all persons who request them—and are signed by tens of thousands of persons who want to exercise some control over the manner and location of their dying.

Other advance directives are more specialized documents provided by health care associations and institutions. For example, at the national level the American Public Health Association has its own form, even though the document is not widely publicized.[15] At the local level, some health care institutions provide specialized forms for patients who are critically or terminally ill. An example of this localized use of advance directives is the "living will declaration" used by oncologists at the University of Kansas Medical Center to elicit the views of their Kansas patients regarding the possible need for resuscitation (the form is an adaptation of the Kansas Natural Death Act, not the SRD form having the same title).[16]

Some of the more interesting specialized documents are intended for use by persons having particular kinds of religious beliefs. Written for persons who believe that decisions to abate treatment can have religious significance, these planning documents are distributed by national health and hospital associations having Catholic and Protestant affiliations.

The first advance directive written to reflect a particular religious perspective was devised by the Catholic Hospital Association in 1974. Concerned that the Euthanasia Educational Council's "Living Will" was thoroughly secular in its orientation, some Catholics developed an alternative advance directive entitled "Christian Affirmation of Life." The original version of this planning document began with a formalized declaration of religious beliefs (worded along the lines of a creedal statement), followed by a treatment directive couched in terminology reflecting Catholic theological concepts as well as making the request that "no extraordinary means" be used to prolong the signer's life.

The current version of "Christian Affirmation of Life" was developed in 1982 and is available through the Catholic Health Association (CHA). This organization, as the successor to the Catholic Hospital Association, is a coordinating body for more than 850 hospitals and long-term care facilities. One of the CHA's many services to these health care institutions is the distribution of its advance directive so that patients in these institutions can be aided, if they wish, in expressing their preferences about the technological prolongation of their dying.

The revised version of the CHA document uses significantly different language from the original form, even though it retains a similar format. The document contains a prologue that affirms the Christian belief in eternal life, the moral and legal right of patients "to choose what will be done to care for them," and the moral claim that "death need not be resisted with every possible means." The prologue also indicates that the CHA form is not a legal document, but "one of moral persuasion." As such, the document's purpose is that of enabling thoughtful Catholics to communicate their "desires regarding treatment for terminal illness" prior to the possible diagnosis of such an illness in the hope that, should they later become nonautonomous, other persons will make decisions regarding treatment "in accordance with the patient's legitimate wishes."

The directive portion of the CHA document consists of three paragraphs worded in quite general terminology. A signer of the document asks to be "fully informed of the fact" of terminal illness should such a condition be diagnosed, requests that "no ethically extraordinary means" be used to prolong the dying process should there be no reasonable expectation of recovery, calls for the alleviation of pain "if it becomes unbearable," prohibits any consideration of euthanasia ("the intention of shortening my life"), and requests that he or she be the object of prayer by concerned Christians before and after death. The document is clearly not designed for legal purposes in that it provides no declaration of the signer's competence, has no place for the signature of witnesses, names no proxy, and makes no mention of specific treatments to be administered or abated during the period of terminal illness. The signer simply calls on responsible parties at the time of terminal illness to refrain from using "treatment that does not offer a reasonable hope of benefit to me or that cannot be accomplished without excessive expense, pain or other grave burden"—the document's definition of "ethically extraordinary means."

The American Protestant Hospital Association also came out with an advance directive in the mid-1970s. Entitled "Instructions for My Care in the Event of Terminal Illness," the document is said to "carry some moral weight" even though it is "a document of reflection and not a legal document." The document consists of two parts. The first part is called "A Personal Statement of Faith" according to which the signer indicates personal belief in God as the creator of human life, the sanctity of human life, the importance of dignity in dying, the wrongness of prolonging life through "artificial and mechanical life-support systems" when there is no reasonable prospect of a patient's recovery, and the right "to die my own death" by refusing "artificial and heroic measures to prolong my dying."

The directive portion of this instruction directive begins with an affirmation that "life is a gift of God" and that "physical death is a part of life and is the completed stage of a person's development." The signer then directs, according to the vague terminology of the form, that life not be prolonged "by artificial or mechanical means" if there is no reasonable expectation of recovery from "physical or mental disability," that pain medication and symptom control be administered, and that all legal means be used to support the choice for treatment abatement. By contrast, euthanasia ("direct intervention . . . to shorten my life") is explicitly rejected. The directive concludes with a statement releasing from legal liability all parties who carry out the signer's requests.

The American Protestant Health Association (APHA), having been formed in 1984 as the coordinating body for approximately 250 Protestant hospitals and health care institutions, now distributes alternative versions of the advance directive originally formulated by the more narrowly defined American Protestant Hospital Association. One version of the APHA's "Instructions for My Care" document is the same explicitly religious directive just discussed: both the confessional prologue and the wording of the instruction directive remain unchanged.

The other version of the APHA document is intended for patients in Protestant facilities who may wish to communicate their preferences regarding treatment abatement without employing theological terminology. Thus, instead of making a religious affirmation concerning God's role in creating and sustaining human life, the signer of this document simply agrees with a formalized "Introductory Statement" declaring that "death is a natural event in the course of human life," that every person has a "human right of autonomy" that includes decisions to refuse medical treatment, and that "artificial and mechanical life-support systems" should be abated when they are unable to "aid the continuation of the quality of my personal and biological life." The directive portion of the document is identical in wording to the other APHA form, except for the omission of the introductory paragraph containing religious claims. Both forms can be signed by two witnesses.

PERSONALIZED DIRECTIVES. For many persons, the advance directives distributed by right-to-die organizations and health care associations provide an adequate means of communicating their preferences regarding treatment abatement.

Agreeing with the wording of a formalized directive, they sign the document, possibly have their signature witnessed by friends or associates, possibly designate a proxy in the event they become nonautonomous (the CFD, SRD, and Hemlock Society refusal-of-treatment forms provide this alternative), and possibly list their individual preferences concerning unwanted treatments or unwanted conditions (the CFD form permits and the SRD form encourages the signer to list such individual choices).

However, many other persons find the standardized advance directives too formal, too brief, too inflexible, too vague, too easily misinterpreted—and unlikely to persuade uncertain relatives and apprehensive physicians to engage in treatment abatement according to the "one-size-fits-all" language used in the documents. Especially given the possibility of losing personal autonomy at some point in the future, thoughtful persons who want to maximize their ability to persuade others to carry out their wishes regarding treatment abatement—even in the event of unconsciousness—frequently find the widely distributed organizational documents to be inadequate instruments for effectively achieving that purpose.

Such persons, given sufficient motivation to do the work involved, often produce personalized directives as a preferable alternative to all of the nationally distributed forms. By means of these personalized directives, thoughtful individuals substantially increase the possibility that, regardless of their neurological status at the time of critical illness, they will be able to guide surrogates and physicians in deciding when to administer life-sustaining medical treatment and when the conditions are appropriate for such treatment to be abated.

Although most persons signing advance directives continue to prefer the convenience of the standardized forms (as well as the name recognition and "support system" provided by the sponsoring organization), personalized directives have numerous advantages. By formulating advance directives themselves, individuals gain at least a dozen advantages over the use of the organizational forms:

1. They can demonstrate the soundness of mind and moral freedom with which they make choices relative to the technological prolongation of life.
2. They can insist on candor and honesty from health care professionals any time medical prognosis, treatment alternatives, or other matters of importance to them are being discussed.
3. They can convey preferences about medical treatment and treatment abatement in their own terminology, instead of using the borrowed language of a universal form.
4. They can reflect on the meaning of life and its approaching end in the context of their own value system.
5. They can define any terms that are susceptible to varying interpretations.

6. They can be as specific as they care to be regarding unwanted treatments and/or unwanted conditions that can be but should not be prolonged through medical technology.
7. They can address the particularities of their own life situation.
8. They can designate one or more trusted individuals as proxies to make decisions on their behalf in the event of personal incapacity.
9. They can indicate whether proxy decision makers are to consider themselves bound by the preferences articulated in the advance directive, or at liberty to make decisions based on their own perception of the nonautonomous patient's best interests.
10. They can communicate preferences regarding the setting in which medical care and other forms of care are to be given during the terminal phase of life.
11. They can express their views concerning the use of pain medication, including circumstances in which the use of certain drugs can become addictive or hasten one's death.
12. They can provide timely guidance for their probable survivors regarding postmortem decisions (cadaver organ donation, preferred type of death service, disposition of the dead body, etc.).

In addition to these advantages concerning the content of an advance directive, individuals doing this type of prospective planning have another advantage over persons signing conventional forms: they can be creative in selecting the medium for communicating all of these preferences, possibly using a nonerasable tape recording or a videotape as a supplement to or substitute for a written directive.

At the present time, however, personalized directives are usually written documents (William Bartling's multiple directives are a notable exception). A number of these directives are primarily intended to provide instructions relative to (1) unwanted treatments or (2) unwanted medical conditions. For example, one personalized directive lists the following unwanted treatments: "Intravenous or forced feeding, hydration or medication, and artificial respiration, cardiac resuscitation and all such heroic or non-heroic measures."[17] Another personalized document stipulates three unwanted treatments: "(a) Electrical or mechanical resuscitation of my heart when it has stopped beating. (b) Nasogastric tube feeding when I am paralyzed or unable to take nourishment by mouth. (c) Mechanical respiration when I am no longer able to sustain my own breathing."[18]

Other persons formulating treatment directives tend to focus more on unwanted medical conditions. For example, Ernest Morgan, an activist in the right-to-die movement, wrote a directive that contains a simply stated preference to avoid prolonged incapacity: "In the event of my incapacity to make such decisions, because of unconsciousness or other condition, for more than 24 hours, that circumstance shall constitute a decision against treatment directed toward recovery or life support."[19] Another person's directive emphasizes the importance of communication:

If intervention involves the loss either of a receiving sense or a form of communication with the rest of the world I wish this to be considered in the following way: I would be willing to risk intervention which might involve my continuing to live blind, alone *or* deaf alone, *or* incapable of movement of the lower half of my body. If further impairment were risked, I would be willing to live blind if I were able to hear and to speak, or deaf if I were able to see and to write. In other words, I would want to be certain of being able to receive communications from others and of communicating with others in appropriately related ways.[20]

Other persons doing prospective planning with advance directives choose to entrust decision making to a relative or friend in the event of personal incapacity. Perhaps not wishing to constrain proxies by enumerating unwanted treatments or unwanted conditions in a directive, and possibly trying to allow for the uncertainty inherent to projecting the future (in advance directives as well as medical prognosis), some individuals select one or more proxies to make treatment-abatement decisions on their behalf should they ever actually become brain-damaged, permanently unconscious, or for some other reason be unable to make decisions themselves about the merits of life-sustaining treatment. Thus one person's directive names his wife as his proxy:

If I become incompetent or so incapacitated as not to be able to communicate my wishes with respect to the application and continuance of my medical treatment, I hereby appoint my wife,_____, as my legal guardian for the purpose of making legal decisions regarding my medical care and giving legal orders, consents and denials of consent relating thereto, and I further grant her power-of-attorney to act in my place on such matters.[21]

Another directive designates a trusted friend as a proxy and then states: "To induce my attorney-in-fact to act hereunder, I for myself and for my heirs, executors, legal representatives and assigns, hereby agree to idemnify and hold harmless my attorney-in-fact from and against any and all claims that may arise against him in such capacity, except as a result of his gross negligence or willful misconduct."[22]

An increasing number of people formulate composite directives, thereby gaining the dual benefit of providing personal instructions regarding treatment abatement and having a trusted relative or friend prepared to interpret those instructions. By using this dual strategy of planning for the possibility of treatment abatement, individuals prepare in advance for variable situations of critical or terminal illness that might arise subsequent to the signer's loss of autonomy through brain damage or prolonged unconsciousness.

Two exemplary composite directives are those drawn up by Sissela Bok and Robert Veatch. Bok, a philosopher at the Harvard Medical School, published her version of a composite directive some years ago. The document, while possibly not Bok's own personal directive, is instructive in illustrating the personal touches that are important in this kind of advance directive. For example, Bok's form emphasizes that the signer's personal instructions are to be followed unless doing so would be unlawful: "If these instructions create a conflict with the desires of my relatives, or with hospital policies or with the principles of those providing my care, I ask that my instructions prevail, unless they are contrary to existing law or would expose medical personnel or the hospital to a substantial risk of legal liability." The document also states that if the signer is irreversibly dying and has no reasonable chance of regaining communicative skills or avoiding prolonged suffering, the signer does not want to be subjected to surgery or resuscitation—or "life support from mechanical ventilators, intensive care services, or other life-prolonging procedures, including the administration of antibiotics and blood products." The document then contains the following statement regarding proxies:

> In order to carry out these instructions and to interpret them, I authorize_____to accept, plan, and refuse treatment on my behalf in cooperation with attending physicians and health personnel. This person knows how I value the experience of living, and how I would weigh incompetence, suffering, and dying. Should it be impossible to reach this person, I authorize_____to make such choices for me. I have discussed my desires concerning terminal care with them, and I trust their judgment on my behalf.[23]

Veatch, an ethicist at the Kennedy Institute of Ethics at Georgetown University, was kind enough to share his personal directive with me following a discussion about advance directives at the Hastings Center in the fall of 1985. The document had been finished less than a month before that discussion; it reflects Veatch's keen grasp of the issues inherent to treatment abatement as well as numerous features of his own life situation. As an example of the latter, Veatch's document requests—since on any given day he is likely to travel by car through portions of Maryland, Virginia, and the District of Columbia—that he be moved from one legal jurisdiction to another in the event of critical illness if such a move should prove necessary to have his wishes respected regarding treatment abatement. In this way, as well as in at least 10 other distinctive ways, Veatch's document demonstrates many of the advantages of personalized directives discussed earlier.[24]

My own personal directive follows. Like the documents formulated by Bok and Veatch, my directive illustrates some of the personalized features that are possible whenever reflective individuals use written documents to plan for the possibility of treatment abatement. The document should be taken not as a model for personalized directives, but simply as an example of one person's statement of preferences, values, and wishes prior to the possibility of critical or terminal illness. Composed in 1987 (years after I had been convinced of the merits of such directives!), the document has been copied and given to several appropriate persons; it will be updated periodically and revised as needed.

ON LIVING AND DYING

I, Robert F. Weir, being of sound mind (to the extent that is true of any university professor), intentionally and voluntarily make the following statements as a directive to be followed if I should ever lose personal autonomy for an extended period of time because of accident or illness. These statements should be taken as a personal expression of my preferences regarding various decisions that will have to be made at such a time.

I love life. I believe that the life we have as individuals is a gift from God, a gift to be cherished, used for the benefit of others as well as ourselves, enjoyed, and extended as long as we are capable of faithfully exercising stewardship over it. My life has been enriched by my loving parents, Frank and Erlene Weir, my loving wife, Jerry; my children, Melinda and Randall; and a number of friends and professional colleagues. My life has also been enjoyable because of my educational experiences, participation in sports, appreciation of music, teaching, writing, and traveling.

I want to continue living a full life, but not at all costs and not when I have lost the cognitive abilities to think, communicate, experience the pleasures of life, and deal with the challenges that also characterize the ongoing experience of individual human lives. Because of my experiences with patients, research in biomedical ethics, and writing on the subject of abating treatment, I know that medical circumstances can develop that would preclude my ability to continue living as a conscious, thinking, and relational subject. Should such circumstances occur and seem, on the basis of the best medical information available, to be beyond the capability of medical technology to restore me to the kind of life I cherish, those circumstances would represent for me a fate worse than death.

Now to be more specific. If I should ever lose consciousness as a consequence of an accident or other medical emergency, I give my consent to being placed on a life-support system (including a ventilator, technological feeding and hydration, antibiotics, and a catheter for elimination purposes) for a limited period of time. Moreover, I give consent to surgery in such an emergency, if that sort of medical intervention is believed by physicians on the scene to be necessary to correct internal organ damage and restore me to a cognitive, relational form of living. However, if after a reasonable period of time (measured in days or weeks, and not to exceed 3 months) the life-support system is not proving beneficial in restoring me to a cognitive, relational form of living, I direct my proxy to request that the system of treatment sustaining my biological existence be discontinued. Stopping life-sustaining treatment in this kind of clinical situation is morally no different from never having started it; therefore, my proxy's request on my behalf should be carried out by the attending physician.

I could also become critically ill for a variety of medical reasons other than an emergency situation. If I should become critically ill and be unable to make decisions about my health care at that time, I direct my proxy and other responsible parties present to ascertain as carefully and accurately as possible the prospects of my recovery from the condition of criticial illness. If the administration of certain modalities of medical technology (including mechanical ventilation, burn therapy, kidney dialysis, antibiotics, surgery, cancer therapy, technological feeding and hydration, and cardiopulmonary resuscitation) would be judged as being beneficial in substantially improving or correcting the condition(s) causing the critical illness, I direct that the appropriate treatment(s) be administered. I would also want appropriate pain medication to be administered. If, however, the treatment being given to me proves to be useless in restoring me to consciousness, futile in restoring me to a relational form of living, or offers disproportionate burdens to benefits to me or my family (in terms of pain, psychological suffering, or financial hardship), I direct that the treatment(s) be discontinued even if I am not terminally ill.

If I should have an incurable injury, disease, or illness certified to be a terminal condition by two physicians, one of whom shall be my attending physician, I direct that no medical treatments be started or continued that will serve merely to prolong my dying. Having been clearly diagnosed as being in the terminal phase of life, I would be more interested in the quality of my remaining time than in the quantity of time to be secured through the application of medical technology. Therefore I request that I continue to be given appropriate pain medication (with no concern being given to the possibility of addiction), oral feeding and hydration, suction, hygienic care, and other forms of palliative care throughout my dying period. In addition, I direct my proxy to take all reasonable steps to ensure that, as the end of my life nears, I be allowed to live out my days under the care of the physicians and nurses of a hospice program, if that is a practical option. Whatever the physical setting of my terminal phase of life—home, hospice program, nursing home, or hospital—I direct that all technological means of sustaining my life (including mechanical ventilation, all forms of technological feeding and hydration, and the other treatments listed in the preceding paragraph) be abated. That done, when cardiac or respiratory arrest occurs, the use of CPR or any other resuscitative procedure would clearly be contrary to my wishes.

I intend these instructions to be an expression of my legal right to refuse medical treatment, including medical treatment that could sustain my life. I expect my family, physicians, friends, and others concerned with my care to regard themselves as morally and legally bound to act in accord with these requests. Any physician carrying out these requests should be free, given the legal status of treatment abatement, from any legal liability for having followed my directions.

To help interpret my instructions and see that they are carried out, I designate Jerry Weir, my wife, as my agent for the purpose of making all medical decisions in the event I no longer have the capacity to make the decisions myself. By designating her as my agent, I grant her full power and authority to consent, refuse consent, or withdraw consent to any medical treatment or medical intervention recommended on my behalf by physicians. I urge her to make such decisions along the lines indicated in the preceding paragraphs. However, if a medical situation arises that I have not anticipated, or if she cannot discern how to apply my values to a particular situation involving medical treatment, she is to make such a decision based on her understanding of my best interests in that situation. Should it be necessary, she should immediately dismiss any physician who fails to comply with her decision on my behalf. If any further action is necessary to ensure that my wishes are carried out, she should be prepared to consult with knowledgeable authorities (I suggest Giles Scofield at Concern for Dying, Fenella Rouse at the Society for the Right to Die, or their associates) and then take legal steps against the physician(s), administrators, and institutions involved in prolonging my life against my wishes.

Should my wife be unable, for whatever reason, to make such decisions on my behalf, I designate_____as an alternate proxy. I have discussed my preferences concerning treatment abatement with him, and he understands my views on medical care in the event I become critically or terminally ill. I trust him to make decisions on my behalf, and authorize him to make any of the decisions discussed in the preceding paragraphs of this document.

Robert F. Weir

The declarant is personally known by me, and I believe the declarant to be of sound mind. I am at least 18 years of age and am not related to the declarant by blood or marriage, entitled to any portion of the declarant's estate, or directly responsible for the financial expenses of the declarant's medical care. I am not the declarant's attending physician, an employee of the attending physician, or an employee of the health facility in which the declarant is a patient.

_____

Witness

_____

Witness

_____

Date of Declaration

Legal status of nonstatutory advance directives

Signers of advance directives unquestionably intend their documents to be morally persuasive in the event they become critically or terminally ill and are unable to make treatment-abatement decisions personally. Whether using standardized forms, more specialized documents, or personalized directives, the numerous persons who have signed nonstatutory advance directives clearly intend their documents to *speak for them* when they can no longer speak for themselves in a conventional manner. Through such documents they anticipate being able to influence relatives, physicians, and any other participants in the decision-making process to carry out their expressed preferences in abating treatment and/or to follow the decisions made on their behalf by their chosen proxies.

In many instances the intended purpose of advance directives is realized: relatives and physicians are persuaded to follow the previously autonomous signer's wishes, and life-sustaining treatment is abated according to those expressed wishes. However, in many other instances advance directives fail to achieve their intended purpose because of disagreement on the part of relatives or physicians. In some cases, responsible relatives and physicians choose not to abide by the expressed preferences of a now-nonautonomous patient because the language in the patient's directive is vague, the patient's prognosis is uncertain, or the conditions envisioned by the previously autonomous patient do not sufficiently fit the clinical conditions that actually exist. In other cases, especially those involving vitalistic physicians or physicians paranoid about the law, the preferences of a now-nonautonomous patient are simply ignored by individuals who summarily dismiss advance directives as "worthless pieces of paper."

Before 1984, the surrogate or relatives of a nonautonomous patient had limited alternatives when dealing with a physician who ignored the patient's advance directive. If they were unable to transfer the patient to the care of another physician who would abate treatment according to the patient's requests, they—and the patient—were caught in the middle of an often-repeated power play: any physician who chose not to be persuaded by a patient's written requests could simply ignore those requests and proceed with the technological prolongation of the patient's dying as though the patient had never expressed opposition to such treatment. Although the *Severns* and the *Eichner* courts had taken the earlier, unwritten views of two nonautonomous patients as having probative value (and the *Colyer* court had agreed, in principle), the generally held view was that nonstatutory advance directives lacked legal authority. If the signers of such documents failed to persuade the decision makers in their cases to follow their requests, they were thought to become indistinguishable in the eyes of the law from other nonautonomous patients who had never expressed any preferences regarding the medical prolongation of life.

Two cases decided in 1984 signified a changing perspective regarding the legal status of nonstatutory directives. In a trial court decision in Arizona, the judge specifically mentioned the "Living Will" executed by Harriet Shulan while she was autonomous as a significant factor in his decision to grant the request of Annabelle Lurie, Shulan's daughter and attorney-in-fact, to have the nonautonomous, terminally ill patient removed from the ventilator that was sustaining her life against her previously expressed wishes.[25] Later that year the Florida Supreme Court issued its decision in the Francis Landy case (see Case 4.15), the first time any state supreme court had addressed the question of an advance directive's validity as a form of evidence in making a "substituted judgment" on the behalf of a nonautonomous patient. In the view of the Florida court, as we discussed in the previous chapter, a nonstatutory advance directive previously signed by a patient now permanently unconscious and terminally ill "would be persuasive evidence of that incompetent person's intention and it should be given great weight by the person or persons who substitute their judgment on behalf of the terminally ill incompetent."[26]

The following year two courts in two other states agreed that a nonstatutory advance directive could, depending on the facts in a case, represent important evidence concerning a previously competent patient's views on the merits of life-sustaining treatment. In the landmark *Conroy* decision, the New Jersey Supreme Court pointed out that even if advance directives are not legally binding apart from a legislative statute to that effect, they nevertheless "are relevant evidence of the patient's intent" in cases involving nonautonomous patients. Especially because such documents can demonstrate "a carefully considered position . . . that a person had maintained over a number of years," they can have considerable probative value in providing "clear evidence" of the patient's wishes. In this way, such documents can be used in meeting the "subjective test": abating treatment when "it is clear that the particular patient would have refused the treatment under the circumstances involved" in the case.[27]

The second 1985 case took place in New York. Although *Saunders* was a lower-court decision, it is important at least in part because it was issued in a state lacking natural death legislation. The case concerned the validity of a personalized directive formulated by a 70-year-old woman suffering from emphysema and lung cancer. The court, in ruling on the validity of the advance directive should the autonomous patient subsequently become nonautonomous, held that such a document can provide "clear and convincing evidence" of a patient's wishes to abate life-sustaining medical treatment.[28]

What, then, is the legal status of nonstatutory advance directives? At the very least, as indicated by these four court cases in different jurisdictions, nonstatutory forms are now widely regarded as representing important evidence for surrogates to use in making informed treatment-abatement decisions on the behalf of nonautonomous patients. In this respect, nonautonomous patients who executed advance directives while they were autonomous are much more likely to have their wishes carried out now than they would have been a few years ago. Moreover, any proxy or surrogate of a nonautonomous patient now confronted with an uncooperative physician who refuses to carry out the patient's requests can initiate court action to override the physician's view. Having taken this step (often a difficult step in terms of time, effort, money, and emotional stress), a proxy or surrogate can be reasonably sure that the court will follow these other courts in regarding the patient's advance directive as *important evidence of the patient's own thoughtful views* on treatment abatement—and, on the basis of that evidence, order treatment to be abated according to the previously autonomous patient's requests.

Beyond the role of nonstatutory advance directives as judicial evidence, their legal status depends on the states in which they are used. Such documents are clearly not legally binding on physicians apart from legislative action in the various states. Consequently, nonstatutory advance directives are not legally binding in states that do not yet have natural death acts (e.g., New Jersey, New York), nor are they legally binding in states having natural death acts that require the use of a specific statutory declaration form (e.g., California, Oregon). However, nonstatutory advance directives can be legally binding if they meet the requirements of the law (e.g., signed by two adult witnesses unrelated to the declarant) in states having natural death acts that permit variable declaration forms to be used (e.g., Maine, Virginia). We now turn to a discussion of these state statutes.

Planning in accordance with legislative statute

The emerging legal status of nonstatutory advance directives is a recent development in case law. Prior to the Arizona and Florida cases discussed in the previous section, the legal status of such planning documents was unknown for a very simple reason: no court had ever addressed the issue.[29] In the absence of such case law, nonstatutory advance directives were for years widely assumed to be without any legal authority.

Yet, as we have seen, numerous individuals in the post-*Quinlan* era were interested in planning for the possible circumstances of their own dying, hoping therby to avoid becoming "another Quinlan." Such persons in the immediate aftermath of *Quinlan* faced what appeared to be a moral and legal dilemma. If they hoped to avoid the judicial system by communicating their views on the technological prolongation of dying through an advance directive (the forms distributed by the Euthanasia Educational Council, the Catholic Hospital Association, and the American Protestant Hospital Association were available at the time) and subsequently lost the capacity to make decisions about their medical care, uncooperative physcians could simply disregard their attempts at moral persuasion without risking any legal penalties. Even if for some reason their cases ended up in court, the *Quinlan* decision indicated that any verbal comments (and, possibly, written statements) they made earlier while they were autonomous would lack sufficient probative value to have any bearing on the actual decision making about prolonging their lives with medical technology.

At the same time, the immediate aftermath of *Quinlan* was fraught with uncertainty for physicians responsible for the medical treatment of critically or terminally ill patients. Prior to the development of the case law we discussed in Chapters 3 and 4, the legal implications of abating treatment in such cases were simply not very clear. For physicians in 1976, at the beginning of the second phase of the ongoing debate over abating treatment, the prospect of deciding to discontinue life-sustaining treatment from some critically or terminally ill patients—especially when those patients lacked personal autonomy—suggested taking unnecessary legal risks. Having some autonomous patients present "Living Wills" or other advance directives in the general context of a claimed "right-to-die" only compounded the anxiety of physicians concerning the legality of withholding or withdrawing life-sustaining medical treatment.

One alternative, for patients and physicians, was to clarify at least some of the questions regarding the legality of abating treatment with critically or terminally ill patients by means of legislative statute. Why not facilitate the legal right of patients to refuse life-prolonging medical treatment by making advance directives legally binding under specified circumstances? Why not clarify some of the obligations and risks of physicians in treatment-abatement cases—at least in some cases—through legislative action?

Statutory alternatives

To the credit of Representative Barry Keene and his colleagues in the California legislature, California became the first state to enact a statutory version of an advance directive. Signed into law in September 1976, the California Natural Death Act permits terminally ill patients to sign a legally binding directive (14 or more days after being diagnosed as terminally ill by two physicians) stipulating that life-sustaining procedures be withheld or withdrawn so that the patients can "die naturally" apart from any "mechanical or other artificial means" of prolonging the moment of death; any physician who refuses to follow the signed directive or transfer a "qualified patient" to another physician can be charged with unprofessional conduct (such a charge can, theoretically, result in the suspension or revocation of a physician's license), but is not civilly or criminally liable for failing to effectuate the directive.

Unfortunately, the California law is much more restrictive than it was originally intended to be. Initial opposition to Keene's legislative bill by the California Conference of Catholic Health Facilities and ongoing opposition to the bill by the Pro-Life Council resulted in the bill's being amended five times in the assembly and four times in the senate. Because of this opposition and the compromises that were made to get the bill passed, the California law is limited to a small group of patients: those who execute or reexecute the directive 2 weeks or more after a terminal diagnosis, who can be said to face "imminent" death, and whose dying is being prolonged only by "mechanical" or "artificial" means.[30] The law does not apply to persons with a life expectancy greater than 5 years (the directive, when signed by a non-terminally ill person, is effective for only 5 years), pregnant women, patients who are critically ill but not terminally ill (e.g., patients who are permanently unconscious, like Karen Quinlan was), patients whose deaths are not imminent, patients who request to be killed, or patients receiving "natural" life-sustaining treatment. The various restrictions of the law, in fact, do more to protect physicians from liability than they help serve the interests of persons who want to do prospective planning for the circumstances of dying.

Supporters of the original legislative bill accepted many of the restrictive amendments, thinking that the amendments could be changed with "cleanup" legislation at a later time. Such changes have not proved possible: the California law retains its 1976 wording, largely because of effective pro-life lobbying since that time. Instead, what has happened is that the California Natural Death Act has, with all of its limitations, been used as a model law in several other states; moreover, the title of the California law has come to be used generically as the name for all state laws providing for statutory advance directives. The challenge confronting legislators in other states since 1976 has been that of simply adopting the California version of natural death legislation, with or without significant modifications, or taking on the harder task of trying to pass legislative statutes (almost always against pro-life lobbying and, frequently, lobbying by conservative religious groups) that will more effectively facilitate the prospective planning by individual citizens for the possibility of treatment abatement should such a need arise later in their lives.

Natural death acts

At the present time, 38 states and the District of Columbia have joined California in passing natural death legislation. Seven states passed laws in 1977, two additional states joined the list in 1979, 13 more states and the District of Columbia passed laws by the end of 1984, 13 states passed laws in 1985 alone, and 3 additional states followed suit in 1986. Of these laws, the legislative statutes passed in Idaho, Oregon, Texas, and Washington most closely followed the California law. No natural death act has been rescinded and, of the 40 laws, eight laws (those in New Mexico, North Carolina, Oregon, Texas, Georgia, Arkansas, Illinois, and Wisconsin) have subsequently been amended to make them less restrictive than the original versions.[31]

The official titles of these laws vary considerably, with a number of them being called "Natural Death Acts," others being called "Living Will Acts," others "Death with Dignity Acts," others "Right to Terminate Treatment Acts," and so on. No two of these legislative statutes are exactly alike, but some of them can be grouped together because of their similarities. For example, in addition to the group of statutes (in their original versions) most closely resembling the California law, three of the earlier laws (Kansas, Alabama, and the District of Columbia) resemble the "Medical Treatment Decision Act" advocated by the SRD, and three of the 1985 laws (Iowa, Maine, and Montana) contain provisions from the "Uniform Rights of the Terminally Ill Act" recommended in 1985 by the National Conference of Commissioners on Uniform State Laws, the NCCUSL (we will discuss these model statutes shortly).

These natural death acts share a number of common features, including three problematic ones for individuals interested in planning for the possibility of treatment abatement. First, most of the statutes (exceptions: New Mexico, Arkansas) limit treatment abatement to conditions of terminal illness, thereby failing to make statutory provisions for abating treatment in other circumstances of critical illness. Second, the majority of the statutes (nine laws are exceptions, to a varying degree) omit any procedures for abating treatment on the behalf of nonautonomous patients (comatose patients and terminally ill minors fall outside the provisions of the laws). Third, many of the newer laws (20 of the laws passed in 1984–1986) exclude or severely restrict technological feeding and hydration as life-sustaining procedures that may be abated, a compromise feature of the newer laws required by pro-life groups.

For a specific, state-by-state comparison of additional features of these statutes, see the Appendix. Some of the more common features are listed here.[32]

legal recognition of an adult's advance directive regarding treatment abatement
   in the event of a terminal condition

specification of the medical evidence (typically, diagnosis of a terminal condition by two physicians) necessary to "qualify" a person to make the requests contained in the advance directive

definition of relevant terms, with (1) "life-sustaining procedure" meaning either "artificial" treatments or treatments that only "prolong the dying process," and (2) "terminal condition" meaning either that death is "imminent" or that death is expected "within a relatively short time"

a declaration form (except in Arkansas, Delaware, and New Mexico) that must be precisely followed (in California, Georgia, Idaho, and Oregon) or "substantially" followed in the other states (most states permit personalized instructions and choice of a proxy)

specification of the procedures necessary for executing the declaration form (typically, the signatures of two adult witnesses)

specification that a declaration is effective until revoked (only California and Idaho still place a time limit on the directive)

easy revocation procedures in case a declarant has a change of mind regarding earlier requests for treatment abatement

specification (in most of the laws) that a patient's current wishes supersede the requests made in the declaration

provision of immunity from civil or criminal liability for physicians and other health care personnel who comply with a patient's advance directive

the requirement (in most states) that any physician unable to honor an advance directive transfer the patient to a physician who will

penalties for forging, intentionally destroying, or concealing the revocation of a patient's directive

an invalidation of the declaration (in 24 states) if the terminally ill patient is pregnant

specification (in all but 10 of the statutes) that the language and provisions of the statute cannot "impair or supersede" other existing rights and responsibilities related to abating treatment and

the stipulation that implementation of a qualified patient's directive does not constitute suicide or assisted suicide, nor does it affect the terms of the declarant's life insurance policy.

Two of the natural death acts stand out, in my judgment, as the best of the legislative efforts thus far; both of them offer lessons for legislators in other states who are interested in helping citizens plan for the possibility of treatment abatement. The Virginia Natural Death Act, signed into law in 1983, was carefully drafted by an interdisciplinary subcommittee chaired by Delegate Bernard Cohen and was supported by a number of diverse groups including the Virginia Medical Society, the Virginia Nurses Association, the Coalition of the Aging, the Catholic Diocese of Richmond, and the Episcopal Diocese of Virginia. This law, which is more comprehensive and more flexible than most natural death legislation, provides for the abatement of life-prolonging procedures for terminally ill patients in any of three categories: autonomous patients who at any time executed a written declaration signed by two witnesses, or made an oral declaration in the presence of a physician and two witnesses; nonautonomous patients who in a declaration made while autonomous previously designated a proxy to make medical decisions on their behalf; and nonautonomous patients who never executed an advance directive of any type. To protect patients in the third category, the law stipulates that the attending physician and at least one of several other persons (listed in order of priority) must agree on the merits of abating treatment in a given case before life-prolonging procedures may be withheld or withdrawn. The life-prolonging procedures that may be abated are defined as any medical treatment or intervention that (1) "utilizes mechanical or other artificial means to sustain, restore or supplant a spontaneous vital function" or are otherwise of "such a nature as to afford a patient no reasonable expectation of recovery from a terminal condition" and (2) serves "only to prolong the dying process" when administered to a patient in a terminal condition.[33]

Legislators in Texas apparently subscribe to the maxim that says, "If at first you don't succeed, try, try again." The original version of the Texas Natural Death Act, enacted in 1977, was patterned after the California law. The Texas law has been amended in three subsequent legislative sessions, thereby removing three restrictions of the 1977 law: the 14-day waiting period after the diagnosis of a terminal condition, the required use of the declaration form contained in the statute, and the 5-year limit to the document's effectiveness. As a consequence, the Texas law, as amended in 1985 with the leadership of Representative Bob Bush, now offers citizens of that state a much improved statutory mechanism for planning for the possibility of treatment abatement. The law now permits written or oral directives, authorizes the selection of a proxy, provides a legal mechanism for treatment-abatement decisions made on the behalf of nonautonomous patients who never executed an advance directive (including patients without guardians), and specifies the legal conditions under which a parent or legal guardian (or adult spouse) may execute a directive on the behalf of a terminally ill patient under the age of 18.[34]

For all of their virtues, the Virginia law and the Texas law (as amended in 1985) are still problematic. Both laws use ambiguous language in referring to death as being "imminent," both laws fail to have a provision accepting advance directives executed out of state, and both laws fail to impose *any* penalty (not even the charge of unprofessional conduct) on physicians who try to thwart the prospective planning of patients by (1) refusing to comply with their requests for treatment abatement and (2) failing to transfer them to physicians who will comply with such requests. In addition, the Virginia law lacks any provision for treatment abatement on the behalf of terminally ill minors, and the Texas law contains the increasingly prevalent statement invalidating an advance directive whenever an otherwise qualified declarant is pregnant.

Of these limitations, the one failing to impose any penalty on uncooperative physicians is the most serious. Of course, legislators interested in passing natural death legislation are much more likely to receive the support of a state medical society if a proposed law does not contain a provision whereby uncooperative physicians are civilly liable or at least can be charged with unprofessional conduct. Unfortunately, the support of a state medical society that is often crucial for the passage of a law can be purchased at too high a price: an unstated grant of immunity for physicians who, for whatever reason, choose to prevent a statutory advance directive from working the way it was intended by the legislators who wrote the law and the persons who executed their own versions of the directive.

Proposed statutes

Given the variability in natural death acts, the problematic features in many of the laws, and the fact that only six states (Arkansas, Arizona, Hawaii, Maine, Maryland, and Montana) recognize the validity of advance directives executed in other states, a need exists for greater uniformity among the states regarding the statutory basis on which citizens can plan for the possibility of treatment abatement. To meet this need, a number of individuals and groups have proposed model statues. Some of these proposals have been around for several years and have been discussed in the literature, but seem to have had limited impact on the shaping of public policy.[35] Other proposals have been influential in shaping some of the statutes that address the issue of treatment abatement (at least with terminally ill patients), and likely will remain influential over the next several years. Four such proposals stand out, for at least two reasons: the substantive content of the proposed statutes, and the significance of the organizations recommending these statutes as models to be adopted.

As mentioned earlier, the "Medical Treatment Decision Act" is a model statute recommended by the SRD. Originally drafted in a 1978 Legislative Services Project at the Yale Law School and revised by the SRD in 1984, this model statute has been influential in the development of at least three state laws. This proposed law is preferable to most of the 40 statutes currently in existence: it avoids the problematic language of "artificial" procedures and "imminent" death, points out that the execution of the declaration is not to be taken as an indication of the declarant's mental incompetency, does not require the use of the declaration form contained in the act, holds physicians civilly liable if they fail to comply with the declaration of a qualified patient, and (following the 1984 revision) specifically provides for the appointment of a proxy in case the declarant is incapable of personally making decisions about medical care during the terminal phase of life. Unfortunately, the proposed law is unduly narrow in that it is limited to adults, limited to persons with terminal conditions, and limited to the use of a written declaration for the purpose of communicating one's wishes regarding treatment abatement. Moreover, while the proposed law now provides for the appointment of a proxy, it fails to give any indication of the criteria that a proxy should use in making decisions on the behalf of a nonautonomous patient.[36]

The second proposed statute is the one developed by the NCCUSL. Drafted by a 12-member committee over a 2-year period and approved by the NCCUSL at its August 1985 meeting, the "Uniform Rights of the Terminally Ill Act" is an attempt to have a simple, uniform act that could, if adopted by the various states, bring desirable uniformity to natural death legislation. Thus far, at least three states have adopted some of the language and some of the provisions of the proposed statute. For states not yet having natural death legislation, and for state legislatures willing to consider amending current natural death legislation, the uniform act has much to offer: considerably clearer terminology than found in most of the 40 laws, the option of personalized instructions, no restrictions concerning the persons who may witness the signing of the declaration, the inclusion of artificial feeding and hydration as forms of life-sustaining treatment that may be withdrawn whenever such treatment serves only to prolong the process of dying without providing comfort care or the alleviation of pain, the provision of criminal liability (in a misdemeanor category) for physicians who willfully fail to comply with the law, and the acceptance of advance directives properly executed in other states. However, the intentionally limited scope of the uniform act means that it has no provisions for minors with terminal conditions, for critically ill adults without terminal conditions, for the appointment of a proxy, or for nonautonomous patients who never made a prior declaration concerning treatment abatement.[37]

Better than either of these statutory proposals, in many respects, is the model law developed by the Legal Advisers Committee of Concern for Dying. Entitled "The Right to Refuse Treatment: A Model Act," this statutory proposal is the work of an 11-member committee of legal scholars, chaired by George Annas, that attempted to move beyond the limitations of the early natural death legislation. In contrast to the SRD and the NCCUSL proposals, the CFD-sponsored model act contains no declaration form because "we believe the individual's wishes will be more likely to be set forth if their own words are used." To facilitate the development of personalized, legally binding directives, the CFD committee sets forth the desirable features of a legislative statute that would permit all functionally autonomous persons to communicate their preferences regarding treatment abatement by means of either a written or oral directive. Such a legislative statute would apply to all autonomous adults and mature minors—not merely terminally ill adults. It would permit the refusal of any medical procedure or treatment (including artificial feeding) and permit individuals to designate a proxy and set forth the criteria according to which the designated person should make decisions about treatment refusal on their behalf. In addition, it would require the continuation of palliative care for patients who have refused other forms of medical intervention, except when palliative care is also refused by a patient. Finally, the statute would contain provisions for civil administrative sanctions (such as professional disciplinary action) to be brought against physicians who refuse to comply with a patient's directive or transfer the patient to another physician.[38]

A quite different statutory proposal is made by the Hemlock Society. Formulated by Derek Humphry and three Los Angeles attorneys, "The Humane and Dignified Death Act" is intended to be a substantial modification and expansion of the California Natural Death Act. First proposed in 1986, the model statute consists of (1) a revised natural death act combined with provisions from the durable-power-of-attorney legislation in California and (2) an advance directive calling for voluntary euthanasia administered by a physician. The proposed law applies only to patients who are terminally ill, as evidenced by the certification by two physicians that an individual has a medical condition expected to result in death within 6 months. If enacted into law, this legislation would require that any terminally ill person wanting to communicate preferences about treatment abatement during the terminal phase of life sign a specifically worded directive to that effect; the declaration form also provides for the naming of a proxy to make health care decisions, should that become necessary. As an alternative, such a patient could sign a second declaration form calling for the attending physician not merely to abate treatment but to "administer aid in dying in a humane and dignified manner." By requesting "aid in dying," the patient would be calling for "any medical procedure that will swiftly, painlessly, and humanely terminate the life of the qualified patient." Such a provision, if enacted into law, would be unprecedented in the United States and constitute a major step beyond any of the current legislation or other statutory proposals. However, the possibility that this proposed statute will actually become law in California or any other state seems unlikely, especially since the bill as currently written imposes a legal obligation on some physicians to engage in the intentional killing of patients without adequate safeguards to protect against the abuses that could accompany such a public policy.[39]

The Hemlock Society and its political action arm, Americans Against Human Suffering (AAHS), tried but failed to get "The Humane and Dignified Death Act" on the November 1988 ballot in California. After a concerted effort to get the 320,000 signatures necessary in the petition drive (the campaign netted

129,764 signatures), Derek Humphry and Robert Risley (the president of AAHS) announced that they would mount another petition drive in 1990.[40]

Durable power of attorney

As indicated throughout this chapter, individuals who plan for the possibility of treatment abatement often choose to supplement their written or oral instructions with the selection of a proxy who can represent their interests and preferences if the time ever comes when they are unable to do so themselves. Persons using nonstatutory advance directives can now designate a proxy if they sign the "Living Will" distributed by CFD or the "Living Will Declaration" distributed by the SRD, since both organizations have added this provision to the current versions of their documents. Individuals preferring to formulate their own personalized advance directives can obviously also designate a proxy, if that planning alternative is important to them.

For persons using statutory advance directives, the possibility of designating a proxy to make health care decisions in the event of personal incapacity largely depends on the states in which such persons live. All 50 states, plus the District of Columbia, now have durable-power-of-attorney statutes that enable an individual (the "principal") to give another person (the "attorney-in-fact," or "agent") authority to carry out designated tasks on the principal's behalf. The power of attorney is "durable" whenever it stipulates that the agent's authority will continue even if the principal becomes nonautonomous or legally incompetent, in contrast to the more customary power of attorney that becomes inoperative if and when the principal becomes incapacitated.[41]

However, the applicability of these durable-power-of-attorney statutes to decisions about medical treatment is not as clear as it could be, especially in that an agent's decision to have treatment abated can sometimes result in the principal's death. Most of these statutes were enacted years before cases of nonautonomous patients became events of importance for the media, the courts, and concerned citizens. Even the "Uniform Durable Power of Attorney Act," the model act promulgated by the NCCUSL in 1979, failed to specify whether the agent's authority includes making decisions on the behalf of the principal regarding the continuation or the abatement of life-sustaining treatment.[42]

Nevertheless, since no court has prohibited the use of durable-power-of-attorney statutes for the purpose of making decisions about medical treatment, and since the New Jersey Supreme Court approved the use of such legislation in *Conroy,* at least some of the durable-power-of-attorney legislation in some states seems to permit decisions about treatment abatement made on the behalf of a nonautonomous patient by that patient's designated agent. To remove any doubt, a few states (e.g., Colorado, Pennsylvania) have recently amended their durable-power-of-attorney statutes to include the authority to make health care decisions.[43] In addition, the natural death legislation in most states permits citizens to designate a proxy, if they choose to do so as a part of their personalized instructions. Only four states (California, Georgia, Idaho, and Oregon) have natural death acts that preclude the naming of a proxy. At least 13 states, including Virginia and Texas, now have specific provisions in their natural death acts that enable citizens to designate a proxy who will have the authority to make decisions on their behalf regarding the abatement of life-sustaining medical treatment.

Five state legislatures and the District of Columbia have recently taken an alternative step by enacting laws specifically applying the durable power of attorney to health care decisions, including decisions concerning the withholding or the withdrawing of life-support systems. From 1985 to 1988, Maine, Rhode Island, Illinois, and Nevada enacted legislation authorizing a durable power of attorney for health care to refuse life-sustaining treatment.[44] The first state to have such a law was, again, California. In 1984 the California legislature, trying to remedy at least one of the problems with its natural death legislation, passed the "Keene Health Care Agent Act," which included a declaration form entitled "Durable Power of Attorney for Health Care."

The California law, already influential in the states just mentioned, will probably represent model legislation to be adopted in additional states not presently having specific provisions for the designation of a proxy to make decisions about treatment abatement. The declaration form contained in the California law can be signed by any adult resident of the state, whether healthy, sick, critically ill, or terminally ill. All the law requires is that the declarant is capable of voluntarily filling out the form, signing it, and having it (1) notarized, or (2) witnessed by two persons (one of whom cannot be related to the declarant), or (3) signed by a patient advocate or ombudsman (if the declarant is a nursing home patient). The document specifically warns that the designated agent (or agents) for health care will have the power, should the declarant become nonautonomous for any reason, "to consent to your doctor not giving treatment or stopping treatment which would keep you alive."

The heart of the California directive for health care decisions is a two-part declaration of one's desires concerning life-sustaining treatment. The first part consists of three formalized statements, one of which is to be initialed to indicate agreement: (1) a statement calling for the abatement of life-sustaining treatment "if the burdens of the treatment outweigh the expected benefits," (2) a statement calling for life-sustaining treatment "unless I am in a coma which my doctors reasonably believe to be irreversible," or (3) a statement calling for the *prolongation of life* "to the greatest extent possible without regard to my condition, the chances I have for recovery or the cost of the procedures" (the third statement was necessary for passage of the law as a compromise with pro-life advocates). The second part of the declaration offers the declarant an opportunity to add a personalized statement regarding treatment or treatment abatement. The entire document is revocable in several ways and is valid for a limited period of 7 years.[45]

Personal planning and public policy

Planning for the possibility of treatment abatement can be, and increasingly is, a matter of public policy. In the years since the passage of the 1976 natural death legislation in California, most states have adopted versions of the same legislation, all states have enacted durable-power-of-attorney legislation, and many states have made specific legislative moves to facilitate the right to refuse life-sustaining treatment on the part of citizens who may subsequently lose the capacity to make such a decision themselves. The recent trend in terms of public policy is thus unmistakeably clear: most citizens in the United States now have legal mechanisms for refusing unwanted medical treatment that were simply not available a few years ago.

Nevertheless, given the ongoing debate over the merits of abating treatment when patients' lives are at stake, any state legislature that in the near future considers a legislative bill affecting the legal right to refuse treatment can expect intense lobbying for and against the bill. Supporting a bill that enhances the right to refuse treatment will be the SRD, advocacy groups for older adults, probably CFD, and an assortment of religious groups. Opposing natural death legislation and any other effort to facilitate individual planning for treatment abatement will be national groups within the pro-life movement (the National Right to Life Committee, the American Life League, Americans United for Life, the Human Life Alliance, National Doctors for Life, The Human Life Center, etc.), state-based groups within the same movement (the California Pro-Life Council, Minnesota Citizens Concerned for Life, etc.), some individual physicians, and an assortment of religious groups. Increasingly unable to prevent natural death legislation and durable-power-of-attorney legislation from becoming state law, pro-life groups will probably continue to oppose such legislation by using one or more of the following strategies now being practiced: (1) the defeat of any amendments to existing natural death legislation that would make such laws more flexible and more easily used by more citizens, (2) the requirement of certain "compromises," the most common one since 1984 being the prohibition of abating artificial feeding and hydration, in order to pass laws facilitating the refusal of life-sustaining treatment, and/or (3) the inclusion of pro-life statements (as in the California law establishing the durable power of attorney for health care) or alternative pro-life declaration forms added to natural death legislation, such as the alternative form in the Indiana law that requests the use of all "life-prolonging procedures that would *extend* my life" in the event a terminal condition is diagnosed.[46]

What shape should public policy take regarding the planning by individual citizens for the possibility of treatment abatement? In my view, such planning needs to be facilitated to a much greater extent than is presently the case in most states. Rather than preventing citizens from having a legally binding planning mechanism, or restricting such a mechanism to a limited group of people, or forcing individuals to go to court to have their legal right of treatment refusal affirmed, state legislatures need to enact laws (or amend existing laws) so that concerned citizens can plan, if they choose to do so, for the possibility of treatment abatement in the event of critical or terminal illness. Such laws should

apply to *all* autonomous adults and mature minors,

permit the refusal of *any* medical treatment or intervention,

permit the designation of a proxy for any extended circumstances of nonautonomy,

allow for either written or oral (or videotaped) declarations,

require the continuation of palliative care (pain medication, oral feeding, hydration, suction, and hygienic care) unless specifically refused by a patient,

have adequate safeguards to protect patients from harm and responsible health care personnel from legal action (when following the law),

have enforceable civil and criminal penalties for physicians who intentionally disobey the law,

have criminal penalties for any person concealing, destroying, or misusing a patient's declaration form, and

provide a legal mechanism (trustworthy relatives or friends as surrogates, or an IEC for patients without guardians) for making decisions to abate treatment on the behalf of critically or terminally ill, nonatuonomous patients who failed to plan for the circumstances in which they are caught.

In addition to its public policy implications, planning for the possibility of treatment abatement can obviously also be, and usually is, an intensely personal enterprise. In the years since the Quinlan case, the number and types of planning alternatives available to reflective individuals have far exceeded the options available at that time. Yet, the availability of planning alternatives is certainly not the whole story, because of several problems connected with trying to do prospective planning in the present for possible circumstances in the future that are, simply put, not pleasant to think about.

Four of these problems need to be mentioned, however briefly. The first problem is that of motivation. Although figures given by CFD, the SRD, and the "Dear Abby" newspaper column indicate that approximately 10 million of the standardized versions of advance directives have been distributed, reliable figures on how many of these documents have actually been executed in the recommended manner are impossible to get. My guess is that only a relatively small percentage of persons receiving such documents actually sign them, and that the percentage of persons executing standardized advance directives is inversely related to both the level of formal education such persons have and their more specific knowledge concerning the uncertainties inherent to the practive of medicine. For persons trained to use words as precisely as possible, the vagueness of the terminology in standardized forms is problematic. Yet, even for persons who understand the benefits of personalized declarations, the task of motivating oneself to do personalized planning—and actually to commit words to paper, tape, or diskette—can be exceedingly difficult because of the "vagueness" of one's personal future as well as the frequent "vagueness" of medical decision making. Thus, to cite one example, 48 percent of the nurses and physicians responding to a recent survey on living wills expressed interest in signing such a document, but only 20 percent of them had actually signed an advance directive or made similar arrangements for the possible circumstances of their own dying.[47]

Another problem has to do with the goal being sought through prospective planning. Unfortunately, the publicity given to the right-to-die movement, the development of hospices, and the passage of natural death acts since 1976 has led many persons to have a romanticized view of what dying involves. Especially for persons not connected with the practice of medicine, the notion of "natural" death evokes images of comfort, tranquility, freedom from pain, and a general sense of peacefulness that may not actually occur when the time for them to die draws near. When such persons engage in prospective planning for the possible circumstances of dying, they are inclined to plan for a "dignified" death in which all forms of medical treatment—including palliative care—are somehow unnecessary. A more realistic approach to planning for the possibility of treatment abatement in the event of a terminal condition is to use personalized instructions, the designation of a proxy, and the help of a cooperative physician to achieve, in the words of Pabst Battin, the goal of "the least worst death" that is possible in the given circumstances.[48]

The third problem involves a fundamental tension inherent to most prospective planning about the possibility of abating treatment. Any person who tries to anticipate the likely circumstances of critical or terminal illness by signing a nonstatutory advance directive, formulating a personalized directive, or executing a statutory declaration form can reasonably be said to do so as an expression of personal autonomy. Not wanting to be victimized by a misplaced application of medical technology, such a person intends to exercise continued self-determination through the advance communication of personal preferences—to the point of influencing the decisions that will actually be made regarding his or her medical care in the event of critical or terminal illness. Yet, in so doing, the person who tries to anticipate the decisions that may have to be made in the future sometimes can cause problems for the family members and medical personnel who actually have to do the decision making in the future. In some instances, the conflict between (1) the circumstances anticipated by an autonomous person and (2) the circumstances that actually come to exist for that individual subsequent to the loss of autonomy is sufficiently great that, as Stuart Eisendrath and Albert Jonsen have pointed out, responsible decision makers interested in promoting the patient's best interests occasionally end up refusing to abide by the patient's previous refusal of medical treatment.[49]

The last problem to be discussed at this point concerns the implementation of plans drawn up by autonomous persons in advance of critical or terminal illness. Although it is certainly possible for responsible physicians (and relatives) to decide to override a nonautonomous patient's previously expressed wishes out of a concern to further that patient's best interests, a more common situation is that of physicians refusing to implement a nonautonomous patient's wishes for other kinds of reasons: a vitalistic personal philosophy, adherence to the "technological imperative," anxiety about legal liablity, or sheer obstinacy. In such situations, especially if transferring the patient to another physician's care is impractical, the prospective planning done by the patient in regard to the possibility of treatment abatement carries little moral or legal weight—unless the patient's proxy or relatives are willing to take the matter to court.

What advice can be given to individuals interested in planning for the possibility of treatment abatement? For what it's worth, my advice is to engage in a five-step approach to prospective planning. First, persons wanting to plan for the possibility of abating treatment should communicate instructions by formulating a personalized advance directive or signing the organizational form that most nearly reflects the value system and preferences of the signer. Second, such persons should designate a trusted relative or friend as a proxy in the event personal autonomy is lost, select an alternate proxy or two, and make sure that all of them understand the circumstances in which various modalities of life-sustaining treatment are to be abated. Third, these nonstatutory planning efforts should be supplemented by executing the forms permitted by the natural death legislation and durable-power-of-attorney legislation in the state of residence. By using statutory directives as a supplementary step, a legally binding directive (or two) is added to the possibly more personalized, but nonstatutory advance directive; any conflict in the provisions of the nonstatutory and statutory documents can be expected to be resolved, on the basis of *Corbett* (see Case 4.18), in favor of the constitutional right of privacy as reflected in the provisions of the nonstatutory directive. Fourth, prospective planning should, whenever possible, involve discussions with an appropriate primary physician so that, should the circumstances of a critical or terminal illness actually occur, a plan of treatment reflective of the patient's personal preferences will be more likely to be carried out. Finally, these four planning steps should be made known to family members and close friends not selected as the proxy, so that multiple persons will know the importance placed on setting ethical and legal limits to the medical prolongation of life.

Notes

1. This quotation is taken from Concern for Dying's (CFD) "Living Will" (1984 version).
2. This quotation comes from the National Conference of Commissioners on Uniform State Laws, "Uniform Rights of the Terminally Ill Act" (August 1985).
3. "Optimum Care for Hopelessly Ill Patients: A Report of the Critical Care Committee of the Massachusetts General Hospital," *The New England Journal of Medicine* 295 (August 12, 1976): 362–64.
4. Severns v. Wilmington Medical Center, Inc., 421 A.2d 1334, 1344 (Del. 1980); and In re Severns, 425 A.2d 156, 158 (Del. Ch. 1980).
5. Leach v. Akron General Medical Center, 68 Ohio Misc. 1, 22 Ohio Ops.3d 49, 51, 426 N.E.2d 809 (Com. Pl. 1980).
6. Eichner v. Dillon, 52 N.Y.2d 363, 438 N.Y.S.2d 266, 420 N.E.2d 64 (1981).
7. Barber v. Superior Court, 147 Cal.App.3d 1006, 195 Cal.Rptr. 484, 493 (1983).
8. Brophy v. New England Sinai Hospital, Inc., 398 Mass. 417, 497 N.E.2d 626, 632 (1986). In addition to *Leach, Eichner,* and *Brophy,* another case involved the enforcement of an oral directive made by a patient when previously autonomous. See In re Lydia E. Hall Hospital, 116 Misc.2d 477, 455 N.Y.S.2d 706 (Sup. Ct. 1982).
9. Bartling v. Superior Court, 163 Cal.App.3d 186, 209 Cal.Rptr. 220 (1984).
10. See the Hastings Center Project, *Guidelines on the Termination of Life-Sustaining Treatment and the Care of the Dying* (Briarcliff Manor, N.Y.: The Hastings Center, 1987).
11. CFD, *The Living Will and Advance Directives: A Legal Guide to Treatment Decisions* (New York: CFD, 1986).
12. CFD, "Newsletter," vol. 11 (Summer, 1985), p. 5.
13. Corbett v. D'Alessandro, 487 So.2d 368 (Fla. Dist. Ct. App.), *review denied,* 492 So.2d 1331 (Fla. 1986); In re Jobes, 108 N.J. 394, 529 A.2d 434 (1987); Brophy, *supra,* 497 N.E.2d 626 (1986); In re Peter, 108 N.J. 365, 529 A.2d 419 (1987); McVey v. Englewood Hospital Association (Palermo), 216 N.J. Super. 502, 524 A.2d 450 (Super. Ct. App. Div.), *cert. denied,* 108 N.J. 182, 528 A.2d 12 (1987); Rasmussen v. Fleming, 741 P.2d 674 (Ariz. 1987); In re Requena, 213 N.J. Super. 475, 517 A.2d 886 (Super. Ct. Ch. Div.), *aff'd,* 213 N.J. Super. 443, 517 A.2d 869 (Super. Ct. App. Div. 1986); In re Gardner, 534 A.2d 947 (Maine 1987); Delio v. Westchester County Medical Center, 129 A.D.2d 1, 516 N.Y.S.2d 677 (App. Div. 2d Dep't 1987); In re Farrell, 108 N.J. 335, 529 A.2d 404 (1987); and In re Drabick, 200 Cal.App.3d 185, 245 Cal.Rptr. 840 (1988).
14. Derek Humphry and Ann Wickett, *The Right to Die: Understanding Euthanasia* (New York: Harper & Row, 1986).
15. See the President's Commission, *Deciding to Forego Life-Sustaining Treatment* (Washington, D.C.: U.S. Government Printing Office, 1983), p. 139.
16. Ronald L. Stephens, " 'Do Not Resuscitate' Orders: Ensuring the Patient's Participation," *Journal of the American Medical Association* 255 (January 10, 1986): 240–41.
17. This statement is taken from a personalized advance directive in the files of CFD.
18. This statement is taken from another personalized advance directive in the files of CFD.

19. Ernest Morgan's "An Alternative Living Will" is published in the tenth edition of his *A. Manual of Death Education and Simple Burial* (Burnsville, N.C.: Celo Press, 1984), p. 109.

20. This passage appears in an anonymous directive entitled "On Medical Intervention," which is printed in Walter Modell, "A 'Will' to Live," *The New England Journal of Medicine* 290 (April 18, 1974): 907–8.

21. This statement appears in one of the personalized advance directives in the files of CFD.

22. This statement is in an advance directive in the files of CFD.

23. Sissela Bok, "Personal Directions for Care at the End of Life," *The New England Journal of Medicine* 295 (August 12, 1976): 367–69.

24. This personalized directive is entitled "Declaration of Robert M. Veatch" and dated October 2, 1985.

25. Lurie v. Samaritan Health Service, No. C510198 (Ariz. Super. Ct. Mariopa Co., March 24, 1984).

26. John F. Kennedy Memorial Hospital, Inc. v. Bludworth, 452 So.2d 921, 926 (Fla. 1984).

27. In re Conroy, 98 N.J. 321, 486 A.2d 1209, 1229, 1230 (1985).

28. Saunders v. State, 129 Misc.2d 45, 492 N.Y.S.2d 510 (1985).

29. For legal commentary on nonstatutory advance directives, see Luis Kutner, "Due Process of Euthanasia: The Living Will, a Proposal," *Indiana Law Journal* 44 (1969): 539–54; Michael T. Sullivan, "The Dying Person—His Plight and His Right," *New England Law Review* 8 (1973): 197–216; John Strand, "The 'Living Will:' The Right to Death with Dignity?" *Case Western Reserve Law Review* 26 (1976): 485–526; Note, "Informed Consent and the Dying Patient," *Yale Law Journal* 83 (1974): 1632–64; James Turner, "Living Wills—Need for Legal Recognition," *West Virginia Law Review* 78 (1976): 370–80; Sidney D. Rosoff, "Living Wills and Natural Death Acts," in A. Edward Doudera and J. Douglas Peters, eds., *Legal and Ethical Aspects of Treating Critically and Terminally Ill Patients* (Ann Arbor, Mich.: Health Administration Press, 1982), pp. 186–193; President's Commission, *Deciding to Forego,* pp. 136–40; John A. Robertson, *The Right of the Critically Ill* (Cambridge, Mass.: Ballinger, 1983), pp. 97–115; Nancy Finnel, "Death with Dignity: The Living Will," *Critical Care Monitor* 3 (January–February 1983): 2–3; Michael Gilfix and Thomas A. Raffin, "Withholding or Withdrawing Extraordinary Life Support," *The Western Journal of Medicine* 141 (September 1984): 387–94; and Ron M. Landsman, "Terminating Food and Water: Emerging Legal Rules," in Joanne Lynn, ed., *By No Extraordinary Means: The Choice to Forego Life-Sustaining Food and Water* (Bloomington, Ind.: Indiana University Press, 1986), pp. 135–49.

30. California Natural Death Act, Calif. Health and Safety Code §§ 7185–95 (1976). For commentary and criticism, see Michael Garland, "Politics, Legislation, and Natural Death," *Hastings Center Report* 6 (October 1976): 5–6; and Karen Lebacqz, "On 'Natural Death,'" *Hastings Center Report* 7 (April 1977): 14. Additional criticism of the California law is found in the President's Commission, *Deciding to Forego,* pp. 142–44.

31. This information is taken from four publications of the Society for the Right to Die (SRD): *1981 Handbook* (New York: SRD, 1981), *Handbook of Living Will Laws*

1981–1984 (New York: SRD, 1984), *Handbook of 1985 Living Will Laws* (New York: SRD, 1986), and *Handbook of Living Will Laws* (New York: SRD, 1987).

32. For more detailed information about the common features of these laws, see SRD, *The Physician and the Hopelessly Ill Patient* (New York: SRD, 1985), pp. 39–41.

33. Virginia Natural Death Act, Va. Code §§54-325.8:1 to 54-325.8:13.

34. Texas Natural Death Act, Tex. Stat. Ann. Art. 4590h (1977, amend. 1979, 1983, 1985).

35. For example, see Robert M. Veatch, *Death, Dying, and the Biological Revolution* (New Haven, Conn.: Yale University Press, 1976), pp. 198–203; Germain Grisez and Joseph M. Boyle, Jr., *Life and Death with Liberty and Justice: A Contribution to the Euthanasia Debate* (Notre Dame, Ind.: University of Notre Dame Press, 1979), pp. 109–20; Arnold S. Relman, "Michigan's Sensible 'Living Will,'" *The New England Journal of Medicine* 300 (May 31, 1979): 270–71; and the President's Commission, *Deciding to Forego*, pp. 147–53, 423–37.

36. The text of the "Medical Treatment Decision Act" is contained in SRD, *Handbook of Living Will Laws 1981–1984*, pp. 35–38.

37. The text of the "Uniform Rights of the Terminally Ill Act" is contained in the SRD, *Handbook of 1985 Living Will Laws*, pp. 35–47.

38. Legal Advisers Committee of CFD, "The Right to Refuse Treatment: A Model Act," *American Journal of Public Health* 73 (August 1983): 918–21.

39. The text of "The Humane and Dignified Death Act" is distributed by the Hemlock Society.

40. Hemlock Society, "Hemlock Quarterly," no. 32 (July 1988), p. 1.

41. CFD, *The Living Will and Advance Directives*, p. 23.

42. The "Uniform Durable Power of Attorney Act" is printed in the President's Commission, *Deciding to Forego*, pp. 391–92. Also printed in the President's Commission report are the texts of the 42 durable-power-of-attorney statutes in existence at the time of the report. See pp. 393–422 of the report.

43. See the report of the Special Committee on Biomedical Ethics, *Values in Conflict: Resolving Ethical Issues in Hospital Care* (Chicago: American Hospital Association, 1985), p. 75.

44. California Durable Power of Attorney for Health Care Act, Cal. Civ. Code §§ 2430-2513 (1984, 1985); Maine Power of Attorney Act, Me. Rev. Stat. Ann. Tit. 18-A, §§ 5-501, 5-502 (1985); Rhode Island Health Care Power of Attorney Act, R.I. Gen. Laws §§ 23-4.10-1 to 23-4.10-2 (1986); District of Columbia Durable Power of Attorney Act, D.C. Code Ann. §§ 21-2081 to 21-2085 (1987); Illinois Power of Attorney Act, Ill. Rev. Stat. Ch. 110½, §§ 804-1 to 804-12 (1987); and Nevada Durable Power of Attorney for Health Care Decisions Act, 1987 Nev. Stat. 396 (1987). These citations come from the SRD, *Physician and the Hopelessly Ill Patient* (1988 suppl.), p. 37.

45. California Durable Power of Attorney for Health Care Act, Cal. Civ. Code §§ 2410–43.

46. Indiana Living Wills and Life-Prolonging Procedures Act, Ind. Code § 16-8-11 (1985). A few nonstatutory advance directives have also been formulated to request *maximum* treatment regardless of a patient's diagnosis or prognosis. For example, see Marshall B. Kapp, "Response to the Living Will Furor: Directives for Maximum Care," *The American Journal of Medicine* 72 (June 1982): 855–59.

47. Gene Cranston Anderson et al., "Living Wills: Do Nurses and Physicians Have Them?" *American Journal of Nursing* 86 (March 1986): 271–75.
48. M. Pabst Battin, "The Least Worst Death," *Hastings Center Report* 13 (April 1983): 13–16.
49. Stuart J. Eisendrath and Albert R. Jonsen, "The Living Will: Help or Hindrance?" *Journal of the American Medical Association* 249 (April 15, 1983): 2054–58.

6

Options among Ethicists

There are medically indicated treatments (these used to be called "ordinary") that a competent conscious patient has no moral right to refuse, just as no one has a moral right deliberately to ruin his health. Treatment refusal is a relative right, contrary to what is believed today by those who would reduce medical ethics to patient autonomy and a "right to die."

Paul Ramsey, Ph.D.[1]

There is nothing wrong with being the cause of someone's death if his death is, all things considered, a good thing. And if his death is *not* a good thing, then *no* form of euthanasia, active or passive, is justified. So . . . we see that the two kinds of euthanasia stand or fall together.

James Rachels, Ph.D.[2]

As we have seen in the last three chapters, the law has addressed the issue of treatment abatement with critically ill patients in a number of ways. The common-law tradition, constitutional law at the state and federal levels, recent case law in state and federal courts, and statutes enacted since 1976 by the majority of the state legislatures have combined to set legal limits on the medical prolongation of life. The law, as interpreted by judges in 25 states and formulated by legislators in the 40 jurisdictions having natural death acts, has emphasized the right of autonomous patients to refuse medical treatment and has established procedures according to which proxies or surrogates can refuse life-sustaining treatment on the behalf of nonautonomous patients. In this manner, the law has tried to protect critically and terminally ill patients from being overtreated by physicians having an unprecedented array of life-prolonging technologies at their disposal. In so doing, the law has enabled such patients to have life-sustaining treatments withheld, decelerated, or withdrawn in most instances when the treatments are unwanted by the patient or regarded as contrary to the patient's best interests.

The law, especially in the court decisions and legislative statutes that have come about in the post-*Quinlan* era, has also tried to protect critically and terminally ill patients from being undertreated or intentionally killed by physicians and other health care professionals. Most of the court decisions have therefore addressed a number of substantive and procedural questions related to

214

the state's interests in preserving individual lives, the possible characterization of treatment abatement as suicide, the possible liability of physicians in such cases to civil and/or criminal penalties, the applicability of major ethical distinctions to the case at bar, and the need for procedural safeguards for critically ill patients whenever life-sustaining treatments are withheld, decelerated, or withdrawn. Most natural death acts have also tried to protect "qualified patients" from having their lives wrongfully terminated by including one or more of the following provisions in the state law: a requirement that the declaration form be witnessed by two adults unrelated to the declarant, a requirement that nutrition and hydration not be abated, alternative ways for a declarant to revoke the declaration, a prohibition of falsifying or forging a directive, and a prohibition of "mercy killing."

As important as these developments are, the law is not the only force in modern society—nor is it the first—to try to protect critically ill patients from the dual dangers of overtreatment and undertreatment. As Alexander Capron points out, some of the distinctions that play pivotal roles in current judicial opinions in treatment-abatement cases are actually "borrowed lessons" relying on traditional concepts and arguments developed by philosophers and theologians working in the field of ethics.[3]

In fact, all persons—ethicists, physicians, attorneys, judges, political activists in pro-life groups, participants in the right-to-die movement, and others—who currently address the issue of treatment abatement and the related issues of suicide and euthanasia as *ethical* issues (not medical or legal issues only) are inheritors of a centuries-old Western intellectual tradition that continues to influence contemporary opinion and decision making. That intellectual heritage, composed of numerous philosophical perspectives and three major religious traditions, contains periodic statements regarding the morality of suicide, intentional killing, and exceptions to the duty of prolonging one's life that were formulated long before the development of modern medical technology. For example, Plato, Aristotle, Seneca, Augustine, Thomas Aquinas, David Hume, Immanuel Kant, and other philosophers addressed the morality of suicide, with the majority of these philosophers concluding that intentional acts of self-destruction cannot be justified. Western religious traditions joined in the prohibition of the intentional killing of oneself or others by private citizens, with Jewish scholars appealing to passages in the Torah (Genesis 9:6, Exodus 20:13, Deuteronomy 32:39, etc.) and the Babylonian Talmud (Shabbat 151b), Christian theologians citing selected biblical passages (usually Exodus 20:13 and Deuteronomy 32:39), and Muslim theologians emphasizing the Quran (sura 3:139) as well as the traditional view of Muhammad's refusal to bury anyone who had committed suicide.[4]

Given this general, but neither unanimous nor uniform prohibition of intentionally killing oneself or others (such killing was often regarded as tragically necessary in self-defense, participation in just wars, or the carrying out of certain official positions in society), numbers of Jewish scholars and Christian theologians deliberated over the centuries regarding possible circumstances in which the deaths of individuals could justifiably be accelerated in ways other than intentional killing. In particular, rabbinic scholars and Christian theologians— especially those in the Roman Catholic tradition—seriously considered (1) exceptions to the moral duty (understood in a theistic context) of prolonging one's life and (2) circumstances in which the unintended hastening of another's death might be justifiable.

For rabbinic scholars, neither of these alternatives was considered permissible. In developing this orthodox Jewish view, rabbis put forth a number of classical examples that now seem quaint and simplistic to persons not belonging to Orthodox Judaism. Nevertheless, the examples serve to illustrate the fundamental importance placed on the preservation of individual human lives by Orthodox Jews. For instance, questions were raised regarding the obligation of a Jew who on the Sabbath found a person buried alive under a house with sufficiently serious injuries that the recovery of health, should the person be pulled from the debris, was virtually impossible. Other questions were raised regarding permissible conduct with a man who had been moribund for a long time, when it was possible that his death was somehow being delayed by the pillow under his head, or the keys of the synagogue that were under his head, or the noise being made by a nearby woodchopper. In the former case, rabbinic opinion was that the Sabbath should be violated if it meant saving a person's life for even an hour, for in that hour the individual might repent and utter a confession. In the second case, rabbinic opinion was that removing the pillow or the keys from beneath the patient's head was forbidden, because even the slightest movement of a dying person's body that hastens death is equivalent to an act of murder. However, the removal of the noisy woodchopper was permissible, because that action was simply the removal of an extraneous factor interfering with the natural deterioration of body functions that results in death.[5]

In contrast, Roman Catholic moral theologians concluded that the prolongation of human life was not an absolute duty. While maintaining that the intentional (or direct) killing of oneself or another person was forbidden on moral grounds, these theologians developed (1) the ordinary/extraordinary distinction as a justifying reason for exceptions to the duty of prolonging life and (2) the rule of double effect as a justifying reason for acts of foreseen, but unintended (or indirect) killing.

The distinction between ordinary and extraordinary means of prolonging life goes back to the sixteenth century. At that time, before the development of antisepsis and anesthesia, surgery was almost always an excruciating ordeal involving considerable pain and disfigurement. In fact, surgical procedures, typically amputations, were often compared with torture. Consequently, questions arose concerning whether a patient's refusal of an amputation or any other very painful procedure should be forbidden by the Church on the grounds that the refusal of possibly life-prolonging treatment was actually suicide, and thus immoral.

Two Spanish theologians maintained that very painful treatments went beyond a reasonable understanding of the duty to prolong one's life. Domingo Soto (1494–1560) argued that religious superiors could require their subjects to use medicine that could be taken without too much difficulty, but could not require them to undergo excruciating pain because nobody is obligated to go to such lengths to prolong life. In 1595 Domingo Báñez (1528–1604) introduced the terms *ordinary* and *extraordinary* into the ongoing discussion about the preservation of life. For him, Christians and other human beings can reasonably be expected to prolong their lives by taking nourishment and medicine "common to all" and by enduring some pain and suffering connected with medical treatment, but nobody can reasonably be expected to endure horrible pain or anguish involved in surgical procedures or to undertake treatments—even lifesaving measures—that are disproportionate to one's condition or state in life.[6]

The following century, during the Spanish Inquisition, questions arose regarding the obligation of a condemned heretic to prolong his or her life. Suppose, so the hypothetical case went, a man was condemned to be burned at the stake for his heretical views (the infamous *auto-da-fé*), the fire was started, the man asked for a goblet of water as the fire began to lick at his feet, and the merciful executioner gave him some water. Was a man in such a situation morally obligated to try to prolong his life by pouring the water on the fire and thus momentarily decreasing the flames? No, according to the theological opinion at the time, because the goblet of water would be an "extraordinary" means of prolonging life in that it would provide no real benefit to the condemned man.[7]

Of course, by the twentieth century surgical procedures had advanced far beyond amputations, life-prolonging treatments did not necessarily involve great pain, and the deplorable practices of the Inquisition were no longer in vogue. Nevertheless, until very recently the ordinary/extraordinary distinction unquestionably continued to be influential in the decisions made in clinical settings about treatment abatement, official policy statements by medical organizations (e.g., the 1973 statement by the A.M.A. House of Delegates, to which we shall return), and treatment-abatement cases that ended up in court.

The ongoing influence of the distinction in this century is largely due to the work of several Roman Catholic moral theologians during the middle decades of the century: Charles McFadden, Gerald Kelly, Edwin Healy, and Thomas O'Donnell.[8] McFadden, whose widely used textbook on medical ethics went through a title change and six editions between 1949 and 1967, passed on the tradition that permitted "extraordinary" means of prolonging life to be withheld or withdrawn. For him, the determination of which means of prolonging life were "ordinary" and which were "extraordinary" required assessments of several factors related to a critically ill patient's medical condition and life situation: reasonable hope of success, excessive pain, possibility of scandal, spiritual good, and expense.[9]

Gerald Kelly, probably the foremost medical ethicist of his time, contributed to the importance placed on the ordinary/extraordinary distinction through his numerous articles and his role in helping formulate the "Ethical and Religious Directives for Catholic Hospitals," published by the Catholic Hospital Association in 1949. His interpretation of the distinction remains one of the most widely quoted statements on any subject in biomedical ethics since it was published in 1951:

Ordinary means are all medicines, treatments, and operations, which offer a reasonable hope of benefit and which can be obtained and used without excessive expense, pain, or other inconvenience. Extraordinary means are all medicines, treatments, and operations, which cannot be obtained or used without excessive expense, pain, or other inconvenience, or which, if used, would not offer a reasonable hope of benefit.[10]

The rule of double effect, more easily criticized and less widely used than the ordinary/extraordinary distinction, has a long history and still influences the thinking of some physicians and ethicists as they consider circumstances in which the deaths of some suffering, critically ill patients can justifiably be hastened.[11] For example, the current "Ethical and Religious Directives for Catholic Health Facilities" (an updated and revised version of the 1949 directives) states that "it is not euthanasia to give a dying person sedatives and analgesics for the alleviation of pain, when such a measure is judged necessary, even though they may deprive the patient of the use of reason, or shorten his life."[12]

The basic premises of the rule of double effect go back to Thomas Aquinas. Believing that the intentional killing of oneself or others is always wrong, Aquinas acknowledged that Christians and other persons are occasionally confronted by unjust aggressors and have to consider the morality of self-defense. What is one to do in such a situation if one believes the intentional killing of another person to be an immoral act? In his analysis of this situation of moral conflict, Aquinas pointed out that a single act can have two "effects," with only one of the effects or consequences being intended by the moral agent. The other effect or consequence is "apart from the intention," but can be foreseen as inextricably linked with the intended consequence if the act is done. In such a situation, the morality of an act is determined by "that which is intended," not by "that which is apart from the intention." Thus, when one is confronted by an unjust aggressor (or aggressors), killing in self-defense is regrettable but morally permissible if necessary to save one's life: the intention is to preserve one's own life (the good effect), whereas the death of the aggressor is merely foreseen as an unintended or indirect consequence (the evil effect) of the act.[13]

Since Aquinas, the rule of double effect has been expanded, revised, updated, interpreted as having three or four necessary conditions, reduced to having a single emphasis, and applied to a range of tragic situations by various philosophers and theologians subscribing to the theory. The more common applications have included justifying the unintended killing of a fetus in a "therapeutic" abortion (the death of the fetus is the indirect result of an effort to save the pregnant woman's life when she has an ectopic pregnancy or a cancerous uterus), the unintended killing of civilians in a just war (their deaths are the indirect result of an attack on a legitimate military target), and one's own unintended death in the pursuit of a noble cause (when death was foreseen as a necessary risk in taking on the cause, the resulting death is not considered a suicide).

The number of conditions necessary for the rule, the interpretation of the conditions, and the numerical order of the conditions were never unanimously agreed on by philosophers and theologians using the theory. However, Jean Pierre Gury (1801–1866), a French Jesuit, is credited with having formulated the modern version of the rule, with four specified conditions. In this century, Gerald Kelly's interpretation of the four necessary conditions is widely accepted as the correct version of the rule of double effect: (1) the action in itself, considered independent of its effects, must not be morally evil; (2) the evil effect cannot be the means of producing the good effect; (3) the evil effect is sincerely not intended by the agent, but only foreseen and tolerated; and (4) there must be a proportionate reason for performing the action that outweighs the action's unintended evil consequences.[14]

As illustrated by the earlier CHA directive, the rule of double effect has been and continues to be used as a theoretical framework of justification by some physicians and ethicists for the hastening of some patients' deaths. For such acts of killing to be justified, the four conditions of the rule must be met:

1. The action in itself (e.g., the administration of graduated doses of morphine to relieve a critically ill patient's pain) has to be regarded as good or at least morally indifferent.
2. The evil effect (in this instance, the patient's death) cannot be causally linked or precede in time the production of the good effect (relief of the patient's pain).
3. The patient's death can only be foreseen and permitted as a possible consequence of increased amounts of the analgesic, but cannot be intended by the agent (the variability of patients in terms of pain perception, pain toleration, and response to pain medication adds an element of unpredictability to the agent's foresight in this situation that is not always present in double-effect situations).
4. There must be a proportionality between good and evil effects, in the sense of a relationship of benefit to harm for the patient that must, on balance, be

regarded as beneficial to the patient. In this manner, the killing of a suffering, critically ill patient is permissible because it does not fall under the prohibition of intentional (or direct) killing. To use the wording of the CHA directive, such indirect killing "is not euthanasia."

The upshot of this theoretical background is that for centuries, up through Gerald Kelly's publications in the early 1950s, most philosophers and theologians were in general agreement that acts of intentional killing—inside clinical settings as well as outside—were morally prohibited. With the exception of a few notable dissenters (especially Hume, followed in the nineteenth century by Jeremy Bentham and John Stuart Mill), the dominant philosophical and theological opinion emphasized the moral obligation of prolonging individual human lives and the moral impermissibility of suicide, assisted suicide, and euthanasia. However, many of the philosophers and theologians, particularly those in the Roman Catholic tradition, accepted one or both of the theories just described: the ordinary/ extraordinary distinction being used to justify the abatement of life-prolonging treatments in certain circumstances, and the rule of double effect being used to justify acts of indirect killing whenever such killing was regarded as "apart from the intention" of relieving the suffering of some patients through the administration of pain medications.

The first important modern dissent from these views was put forth by Joseph Fletcher with the publication of his *Morals and Medicine* in 1954. Writing from his perspective as a Protestant professor of theological ethics and hoping that his views were "within the range and provision of Christian theology," but using some of the humanistic and utilitarian themes that would characterize his later works, Fletcher challenged the dominant view that intentional killing in clinical contexts is always wrong. For him, at the time a director of the Euthanasia Society of America, the traditional philosophical and theological arguments against suicide and voluntary euthanasia simply did not work. Rejecting the classical arguments of Augustine and Aquinas, dismissing 10 of the more common objections to voluntary euthanasia, and using the example of Jonathan Swift's 8-year ordeal of agonized suffering and dying to emphasize the need for voluntary euthanasia, he defended the morality of voluntary euthanasia as a necessary part of a "freedom ethic" and called for the passage of the Euthanasia Society's model bill for the legalization of voluntary euthanasia for terminally ill, adult patients requesting a merciful end to their suffering.[15]

Fletcher's published views provoked a storm of protest from Catholic theologians in the United States. Gerald Kelly and several other Catholic writers said Fletcher's book came under canon 1399 (an ecclesiastical law forbidding Catholics from reading certain books), and thus should not be read by Catholics without permission.[16] Even one of the more sympathetic Catholic reviewers stated that the book "contains vicious errors which forbid its being placed on open library shelves."[17]

First phase of the debate about abating treatment: 1957–1975

That, simply put, is the philosophical and theological background to Pope Pius XII's famous allocution in 1957 regarding the moral limits to the prolongation of life. When Bruno Haid initiated the first phase of the contemporary debate over treatment abatement (see Chapter 1), he gave Pius XII an opportunity to validate and update the Western intellectual tradition regarding the morality of forgoing life-prolonging treatment when such treatment is unwanted, seems to be futile, and/or fails to offer a proportionate balance of benefits to burdens to the patient.

In addressing the questions put to him by Dr. Haid, Pius XII, who (in Albert Jonsen's words) "has never been accused of being a liberal," affirmed the importance of the ordinary/extraordinary distinction.[18] Pointing out that "natural reason and Christian morals" agree that patients have a duty "to take the necessary treatment for the preservation of life and health," the Pope proceeded to declare: "Normally one is held to use only ordinary means—according to circumstances of persons, places, times and culture—that is to say, means that do not involve any grave burden for oneself or another." He went on to state, specifically in regard to the withholding or withdrawing of mechanical ventilation, that such acts of treatment abatement do not constitute cases of "direct disposal of the life of the patient, nor of euthanasia in any way," for any direct causation of death "would never be licit."[19]

In one sense, this papal address marked the end of a long period during the first part of this century in which serious reflection about the ethics of death and dying was largely the enterprise of Catholic moral theologians. For the most part, they updated and revised the dominant views of the past: the sanctity of human life, the immorality of intentional killing, the general obligation to prolong individual lives, the ordinary/extraordinary distinction (sometimes using outmoded examples that did not square with the advances of twentieth-century medicine), the resulting distinction between killing and letting die, and the rule of double effect. Meanwhile, with the exception of Fletcher, the few Protestant theologians addressing ethical issues in medicine before 1957 tended to repeat the traditional views regarding the sanctity of human life, the moral obligation of prolonging individual lives, and the moral impermissibility of suicide and euthanasia (usually without using the distinctions common to Catholic thinkers). Philosophers without professional religious affiliations devoted their energies to theoretical matters generally lacking practical import, with virtually no one addressing the philosophical issues connected with life-threatening illness, dying, and death.

In another sense, the papal address signaled the beginning of a new era in which the ethics of death and dying would be addressed more than ever before, with ethicists and other reflective persons following Haid in raising serious questions about the need for moral and legal limits to the medical prolongation of life. However, in the post-1957 era the questions would neither be addressed to the Pope nor would they be bound by the traditional views of philosophers and theologians in earlier historical periods. Rather, the new era would see an unprecedented, wide-open, ongoing debate about the morality and legality of treatment abatement and the related issues of suicide and euthanasia in the light of new developments in medicine, law, and other spheres of life.

The first phase of the debate was marked by numerous developments that influenced the morality, legality, and medical practice of treatment abatement. Some of the developments, as we have seen in earlier chapters, had to do with advances in medical technology, surgery, biochemistry, resuscitation methods, the medical administration of nutrients, intensive care, and medical institutions that earlier generations would not have imagined possible. Other developments took place in law, beginning with widely read publications in the late 1950s by Glanville Williams and Yale Kamisar concerning the merits of legalizing euthanasia and followed by significant articles on treatment abatement by George Fletcher (1967) and Norman Cantor (1973), a major effort to get a voluntary euthanasia bill passed by the British Parliament (1969), debates in several state legislatures in the 1960s and early 1970s concerning the possible legalization of euthanasia, several important legal cases involving treatment abatement with autonomous patients (*Brooks, Heston, Osborne,* and *Yetter* are discussed in Chapter 3), and the decriminalization of suicide in the various states in the early-to mid-1970s.[20] Other developments involved serious, influential studies of critically and terminally ill patients by Elisabeth Kübler-Ross, Avery Weisman, Diana Crane, and Ruth Russell.[21] Still other developments had to do with the emergence of the interdisciplinary field of biomedical ethics, beginning with the establishment of the Hastings Center in 1969 and the Kennedy Institute of Ethics in 1971, and followed by a number of important publications on treatment abatement, suicide, and euthanasia by religious ethicists (Paul Ramsey, Robert Veatch, Daniel Maguire, Arthur Dyck, and others) and philosophers in Great Britain and the United States (Anthony Flew, R. M. Hare, Sissela Bok, Marvin Kohl, Richard Brandt, James Rachels, and others).[22]

Of the articles and books by ethicists, four publications stand out in terms of their influence on subsequent thinking about the appropriate ethical and legal limits to be placed on the medical prolongation of life. The first of these publications, Paul Ramsey's *The Patient as Person,* published in 1970, had an impact on the ethics of death and dying that rivaled the earlier work of Joseph Fletcher, to the point that Ramsey's book was the most frequently cited work in biomedical ethics during the 1970s.[23] Writing as a Protestant Christian ethicist,

Ramsey used several of the concepts and distinctions long associated with Catholic moral theologians, provided an important alternative position in religious ethics to that of Fletcher, and succeeded in bringing considerable credibility to the emerging field of biomedical ethics.

In the major chapter of the book devoted to treatment abatement, entitled "On (Only) Caring for the Dying," Ramsey employed three distinctions as the foundation blocks for his ethical position: ordinary/extraordinary, prolonging life/prolonging dying, and killing/allowing to die. Taken together, these distinctions led to a further distinction between nondying and dying patients: nondying patients should have their lives prolonged with medically indicated treatment, whereas dying patients require neither curing (because of its futility in such circumstances) nor killing (because direct killing is immoral), but ongoing care during the terminal phase of life. For Ramsey, such an "ethics of only caring for the dying" is clearly preferable to two alternative, extreme positions: one held by "advocates of relentless efforts to save life" who refuse to recognize that medical treatment is sometimes useless in preventing death, and the other held by advocates of "the direct killing of terminal patients" (Joseph Fletcher is singled out as an example) who reject the "discriminating concepts of traditional medical ethics."[24]

Daniel Maguire's *Death by Choice*, first published in 1973, was an attempt to demonstrate that euthanasia could be morally permissible—even for Christians. Writing as a Catholic moral theologian, Maguire argued that the traditional prohibition of the direct killing of innocents was flawed, for two reasons: it had too often been interpreted in such an artificial manner that exceptional circumstances of "indirect" killing had been readily permitted (e.g., in just wars, in capital punishment), and it had led to "an unnuanced absolutism" that simply rejected a priori any other termination of innocent lives for good reasons other than self-defense. He proposed, using the omission/commission distinction that goes back to Aquinas, that both "passive" (or "negative") euthanasia and "active" (or "positive") euthanasia could be justified in some cases of terminal illness. Rejecting a number of objections to euthanasia, he concluded that "death by choice"—in either a passive or active mode—is a permissible option for dying patients with unrelieved pain, even though suicide outside medical settings remains the wrong alternative for persons who are not terminally ill.[25]

Marvin Kohl's *The Morality of Killing*, published in 1974, was a straightforward attempt to move beyond the justification of abating treatment to justify the intentional killing of some terminally ill patients. Writing as a philosopher, Kohl rejected several versions of the sanctity-of-life principle that had been put forward by religious and secular writers. For him, the "absolutist" claim (in either a religious or nonreligious formulation) that one ought never to kill an innocent human being is simply wrong, because it sometimes is contrary to the principle of beneficence, sometimes is contrary to the principle of justice, and can lead to the absurdity of saying (in nonmedical settings) that it is better to allow a thousand innocent persons to die than to kill one innocent person. In medical settings, the sanctity-of-life perspective (at least when elevated to the status of an exceptionless principle) is problematic in terms of a paradigm case in which a patient experiencing excruciating pain from metastatic cancer is undoubtedly going to die, favors an "easy death," and is in the presence of someone else who desires to help the suffering patient. In such a situation, Kohl argued, it would "be kind to kill" the patient by means of some form of "beneficent euthanasia." For an act of intentional killing to count as beneficent euthanasia, it would have to (1) involve the painless inducement of a quick death, (2) result in "beneficial treatment" for the recipient, (3) be intended to be helpful, and (4) bring to the agent no remuneration or financial gain.[26]

James Rachels published an article the following year that received unusual attention, partially because he attacked the widely held distinction between killing patients and allowing them to die and partially because he criticized an official policy of the A.M.A. (the 1973 statement by the House of Delegates) that was based on the traditional distinction. In the article, entitled "Active and Passive Euthanasia," Rachels argued that allowing patients to die can sometimes be a slow and painful process for the patient and everyone connected with the case, that the cessation of treatment can itself constitute "the intentional termination of a life," and that "the bare difference" between killing and letting die is morally insignificant. Using a now-famous illustration of two uncles (Smith and Jones) contributing to the deaths of their 6-year-old cousins, he maintained that killing someone is not necessarily worse than letting someone die. Moreover, he argued that in medical settings some instances of "active" euthanasia are actually preferable to "passive" euthanasia.[27]

Second and Third Phases: 1976–1984, 1985–present

When compared to the earlier philosophical and theological discussions of the moral obligation to prolong life and the limited circumstances in which that obligation was overridden by other considerations, the post-1957 debate about the morality of abating treatment represented a dramatic change: traditional appeals to authoritative answers were questioned, traditional ethical distinctions and principles were revised and sometimes rejected, and the traditional prohibition of intentional killing was challenged by at least a few philosophers and theologians. However, viewed from our current vantage point, the post-1957 debate pales in contrast to the debate that ensued in 1976 and the years following that remarkable year.

The three events in 1976 that were mentioned in Chapter 1—the Karen Quinlan case, the publication of two sets of institutional policies on treatment abatement in *The New England Journal of Medicine,* and the passage of the California

Natural Death Act—marked 1976 as a watershed year in the ongoing debate about treatment abatement and signaled the beginning of an unprecedented expansion of the debate into the public forum. In the 9 years that followed, the morality of abating treatment, the legality of abating treatment, and (less frequently) the morality and legality of intentional killing became the focal points for discussion and debate in numerous clinical settings, in courtrooms and legislative chambers in a number of states (as discussed in Chapters 3–5), and through a variety of efforts to influence public opinion.

Some of the attempts to shape public opinion regarding the morality and legality of abating treatment took place in widely read publications such as the President's Commission's *Deciding to Forego Life-Sustaining Treatment* (sometimes criticized by pro-life advocates as "the euthanasia Bible"), the *Report on Euthanasia, Aiding Suicide and Cessation of Treatment* by the Law Reform Commission of Canada, the American Society of Law and Medicine's *Legal and Ethical Aspects of Treating Critically and Terminally Ill Patients,* a *New England Journal of Medicine* article written by 10 distinguished physicians, and a number of important works by ethicists and attorneys.[28] Other attempts to shape public opinion took the form of educational activities by Concern for Dying (CFD) and the lobbying and litigative efforts on the part of the Society for the Right to Die (SRD). In Great Britain, efforts to influence public opinion included stage productions, with Brian Clark's critically acclaimed *Whose Life Is It Anyway?* being countered in London theatres with Malcolm Muggeridge's and Alan Thornhill's *Sentenced to Life.*[29]

The current phase of the debate over the morality and legality of abating treatment, as well as the relationship of treatment abatement to suicide and euthanasia, began to attract public attention in 1985. That year, as previously mentioned, three trends of the post-1976 period escalated in dramatic ways: the *Conroy* decision brought the question of abating medical nutrition and hydration on the behalf of nonautonomous patients to the forefront of case law, the 13 natural death acts passed that year specifically addressed the abatement of artificial feeding, and some of the activist groups within the pro-life movement and the right-to-die movement further polarized the debate over the morality and legality of abating treatment by characterizing the opposition's view in the conflict over artificial feeding as advocacy of either "mercy killing" or "force-feeding." As a consequence of these developments, the third phase of the debate over abating treatment has been symbolized by serious disagreements over medical nutrition and hydration in much the same way that the earlier periods of the debate were symbolized more by disagreements over mechanical ventilation than over any of the other modalities of life-sustaining treatment.

Like the post-1976 period of the debate, the post-1985 phase includes a number of significant court cases (see Chapter 4), an expansive body of literature (much of it focusing on the specific issue of abating medical nutrition and hydration), and frequent uses of the media by pro-life groups and right-to-die groups as a means of influencing public opinion.[30] Unlike the two earlier periods, the current phase of the debate is characterized by several features not commonly encountered in the past: an intensity of argumentation, a choosing-up of sides, a pejorative use of labels, a tendency to take on opponents by name, a bottom-of-the-ninth-one-run-behind-bases-loaded-two-outs urgency, and a passion for winning. Put another way, the stakes in the debate are now greater than in the past because the advocates of abating medical feeding (when medically and morally appropriate) have been victorious in a number of fiercely contested legal cases since *Conroy,* and several nonautonomous patients have subsequently died following the removal of NG and G-tubes. In response, the strategy of the opponents of this form of treatment abatement (and perhaps other forms as well) is now to circumvent this emerging case law by getting a "Patients' Rights Act" (promoted by the National Right to Life Committee—NRLC) passed by state legislatures and possibly some type of "Granny Doe" legislation passed by Congress.[31]

Indicative of this change (in mood and approach) is an ongoing effort by individuals and organizations to influence clinical decisions, case law, legislative action, and public opinion regarding the morality/immorality of abating medical nutrition and hydration with some critically ill patients. In addition to the various pro-life groups and right-to-die organizations, participants in this effort include some practicing physicians (e.g., Joanne Lynn, Ronald Cranford, Bernard Lo, and Mark Siegler), a number of attorneys working in the field of health law (George Annas, Norman Cantor, Alexander Capron, Rebecca Dresser, Edward Grant, Dennis Horan, Alan Weisbard, and others), some of the judges who have written opinions on the abatement of medical feeding, a number of Catholic scholars vying for the "heart" of that religious tradition, and several organizations that have put out position papers on the subject (e.g., the A.M.A. and the National Conference of Catholic Bishops).[32]

The importance of the conflict over the morality and legality of abating medical feeding—and its divisiveness—can be illustrated by two judicial opinions issued in September 1986. As previously indicated (see Case 4.19), the Supreme Judicial Court of Massachusetts ruled that month, in a 4–3 split decision, that the G-tube sustaining Paul Brophy's irreversibly comatose life could be removed. In a dissenting opinion to that decision, Justice Nolan stated:

In the forum of ethics, despite the opinion's high-blown language to the contrary, the court today has endorsed euthanasia and suicide. Suicide is direct self-destruction and is intrinsically evil. No set of circumstances can make it moral. Paul Brophy will die as a direct result of the cessation of feeding. The ethical principle of double effect is totally inapplicable here. This death by dehydration and starvation has been approved by the court. . . . I can think of nothing more degrading to the human person than the balance which the court struck today in favor of death and against life. It is but another triumph for the forces of secular humanism (modern paganism) which have now succeeded in imposing their anti-life principles at both ends of life's spectrum.[33]

Two weeks later, Reginald Stanton, a judge of the Superior Court of New Jersey, issued his opinion in the case of Beverly Requena (see Case 3.10). In deciding that this autonomous woman dying of ALS could refuse technological feeding, and have that refusal upheld in spite of the hospital's objections, Judge Stanton commented:

One of the problems in the case before me is that there has been a tendency on the part of the Hospital to find a "pro-life" versus "anti-life" issue where one does not truly exist. . . . This poor woman is not anti-life and her decision is not anti-life. She would dearly like to be well and to have a decent life. Unfortunately, a decent life is not hers to have. She has suffered much. . . . "Denial" of food connotes a refusal to give food to someone who wants it. Honoring Beverly Requena's request not to be fed artificially is not denying her anything. It is not an infliction of harm upon her by the Hospital. On the contrary, it is recognizing her dignity and worth as a human being.[34]

Again, "borrowed lessons" from ethics being used in two courts of law in different states: the rule of double effect in the first case, the principle of non-maleficence in the second. So it is during the third phase of the debate over abating treatment, with justices and numerous other concerned persons trying to decide when treatment abatement is permissible with critically and terminally ill patients.

Ongoing Ethical Options

In the midst of this post-*Quinlan* and post-*Conroy* ferment, ethicists have joined with patients, physicians, attorneys, judges, and other reflective persons to address the central ethical question in any effort to place limits on the medical prolongation of life: under what circumstances is abating treatment *morally* justifiable? Related to this question are numerous other questions, including the following ones. What limits (in terms of types of treatments, categories of patients, ethical distinctions) should be placed on abating treatment? Is the abatement of life-sustaining treatment justifiable only with dying patients, or also in the cases of some nondying patients? Are some judicially permitted cases of treatment abatement with nonautonomous patients morally wrong? How, and to what extent, do traditional ethical principles apply to contemporary cases of life-sustaining treatment? Is there any significant moral difference between abating life-sustaining treatment and intentionally killing patients with potassium chloride, a bolus of air, or some other death-dealing agent? Is the abatement of technological feeding with a nonautonomous patient a step down the "slippery slope" toward nonvoluntary euthanasia? Can the intentional killing of a patient ever be morally justifiable?

In wrestling with these questions and the cases of critically ill patients to which they pertain, some ethicists try to interpret appropriate conduct in the light of traditional ethical principles and distinctions; others revise traditional theories (e.g., the ordinary/extraordinary distinction) in the light of contemporary technological developments, and still others reject traditional principles and distinctions (e.g., the prohibition of intentional killing) as no longer being applicable to some of the clinical settings of modern medicine. Along the way, as ethicists respond to the realities of clinical medicine and the developments in law, some distinguishable ethical positions emerge.

Six of these positions will be discussed in this section. Three of the positions represent variations within what is commonly regarded as a "pro-life" view of abating treatment, and the other three positions represent variations within what is often called a "right-to-die" perspective on treatment abatement and the related issues of suicide and euthanasia. Taken together, the positions demarcate ethical options that have been developed since 1976 on a conservative-to-liberal philosophical spectrum, as such a spectrum applies to end-of-life ethical issues. The options to be discussed are not "pure types," because of the inevitable overlapping and blending that sometimes occurs as serious thinkers deal with complex issues—and try to influence the thinking of others—over a period of several years. Nevertheless, I will try to sort out the differences between the positions as well as discuss similarities and differences among individual ethicists who come down in approximately the same place regarding the morality of abating treatment and related ethical issues. Each of the positions will be presented by discussing the views of one or two representative thinkers, with other ethicists holding variations of the same position receiving less attention.

Position 1.   Never abate life-sustaining treatment

The most conservative position on the morality of abating treatment has been around a long time—centuries before the development of mechanical ventilation, feeding tubes, or any of the other life-sustaining technologies of our time. That position, simply put, is that each human life is of infinite and inestimable value, that the value of a life is not dependent on its duration or quality, and that any shortening of a life is morally unacceptable. According to this view, all medical means of extending the length of an individual's life are not only morally permissible, but morally obligatory.

This ethical option, as indicated earlier, is the position of Orthodox Judaism. In earlier centuries, Jews "were the original right-to-life advocates, unequivocally opposed to suicide, infanticide, and euthanasia except in the most extenuating circumstances."[35] Today, although not widely known in the United States (perhaps because there are only half a million Orthodox Jews among the 6 million American Jews), the position of traditional Judaism is still the most straightforward, thoroughgoing, and extreme "pro-life" option available on the moraltiy of treatment abatement and related issues.

The foundation stone for this sanctity-of-life position is a fundamental religious belief that individual human lives are, correctly understood, gifts from God. With this "givenness" of life comes the view that human bodies are, in an ultimate sense, divine property—residences, if you will, in which we are tenants—that must be maintained with care, prolonged as long as possible, and, when the time comes, returned to the rightful Owner. To shorten one's "lease on life" through suicide or euthanasia, or simply by giving up too early on medical efforts to prolong life, is to deny divine ownership and fail to exercise responsible stewardship over that which has been given by God. In this perspective, as Michael Nevins points out, the answer to the familiar question "Whose life is it anyway?" is clear: "It's not yours."[36]

Because of this perspective on life, most Jewish rabbis have traditionally encouraged every possible means of prolonging life (rubbing salt in wounds, making noise near a sick person's bed, saying audible prayers at the bedside of a dying person) and equated virtually any shortening of life with murder, even if a life was shortened by merely moving a patient's head (the pillow and synagogue key examples given earlier) or closing a dying patient's eyes. The preservation of human life was regarded with such overriding importance that the Sabbath could be violated, the Day of Atonement desecrated, and any of the commandments in the Torah broken (with the exceptions of murder, idolatry, and sexual offenses such as incest and adultery) if necessary to do so. The transcendent importance of saving a person's life meant that ethical distinctions used by other people—such as the development of the ordinary/extraordinary distinction and the rule of double effect by Catholic theologians—were simply not acceptable as justifying reasons for shortening human lives no matter what the medical prognosis might be in individual cases. The only possible exception to this fundamental obligation of preserving life as long as possible was the distinctly Jewish concept of a *goses:* a dying person whose death was so imminent that it was believed about to occur in a matter of hours.

Of course, not all rabbis hold this traditional perspective on life in the age of modern medicine. Rabbis in the Conservative and Reform divisions of modern Judaism certainly do not have this position on the morality of abating treatment, and at least some Orthodox rabbis and physicians vary somewhat from this traditional position.[37] However, among rabbis who have addressed the issue of abating treatment in the post-*Quinlan* era, David Bleich stands out as the unofficial standard-bearer for the traditional ethical position of Judaism.

Bleich, a professor of Talmud at Yeshiva University, first addressed the issue of abating treatment while the Quinlan case was being appealed. Responding to Judge Muir's decision in the New Jersey Superior Court, but writing before the New Jersey Supreme Court's decision, Bleich commented:

The physicians at St. Claire's Hospital are to be commended for not opting for the path of least resistance and for their tenacity in scrupulously discharging the moral and professional duties with which they are charged. The controversy surrounding the care of Karen Quinlan has called attention to and sharpened the question which will be posed over and over again: Who is the arbiter of life and death, man or God?[38]

In answering his own question, Bleich observes that according to the traditional perspective of Judaism, "man does not enjoy the right of self-determination with regard to questions of life and death." Judaism "has always taught that life, no less than death, is involuntary." Moreover, in Jewish law and moral teaching "life is a supreme value and its preservation takes precedence over virtually all other considerations."

For Bleich, the implications of this perspective are very clear and are repeated in several of his publications. The category of *pikku' ah nefesh* (preservation of life) extends to all human beings "of every description and classification" (including patients in a PVS), precludes the ethical distinctions found in the Catholic tradition, and makes mandatory the use of life-sustaining technology "even when it is known with certainty that human medicine offers no hope of a cure or restoration to health." The extent to which life-sustaining treatment is morally required—even in cases involving hopelessly ill patients—is illustrated with a story about the nineteenth-century Polish scholar popularly known as Reb Eisel Charif:

The venerable Rabbi was afflicted with a severe illness and was attended by an eminent specialist. As the disease progressed beyond hope of cure, the physician informed the Rabbi's family of the gravity of the situation. He also informed them that he therefore felt justified in withdrawing from the case. The doctor's grave prognosis notwithstanding, Reb Eisel Charif recovered completely. Some time later, the physician chanced to come upon the Rabbi in the street. The doctor stopped in his tracks in astonishment and exclaimed, "Rabbi, have you come back from the other world?" The Rabbi responded, "You are indeed correct. I *have* returned from the other world. Moreover, I did you a great favor while I was there. An angel ushered me in to a large chamber. At the far end of the room was a door and lined up in front of the door were a large number of well-dressed, dignified and intelligent-looking men. These men were proceeding through the doorway in a single file. I asked the angel who these men were and where the door led. He informed me that the door was the entrance to the netherworld and that the men passing through those portals were those of whom the Mishnah says, "The best of physicians merits *Gehinnom.*" Much to my surprise, I noticed that you too were standing in the line about to proceed through the door. I immediately approached the angel and told him: "Remove that man immediately! He is no doctor. He does not treat patients; he abandons them!"[39] (Reprinted by permission of the Publishers, Hebrew Publishing Company, Copyright © 1979. All Rights Reserved.)

Bleich uses this example and other rabbinic examples to emphasize that in the traditional Jewish perspective on life, *every moment of life* is of infinite value. Even though an individual patient's life may be in its terminal phase, even though it may be characterized by unbearable pain, and even though the patient cries out for someone to bring an end to such a torturous existence—neither treatment abatement nor euthanasia is a moral option. Likewise, even though an individual patient is in an irreversible coma, had signed an advance directive before losing consciousness, had chosen a proxy in advance, and now has everyone involved in the case in agreement that continued life support is no longer in the patient's best interests—neither treatment abatement nor euthanasia is a moral option. To withhold, decelerate, or withdraw life-sustaining treatment in such cases is morally the same as intentionally killing the patients. Why? Any omission of life-prolonging treatments and any deliberate act of "mercy killing" are both equally prohibited by Jewish law and ethics because, as long as a patient is "endowed with a spark of life," such choices represent an "unwarranted intervention in an area which must be governed only by God Himself."[40]

To have any exception to the requirement of prolonging life as long as possible requires some kind of objective, empirical criterion or test that effectively demonstrates—without moral deliberation, intervention in hastening the patient's death, or a shadow of doubt—that a patient is "actually in the clutches of the angel of death and the death process has actually begun."[41] Simply classifying a patient as being terminally ill, dying, or even imminently dying is not sufficient. Rather, what is required is "conclusive evidence . . . that the state [of the patient] is not only irreversible but also not prolongable even by artificial means."[42]

Such an objective, undeniable standard is provided, Bleich believes, by the concept of a *goses*. For a dying person to be a *goses,* or to be in a state of *gesisah,* means either (1) that the patient cannot, under any medical circumstances, be maintained alive for a period of 72 hours or (2) that the patient has started making a "death rattle" (a sound caused by a buildup of oral secretions in the back of the patient's mouth). If a dying patient's life can be prolonged for more than 3 days, such a patient is by definition not a *goses* and should receive whatever treatment modalities are medically feasible. However, once a patient is identified as a *goses,* that patient's life is, according to the Talmud, like the "flickering flame" of a candle. At this time, and only at this time, the distinction between acts and omissions becomes morally significant: one may withdraw treatment to permit a moribund patient to have an unimpeded death, but one may not move the patient, manipulate the patient's body, or hasten death in any other way "even by a matter of moments," because that is "tantamount to murder." Again, the Talmudic analogy: "The matter may be compared to a flickering flame; as soon as one touches it, the light is extinguished."[43]

In Bleich's view, the morality of abating treatment therefore has nothing to do with a patient's preferences, the legal right to refuse medical treatment, court decisions in treatment-abatement cases (the final *Quinlan* decision is "antithetical to Jewish teaching"), the signing of nonstatutory advance directives, natural death acts, the burdens sometimes imposed by medical technology, or considerations of whether life-sustaining treatment is in the best interests of a patient in a given case. Rather, the morality of abating treatment has to do with the prolongation of any and all lives until God indicates, through some objective sign, that a "flickering flame" may be allowed to go out. The "reading" of that sign is best done by a qualified rabbinic authority on a case-by-case basis.[44]

Position 2. Never abate treatment with nondying patients

A second ethical option shares much common ground with the position just described. Like the position of Orthodox Judaism, this second perspective is rooted in a religious understanding of human life, has a strong duty-based deontological orientation toward moral conduct, claims that individual human lives have inestimable value independent of and transcendent to their duration and quality, supports medical paternalism over the desires and wishes of patients, and maintains that all attempts to hasten the deaths of patients are morally unacceptable. Unlike the position of Orthodox Judaism, this second option makes considerable use of the ethical distinctions developed in the Christian tradition and attempts to relate ethical reflection to the developments in contemporary medicine and law instead of simply dismissing such developments as being antithetical to a religious perspective on life.

In terms of the morality of abating treatment, the philosophers and religious ethicists who hold this second view agree with Bleich and traditional Judaism regarding the importance of an objective standard that clearly demarcates cases in which abating treatment is morally justifiable from cases in which the withholding, decreasing, or withdrawing of life-sustaining treatment is wrong. For the Christian thinkers identified with this second sanctity-of-life position, some kind of physiologically based standard (for cases involving autonomous patients) or factually based standard (for cases with nonautonomous patients) is necessary to prevent an unbridled subjectivism from dominating decisions to abate treatment.

Like Bleich, the proponents of this second ethical option believe that an objective standard is necessary as a moral "wall" to hold back the tide of unwarranted wishes, suicidal desires, substituted judgments, quality-of-life assessments, and calculations of patients' best interests that could lead to the societal acceptance of voluntary and nonvoluntary euthanasia. However, these ethicists think that erecting such a wall at the point in time when, according to the teachings of Judaism, a dying patient becomes identified as a *goses* is *much too restrictive*—it indicates a refusal to admit that medical treatment can become useless prior to that point in a dying patient's irreversible trajectory toward death. Instead, a more satisfactory way of constructing a moral wall between the permissible abatement of treatment and the impermissible termination of patient's lives is by emphasizing the different obligations imposed by caring for the dying and caring for the nondying. For them, therefore, the morality of abating treatment depends on a distinction between dying and nondying patients.

The best-known representative of the second position is Paul Ramsey. As previously indicated, Ramsey's *The Patient as Person* was the most influential publication on the morality of abating treatment in the years immediately prior to the Quinlan case.[45] Ramsey, a professor of Christian ethics at Princeton until his retirement in 1982, responded to the Quinlan case soon after Judge Muir's trial court decision and several times subsequent to the New Jersey Supreme Court's decision in the case.[46] Having previously written about the obligation to care for patients in prolonged comas, Ramsey found the case, in both its medical and legal forms, to be of crucial importance in his ongoing efforts to address the ethical and legal issues connected with the categorical imperative enunciated in his earlier book: "Never abandon care!"[47]

In 1978, Ramsey published *Ethics at the Edges of Life,* another widely acclaimed book dealing with beginning-of-life and end-of-life ethical issues.[48] In this book, along with several articles, he updated his pre-*Quinlan* views on the morality of abating treatment, revised earlier comments regarding the usefulness and limitations of traditional ethical distinctions, considered the morality of euthanasia in exceptional circumstances, and criticized the judicial opinions in *Quinlan* and some of the other early cases involving treatment abatement with nonautonomous patients.[49]

Ramsey's post-*Quinlan* publications reflect two changes in his views regarding the applicability of the ordinary/extraordinary distinction to cases of treatment abatement. Having emphasized the distinction in his earlier book more than any ethicist since Gerald Kelly—and probably more than *any* other Protestant ethicist—he acknowledged in 1978 that his earlier interpretation of the distinction had been flawed. He had applied the distinction almost exclusively to dying patients who were both conscious and autonomous. In doing so, he had misinterpreted the Catholic moral theologians who originally formulated the distinction as a way for individuals to decide about radical life-prolonging measures but who did not have in mind persons who were already dying: "I suppose . . . that these past thinkers never imagined it could be a medical duty to aimlessly prolong dying."[50] Moreover, Ramsey realized that his earlier emphasis on the distinction had influenced others to apply the distinction "to cases for which it was never intended," thereby leading to "quality-of-expected-life judgments" in cases involving "the desperately ill or 'incurables' who are voiceless."

Precisely because voiceless patients need continuing care, as well as protection from having their lives terminated arbitrarily, Ramsey decided to *replace* the ordinary/extraordinary distinction with other ethical standards. In his first replacement proposal, he suggested that "the morally significant meaning" of the traditional distinction "can be reduced almost without remainder to two components": a comparison of treatments that are "medically indicated," and a patient's right to refuse treatment.[51] He subsequently revised that proposal in a discussion of five optional medical and moral standards for making decisions to abate treatment: (1) the ordinary/extraordinary distinction, (2) a standard-medical-care policy, (3) a patient's right to refuse treatment, (4) a medical indications policy, and (5) a quality-of-expected-life policy. Given these options, he argued that "the significant moral meaning" of the various standards "can be reduced almost without significant remainder to a medical indications policy."[52]

Why the change in the second replacement proposal? Why jettison the earlier emphasis on the right of patients to refuse medical treatment and end up with a medical indications policy as the exclusive test for justifying treatment abatement? The first reason is abundantly clear: a medical indications policy provides an *objective standard* for deciding about treatment abatement in cases "of the dying and the ill or incurable (without confusing them)." In fact, Ramsey believes that the original terms "ordinary" and "extraordinary" directed the attention of decision makers "to *objective* consideration of the patient's condition and of the armamentarium of medicine's remedies." The benefits of having such an objective standard are threefold: it serves as a check against the "arbitrary freedom," "subjective decisions," and "voluntaristic determination" of autonomous patients by making their claimed "right to die" only a relative right (relative to their medical status); it protects the ethical integrity of physicians by giving them an empirical reason not to be turned into "animated tools" (to use Aristotle's definition of a slave) that simply assist a patient to attain anything he wishes; and it protects nonautonomous patients by imposing an "obligation to use the treatment indicated among the available alternatives . . . in the management of unconscious nondying patients."

Specifically in regard to nonautonomous patients, the objectivity provided by a medical indications policy—at one point referred to as "biological indices for medical help"—is considerably preferable to the subjectivism of alternative ways of making decisions to treat or to abate treatment on the behalf of patients who lack the capacity to make such decisions themselves. One rejected alternative is Robert Veatch's standard of "reasonableness" for such decisions. To Ramsey, the Veatch proposal is unacceptable because it has "very little objective reference," allows nonmedical value judgments into decisions about medical treatment, and permits substituted judgments to be made without any medical "chart or compass." Another rejected alternative is Richard McCormick's standard of "minimum personal relatedness." When applied to adult, nondying patients, the McCormick proposal allows for quality-of-life criteria to be used in decision making, erodes the distinction between voluntary and nonvoluntary euthanasia, and permits "a geriatric patient's lost further potential" to become a factor in decisions to abate treatment.[53]

For Ramsey, a medical indications policy is necessary to counter the use of "quality-of-expected-life" criteria by McCormick, physicians, patients' surrogates, or anyone else. Such criteria are impermissible because they fail to reflect the fundamental Christian notion that "an individual human life is absolutely unique, inviolable, irreplaceable, noninterchangeable, not substitutable, and not meldable with other lives."[54] A medical indications policy is consistent with this religious perspective in that it "requires simply a *comparison of treatments* to determine whether any are likely to be beneficial in any way other than prolonging dying"—not a comparison of "patient-*persons* or of different stages or conditions of the same patient-person in order to determine his quality-of-life struggles or prospects."

Moreover, a medical indications policy is necessary as a means of distinguishing between dying patients and nondying patients, and of determining the moral requirements of caring for patients in the two categories. For patients identified by their physicians as dying—whether they are conscious or unconscious, autonomous or nonautonomous—the responsible moral choice is for some variation of abating treatment. Such a choice does not mean passivity, nor does it mean some kind of "omission" as opposed to an "act." Rather, the decision to abate curative treatment "is followed immediately by an exceedingly active practice of medicine involving 'commissions' of many sorts in caring for the dying." For patients in the second category, however, physicians are obligated to use whatever medical treatments are indicated by the patients' physiological conditions. If such patients have a prognosis of terminal illness (but are not yet dying) or have a severe disabling condition (to the point that they are "voiceless nondying patients"), physicians and surrogates have "an undiminished obligation first of all to sustain life." Only in those cases where no medical interventions are helpful in improving the patients' conditions is it morally appropriate "to use palliative treatments where possible." The dying/nondying distinction thus represents an ethical *rule of practice* for caring for the critically ill: "favoring life when the patient has no capacity to refuse treatment or to share in physicians' or family decisions to omit or neglect treatment or otherwise initiate the incompetent, incurable patient's dying."

The distinction between dying patients and nondying (but possibly incurable) patients is "crucial for the morality of substituting the judgments of the well for those of the ill." Because a medical indications policy makes this distinction possible in clinical settings, such a policy "is the only way to take a middle path between relentless treatment of the voiceless dying, which refuses to let them die even when disease or injury has won, and killing or hastening death or neglecting to sustain those who simply are voiceless incurables."

Ramsey also believes that a medical indications policy should be used in judicial decisions about cases involving treatment abatement. Such decisions should be based on "the objective condition of the patient," not on "the wishes of any of the parties concerned." Treatments are "not electable because elected, desirable because desired." Thus in commenting on the trial court decision in

Quinlan, he focused on the opposing views of Karen Quinlan's parents and physicians: the former wanted mechanical ventilation stopped but IV feedings continued, whereas the latter thought both modalities of treatment should be continued. In Ramsey's judgment, both parties were wrong: "Treatments that were potentially lifesaving (or reasonably believed to be so) when first begun have now become means for aimlessly prolonging Karen's dying." In other words, both forms of treatment are "no longer indicated."[55]

Unfortunately, in Ramsey's view, the final decision in *Quinlan* was flawed, as were the final decision in *Saikewicz* and the appellate decision in *Eichner:* "*Quinlan* was the right decision for the wrong reasons . . . *Saikewicz* was a wrong decision for wrong reasons [and] *Eichner* was the right decision for a mixture of wrong reasons."[56] Ramsey is critical of *Quinlan* (see Case 4.1) because, while he thinks the decision to terminate mechanical ventilation was correct in this case of a patient believed to be *dying,* he argues that the New Jersey Supreme Court decision "shows the folly of failure to give legal effect to a medical indications policy," opens the legal door to the abatement of treatment with other unconscious, but *nondying* patients, obliterates the distinction between voluntary euthanasia and nonvoluntary euthanasia, and diffuses professional decision-making responsibility by means of a strange and questionable "ethics committee."[57] He disagrees with the *Saikewicz* decision (see Case 4.2) for a number of reasons: the court's opinion is based on quality-of-life judgments, fails to distinguish between "letting the dying die" and letting nondying patients (who may be retarded and incurable) die, pretends to use the substituted-judgment test for a never-competent patient, treats Saikewicz *as if* he were a competent patient, and permits "court-supervised involuntary euthanasia."[58] He agrees with the *Eichner* decision (see Case 4.8), but again criticizes the reasons given by the court. Instead of using an objective, factually based standard available to it (Brother Fox's earlier statements about treatment abatement), the court employs a variety of questionable subjective standards: "privacy," "best interests," and "quality of life." For Ramsey, such subjective standards are inherently wrong ways of making decisions about the appropriate care due to nonautonomous patients. Instead, he argues that decision making should be limited to what "we objectively know to do, namely, to cease treatment when, and only when, to continue would only prolong the dying of the dying."[59]

In addition, Ramsey addresses three other aspects of the issue of abating treatment. Is the abatement of medical feeding and hydration morally different from the abatement of mechanical ventilation and other life-prolonging technologies? No, he says, as long as the patient in question is *dying.* Thus he regarded the respirator and the IV feeding tube as being "no longer indicated" in the care of Karen Quinlan and offered to accompany her parents and their priest "to Karen's room . . . to pray while Joseph and Julia Quinlan disconnect both the respirator and the IV and hold Karen in their arms while she dies."[60] Nevertheless, "to be on the safe side," he repeatedly suggests that physicians continue a glucose drip—"to give the comfort of a cup of cool water" to a dying patient—while they discontinue high-caloric tube feedings that merely prolong the dying process.[61] In his most recently published comments, he updates his earlier distinction of continuing hydration/ discontinuing calories by expressing concern over the care being given to nonautonomous patients who are "at a way-station in their dying." Specifically addressing the cases of Nancy Jobes and Paul Brophy (Cases 4.17 and 4.19), he compares the Quinlan case ("my equation of intravenous feeding with ventilation was in the context of the trial court's finding that Karen Quinlan was *dying*") with *Jobes, Brophy,* and other recent cases involving the abatement of medical feeding *and* hydration:

No one had yet thought [in 1976] of using a patient's need for food and water as a means to start the dying process again or to bring on the death of patients who "refuse" to die. . . . To contemplate bringing on death slowly by dehydration requires, I should think, the *exclusion* of possible pain. . . . Startling the death angel into flying slowly is, in any case, a strange idea in need of explanation. The explanation could be our lack of confidence in caring. Another explanation may be the ascendency of proportionalism and/or consequentialism in determining "net benefits" over the intention of a moral agent in bringing on death or in refraining from doing so. If proportional benefit is a good reason, then a quick death seems the best thing to do.[62]

What is the moral status of natural death acts? For Ramsey, writing in anticipation that other states would follow California's lead in enacting natural death acts, statutory advance directives offer "portentous issues" to the citizens of this country. If carelessly drafted, or if patterned after the model statutes of right-to-die organizations, natural death acts could legalize "arbitrary treatment refusals," limit the discretion of physicians, and be a "giant step" toward the acceptance of euthanasia in medical practice and public policy. However, carefully worded statutes that clearly limit the refusal of treatment to dying patients may be "the last, best chance we have" to stop the movement toward voluntary and nonvoluntary euthanasia. In fact, "no better place is likely to be found at which to build a holding wall to protect the foundations of the Venice of Western law and morals from the daily watery bombardment that now threatens to take that city into the sea."[63]

Is euthanasia ever morally acceptable? To the surprise of many people, Ramsey answers in the affirmative. At one point he expresses regret for having earlier suggested two exceptions to the duty always (and only) to care for the dying: deep coma or intractable pain, either of which could bring about a patient's "impenetrable inaccessibility to care."[64] Nevertheless, he leaves the door slightly open to the *exceptional case* in which intentional killing would be morally justifiable as an *extension* of care. He points out that "the entire *moral* reason for prohibiting direct killing or accelerating dying" is not because of an omission/commission distinction or a direct/indirect action distinction, but solely because of "our obligation always to care for the dying." To that end, he warns against killing unconscious patients who may be at "a penultimate stage" of dying: "beyond showing response to us [but] not altogether in God's keeping [and thus] within reach of violation at our hands." However, if (1) a patient is clearly dying, (2) such a patient seems truly unreachable by any agent's care, (3) no quality-of-life judgments are made regarding the patient, and (4) the agent claims conscientious objector status in this particular case against the moral rule regarding killing in medical practice, then "it would be right to hasten death, if there is such a case."

Arthur Dyck, a professor of population ethics at the Harvard School of Public Health and Harvard Divinity School, agrees that treatment should never be abated with nondying patients, nor should any patients ever be intentionally killed. For him, the moral difference between permitting dying patients to die and intentionally killing patients is a difference between two perspectives on life. One perspective, which he terms "euthanasia" or "mercy killing" and identifies with Joseph Fletcher, Marvin Kohl, and James Rachels, is based on the view that lives not worth living can sometimes be terminated to the benefit of the person killed. The other perspective, which he labels "benemortasia," is based on the view that no lives are ever not worth living or prolonging whenever possible by medical treatment, even when a nondying but "desperately sick" patient expresses a wish to die. In terms of irreversibly comatose patients, "there is a strong presumption to continue to support the comatose and the severely brain damaged until there is no reasonable hope of improving or reversing their condition."[65] Given this exceptionless duty to sustain the lives of nondying patients—a duty he describes as "making every effort to save and repair life"— he argues that Joseph Saikewicz should have been given chemotherapy and that patients with Alzheimer's disease should, if they refuse food, be fed by means of a G-tube, unless they are clearly dying and cannot experience even the "primitive" joys and satisfactions of life.[66]

For Germain Grisez, now a professor of Christian ethics at Mount St. Mary's College, the dying/nondying distinction is very important in determining the morality and legality of treatment abatement, especially when the lives at stake are those of nonautonomous patients.[67] Identifying himself as one of the "friends of life" and an opponent of euthanasia, he says that the most effective way of countering the proponents of euthanasia is not by defending some version of a vitalistic philosophy, but by drawing "a reasonable line beyond which . . . efforts to prolong life" are not morally necessary.[68] The distinction between dying and nondying patients provides such a line. This distinction is repeatedly used in his *Life and Death with Liberty and Justice,* a book he coauthored with Joseph Boyle, Jr. According to them, the "question whether a person is dying is a matter of fact to be determined by evidence."[69] With the objectivity provided by this evidence, Grisez arrives at the following conclusions (with agreement by

Boyle) regarding the morality of abating treatment with nonautonomous patients: a nondying patient should be given life-sustaining treatment even if the patient's surrogate and physicians believe otherwise, a dying but conscious patient should be given ordinary nursing care and palliative medical care, and a patient who is both permanently unconscious and dying should be given only ordinary nursing care (excluding mechanical ventilation, antibiotics, and "the feeding of a special formula by tube").[70]

Such treatment abatement is unquestionably legal, according to Grisez (and Boyle), and could be formulated into a workable statutory directive that would emphasize the principles of liberty and justice. However, the eight natural death acts in existence by 1978 only furthered the goals of the "pro-euthanasia movement" by making homicide by omission an easier medical option, creating a climate of public acceptance for several false concepts ("death with dignity," "a right to privacy," and "a right to die"), opening the door to a quality-of-life ethic, and taking our "anti-life" society down the road to voluntary and non-voluntary euthanasia.[71]

Position 3.   Never abate life-sustaining nutrition and hydration

A third position is, in many respects, closely aligned with the ethical position articulated by Ramsey, Dyck, and Grisez. In some respects, in fact, this third perspective on the morality of abating treatment is simply an updating of the perspective just discussed. Ethicists holding either of these two views emphasize the sanctity of human life, the difficulties and dangers inherent in quality-of-life judgments, the immorality of euthanasia, and the ongoing need to use and, when necessary, to revise traditional ethical distinctions (especially the distinctions of ordinary/extraordinary means, direct/indirect actions, and let die/kill) developed by Catholic moral theologians.

All of the ethicists holding these two positions agree that some kind of objective standard is necessary to guide decisions about abating treatment so that autonomous patients may be prevented from inflicting harm on themselves and others and, more importantly, so that nonautonomous patients can be protected from having their lives intentionally terminated. They believe that this objective standard has to be grounded in medicine and ethics, not law, because a number of courts have made the wrong decision in cases involving treatment abatement with nonautonomous patients, and the various natural death acts fail to provide sufficient legal protection for nonautonomous patients.

Position 3, however, differs from position 2 in several ways. First, the ethicists identified with the two positions interpret the issue of treatment abatement somewhat differently because they address the morality of abating treatment in the context of different cases involving the employment of different life-sustaining technologies. Ramsey, Dyck, and Grisez concentrate on the morality of abating mechanical ventilation and chemotherapy, with less attention given to questions related to the abatement of medical feeding and nutrition, because of the impact the cases of Karen Quinlan and Joseph Saikewicz had on their thinking. The ethicists now to be discussed, by contrast, focus almost exclusively on the morality of abating nutrition and fluids because of the centrality of that modality of life-sustaining technology in the cases of Claire Conroy, Paul Brophy, and several other nonautonomous patients in the post-*Conroy* era.

Second, the ethicists identified with the third position disagree with Ramsey, Dyck, Grisez, and others who think that the objective ethical standard to be used in cases of abating treatment is the one that distinguishes dying from nondying patients. Rather than drawing a line between two categories of critically ill patients, these ethicists think that a more appropriate—and more easily defended—ethical standard permits a line to be drawn between *two categories of life-sustaining care:* medical treatments and nonmedical forms of care. Consequently, they draw the line at providing life-sustaining nutrition and hydration, a form of care they regard as being nonmedical in nature. Depending on relevant factors in various cases of critically ill patients, they think that all modalities of life-sustaining *medical* treatment may, perhaps, be abated on moral grounds. But food and water may never be abated, because (among other reasons) this manner of sustaining patients' lives is morally different from mechanical ventilation, chemotherapy, antibiotics, burn therapy, and all other modalities of medical treatment.

Third, some of these ethicists—along with some attorneys and members of some politically active pro-life groups—regard the unabated administration of nutrition and fluids as a kind of litmus test according to which all participants and all forms of participation in the contemporary debate over treatment abatement are to be judged. In contrast to the limited flexibility of, say, Paul Ramsey, who is willing to consider the abatement of at least life-sustaining food with some patients thought to be dying, some of the advocates of this ethical perspective use the ongoing provision of nutrition and hydration to critically ill patients (whether dying or not) as an inflexible, exceptionless test for determining the correct interpretation of traditional Catholic teaching on abating treatment (especially the ordinary/extraordinary distinction), as well as the acceptability of court decisions, natural death acts, and all other public manifestations of the debate over the morality and legality of abating treatment.

The most prolific and visible representative of this ethical position is Robert Barry, O.P., an assistant professor of religious studies at the University of Illinois. With a number of publications on the abatement of nutrition and fluids, and with several appearances on nationally televised discussions and debates over the morality and legalization of euthanasia, Barry consistently argues that life-sustaining food and fluids should never be abated in the care of critically ill patients. To accept the abatement of such "normal, routine care" is, he fears, an acceptance of medical killing that will lead society toward the legalization of voluntary and nonvoluntary euthanasia.

For Barry, abating treatment with critically ill patients is sometimes justifiable, as long as the treatment being abated is mechanical ventilation or some other modality of treatment that is clearly medical in nature. However, "failing to provide nutrition and fluids that will sustain life is never a responsible moral decision."[72] Food and fluids "should be given to all patients until a certain determination of death has been made because denying life-sustaining nutrition and fluids imposes harm on them."[73] The only sound reason, in his judgment, for "denying life-sustaining nutrition and fluids is medical impossibility."[74] By contrast, there could "never be anything immoral in providing life-sustaining and medically providable nutrition and fluids to patients."[75]

Why is this the case? Why defend an ethical position that says the provision of life-sustaining food and fluids is *always* moral and any abatement of food and fluids is immoral? Barry provides a number of reasons. First, he repeatedly argues that "assisted feeding" is not a form of medical treatment. Eschewing terms such as "artificial," "medical," and "technological" in reference to the feeding and hydrating of patients in clinical settings, he maintains that assisted feeding—or "medically providable" food and fluids—is not medical treatment because it does not have the purpose that medical treatments have, does not require the same level of professional skill in maintenance that medical treatments do, and does not leave patients alive when withdrawn as medical treatments often do.

The purpose of medical treatments, according to Barry, is as follows: they "directly, proximately, and immediately cure, remedy, or palliate clinically diagnosable conditions, and unlike nutrition and fluids, are only indirectly and remotely natural extrinsic resources of the body." Given this purpose, medical treatments such as appendectomies, coronary bypasses, antibiotics, and vaccines are provided to impede "previously existing pathological conditions or . . . future possible lethal conditions." By contrast, nutrition and fluids "directly, proximately, and immediately . . . do not cure any clinically diagnosable pathological conditions, and they meet the need of the body for basic resources." Although nutrition and fluids sometimes alleviate pain and "indirectly have some neurological impact," they do so "only because they meet a need of the body for basic and extrinsic resources."[76]

Assisted feeding also differs from medical treatments in terms of the professional skills required for administering nutrition and fluids. Although hyperalimentation is one form of assisted feeding that requires "more than ordinary competent nursing skill to be administered"—and thus should be classified as an ordinary medical treatment—the other forms of assisted feeding can be maintained in most clinical situations by skilled nursing care. In this respect, assisted feeding by means of IV line, NG tube, or G-tube is comparable to urinary catheter tubes in that, once in place, all of these tubes are merely "passive conduits" that require "little more than ordinary care and caution."[77]

Moreover, assisted feeding differs from medical treatments in that, when nutrition and fluids are "definitely and absolutely" denied to patients, those patients die. Whereas patients often continue to live—sometimes to the surprise of their physicians—when medical treatments are abated, the withholding or withdrawing of nutrition and fluids from patients "universally causes debilitation and death within a certain period of time."[78]

A second reason for saying that assisted feeding is always morally required is clear-cut: it provides an objective standard that can be used to combat other, more subjective ethical standards used in the debate over abating treatment. In contrast to the claims about the "uselessness" and "burdensomeness" of some instances of assisted feeding that one finds among ethicists subscribing to other standards—the "pure contentless patient autonomy" standard, the "quality-of-life" standard, and the "best interests" standard—building an ethical position on the mandatory feeding and hydrating of all patients leaves little room for doubt or debate. In fact, one could hardly ask for a more decisive standard than simply stating: "when it is likely that food and water will sustain life, they should be given when medically possible."[79]

Third, abating assisted feeding is tantamount to the intentional killing of patients. In fact, the certitude of patient deaths following the abatement of assisted feeding is one of the features that distinguishes the abatement of nutrition and hydration from the abatement of mechanical ventilation. Ventilators, in providing *active* therapy, being *invasive,* and *replacing* the breathing function of the body, also differ from assisted feeding in that they can sometimes be withdrawn to the benefit and continued life of a patient. By contrast, the withdrawal of food and fluids "is morally identical to placing a plastic bag over a person's head because they both guarantee death in a relatively short period of time."[80]

Fourth, abating assisted feeding inflicts harm on critically ill patients and on the society in which those patients live. In terms of the harm done to patients denied nutrition and hydration, Barry thinks that "death by starvation and dehydration" is cruel, revolting, and irrational. To make his point he cites a litany of painful conditions that were described in the trial court decision in *Conroy:* burning of the lips, ulcerations, crusting, and so forth.[81] In terms of the long-term harm that awaits a society that permits the abatement of food and fluids from critically ill patients, he develops his own litany of moral disasters: "starvation of the comatose . . . will become as widely accepted as is contraception at the present time," the 500,000 people receiving parenteral nutrition and 780,000 people receiving enteral nutrition each year in the United States will become "medically vulnerable persons," and our society will experience acts of mercy killing "comparable to the Nazi period."[82]

Fifth, abating assisted feeding is contrary to the traditional teachings of Catholic moral theologians. In making this point, Barry criticizes several contemporary Catholic theologians who are willing, in rare circumstances, to justify the abatement of nutrition and hydration in the care of some critically and (possibly) terminally ill patients: John Paris, Richard McCormick, Kevin O'Rourke, and John Connery. O'Rourke is singled out for having endorsed the March 1986 statement on the abatement of food and water by the Judicial Council of the A.M.A.[83] In arguing that Paris, McCormick, and O'Rourke, in particular, have departed from traditional Catholic teachings, Barry maintains that Aquinas, Francisco Vitoria, Juan Cardinal De Lugo, Joseph Sullivan, Charles McFadden, and Gerald Kelly all developed positions in opposition to the abatement of food and fluids, even though he has to criticize a basic "inconsistency" in Kelly's thought to make his claim.[84] To demonstrate further that his position is the correct version of the Church's teachings, Barry cites the *amicus curiae* brief of the New Jersey Catholic Conference in the Nancy Jobes case, the policy statement of the Catholic hospital in the Beverly Requena case, two policy statements by the Committee for Pro-Life Activities of the National Conference of Bishops, and selected comments by three American cardinals and two American bishops.[85]

Are there exceptions to the requirement of providing life-sustaining nutrition and hydration? Barry mentions only two such possibilities: when assisted feeding is medically impossible, and when "the mode of provision would itself cause radical and extreme pain for the recipient."[86] Otherwise, he argues that all critically ill patients—conscious and unconscious, autonomous and nonautonomous, dying and nondying—should be given food and water. That an autonomous patient such as Elizabeth Bouvia does not want to be fed with an NG tube is immaterial.[87] That some combination of patient surrogates, physicians, and judges agree that continued feeding and hydration is no longer in the best interests of a nonautonomous patient also is immaterial, as he clearly indicates in his criticisms of the legal decisions in *Conroy, Brophy, Jobes, Requena, Rasmussen,* and *Rodas.*[88] Even patients who are diagnosed as being *brain dead* should be given food and fluids because "they are only in the final stages of dying, but are not yet dead."[89]

How far is Barry willing to go to prevent life-sustaining nutrition and hydration from being abated with critically ill patients? Quite far, it seems. He takes Kelly's "principle of the common good" and expands on it to argue that "the common good can require a person to accept assisted feeding in order to prevent the social and legal endorsement of euthanasia by omission which would pose a clear threat to the handicapped, immature, unstable, and medically vulnerable from mercy killing."[90] Moreover, he proposes countering the "pro-euthanasia movement" and preventing "fully legalized mercy killing" by having state and federal legislation enacted "to remove life-sustaining medically providable nutrition and fluids from the legal class of medical treatments that can be declined by patients."[91] As we have seen, a number of state legislatures have now enacted such laws.

Two other ethicists share Barry's concern about the moral implications of justifying the abatement of life-sustaining nutrition and hydration. In contrast to him, however, neither of them is interested in legally preventing the abatement of food and fluids, neither makes apocalyptic predictions about the future, and neither tries to "show the flag" of the Catholic tradition. Instead, both of them address the question whether the abatement of life-sustaining nutrition and hydration is tantamount to the intentional killing of patients.[92]

Daniel Callahan, the director of the Hastings Center, raises questions about the morality of abating food and fluids in an article written before the New Jersey Supreme Court decision in the Claire Conroy case. For him, responding in part to the controversy surrounding the Conroy case, proposals to abate life-sustaining nutrition and hydration pose two problems: one involving emotion and symbolism, the other involving concern about the moral reasoning behind efforts to abate food and fluids in the care of patients such as Conroy. He thinks that both of these problems suggest that abating life-sustaining nutrition and hydration is rarely if ever justifiable.

The problem of emotion and symbolism has to do with what Callahan describes as his (and other persons') "stubborn emotional repugnance against a discontinuance of nutrition." If artificial respiration and artificial feeding are taken to be morally identical, then "the only impediment" to the enactment of a social policy of abating food and fluids "is a cluster of sentiments and emotions that is repelled by the idea of starving someone to death, even in those cases where it might be for the patient's own good." Acknowledging that this view is hard to defend rationally, he still holds out for the symbolic importance of feeding the hungry as "the most fundamental of all human relationships."[93]

The other problem is, if anything, more serious. Responding to an article written by Joanne Lynn and James Childress, Callahan reluctantly admits that he cannot "deny the moral licitness of the discontinuation of feeding under some circumstances," such as those put forth by Lynn and Childress.[94] Nevertheless, he voices a suspicion that the debate over the feeding issue has arisen "because a denial of nutrition may in the long run become the only effective way to make certain that a large number of biologically tenacious patients actually die." Given the increasing number of "superannuated, chronically ill, physically marginal elderly," he wonders if the abatement of food and fluids will become "the nontreatment of choice."[95]

Gilbert Meilaender, a professor of religion at Oberlin College, picks up on Callahan's statement regarding the certitude of death following the withdrawal of nutrition from "biologically tenacious patients." Having written in an earlier article that intentional killing—"aiming at death"—is incompatible with Christian love, Meilaender enters the debate about nutrition and hydration by stating that the policy toward which we are moving (after *Barber, Hier,* and the first two decisions in the Conroy case) is "not merely one of 'allowing to die': it is one of aiming to kill."[96]

Focusing primarily on cases of permanently unconscious patients and using two ethical distinctions along the way (let die/kill, and the intention/foresight distinction that lies at the heart of the rule of double effect), Meilaender makes a number of points in trying to build a case against the abatement of food and fluids on the behalf of nonautonomous patients. He argues that patients in a PVS are "not dying," that the provision of food and drink is "the sort of care that all human beings owe each other," and that abating food and fluids is not morally equivalent to abating mechanical ventilation because of the difference in the certitude of death as the result of these two actions. Consequently, when nutrition and hydration are abated in the care of permanently unconscious patients, "we cease no treatment aimed at disease." Rather, "we withdraw the nourishment that sustains all human beings whether healthy or ill, and we do so when the only result of our action can be death."[97]

Even if the provision of food and fluids is regarded as medical treatment, a view that Meilaender rejects, the abatement of such treatment cannot be justified as being either useless (because it sustains "embodied persons" who are not dying) or burdensome (because PVS patients are unlikely to experience feeding or other treatment in this manner). However, because the provision of food and fluids *may* be experienced as burdensome by conscious but severely demented patients, a reasonable trial period should be used to demonstrate whether such a patient actually finds such care "excessively burdensome."

Meilaender's conclusion is straightforward: life-sustaining nutrition and hydration should never be abated in the care of permanently unconscious patients, in spite of claims to the contrary by persons using the quality-of-life or best-interests standards. For him, the abatement of such "ordinary human care" can be understood correctly only as "aiming to kill," and any such act is morally wrong because of the fundamental moral conviction that "it is wrong to aim to kill the innocent."[98]

Position 4. *Abate all life-sustaining medical treatment when warranted*

The ethicists to whom we now turn differ on the morality of abating treatment from the ethicists just discussed, for a number of reasons to be developed later. At this point, the most obvious difference is their interpretation of the status of assisted feeding, and the moral implications they derive from that interpretation. The ethicists identified with position 3 think that the use of IV lines, NG tubes, and G-tubes constitutes "normal, routine care" that is morally comparable to bringing food and drinks on hospital trays to patients who can eat and drink in a normal manner. Consequently, they regard assisted feeding as involving an obligation to "feed the hungry" that compels compassionate, humane persons to respond in a manner not unlike that of parents feeding their hungry children, altruistic individuals feeding hungry citizens in soup kitchens, missionaries and relief-agency workers feeding starving people in drought-stricken areas of the world, and so on. To abate this fundamental form of human care is, from this perspective, an unthinkable choice.

The ethicists now to be discussed think that the use of IV lines, NG tubes, and G-tubes to provide nutrition and hydration for some autonomous patients and many nonautonomous patients in hospitals is morally comparable to using other technological delivery systems to provide patients with oxygen, antibiotics, cleansed blood, and so forth. Consequently, they refer to the technological provision of nutrients and fluids as being "artificial" or "medical" feeding and regard such feeding as a form of medical treatment that, like all medical treatments, is not always wanted or needed by patients, is not always beneficial on balance to critically ill patients, and is not always in the best interests of autonomous or nonautonomous patients. To abate this technological form of feeding and hydration is, from this perspective, a choice that is similar to other decisions to abate treatment, though perhaps less common. To make such a decision as a way of acting in a patient's best interests is not, in their view, the same as intending to kill the patient.

John Paris, S.J., a professor of medical ethics at the College of the Holy Cross and the medical schools of Tufts University and the University of Massachusetts, is the first representative of position 4. As a consultant to the President's Commission, an expert witness in *Barber* and *Brophy*, and a consultant to the plaintiff's attorney in *Conroy*, he has dealt in several settings with questions related to the abatement of all forms of medical treatment, including technological feeding and hydration. He has also addressed these questions in a number of articles, some of them coauthored with other professionals in medicine, law, and ethics.

For Paris, developing a reasoned position on the abatement of all forms of medical treatment when the circumstances warrant is complicated by the ongoing need to deal with opposing views. One of the opposing views is held by persons enamored with the possibilities of modern medical technology to the point that they feel compelled to follow the "technological imperative" discussed in Chapter 2. In response to this view, Paris points out that in some cases (he uses the example of Paul Brophy) the medical interventions that are done to sustain a patient's life actually turn out to be "half-way technology" (to borrow Lewis Thomas' terminology): the technologies available are capable of sustaining an individual's organic functions for 20 or 30 years, but cannot reverse the brain damage or restore the patient to a functioning condition. In such cases, to continue the medical intervention once the technology has proved futile in overcoming the patient's disease is to "rob us of our capacity to make human moral judgments and make us captives of our technology."[99]

Another, closely related opposing view is that of physicians, hospital administrators, and other persons who subscribe to the philosophy of vitalism. An example of this view is evident in the testimony of Dr. Marshall Brummer, a pulmonary specialist, before the President's Commission. Asked if physicians have the duty "to do everything for [a] patient until that patient is called to his or her reward," Dr. Brummer responded with an affirmative answer.[100]

In trying to combat this sort of vitalist perspective, Paris runs into another kind of opposition: that of pro-life activists, some of whom subject him to "virulent attacks." He attributes the difficulty of passing effective natural death acts to the long-standing opposition of right-to-life groups such as the Connecticut Right-to-Life Commission, an organization that successfully defeated efforts in that state for natural death legislation until 1985. He also believes that the more radical right-to-life advocates—those with a "life-at-any-cost mind-set"—threaten to undermine traditional Catholic teachings regarding appropriate care of the dying, as illustrated by the case of a Catholic wife in New York who said she would "never, never" consent to the removal of her brain-dead husband's respirator because "it is against my religion."[101]

Physicians, hospital administrators, and administrators of nursing homes sometimes present yet another opposing view when they refuse to abate life-sustaining treatment apart from a court order. Illustrative of this undue anxiety over liability is the physician in the Melanie Bacchiochi case. Bacchiochi, a young Connecticut woman, was judged by her physician to be brain-dead on the basis of repeated flat EEGs over a period of several days subsequent to her cardiopulmonary arrest. However, since Connecticut lacked a brain-death statute, her physician announced that "if he lived to be 150" he would not remove the respirator from a brain-dead patient without a court order.[102] This kind of attitude, which also brought on lengthy court proceedings in *Spring, Brophy,* and other cases, imposes on patient surrogates "costly, cumbersome, and traumatic" court hearings that sometimes seem quite unnecessary.

Thus, in a variety of ways, physicians, administrators, pro-life activists, and others often oppose the abatement of life-sustaining treatment because they mistakenly believe that "not doing everything to extend life as long as is physically possible is equivalent to killing the patient."[103] In sharp contrast, a final opposing view comes from the opposite direction in the form of utilitarian arguments advocating suicide and euthanasia. Paris constantly rejects such arguments, maintaining that "a crass utilitarianism that would write off the confused, the incompetent and the senile" is as wrong as the "save at all cost" mentality. In response to the influential *New England Journal of Medicine* article written by Sidney Wanzer and nine other physicians (see earlier text and note 28), an article with which Paris is in substantial agreement, he and Andrew Varga sound an important cautionary note:

There are forces in our society—forces actively promoting their cause—who would be all too ready to read the physician guidelines as an open invitation to withhold such basic treatments as antibiotics and hydration from the demented or the mildly senile whenever they experience a life-threatening episode, rather than when, as the authors direct, such patients have reached an acute crisis at the end stages of a terminal illness.[104]

In contrast to all of these opposing views, Paris defends a middle-of-the-road position that is "not new, novel, or unprecedented": the view that *all* modalities of medical treatment, including technological feeding and hydration, may be abated in appropriate circumstances of life-threatening illness. He regards this position as a "consensus view" developed by Catholic moral theologians since the sixteenth century, articulated by the President's Commission in 1983, held by the nation's leading physicians (e.g., the authors of the *New England Journal of Medicine* article mentioned earlier), written into recent case law in a number of judicial opinions from *Barber* to the present. As he and Richard McCormick describe the position, this ethical option

recognizes that there are certain circumstances in which the patient's condition is so debilitated that any treatment would be futile or, if not futile, would prove so burdensome as to be nonobligatory. In those limited situations, the withholding of nutrition and hydration is designed not to hasten the death by starvation or dehydration, but to spare the patient the prolongation of life when the patient can derive no benefit from such prolongation.[105]

Central to this position are three claims: that quality-of-life judgments are inescapable in making decisions to abate treatment, that artificial feeding and hydration is correctly understood as a modality of medical treatment, and that the burdens of artificial feeding and hydration occasionally outweigh the benefits of such treatment to the patient. In regard to the first claim, Paris thinks that patient surrogates and physicians must move beyond asking, "Can we keep this patient alive?" to asking a more difficult question, "What kind of life are we saving?" The attempt by pro-life advocates to make quality-of-life judgments incompatible with a sanctity-of-life perspective is simplistic and can lead, when "quality of life" is turned into a political slogan to criticize opponents' views, to a heretical interpretation of the dignity and value of human lives. Rather than following the "right-to-lifers" in having an "idolatry of life," he maintains that a correct usage of quality-of-life judgments—not the aberrant form in which individuals are judged according to their social utility—is grounded in the teachings of the Catholic moral theologians. In his words:

The common teaching that a patient with widely disseminated metastatic disease need not receive antibiotics for an intercurrent pneumonia is precisely the type of quality-of-life standard which prevails in traditional Catholic medical ethics. Absent the quality-of-life judgment, there could be no moral warrant for the withholding of such a simple, inexpensive, and effective treatment for a life-threatening condition. Likewise, it is only on a quality-of-life assessment that the judge in the Brophy case could write, as he did, that no life-threatening infection need be treated.[106]

As to the second claim, Paris disagrees with Barry, Callahan, Meilaender, and others who believe that assisted feeding is not a form of medical treatment. For him, that interpretation is simply false, as demonstrated by the President's Commission and the opinions of the *Barber, Hier,* and *Conroy* courts. Without feeling the need to belabor the point, he simply repeats the consensus view: namely, "the artificial provision of nutrition and fluids is not the same as providing ordinary food and water to a patient."[107]

The third claim, of course, is crucial in justifying the abatement of life-sustaining nutrition and hydration. Like the administration of all medical treatments, the administration of artificial food and fluids produces a mixed record of success and failure: beneficial on balance in the great majority of cases, but occasionally more burdensome than beneficial to some patients. It is this minority of cases that concerns Paris. To deal with such cases, he thinks the traditional ordinary/extraordinary distinction needs to be understood in terms of a proportionate benefit/burden test, as the *Barber, Hier,* and *Conroy* courts did, thereby focusing on the condition of the patient instead of the medical techniques used to treat the patient.[108] When applied to the medical condition of patients receiving artificial feeding, the implications of assessing benefits and burdens are the same as with other modalities of medical treatment: "No matter how simple, inexpensive, readily available, noninvasive, and common the procedure, if it does not offer substantial hope of benefit to the patient, he has no moral obligation to undergo it, nor the physician to provide it, nor the judge to order it."[109]

Precisely because he believes this ethical position is "not new," but an updating of the traditional Catholic teaching on the morality of treatment abatement prior to the 1960s ("when the development of high-technology medicine outstripped moral reflection and analysis"), Paris is particularly bothered by some contemporary Catholics who obscure this point to score points with their right-to-life allies. Consequently, he and McCormick single out the writers of the *amicus curiae* brief of the New Jersey Catholic Conference in the Nancy Jobes case, the hospital administrators in the Beverly Requena case, and Robert Barry for particular criticism. Contrary to Barry's claims, they argue that the views of Báñez, Vitoria, Gerald Kelly, and Daniel Cronin demonstrate that, prior to the Quinlan case, "there was little ambiguity or hesitancy about ending artificial feeding for dying patients." Among contemporary Catholic ethicists, they list 10 scholars who have written on the morality of abating treatment, and all of them agree that artificial feeding and fluids may be abated whenever the burdens outweigh the benefits to the patient. They conclude:

It is this bedrock teaching of theology on the meaning of life and death—neither of which in the Christian framework ought to be made absolute—and not a misplaced debate on "the casuistry of means" that should guide our judgments on the difficult and sometimes trying decisions cast up by modern medical technology. To do otherwise—or to count mere vegetative existence as a patient-benefit—is to let slip one's grasp on the heart of Catholic tradition in this matter. It is that tradition, developed over centuries of living out the Gospel message on the meaning of life and death—and not some immediate political "pro-life" agenda—that ought to be the source of our advice and guidance to the courts.[110]

How does Paris think cases involving the abatement of nutrition and hydration with nonautonomous patients should be handled? First, he emphasizes the importance of getting the facts unique to each case, including, where available, the previous views on treatment abatement held by the now-nonautonomous patient. Second, he believes that such cases should be handled in a manner consistent with the views put forth by the President's Commission and all courts of final decision in such cases since *Barber*. Third, he recommends the use of IECs as an alternative to the courts. Fourth, when the burdens of artificial feeding are judged to outweigh the benefits to the patient, he recommends, following the President's Commission, supportive care of the dying through the provision of comfort, company, and sedation from pain. Finally, he opposes any form of "active euthanasia" in these or any other cases.

Richard McCormick, S.J., as indicated in the discussion of Paris, is also a representative of position 4. Now the John A. O'Brien Professor of Christian Ethics at Notre Dame, McCormick defends the abatement of all forms of medical treatment in several publications. One of the more influential of those publications was coauthored with Paris. Having criticized the natural death legislation enacted in the late 1970s, McCormick and Paris reconsidered and changed their views on the use of advance directives. Although natural death legislation remains problematic, the legislative bills under consideration in 1981 were thought to have adequate safeguards to protect patients' preferences and guard against the possibility of euthanasia. Such legislation was also regarded as necessary to combat radical right-to-life groups intent on preventing patients from refusing life-sustaining treatment. In addition, nonstatutory advance directives such as the one proposed by Sissela Bok (see Chapter 5) were considered "helpful and fully Christian."[111]

McCormick's views on the morality and legality of abating treatment appear in his responses to *Quinlan, Saikewicz, Eichner, Barber,* and *Conroy*.[112] For him, *Barber* and *Conroy*, as well as the expansive ethical literature that has focused on artificial feeding and hydration, produce five key issues: the notion of a dying patient, the nature of artificial nutrition and hydration, the intention of death, the burden/benefit calculus, and the ongoing need to protect nonautonomous patients from nonvoluntary euthanasia. He thinks the concept of "the dying patient" is important but often ambiguous, considers artificial feeding and hydration to be a form of medical treatment, and argues against Meilaender that the abatement of such feeding and fluids need not be construed as "aiming at death." Rather, if artificial feeding is "foreseeably permanent" in the care of permanently unconscious patients or "profoundly incompetent ones . . . said to be dying," the removal of the feeding need not "involve a death-aim [but] only a thoroughly Christian assertion that there are values greater in life than living, that we all retain the right to decide how we shall live while dying."[113]

McCormick agrees with the Vatican's *Declaration on Euthanasia* and the President's Commission in moving away from the terminology of the ordinary/ extraordinary distinction to focus on the benefits and burdens of life-sustaining treatment. He thinks that the sort of calculation necessary to assess benefits and burdens "unavoidably" involves focusing on the "quality-of-life component . . . present in some of these decisions." However, assessments of (1) the burden of the treatment itself (in terms of pain and expense) and (2) the burden of continued existence need to be based on clear criteria, lest the door be opened to the abuse of euthanasia. He summarizes his position in the following manner:

> The permanently comatose and *some* noncomatose but elderly incompetent patients may be classified broadly as dying; . . . feeding by IV lines and nasogastric tubes is a medical procedure; . . . its discontinuance need not involve aiming at the death of such patients; and . . . the burden–benefit calculus may include, indeed often unavoidably includes, a quality-of-life ingredient, providing we draw the line at the right place.[114]

Albert Jonsen, a professor of medical ethics at the University of Washington School of Medicine, is in basic agreement with Paris and McCormick. Like them, he uses several of the ethical distinctions developed in earlier centuries by Catholic moral theologians, revises the ordinary/extraordinary distinction to mean proportionate/disproportionate care, thinks quality-of-life judgments are compatible with a sanctity-of-life perspective, favors the use of advance directives, and maintains that all medical treatments can be abated in certain circumstances. As a member of the President's Commission in the early 1980s, he advocates a position on treatment abatement that is generally consistent with the commission's *Deciding to Forego Life-Sustaining Treatment,* as well as most of the recent court decisions concerning treatment abatement.[115]

In *Clinical Ethics,* an influential book he coauthored with Mark Siegler and William Winslade, Jonsen and the others discuss treatment abatement from the perspectives of medicine, law, and ethics. In terms of the medical practice of abating treatment, they point out that physicians seem inclined to discontinue medical interventions in a certain order:

> Roughly speaking, this order seems to be as follows: the withdrawal of experimental therapy . . . ; the decision not to perform CPR; the discontinuation of breathing support such as a respirator; the discontinuation of agents that artificially maintain blood pressure and cardiac output; the decision not to intervene in the face of infections with antibiotic treatment; the decision to discontinue unusual forms of alimentation such as tube feeding

or parenteral hyperalimentation; and finally the decision to reduce intravenous fluids to a maintenance or even, at times, a below-maintenance level.[116]

Jonsen thinks that all of these forms of abating treatment are sometimes warranted. In cases of autonomous patients, he says, along with Bernard Lo, that any of four factors may present a sufficient reason for abating life-sustaining treatment: the treatment is futile, the patient declines the treatment, the quality of the patient's life is unacceptable to the patient, and the costs of continuing the treatment are judged to be excessive. However, "withholding medical therapy does not mean withholding care." Rather, "aggressive" supportive care should be provided to patients as they are dying: "adequate pain control, attention to bladder and bowel function, discontinuation of 'routine' tests, unlimited visiting hours, opportunities to talk or be silent, and assistance [in] arranging personal affairs."[117]

Of course decisions to abate treatment with nonautonomous patients are more difficult to justify on moral and legal grounds. However, Jonsen says, along with Siegler and Winslade, that such decisions are morally justifiable whenever three features of a case are in conjunction: (1) no goals of medicine "other than support of organic life are being or will be accomplished," (2) the patient's preferences are unknown or are believed to favor abating treatment in the circumstances of the case, and (3) the patient's quality of life has "fallen irretrievably below the threshold considered minimal" (e.g., whenever a patient is diagnosed with PVS, "a 'person' no longer exists in any significant sense of the term"). In some cases, these three features are joined by an important "external factor" (such as the excessive cost of the treatment). When all four of these variables come together in a case, abating treatment is not only permissible but obligatory. Moreover, abating treatment in such cases is clearly "within the law."[118]

As to the specific question of abating artificial feeding and hydration, Jonsen thinks that the abatement of IV lines, NG tubes, G-tubes, and parenteral hyperalimentation through central venous catheters is justifiable in some cases. For illustration purposes, he, Siegler, and Winslade present a case of a 94-year-old male nursing home patient who is nonautonomous, has had several bouts with aspiration pneumonia, has been treated with antibiotics and fluids, has frequently choked and expelled food, and regularly has a fever and severe coughs. If the patient has another episode of pneumonia, they recommend refraining from treating the disease, thereby permitting pneumonia once again to be "the old man's friend." As a part of this recommendation, they state that in this case, "there is no obligation to proceed with measures such as gastrostomy or gastrogavage."[119]

What about the morality of euthanasia? Here Jonsen varies from Paris and McCormick. Whereas they consistently reject euthanasia as being immoral, he explores several arguments for and against euthanasia; in addition, he points out that physicians who give patients high doses of morphine or diazepam engage in intentional killing in a manner "similar to administering an intravenous air bubble or an intravenous bolus of potassium."[120] For him, euthanasia in its "active" form is "undesirable" largely because "acceptance of the practice as ethical may bear the seeds of unacceptable social consequences." If, however, a physician concludes in a particular case "that he or she should accede to the plea of a sufferer who requests death, such a decision would be a sort of 'conscientious objection' to the prevailing ethical and legal view."[121]

Douglas Walton, a professor of philosophy at the University of Winnipeg, is in substantial agreement with Paris, McCormick, and Jonsen. Focusing on ICU patients, he argues that "constructive negotiation" is desirable in an ICU between autonomous patients and their physicians. By arriving at "a middle point . . . between paternalism and patient autonomy," the decision makers in a case can jointly agree on continuing treatment or abating any of the treatments that are used to sustain patients' lives. For permanently unconscious patients, the first requirement is to determine if they are brain-dead (using whole-brain criteria), have the apallic syndrome (e.g., Elaine Esposito survived for more than 37 years with this condition), or have some other form of irreversible unconsciousness. Once a patient has been diagnosed as having an irreversible illness that cannot be cured or remedied with medical treatment, decisions have to be made regarding the abatement of any medical treatments (including tube feedings) that are either extraordinary ("especially demanding and burdensome") or harmful to the patient.[122]

Position 5. Intentional killing as an exceptional moral alternative

Albert Jonsen's views on the morality of euthanasia provide a transition step between positions 4 and 5 and also point to the fundamental difference between these positions. The other ethicists identified with the fourth position—and virtually all of the ethicists identified with the first three positions—believe that the letting die/killing distinction is valid, that the moral and legal prohibition of euthanasia is very important, and that exceptions to the prohibition of intentional killing in clinical contexts are not permissible.

By contrast, Jonsen is willing to consider euthanasia as a possible moral alternative for physicians caring for patients who request death as a form of relief from their suffering. In his most extended comments on euthanasia, he (and Bernard Lo) discuss the morality of euthanasia as an option in the care of a terminally ill patient with recurrent metastatic carcinoma, a patient who had refused several modalities of treatment and then requested that his physician "speed up" his death.[123] In his comments on that case, as well as in his more general comments elsewhere on euthanasia, Jonsen never condones or justifies the intentional killing of patients; yet he also never completely shuts the door to that option. Instead, he indicates that a policy of euthanasia would be undesirable because of its long-term consequences, yet suggests—as does Paul Ramsey, for exceptional circumstances—that some physicians may feel compelled on occasion to engage in individual acts of euthanasia as a form of conscientious objection to laws prohibiting the intentional killing of patients even for reasons of mercy.

Two other ethicists, Robert Veatch and James Childress, defend the ethical position suggested (almost as an aside) by Jonsen and Ramsey. Veatch, already mentioned in Chapter 5, analyzes the morality of treatment abatement and intentional killing in numerous publications. Especially in *Death, Dying, and the Biological Revolution,* originally published in 1976, and scheduled for a second edition as this is being written, he maintains that the abatement of all medical treatment is sometimes justifiable. He also states that "allowed" deaths and "double-effect" deaths are morally preferable to the intentional killing of patients. Nevertheless, with great reluctance, he says that intentional killing can be occasionally justified as an exceptional moral alternative in the care of critically ill patients.[124]

Veatch arrives at these conclusions by approaching the issue of abating treatment from a "patient-centered perspective." That perspective, which he consistently maintains is needed as a corrective to the "technological priesthood" of scientists and physicians, emphasizes the importance of patient autonomy and interprets physicians and other health professionals in the context of being "invited into the patient's world." In order to combat the fallacy of the generalization of expertise—a false view that tends to regard physicians as experts in making moral decisions in clinical settings—Veatch constantly stresses that patients and their agents, not physicians, are the appropriate persons to make decisions about initiating, continuing, or abating treatment.

The problem, in Veatch's view, is that physicians frequently approach the issue of abating treatment from the wrong direction: they assume the right to "order" treatments for patients, to do whatever they regard as being beneficial for patients, to prolong patients' lives as the ultimate goal of medicine, to combat patients' deaths whenever and however they can, and, when they can no longer prevent patients from dying, to issue a DNR "order."[125] All of these decisions are framed in terms of "what should we, as medical professionals, do with regard to the patient who is lying in our hospital bed?" Working out of this perspective, physicians consider questions related to medical care ("Should we treat; should we stop the respirator; should we discuss the matter with the family; should we mercifully inject the air bubble?") as if they, both literally and figuratively, "were standing above the patient . . . trying to decide what is best for him."[126]

This false and harmful perspective, which minimizes and belies the importance of patient self-determination and consent to medical treatment, is aided by ethicists who emphasize the need to have an objective standard for making decisions about administering treatment and abating treatment. Responding in particular to Ramsey's proposal concerning "medically indicated" treatments, Veatch says the proposal is "wishful thinking on the part of one who does not know the enormous ambiguity of the term." Rather than using a "pseudoscientific term" that suggests moral approval of any medical intervention physicians recommend, "whether it is helpful or moral or tolerable by the patient," he suggests that ethicists and others candidly admit that the quest for objectivity in decision making through "technical, medical facts" is doomed to failure.[127] Consequently, he thinks that proposed distinctions such as dying/nondying patients, medically indicated/not medically indicated treatment, or medical/nonmedical feeding are rarely decisive and often bring about misplaced debates.

To Veatch, decisions about continuing or abating medical treatment are inescapably subjective in nature. Misleading distinctions such as those just mentioned and misleading descriptions (such as "inevitably dying") fail to reflect the fact that, in spite of technological monitoring equipment, laboratory reports on blood gases and electrolytes, and so forth, decisions about the morality of abating treatment are "inherently evaluative." The task is not to determine whether a recommended treatment can be done, but whether that treatment is useless or gravely burdensome to a particular patient—from that person's perspective, if possible.

To emphasize the subjective nature of decisions about useful medical treatment, Veatch uses the example of a permanently vegetative patient who would die without a ventilator, but who might live years with mechanical ventilation. Whether the ventilator is to be judged useful or useless depends on "whether it serves some useful purpose to preserve vegetative life." Different people, such as an Orthodox Jew and a Roman Catholic, are likely to give different answers. Moreover, they "ought to give different answers if they are reflecting their traditions."[128] To emphasize the subjective nature of decisions about burdensome treatment, he uses an example of two medically identical patients on hemodialysis. It is quite possible that one patient will judge that the life-sustaining requirement of being attached to a dialysis machine 6–8 hours a day for 2–3 days a week for the remainder of his or her life is an excruciating, unbearable burden, whereas the other patient may regard the required dialysis unpleasant, but beneficial on balance. To make such decisions about the benefits and burdens of life-sustaining treatment requires, for competent patients, the "inherently nonmedical determination of how valuable it is to continue living."[129]

Veatch does not think his views lead to an unlimited subjectivism, as Ramsey has charged, because of his use of ethical principles and ethical distinctions. Central to his deontological position are several ethical principles he believes to be nonconsequentialist in nature and coequal in rank: autonomy, honesty, contract keeping, justice, and avoiding killing.[130] In addition, while rejecting some proposed ethical distinctions, he believes that at least three ethical distinctions remain important in assessing the morality of abating treatment and other end-of-life issues. The *direct/indirect action distinction* is problematic and easily criticized, but possibly useful in some clinical situations. The other two distinctions, properly interpreted, have particular importance to the ethical issues of treatment abatement and intentional killing. The traditional *ordinary/ extraordinary distinction* is helpful, once the misleading terms "ordinary" and "extraordinary" are dropped, as a way of distinguishing between reasonable and unreasonable treatments. Possibly acknowledging that reasonableness, like beauty, can be in the eye of the beholder, Veatch proposes three "rational criteria" for making judgments about reasonable (and thus obligatory) treatment, with all of the criteria being applied from the patient's perspective: (1) useful versus useless, (2) grave burden, and (3) proportionality of usefulness and burdensomeness. The *let die/kill distinction* is helpful in distinguishing between treatment abatement and euthanasia, at least for ethicists (and other people) who do not accept "the consequentialist's premise that all that counts in morality is consequences." Among the several ways of trying to establish that the often-claimed difference between letting die and killing is a real difference, Veatch finds only two arguments satisfactory: (1) the *long-term* consequences differ in that the practice of letting die is self-limiting ("only certain members of the society will die if left untreated"), whereas "a practice of merciful killing could potentially include all humans within its scope"; and (2) active killing is "deontologically wrong" in that "killing another human being . . . is always a wrong-making characteristic" of actions, whereas letting another human being die is not always wrong.[131]

When, then, is a refusal of treatment acceptable? For Veatch, such decisions by autonomous patients are acceptable as long as they are reasoned. In other words, autonomous patients have an *absolute* right "to refuse treatment for themselves whenever they can offer reasons valid to themselves."[132] The more difficult problem is extending autonomy to surrogate decision makers without giving them unlimited discretion to make foolish or malicious decisions. To deal with the morally important differences among cases involving nonautonomous patients, and to extend the principle of autonomy to surrogates in at least some of these cases, Veatch makes an important and novel proposal to distinguish between two types of surrogates: (1) those who are strangers to the nonautonomous patient, and (2) those who can be "bonded guardians" because they have a preexisting relationship with the nonautonomous patient as relatives or close friends. Bonded guardians, in contrast to "nonbonded" or "stranger" guardians, can be granted at least some discretion (or "familial autonomy") in making decisions to abate treatment on the behalf of a nonautonomous patient, and thus need only follow what Veatch calls the "standard of reasonableness." That standard, or test for surrogate treatment-abatement decisions, stipulates that a treatment refusal is *unreasonable* (and thus treatment morally required) whenever

the treatment is useful in treating a patient's condition (though not necessarily lifesaving) and at the same time does not give rise to any significant patient-centered objections based on physical or mental burden; familial, social or economic concern, or religious belief.[133]

Can the medical administration of nutrition and hydration be disproportionately burdensome, and therefore expendable? Veatch answers in the affirmative, but with caution. For him, the debate over whether such feeding is medical or nonmedical is misplaced, because the characterization of the feeding is irrelevant: even nonmedical forms of care are expendable whenever they are judged to be useless or disproportionately burdensome. However, he believes that Callahan is "on to something" in regard to the symbolism of providing food and fluids, and thinks the "revulsion" over abating this form of care "should remain as a way of requiring excruciatingly careful justification for withholding nutrition and hydration." Moreover, while the abatement of nutrition and hydration are "within the rights of the competent patient" and also "acceptable for the properly established surrogate acting within reason," he cautions against the potential long-term harm of abating nutrition as a "backdoor approach to active killing." Because of the certitude of death following the abatement of artificial feeding and fluids, the "potential harms of a policy tolerating forgoing nutrition are much like those of tolerating active killing."[134]

As to the acceptability of euthanasia ("active killing" in Veatch's terminology) as an exceptional moral alternative, he concludes that such actions can occasionally be justifiable. Although he describes his view as an "essentially pacifist anti-killing position" in *A Theory of Medical Ethics*, he states (in both editions of *Death, Dying, and the Biological Revolution*) that active killing can be a moral option in rare situations.[135] Even though killing another human being obviously violates the principle of avoiding killing and therefore is always "*prima facie* wrong," such acts of killing in rare cases could be "moral on balance" in meeting the request for relief from a patient in intractable pain. In such a case, however, the justifying reason would be justice (to meet the needs of "the least well off") rather than mercy, because mercy has consequentialist implications that could open the door to "other killings . . . that seem clearly unacceptable."[136]

Having accepted active killing as an exceptional—*very* exceptional—moral alternative, Veatch rejects the option of making these actions legal. Because such cases are quite rare, and because a legal policy in favor of active killing would involve "great danger," he thinks that prudence calls for the continued criminalization of all active killings. For physicians and any other moral agents who nevertheless feel compelled to kill a patient in extreme pain for reasons of mercy or justice, he advises "an appeal to civil disobedience." If such a killing can be justified as an act of civil disobedience, the courts always have the option of showing leniency in their judgments—without accepting active killing as a matter of legal policy.[137]

James Childress, a professor of religious studies and medical education at the University of Virginia, analyzes the morality of treatment abatement, assisted suicide, and euthanasia in several books and articles. Like Veatch, he begins with a presumption in favor of prolonging life and updates the traditional distinctions of ordinary/extraordinary means, let die/kill, and direct/indirect actions in an ongoing effort to bring ethical insight to end-of-life issues as they arise in contemporary clinical settings. Also like Veatch, he supports the abatement of all medical treatment when warranted, goes beyond that view to justify acts of euthanasia as an exceptional moral alternative in some circumstances, and argues that the intentional killing of patients should not be legalized as a social policy.

Unlike Veatch, he uses the principle of respect for persons as a way of emphasizing patient autonomy; supplements that principle with the principles of beneficence and nonmaleficence, as well as justice; deals much more extensively with the abatement of artificial feeding and hydration; and thinks that weak paternalism is occasionally justified in overriding treatment-abatement decisions made by questionably autonomous patients or the surrogates of nonautonomous patients. Also in contrast to Veatch, Childress has a mixed deontological perspective in ethics that allows some consideration of consequences in determining the morality of actions, and he is therefore willing to justify occasional acts of intentional killing done for reasons of mercy in a way Veatch finds unacceptable.

Childress thinks that all autonomous persons, inside or outside hospital settings, "have the moral right and have, or should have, the legal right to refuse lifesaving medical treatment for whatever reasons they find appropriate."[138] This right to refuse treatment is more than a "relative right" (Ramsey), but it is not absolute, as Veatch suggests. Instead, the right to refuse treatment involves interaction among the principles of respect for persons, beneficence, and nonmaleficence. The general "presumption" that an adult patient has the autonomous status to make a decision about treatment abatement can be "rebutted under certain conditions," such as (1) a determination that the patient lacks decision-making capacity or (2) a judgment that the patient's refusal of life-sustaining treatment would impose serious burdens on others (such as a minor child left without a mother). In these circumstances, Childress believes that a decision to abate treatment can and should be overridden through a form of limited or constrained paternalistic action.

When decisions to abate treatment involve nonautonomous patients, Childress is concerned about substantive and procedural aspects of the decisions. In terms of the substantive features of these "hard cases," he argues that the "range of reasons" permitting treatment abatement on the behalf of others needs to be restricted. Standards of "quality of life," "meaningful life," or "humanhood"

(Joseph Fletcher) are all problematic in that they tend to move toward "insidious judgments of social worth."[139] To allow physicians or patients' surrogates to use such standards is to open the door to inherently vague standards that can be corrupted by judgments of social worth and can easily be directed in abusive ways against the senile and mentally retarded. Consequently, such slogans or standards should be replaced by "the patient's best interests," especially if the patient has never been autonomous.

In terms of procedure, Childress thinks that family members or close friends are the preferable decision makers whenever a nonautonomous patient has previously been autonomous, because the patient's wishes or values are likely to be more accessible to these persons. In cases of nonautonomous patients who have never been autonomous, or nonautonomous patients whose preferences regarding treatment abatement are not known, the best-interests standard should be employed by surrogates according to a serial or lexical ordering of decision makers: family members, physicians and other health care professionals, hospital committees, and the courts.[140]

When may medical nutrition and hydration be abated? Childress was one of the first ethicists to address the morality of abating life-sustaining food and fluids, and he argues much more forcefully than Veatch does for the abatement of this modality of medical treatment whenever the discontinuation of such treatment is in a patient's best interests. In a widely read article coauthored with Joanne Lynn, he argues that three rare kinds of situations call for the abatement of food and fluids: when such treatment is futile, when such treatment offers no possibility of benefit to permanently unconscious patients, and when such treatment is, on balance, disproportionately burdensome to the patient. According to Childress and Lynn, medical nutrition and hydration "do not appear to be distinguishable in any morally relevant way from other life-sustaining medical treatments that may on occasion be withheld or withdrawn."[141]

In two subsequent articles Childress elaborates on the morality of abating medical nutrition and hydration. In an article coauthored with Steven Dalle Mura, Childress rejects three opposing views: that abating food and fluids is tantamount to killing patients, that such treatment is always necessary for the comfort and dignity of patients, and that such treatment is symbolically important. The last of these arguments, identified with the "symbol or sentiment utilitarianism" of Daniel Callahan, is particularly criticized for allowing "the possibility of damage to a symbol's 'interests' to outweigh actual, palpable damage to or violation of the central interests of actual (and not symbolic) persons."[142]

The same arguments against Callahan's views appear in a third article on medical nutrition and hydration. In addition, Childress revises the ordinary/extraordinary distinction by discussing "obligatory" and "optional" treatments. For him, the administration of medical nutrition and hydration, like other forms of life-sustaining medical treatment, is correctly understood in the context of a physician's obligation to care for a patient, an "obligation of care [that] should be shaped by the patient's needs and preferences." Consequently, the administration of life-sustaining nutrition and hydration is (1) usually obligatory, (2) sometimes optional (in two senses: indifference, or praiseworthiness as a heroic act), and (3) *sometimes wrong*. When an autonomous patient, or a previously autonomous patient whose views are known, has unambivalently refused medical nutrition and hydration without violating anyone else's rights, the provision of such treatment—even if based on benevolence—"is a form of disrespect and an insult to the patient as a person." Likewise, whenever a physician or surrogate of a nonautonomous patient concludes that medical feeding of the patient is futile, of no benefit to the patient, or disproportionately burdensome to the patient, the continuation of medical feeding represents a violation of the patient's interests. In such a situation, the treatment is "not only optional but also wrong," and the physician has an obligation not to provide the treatment.[143]

Childress also discusses the let die/kill distinction at some length, often in response to James Rachels' rejection of the distinction. For Childress, Rachels' examples of Smith and Jones (discussed earlier, under "First Phase of the Debate"), are "so markedly disanalogous" to medical situations of allowing patients to die that "it is not clear what Rachels' argument shows."[144] In any case, Childress believes that "the distinction is worth retaining" because of its embodiment in current medical practices, its importance in sustaining relationships of trust between patients and physicians, and the practical difference in the certitude of patients' deaths when acts of intentional killing are compared with acts of abating treatment. Nevertheless, he emphasizes that

acceptance or rejection of the *distinction* does not necessarily determine *moral conclusions* about particular cases. . . . Even if the distinction is morally significant, the label "killing" or the label "letting die" should not dictate a conclusion about a particular case. For example, it would be absurd to affirm the moral significance of the distinction and then to accept *all* cases of letting die as morally fitting. Even instances of letting die must meet other criteria such as the detriment–benefit calculation, and some cases of allowed death involve egregious negligence.[145]

In a similar manner, Childress argues that *not all* acts of intentionally killing patients are morally blameworthy. Continuing to affirm the let die/kill distinction, he says that individual acts of intentional killing for reasons of mercy "may well be right, and perhaps even praiseworthy" in rare clinical cases in which a patient's pain cannot be effectively controlled, and the patient expresses a wish to be "put out of his misery."[146] Moreover, specifically in contrast to Arthur Dyck's views, he states that "killing may not always violate the duty of nonmaleficence, and it may be an expression of love, mercy, kindness, and care."[147]

Nevertheless, Childress thinks that abating treatment is morally preferable to intentional killing, that hospices offer an effective alternative to the ineffective care terminally ill patients often get in hospitals, and that, even though intentional killing for reasons of mercy can occasionally be justified on moral grounds, such acts of killing patients should remain illegal. Emphasizing the distinction between *acts* and *practices,* he maintains that a practice of euthanasia should not become social policy even if some acts of euthanasia "do indeed express mercy, are beneficent, are not nonmaleficent (at least in the sense of net harm), [and] are not unjust and disrespectful (because they are in accord with a competent person's wishes)."[148] Because no one has a "positive right to be killed," and because a practice of euthanasia would be open to abuse, he thinks it is necessary "to prohibit by rule and policy some acts that do not appear to be wrong in some circumstances in order to maintain a viable practice that, for the most part, expresses our principles and avoids seriously undesirable consequences."[149] He therefore states that the "legal rule against 'mercy killing'—and its counterpart in professional ethics—is, I would argue, morally justified."[150]

How, then, should illegal but possibly moral acts of euthanasia be handled? Pointing out that Veatch and Ramsey have both suggested civil disobedience as a possible legal framework for such acts, Childresss suggests conscientious objection as a preferable legal framework. Both civil disobedience and conscientious objection are, according to him, (1) public, (2) nonviolent (with violence being defined as "intentional and unauthorized harm or injury to a person against his/her will"), and (3) submissive violations of law. The two forms of protest differ in that conscientious objection (4) is based on personal moral convictions that are often religious rather than political in nature, and (5) is intended primarily to witness to those moral convictions rather than promote social and legal change.[151] An example of euthanasia as an act of conscientious objection is the case of Lester Zygmanik, who in 1973 carried out his paralyzed brother's request to be killed by shooting him with a sawed-off shotgun. Childress approves of the way the jury handled the Zygmanik case in that they *excused* his action (by ruling him not guilty by reason of temporary insanity) without *justifying* the act of killing or suggesting that the law of the land should be changed.[152]

Position 6.   Intentional killing as a moral and legal alternative

The most liberal position on the morality of abating treatment is relatively new compared with the positions at the opposite end of the spectrum. With its utilitarian roots going back to Jeremy Bentham and John Stuart Mill, and with Joseph Fletcher getting credit as the first contemporary advocate of voluntary euthanasia as a moral and legal option, this ethical position clearly lacks the kind of claim to "tradition" that one finds among Jewish rabbis, Roman Catholic

moral theologians, and philosophers and religious ethicists who have been significantly influenced by these religious perspectives on life and death. However,
many philosophers are convinced that this last position, in its utilitarian and
libertarian forms, is a needed corrective to the traditional ways of thinking about
treatment abatement and euthanasia.

In some respects, despite their major differences, position 6 is like position 1.
In contrast to all of the intervening positions, these two positions on opposite
ends of the spectrum share a certain kind of clarity and simplicity. Representatives of both views regard treatment abatement and euthanasia as being morally
equivalent, reject the ethical distinctions believed to be important by ethicists
identified with the other positions, and place the contemporary controversy over
the abatement of nutrition and hydration in the Shakespearian category of "much
ado about nothing."

Beginning with Fletcher's dissenting opinion in the 1950s, and continuing
with the publications of Marvin Kohl, James Rachels, and a few other philosophers in the mid-1970s, this ethical option came into prominence during the
second and third phases of the debate over the morality of abating treatment. As
evidenced by the controversy engendered by proposals to abate mechanical ventilation, medical nutrition and hydration, and other modalities of life-sustaining
treatment from Karen Quinlan, Claire Conroy, and other nonautonomous patients, some of the traditional ethical "answers" simply did not seem to fit the
questions brought about by technological medicine. Moreover, the increasing
ability of physicians to use various medical technologies to prolong the lives of
many patients—autonomous and nonautonomous, conscious and permanently
unconscious—for indeterminate periods of time emphasized the importance of
other ethical questions related to the *purpose* of such technologies, the *quality* of
the lives being prolonged, and the financial and emotional *costs* of vitalistic
approaches to medicine.

For many philosophers, the combination of (1) outdated ethical theories and
(2) unprecedented moral problems in technological medicine requires new philosophical approaches to the cluster of ethical issues at the end of life. Consequently, philosophers working out of utilitarian and/or libertarian perspectives on
life and death regularly challenge the "moral absolutism" that is represented by
more conservative ethicists, promulgated through policy statements of medical
societies, and embodied in laws prohibiting the killing of suffering patients even
at those patients' requests. To these philosophers, each human life is *not* correctly understood as a gift from god, is *not* of infinite and inestimable worth, and
is *not* to be prolonged indefinitely merely because advances in biomedical en-
gineering, biochemistry, and pharmacology make the continued biological existence of some patients medically possible. Rather, the value of individual lives
obviously depends on the quality and duration of those lives, the suffering and
debilitating conditions endured as a part of those lives, and the ongoing possi-

bility of those lives being meaningful instead of merely existing at an organic level. Also obvious from these philosophical perspectives is the answer to the question "Whose life is it anyway?" The answer: "not God's, not the state's, not the hospital's, not the physician's, but mine."

James Rachels, a professor of philosophy at the University of Alabama at Birmingham, is a leading representative of this ethical perspective on treatment abatement and related end-of-life ethical issues. Beginning with his influential *New England Journal of Medicine* article discussed earlier, he has continued to criticize widely held intuitions and widely used arguments regarding the alleged differences between allowing patients to die and killing them. For him, all attempts to show that the let die/kill distinction is morally significant are "muddled," "irrational," and often "cruel" in their practical consequences.[153]

In contrast to the views of Veatch and Childress, Rachels is convinced that deliberately allowing patients to die and intentionally killing patients are "morally the same thing," that both voluntary and nonvoluntary euthanasia are easily justified, and that euthanasia or "mercy killing" should be legally acceptable as a defense against the charge of homicide. To arrive at this position regarding euthanasia as a moral and legal option, he rejects the "traditional view," puts together several arguments concerning the morality of euthanasia, supports these philosophical arguments with several case presentations (the paradigm case being "Jack," a cancer patient at NIH) and proposes a way of legalizing euthanasia.[154]

Rachels identifies the "traditional view" with Christianity, all sanctity-of-life views (including Jainism and Albert Schweitzer), and, most specifically, the ethical distinctions developed by Roman Catholic moral theologians. Rejecting all sanctity-of-life views that value humans for merely "being alive" (in a biological sense), he proposes "a new understanding of the sanctity of life" according to which humans (and some nonhuman animals) are to be valued only when they "have a life" in a biographical sense. For him, "the value of life is the value it has *for the beings who are the subjects of lives.*" By emphasizing the being alive/having a life distinction, he maintains that the crucial question in deciding questions of life and death is this one: "Is a *life,* in the biographical sense, being destroyed or otherwise adversely affected?" In comparison to this question, other ethical questions traditionally thought important are really not important: "the species of the subject of the life, and the means that are used [to bring about death], as well as the intention with which the act is done, are all more or less irrelevant."[155]

To make his case, Rachels proceeds to "debunk" irrelevant ethical distinctions associated with the traditional view. The intentional/nonintentional termination of life, the ordinary/extraordinary means of treatment, and the let die/kill distinctions are all "a muddle of indefensible claims, backed by tradition but not by reason."[156] The first two distinctions are dismissed fairly quickly. Using an argument-by-analogy methodology (e.g., Jack and Jill go to visit their grand-mother), he argues that a difference in intention between two moral agents is irrelevant when they "do the same thing" to produce "the same consequences." For him, "*the rightness or wrongness of an act is determined by the reasons for and against it*"—and intention is often "not among the reasons" for or against an action.[157] Then, interpreting the ordinary/extraordinary distinction in a defi-nitional manner to apply to specific treatments, he rejects the second distinction as being both false and useless. The reason is simple: "the definitions require that we must *already* have decided the moral questions of life and death—we must already have decided whether the use of the treatment is a good thing—*before* we can answer the question of whether the treatment is extraordinary."

The heart of Rachels' position lies in his rejection of the third distinction. In fact, most of his publications represent an expansion and updating of the two themes developed in his initial article on the subject: the "bare difference" between killing and letting die is morally insignificant, and in some circum-stances "active" euthanasia is morally preferable to "passive" euthanasia. Re-sponding to various critics of his position, he now uses two principal arguments to support the "Equivalence Thesis": "the bare fact that one act is an act of killing, while another act is an act of 'merely' letting someone die, is not a morally good reason in support of the judgment that the former is worse than the latter."[158] The first of the arguments is called the "Bare Difference Argument." Trying to parry criticisms by Judith Jarvis Thomson and Philippa Foot, Rachels uses additional analogies (e.g., head-chopping versus nose-punching, an analogy borrowed from Thomson and used against her) to demonstrate that if two actions *have the same consequences* there can be no intrinsic difference between the two actions that has moral significance. Having completed the demonstration that killing and letting die are morally equivalent, he moves to a second argument. The "No Relevant Difference Argument" is an attempt to show *why* the two actions are morally equivalent. Responding to criticisms by Richard Trammell, Rachels argues that killing and letting die are morally equivalent because the consequences they produce are equally wrong. In his words: they both put "an end to one's biographical life," or "the victim ends up dead."

Rachels thus thinks that in a strictly formal or analytical sense the conse-quences produced by letting patients die and killing them makes the two actions morally equivalent. However, when he applies the equivalence thesis to cases of critically ill patients in clinical settings, he consistently says that intentionally killing some of these patients ("active euthanasia") is morally preferable to abating life-sustaining treatment so that they may die ("passive euthanasia"). The reason for the difference is some other feature of the cases, usually the suffering of the patient. For instance, he puts forth the case of a patient who is terminally ill with throat cancer. To Rachels, the physician in charge of such a case has three alternatives: (1) continue unabated treatment until the suffering patient finally dies days later; (2) terminate treatment and "do nothing else" until the suffering patient dies, possibly within a matter of hours; and (3) give the patient a lethal injection upon the patient's request so that death will occur immediately. In his view, the first alterantive is "patently inhumane" but at least has "a certain kind of integrity." The third alternative is "the morally decent position." And the second alternative, the alternative of terminating treatment but not killing the patient? That alternative—widely thought to be a "moderate" view—is "sheer nonsense from both the point of view of logic and of morals."[159]

When discussing the morality of euthanasia, Rachels' favorite case is the case of "Jack," Stewart Alsop's dying roommate at the NIH in the early 1970s. Jack was 28, had a melanoma in his stomach "about the size of a softball," suffered constantly from the pain associated with the cancer, and consequently would regularly "moan, or whimper . . . then he would begin to howl, like a dog."[160] For Rachels, "Jack" is a representative of an unknown number of terminally ill patients who suffer from ineffectively controlled pain, continue to suffer point-lessly, and would suffer less if they were killed quickly with a lethal injection. That such killing is morally preferable in such circumstances seems clear to him:

If we simply withhold treatment, it may take him *longer* to die, and so he will suffer *more* than he would if we were to administer the lethal injection. This fact provides strong reason for thinking that, once we have made the initial decision not to prolong his agony, active euthanasia is actually preferable to passive euthanasia rather than the reverse. It also shows a kind of incoherence in the conventional view: to say that passive euthanasia is preferable is to endorse the option which leads to more suffering rather than less, and is contrary to the humanitarian impulse which prompts the decision not to prolong his life in the first place.[161]

In order for the case of "Jack" to be "the clearest possible case of euthana-sia," five features have to be present in the case: (1) the patient would have been deliberately killed, (2) the patient was going to die soon anyway, (3) the patient was suffering terrible pain, (4) the patient would have asked to be killed, and (5) the reason for the killing was mercy.[162] When Rachels considers the philosoph-ical arguments for and against euthanasia in this type of case, he rejects a cluster of arguments against "active" euthanasia and says that two arguments for the morality of such killing are cogent: (1) the argument from the Golden Rule, as developed by R.M. Hare; and (2) the classical argument from mercy. For him, the argument from mercy is "the single most powerful argument" in support of "active" euthanasia, especially in his updating of the utilitarian version of the argument. Simply put, his argument for euthanasia calls for "doing what is in everyone's best interests" (in the case of "Jack," a consideration of everyone's best interests would include Jack, Jack's wife, physicians, nurses, and other patients). By focusing on the best interests of all parties in a case, he believes that he "proves that active euthanasia *can* be justified":

1. If an action promotes the best interests of *everyone* concerned and violates *no one's* rights, then that action is morally acceptable.
2. In at least some cases, active euthanasia promotes the best interests of everyone concerned and violates no one's rights.
3. Therefore, in at least some cases, active euthanasia is morally acceptable.[163]

Yet, in contrast to the legality of "nonvoluntary passive euthanasia" since 1976 (as illustrated by the Quinlan, Herbert, and Conroy cases), "active" euthanasia remains illegal—even though juries sometimes refuse to convict "mercy killers." Should there continue to be "a considerable gap between the official position of the law . . . and what actually happens" in courts of law? Rachels, in contrast to Veatch and Childress, thinks not. For him, "it is at least *prima facie* undesirable for there to be such a wide gap here, for if we deem a type of behavior not fit for punishment, why should we continue to stigmatize that behavior as criminal?"[164]

Rachels thinks that the "slippery-slope argument," the most widely used argument against the legalization of euthanasia, does not work, in either its logical or psychological versions. Would legalizing euthanasia in clinical settings actually lead to undesirable consequences? He thinks not, suggesting that the abuses that would inevitably occur would not be "*so* numerous as to outweigh the advantages of legalization." Even extending the legalization of euthanasia to cases of *nonvoluntary* euthanasia, a legal change he favors, would still have beneficial consequences for society. By simply prohibiting *involuntary* euthanasia, but legalizing voluntary *and* nonvoluntary euthanasia, society would thereby permit justifiable killing in "a variety of cases": "Hans Florian's wife" (a patient with Alzheimer's disease), "Repouille's son" (a brain-damaged teenager), "Baby Jane Doe" (an infant with spina bifida and microcephaly), and patients "in irreversible coma." In this manner, "active" euthanasia would be a legal option whenever "a person's biographical life is over" or whenever "there is no prospect of a biographical life."[165]

Rachels therefore proposes that "active" euthanasia be legalized as an expression of "the argument from liberty." Expanding on Bentham and Mill, he maintains (1) that "a terminal patient who wishes to end his or her life rather than continue suffering has the right to do so" (as do, he thinks, a range of nonautonomous patients), and (2) that a physician or other third party may kill such a patient whenever both patient and physician are "consenting adults" engaged in "a private affair" in which "others have no right to interfere." To make this type of killing actually work as a legal option does not require the cumbersome procedures proposed in earlier years by euthanasia societies in Britain and the United States. Instead, he simply proposes that "a plea of mercy killing be acceptable as a defense against a charge of homicide in much the same way that a plea of self-defense is acceptable.'' He concludes: ''the main consequence of my proposal would be to sanction officially what . . . juries already do.''[166]

Jonathan Glover, a Fellow in Philosophy at New College, Oxford, agrees with many of Rachels' views. Glover rejects the sanctity-of-life principle in favor of quality-of-life judgments, arguing that such judgments sometimes necessarily lead to a justification of killing in order to avoid greater evils. Rather than being intrinsically wrong, killing is (1) *directly* wrong whenever it ''reduces the length of a worth-while life'' or overrides an autonomous person's desire to go on living, and (2) *indirectly* wrong whenever it produces harmful side effects for other people.[167]

When he discusses the morality of killing in clinical settings, Glover rejects the let die/kill distinction, the rule of double effect (''intellectually dubious rigmarole''), and the distinction between ordinary and extraordinary means of prolonging life. Instead of using these ''conservative'' distinctions to prohibit killing or limit acts of justifiable killing, he prefers to focus on the consequences produced by killing to see which acts of killing are permissible and which acts are directly or indirectly wrong. Using this approach, he concludes that acts of assisted suicide and acts of voluntary euthanasia are often justifiable. Assisted suicide is ''always to be preferred,'' but voluntary euthanasia ''is justified in those cases where we know that the person would commit suicide if he could.''[168]

Moreover, when acts of voluntary euthanasia do not produce ''overridingly bad side-effects,'' they should be legal. However, Glover does not propose a legal mechanism for handling such acts of killing. Rather, stating that he believes in ''trusting doctors not to take life unjustifiably,'' he makes a simple proposal: have a trial period to gather empirical data on legalized medical killing upon patients' requests to see whose ''guesses and intuitions'' are correct regarding such a policy, his optimistic predictions or the pessimistic predictions of the opponents of legalized voluntary euthanasia.[169]

Glover believes that the morality of nonvoluntary euthanasia hangs on the answers to two questions: ''When, if ever, is it justifiable to conclude that someone's life is not worth living?'' and ''What should our policy be'' in the event of such cases? For him, the only way of answering the first question, an admittedly unsatisfactory approach, is to substitute ourselves in the place of a nonautonomous patient and ask ''whether we ourselves would find such a life preferable to death.'' Of course, in trying to judge that ''someone would, if able to choose, prefer to be dead'' one always runs the risk of being wrong. But, according to Glover, one runs risks the other way as well, in preserving nonautonomous lives that are characterized by pain, paralysis, loneliness, claustrophobia, and ''boredom to the point of madness.'' In such instances, when one concludes that (1) a patient does not have ''a life worth living'' and (2) ''this kind of life" does not justify the effort necessary to preserve it or "the effects on other people that its preservation is having," an "intentional and undiluted act of killing" is the preferable alternative. Such an act of killing may not only be justifiable, but may be an act of "a decent and generous person" who should receive respect rather than moral or legal condemnation.[170]

Two philosophers at the Centre for Human Bioethics at Monash University (Australia) have views similar to those held by Rachels and Glover. Peter Singer, the director of the centre, provides utilitarian arguments for non-voluntary and voluntary euthanasia. For him, there is no intrinsic moral difference between allowing patients to die and killing them, even though he acknowledges (in contrast to Rachels) that extrinsic factors in some cases preclude an equivalence thesis applied to cases of letting die and cases of killing. Nevertheless, he thinks that "active" euthanasia is morally preferable to the "drawn-out death" of "passive" euthanasia, as indicated by his comments regarding the morality of nonvoluntary euthanasia. He argues that "a swift and painless death" is called for in the medical management of nonautonomous patients in two sets of circumstances: (1) when patients are in irreversible coma ("their lives have no intrinsic value . . . They are, in effect, dead"), and (2) when conscious but not self-conscious patients experience more pain than pleasure ("it is difficult to see the point of keeping such beings alive if their life is, on the whole, miserable").[171]

Singer thinks the case for voluntary euthanasia is much stronger. Voluntary euthanasia is justifiable whenever a rational and self-conscious patient requests to be killed rather than having to endure severe pain or "other distressing conditions" (such as fragile bones, incontinence of bowel or bladder, or difficulty in breathing). Acts of voluntary euthanasia should also be legal and, if the provisions of the law follow the proposals made by voluntary euthanasia societies (incurable illness diagnosed by two physicians, a written request for euthanasia witnessed by two other persons, and a 30-day waiting period before the act of killing), the benefits of legalized medical killing will far outweigh the "very small number of unnecessary deaths that might occur."[172]

Helga Kuhse, the deputy director of the Centre for Human Bioethics, has a virtually identical position. Rejecting the sanctity-of-life principle and all of the ethical distinctions discussed in this chapter, she argues that "both active and passive euthanasia are instances of the intentional termination of life," that "active" euthanasia is morally preferable to letting nature "take her sometimes cruel course," and that "active" euthanasia should be legalized. If other countries would follow the Netherlands in legalizing this type of killing in clinical settings, she thinks that the practice of helping patients die upon their request would "decrease, not increase, the scope of abuse" now found in the medical management of critically ill patients.[173]

Assessment

What can be made of these six different positions and the variations within them? It is clear, at the very least, that ethicists disagree as much among themselves on the issue of abating treatment as physicians, attorneys, and other reflective persons do. I do not plan to unpack all the reasons for the disagreements among ethicists, nor do I plan to do an exhaustive analysis and comparison of the positions just presented. What I do want to do, as a transitional step to the presentation of my own views in the last three chapters, is to comment briefly on some of the major differences among ethicists as they address end-of-life issues, expand the conservative-to-liberal philosophical spectrum beyond the ethicists just discussed, and assess each of the six typological positions we have discussed.

The philosophical spectrum mentioned earlier moves from an extreme "pro-life" position (1) to moderate "pro-life" positions (2–3) to moderate "right-to-die" positions (4–5) to an extreme "right-to-die" position (6). At times, depending on which ethicist is being discussed, the differences between two adjacent positions do not seem monumental: it is as though normally friendly professional colleagues are simply having a temporary disagreement. Other times, depending on the personalities, combativeness, methodologies, and world views of individual ethicists, the differences between two or more positions seem to constitute a chasm of some size: it is as though inflexible opponents are engaged in a struggle to the end, with truth, justice, and the future of society all at stake at the same time.

How are the differences in perspective on the morality of treatment abatement to be explained? In one respect, the differences can be explained through the use of metaphor. Virtually all of these ethicists occasionally draw a "line," build a "wall," construct a "barrier," or engage in some other metaphorical activity to demarcate a portion of philosophical "territory" they regard as being of vital importance. For example, Ramsey describes the development of natural death acts as "a holding wall to protect the foundations" of the civilized world from the threat of euthanasia, McCormick emphasizes the importance of "drawing a line at the right place" in making quality-of-life judgments, and Childress says in regard to technological feeding that "we need strong barriers to prevent the triumph of a narrow and hard economic rationality, but the barriers themselves will not hold if we erect them hastily and in the wrong places." In this manner Bleich "draws a line" between himself and all others who are willing to justify treatment abatement prior to the beginning of the actual "death process," Rachels puts up a barrier between himself and all others who persistently hold the "irrational" view that letting patients die and killing them is morally different, and ethicists between these two extreme positions sometimes construct metaphorical borders *on both sides* of them to differentiate their positions from the

positions of other ethicists on the matters of quality-of-life judgments, technological feeding and hydration, intentional killing, and so on.

In another respect, the differences among the various ethicists are more subtle.
As one moves from one end of the spectrum to the other, differences emerge in
numerous ways: the importance of religious references, the emphasis placed on
the sanctity-of-life principle, the use of traditional ethical distinctions, the need
for quality-of-life judgments, the relative importance of patient autonomy and
medical paternalism, the objectivity or subjectivity of moral judgments, the
attention given to actual clinical cases, the familiarity with recent case law
(especially in the United States), the interpretation of technological feeding and
hydration as a form of medical or nonmedical care, the relationship between
treatment abatement and other end-of-life issues (brain death, suicide, assisted
suicide, and euthanasia), and the moral reasons given for or against treatment
abatement in particular cases. How these various matters are handled determines
not only where an individual ethicist ends up on the spectrum, but also the
audience most likely to be receptive to the ethicist's views and the general impact
or persuasiveness of the ethicist's arguments concerning the appropriate moral
limits to be placed on the technological prolongation of life.

Because the debate over the morality of treatment abatement extends far
beyond professional ethicists, and because the issue has become the focal point
for many educational efforts and considerable political activity in recent years,
the spectrum of differing ethical positions need not be limited to the views of
individual ethicists. As illustrated by Figure 6.1, a number of pro-life groups,
right-to-die organizations, governmental commissions, courts, and professional
organizations have issued policy statements or otherwise taken official positions
concerning the morality (and legality) of abating treatment. Although some of
these groups have identified their positions in fairly general terms, others have
issued carefully worded policy statements on specific aspects of abating treatment such as DNR policies, quality-of-life judgments, and the abatement of
technological feeding. The inclusion of these groups and organizations on the
spectrum of ethical positions is intended to highlight the breadth and diversity of
the ongoing debate over treatment abatement and related end-of-life issues.

Now, in concluding this chapter on ethical options, it may be helpful to point
out certain strengths and weaknesses in each of the six typological positions
discussed earlier. The strengths of the first position are to be found in its emphasis on the "givenness" of life and our role as stewards of the lives given to
us. As best articulated by Bleich, the perspective of Orthodox Judaism serves as
an important reminder to all religious believers—especially theists—that human
life in general and our own individual lives in particular are fundamentally
dependent on God's creative and sustaining power. Given this religious perspective, the issue of treatment abatement is best understood in the context of stewardship: of our lives, the skills physicians have in prolonging life and relieving

INDIVIDUAL   POSITIONS

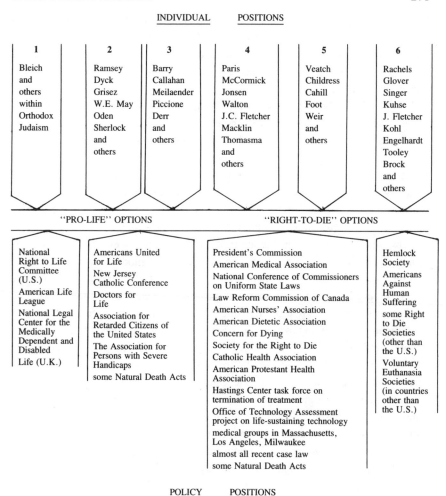

1	2	3	4	5	6
Bleich and others within Orthodox Judaism	Ramsey Dyck Grisez W.E. May Oden Sherlock and others	Barry Callahan Meilaender Piccione Derr and others	Paris McCormick Jonsen Walton J.C. Fletcher Macklin Thomasma and others	Veatch Childress Cahill Foot Weir and others	Rachels Glover Singer Kuhse J. Fletcher Kohl Engelhardt Tooley Brock and others

"PRO-LIFE" OPTIONS   "RIGHT-TO-DIE" OPTIONS

| National Right to Life Committee (U.S.) American Life League National Legal Center for the Medically Dependent and Disabled Life (U.K.) | Americans United for Life New Jersey Catholic Conference Doctors for Life Association for Retarded Citizens of the United States The Association for Persons with Severe Handicaps some Natural Death Acts | President's Commission American Medical Association National Conference of Commissioners on Uniform State Laws Law Reform Commission of Canada American Nurses' Association American Dietetic Association Concern for Dying Society for the Right to Die Catholic Health Association American Protestant Health Association Hastings Center task force on termination of treatment Office of Technology Assessment project on life-sustaining technology medical groups in Massachusetts, Los Angeles, Milwaukee almost all recent case law some Natural Death Acts | Hemlock Society Americans Against Human Suffering some Right to Die Societies (other than the U.S.) Voluntary Euthanasia Societies (in countries other than the U.S.) |

POLICY   POSITIONS

FIGURE 6.1. Ethical options regarding treatment abatement and euthanasia.

suffering, the skills nurses and other health care professionals have in caring for critically and terminally ill patients, and the ability we have as persons to make the often difficult decisions related to life and death.

Unfortunately, the strengths of this position are outweighed by its weaknesses, as evidenced by the traditional perspective of Orthodox Judaism regarding the extreme steps to be taken to prolong the lives of dying persons and the extreme views of Bleich on the issue of treatment abatement. The weaknesses of this extreme "pro-life" position are most noticeable in the alarmist views trumpeted by other persons and groups in the radical wing of the pro-life movement in the United States and the United Kingdom. The most outspoken representatives of this radical "right-to-life" position (e.g., the NRLC, the American Life League, and Life) usually have no connection with Orthodox Judaism, yet for other reasons (usually conservative or fundamentalist Christian reasons) advocate the same approach to the issue of abating treatment found in traditional Judaism— that is, sustain life at all costs.

This position, whether rooted in traditional Judaism or newly developed out of some other radically conservative perspective on life, is fraught with problems. I will mention only a few of them. The first one has to do with the simplicity of the position. As Ronald Green points out, contemporary Jewish rabbis who try to apply traditional rabbinic teachings to the ethical issues of technological medicine often seem unaware of how complicated modern medicine is.[174] Likewise, when the NRLC suggests that the only ethical options available are (1) theirs and (2) "euthanasia proponents," they oversimplify and intentionally polarize divergent views on the appropriate care to be given critically and terminally ill patients.[175] Either way, the complexity of modern medicine and the complexity of some of the ethical issues posed by technological medicine are falsely reduced to a simplistic perspective out of touch with the real world.

A second problem is that of vitalism. When Bleich refuses to justify treatment abatement until a dying patient is "actually in the clutches of the angel of death," and when the NRLC-sponsored "Patients' Rights Act" calls for the unabated prolongation of life until "the *final stage* of a *terminal illness*" (emphasis added), they are equating the value of individual human lives with the maintenance of biological organ systems. Whether terminally ill patients are conscious or unconscious, autonomous or nonautonomous, pain-free or suffering from unmitigated pain does not seem to matter. What does matter, in Bleich's words, is "conclusive evidence" that a patient's life is "not prolongable even by artificial means." In this manner, strangely enough, extreme pro-life advocates engage in a type of *idolatry of organic existence* and suggest that *no patient should ever be allowed to die* until God (apparently in the role of Puppeteer) "pulls" that patient's "string."

A third problem is that a number of important moral and legal concepts simply disappear when Bleich and other advocates of this position address the issue of abating treatment. The principle of autonomy, the right to self-determination, the right of privacy, the right of autonomous patients to refuse medical treatment, the concept of patient best interests, and the right of surrogates to make decisions to abate treatment on the behalf of nonautonomous patients are not to be found within the intellectual framework of this radical position. Instead, representatives of this view dismiss certain legal rights (the right of privacy is the first one tossed out) and simply ignore patient-centered concepts as they emphasize the importance of life-sustaining, paternalistic stands taken by "pro-life" physicians, judges, and institutions. Illustrative of this perspective is a statement by Judie Brown, the president of the American Life League: "The USA . . . is now a nation where each citizen can be a god, a personal deity who rejects suffering, rejects inconvenience, [and has] a legalized right to privacy that leads directly to hell. . . . Reversing this sadistic trend would be a simple matter for the judiciary, the medical profession, the citizenry."[176]

A fourth problem is that representatives of this position would, if they had the power, turn back the clock to the pre-*Quinlan* era. According to this view, all of the court decisions affirming treatment abatement for autonomous or nonautonomous patients—from *Quinlan* to the present—are antithetical to the imperative of prolonging life as long as technologically possible. In a similar manner, all natural death acts should be repealed, all durable-power-of-attorney statutes that include treatment-abatement decisions should be repealed, and all nonstatutory advance directives should have no legal standing in court. In this way extreme "right-to-lifers" would combat the dangers of euthanasia by using all modalities of medical technology to prolong the biological existence of all patients for as long as possible, regardless of whether such life-sustaining measures are wanted by the patients or can reasonably be said to be in the patients' best interests.

Given the similarity of positions 2 and 3, the strengths of these two moderate "pro-life" positions can be presented at the same time. Those strengths, for which Ramsey deserves a disproportionate share of credit, include an emphasis on a religious understanding of human existence, an awareness that relentless efforts to prolong life are sometimes futile, a careful effort to use ethical distinctions in the analysis of treatment abatement and other end-of-life issues, an unwavering call for medical *and* nonmedical forms of care to be given to dying patients, and an ongoing concern about the abuses that can accompany a moral and legal acceptance of the intentional killing of patients. In addition, as illustrated by the published views of Ramsey, Dyck, Grisez, Barry, Callahan, and Meilaender, there is a recognition that consequences are not the only right-making feature of moral actions. Rather, as each of them points out in a number of ways, the motivation, intention, and means used to produce consequences also have a bearing—sometimes decisively so—on the morality of actions.

Along with these strengths, there are a number of problems connected with the second and third positions. Position 2, especially as this view appears in Ramsey's publications, is built on a distinction between *two categories of patients* that simply does not work when subjected to close analysis. To build an ethical position concerning treatment abatement on a nondying/dying patient distinction—and not even try to define "dying" in terms of diagnostic features, prognostic criteria, or time remaining before death—is to rest the position on a distinction that is conceptually vague and, in some instances, medically uncertain. Ramsey acknowledges the conceptual vagueness of the distinction but tries to circumvent the problem of medical uncertainty by simply declaring that "this is a *medical* judgment and that physicians can and do determine—in human, no doubt fallible judgment—the difference between dying and nondying terminal patients."[177]

Another problem with position 2, given the emphasis placed on the nondying/ dying patient distinction, arises in cases of patients with PVS or some other form of unconsciousness from which they are not expected to recover. Such patients clearly cause problems for Ramsey (and a lot of us), since he refers to them in various places as "dying," "not categorically dying," at "a way-station in their dying," and in the "penultimate stage" of dying. Indicative of Ramsey's uncertainty in how to characterize such patients is his differing assessment of the Quinlan and Jobes cases. These two cases, separated by 10 years, involved two young patients in PVS, both of whom could breathe spontaneously but required technological feeding and hydration. Yet in these medically similar cases, Ramsey supported the abatement of medical feeding with Quinlan (because he believed she was dying) but opposed the same sort of treatment abatement in the Jobes case. Furthermore, position 2 is problematic because, while justifying treatment abatement in far more cases than the advocates of the extreme "pro-life" position are willing to do, representatives of this more moderate position still impose serious constraints on abating treatment with both autonomous and nonautonomous patients. Ramsey, Dyck, Grisez, and other "pro-life" advocates who can be identified with this ethical position (e.g., Edward Grant, the executive director, and Dennis Horan, the chairman of the board of Americans United for Life Legal Defense Fund)[178] believe that the right to refuse treatment is only a relative right. The right is relative, they think, in a dual sense: relative to the paternalistic views of physicians, and relative to the purported benefits of all life-sustaining medical treatment (including artificial feeding) that is "medically indicated."

The problems connected with position 3 are more narrowly focused, given the emphasis placed on artificial feeding and hydration as a particular form of life-sustaining care. This position, especially as articulated by Barry and (to a lesser degree) Meilaender, is built on a distinction between *two categories of care* that is both misleading and, in some cases, pointless. Additional criticism of this position will be presented in Chapter 9. At this point it should suffice simply to say that I am in agreement with the majority of ethicists (and courts) concerning artificial feeding and hydration: that the various medical procedures for administering foods and fluids are modalities of life-sustaining technology not unlike other technologies used to prolong patients' lives, that the characterization of such technology as "normal, routine care" simply does not persuasively distinguish these forms of treatment from other medical treatments, and that in some cases the abatement of such life-sustaining treatment is justifiable because the continuation of medicalized feeding is contrary to some patients' best interests.

The strengths of positions 4 and 5 can also be presented together, given the numerous points of agreement among the ethicists holding either of these positions. For Paris, McCormick, Jonsen, Walton, Veatch, and Childress, the issue of treatment abatement calls for a substantial departure from the three ethical positions just discussed. For these ethicists, the morality of abating treatment is correctly understood only from a moderate "right-to-die" perspective that includes an interpretation of life as a relative (not absolute) good and death as a relative (not absolute) evil, an emphasis on patient autonomy (or respect for a critically ill patient as a person) within the context of decisions made about life and death, and a limitation to the medical or judicial paternalism that would sometimes attempt to override decisions for treatment abatement made by autonomous patients and more frequently try to override such decisions when made by surrogates on the behalf of nonautonomous patients. In addition, these ethicists agree that a responsible and defensible position on the morality of abating treatment includes a careful effort to assess traditional ethical distinctions in the light of developments in technological medicine, an acceptance of several morally permissible reasons for abating treatment depending on the circumstances of particular cases, an awareness of the necessity of making quality-of-life judgments *and* the need to restrain such judgments from considerations of social utility, a recognition of the need to consider the proportionality of benefits and burdens provided by life-sustaining medical treatment, a willingness to justify the abatement of technological feeding and hydration in a minority of cases of critical illness, and an ongoing concern regarding the abuses that might accompany a social policy open to the intentional killing of patients. On all of these general, thematic points, I am in agreement with the ethicists identified with the fourth and fifth positions.

However, position 4 is not without problems, nor is position 5. One of the difficulties with the fourth position is that the ethicists identified with the position, especially Paris and McCormick, reject the general position held by Barry and like-minded ethicists regarding artificial feeding, but rarely address the specific arguments put forth by Barry, Callahan, or Meilaender. Another problem is that, with the exception of Jonsen, the other three ethicists discussed in connection with the fourth position reject the option of euthanasia, yet fail to address the serious moral problem presented by patients whose intolerable suffering is impervious to medical management, whose lives are not being sustained by mechanical ventilation or technological feeding, who are unable to commit suicide, and who request to be killed. Still another problem is unique to this position. Just as Barry and other "pro-life" ethicists sometimes try to score points by taking potshots at the President's Commission report on forgoing treatment, so Paris and Jonsen occasionally "show the flag" by citing the same report as though it has a special handle on the truth. That Paris and Jonsen take pride in the work of the commission is understandable, given their extensive personal involvement in the commission's several important publications, but commission-affirming comments need not be a substitute for carefully reasoned arguments any more than commission-bashing comments are.

The difficulties with the fifth position can be placed in two separate categories. On the one hand, there are difficulties inherent to the placement of the position on the philosophical spectrum. More conservative ethicists criticize this position because Veatch, Childress, and others sharing their views are willing to justify occasional acts of intentional killing, a move most of the ethicists just discussed regard as either (1) intrinsically immoral or (2) wrong because of the abuses that predictably will accompany the moral acceptance of such killing in clinical settings. More liberal ethicists criticize this position because Veatch and Childress retain some of the traditional ethical distinctions and do not call for the legalization of euthanasia. On the other hand, there are difficulties specific to the individually developed positions of Veatch and Childress. For example, Veatch emphasizes the "patient-centered perspective" to the point that the professional role of physicians is seriously devalued, Childress goes to great lengths to justify the abatement of technological feeding without really addressing the criticism (put forth by Meilaender and others) that this form of treatment abatement entails intentional killing, and neither of them sufficiently indicates when euthanasia *is* and *is not* justifiable. Since my own views on treatment abatement and euthanasia are to be identified with position 5, the next three chapters will contain my efforts to expand, revise, and possibly improve on the work already done by Veatch and Childress.

Position 6 also brings an assortment of strengths and weaknesses to the debate about the morality of treatment abatement and euthanasia. The strengths of the position are several. Rachels, Glover, Singer, and Kuhse rightly emphasize the irremediable suffering of some critically ill and terminally ill patients, the necessity of considering the quality of patients' lives in making life-and-death decisions, the questionability of sustaining all permanently unconscious bodies as long as technologically possible, and the legitimacy of some patients' requests for euthanasia. In addition, these philosophers, along with Joseph Fletcher, Marvin Kohl, and others, contribute an important element to the ongoing debate over the morality of treatment abatement and euthanasia: namely, the challenges and criticisms they advance against long-held ethical concepts and principles necessitate a reassessment of traditional views and a rethinking of whether and how such views still apply in the age of technological medicine.

However, this position also has numerous problems. The first problem is the extremity of the position, both in the sense of the ethical views put forward and the manner with which they are put forward. Rachels, Singer, and Kuhse—more so than Glover—sometimes advance ideas that gain attention because they are different, not because they are well reasoned. In this manner, for example, Rachels calls for the legalization of nonvoluntary euthanasia in a significantly differing "variety of cases," Singer casually states that irreversibly comatose patients are already dead, Kuhse asserts that current medical practices are more abusive than would be the legalization of medical killing, and each of them rushes to a moral justification of euthanasia without acknowledging the seriousness of this step. Likewise, these philosophers share the tendency of being extremely negative toward others' views at times—to the point of condescension. Thus, instead of simply criticizing ideas with which they disagree, they occasionally choose to ridicule the ideas as being "irrational," "sheer nonsense," and so forth.

A second problem has to do with their handling of ethical distinctions. All of the philosophers identified with the sixth position go to great lengths to "debunk" (as Rachels says) several ethical distinctions they find flawed. That, of course, is legitimate, and I will try to deal with some of their criticisms of the let die/kill distinction in the next chapter. However, at the same time that they are rejecting *some* ethical distinctions, they (Rachels more than the others) use the adjectival distinction of "passive"/"active" euthanasia without (1) explaining the usage of these adjectives, (2) showing any relationship between these adjectives and the omission/commission distinction or the let die/kill distinction, or (3) demonstrating how the use of these adjectival distinctions adds clarity to the philosophical analysis of euthanasia. Of course, it is possible that the unargued usage of "passive" and "active" is intended to blur through labeling any possible moral difference between treatment abatement and euthanasia, which is precisely what some pro-life advocates claim that the "pro-euthanasia movement" does as a matter of strategy.

A third problem involves the thoroughgoing consequentialism embraced by these ethicists. Writing from the general perspective of utilitarianism, they are convinced that the only right-making feature of an action is the consequence produced by that action. That is the reason, obviously, for their rejection of any morally significant difference between treatment abatement and euthanasia. That is the reason they place little if any importance on the motives, intentions, and means involved in the deaths of patients following an act of treatment abatement or an act of euthanasia. That is the reason Singer can somewhat casually dismiss the "unnecessary deaths" that would come about through the legalization of euthanasia. And that is at least partially the reason why Rachels, Glover, and Kuhse, in contrast to the Hemlock Society and voluntary euthanasia societies in several countries, pay amazingly little attention to (1) the *conditions necessary to justify euthanasia* or (2) the *procedural mechanisms* that could most effectively minimize any abuses connected with the legalization of voluntary euthanasia and especially the legalization of nonvoluntary euthanasia.

Finally, these philosophers, in a way somewhat similar to the position of Orthodox Judaism, seem strangely out of touch with recent developments in law and medicine as these developments relate to the care of critically ill patients. Glover and Singer can possibly be excused, because their published works discussed earlier are now several years old. But the works by Rachels and Kuhse are recent, yet both philosophers pay insufficient attention to recent case law or statutory law in the United States, Australia, or elsewhere. In particular, they seem unaware that much recent case law recognizes—as they do not—that abating treatment is not always equivalent to "letting die." Even more significant is the absence of any references to recent medical developments in the areas of pain management, palliative care, and hospice care. For some opponents of euthanasia, these recent developments in the care of critically ill and terminally ill patients provide the main reason for believing that many of the arguments put forth by Rachels, Glover, Singer, and Kuhse are misplaced.

NOTES

1. Paul Ramsey, *Ethics at the Edges of Life* (New Haven: Yale University Press, 1978), p. 156.
2. James Rachels, "Euthanasia, Killing, and Letting Die," in John Ladd, ed., *Ethical Issues Relating to Life and Death* (New York: Oxford University Press, 1979), p. 157.
3. Alexander Morgan Capron, "Borrowed Lessons: The Role of Ethical Distinctions in Framing Law on Life-Sustaining Treatment," *Arizona State Law Journal* 1984 (1984): 647–60.
4. See Fred Rosner, "The Jewish Attitude toward Euthanasia," in Fred Rosner and J. David Bleich, eds., *Jewish Bioethics* (Brooklyn, N.Y.: Hebrew Publishing Company, 1979), pp. 253–65; and David H. Smith and Seymour Perlin, "Suicide," in Warren T. Reich, editor-in-chief, *Encyclopedia of Bioethics* 4 (New York: The Free Press, 1978), pp. 1618–27.
5. Basil F. Herring, *Jewish Ethics and Halakhah for Our Time: Sources and Commentary* (New York: KTAV Publishing House, 1984), pp. 67–90.
6. James J. McCartney, "The Development of the Doctrine of Ordinary and Extraordinary Means of Preserving Life in Catholic Moral Theology before the Karen Quinlan Case," *Linacre Quarterly* 47 (August 1980): 215–24; Gary M. Atkinson, "Theological History of Catholic Teaching on Prolonging Life," in Donald G. McCarthy and Albert S. Moraczewski, eds., *Moral Responsibility in Prolonging Life Decisions* (St. Louis: Pope John XXIII Center, 1981), pp. 95–115; and John J. Paris and Richard A. McCormick, "The Catholic Tradition on the Use of Nutrition and Fluids," *America* 156 (May 2, 1987): 358.
7. Albert R. Jonsen, "Traditional Distinctions for Making Ethical Judgments," *Arizona State Law Journal* 1984 (1984): 665. Paul Ramsey earlier made use of the same case in *The Patient as Person* (New Haven, Conn.: Yale University Press, 1970), p. 128.
8. Charles J. McFadden, *Medical Ethics for Nurses* (Philadelphia: F.A. Davis, 1946), title changed to *Medical Ethics* for subsequent editions (Philadelphia: F.A. Davis, 1949, 1953, 1956, 1961, 1967); Gerald Kelly, *Medico-Moral Problems,* published in five parts (St. Louis: Catholic Hospital Association, 1949–1954), then published in a single volume (St. Louis: Catholic Hospital Association, 1958); Edwin F. Healy, *Medical Ethics* (Chicago: Loyola University Press, 1956); and Thomas J. O'Donnell, *Morals in Medicine* (Westminster, Md.: Newman Press, 1956).

9. For a very helpful interpretation of McFadden's work and the contributions of other moral theologians, see David F. Kelly, *The Emergence of Roman Catholic Medical Ethics in North America* (New York and Toronto: The Edwin Mellen Press, 1979).

10. Gerald Kelly, "The Duty to Preserve Life," *Theological Studies* 12 (December 1951): 550. Also see idem, "The Duty of Using Artificial Means of Preserving Life," *Theological Studies* 11 (June 1950): 203–20. For a contemporary interpretation of the distinction, see The Linacre Centre for the Study of the Ethics of Health Care, *Prolongation of Life: Ordinary and Extraordinary Means of Prolonging Life* (London: The Linacre Centre, 1979).

11. See Joseph T. Mangan, "An Historical Analysis of the Principle of Double Effect," *Theological Studies* 10 (1949): 41–61; Jonathan Bennett, "Whatever the Consequences," *Analysis* 26 (1966): 83–102; Philippa Foot, "The Problem of Abortion and the Doctrine of Double Effect," *Oxford Review* 5 (1967): 5–15; Richard A. McCormick, *Ambiguity in Moral Choice* (Milwaukee: Marquette University Press, 1973); William E. May, "Double Effect," in Reich, *Encyclopedia of Bioethics,* pp. 316–20; Paul Ramsey and Richard A. McCormick, eds., *Doing Evil to Achieve Good* (Chicago: Loyola University Press, 1978); Joseph M. Boyle, Jr., "Toward Understanding the Principle of Double Effect," *Ethics* 90 (July 1980): 527–38; and Tom L. Beauchamp and James F. Childress, *Principles of Biomedical Ethics,* 2nd ed. (New York: Oxford University Press, 1983), pp. 113–15.

12. Quoted by Beauchamp and Childress, *Principles of Biomedical Ethics,* p. 114.

13. This justification of self-defense appears in the *Summa Theologica,* II-II, Q. 64, Art. 7. My interpretation is largely based on the material in David Kelly, *Emergence of Roman Catholic Medical Ethics,* p. 250.

14. David Kelly, *Emergence of Roman Catholic Medical Ethics,* p. 251.

15. Joseph Fletcher, *Morals and Medicine* (Princeton, N.J.: Princeton University Press, 1954), pp. 172–210. For some of his later views on euthanasia, see idem, *Moral Responsibility* (Philadelphia: Westminster Press, 1967), pp. 141–60; idem, "The Patient's Right to Die," in A.B. Downing, ed., *Euthanasia and the Right to Death* (Los Angeles: Nash Publishing, 1969), pp. 61–70; idem, "Ethics and Euthanasia," in Robert H. Williams, ed., *To Live and to Die* (New York: Springer-Verlag, 1974), pp. 113–22; idem, "The 'Right' to Live and the 'Right' to Die," in Marvin Kohl, ed., *Beneficent Euthanasia* (Buffalo, N.Y.: Prometheus Books, 1975), pp. 44–53; idem, *Humanhood: Essays in Biomedical Ethics* (Buffalo, N.Y.: Prometheus Books, 1979), pp. 149–58; and idem, "The Courts and Euthanasia," *Law, Medicine, and Health Care* 15 (Winter 1987–1988): 223–30.

16. David Kelly, *Emergence of Roman Catholic Medical Ethics,* p. 378.

17. Quoted by LeRoy Walters, "Religion and the Renaissance of Medical Ethics in the United States: 1965–1975," in Earl Shelp, ed., *Theology and Bioethics* (Dordrecht, the Netherlands, and Boston: D. Reidel, 1985), p. 5.

18. Jonsen, "Traditional Distinctions," p. 664.

19. Pope Pius XII, "The Prolongation of Life," in Stanley Reiser, Arthur Dyck, and William Curran, eds., *Ethics in Medicine* (Cambridge, Mass. and London: MIT Press, 1977), pp. 502–3.

20. See Glanville Williams, *The Sanctity of Life and the Criminal Law* (London: Faber & Faber, 1958); Yale Kamisar, "Euthanasia Legislation: Some Nonreligious Objections," *Minnesota Law Review* 42 (May 1958): 969–1042; Glanville Williams, " 'Mercy-Killing' Legislation—A Rejoinder," *Minnesota Law Review* 43 (November 1958): 1–12; George P. Fletcher, "Prolonging Life," *Washington Law*

Review 42 (1967): 999–1016; and Norman L. Cantor, "A Patient's Decision to Decline Lifesaving Medical Treatment: Bodily Integrity versus the Preservation of Life," *Rutgers Law Review* 26 (Winter 1973): 228–64.

21. Elisabeth Kübler-Ross, *On Death and Dying* (New York: Macmillan, 1969); Avery Weisman, *On Dying and Denying* (New York: Behavioral Publications, 1972); Diana Crane, *The Sanctity of Social Life: Physicians' Treatment of Critically Ill Patients* (New York: Russell Sage Foundation, 1975); and O. Ruth Russell, *Freedom to Die* (New York: Human Sciences Press, 1975).

22. Paul Ramsey, *The Patient as Person;* Robert M. Veatch, "Choosing Not to Prolong Dying," *Medical Dimensions* (December 1972): 8–10; Daniel Maguire, *Death by Choice* (New York: Doubleday, 1973); Arthur Dyck, "An Alternative to the Ethic of Euthanasia," in Williams, ed., *To Live and to Die,* pp. 98–112; Anthony Flew, "The Principle of Euthanasia," in Downing, *Euthanasia and the Right to Death,* pp. 30–48; R.M. Hare, "Euthanasia: A Christian View," *Philosophic Exchange* 2 (Summer 1975): 43–52; Sissela Bok, "Euthanasia and the Care of the Dying," *BioScience* 23 (August 1973): 461–66; Marvin Kohl, *The Morality of Killing* (Atlantic Highlands, N.J.: Humanities Press, 1974); Richard B. Brandt, "The Morality and Rationality of Suicide," in Seymour Perlin, ed., *A Handbook for the Study of Suicide* (New York: Oxford University Press, 1975), pp. 61–75; and James Rachels, "Active and Passive Euthanasia," *The New England Journal of Medicine* 292 (January 9, 1975): 78–80.

23. Walters, "Religion and the Renaissance," p. 11.

24. Ramsey, *The Patient as Person,* pp. 113–64.

25. Maguire, *Death by Choice,* pp. 131–221.

26. Kohl, *Morality of Killing,* pp. 3–35, 71–110. These views are expanded in his subsequent response to an article by Arthur Dyck entitled "Beneficent Euthanasia and Benemortasia: Alternative Views of Mercy." Kohl's article is entitled "Voluntary Beneficent Euthanasia." Both articles are in Kohl, *Beneficent Euthanasia,* pp. 117–29 and 130–41.

27. Rachels, "Active and Passive Euthanasia," pp. 78–80. The article has been reprinted a number of places, including the second edition of my anthology *Ethical Issues in Death and Dying* (New York: Columbia University Press, 1986), pp. 249–56.

28. President's Commission, *Deciding to Forego Life-Sustaining Treatment* (Washington, D.C.: U.S. Government Printing Office, 1983); Law Reform Commission of Canada, *Working Paper 28: Euthanasia, Aiding Suicide and Cessation of Treatment* (Ottawa: Minister of Supply and Services, 1982) and idem, *Report on Euthanasia, Aiding Suicide and Cessation of Treatment* (Ottawa: Minister of Supply and Services, 1983); A. Edward Doudera and J. Douglas Peters, eds., *Legal and Ethical Aspects of Treating Critically and Terminally Ill Patients* (Ann Arbor, Mich.: Health Administration Press, 1982); Sidney H. Wanzer et al., "The Physician's Responsibility toward Hopelessly Ill Patients," *The New England Journal of Medicine* 310 (April 12, 1984): 955–59; Robert M. Veatch, *Death, Dying, and the Biological Revolution* (New Haven, Conn.: Yale University Press, 1976); Ramsey, *Ethics at the Edges of Life;* Beauchamp and Childress, *Principles of Biomedical Ethics;* Albert R. Jonsen, Mark Siegler, and William J. Winslade, *Clinical Ethics* (New York: Macmillan, 1982); Douglas N. Walton, *Ethics of Withdrawal of Life-Support Systems* (Westport, Conn.: Greenwood Press, 1983); David W. Meyers, *Medico-Legal Implications of Death and Dying* (Rochester, N.Y. and San Francisco: The

Lawyers Co-Operative Publishing Co. and Bancroft-Whitney Co., 1981); John A. Robertson, *The Rights of the Critically Ill* (Cambridge, Mass.: Ballinger, 1983); and Norman L. Cantor, *Legal Frontiers of Death and Dying* (Bloomington, Ind.: Indiana University Press, 1987).

29. Brian Clark, *Whose Life Is It Anyway?* (New York: Dodd Mead, 1979); and Malcolm Muggeridge and Alan Thornhill, *Sentenced to Life* (Nashville, Tenn. and New York: Thomas Nelson Publishers, 1983).

30. The three most influential publications thus far are Joanne Lynn, ed., *By No Extraordinary Means: The Choice to Forgo Life-Sustaining Food and Water* (Bloomington, Ind. Indiana University Press, 1986); Office of Technology Assessment (OTA), *Life-Sustaining Technologies and the Elderly* (Washington, D.C.: U.S. Government Printing Office, 1987); and the Hastings Center project, *Guidelines on the Termination of Life-Sustaining Treatment and the Care of the Dying* (Briarcliff, Manor, N.Y.: The Hastings Center, 1987).

31. Oklahoma was the first state to pass legislation along these lines. Although not the "Patients' Rights Act" sponsored by the NRLC, the "Hydration and Nutrition for Incompetent Patients Act" is a law that significantly limits the treatment-abatement options of physicians, guardians, and courts. Codified as Section 3080.1–3080.5 of Title 63 O.S., the law went into effect November 1, 1987.

32. The rapidly expanding literature on the abatement of medical feeding and hydration was catalogued in 1986 by the National Reference Center for Bioethics Literature. See Pat Milmoe McCarrick, "Scope Note 7: Withholding or Withdrawing Nutrition or Hydration," Kennedy Institute of Ethics, November 1986. For organizational statements on artificial feeding and hydration, see the following: Council on Ethical and Judicial Affairs, A.M.A., "Withholding or Withdrawing Life-Prolonging Treatment," March 15, 1986; Committee on Biomedical Ethics of the Los Angeles County Medical Association and the Los Angeles County Bar Association, "Principles and Guidelines Concerning the Foregoing of Life-Sustaining Treatment for Adult Patients," January 6, 1986; Massachusetts Medical Society, "Resolution," July 17, 1985; Medical Society of Milwaukee County, "Withdrawal of Nutrition and Hydration in Terminal Adult Patients," 1985; Committee for Pro-Life Activities of the National Conference of Catholic Bishops, "Guidelines for Legislation on Life-Sustaining Treatment," November 10, 1984; and Committee for Pro-Life Activities of the National Conference of Catholic Bishops, "Statement on Uniform Rights of the Terminally Ill Act," June 1986.

33. Brophy v. New England Sinai Hospital, Inc., 398 Mass. 417, 497 N.E.2d 626, 640 (1986) (J. Nolan dissenting).

34. In re Requena, 213 N.J. Super. 443, 517 A.2d 869.

35. Michael Nevins, "Perspectives of a Jewish Physician," in Lynn, *By No Extraordinary Means,* p. 100.

36. Ibid., p. 105.

37. For modern, but pre-*Quinlan* Jewish views held by some rabbis and physicians, see Immanuel Jakobovits, *Jewish Medical Ethics* (New York: Bloch Publishing Co., 1959, 1975); Moses Tendler, *Medical Ethics,* 5th ed. (New York: Committee on Religious Affairs of the Federation of Jewish Philanthropies, Inc., 1975); and Fred Rosner, *Modern Medicine and Jewish Law* (New York: Yeshiva University Press, 1972). For some post-*Quinlan* Jewish views on treatment abatement, see Seymour Siegel, "Medical Ethics, History of," in Reich, *Encyclopedia of Bioethics,* pp. 895–97; Fred Rosner and J. David Bleich, eds., *Jewish Bioethics* (New York:

Hebrew Publishing Co., 1979), pp. 253–348; and Levi Meier, "Code and No-Code: A Psychological Analysis and the Viewpoint of Jewish Law," in Doudera and Peters, *Legal and Ethical Aspects*, pp. 90–97.

38. J. David Bleich, "Karen Ann Quinlan: A Torah Perspective," *Jewish Life* (Winter 1976). This article is reprinted in Menachem Marc Kellner, ed., *Contemporary Jewish Ethics* (New York: Sanhedrin Press, 1978), pp. 296–307. It is reprinted under the title "The Quinlan Case: A Jewish Perspective," in Rosner and Bleich, *Jewish Bioethics*, pp. 266–76, with only two footnotes making any reference to the New Jersey Supreme Court decision. The unfootnoted quotations that follow come from the reprinted article in *Jewish Bioethics*.

39. Bleich, "Quinlan Case," p. 272.

40. J. David Bleich, *Judaism and Healing* (New York: KTAV Publishing House, 1981), p. 136.

41. Ibid., p. 140.

42. Ibid., p. 142.

43. J. David Bleich, "The Obligation to Heal in the Talmudic Tradition: A Comparative Analysis," in Rosner and Bleich, *Jewish Bioethics*. p. 33.

44. Bleich, *Judaism and Healing*, p. 144.

45. For some of Ramsey's other views prior to the Quinlan case, see his "The Indignity of 'Death with Dignity,'" *Hastings Center Studies* 2 (May 1974): 47–62.

46. Paul Ramsey, "Pronlonged Dying: Not Medically Indicated," *Hastings Center Report* 6 (February 1976): 14–17; idem, "The Right Care of Karen Quinlan," *Crucible* (April–June, 1976): 66–71; and idem, " 'Euthanasia' and Dying Well Enough," *Linacre Quarterly* 44 (February 1977): 37–46.

47. Ramsey, *The Patient as Person*, p. 153.

48. Ramsey, *Ethics at the Edges of Life*, pp. 145–88, 268–99.

49. For example, see Paul Ramsey, "The *Saikewicz* Precedent: What's Good for an Incompetent Patient?" *Hastings Center Report* 8 (December 1978); 36–42; and idem, "The Two-Step Fantastic: The Continuing Case of Brother Fox," *Theological Studies* 42 (March 1981): 122–34.

50. Ramsey, *Ethics at the Edges of Life*, p. 155. Unless otherwise noted, the quotations in the next several paragraphs come from Chapter 4 of this book.

51. Ramsey, "Prolonged Dying," p. 15. The same view is expressed in idem, " 'Euthanasia' and Dying Well Enough," p. 44. This view is revised in the later version of this article that appears as Chapter 4 of *Ethics at the Edges of Life*.

52. Ramsey, *Ethics at the Edges of Life*, p. 155.

53. Ramsey's criticisms are directed against Veatch's *Death, Dying, and the Biological Revolution* and McCormick's "To Save and Let Die: The Dilemma of Modern Medicine," *Journal of the American Medical Association* 229 (July 8, 1974): 172–76.

54. Ramsey, *Ethics at the Edges of Life*, p. xiv.

55. Ramsey, "Prolonged Dying," p. 16.

56. Ramsey, "Two-Step Fantastic," p. 133.

57. Ramsey, *Ethics at the Edges of Life*, pp. 268–99.

58. Ibid., pp. 300–17, 335.

59. Ramsey, "Two-Step Fantastic," p. 133.

60. Ramsey, "Prolonged Dying," p. 17.

61. Ramsey, *The Patient as Person*, pp. 128–29; idem, "Prolonged Dying," p. 16; and idem, *Ethics at the Edges of Life*, p. 270.

62. Paul Ramsey, "Speeding or Slowing the Angel of Death" (Letter to the Editor), *America* 156 (May 30, 1987): 449–50.

63. Ramsey, *Ethics at the Edges of Life,* p. 329.

64. Ibid., pp. 219–25. See especially n. 44 on p. 220. The unfootnoted quotations that follow come from these pages.

65. Arthur J. Dyck, *On Human Care: An Introduction to Ethics* (Nashville, Tenn.: Abingdon Press, 1977), p. 85. For two earlier articles on this issue by Dyck, see idem, "An Alternative to the Ethic of Euthanasia," in Williams, *To Live and to Die,* pp. 98–112; and his "Beneficent Euthanasia and Benemortasia," in Kohl, *Beneficent Euthanasia,* pp. 117–29.

66. Arthur J. Dyck, "Ethical Aspects of Care for the Dying Incompetent," *Journal of the American Geriatrics Society* 32 (September 1984): 661–64.

67. Other ethicists emphasizing the distinction between dying and nondying patients include Thomas C. Oden, William E. May, and Richard Sherlock. For Oden's views on the morality of treatment abatement, see his "Beyond an Ethic of Immediate Sympathy," *Hastings Center Report* 6 (February 1976): 12–14; and idem, *Should Treatment Be Terminated?* (New York: Harper & Row, 1976). For May's views, see his *Human Existence, Medicine and Ethics* (Chicago: Franciscan Herald Press, 1977). For Sherlock's views, see his "For Everything There Is a Season: The Right to Die in American Law," *Brigham Young Law Review* 2 (1982): 545–616; and idem, *Preserving Life* (Chicago: Loyola University Press, 1987), pp. 117–71.

68. Germain Grisez, "Suicide and Euthanasia," in Dennis J. Horan and David Mall, eds., *Death, Dying, and Euthanasia* (Washington, D.C.: University Publications of America, 1977), p. 753.

69. Germain Grisez and Joseph M. Boyle, Jr., *Life and Death with Liberty and Justice* (Notre Dame, Ind.: University of Notre Dame Press, 1979), p. 290.

70. Ibid., pp. 266–75.

71. Germain Grisez and Joseph M. Boyle, Jr., "An Alternative to 'Death with Dignity,'" *Human Life Review* 4 (Winter 1978): 26–43. For some of Boyle's views, see his "The Patient/Physician Relationship," in McCarthy and Moraczewski, *Moral Responsibility in Prolonging Life Decisions,* pp. 80–94; and idem, "On Killing and Letting Die," *New Scholasticism* 51 (1977): 433–52.

72. Robert L. Barry, "The Ethics of Providing Life-Sustaining Nutrition and Fluids to Incompetent Patients," *The Journal of Family and Culture* 1 (Summer 1985): 31.

73. Ibid., p. 34.

74. Robert L. Barry, "Ethics and Brain Death," *New Scholasticism* 61 (Winter 1987): 95.

75. Robert L. Barry, "Facing Hard Cases: The Ethics of Assisted Feeding," *Issues in Law and Medicine* 2 (1986): 103.

76. Ibid., p. 101.

77. Ibid., p. 102.

78. Barry, "Ethics of Providing Life-Sustaining Nutrition," pp. 27–31.

79. Robert L. Barry, "Pulling the Tube: Mercy or Manslaughter," *Medical Ethics for the Physician* 1 (August 1986): 11.

80. Barry, "Facing Hard Cases," p. 102.

81. Barry, "Ethics of Providing Life-Sustaining Nutrition," p. 25.

82. Robert L. Barry, "Closing the Circle: *Humanae Vitae* and Feeding the Comatose," *Homiletic and Pastoral Review* (July 1986): 56; and idem, "Euthanasia: The Domino Falls," *National Catholic Reporter,* February 1, 1987.

83. Robert L. Barry, "Catholic Ethics and Feeding the Comatose," unpublished manuscript. Barry's criticism is directed toward Kevin O'Rourke's "The A.M.A. Statement on Tube Feeding: An Ethical Analysis," *America* 155 (November 22, 1986): 321–23, 331.

84. Robert L. Barry, "Feeding the Comatose and the Common Good in the Catholic Tradition," unpublished manuscript.

85. Barry, "Catholic Ethics and Feeding the Comatose," unpublished manuscript; and idem, "The Broadening Scope of Euthanasia," *The Journal of Family and Culture* 3 (Summer 1987): 35–52.

86. Barry, "Ethics of Providing Life-Sustaining Nutrition," pp. 31–32.

87. Robert L. Barry, "The Elizabeth Bouvia Case: Legalizing Euthanasia by Lethal Injection," *Linacre Quarterly* 53 (August 1986): 13–21.

88. Especially see Barry, "Broadening Scope of Euthanasia," pp. 35–52.

89. Barry, "Ethics of Providing Life-Sustaining Nutrition," p. 36, n. 22.

90. Barry, "Catholic Ethics and Feeding the Comatose," unpublished manuscript.

91. Barry, "Elizabeth Bouvia Case," p. 19.

92. Joseph Piccione, J.D., author of several public policy monographs and currently a staff member at the National Forum Foundation in Washington, D.C., holds a position quite similar to that of Barry. Piccione's monograph entitled *Last Rights: Treatment and Care Issues in Medical Ethics* (Washington, D.C.: Free Congress Research and Education Foundation, 1984) is quite influential in some pro-life groups. Also see Patrick G. Derr, "Why Food and Fluids Can Never Be Denied," *Hastings Center Report* 16 (February 1986): 28–30.

93. Daniel Callahan, "On Feeding the Dying," *Hastings Center Report* 13 (October 1983): 22.

94. See Joanne Lynn and James F. Childress, "Must Patients Always Be Given Food and Water?" *Hastings Center Report* 13 (October 1983): 17–21.

95. Callahan, "On Feeding the Dying," p. 22. Callahan has expanded his views and defended them in his "Feeding the Elderly Dying," *Generations* 10 (Winter 1985): 15–17; idem, "Public Policy and the Cessation of Nutrition," in Lynn, *By No Extraordinary Means*, pp. 61–66; and idem, *Setting Limits* (New York: Simon & Schuster, 1987), pp. 187–93. Similar views appear in Ronald A. Carson, "The Symbolic Significance of Giving to Eat and Drink," in Lynn, *By No Extraordinary Means*, pp. 84–88.

96. Gilbert Meilaender, "On Removing Food and Water: Against the Stream," *Hastings Center Report* 14 (December 1984): 11. For the earlier article, see idem, "Euthanasia and Christian Vision," *Thought* 57 (December 1982): 465–75. Also see idem, "The Distinction between Killing and Allowing to Die," *Theological Studies* 37 (1976): 467–70.

97. Meilaender, "On Removing Food and Water," p. 12.

98. Ibid., p. 13. An abbreviated version of this article was reprinted as "Caring for the Permanently Unconscious Patient," in Lynn, *By No Extraordinary Means*, pp. 195–201.

99. John J. Paris, "The Withdrawal of Intravenous Feeding: Murder or an Acceptable Medical Practice?" in Patricia H. Werhane et al., eds., *Philosophical Issues in Human Rights* (New York: Random House, 1986), p. 94.

100. John J. Paris and Richard A. McCromick, "Living-Will Legislation, Reconsidered," *America* 145 (September 5, 1981): 88.

101. Ibid., p. 88.

102. John J. Paris, "Brain Death, Death, and Euthanasia," *Thought* 57 (December 1982): 477.

103. John J. Paris, "The Decision to Withdraw Life-Sustaining Treatment and the Potential Role of an IEC: The Case of *People v. Barber and Nejdl,*" in Ronald E. Cranford and A. Edward Doudera, eds., *Institutional Ethics Committees and Health Care Decision Making* (Ann Arbor, Mich.: Health Administration Press, 1984), p. 205.

104. John J. Paris and Andrew C. Varga, "Care of the Hopelessly Ill," *America* 151 (September 22, 1984): 144.

105. John J. Paris and Richard A. McCormick, "The Catholic Tradition on the Use of Nutrition and Fluids," *America* 156 (May 2, 1987): 358.

106. Judy Cassidy, "Withholding or Withdrawing Nutrition and Fluids: What Are the Real Issues?," an interview with John Paris in *Health Progress* 42 (December 1985): 23.

107. John J. Paris, "When Burdens of Feeding Outweigh Benefits," *Hastings Center Report* 16 (February 1986): 31.

108. John J. Paris and Frank E. Reardon, "Court Responses to Withholding or Withdrawing Artificial Nutrition and Fluids," *Journal of the American Medical Association* 253 (April 19, 1985): 2243–45.

109. Paris, "When Burdens of Feeding Outweigh Benefits," p. 32.

110. Paris and McCormick, "Catholic Tradition," p. 361.

111. Paris and McCormick, "Living-Will Legislation," pp. 86–89.

112. Richard A. McCormick, "Care of the Dying and Euthanasia," in his *Notes on Moral Theology 1965 through 1980* (Washington, D.C.: University Press of America, 1981), pp. 592–612; Richard A. McCormick and Andre E. Hellegers, "The Case of Joseph Saikewicz," *America* 138 (1978): 257–60; Richard A. McCormick and Robert Veatch, "The Preservation of Life and Self-Determination," *Theological Studies* 41 (June 1980): 390–96; Richard A. McCormick, "Notes on Moral Theology: 1983," *Theological Studies* 45 (1984): 115–19; and idem, "Caring or Starving? The Case of Claire Conroy," *America* 152 (April 6, 1985): 269–73.

113. McCormick, "Caring or Starving?," p. 272.

114. Ibid., p. 273.

115. See Albert R. Jonsen and George Lister, "Life-Support Systems," in Reich, ed., *Encyclopedia of Bioethics,* pp. 840–48; Albert R. Jonsen, "Do No Harm," *Annals of Internal Medicine* 88 (1978): 827–32; Bernard Lo and Albert R. Jonsen, "Ethical Decisions in the Care of a Patient Terminally Ill with Metastatic Cancer," *Annals of Internal Medicine* 92 (1980): 107–11; idem, "Clinical Decisions to Limit Treatment," *Annals of Internal Medicine* 93 (1980): 764–68; John D. Baxter and Albert R. Jonsen, "What Is Extraordinary Life Support?" *Western Journal of Medicine* 141 (September 1984): 358–63; Albert R. Jonsen, "Traditional Distinctions for Making Ethical Judgments," pp. 661–66; and Robert A. Pearlman and Albert R. Jonsen, "The Use of Quality-of-Life Considerations in Medical Decision Making," *Journal of the American Geriatrics Society* 33 (May 1985): 344–52.

116. Jonsen, Siegler, and Winslade, *Clinical Ethics,* p. 35.

117. Lo and Jonsen, "Clinical Decisions to Limit Treatment," p. 767.

118. Jonsen, Siegler, and Winslade, *Clinical Ethics,* pp. 114–18, 144–45.

119. Ibid., pp. 120–21.

120. Lo and Jonsen, "Ethical Decisions in the Care of a Patient," p. 109.

121. Jonsen, Siegler, and Winslade, *Clinical Ethics,* p. 127.

122. Walton, *Ethics of Withdrawal*, and the chapter on cessation of treatment in idem, *Physician–Patient Decision-Making* (Westport, Conn.: Greenwood Press, 1985), pp. 141–59. Other ethicists who can be identified with the fourth position include John C. Fletcher, David C. Thomasma, and Ruth Macklin. For some of their views, see John Fletcher, "Is Euthanasia Ever Justifiable?," in Peter H. Wiernik, ed., *Controversies in Oncology* (New York: John Wiley & Sons, 1982), pp. 297–321; David Thomasma, "Ethical Judgments of Quality of Life in the Care of the Aged," *Journal of the American Geriatrics Society* 32 (July 1984): 525–27; David Thomasma, Kenneth C. Micetich, and Patricia H. Steinecker, "Continuance of Nutritional Care in the Terminally Ill Patient," in James P. Orlowski and George A. Kanoti, guest eds., *Critical Care Clinics: Ethical Moments in Critical Care Medicine* 2 (January 1986): 61–71; and Ruth Macklin, *Mortal Choices* (New York: Pantheon Books, 1987), pp. 49–81.

123. Lo and Jonsen, "Ethical Decisions in the Care of a Patient," pp. 107–10.

124. Robert M. Veatch, *Death, Dying, and the Biological Revolution*, 2nd ed. in press. Unless otherwise noted, the references made to this book are references to the second edition.

125. See Robert M. Veatch, "From Cases to Rules: The Challenge in Contemporary Medical Ethics," in Virginia Abernethy, ed., *Frontiers in Medical Ethics* (Cambridge, Mass.: Ballinger, 1980), pp. 43–61; idem, *A Theory of Medical Ethics* (New York: Basic Books, 1981), pp. 164–69, 207–8; and idem, " 'Do Not Resuscitate' Orders: A Dangerous Innovation," an unpublished paper.

126. Robert M. Veatch, "Caring for the Dying Person—Ethical Issues at Stake," in David Barton, ed., *Dying and Death: A Clinical Guide for Caregivers* (Baltimore: Williams & Wilkins, 1977), p. 163.

127. Robert M. Veatch, "Prolonging Living and Prolonging Dying: A Distinction that is not Decisive," in Aubrey Milunsky and Geroge J. Annas, eds., *Genetics and the Law II* (New York: Plenum Press, 1980), pp. 184–85.

128. Veatch, *Death, Dying, and the Biological Revolution*, in press.

129. Ibid., in press.

130. Veatch, *Theory of Medical Ethics*, pp. 141–305.

131. Veatch, *Death, Dying, and the Biological Revolution*, in press.

132. Ibid., in press.

133. Ibid., in press. For the development of Veatch's views on surrogate decision making, see McCormick and Veatch, "Preservation of Life and Self-Determination," pp. 390–96; Robert M. Veatch, "An Ethical Framework for Terminal Care Decisions," *Journal of the American Geriatrics Society* 32 (September 1984): 665–69; idem, "Limits of Guardian Treatment Refusal: A Reasonableness Standard," *American Journal of Law and Medicine* 9 (Winter 1984): 427–68; and the second edition of *Death, Dying, and the Biological Revolution*.

134. Veatch, *Death, Dying, and the Biological Revolution*, in press.

135. Compare Veatch, *Theory of Medical Ethics*, pp. 233–35 with the first edition of *Death, Dying, and the Biological Revolution*, pp. 89–90, 93–99, and the second edition of the same book, in press. Also see Robert M. Veatch, "Ethics and the Dying," in David J. Schnall and Carl L. Figliola, eds., *Contemporary Issues in Health Care* (New York: Praeger Publishers, 1984), pp. 98–101.

136. Veatch, *Death, Dying, and the biological Revolution*, in press.

137. Ibid., in press.

138. James F. Childress, *Who Should Decide?* (New York: Oxford University Press, 1982), p. 164.
139. James F. Childress, *Priorities in Biomedical Ethics* (Philadelphia: Westminster Press, 1981), p. 45. Also see idem, "On Ending Life," *Criterion* (Summer 1978): 4–8, an article published by the University of Chicago Divinity School that is an earlier version of the second chapter in *Priorities*.
140. Childress, *Who Should Decide?*, pp. 172–75.
141. Lynn and Childress, "Must Patients Always Be Given Food and Water?" p. 21.
142. James F. Childress and Steven L. Dalle Mura, "Caring for Patients and Caring for Symbols: Reflections on Artificial Nutrition and Hydration," *BioLaw* 1 (August 1986): S: 4.
143. James F. Childress, "When Is It Morally Justifiable to Discontinue Medical Nutrition and Hydration?," in Lynn, *By No Extraordinary Means*, pp. 77–79.
144. Beauchamp and Childress, *Principles of Biomedical Ethics*, p. 117. Also see Childress' discussion of Rachels' views in *Priorities in Biomedical Ethics*, pp. 36–39.
145. Beauchamp and Childress, *Principles of Biomedical Ethics*, pp. 116–17. Also see Childress, "To Kill or Let Die," in Elsie L. Bandman and Bertram Bandman, eds., *Bioethics and Human Rights* (Boston: Little, Brown, 1978), pp. 128–31.
146. James F. Childress, Ruth L. Roettinger, Mark Siegler, and Oscar A. Thorup, "Voluntary Exit: Is There a Case for Rational Suicide?," *The Pharos* 45 (Fall 1982): 30.
147. James F. Childress, "Love and Justice in Christian Biomedical Ethics," in Shelp, *Theology and Bioethics*, p. 227.
148. Ibid., p. 227.
149. Beauchamp and Childress, *Principles of Biomedical Ethics*, pp. 119–20.
150. James F. Childress, "Civil Disobedience, Conscientious Objection, and Evasive Noncompliance: A Framework for the Analysis and Assessment of Illegal Actions in Health Care," *Journal of Medicine and Philosophy* 10 (1985): 73.
151. Ibid., pp. 68, 75.
152. Ibid., pp. 75–76. Also see Childress, *Who Should Decide?*, pp. 179–80. Other ethicists who can be identified with the fifth position include Philippa Foot and Lisa Sowle Cahill. See Philippa Foot, "Euthanasia," *Philosophy and Public Affaris* 6 (Winter 1977): 85–112; and Lisa Sowle Cahill, "A 'Natural Law' Reconsideration of Euthanasia," *Linacre Quarterly* 44 (February 1977): 47–63.
153. See James Rachels, "Active and Passive Euthanasia," pp. 78–80; idem, "Euthanasia, Killing, and Letting Die," in Ladd, *Ethical Issues Relating to Life and Death*, pp. 146–63; and a slightly different article under the same title in Wade L. Robison and Michael S. Pritchard, eds., *Medical Responsibility* (Clifton, N.J.: The Humana Press, 1979), pp. 153–68.
154. The most complete presentations of his position are found in Rachels, "Euthanasia," in Tom Regan, ed., *Matters of Life and Death*, 2nd ed. (New York: Random House, 1986), pp. 35–76; and idem, *The End of Life: Euthanasia and Morality* (Oxford: Oxford University Press, 1986).
155. Rachels, *End of Life*, pp. 38, 5–6. Unless indicated otherwise, the unfootnoted quotations that follow are taken in a sequential manner from this book.
156. James Rachels, "More Impertinent Distinctions," in Thomas A. Mappes and Jane S. Zembaty, eds., *Biomedical Ethics*, 2nd ed. (New York: McGraw-Hill, 1986), p. 396.

157. Rachels, *End of Life*, p. 95.
158. Ibid., p. 111. Also see idem, "Killing and Starving to Death," *Philosophy* 54 (1979): 159–71; and idem, "Reasoning about Killing and Letting Die," *Southern Journal of Philosophy* 19 (1981): 465–73.
159. See Rachels, "Euthanasia, Killing, and Letting Die," p. 159.
160. Rachels, "Euthanasia," pp. 49–50; and idem, *End of Life*, p. 153. The case comes from Stewart Alsop, "The Right to Die with Dignity," *Good Housekeeping*, August 1974.
161. Rachels, "Euthanasia, Killing and Letting die," pp. 151–52.
162. Rachels, "Euthanasia," p. 36.
163. Ibid., p. 52.
164. Rachels, *End of Life*, p. 170.
165. Ibid., p. 179.
166. Ibid., p. 187. Also see Rachels, "Barney Clark's Key," *Hastings Center Report* 13 (April 1983): 17–19.
167. Jonathan Glover, *Causing Death and Saving Lives* (Harmondsworth, England and New York: Penguin Books, 1977), pp. 113–14.
168. Ibid., pp. 184–85.
169. Ibid., pp. 188–89.
170. Ibid., pp. 192–200.
171. Peter Singer, *Practical Ethics* (Cambridge: Cambridge University Press, 1979), p. 139.
172. Ibid., pp. 140–46.
173. Helga Kuhse, "The Case for Active Voluntary Euthanasia," *Law, Medicine and Health Care* 14 (September 1986): 145–48. Also see her comments in "Debate: Extraordinary Means and the Sanctity of Life," *Journal of Medical Ethics* 7 (1981): 74–79; idem, "Extraordinary Means and the Intentional Termination of Life," *Social Science and Medicine* 15F (1981): 117–21; and idem, *The Sanctity-of-Life Doctrine in Medicine* (Oxford: Oxford University Press, 1987). Other ethicists who can be identified with the sixth position include Joseph Fletcher, Marvin Kohl, Michael Tooley, H. Tristram Engelhardt, Jr., and Dan Brock. Some of the relevant publications by Fletcher and Kohl have already been cited in nn. 15 and 26. For Tooley's views, see his "Decisions to Terminate Life and the Concept of Person," in Ladd, *Ethical Issues Relating to Life and Death*, pp. 62–93. For Engelhardt's views, see Engelhardt and Michele Malloy, "Suicide and Assisting Suicide: A Critique of Legal Sanctions," *Southwestern Law Journal* 36 (November 1982): 1003–37; and Engelhardt, *The Foundations of Bioethics* (New York: Oxford University Press, 1986), especially pp. 312–17. For Brock's views, see his "Moral Rights and Permissible Killing," in Ladd, *Ethical Issues Relating to Life and Death*, pp. 94–117; idem, "Taking Human Life," *Ethics* 95 (July 1985): 851–65; and idem, "Forgoing Life-Sustaining Food and Water: Is It Killing?" in Lynn, *By No Extraordinary Means*, pp. 117–31.
174. Ronald M. Green, "Comtemporary Jewish Bioethics: A Critical Assessment," in Shelp, *Theology and Bioethics*, pp. 245–266 at 254.
175. See the National Right to Life Committee's "Position Statement on Euthanasia," first approved January 21, 1980, and amended April 14, 1984. The committee drawing up the document was chaired by James Bopp, Jr., J.D.
176. Judie Brown, "Using 'Right to Die' Is Sign of Sick Society," Opinion Page of *USA Today*, January 29, 1987, p. 8A.

177. Ramsey, *Ethics at the Edges of Life,* p. 187.
178. See Dennis J. Horan and Edward R. Grant, "Prolonging Life and Withdrawing Treatment: Legal Issues," *Studies in Law and Medicine* No. 15 (1983): 1–18; idem, "The Legal Aspects of Withdrawing Nourishment," *The Journal of Legal Medicine* 5 (1984): 595–632; idem, "Suicide: The Next Pro-Life Frontier," *Studies in Law and Medicine* No. 22 (1985): 1–11; C. Everett Koop and Edward R. Grant, "The 'Small Beginnings' of Euthanasia: Examining the Erosion in Legal Prohibitions against Mercy-Killing," *Notre Dame Journal of Law, Ethics and Public Policy* 2 (1986): 585–634; Dennis J. Horan and Edward R. Grant, "Catholic Ethical Teaching and Public Policy: How Do They Relate?," *Linacre Quarterly* 53 (November 1986): 28–38; and idem, "Hydration, Nutrition, and Euthanasia: Legal Reflections on the Role of Church Teaching," unpublished manuscript.

7

Treatment Abatement and Other End-of-Life Issues

Many of our *moral* views turn in significant respects on our conceptual (or definitional) views. For example, many physicians and theologians believe that suicide and assisting a suicide fall wholly outside the boundaries of permissible practice in medicine, and yet these physicians and theologians are quick to add that health professionals often morally should permit terminally ill patients to refuse medical treatment if its continuation is burdensome, painful, risky, or costly, even though the refusal will bring death more quickly. One's ability to implement this moral perspective will turn in important ways on how one defines the boundary (if it can be defined) between suicide and refusal of treatment.

TOM L. BEAUCHAMP, PH.D.[1]

The ethical question here about facilitating dying is whether those who would limit medical actions to acts of omission only, excluding all acts of commission, are on defensible grounds when they make that distinction. It is, of course, a distinction widely made, but is it logically or rationally tenable? . . . I want to contend that the distinction is vacuous, that there is no moral difference between contriving death by indirect means and doing it by direct means. Look, for instance, at a recent ethical directive of the Judicial Council of the American Medical Association that approves of stopping artificially provided nutrition and hydration for irreversibly comatose patients, *even if death is not imminent*. In short, they say it is morally licit to end the life of a patient who is not at this moment dying. Is this not what some call "active" euthanasia, as distinct from "passive"?

JOSEPH FLETCHER, S.T.D.[2]

As described in the first chapter, the concept of treatment abatement includes three possibilities: the withholding of treatment, the selective or complete deceleration of treatment, and the withdrawing of treatment previously started. When a patient does not have a life-threatening condition and recommended treatment is therefore unnecessary for the sustaining of the patient's life, treatment abatement is commonplace and far from controversial. Thousands of persons each day decide for any number of reasons to abate recommended treatment as they opt not to have a physician's prescription filled at the pharmacy, choose to take less than the recommended dosage of a liquid medication or fewer than the recommended number of pills, or simply decide to discontinue taking prescribed medicine or participating in a recommended diet and exercise program.

However, when a patient is critically ill and perhaps dying, when the patient is in a hospital or nursing home, and when medical treatment is available that could forestall the patient's death, any decision to abate that treatment is obviously a serious moral and legal matter. To withhold, reduce, or with sustaining treatment in the face of a patient's probable or certain dead pending on the patient's condition and the modality of treatment being abate is not a step to be taken lightly by physicians and other health care professional Consequently, as we have seen in earlier chapters, numerous persons sometimes get involved in decisions to abate life-sustaining treatment: an autonomous patient or the surrogate of a nonautonomous patient, the attending physician and other physicians and nurses caring for the patient, the patient's family or guardian, the administrator of the hospital or nursing home, one or more court justices, a guardian *ad litem,* pro-life and right-to-die groups, and so on.

Several features of such decisions lead to questions about the conceptual relationship of treatment abatement and other ethical issues that occasionally arise at the end of life. Among these features are the possible ambiguity of motives and intentions on the part of an autonomous patient who refuses life-sustaining treatment, a condition of permanent unconsciousness or some other condition that prevents a patient from having the capacity to make a decision regarding the administration or abatement of life-sustaining treatment, the possible ambiguity of motives and intentions on the part of the surrogate making a decision to abate treatment on the behalf of a nonautonomous patient, the possible ambiguity of motives and intentions on the part of physicians and nurses who implement the decision to abate treatment, the probable if not certain death of the patient following the abatement of life-sustaining treatment, and the omnipresent threat of civil or criminal action against the health care professionals who participate in implementing such decisions.

Given these complicating factors, some persons inside and outside medicine occasionally confuse the issue of treatment abatement with one or more of these other end-of-life issues: (1) brain death, (2) suicide, (3) assisted suicide, and (4) euthanasia, in either its voluntary or nonvoluntary form. Whether the confusion of treatment abatement and these other issues is accidental or intentional is often difficult to discern. Surely the conceptual similarities among several of these issues can be a sufficient cause for confusion, especially for persons lacking the time and inclination to think seriously about the differences among these issues. Some physicians, for instance, may blur the conceptual differences among these issues either because their time for thinking about such matters is severely limited, or because they lack the philosophical skills that could be helpful in such an analysis. Alternatively, some physicians may blur these differences because they want to camouflage their reasons for being uncooperative with a request to abate treatment made by an autonomous patient or by the surrogate of a nonautonomous patient.

For some pro-life advocates and also for some advocates of euthanasia as a standard moral and legal option, the blurring of whatever conceptual differences there may be between treatment abatement and these other issues seems part of

That strategy, simply put, is intentionally to blur the possible
this issue and the other end-of-life issues in order to score
over the morality of several of these actions. Thus some (but
e advocates, who may be identified with any one of the first
sed in the preceding chapter, seem unnecessarily to blur the
tween treatment abatement and the other end-of-life issues
abating treatment can be rejected as wrong for the same
..., assisted suicide, and euthanasia are held to be morally
unacceptable. Likewise, the philosophers identified with the sixth position in the
previous chapter seem unnecessarily to blur the relevant differences between
abating treatment and the other issues so that they can argue that suicide, assisted
suicide, voluntary euthanasia, and nonvoluntary euthanasia are as acceptable on
moral and legal grounds as treatment abatement is.

Without doubt, there are overlapping features among some of these ethical
issues at the end of life. Even if one subscribes neither to the vitalistic perspective of the more extreme pro-life advocates nor to the consequentialist thinking
of the utilitarians and libertarians at the other end of the spectrum, the most
obvious feature that most acts of abating treatment with critically ill patients have
with many acts of attempted suicide, assisted suicide, and euthanasia is undeniable: the death of the patient. However, to stop the analysis of these issues at
that point is to omit other features of these acts that may help to distinguish
treatment abatement in important ways from the other issues. Of course, even if
there are distinguishing features between treatment abatement and the other
end-of-life issues that can stand up to challenge, the identification of such features *does not entail any particular conclusions* about the morality of these
actions in individual cases. Nevertheless, the sorting out of relevant differences
among these issues can enhance and strengthen any effort to set forth the general
conditions under which abating treatment with critically ill patients is morally
justifiable.

Brain death

The first end-of-life issue to be discussed is the definition and determination of
death. This issue has two related parts, both brought about in the 1960s by the
unprecedented technological capacity of medicine to sustain the respiratory and
circulatory functions of some ICU patients for prolonged periods of time. The
first part of the issue consists of a conceptual or philosophical interpretation of
what death means in the age of technological medicine, since the traditional
understanding of death as the cessation of spontaneous cardiopulmonary activity
is sometimes clouded by technological means of prolonging those functions in
patients. The second part focuses on the appropriate clinical tests to be used in
determining that a former patient is now dead, especially if that patient's life has

been prolonged by technological means. Taken together, the two parts of this issue have utmost importance, as evidenced by the attention given the issue by physicians, legal scholars, philosophers, state legislators, journalists, and other concerned persons over the past two decades.

The debate over the definition and determination of death during the 1970s involved competing philosophical perspectives on the meaning of death (especially between the advocates of neocortical death and the advocates of whole-brain death), numerous medical proposals aimed at updating the clinical criteria put forth in 1968 by an ad hoc committee of the Harvard Medical School, and an extraordinary variety of new state laws as legislators in many states followed the 1970 effort of the Kansas legislature to update the legal definition of death in the light of technological developments in medicine. To a great extent, the 1981 report of the President's Commission entitled *Defining Death* produced consensus on these philosophical, medical, and legal matters.[3] The clinical guidelines produced by the commission's medical consultants have received wide acceptance, and the proposed Uniform Determination of Death Act has become law in 17 states and is pending in several others.[4] In spite of this progress toward agreement, however, some critics of the positions advocated by the President's Commission remain outspoken in calling for alternative philosophical definitions of death and better legal definitions of death.[5]

The intricacies of this unfinished debate over the definition and determination of death are beyond the purview of this book. What is of concern at this point, however, is the tendency on the part of some persons to confuse this issue with the issue of treatment abatement. Some physicians, for instance, use their own confusion over these two issues as a reason for refusing to abate treatment with critically ill patients. Such physicians, when asked why they refuse to terminate the mechanical ventilation or technological feeding being used to sustain the life of a patient with PVS, occasionally respond with a completely irrelevant statement: "But the patient isn't dead yet!" Likewise, some health care institutions confuse the two issues in their policy statements. For example, the Worcester (Massachusetts) Hahnemann Hospital has had a policy whereby the only acceptable reason for abating life-sustaining treatment in the care of any patient is that the patient be dead according to the "Harvard criteria" for death![6]

Some attorneys and ethicists also confuse the two issues on occasion and thus make puzzling statements about treatment abatement. Katherine Benesch, for instance, puts forth this legal advice regarding the termination of life support: "There should be no liability for terminating the life-support systems of a brain-dead patient, as long as this takes place in a state where brain-based criteria have been recognized as one standard for determining death."[7] Robert Barry, as was noted in the previous chapter, goes even further by suggesting that brain-dead patients should continue to be given technological feeding and hydration!

The response to such signs of confusion (or category mistakes, if you will) is twofold. First, it is true that certain surface similarities between the two issues can possibly be confusing: both issues have been widely publicized in the media, both issues have been the focal point of court cases, both issues have been the subject of new statutes in the majority of the 50 states, both issues have been controversial for overlapping periods of time, and so on. Moreover, each issue often impinges on the other one: most patients who have life-sustaining treatment abated subsequently die and are quite possibly declared dead on the basis of some formulation of brain-death criteria, and many patients declared dead in institutional settings subsequently are separated from some medical technologies that previously had provided life-sustaining treatment while the patients were alive.

However, no matter how many surface similarities and related aspects are involved, the two issues are not the same and should not be confused with one another. The most obvious difference between the two issues—bordering on the self-evident—is the *difference between life and death*. The subject of a decision to abate treatment is unquestionably still alive (even though perhaps permanently unconscious) according to a whole-brain interpretation of death, but has a deteriorating medical condition that calls for less than maximal treatment. By contrast, the subject of a declaration-of-death decision is an unburied corpse that calls for no medical treatment whatever unless for the temporary purpose of sustaining organs in that cadaver so that they can be transplanted into the body of another critically ill or otherwise impaired patient.

The difference between the two issues also has to do with a *difference in the use of technology*. In decisions to abate treatment, the decision is usually *about* a modality of technology that is being used or could be used to sustain a patient's life for an indeterminate period of time. By contrast, in decisions focused on the determination and declaration of death, various technologies (for example, EEGs) are frequently used to *help make the decision* whether a patient is alive or dead.

Furthermore, the difference between the two issues is evident in the *role of surrogates for patients*. In decisions to abate treatment made on the behalf of nonautonomous patients, surrogates for the patients have a central decision-making role. By contrast, no physician would think of turning to a patient's surrogate for the purpose of asking the surrogate to make the decision whether the patient is still alive or has died. Even the possibility of a physician's involving a relative or friend of a patient in this manner is ludicrous (Physician: "I can't tell if the patient is dead. What do you think?").

Finally, the difference between the two issues can be seen in the *nature of the questions asked*. In decisions to abate treatment, decision makers usually wrestle with some version of this question: "Is abating treatment morally justified in this case, and is it legally permitted?" In decisions concerning a patient's aliveness or lack of aliveness, a very different question is posed: "Is this patient now dead, and how do we know that?"

Suicide

Although laws making suicide a crime were repealed in most if not all jurisdictions in the United States in the 1970s, questions about the relationship between suicide and the abatement of life-sustaining treatment often arise in treatment-abatement cases that end up in court. Are there significant differences between acts of suicide and acts of abating treatment? Do autonomous patients sometimes have suicidal motives in refusing life-sustaining treatment? If so, does the apparent presence or the unquestionable presence of suicidal motives in an autonomous patient's decision to abate treatment make a moral or legal difference? If a disabled but autonomous patient requests aid from health care personnel in carrying out a suicide attempt, are those health care professionals morally obligated and legally permitted to carry out the request? If life-sustaining treatment is abated in the care of a nonautonomous patient, are the decision makers in the case at risk for prosecution for having assisted in a suicide?

Several of the cases presented in earlier chapters contain judicial opinions on these questions, frequently in the context of considering the prevention of suicide as one of the state's legitimate interests in such cases. Of course the notion that the state has a legitimate interest in preventing suicide is open to question, especially in cases involving autonomous patients residing in jurisdictions that no longer consider suicide a criminal act. Less questionable is a court's concern over the possibility that a decision to abate treatment on the behalf of a nonautonomous patient is actually an attempt to assist in the suicide of that patient, since aiding in an attempt at suicide is still a criminal act in many jurisdictions. We will return to this matter momentarily.

For the present, the major question before us is whether there are conceptual features of acts of suicide and acts of abating treatment that are sufficiently different to warrant the claim that most decisions for treatment abatement made by autonomous patients (or by surrogates for previously autonomous patients whose wishes are clearly known) are not acts of suicide. Several of the courts of final decision in the cases presented in Chapter 3 dealt with the question of suicide, and all of them judged that the patients in those cases were not trying to commit suicide in their refusals of life-sustaining treatment.

Two reasons commonly appear in these judicial opinions for rejecting the claim that these patients are actually engaged in suicide: (1) the patient's intention in refusing treatment, and (2) the "underlying cause" of the patient's death when the patient dies without the treatment. Regarding the first reason, the *Perlmutter* court emphasized Perlmutter's "basic wish to live" even though he refused the continuation of mechanical ventilation.[8] The *Bartling* court quoted the patient's personal statement concerning his not wanting to die and agreed that Bartling had no "specific intent to die."[9] Judge Stanton, in his opinion in *Requena* that was partially quoted in the preceding chapter, stated that this patient with ALS "is not anti-life" and that she "would dearly like to be well and to have a decent life."[10]

As to the second reason, the *Myers* court rejected the claim of self-inflicted death should Myers subsequently die after refusing treatment. The court argued that Myers' death would result from "natural causes" (his kidney condition), a "death-producing agent" the prisoner had not set in motion.[11] Likewise, the *Perlmutter* court claimed that any charge of suicide would not be accurate, since Abe Perlmutter obviously did not "self-induce his horrible affliction."[12] And Judge Stanton said that Beverly Requena's refusal of technological feeding did not involve "any positive act to terminate life" but simply amounted to "acquiescence in the natural shutting down of a critical bodily function."[13]

The question of the relationship between the refusal of life-sustaining treatment and an act of suicide was particularly important in the Bouvia case (see Case 3.9). What was different, the justices of the court of appeal asked, in Elizabeth Bouvia's refusal of an NG tube in 1986, compared with her refusal of oral feeding, fluids, and other nutrients in 1983? Beyond the differences in medical settings and her worsening medical condition, the justices found a difference in Bouvia's intention. Whereas she had earlier clearly displayed the desire to terminate her life with the assistance of health care professionals, she seemed in 1986 no longer determined to hasten the ending of her life. Rather, she simply wanted to receive effective pain medication without the insertion of a "hated and unwanted device" to supplement her oral intake of food. On the basis of this difference in intention, the justices concluded that Bouvia's "decision to allow nature to take its course" (her condition of cerebral palsy had degenerated in 3 years to the point of quadriplegia, crippling arthritis, and continual pain) "is not equivalent" to a decision to commit suicide.[14]

Similar comments have been made by courts handling cases of nonautonomous patients. For example, the *Delio* court reasoned that the state's interest in preventing suicide and assisted suicide did not apply to the case at bar. The court argued that Daniel Delio, a patient in PVS following unexpected cardiac arrest, was not being aided in committing suicide through the removal of technological feeding and hydration. The court maintained that "suicide requires a specific intent to die," whereas Delio and other patients opposed to the technological prolongation of their lives usually display "only an intent to live free of unwanted mechanical devices and permit the processes of nature to run their course."[15] The *Gardner* court took a similar position regarding another PVS patient. Joseph Gardner, permanently unconscious following a fall from a pickup, "in no sense has decided to kill himself." Gardner did not intentionally place himself "in such a position that his continued biological existence would depend upon the provision of life-sustaining procedures.'' Rather, having been placed in that situation as a consequence of a tragic accident, he ''is simply exercising his right to control the course of his medical care.''[16]

Are these courts correct? Does an analysis of a person's intention and the underlying cause of that person's impending death provide sufficient grounds for distinguishing between decisions to abate life-sustaining treatment and decisions to commit suicide? If not, is there any feature of these acts that makes them intrinsically different?

The appropriate answers to these questions seem to be, in order, ''to a large extent,'' ''frequently,'' and ''no.'' Given the ongoing debate about the concept of suicide and about the psychological makeup of persons who attempt suicide or commit suicide, any attempt to argue for an intrinsic difference between treatment abatement and suicide is doomed to failure. The simple fact is that a refusal to allow a blood transfusion, or the amputation of a limb, or the continuation of kidney dialysis, or the initiation/continuation of mechanical ventilation, or the initiation/continuation of technological feeding cannot be defined in such a way as to rule out the possibility of suicidal interests on the part of the autonomous patient who is refusing life-sustaining treatment. As Tom Beauchamp points out: ''These acts *can* be suicides, because *any* means productive of death can be used to the end of suicide.''[17]

The difficulty in sorting out the differences between these two acts is due to two sorts of ambiguity. On the one hand, the concept of suicide itself is ambiguous. Most persons, I think, will agree that a minimalist definition of suicide involves three features: (1) the death is intentional on the part of the person who dies, (2) the death is caused by that person, and (3) the decision to engage in self-destruction is noncoerced. Beyond this minimalist definition, the dispute over the concept of suicide includes differences over a number of other factors that have bearing on a comprehensive definition of suicide: the rationality or irrationality of the person's decision, the motives connected with the decision, the time involved in self-destruction (life-styles known to be hazardous are sometimes referred to as ''slow suicides''), the requirement that the person not have a fatal medical condition, the directness or indirectness of the act of self-destruction, the possible roles of altruism and sacrifice, and so on.[18]

On the other hand, the motivation and intention of the person who refuses life-sustaining treatment are sometimes unclear, even when the analysis of the patient's motivation and intention is done by a psychiatrist. Although these psychological factors are sufficiently clear in most cases, they remain elusive or debatable in some instances. Thus even if everyone involved in a case agrees that the patient has the *capacity* to refuse treatment, they may not be able to agree on exactly *why* the patient has refused treatment or precisely *what* he or she primarily intends to be the consequence of that decision.

Nevertheless, as the courts have correctly indicated, there are some differences between these two legal acts that are sufficiently clear in enough cases to enable physicians, relatives of the patients, and all other participants in treatment-abatement cases to avoid confusing a patient's choice to forgo life-sustaining treatment with a decision to commit suicide. At least three such differences provide the basis for claiming that *most* decisions made by autonomous patients to abate life-sustaining treatment *are not acts of suicide*.

First, autonomous patients opting for the abatement of life-sustaining treatment *do not usually have suicidal motives*. In contrast to persons bent on self-destruction, persons choosing to forgo the prolongation of their lives through various medical interventions are not usually motivated by guilt, self-hatred, a desire to punish someone else, a desire to show contempt for the world, a desire to contribute to some noble cause, or any of the other motivating reasons often connected with suicides.[19]

Second, autonomous patients who refuse life-sustaining treatments *do not usually intend to die*. Instead, they intend through their decision merely to be relieved of technological procedures and medical interventions they find abhorrent, contrary to their chosen life-styles, futile in restoring them to a meaningful quality of life, or contrary to their best interests. They often genuinely do not want to die, but are willing to accept a "natural" end to their lives if that is the necessary price to pay for freedom from some technological prolongation of their lives that seems to have no ending point short of their deaths.

Third, such patients *cannot correctly be said to have caused their own deaths* when they decide to have life-sustaining treatment withheld, decelerated, or withdrawn. All of these patients have one or more serious medical conditions that have caused them to be critically ill or dying in the first place. All of them would have died from those underlying conditions if they had been so afflicted prior to the technological age of medicine. Thus, in contrast to persons who use guns, poisons, knives, ropes, pills, or other lethal devices to kill themselves, patients who choose to forgo medical treatments that could prolong both their lives and their pathological conditions for an indefinite period of time do not inflict death on themselves. Rather, they merely "say no" to some version of technological medicine's multifaceted attempt at turning a critically ill patient's body into a perpetual-motion machine. In so doing, they assent (in Judge Stanton's words) to "the natural shutting down" of their biological systems.

Assisted suicide

The concept of assisted suicide is problematic not only because it can be confused with the abatement of life-sustaining treatment, but also because of its relatedness to the concepts of suicide and voluntary euthanasia. As with suicides done without assistance from another person, an assisted suicide involves a patient in a clinical setting or a person outside a clinical setting who has suicidal motives, clearly intends to die, and is noncoerced in deciding to hasten his or her own death. In contrast to "normal" suicides, an assisted suicide requires aid from a physician, a relative or friend of the person wanting to commit suicide, or some other person who carries out the role of "enabler." The enabler can supply information on the most effective ways of committing suicide, provide a lethal dosage of pills or some other means of producing death, give the suicidal person encouragement in performing the act of self-destruction, or help in the actual act of killing (e.g., by helping the person take the pills, pull the trigger of a gun, or turn on the gas). Also in contrast to suicide, any act of assisted suicide is an illegal act in many jurisdictions punishable by fines and/or short-term imprisonment.

Assisted suicide also has many of the same features as voluntary euthanasia. Like acts of voluntary euthanasia, acts of assisted suicide involve helping to bring about the death of a person who has intractable pain or some other intolerable condition, who is unable for physical or psychological reasons to commit suicide without assistance, who prefers death to the continuation of an intolerable life, and who requests aid in bringing about an end to his or her life. Acts of assisted suicide differ from acts of voluntary euthanasia in two major ways: final agency and legal liability. In acts of assisted suicide, the person who does the actual killing is the person who wants to die, and the enabler who assists in that deed runs the risk of a relatively mild legal penalty or, in some jurisdictions, no legal penalty at all. In acts of voluntary euthanasia, the person who does the actual killing is someone other than the person who wants to die, and that person who kills—even for reasons of mercy—runs the risk of being prosecuted for having committed murder or manslaughter.

The widespread illegality of assisted suicide—no matter the relative mildness of the punishment compared with the possible punishment for an act of euthanasia—is one reason why many of the courts that have handled treatment-abatement cases have pointed out that the specific act(s) of abating treatment under consideration in those judicial proceedings are not to be interpreted as acts of suicide. In cases involving autonomous patients and especially in cases involving nonautonomous patients, a number of courts have addressed the distinction between treatment abatement and suicide not only to make clear which of these legal acts is involved in the case at bar but also to demonstrate that state statutes prohibiting the "aiding and abetting" of suicide do not apply to the case.

Another reason that the *Quinlan, Saikewicz, Perlmutter, Colyer, Bartling, Conroy, Bouvia,* and other courts have distinguished between the abatement of life-sustaining treatment and an act of suicide is the differing moral assessment given by many people to efforts at assisting in these actions. Assisting someone to commit suicide, even more than an act of suicide itself, is widely regarded in the United States as morally impermissible. For instance, all of the individual ethicists and groups identified with the first three positions in the previous chapter reject both suicide and assisted suicide on moral grounds, in part because both of these acts go counter to religious perspectives that interpret individual lives as gifts from God. Most of the ethicists and groups identified with the fourth position also find suicide and assisted suicide to be morally unacceptable, but direct much more criticism at acts of assisted suicide and reject all such acts for policy reasons as well as substantive reasons having to do with the acts themselves.

Although acts of abating life-sustaining treatment *can* be acts of assisting a patient to commit suicide, these two acts are usually distinguishable in several ways. First, there are the differences that we have already discussed pertaining to the *motivation, intention, and causative role* of the person whose life is at stake. An autonomous, critically ill patient who refuses life-sustaining treat-ment—with little or no doubt that such a refusal if carried out will probably hasten his or her death—cannot usually be said to have suicidal motives, actually intend to die, or be the cause of his or her own death. By contrast, a person who requests assistance in committing suicide—and follows through by killing him-self or herself—does play an active role in that event in terms of motivation, intention, and causation.

Another difference between the abatement of life-sustaining treatment and an assisted suicide has to do with *different kinds of moral rights* involved in the relationship between a patient and that patient's physician. A decision made by an autonomous patient or by the surrogate of a nonautonomous patient to forgo chemotherapy, mechanical ventilation, or some other life-sustaining treatment involves the *negative* right (or liberty right) of treatment refusal, backed up by claims concerning self-determination, religious liberty, privacy, or some com-bination of these legal rights. A correlate of this negative right is an obligation on the part of the patient's physician not to interfere with or thwart that negative right, sometimes interpreted as the right to be left alone or the right to nonin-terference, unless the physician has some overriding obligation of another sort. In contrast, a request by a patient to have a physician's assistance in committing suicide involves a *positive* right (or welfare right), or at least a claim to that effect. Not merely calling on the physician to refrain from a medical intervention of some sort during critical illness or the terminal phase of life, the patient tries to impose an obligation on the physician actually to help the patient commit suicide. However, this attempt generally fails, as it should, because few physi-cians perceive themselves to have a moral obligation to help someone else engage in self-destruction.

Euthanasia

The conceptual and moral relationship between treatment abatement and eutha-nasia has been widely discussed for a number of years, often with more heat being generated than progress made toward greater understanding. The literature on the subject is vast, the dispute over the relationship has every sign of continuing without resolution, and the disputants tend to pass by one another (in their publications) like ships in the night.[20]

Three examples should suffice to illustrate the conceptual confusion that is often displayed when euthanasia is discussed. Years ago Joseph Fletcher proposed a typology of forms of euthanasia that demonstrated his confusion regarding the rule of double effect. Interpreting euthanasia as a "good death," he suggested that euthanasia can be (1) voluntary and direct, (2) voluntary but indirect, (3) direct but involuntary, and (4) both indirect and involuntary.[21] More recently, two persons added to this conceptual confusion in their comments on the infamous "Debbie" case of euthanasia (a real or fictitious case of a gynecology resident killing a cancer patient who said, "Let's get this over with") published in the *Journal of the American Medical Association* (*JAMA*). Kenneth Vaux, an ethicist, distinguished among (1) passive euthanasia, (2) double-effect euthanasia, and (3) active euthanasia.[22] George Lundberg, the editor of *JAMA*, presented a vague definition of euthanasia and then said there are six major types of euthanasia: (1) passive, (2) semipassive, (3) semiactive, (4) accidental, (5) suicidal, and (6) active.[23]

I have no particular reason to believe that I will succeed where Fletcher, Vaux, Lundberg, and others have failed, but think that even a small measure of conceptual clarity will contribute to a better understanding of the morality of abating treatment with critically ill patients. Briefly put, the difficulty in achieving conceptual clarity in regard to treatment abatement and euthanasia exists for a wide variety of reasons:

the variety of cases that involve the abatement of treatment, including the abatement of treatments that prolong patients' lives;

the terminological problems connected with "euthanasia," with that term etymologically signifying a "good death" and through modern usage signifying "killing a hopelessly ill patient for reasons of mercy";

the tendency of some persons to confuse treatment abatement *and* euthanasia with double-effect deaths;

the widespread use of three distinctions (active/passive, omission/commission, and withhold/withdraw) that may once have been helpful in the ethical analysis of end-of-life issues, but now need to be placed in the historical archives of biomedical ethics;

the tendency of some persons regularly and simplistically to invoke the ordinary/extraordinary distinction, thereby confining the ethical analysis of treatment abatement to the debatable category of "extraordinary" or "heroic" means of prolonging life;

the frequent failure to distinguish among the forms of euthanasia, not on the
misleading basis of "active" and "passive" euthanasia (or "positive" and
"negative" euthanasia) but on the basis of patient preferences and choices;
the tendency of some consequentialists to blur any possible differences between
abating treatment and euthanasia by interpreting treatment abatement synony-
mously with "letting die"; and
the inherent vagueness of the two central concepts—intention and causation—
necessary to distinguish some acts of treatment abatement from all acts of
euthanasia.

Four steps can be taken to move beyond this conceptual confusion regarding
treatment abatement and euthanasia. The first step can be simply stated, but is
exceedingly difficult to bring about: we need to stop using ethical categories and
distinctions that have outlived their usefulness! In particular, unless certain aspects of the debate about the relationship of treatment abatement and euthanasia
are to be perpetuated ad nauseam, we must get to the point of excising them from
philosophical discussions of these two end-of-life issues. My candidates for
expulsion to the archives mentioned previously are as follows: (1) repetitious
references to the etymology of "euthanasia," (2) the language of "ordinary"
and "extraordinary" means (unless this terminology is "translated" into the
language of proportionate benefit and burden, or limited to specific clinical
settings such as the ICU), (3) the adjectival distinctions of "active" (or "positive") and "passive" (or "negative") euthanasia, and (4) the two other ethical
distinctions just mentioned (omission/commission, withhold/withdraw) that have
limited if any applicability to these end-of-life issues in technological medicine.

This done, the second step is to gain greater clarity about the possible forms
that treatment abatement can take. In addition to the three features of the concept
of treatment abatement that have been discussed earlier (i.e., the withholding,
decelerating, and withdrawing of treatment), acts of treatment abatement can
take any one of three forms. When individuals who are not patients in a health
care setting decide to forgo recommended treatment, the decision upon being
carried out can be classified as *personal* (or self-administered) *treatment abatement.* Although such behavior goes counter to medical advice, this form of
abating treatment is voluntary, commonplace, uncontroversial, done without the
cooperation of any health care professional (or anyone else), and based entirely
on one's autonomy as a health care consumer.

In sharp contrast, the abatement of treatment in a clinical setting is another
matter entirely, especially when the treatment is known to be life-sustaining,
wanted by an autonomous patient, and/or clearly in the best interests of a critically ill patient whether autonomous or nonautonomous. When mechanical ventilation, medical feeding and hydration, or some other life-sustaining treatment
is not administered to a critically ill patient in these circumstances—or is re-

moved from such a patient—the action can be classified as *imposed treatment abatement*. If a patient dies after this type of treatment abatement, the person who abated treatment in this manner is liable for prosecution under the charge of murder or manslaughter.

The third form of treatment abatement, *cooperative treatment abatement,* is the subject of this book. Based on the choice of an autonomous, critically ill patient or on the best interests of a critically ill patient whether autonomous or nonautonomous, this form of abating treatment requires cooperation on the part of health care professionals. If the treatment that is withheld, decelerated, or withdrawn usually sustains patients' lives, and even if a particular patient dies following the abatement of such treatment, a cooperative act of abating treatment is nevertheless not the moral or legal equivalent of acts of assisted suicide or euthanasia. If such a case is taken to court, as we have seen in earlier chapters, the act of cooperative treatment abatement never—as of this writing—involves conviction of the health care professionals on either civil or criminal charges.

The third step toward greater conceptual clarity is to distinguish among the forms of euthanasia. When an autonomous, hopelessly ill patient decides that death is preferable to a continually painful or otherwise intolerable existence and requests that he or she be killed, the subsequent intentional killing of the patient for reasons of mercy by the attending physician (or someone else) is *voluntary euthanasia*. The second form of euthanasia applies to permanently unconscious or otherwise nonautonomous patients who have never expressed preferences regarding the technological prolongation of their lives. If and when such nonautonomous patients are intentionally killed for reasons of mercy, the causation of their deaths is correctly described as *nonvoluntary euthanasia* because they were unable to express a desire or preference concerning the continuation or termination of their lives. When autonomous patients express a desire to continue living, or when a now-nonautonomous patient previously expressed such a desire in a clear fashion when thinking about the possibility of medical circumstances similar to the circumstances that now exist, any subsequent killing of such patients by someone else is *involuntary euthanasia* (in moral terms) or murder (in legal terms).

These forms of treatment abatement and euthanasia often differ in terms of the seriousness of the patient's medical condition, the patient's decision-making capacity, the patient's motivation, the patient's intention, and the consequence of an act of treatment abatement or euthanasia on the patient's continued life or likelihood of death. In addition, these forms of treatment abatement and euthanasia can and often do differ in terms of the physician's motivation, the physician's intention, the physician's action, and the physician's legal liability for an act of abating treatment or killing a critically ill patient. See Table 7.1 for a comparison of these differences.

TABLE 7.1   Characteristic Features of Treatment Abatement and Euthanasia

Personal treatment abatement (PTA)	Cooperative treatment abatement (CTA)	Imposed treatment abatement (ITA)
1. Individual is neither critically ill nor a patient in a health care facility.	1. Patient's medical condition is critical and appears irreversible.	1. Same as CTA
2. Individual has decision-making capacity.	2. Patient can be autonomous or nonautonomous.	2. Same as CTA
3. Individual is not in great pain or discomfort.	3. Amount of pain, physical suffering, and psychological suffering can vary.	3. Same as CTA
4. Individual does not intend to die.	4. Patient does not usually intend to die.	4. Patient does not intend to die.
5. Individual prefers life to death, wellness to illness, "normalcy" to medical intervention.	5. Same as PTA	5. Same as PTA and CTA
6. Individual voluntarily abates treatment.	6. Patient or patient's surrogate requests abatement of treatment, even if life-sustaining.	6. Neither the patient nor the patient's surrogate makes such a request.
7. Physician is not involved.	7. Physician withholds, decelerates, or withdraws treatment, even if life-sustaining.	7. Same as CTA
8. No one else is involved.	8. Physician's motive can vary, but includes promotion of patient's preferences and best interests.	8. Physician's motive is something other than promotion of patient's best interests.
9. Individual's motive can vary, but self-determination is central.	9. Physician's intention is usually to promote patient's best interests.	9. Physician intends death of patient.
10. Individual continues to live.	10. Probability of patient's death depends on modality of treatment abated.	10. Patient probably dies.

Legal implications

Law not a factor	Action legal, given factors above	Probable charges of manslaughter or murder

(Continued)

TABLE 7.1 (Continued)

Voluntary euthanasia (VE)	Nonvoluntary euthanasia (NE)	Involuntary euthanasia (IE)
1. Patient's medical condition is critical and appears irreversible.	1. Same as VE	1. Patient's medical condition can vary.
2. Patient has decision-making capacity.	2. Patient is nonautonomous.	2. Patient can be autonomous or nonautonomous.
3. Patient has intractable pain or other intolerable condition.	3. Amount of pain and discomfort for patient is unclear.	3. Amount of pain and discomfort can vary.
4. Patient is unable to commit suicide.	4. Same as VE	4. Patient is not interested in committing suicide.
5. Patient perfers death to continuation of intolerable life.	5. Patient preferences are unknown and perhaps unknowable.	5. Patient prefers life to death.
6. Patient requests to be killed.	6. Patient is unable to request to be killed.	6. Patient does not request to be killed.
7. Physician (or someone) intends to kill patient.	7. Same as VE	7. Same as VE and NE
8. Physician (or someone) causes patient's death.	8. Same as VE	8. Same as VE and NE
9. Physician's motive in killing is compassion or mercy.	9. Same as VE	9. Motive for killing is something other than mercy.
10. Patient is dead.	10. Same as VE	10. Same as VE and NE

Legal implications

Possible charges of manslaughter or murder	Possible charges of manslaughter or murder	Probable charges of manslaughter or murder

When the forms of treatment abatement and euthanasia are compared, any act of *personal* treatment abatement clearly belongs in a category separate from the others: the individual abating treatment is not a patient in an institutional setting, no physician or nurse helps with or is immediately aware of the treatment abatement, and the person usually is not likely to die as a consequence of never starting, cutting back on, or stopping recommended treatment. By contrast, *imposed* treatment abatement and *involuntary* euthanasia are largely indistinguishable and thus fall into the same moral and legal categories. Although some people try to distinguish between these two life-ending events on the basis of the omission/commission distinction, I fail to see the moral relevance of the distinction in these clinical situations. Given that the patients in both situations want to live (as far as anyone knows), make no decision for death, will probably live with effective medical treatment, and will almost certainly die as a consequence of either type of intervention under discussion, any attempt to impose the abatement of life-sustaining treatment or administer a death-dealing agent under these conditions with the intention of causing the patient's death is morally unjustifiable and legally punishable under homicide statutes.

That leaves *cooperative* treatment abatement (or simply "treatment abatement," unless specified otherwise), voluntary euthanasia, and nonvoluntary euthanasia. As previously mentioned, some pro-life advocates and some advocates of euthanasia as a standard moral and legal option argue that all of these actions are morally indistinguishable—except for the important difference between autonomous and nonautonomous patients. They go on to argue that, even though the law presently does not regard all of these actions in the same manner, it should, once the distinction is made between autonomous and nonautonomous patients.

I find these views simplistic, seriously mistaken, and open to harmful practices if enacted into public policy. In contrast to the religious and philosophical views identified as positions 1 and 6 in the previous chapter, I am convinced that treatment abatement is conceptually different from both voluntary and nonvoluntary euthanasia. The moral implications of these conceptual differences will be developed later in this chapter and in Chapter 9. At this point, it should suffice merely to point out that a description of these conceptual differences between cooperative treatment abatement and the remaining forms of euthanasia (the only two forms of euthanasia that anyone seriously tries to justify on moral grounds) does not entail any particular moral conclusion about any particular case. Simply because an action can correctly be described as "cooperative treatment abatement" does not automatically make the action morally justifiable, nor does the correct labeling of an action as "voluntary euthanasia" automatically make the action wrong on moral grounds. For instance, a physician's cooperation with the surrogate of a critically ill patient in abating life-sustaining treatment does not necessarily mean that the treatment abatement is in the patient's best interests. Rather, to determine the moral licitness of any of these actions requires analysis of the morally relevant factors in a given case.

The fourth step toward greater conceptual clarity is therefore to distinguish between (1) treatment abatement, particularly when the treatment being abated is capable of prolonging a patient's life, and (2) euthanasia, in either its voluntary or nonvoluntary form. To suggest such a distinction is, of course, hardly novel. Numerous persons, including all of the ethicists identified with positions 2–5 in the previous chapter, have held that important conceptual (and moral) differences exist between these actions. The President's Commission stated: "Although declining to start or continue life-sustaining treatment is often acceptable, health care providers properly refuse to honor a patient's request to be directly killed."[24] More recently, the members of the Hastings Center project on the termination of life-sustaining treatment made the following comment:

Under the rubric of "termination of treatment," we do not include active euthanasia ("mercy killing") or assisted suicide. These Guidelines have been formulated in the belief that *a reasonable, if not unambiguous, line* can be drawn between forgoing life-sustaining treatment on the one hand, and active euthanasia or assisted suicide on the other."[25]

I agree that "a reasonable, if not unambiguous, line" can be drawn between acts of abating life-sustaining treatment and acts of euthanasia. To defend this position requires, first of all, a narrowing of the terrain that will be covered. Although the philosophers and religious ethicists who have written on this conceptual issue often couch their views in the larger context of the perennial debate over the killing/letting die distinction, I do not plan to venture beyond the clinical settings in which this issue most frequently arises.[26] The wider implications of the debate over the killing/letting die distinction do not lack intrinsic interest, but many of the imaginative, exotic, and downright strange cases and pairs of cases discussed in the literature often have little relevance to the more specific issue of the conceptual and moral relationship of treatment abatement and euthanasia that one encounters in the "real-world" settings of ICUs, geriatric centers, and hospices.

To defend the conceptual differences between treatment abatement and euthanasia (voluntary and nonvoluntary) also requires a certain realism about the limitations of rational argument. Unfortunately, the debate over (1) whether there are important conceptual differences between treatment abatement and euthanasia and (2) whether one or more of these conceptual differences has any "moral bite" usually results in a stalemate, with each side "preaching to the converted" and claiming that the other side has the burden of proof in this matter.

In part, the continuing debate about the conceptual and moral relationship of treatment abatement and euthanasia is traceable to the fundamental way in which ethical theory colors one's "vision." Many utilitarians and other consequentialists simply cannot "see" how the abatement of life-sustaining treatment and acts of euthanasia are different in any morally significant way, because both actions tend to have the same consequences. In James Rachels' words, "the victim ends up dead" either way. Although factually untrue in some clinical cases, Rachels' statement emphasizes the firmly held view of consequentialists that the only right-making feature of an action is the consequence it produces. Because of this perspective, utilitarians and other consequentialists tend to interpret *all* acts of abating life-sustaining treatment as acts of "allowing to die."

In a similar manner, deontologists of various types—strict or mixed, duty-based or rights-based—have great difficulty "seeing" how the means used to bring about a particular consequence are not themselves fundamentally important. From this perspective, the mere fact that the death of a particular critically ill patient cannot be prevented medically, or is acceptable to the patient and other persons involved in the case, or is the probable outcome of abating treatment, or is the certain outcome of abating treatment, does not mean that the manner (or means) by which that death occurs is morally insignificant. Deontologists find it difficult to understand why features of actions other than consequences—motives, intentions, and the moral status of the persons being acted on—are not thought morally significant by some consequentialists who address the morality of various actions that can and do bring an end to individual human lives. In fact, many deontologists think that a moral agent's intention is the crucial feature in determining the morality of an action resulting in another person's death. For this reason many deontologists regard *any* act of intentional killing as intrinsically immoral, no matter what other consequences may follow from the act of killing (or refraining from such an act).

As already indicated by some of the foregoing material, I think that a correct understanding of the *conceptual* relationship of treatment abatement and euthanasia requires a compromise position between the frequently stalemated positions described previously. The truth, I think, lies somewhere between the increasingly hardened positions of the disputants on either side. The ethicists identified with positions 2–4 in the previous chapter, most of whom are deontologists of some sort, are correct up to a point: there are *important conceptual* (and *practical*) *differences* between abating life-sustaining treatment and engaging in acts of euthanasia. Likewise, the ethicists identified with position 6, all of whom are consequentialists, are correct up to a point: the conceptual differences between these actions cannot accurately be said to be *intrinsic,* nor can the conceptual and practical differences accurately be said to be of *absolute* moral importance.

The heart of the compromise position I propose is the recognition of conceptual and practical differences that *usually* distinguish forms of treatment abatement from each other as well as from the variable forms of euthanasia, as indicated by Table 7.1. Then, by focusing on the forms of treatment abatement and euthanasia that are most alike and therefore most often confused—cooperative treatment abatement, voluntary euthanasia, and nonvoluntary euthanasia—one can sort out the conceptual differences that usually distinguish these actions with critically ill patients. The crucial test, of course, is whether any of the conceptual and practical differences that generally exist among these actions remain as important differences when the category of cooperative treatment abatement is restricted to the abatement of *life-sustaining* treatments. Finally, lest all of this process seem to be only intellectual gamesmanship, it is necessary to draw out the moral implications of these differences, a task to which we shall return shortly.

Five differences usually distinguish cooperative acts of abating life-sustaining treatment from acts of voluntary or nonvoluntary euthanasia (it is important to retain the category of nonvoluntary euthanasia at this point as a parallel to some acts of treatment abatement with some nonautonomous patients). Of these differences, two have to do with the concepts of the acts involved: agent intention, and the cause of the patient's death. The remaining differences are more practical in nature, and have to do with short- and long-term consequences of treatment abatement and euthanasia.

One of the widely claimed (and widely disputed) differences between the abatement of life-sustaining treatment and acts of voluntary or nonvoluntary euthanasia is that of the agent's intention. In fact, of course, there is a dual aspect to the question of intentionality in such cases: the intention of the patient, and the intention of the physician (or other agent) who abates treatment or kills the patient at the patient's request. The difference in the patient's intentionality is similar to the point made earlier when we discussed suicide: many autonomous patients who decide to forgo life-sustaining treatment do so not because they want to die or intend to die, but because they intend through their decision to refuse technological procedures and medical interventions they find useless, intolerable, harmful, or contrary to their best interests as they perceive those interests.

The more important aspect of the question of intentionality has to do with the intention of the physician (or other agent). No one disputes that a physician who gives a critically ill patient a lethal injection intends to kill that patient, whether requested by the patient to do so or not. In fact, the role of agent intention is so clear in cases of euthanasia that some persons (including me) often use ''intentional killing'' as a synonym for euthanasia. Similarly, no one can seriously argue that a physician who *imposes* the abatement of life-sustaining treatment on a critically ill patient who has not personally (or through a surrogate) opted to abate such treatment intends to do anything other than terminate the patient's life. Consequently, a difference in agent intention cannot correctly be said to be an intrinsic difference between all acts of abating life-sustaining treatment and all acts of euthanasia.

The crux of the dispute over intentionality is found in the form of treatment abatement that I have labeled ''cooperative treatment abatement.'' When a physician cancels surgery, or does not initiate burn therapy, or stops hemodialysis, or turns off a ventilator, or does not administer antibiotics for pneumonia, or in some other way abates life-sustaining treatment in cooperation with an autonomous, critically ill patient's request or in the perceived best interests of a nonautonomous, critically ill patient, what is the most reasonable way of characterizing the physician's intention in such a situation? Does the physician thereby usually intend to kill the patient? I think not. To sharpen the question, does a physician who abates a form of life-sustaining treatment with the knowledge that the patient will certainly die as a consequence of that act necessarily intend or "aim" to kill the patient? Again, I think not. Simply because a physician understands that a patient's death will follow the abatement of such treatment, does not mean the physician *intends* that death as a result of his or her action in abating treatment.

Surely an equally reasonable way of interpreting a physician's intention in such cases—and, I think, a more reasonable way—is to say that the physician intends only to respect and support an autonomous patient's request not to have medical treatment that the patient regards as useless or gravely burdensome. Likewise, a physician who abates life-sustaining treatment with a nonautonomous, critically ill patient based on a reasonable request from that patient's surrogate need not—and usually does not—intend through that action to kill the patient. Rather, the physician intends to promote the patient's best interests by withholding, decelerating, or withdrawing one or more forms of treatment regarded as being pointless, offering more burdens than benefits to the patient, or simply perpetuating the patient's suffering. In this respect, therefore, cooperative acts by physicians to abate life-sustaining treatment while caring for critically ill patients do not necessarily involve an intention to kill the patients, even when the physicians know that the patients are likely to die earlier than they would have if the treatment had not been abated.

Lest I be misunderstood, I am not trying to resolve the dispute over agent intentionality in treatment-abatement cases merely through definitional or conceptual categories. Even though use of the category of imposed treatment abatement greatly reduces the dispute over agent intentionality, the intentional killing of patients through the abatement of life-sustaining treatment is not necessarily limited to that category. A physician who cooperates with the request by an autonomous patient or by the surrogate of a patient for the abatement of life-sustaining treatment *can* intend thereby to terminate the patient's life. My claim is simply that, given the set of circumstances normally found in cases of cooperative treatment abatement, physicians who abate life-sustaining treatment in such circumstances *do not usually intend to kill* their patients. The same statement cannot be made in regard to physicians who give their patients potassium chloride, a bolus of air, or some other lethal dose or injection.

A related, and equally controversial, difference between the abatement of life-sustaining treatment and acts of euthanasia has to do with the causation of death. No one disputes that a physician (or other agent) who gives a patient a lethal injection actually causes the patient's death, whether requested by the patient to do so or not. If the act of killing is reported to the authorities, the physician (or other person) is likely to be charged under a state homicide statute. If the case ends up in court, the prosecuting attorney predictably will try to prove that the person who administered the lethal injection was the "proximate cause" of the patient's death, no matter what type of injury or disease had necessitated the patient's being in the hospital and thus subject to the agent's action. Whether conviction will follow such a trial is entirely another matter, with conviction much less likely if the person being prosecuted is a physician.

By contrast, as we have observed in cases involving autonomous patients, courts dealing with acts of abating life-sustaining treatment have regularly and (in the courts of final decision) consistently used a different theory of causation to rule that the patients in such cases are not suicidal nor are the physicians who cooperate with them in abating treatment guilty of assisting acts of suicide. The *Perlmutter, Bartling, Requena,* and other courts handling such cases (with the exception of the 1983 Bouvia case) have all concluded that these critically ill patients' medical conditions were a "natural cause" or an "underlying cause" of the patients' deaths.

Likewise, courts handling cases involving nonautonomous patients have regularly concluded that the role of the physician in abating life-sustaining treatment was not one of causing the patients' deaths. For example, in a statement quoted in Chapter 4 (and often cited in subsequent court decisions), the *Colyer* court declared in 1983 that "a death which occurs after the removal of life support systems is from natural causes . . ."[27] The *Conroy* court, in a previously quoted comment from its 1985 decision, stated that the patient's death following the removal of an NG tube "would result, if at all, from her underlying medical condition, which included her inability to swallow."[28] The same court, in *Peter,* compared the abatement of technological feeding and hydration with other types of treatment abatement. The court stated that a kidney patient on dialysis does not die "because of the withdrawal of a kidney dialysis machine," but because "his underlying disease has destroyed the proper functioning of his kidneys." In the same way, "Hilda Peter will not die from withdrawal of the nasogastric tube," but because of her "underlying medical problem, i.e., an inability to swallow." Abating this form of medical treatment, like abating other forms of life-sustaining treatment, "merely acquiesces in the natural cessation of a critical bodily function." The "cessation is the cause of death, not the acquiescence."[29]

Why is judicial reasoning about the causation of death different in cases of treatment abatement compared with cases of euthanasia? One possibility is that some of the courts have been addressing the psychological problem many physicians have in abating life-sustaining treatment that has already been started in the care of a critically ill patient. By rejecting any moral or legal difference between withholding or withdrawing life-sustaining treatment, the courts may have been communicating to physicians that neither withholding life-sustaining treatment nor withdrawing life-sustaining treatment from critically ill patients is tantamount to homicide—as long as the available treatment is reasonably regarded as futile or contrary to the patient's best interests.[30]

Another possibility is that the courts are very aware that the determination of causation is not always easy (in many cases at bar, not only those arising in clinical settings), that causation often involves multiple factors, that "cause" is not a legal constant, and that competing theories of causation are available and widely used. Given these complicating aspects of determining causation, the courts may simply presuppose that certain kinds of actions or omissions resulting in patients' deaths are acceptable on moral and legal grounds, whereas other actions or omissions resulting in patients' deaths are not. In this manner, the courts may—without adequate argumentation—simply fall back on the disease theory of causation in cases of treatment abatement to reflect the courts' view that abating life-sustaining treatment judged contrary to a patient's best interests is not morally or legally blameworthy.[31]

A third possibility is that the judicial reasoning in cases involving treatment abatement is simply wrong on the matter of causation of death. This view, put forth most sharply by Joseph Fletcher, is that a number of court justices simply do not want to admit that the abatement of life-sustaining treatment with non-dying patients constitutes suicide on the part of the patients and euthanasia on the part of the physicians who help them by abating treatment. Using the Bouvia, Rodas, and Brophy cases as examples (see Cases 3.9, 3.11, and 4.19), he rejects the theory of causation used in the court decisions. In this view, to claim that a critically ill, but not imminently dying patient's death subsequent to the abatement of life-sustaining treatment is due to natural causes "is baldly contrary to fact."[32] Instead of such "fork-tongued semantics and verbal evasions" on the matter of causation of death, he claims that death in such cases "is not due to an 'underlying' and ultimately fatal disease or disorder [but] due to or a consequence of the decision to die."[33]

Much could be said regarding Fletcher's reiteration of his long-held views, as well as his continued misinterpretation of the kill/let die distinction, the rule of double effect, and some other ethical concepts that we have previously discussed. I will not do that here. However, Fletcher's basic claim needs to be addressed, for two reasons: it reflects a fairly widely held view, especially among the philosophers identified with position 6 in the previous chapter, and it represents a complete rejection of the view that the causation of death provides a conceptual difference between acts of abating life-sustaining treatment and acts of voluntary or nonvoluntary euthanasia.

In contrast to Fletcher and like-minded persons, I think the judicial reasoning about causation of death is correct in the cases presented in Chapters 3 and 4. The defense of that reasoning (something the justices have failed to do adequately) requires three steps. First, I want to be clear about the limited claim I am making regarding the causation of death in such cases. Once again, I am not trying to defend the claim that a difference in the causation of death represents an *intrinsic* conceptual difference between acts of abating life-sustaining treatment and acts of euthanasia. Obviously acts of abating life-sustaining treatment *can* be "the cause" of a patient's death, as in a case of an otherwise healthy patient who contracts a routine bacterial respiratory infection and dies following a physician's negligent or intentional failure to treat a resulting pneumonia.[34] What I am claiming is that there is *usually* a difference in the causation of death—with moral and legal implications—between acts of abating life-sustaining treatment and acts of euthanasia.

Second, the difference in causation of death is most obvious when we concentrate on the kinds of cases that belong to the category labeled "cooperative treatment abatement." The refusal of life-sustaining treatment by an autonomous patient or the request for the abatement of life-sustaining treatment made by a patient's surrogate clearly has no *logical* connection to the matter of causation of death: a physician or other agent can still play a causative role in the patient's death. However, if the features that characterize cooperative treatment abatement are present in a particular case, it is *much more likely* that the patient's death will result from the "underlying condition" that has brought about the critical illness than from a specific omission or action on the part of the physician caring for the patient. To make the point another way, a reasonable determination that the initiation or continuation of one or more life-sustaining medical interventions is contrary to the patient's best interests strongly suggests that the injury or disease process already at work will cause the patient's death. In such cases, one can argue that the physician's omission or action (for instance, in either not starting, or stopping mechanical ventilation) was *a* causative factor in bringing about the patient's death, but certainly not "the cause" of the patient's death.

Third, arriving at "the cause" of a patient's death subsequent to the abatement of life-sustaining treatment requires an interpretation of the relationship between the two (or possibly more) causative factors in the case. In the kinds of cases under discussion, the patient's death is caused by (1) a physiological or pathological factor and (2) a decisional factor, usually in regard to a biochemical or technological intervention in the course of the physiological/pathological process. Although both of these factors can be interpreted as having a role in causing the patient's death, only one of them can correctly be said to have played the *primary* role in causation. The underlying medical condition brought about by injury or disease is this primary cause—in the dual sense of precedence and importance—of the patient's death subsequent to the abatement of life-sustaining treatment. The omission or action by the physician that constitutes the abatement of life-sustaining treatment is no more than a secondary cause of the patient's death. By contrast, the same statement regarding secondary cause simply cannot be made about a physician's injection of a lethal substance into a patient's body, given that the substance will cause the patient to die quickly no matter what the patient's "underlying" medical condition is.

Why is this the case? The fundamental reason has to do with the theory of causation that applies to such cases. Cooperative treatment-abatement cases are "allowing to happen" cases, whereas voluntary or nonvoluntary euthanasia cases are "causing to happen" cases. An "allowing to happen" case, as pointed out by Anthony Woozley, can involve either an omission or an action: "I allow something to happen if I do not put in the way an obstacle which would prevent its happening or if I remove an obstacle which is now preventing its happening."[35] Joel Feinberg observes that "allowing to happen" cases also require a context of legitimacy, as I have previously suggested by means of my cooperative/imposed treatment-abatement distinction. Feinberg then applies this theory of causation to the action of "letting die" by disconnecting a ventilator: "To be a 'letting die' merely, the act of disconnecting must permit the resumption of *a previously blocked causal process* as opposed to being the initiating of a new one (as e.g. by a lethal injection), *and* it must be done legitimately."[36]

David Meyers offers another reason for interpreting the "underlying" medical condition as the primary cause of a patient's death in cases of cooperative treatment abatement. He makes the point that in cases of terminal and incurable illness, the patient dies sooner or later regardless of the medical treatment received. In such cases, he argues that "medical care may *change the time of death* to some degree," but "it is the underlying illness which is the true cause of death." He continues by saying that a physician's decision concerning treatment abatement, if "undertaken to benefit and care for the patient," may also change the "actual time of death" but not cause the death.[37]

A physician's role in a cooperative treatment-abatement case (i.e., abating treatment on the basis of a critically ill patient's preferences or best interests) is therefore not to be interpreted as "the cause" or "the primary cause" of the patient's death, if such a death actually occurs in a reasonably short period of time following the abatement of life-sustaining treatment. Instead, the physician's role in such a case is correctly interpreted as merely allowing either (1) the *continuation* of a causal process involving one or more pathological conditions (e.g., by not initiating burn therapy or mechanical ventilation) or (2) the *resumption* of a previously blocked causal process involving one or more pathological conditions (e.g., by stopping mechanical ventilation or technological feeding and hydration). Either way, whether by "omission" or "commission," the physician in such a situation possibly changes the time of the patient's death, but does not cause it. Put another way, the physician in such a situation merely assents to the decision by an autonomous patient or the surrogate of a nonautonomous patient (again using Judge Stanton's words) to "acquiescence in the natural shutting down" of the patient's biological system.

But what about patients whose deaths cannot be said to be "imminent," given their medical conditions? What about the hypothetical patient mentioned earlier, the one who contracted a routine bacterial respiratory infection and subsequently died from untreated pneumonia? What about other patients who cannot reasonably be said to be terminally ill, even though their continued living is dependent on widely used technological and pharmacological interventions (e.g., patients dependent on cardiac pacemakers or cardiac medications)? What about patients situated similarly to Elizabeth Bouvia, Paul Brophy, and Hector Rodas, none of whom could be classified as imminently dying or terminally ill, but who with tubal feeding could have their biological lives sustained for 10 years or longer? Can the deaths of *all* of these patients subsequent to the abatement of life-sustaining treatment reasonably be attributed to an "underlying" pathological condition? If not, where should one draw the line regarding causation between (1) physician-caused deaths subsequent to the abatement of life-sustaining treatment and (2) disease- or injury-caused deaths subsequent to the abatement of life-sustaining treatment?

The classification scheme developed earlier helps in answering these questions. Clearly, there are cases—both hypothetical and real—in which the abatement of life-sustaining treatment by a physician can correctly be interpreted as "the cause" or "the primary cause" of a patient's death, when a patient dies following the abatement of treatment. Such cases fall under the category of *imposed* treatment abatement, and include all cases in which life-sustaining treatment is abated from patients who are in otherwise healthy conditions, may even be ambulatory, and certainly do not have a medical condition that could reasonably be said to be terminal, fatal, or involve "imminent" death.

By contrast, acts of cooperative treatment abatement by physicians are limited to cases involving patients who have one or more medically serious conditions that appear to be irreversible. Such patients may be regarded as imminently dying, or terminally ill, or critically ill, or gravely impaired. Whatever the medical classification, such patients have pathological conditions that will represent the "underlying" or "primary" or "natural" causes of their deaths subsequent to the abatement of life-sustaining treatment, should they or their surrogates (in cases of nonautonomy) choose on the basis of patient preferences or best interests no longer to resist death. The degree to which the medical conditions can correctly be interpreted in this manner depends in large part on the severity of the medical conditions.

Perhaps an analogy will be helpful at this point. Chances are quite good that you and other readers of this book have owned several cars over a period of years. Let us think about the "deaths" of two of those cars. I am not referring to those frustrating times in which one of the cars sporadically "died" because of poor maintenance, cold temperature, or a poor mixture of gasoline (at most, such mechanical failures might loosely be likened to human "near-death experiences"; more realistically, they might be compared to temporary losses of consciousness by humans and other animals). No, I am referring to the times when these two cars "died" in the sense that neither you nor any potential buyer nor any used-car dealer nor any automotive salvage yard operator could make the cars drivable again.

Let us suppose that you were the only owner—or the last owner—of the cars. Let us also suppose that car number 1 had performed reasonably well and had normal mileage for its years. However, you regularly withheld or (if other persons had previously owned the car) withdrew "life"-sustaining treatment: cleaning and polishing the car's body, providing necessary maintenance and repairs, purchasing new tires, and so on. At some point the car "died"—with rusted body, broken parts, unusable motor—never to "live" again except as a limited source of replacement parts for other cars and possibly a source for recycled steel.

By contrast, you took reasonably good care of car number 2. You washed and waxed the body, kept up in a reasonable fashion with recommended maintenance, repaired it when needed, purchased new tires as needed, and so forth. However, because of some combination of the car's years, high mileage, uncompensable damage to mechanical and body parts due to poor maintenance by previous owners, the "lemon factor," and sheer bad luck (I have in mind a low-priced, "pre-owned" car I purchased some months ago for use by my teenage son, after having it inspected by two mechanics), the car's performance steadily declined and its "health" deteriorated. With the deterioration of the car—and your knowledge of the predictable and unavoidable outcome—you finally decided to forgo any further repair expense. At some subsequent point the car "died" as a usable mechanical vehicle, never to "live" again except as a limited source of replacement parts for other cars and possibly as a source for recycled steel.

What causative role did you have in these automotive "deaths"? In the case of car number 1, it makes sense to say that you—by intention or negligence—were "the cause" or "the primary cause" of the car's "death." In the case of car number 2, you surely did not have the same kind of causative role. Rather, car number 2 had an "underlying condition" that was the primary cause of its "death." Your causative role was secondary only, involving your allowing (possibly with great reluctance) the continuation of a causal process of mechanical deterioration that you finally chose no longer to resist.

We will now briefly turn to three other differences between acts of treatment abatement and acts of euthanasia that are more practical in nature than the matters of intention and causality. Each of the differences has to do with the short- or long-range consequences of these actions (or omissions) in the care of critically ill and hopelessly ill patients.

In contrast to acts of voluntary or nonvoluntary euthanasia, acts of abating treatment *do not always result in the patient's immediate death*. In fact, the rapidity of a patient's death following the abatement of life-sustaining treatment depends on the modality of treatment abated as well as the patient's medical condition. Obviously if CPR is abated, a patient who has experienced cardiac or respiratory arrest quickly dies—if he or she was not already dead. A major reason for the concern by pro-life representatives over the abatement of medical feeding and hydration is the certitude, in most cases, of the patient's death within a short period of time following the abatement of technologically provided nutrients and fluids. In a similar fashion, health care professionals become concerned when patients with life-threatening bleeding refuse transfusions, because of the predictable quickness of their deaths without an adequate blood supply.

However, the abatement of life-sustaining treatment often leaves patients with days, months, and even years of life remaining after the decision to forgo a particular modality of treatment. Simply because a gravely impaired, critically ill, or terminally ill patient (or the surrogate of such a patient) refuses treatment or requests that a form of treatment be abated does not mean that the patient has a short-term "death sentence." Decisions to abate chemotherapy, surgery, dialysis, mechanical ventilation, some life-sustaining medications, and (in some instances) technological feeding do not necessarily mean that the patient will die in the immediate future. Examples include Karen Quinlan, who lived for 9 years in a PVS after the abatement of her mechanical ventilation, and Elizabeth Bouvia, who is still alive more than 3 years after the abatement of an NG tube that was used to supplement her oral intake of food. It is therefore simply not true that the abatement of life-sustaining treatment is always to be equated with allowing patients to die, much less that such acts are to be equated morally with intentional killing.

In contrast to acts of voluntary or nonvoluntary euthanasia, acts of abating treatment generally *provide opportunities for additional forms of care prior to a patient's death*. Because an interval of varying length usually follows the abatement of life-sustaining treatment and precedes the patient's death, relatives of the patient, friends of the patient, physicians, nurses, and other health care professionals can work to meet the patient's needs in ways other than aggressive efforts at prolonging the patient's life. Instead of offering maximal treatment, they can take on the challenge of trying to provide medical treatment and nonmedical care that is appropriate to the patient's needs, preferences, and circumstances.

This challenge is often referred to as "caring for the dying," but it is surely not limited to patients whose deaths are imminent. In some instances, the challenge of providing appropriate care means getting the patient out of a highly technological clinical setting to a less stressful setting such as a private home, geriatric center, or hospice. In many other instances, the challenge of providing appropriate care means providing the patient with various forms of palliative care aimed at controlling pain, relieving discomfort, and aiding dysfunction of various sorts. Often the provision of appropriate care means a number of simple, but important, human touches: offering food (by spoon) and liquids that the patient can take orally, turning the patient in bed to minimize the problem of decubitus ulcers, finding ways of enhancing communication between the patient and others, doing finger rolls to provide temporary comfort from localized pain, dabbing dry lips with a cool washcloth, giving ice chips by spoon to relieve the problem of dry mouth, and so on. The point of these acts is not to prolong the patient's life, but to make the patient's remaining time as comfortable and meaningful as possible. Regularly done by professionals and volunteers in geriatric and hospice settings, such acts of caring invalidate the views of some physicians, ethicists, and others who seem to think that there is "nothing to be done" short of intentional killing for patients who cannot be cured.

In contrast to acts of voluntary or nonvoluntary euthanasia, acts of abating treatment *do not present long-term problems of abuse* as they increasingly become recognized *as general practices* in the care of critically and terminally ill patients. The distinction between acts and practices is important at this point.[38] Individual acts of voluntary euthanasia may occasionally and infrequently be justified on moral grounds, as we will discuss in Chapter 9. However, the inherent problems of abuse that would attend a societal recognition of intentional killing by physicians raise serious questions about the merits of building into medical practice a provision whereby physicians could legally kill their patients in order to relieve intractable pain or some other intolerable condition on the part of the patient. In my view, two such problems stand out: the pragmatic difficulties of limiting the practice to cases of *voluntary* euthanasia, and the threat such a legalized practice of intentional killing would represent to the fiduciary relationship of physicians and patients.

The societal acceptance of treatment abatement, both morally and legally, does not represent the same kind of abusive possibilities. I am not claiming that the practice of abating treatment, especially life-sustaining treatment, represents *no* threat of abuse. In fact, I think that, up to a point, pro-life opposition to certain kinds of treatment abatement with critically and terminally ill patients is a healthy reminder to the rest of us that some acts of abating treatment can, when done for the wrong reasons, unjustifiably result in patients' deaths. However, as long as treatment abatement is done in the appropriate moral context—generally speaking, the context articulated by members of the President's Commission, the members of the Hastings Center project on treatment termination, and the ethicists identified with positions 4 and 5 in the previous chapter—the possibilities of abusive practices are substantially less than with a general practice of euthanasia.

One final word is in order. I am aware of some of the limitations of the views put forth in this chapter. It would be nicer, neater, and more satisfying to present a firm, black-and-white argument regarding the relationship of treatment abatement and euthanasia than to fall back on the it-is-usually-the-case form of argumentation. But the "real world," inside or outside clinical settings, is not always that sharply defined. I think the quotation given earlier from the Hastings Center group comes very close to the truth. The various differences between treatment abatement and euthanasia can be put forth in a reasonably clear fashion, but they are "not unambiguous."

Notes

1. Tom L. Beauchamp, "Suicide," in Tom Regan, ed., *Matters of Life and Death,* 2nd ed. (New York: Random House, 1986), p. 89.
2. Joseph Fletcher, "Medical Resistance to the Right to Die," *Journal of the American Geriatrics Society* 35 (1987): 680 (emphasis in the original).
3. President's Commission for the Study of Ethical Problems in Medicine, *Defining Death* (Washington, D.C.: U.S. Government Printing Office, 1981).
4. One indication of the support for the guidelines developed by the commission's 56 medical consultants is the report of the Hastings Center group in 1987. In the section of the report proposing guidelines for the declaration of death, the members of the Hastings Center group simply reprinted the original report of the medical consultants to the President's Commission. See the Hastings Center project, *Guidelines on the Termination of Life-Sustaining Treatment and the Care of the Dying* (Briarcliff Manor, N.Y.: The Hastings Center, 1987), pp. 91–98.
5. See James L. Bernat, Charles M. Culver, and Bernard Gert, "Defining Death in Theory and Practice," *Hastings Center Report* 12 (February 1982): 5–9; Karen Grandstrand Gervais, *Redefining Death* (New Haven, Conn., and London: Yale University Press, 1986); Robert F. Weir, ed., *Ethical Issues in Death and Dying,* 2nd ed. (New York: Columbia University Press, 1986), pp. 53–111; and Robert M. Veatch, *Death, Dying, and the Biological Revolution,* 2nd ed. (New Haven, Conn., and London: Yale University Press, in press).
6. John Paris and Richard McCormick, "Living-Will Legislation, Reconsidered," *America* 145 (September 5, 1981): 88.
7. Katherine Benesch, "Legal Aspects of Brain Death Certification and Withdrawal of Life Support," in William C. Shoemaker et al., eds., *Textbook of Critical Care* (Philadelphia: W.B. Saunders, 1984), p. 977.
8. Satz v. Perlmutter, 362 So.2d 160, 163 (Fla. Dist. Ct. App. 1978).
9. Bartling v. Superior Court, 163 Cal.App.3d 186, 209 Cal.Rptr. 220, 226 (1984).
10. In re Requena, 213 N.J. Super. 475, 517 A.2d 886, 891 (N.J. Super. Ch. Div. 1986).
11. Commissioner of Corrections v. Myers, 399 N.E.2d 452, 456 (Mass. 1979).
12. Perlmutter, *supra,* 362 So.2d 160, 163.
13. In re Requena, 517 A.2d 886, 888 (1986).
14. Bouvia v. Superior Court of the State of California for the County of Los Angeles, 225 Cal.Rptr. 297, 306 (Cal. App.2d Dist. 1986).
15. Delio v. Westchester County Medical Center, 129 A.D.2d 1, 516 N.Y.S.2d 677, 692 (App. Div. 2d Dep't 1987).
16. In re Gardner, 534 A.2d 947, 955 (Maine 1987).
17. Beauchamp, "Suicide," p. 83. He makes the same point in an earlier version of this article that is reprinted in Weir, *Ethical Issues,* 2nd ed., p. 324.
18. See Beauchamp, "Suicide," pp. 77–122; Joseph Margolis, *Negativities: The Limits of Life* (Columbus, Ohio: Merrill, 1975), Chapter 2; M. Pabst Battin and David J. Mayo, eds., *Suicide: The Philosophical Issues* (New York: St. Martin's Press, 1980);

M. Pabst Battin, *Ethical Issues in Suicide* (Englewood Cliffs, N.J.: Prentice-Hall, 1982); and James F. Childress, *Who Should Decide?* (New York: Oxford University Press, 1982), pp. 157–85.

19. See James R. McCartney, "Suicide vs. Right to Refuse Treatment in the Chronically Ill," *Psychosomatics* 19 (September 1978): 548–51.

20. W. Bruce Fye, "Active Euthanasia: An Historical Survey of Its Conceptual Origins and Introduction into Medical Thought," *Bulletin of the History of Medicine* 52 (Winter 1978): 492–503; James Rachels, "Active and Passive Euthanasia," *The New England Journal of Medicine* 292 (January 9, 1975): 78–80; idem, *The End of Life: Euthanasia and Morality* (Oxford: Oxford University Press, 1986), pp. 106–28; K. Danner Clouser, "Allowing or Causing: Another Look," *Annals of Internal Medicine* 87 (1977): 622–24; Richard Trammell, "Saving Life and Taking Life," *Journal of Philosophy* 72 (1975): 131–37; Bonnie Steinbock, "The Intentional Termination of Life," *Ethics in Science and Medicine* 6 (1979): 59–64; Richard A. O'Neil, "The Moral Relevance of the Active/Passive Euthanasia Distinction," in David H. Smith and Linda Bernstein, eds., *No Rush to Judgment* (Bloomington, Ind.: The Poynter Center, 1978), pp. 177–202; Tom Beauchamp, "A Reply to Rachels on Active and Passive Euthanasia," in Tom L. Beauchamp and Seymour Perlin, eds., *Ethical Issues in Death and Dying* (Englewood Cliffs, N.J.: Prentice-Hall, 1978), pp. 246–58; Natalie Abrams, "Active and Passive Euthanasia," *Philosophy* 53 (1978): 257–63; Philippa Foot, "Euthanasia," *Philosophy and Public Affairs* 6 (Winter 1977): 85–112; Helga Kuhse, "Extraordinary Means and the Intentional Termination of Life," *Social Science and Medicine* 15F (1981): 117–21; Thomas D. Sullivan, "Active and Passive Euthanasia: An Impertinent Distinction?" *Human Life Review* 3 (1977): 40–47; and Bruce R. Reichenbach, "Euthanasia and the Active–Passive Distinction," *Bioethics* 1 (1987): 51–73.

21. One of the places Fletcher used this typology was in his "Ethics and Euthanasia," in Robert H. Williams, ed., *To Live or To Die* (New York: Springer-Verlag, 1973), pp. 113–22.

22. Kenneth L. Vaux, "Debbie's Dying: Mercy Killing and the Good Death," *Journal of the American Medical Association* 259 (April 8, 1988): 2140.

23. George D. Lundberg, " 'It's Over, Debbie' and the Euthanasia Debate," *Journal of the American Medical Association* 259 (April 8, 1988): 2143.

24. President's Commission, *Deciding to Forego Life-Sustaining Treatment* (Washington, D.C.: U.S. Government Printing Office, 1983), p. 63.

25. Hastings Center project, *Guidelines*, p. 6 (emphasis added).

26. See James Rachels, "Euthanasia, Killing, and Letting Die," in John Ladd, ed., *Ethical Issues Relating to Life and Death* (New York: Oxford University Press, 1979), pp. 146–63; idem, "Killing and Starving to Death," *Philosophy* 54 (1979): 159–71; Gilbert Meilaender, "The Distinction between Killing and Allowing to Die," *Theological Studies* 37 (1976): 467–70; Richard O'Neil, "Killing, Letting Die, and Justice," *Analysis* 38 (1978): 124–25; Bonnie Steinbock, ed., *Killing and Letting Die* (Englewood Cliffs, N.J.: Prentice-Hall, 1980); James Childress, "To Kill or Let Die," in Elsie Bandman and Bertram Bandman, eds., *Bioethics and Human Rights* (Boston: Little, Brown, 1978), pp. 128–31; Tom L. Beauchamp and James F. Childress, *Principles of Biomedical Ethics,* 2nd ed. (New York: Oxford University Press, 1983), pp. 115–26; Judith Jarvis Thomson, "Killing, Letting Die, and the Trolley Problem," *Monist* 59 (1976): 204–17; Gary M. Atkinson, "Ambiguities in 'Killing' and 'Letting Die,' " *Journal of Medicine and Philosophy* 8 (1983):

159–68; idem, "Killing and Letting Die: Hidden Value Assumptions," *Social Science and Medicine* 17 (1983): 1915–25; Linacre Centre Paper 2, "Is There a Morally Significant Difference between Killing and Letting Die?" *Prolongation of Life* (1978): 1–19; and Douglas Walton, "Splitting the Difference: Killing and Letting Die," *Dialogue* 20 (1981): 68–78.

27. In re Colyer, 660 P.2d 738, 743 (1983).

28. In re Conroy, 486 A.2d 1209, 1226 (1985).

29. In re Peter, 108 N.J. 365, 529 A.2d 419, 428 (1987).

30. For a novel way of addressing problematic aspects of the false withhold/withdraw distinction, see Dan W. Brock, " 'Stuck on Machines'—Is Stopping Worse than Not Starting?" *Medical Ethics for the Physician* 1/4 (October 1986): 11–12.

31. President's Commission, *Deciding to Forego*, pp. 68–70.

32. Joseph Fletcher, "The Courts and Euthanasia," *Law, Medicine, and Health Care* 15 (Winter 1987–1988), p. 224.

33. Ibid., pp. 224–25.

34. This example is discussed by the President's Commission in *Deciding to Forego*, p. 69; and by Joel Feinberg in his *Harm to Others* (New York: Oxford University Press, 1984), p. 179.

35. Anthony Woozley, "A Duty to Rescue: Some Thoughts on Criminal Liability," *Virginia Law Review* 69 (1983): 1295, as quoted by Feinberg, *Harm to Others*, p. 259n.

36. Feinberg, *Harm to Others*, p. 259n (first emphasis added, second emphasis in the original). For additional discussion of causation theories, see the President's Commission, *Deciding to Forego*, pp. 68–73; and the classic text of H.L.A. Hart and Tony Honore, *Causation in the Law*, 2nd ed. (Oxford: The Clarendon Press, 1985), especially pp. 26–61, 84–108.

37. David W. Meyers, *Medico-Legal Implications of Death and Dying* (Rochester, N.Y.: The Lawyers Co-operative Publishing Company, 1981), p. 128 (emphasis added).

38. Beauchamp and Childress, *Principles of Biomedical Ethics*, pp. 119–25.

8

The Ethical Context for Abating Treatment

The Commission has found that nothing in current law precludes ethically sound decision-making. Neither criminal nor civil law—if properly interpreted and applied by lawyers, judges, health care providers, and the general public—forces patients to undergo procedures that will increase their suffering when they wish to avoid this by foregoing life-sustaining treatment.

THE PRESIDENT'S COMMISSION[1]

Questions about foregoing life-sustaining treatment will ordinarily arise when death is the predictable or unavoidable outcome of the patient's underlying medical condition. However, a patient need not be terminally ill or imminently dying for these decisions to be ethically permissible. Hence these Guidelines cover a broad class of gravely impaired or critically ill patients and others who are not necessarily in danger of imminent death, but who are facing a decision about the use of a life-sustaining treatment.

THE HASTINGS CENTER PROJECT[2]

The published views of the two groups quoted here indicate how far the debate about abating treatment has come in recent years. The report by the President's Commission, published in March 1983, brought the issue of treatment abatement into the public spotlight in an unprecedented manner. Thousands of copies of the report on forgoing life-sustaining treatment were published; numerous copies were distributed to influential persons and groups (including the chief justices of the state supreme courts at their 1984 conference). In addition, countless books, articles, and court decisions subsequently included favorable quotations from the commission's report. To the credit of the commissioners and their staff, the report focused national attention on many of the ethical, medical, and legal aspects of decisions to abate treatment.

In September 1987, the Hastings Center published its report on ethical guidelines for terminating life-sustaining treatment and caring for the dying. Reflecting the virtually unanimous consensus of 20 project members, the report was the outgrowth of a 2-year project that enlisted the help of dozens of professionals in a number of relevant professional areas. Having also contacted numerous medical organizations, health care organizations, pro-life groups, right-to-die groups, religious organizations, and almost any other group reasonably thought to be interested in the project, the directors of the project subsequently coordi-

322

nated the dissemination of the report to these same groups. To the credit of Susan Wolf, Daniel Callahan, and the other members of the project staff, the guidelines—along with a separate casebook edited by Cynthia Cohen[3]—succeed in providing an integrated, comprehensive framework for treatment-abatement decisions that is much more detailed and practical than the earlier, more theoretical work of the President's Commission. The two reports are largely complementary, yet differ in purpose, funding (the Hastings Center project was privately funded), organization, methodology, and authorship (only Dan Brock and Joanne Lynn were members of both groups).

Nevertheless, in spite of the legitimate prestige of these two publications, the reports have not settled the ongoing debate about the morality of abating treatment. Individuals and groups having explicit ''pro-life'' perspectives (identified as positions 1–3 in Chapter 6) are critical of the reports because the President's Commission and the Hastings Center group (1) include technological feeding and hydration as a form of medical treatment that can appropriately be abated in some circumstances, (2) extend treatment abatement beyond dying patients to include critically ill and gravely impaired patients, (3) do not sufficiently emphasize the ethical distinction between treatment abatement and euthanasia, and (4) put too many nonautonomous patients at risk of having their lives terminated. Critics from the other end of the spectrum (especially persons holding the ''right-to-die'' perspective identified as position 6 in Chapter 6) are convinced that the two reports are seriously flawed because both groups (1) fail sufficiently to emphasize utilitarian considerations in treatment-abatement decisions made in regard to nonautonomous patients, (2) put too much weight on the paternalistic decision-making role of physicians in determining appropriate surrogates and appropriate treatment in cases involving nonautonomous patients, (3) accept the ethical distinction between abating life-sustaining treatment and intentionally killing patients, and (4) refuse to accept euthanasia as an occasionally justifiable moral alternative (much less a legal alternative) in the care of critically ill or terminally ill patients.

I agree that the authors of the two reports have not said the final word on the ethics of treatment abatement, although they have greatly enhanced our understanding of this issue. My purpose in writing this book is to add my voice to the crescendo of voices inside and outside medicine calling for reasonable ethical and legal limits to be placed on the technological prolongation of life. To that end, this chapter, combined with Chapter 7 and Chapter 9, is intended to expand on the work of the President's Commission, the Hastings Center group, and the ethicists identified in Chapter 6 as advocating position 4 and especially position 5.

The previous chapter represents the first part of my attempt to move beyond these formative thinkers (whether writing collectively or as individuals) by addressing the conceptual relationship between treatment abatement and other end-of-life issues with which it is frequently confused. As the numerous cases discussed in earlier chapters clearly indicate, greater conceptual clarity is urgently needed—at the bedside, in the hospital corridor, in the legislative chamber, in the courtroom, and in the media—if we are to move toward greater consensus on precisely how and where to set ethical and legal limits on technological medicine's continually expanding capacity to prolong individual biological lives.

This chapter is the second part of my attempt to put forth a responsible position on the ethics of abating treatment. Having distinguished between treatment abatement and some of the other ethical issues that occasionally arise toward the end of life, I now need to discuss the ethical context for decisions to abate treatment. I will first describe some of the social and political aspects of such cases, and then show how ethical theory applies to the cases. With the general ethical context established, I will discuss the centrality of the patient's best interests in the cases.

The complex and controversial nature of treatment abatement

As should be clear by now, treatment abatement—especially the abatement of life-sustaining treatment—is a complex and controversial issue. As such, it evokes strongly felt emotions and beliefs, tempts some persons to engage in oversimplification and stereotyping of alternative views, and challenges all of us to be as conceptually clear, morally sound, and intellectually persuasive as we can be.

At the "macro" level (i.e., the level of state and federal policy), the issue of treatment abatement is increasingly divisive as various groups attempt to shape policy. On the one hand, Concern for Dying (CFD), the Society for the Right to Die (SRD), and other "moderate" groups within the right-to-die movement have now achieved a considerable measure of success: nonstatutory advance directives are increasingly used by individuals and accepted as legal evidence in courts, almost 80 percent of the states have natural death acts, a string of court decisions in a number of jurisdictions has affirmed the moral and legal right of patients (both autonomous and nonautonomous) to have life-sustaining treatment abated on the basis of personal choice or best interests, and a growing number of hospitals and nursing homes have established institutional policies that support the abatement of all forms of life-sustaining treatment under appropriate circumstances. Beyond these changes, other possible changes are being promoted by the Hemlock Society, Americans Against Human Suffering, and other more "extreme" members of the right-to-die movement. At the present time, these groups are actively trying to get "The Humane and Dignified Death Act" passed at the state (beginning in California) and federal levels so that medically assisted suicide and voluntary euthanasia will be legal alternatives for terminally ill patients.

On the other hand, a number of pro-life groups are hard at work trying to prevent additional victories by the "pro-euthanasia movement" (a catchall category used by some pro-life advocates to criticize all persons supportive of the right to die) and, if possible, to thwart successes already gained by right-to-die forces in legislative statutes and court decisions. Representatives of Americans United for Life, organizations of pro-life physicians and nurses, some Catholic pro-life groups, and other "moderate" groups within the pro-life movement regularly put forth their views on appropriate care for the critically and terminally ill by means of *amici curiae* briefs, journal articles, professional conferences, and other exercises of rational persuasion. More "extreme" groups within the pro-life movement are increasingly using another strategy: convinced that rational persuasion is severely limited, they are effectively using power with elected representatives at the state and federal levels to try to enact laws that will prevent autonomous patients from refusing technological feeding and hydration, prohibit surrogates (or any third party) from abating life-sustaining treatment on the behalf of nonautonomous patients, and even preclude state courts from approving the abatement of medical feeding and hydration in cases of nonautonomous patients. With these ends in mind, representatives of the NRLC, the National Legal Center for the Medically Dependent and Disabled, and numerous state-based pro-life groups are actively trying to have the "Patient's Rights Act" (beginning in Ohio) or the more narrow "Nutrition and Hydration for Incompetent Patients Act" (beginning in Oklahoma) passed at the state level, and hope to get similar legislation passed at the federal level as well so that the lives of future "Karen Quinlans" and "Claire Conroys" will be prolonged apart from the abatement of life-sustaining treatment.

At the "micro" level—where individual lives are at stake in ICUs, the surgical-medical areas of hospitals, and various geriatric settings—the issue of abating treatment is sometimes complicated by competing interests and conflicting perceptions of the morally correct course to take. Fortunately, many cases involving the abatement of life-sustaining treatment (especially in, but certainly not limited to, hospice settings) are resolved to the satisfaction of all parties concerned. However, as we observed in Chapter 3, occasionally even the simple cases (e.g., an unquestionably autonomous patient trying to refuse life-sustaining treatment, with no children or with unanimous support by members of an adult family) can run into problems brought about by uncooperative physicians or inflexible institutional policies. In such instances, a physician (or institutional administrator) with a vitalistic philosophy, undue concern about the law, strong monetary interests, or great uncertainty about the appropriate course of action can create serious problems for a patient trying to refuse treatment. When the patient is already on a life-support system, and especially when the patient has difficulty communicating, the problems in refusing treatment can be tantamount to involuntary incarceration in a health care setting.

Considerably more difficult problems arise when the patient is nonautonomous because of mental illness, senility, mental retardation, brain damage, permanent loss of consciousness, or young age and immaturity. Many of the problems in such cases relate directly to the patient and have to do with the patient's underlying medical condition, personal background, and current family circumstances. If the patient's medical condition predictably will result in death in a matter of days or weeks, if that death can be briefly forestalled but not prevented by continuing medical interventions, if the patient was previously autonomous and expressed preferences regarding the future possibility of treatment abatement, and if the patient has a family in agreement concerning the merits of abating life-sustaining treatment, the decision to abate treatment can be reasonably clear from the patient's perspective. Change one or more of these variables, however, and the correctness of the decision to abate treatment from the patient's perspective becomes much more ambiguous, as illustrated by the cases of Joseph Saikewicz, Bertha Colyer, and Nancy Jobes, as well as several other cases presented earlier.

Other problems in these cases often have to do with the attending physician's perspective on abating treatment. If the physician (possibly supported by other physicians in the case) subordinates the other goals of medicine to the single goal of prolonging life, if the physician regards effective pain management and symptom control as less important than dealing aggressively with a patient's underlying medical condition, and if the physician equates the withdrawal of life-sustaining treatment with killing a patient, he or she has substantial (even though wrong) personal reasons for never wanting to "give up" in trying to keep a patient alive. Moreover, the physician caring for a nonautonomous patient may be reluctant to abate life-sustaining treatment for any number of additional reasons: strongly held religious beliefs, anxiety about criminal or civil liability, the desire for personal monetary gain, concern about the motivation of the patient's surrogate or family, or genuine uncertainty about the appropriate medical and moral course of action.

Additional problems in some cases have to do with nonautonomous patients' families. Although family-related complications rarely result in litigation over decisions to abate treatment, such situations occur fairly commonly and make appropriate decision making much more difficult than it would be otherwise. At least six such situations occur with some frequency.

1. Sometimes family members create problems by adamantly maintaining that they want "everything to be done" to save the patient's life, even when the medical evidence and moral perception of other parties in the case clearly indicate that continuing the treatment being administered is at least futile and possibly harmful to the patient.

2. Sometimes family members oppose the continuation of life-sustaining treatment out of ignorance or for questionable reasons, with physicians, nurses,

and other health care professionals suspecting that the motivation behind the family's decision has to do with indifference, personal financial gain, revenge, or some other reason that is contrary to decision making in the patient's best interests.[4]

3. Sometimes families are seriously divided regarding what the patient would prefer and what the appropriate course of action is, thereby adding family turmoil and the possibility of subsequent legal action to the medical and moral uncertainty that may already exist in the case.

4. Sometimes families create problems, especially in cases involving older adult patients, because they have had little if any personal contact with the patient in recent years (a situation known as the "Florida syndrome"), arrive on the hospital scene basically uninformed about the relevant facts in the case, do not know the patient's preferences about continuing or abating treatment, and try to assuage their feelings of guilt by having the medical team go "all out" to save "Granny's" life.

5. Sometimes families and health care providers have to confront the unwelcome fact that no member of the family is the most knowledgeable surrogate decision maker available, because the patient has for years lived with and confided in a homosexual companion, another resident of a nursing home, or some other friend who lacks legal standing as a relative.

6. Sometimes patients, as illustrated by the Joseph Saikewicz and Joseph Hamlin cases, are without family members on the scene, thereby leaving the patient with no guardian or surrogate to speak on his or her behalf until a court-appointed guardian assumes responsibility for decisions regarding the continuation or abatement of treatment.[5]

Occasionally problems arise in cases of nonautonomous patients because of other third-party involvement in the cases. Of the cases presented earlier, several illustrate the problems brought on by third parties who joined physicians in opposing the requests by family members or friends to abate life-sustaining treatment. The Mary Severns case (Case 4.7) was complicated by the Delaware attorney general's contention that the abatement of antibiotics would constitute murder under state law. The Joseph Fox case (Case 4.8) became a legal battle when the guardian *ad litem* and a district attorney opposed abating mechanical ventilation. The Nancy Jobes case (Case 4.17, one of several cases in which the guardian *ad litem* supported abating treatment) took 14 months in litigation because administrators of the nursing home in which she resided opposed the removal of her feeding tube. The Paul Brophy case (Case 4.19) became a *cause célèbre* when hospital administrators supported physicians in the case in claiming that removal of Brophy's G-tube would violate the moral integrity of the medical profession. And the Helen Corbett case (Case 4.18) demonstrates that third parties (in this instance, the state attorney general) sometimes intervene in the cases of nonautonomous patients even when family members *and* physicians are in agreement that abating treatment is morally correct, but perhaps are unsure about the legality of the action.

Numerous additional cases not presented earlier illustrate the complex and controversial nature of treatment abatement. The three cases that follow clearly indicate—in spite of the changing views of clinicians, the development of case law, and the publications of ethicists on abating treatment in the post-*Quinlan* and post-*Conroy* eras—that serious problems continue to appear in cases involving nonautonomous patients.

Case 8.1

Jacqueline Cole, aged 44 and the mother of four young-adult children, suffered a massive stroke from a cerebral hemorrhage in late March 1986. Having watched her own mother slowly die from a brain tumor, Cole had previously informed her husband and children that she would never want to be kept alive by machines. Even as she realized that she was having a stroke, she reminded two of her children of her desire not to be kept alive by artificial means.

Nevertheless, Cole was taken by ambulance from her home in Baltimore to the Maryland General Hospital. There, in a comatose state, she was placed on mechanical ventilation. When Harry Cole, her husband, arrived at the hospital later that day, he was informed by Thaddeus Pula, the head of neurology at the hospital, that the patient was not expected to survive the day.

Jackie Cole did survive that day, and 40 more days. During that time she remained unconscious and her condition deteriorated as she developed a serious lung infection, had one lung collapse, had a tracheostomy to assist her breathing, suffered cardiac arrest during the tracheostomy procedure, was resuscitated, developed pneumonia, and entered into what Dr. Pula described as "a vegetative state." Apparently not distinguishing between "permanent coma" and "persistent vegetative state," Dr. Pula left the family members uncertain as to whether Jackie was going to die soon, remain in her comatose condition for months or years, or have a remote chance of regaining some level of consciousness accompanied by mental impairments.

Harry, a United Presbyterian minister, became convinced that the treatment sustaining Jackie's life should be stopped. He "could see nothing in her future besides misery," he "knew what she wanted," and he perceived "very little sanctity, very little decency or dignity, in the life Jackie had" in the ICU. He became convinced that "our attempts to keep her alive were getting in the way of God's providence."

He requested that the ventilator be turned off and that no further resuscitative efforts be made. The four children and Jackie's sister agreed with the decision. Dr. Pula, however, refused to carry out the request, saying that he had no legal right to shut off the life supports of a patient whose brain was still functioning somewhat. The Coles then sought a court order to have the mechanical ventilation terminated.

On May 9, 41 days after the onset of the comatose condition, Judge John Carroll Byrnes refused the request. As a Baltimore City Circuit Court judge, he was convinced that the law in Maryland "is that a person is alive if she has brain function, and so granting permission to take that life would have been wrong." With that decision, the Coles began planning to transfer Jackie to a nursing home. They were convinced that they had failed in a dual sense: to carry out her wishes, and to do what they believed to be in her best interests.

Six days later they were amazed when Jackie opened her eyes, looked at Harry, smiled, and returned his kiss. Her subsequent recovery amazed everyone connected with the case. Over a period of 5 months, she learned to move her head, arms, and legs. Her infections cleared up. She was weaned off the heart monitor, catheters, ventilator, and artificial feedings. She started physical therapy. By mid-September, she was able to go home on weekends. She did not, however, regain mental normalcy. Even though she could communicate, she could not retain new information or remember much of the past.

For Harry, Jackie's awakening is "a true act of deliverance, God's redemptive work in action." For the children, Jackie is no longer the same person. They continue to think that the decision to abate treatment was correct, based on what they knew about her wishes and about her medical condition at the time. For Dr. Pula, the surprise and pleasure over Jackie's unexpected recovery is tempered by the realization that she is not normal: "She has persistent intellectual impairments and is likely to remain completely dependent." And for Jackie? She is glad to be alive—but supports the family's decision for treatment abatement. In her words: "I support what they did . . . I had told them if I was ever that sick, I'd want to die with a little dignity."[6]

Case 8.2

Anna Hirth, aged 92 and suffering from Alzheimer's disease, was a patient in Hacienda de La Mesa, a nursing home in San Diego. Also suffering from an assortment of other medical problems, Mrs. Hirth had been a patient of Dr. Alan Jay since 1979. In February 1986, Mrs. Hirth choked on food and incurred brain damage that left her at least "semicomatose," unresponsive to her environment and unable to hear, speak, or understand. Dr. Jay, however, believed that the patient reacted to some stimuli, such as pinching, and that she should be kept alive through technological feedings.

The battle lines over abating technological feeding were drawn when Helen Gary, the patient's daughter, requested that the NG tube sustaining her mother's life be withdrawn. Gary was unanimously supported in this request by the patient's family, including a 78-year-old sister of Mrs. Hirth and all of Mrs. Hirth's grandchildren.

Dr. Jay refused, saying that removing the life-sustaining feeding would violate his Jewish faith and his professional beliefs. He reasoned: "Feeding a patient through a nasogastric tube is not dissimilar from feeding a quadriplegic who cannot lift his arms. You wouldn't let a quadriplegic starve himself."

The administrators of Hacienda de La Mesa contended that acceding to Ms. Gary's wishes would make the nursing home and its employees liable for civil or criminal prosecution. They were supported by James Clark, a temporary special conservator appointed for Mrs. Hirth's welfare, who agreed that treatment should be continued for legal and ethical reasons.

Judge Milton Milkes handled the case in the superior court. Having earlier denied Gary's request for a preliminary injunction against the technological feeding, he issued his ruling in the case on March 5, 1987. That ruling named Gary as her mother's guardian, gave her the right to direct Dr. Jay to discontinue the tube feeding, and granted the nursing home legal protection for the treatment abatement to be carried out on its premises. If Dr. Jay and other physicians should refuse to discontinue the feeding, Judge Milkes ruled that the nursing home had the responsibility to stop the treatment.

Dr. Jay refused to follow the judge's ruling. Staff members at Hacienda de La Mesa refused to follow the judge's ruling, and no other physician would terminate the technological feeding of Mrs. Hirth at Hacienda de La Mesa, at least partially because of the publicity the case received in Jewish, Catholic, conservative Protestant, and medical publications in the San Diego area.

On April 15, Judge Milkes seemed to succumb to media pressure by issuing a new, surprise ruling in the case. Still affirming the right of the patient to have the NG tube removed, he nevertheless declared that neither Dr. Jay nor the nursing home staff would have to execute that decision.

Helen Gary, her family, and her attorney responded to the judge's decision in two ways. First, Gary removed her mother from Hacienda de La Mesa, found a physician in Los Angeles County who was willing to remove the NG tube, and then declared on May 21 that her mother had died peacefully. Second, Gary and her attorney have appealed Judge Milkes' April 15 decision.[7]

Case 8.3

Thomas Wirth, aged 47 and suffering from AIDS-related complex (ARC), worked on an advance directive with an attorney's assistance in April 1987.

Declaring that he wished to have no medical treatment if he could not be restored to a "meaningful quality of life," he signed the written document in the presence of several witnesses.

By July 1987, Wirth was the subject of a court battle in New York City. John Evans, the guardian of Mr. Wirth, was joined by Wirth's friends, attorney, and the SRD in a suit against Bellevue Hospital in Manhattan. Wirth was suffering from an AIDS-related brain infection, was in a stuporous condition in Bellevue's AIDS ward, and was being given drug treatments for the infection. Evans and Wirth's other supporters argued in a court hearing that Wirth should be allowed to die from the infection, based on his earlier written instructions and the meager quality of life he would have even if the drug therapy proved effective against the brain infection.

The physicians in the case and the Bellevue attorneys countered by saying that Mr. Wirth should be treated for the infection. They gave several reasons for their position: the infection was subject to treatment, the patient could recover at least partial health, the advance directive was vaguely worded and did not fit this situation, and they were not legally bound to follow the advance directive.

On July 27, Justice Jawn Sandifer issued his opinion in the state supreme court in Manhattan. Sandifer stated that the law could not be concerned with Mr. Wirth's long-term prognosis, but only the immediate illness. Consequently, he ruled that the case was significantly different from earlier right-to-die cases involving PVS patients with no hope of recovery. Mr. Wirth should continue to be treated for the brain infection, the judge declared, because "the immediate prognosis . . . envisions a possibility for recovery."[8]

These cases illustrate numerous points made throughout this book: decisions to abate treatment involve patients with significantly different personal and family situations, such decisions have to be made about a variety of medical conditions and a variety of life-sustaining treatments, such decisions often have to be made on the behalf of patients who lack decision-making capacity themselves, such decisions can be seriously complicated by uncooperative physicians and institutional administrators, and conflicts over these decisions sometimes have to be resolved in one or more courts. Moreover, these cases illustrate the several "fronts" on which the debate about the morality and legality of abating life-sustaining treatment takes place: numerous clinical settings, legislative chambers (the Wirth case could have been different if the New York legislature had already passed a natural death act), courtrooms, and public opinion, especially as public opinion is reflected by and influenced by the media.

These cases are important because each of them represents a recent (even if short-lived) victory for pro-life opponents of abating treatment. The Jacqueline Cole case is the best kind of case imaginable for the pro-life cause: it clearly illustrates that physicians are fallible when making prognostic judgments, that unexpected medical recoveries do occasionally occur (even when the odds in favor of such recoveries are infinitesimal), that decisions based on patient preferences *and* patient best interests can be wrong, and that individual pro-life advocates (such as Judge Byrnes) can sometimes save a life that otherwise would have died. The Anna Hirth case is an important one for opponents of treatment abatement, especially individuals and groups opposing the abatement of technological feeding, because it suggests that even the judiciary can be made to buckle under when confronted by sufficient pressure from pro-life physicians, administrators, and journalists. The Thomas Wirth case is important because Justice Sandifer joined the physicians at Bellevue in rejecting the validity of two kinds of planning steps that Wirth had taken in regard to treatment abatement—his written advance directive and the informed views of his close friend and guardian—and thus left him to receive treatment he did not want and apparently would benefit from only marginally.

Another reason for presenting these cases is that they, to an even greater extent than some of the cases discussed in previous chapters, highlight the importance of formulating a comprehensive, responsible ethics of treatment abatement. These three cases, like the earlier ones, call for the development of an ethics of abating treatment that can inform and guide physicians, patients and their surrogates, legislators, judges, representatives of the media, and all other thoughtful persons concerned about matters of life and death in the context of critical illness. If such an ethics of treatment abatement were more widely accepted already, the cases of Jacqueline Cole, Anna Hirth, and Thomas Wirth might have been handled differently: by getting the medical facts straight before opting to abate treatment in the Cole case, by steadfastly affirming the primacy of the patient's interests compared to the interests of the physician and institution in the Hirth case, and by emphasizing the moral and legal right of Wirth's proxy to refuse all life-sustaining treatment on his behalf.

Centrality of the patient's best interests

How should an ethics of treatment abatement be formulated, especially if one is interested in establishing an ethical position that is medically realistic, philosophically sound, and legally viable? As we discussed in Chapter 6, ethicists themselves are divided on some of the fundamental features of an ethics of treatment abatement (see Table 6.1). Although the views described as position 4 in that chapter come close to representing a consensus or "mainstream" position, that position is frequently attacked from the right and the left by religious ethicists and philosophers who formulate an ethics of treatment abatement in significantly different ways.

Simply put, ethicists on the "pro-life" side of position 4—especially those whose views are strongly influenced by conservative religious views—think that the *sanctity-of-life doctrine* is crucial in developing an ethics of treatment abatement. For David Bleich, Paul Ramsey, Arthur Dyck, Robert Barry, and other ethicists defending some version of a pro-life philosophy, the centrality of the sanctity-of-life doctrine means that each individual life at stake in decisions to abate treatment is unique and of inestimable value, that such decisions are correctly interpreted only in the context of the divine "givenness" of life, that some medically objective standard is necessary for determining which of these decisions are morally correct, and that quality-of-life judgments are always inappropriate because of their hopeless subjectivity.

By contrast, the ethicists identified with position 4 agree with the religious ethicists and philosophers on the more liberal side of the philosophical spectrum that *quality-of-life judgments* are crucial in developing an ethics of treatment abatement. For these advocates of some version of a right-to-die perspective, the centrality of quality-of-life judgments is clear once one recognizes that medical evidence can be and is interpreted differently by different people, that perception of pain and toleration of suffering vary from person to person, and that the same medical treatment can be regarded as offering a welcome extension of life to one patient and as being gravely burdensome to another patient. The reasons for these divergent views are multiple, but surely include the pluralism of religious traditions and nonreligious values that distinguish persons from one another, the differing weight people place on life itself (including life in the sense of some kind of unconscious, technologically sustained biological existence), and the differing meanings they give to death.

However, the ethicists on the right-to-die end of the spectrum do not agree on the relationship between the sanctity-of-life doctrine and the role of quality-of-life judgments. For John Paris, Richard McCormick, Albert Jonsen, Robert Veatch, and most of the other ethicists identified with position 4 or 5, the belief that each human life has transcendent value is compatible with the recognized need to make quality-of-life judgments pertaining to the abatement of life-sustaining treatment. James Rachels, Peter Singer, Helga Kuhse, and others identified with position 6 disagree. They claim, in an unusual point of agreement with many pro-life advocates, that the sanctity-of-life and quality-of-life perspectives are in irreconcilable conflict. Moreover, they argue that the quality-of-life view must replace the traditional religion-based view. Once that is done, they think we will be able to move beyond the kinds of conservative religious opposition to abating treatment that surfaced in the William Bartling, Nancy Jobes, and Anna Hirth cases—and also, they hope, open the moral and legal door to the practice of euthanasia as well.

In my view, the compatibility of the sanctity-of-life and quality-of-life views depends on how each of these perspectives is interpreted. If belief in the sanctity of life is interpreted in such a conservative and narrow manner as to rule out any decision making or actions that would result in the shortening of any patient's life, then Singer's call for the "unsanctifying" of life is understandable. Likewise, if quality-of-life judgments are interpreted in such a broad and judgmental manner as to put many critically and terminally ill patients at risk of having the continuation of their lives determined on the basis of their social usefulness, then Paris' rejection of a "crass utilitarianism" is also understandable.

Neither of these extreme interpretations is necessary. One can surely have a religious perspective on life according to which one affirms that individual human lives are gifts from God, that these lives have meaning and value beyond the assessments of other persons, and that these lives are rightly lived only when individuals understand themselves to be exercising stewardship over something precious, fragile, and transitory. *At the same time* one can have a philosophical perspective on life according to which neither life nor death is absolutized, the tragic occurrence of lives that are no longer worth living is admitted, and the occasional need for decisions having life-and-death implications is recognized.

An alternative standard for decisions is helpful in moving us beyond the false, dichotomous emphasis on either the sanctity-of-life doctrine or quality-of-life judgments alone. That standard, especially for decision makers in cases involving nonautonomous patients, is the patient's-best-interests (PBI) standard. By focusing on *the patient's* best interests, decision makers can incorporate much of the sanctity-of-life perspective without erring, as some pro-life advocates do, in the direction of recommending overtreatment merely because a particular patient is not imminently dying (position 1), is not clearly diagnosed as a dying patient (position 2), or is being sustained by technological feeding and hydration (position 3). By emphasizing the patient's *best interests,* decision makers can make appropriate quality-of-life judgments without erring, as utilitarian right-to-die advocates do (position 6), in the direction of recommending undertreatment and precipitous killing simply because "there's nothing more to do" medically, or because "the victim" is going to die anyway, or because the patient's continued existence runs counter to the financial (and other) interests of family members and society, or because it is easier for some people to kill than to continue caring for a patient who cannot be cured.

A responsible ethics of treatment abatement is thus based on the centrality of the patient's best interests. In adopting this standard, decision makers base decisions about the initiation, continuation, or abatement of life-sustaining treatment on a standard that is firmly rooted in traditional medical practice, pivotal in biomedical ethical theory, and consistent with recent case law. Having presented the relevant case law in earlier chapters, we will now discuss the PBI standard in terms of medical practice and ethical theory.

The continuum of medical care

The centrality of the patient's best interests in determining appropriate medical care is clear whenever medicine is understood as offering a continuum of treatment options for critically and terminally ill patients. This continuum can be demonstrated in two ways. First, we turn to the medical maxim that was briefly mentioned in Chapter 2. Dating from the fifteenth century, the maxim states that the goals of medical care for physicians (and, presumably, members of other health care professions that developed later) are correctly understood as representing a continuum of options that vary in terms of personal challenge and achievability: "cure sometimes, relieve often, comfort always."[9] As updated by Robert Twycross and Sylvia Lack, the continuum now contains a fourth option for physicians caring for patients with advanced cancer or for other terminally ill patients in the age of technological medicine: "give death a chance."[10]

How should this maxim be interpreted? From the perspective of physicians, the maxim clearly emphasizes the multiple goals of medicine, the limitations of medicine in curing illness and prolonging life, the ongoing need to provide medical care that is appropriate to the needs of patients, and the expectation that physicians will continue to provide effective care for their patients when they can no longer expect to cure them. Stated another way, the maxim calls for physicians to provide appropriate medical and nonmedical care for their patients during the "best" and "worst" of times—in times of routine illness, in times of critical illness, and in times of terminal illness.

From the perspective of patients, this traditional medical maxim (with or without its twentieth-century update) points to the appropriateness of using the patient's best interests as the standard for decision making. For many patients, of course, the first of the listed goals is unquestionably in their best interests. They prefer health to illness, life to death, normal activities at work and home to the confining aspects of a room in a hospital or nursing home. However, precisely because cure is not always medically possible, continually aggressive efforts to cure all patients not only represent medical nonsense but courses of action that are clearly contrary to some patients' best interests. Once physicians, patients, patients' families, and others involved in particular cases move beyond medical gamesmanship and psychological denial to recognize that cure is not a statistically probable outcome, the strategy of indefinitely prolonging the lives of patients who cannot be cured also becomes questionable in terms of the patient's best interests.

The medical and moral reason for always trying to provide comfort to patients and occasionally giving death a chance—particularly when cure *and* effective pain relief cannot be achieved—is that it is in the best interests of patients to do so. Otherwise, critically and terminally ill patients may be forced to endure unmitigated pain, unrelieved suffering, and ineffectively controlled symptoms of their underlying medical conditions merely in order to satisfy the interests and desires of other parties: never-give-up physicians, do-everything-possible relatives, and liability-conscious administrators of the institutions in which they reside.

Second, we turn to a much more recent interpretation of the continuum of medical care for critically and terminally ill patients. This account, appearing in a widely discussed article written by 10 physicians, describes the continuum in terms of four "levels" of care to be given to "hopelessly ill" patients.[11] The levels of care are as follows:

1. emergency lifesaving interventions (with CPR techniques);
2. intensive care and advanced life support (with mechanical ventilation and other life-sustaining technologies);
3. general medical care (including antibiotics, other drugs, surgery, cancer chemotherapy, and technological hydration and nutrition); and
4. general nursing care for comfort (including pain medications, technological hydration and nutrition, and hygienic care).

Why divide medical care for critically and/or terminally ill patients in this manner? Why not put all such patients in the same category, that of prolonging life as long as you can, any way you can? According to these physicians, the answer is obvious: "differences in patients' disabilities dictate differences in the appropriate form and intensity of their care."[12] Stated another way, the provision of appropriate medical care means the provision of care individualized according to the best interests of various patients. Consequently, monitoring procedures (temperature, pulse, and blood pressure readings) that are routine for most patients "may be discontinued" for patients requiring only the fourth level of care, precisely because they are in the terminal phase of an irreversible illness. Likewise, blood tests, X-ray examinations, surgical interventions, antibiotics, mechanical ventilation, and technological feeding and hydration may all be discontinued, according to these physicians, unless the medical procedures meet one of two criteria: honoring the patient's wishes, or promoting the patient's best interests by making the patient comfortable.

Role of ethical principles

The standard of the patient's best interests is a converging point for four ethical principles that apply to decisions to abate treatment: the principle of respect for autonomy, the principle of beneficence, the principle of justice, and the principle of nonmaleficence. Two of these principles—respect for autonomy and beneficence—stand out in terms of their importance in helping to determine whether abating treatment is in a patient's best interests. As we have seen repeatedly in cases presented in earlier chapters, the core of the conflict over the abatement of

life-sustaining treatment frequently concerns a conflict between these two principles, as evidenced by (1) the refusal of life-sustaining treatment by an autonomous patient or the rejection of such treatment on the behalf of a previously
autonomous patient, and (2) the judgment by one or more physicians (or other
parties in a case) that the continuation of life-sustaining treatment is the best way
of promoting the patient's well-being. The other two principles serve as important "tests" for determining the limits or boundaries for actions based on the first
two principles, with the principle of justice offering a counterbalance for the
principle of respect for autonomy, and the principle of nonmaleficence providing
an outer limit beyond which actions guided by the principle of beneficence
should not go. Taken together, the four principles provide a broad, but helpful
conceptual framework for determining a patient's best interests in any given
case. That conceptual framework can be illustrated in the following manner:

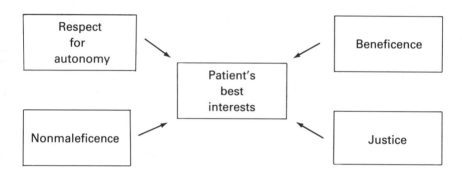

The first principle goes to the heart of decisions to abate treatment by requiring
all persons involved in the decision-making process to consider the merits of
physician-recommended life-sustaining treatment *from the perspective of the
patient* who would be on the receiving end of that treatment. In this manner, the
principle of respect for autonomy brings a subjective component to the determination of the patient's best interests, a component that should not be minimized
because, after all, the illness, pain, suffering, chance for restored health, continued existence, and possible death of the patient that physicians and other
parties in a case deliberate about are hardly objective factors to the patient
involved. Instead, to state the obvious, the illness or disease process is an
existential reality to a conscious patient, probably unlike any experience he or
she has ever had. Likewise, the possibilities of restored health, or at least improved health, or further deterioration of health, or suffering without relief, or
the end of one's existence are intensely personal matters to the patient that color
in an indelible manner the patient's perspective on whether life-sustaining treatment should be initiated, continued, or abated.

The patient's perspective is therefore of great importance in any effort to use the patient's best interests as the standard for treatment-abatement decisions, especially when the patient is or has previously been capable of thinking through the life-and-death implications frequently involved in such decisions. Yet the very fact that patients can and sometimes do opt for treatment abatement contrary to the opinions of physicians (and other parties in cases) raises questions about the meaning and weight to be attached to "the patient's perspective." Does the patient really know what he or she is choosing? Has the patient been adequately informed about treatment possibilities, the likely benefits of treatment, and the predictable outcome apart from the recommended treatment? Does the patient understand that by forgoing certain modalities of life-sustaining treatment, he or she will almost certainly die? In cases of patients who are no longer capable of making decisions relative to treatment recommendations, did the patient sufficiently understand the risks of abating treatment months or years earlier when he or she communicated that preference verbally or in an advance directive?

All of these questions address the important issue of the patient's mental and emotional status when opting for treatment abatement. Simply put, the questions force other parties in particular cases to decide if the patient was "autonomous," "competent," or "decisionally capable" when he or she communicated the preference to have one or more medical treatments withheld, decelerated, or withdrawn. For example, did Karen Quinlan have adequate information and understanding about the long-term prolongation of life by mechanical ventilation when she voiced opposition to such treatment in conversations with friends months before becoming permanently unconscious? Were Delores Heston and her mother acting freely, without internal or external constraints, and consistently with their beliefs as Jehovah's Witnesses when they both refused a blood transfusion for Delores in connection with the surgery necessary to repair her ruptured spleen? Did Rosaria Candura understand that she would soon die unless she consented to have her gangrenous leg amputated? Was Abe Perlmutter cognizant of what would happen to him apart from mechanical ventilation when he asked to be removed from the ventilator? Did Elizabeth Bouvia understand the medical risks she was taking when she refused the NG feedings that supplemented her oral intake of food? Was Patricia Brophy acting consistently with Paul Brophy's value system and verbalized opinions when she requested on his behalf that the G-tube providing him nourishment be removed?

Of course all of these examples are cases that ended up in court. All of them, in one way or another, involved judicial determinations of these patients' competency or incompetency. However, many other cases that are never adjudicated in court hearings involve questions about the decision-making capacity of individual patients. Usually the questions about a particular patient's capacity to make decisions about his or her health care are framed in the psychiatric-legal language of "competency," with little or no reference to the philosophical language of "personhood" and "autonomy." Nevertheless, as I noted in Chapter 3, the concepts of personhood and autonomy are closely related to the concept of competency, and provide the philosophical and psychological foundation on which the more widely used (but also more limited) concept of competency is based.

We need not repeat the discussion of the *concept* of autonomy here. We do, however, need to discuss the dual manner in which the autonomy (or previous autonomy) of critically ill patients functions as an ethical factor in decisions to abate treatment. First, the autonomous choice of a patient to forgo one or more treatment options, or the undeniable previous decision by a now-nonautonomous patient to do the same, provides physicians and other parties to the case an opportunity to exercise the virtue of respectfulness toward others. To the degree that they affirm and abide by the free, rational, and consistent choice of the patient not to start or not to continue life-sustaining treatment, they exhibit the morally appropriate *attitude* of respect for autonomy.[13] In so doing, of course, they also reveal something important about themselves as morally sensitive persons.

Second, the *principle* of respect for autonomy calls for physicians and other parties to a case to abide by the free and rational choice of a patient to forgo treatment whenever (1) that choice is consistent with the patient's value system and (2) that decision will not bring significant harm to one or more minor children of the patient. This principle, sometimes construed more narrowly as the "principle of autonomy" or more broadly as the "principle of respect for persons," focuses on the moral right of autonomous patients to choose how they prefer to live and die. The principle of respect for autonomy therefore requires that physicians and other parties to a case recognize that they have a duty at least to respect the *negative right* of an autonomous patient to refuse treatment, and possibly (in rare cases) to respond affirmatively to an autonomous, critically ill patient's *positive right* to ask for assistance in bringing about his or her death. At its core, the principle of respect for autonomy means that physicians and other parties to a case should practice noninterference whenever a patient's decision to refuse treatment appears to be voluntary, informed, and consistent with the beliefs and values that he or she has held in life. In this manner the principle of respect for autonomy functions as a *constraint* on the pursuit of other goals (e.g., improvement of the patient's health, prolongation of the patient's life) by physicians, other health care personnel, and relatives of the patient.[14]

The importance of this principle has become increasingly clear as the debate over abating treatment has moved from its first to its second and now to its third phase. With the decisions of several courts in the early Jehovah's Witnesses cases, the consistent handling of other legal cases of autonomous patients at the final appellate level, the published reports of the President's Commission, the nationally televised spectacle (on "60 Minutes") of the William Bartling trag-

edy, and the filmed versions of the Dax Cowart case and the Emily Bauer case
(see Chapter 1), numerous persons inside and outside medicine have become
more sensitized to the moral obligation health professionals have to respect the
autonomous choices of their patients—even when some of those choices will
result in the patients' deaths.

In fact, the increased awareness of the importance of respect for the choices of
autonomous patients has led to a public outcry over the handling of a few
publicized cases that have gone contrary to this ethical perspective. The Peter
Cinque case will illustrate the point. Cinque, suffering from the terminal phases
of diabetes in 1982, was a patient in the Lydia E. Hall Hospital in Freeport, New
York. Blind, no longer having either leg, suffering from unmitigated pain, and
receiving continuous maintenance on a kidney dialysis machine, Cinque requested that the dialysis treatment be discontinued. His request was denied, even
after his mental competency was certified by two psychiatrists. Subsequently the
hospital obtained a court order to continue treatment, he experienced irreversible
brain damage after he stopped breathing for an unspecified time in the ICU, and
two bedside court hearings finally resulted in the discontinuation of the dialysis—but in such a rapid manner that he died before his family arrived at the
hospital. Among the persons dismayed at the hospital's refusal of an autonomous
patient's request was Willard Gaylin, M.D., who asked: "How did we get into
this Alice-in-Wonderland world, where a man must beg for his legal rights,
prove his sanity, endure court hearings and finally be reduced to a living cadaver
to do that which has been generally accepted as his privilege?"[15]

The second ethical principle provides a perspective on decisions about medical
treatment in which the benefits of administering treatment and the risks of abating treatment are approached *from the standpoint of the physician* (or physicians)
who bears moral and legal responsibility for providing care to the patients whose
lives and possibly premature deaths are the focal point of such decisions. By
following the ancient principle of beneficence, physicians adhere to an ethical
principle that requires moral agents to advance the important interests of other
persons whenever their own proximity, abilities, and efficient alternatives allow
them to do so with only minimal risk to themselves. In the context of medicine,
the principle of beneficence calls on physicians (and other health care professionals) to advance the multiple important interests of the patients who come
their way, interests generally understood to include the prevention of disease, the
promotion and restoration of health, the amelioration of disabling conditions, the
relief of pain and other forms of suffering, the effective management of disease-
related symptoms, and the prolongation of life. In other words, physicians are
morally obligated to promote the well-being of their patients by providing medical care (and nonmedical care) appropriate to the needs and circumstances of the
patients.

By emphasizing the importance of the patient's well-being, the principle of beneficence brings an objective component to the determination of the patient's best interests. The principle calls for decisions and actions that are "objective" in two quite different ways. In one way, the principle calls for recommendations of and decisions about medical treatment that are independent of any particular patient's idiosyncratic beliefs, ignorance about medicine, fears, prejudices, limited experiences, or other factors that can and do influence patients' decisions to consent to recommended treatment or to refuse to consent to such treatment. If the patient in question is autonomous, this objective approach to promoting the patient's well-being necessitates time, effort, and persuasiveness on the part of a physician to convince an uncooperative patient that the recommended treatment is actually in his or her best interests. If the patient in question is nonautonomous, this approach to promoting the patient's well-being is objective in either of two senses: (1) the physician's making a recommendation regarding beneficial treatment apart from any reliance on what the patient might have chosen if able to do so, or (2) the physician's making a recommendation regarding beneficial treatment that is known to be different from or contrary to the patient's previously expressed preferences while autonomous. Each of these medical approaches to the promotion of nonautonomous patients' well-being is evident in some of the legal cases presented earlier in Chapter 4.

The principle of beneficence also calls for decisions and actions that are objective in a second way. Because individual physicians can have uncertainty, idiosyncratic beliefs, limited knowledge of specialized areas of medicine outside their expertise, fears (e.g., fear of their own deaths, or fear of failure whenever their patients die), prejudices, limited experiences, or other factors that can and sometimes do influence their views of a particular patient's case, the principle of beneficence calls for medical decision making that transcends the possibly provincial and certainly fallible perspective of any individual physician. In a related fashion, the principle requires medical decision making that transcends the possible emotional involvement any individual physician can have with personally significant patients or particularly tragic cases. In this manner the principle sets forth an objective approach to the promotion of the patient's well-being that relies less on the objectivity of any individual physician than on the *collective objectivity* of all persons in the field of medicine. This collective objectivity is gained through time-tested scientific knowledge about the health and diseases of the human body, the "community" standard of appropriate medical practice, the practices of clinical consultations and referrals to physicians in specialized medical areas, technological advances in monitoring patients' conditions and formulating accurate diagnoses of those conditions, the use of computers, and the communal wisdom and experience gained from discussing the matters of diagnosis, prognosis, and treatment options in the context of clinical rounds.

The objectivity sought by physicians in defining and promoting the well-being of patients is therefore obviously important in any effort to use the patient's best interests as the standard for decisions to abate treatment, especially in cases involving nonautonomous patients. Precisely because of the objectivity that seems attainable through the use of expensive diagnostic equipment, laboratory tests, computers, and consultations with medical experts, many physicians function easily in a paternalistic mode that conveys the message "doctors know best" to all other parties to a case who lack a medical degree. To a certain extent, this perspective is understandable and justifiable. By the very nature of their repeated experiences with patients having the same medical conditions (as well as with the surrogates of such patients), physicians have a certain objectivity regarding health and disease that the rest of us do not possess.

It is this objectivity—or at least the quantifiable scientific and mathematical data that help physicians make diagnostic decisions and prognostic predictions— that is attractive to some persons outside medicine. As we have seen in earlier chapters, some pro-life ethicists, attorneys, and legislators think that (1) acceptable decisions by autonomous patients in regard to abating life-sustaining treatment should be limited to certain categories of patients (those whose deaths are "imminent," or those at least diagnosed as dying), and/or (2) the choices of autonomous patients and previously autonomous patients in regard to abating treatment should be limited to certain categories of life-sustaining treatment (with feeding tubes not on the acceptable list), and/or (3) the decisions to abate life-sustaining treatment on the behalf of nonautonomous patients should never be based on quality-of-life judgments. Each of these views represents an attempt to ground justifiable decisions to abate treatment in some kind of objective, medically definable standard that is external to the individual judgments made by autonomous patients or by surrogates of nonautonomous patients. Such efforts to define the patient's well-being in terms of an objective standard are best illustrated by Paul Ramsey's well-known view that the only way of justifying decisions to abate life-sustaining treatment is when such treatment is "not medically indicated."

The relative objectivity of medical data and medical judgments also contributes to the emphasis on the ethical integrity of the medical profession, at least as this view is occasionally put forth by physicians and institutional administrators who oppose abating life-sustaining treatment in particular cases. Such defenders of the integrity of physicians do not merely want to prevent physicians from being turned into medically educated robots (an updated version of Aristotle's "animated tools"), nor do they defend the important idea of conscientious objection for physicians who have serious moral reservations about abating treatment in particular cases and who consequently want to withdraw from these cases by transferring the care of the patients to other physicians. Instead, such defenders of the integrity of physicians sometimes try to argue (as in *Bartling, Jobes,* and several other cases) that the physicians in these cases are *objectively right* in their view of the treatment that is beneficial for these patients, and that anyone who disagrees with them on moral or legal grounds is wrong by definition. For example, one physician was adamantly uncompromising in his criticism of an autonomous Jehovah's Witness patient who refused a blood transfusion and died from total exsanguination following the rupture of her uterus during parturition: "The patient, her husband, and above all, the adviser, must accept responsibility for this needless death."[16] Another physician, reporting on another Jehovah's Witness case, appealed for legal help in promoting the patient's well-being against her will: "Is there any legal mechanism—or can there ever be—for overriding a cult that forbids medical experts to act?"[17]

Such reasoning is wrong, even though the frustration and anger of the physicians in these cases is surely understandable. It is one thing to emphasize the objectivity in medicine that is made possible by the scientific and technological foundation on which this professional field rests, and to value the increased certainty in decision making that such objective facts make possible whenever physicians make diagnoses of pathological conditions, determine that brain death has occurred, or know that certain types of medical conditions (such as those in the two Jehovah's Witnesses cases just mentioned) do not have to result in a patient's death. It is another thing to move from that scientific and statistical base to make health care decisions that have as much to do with one's value system— and the pluralism of such value systems in health care settings—as with the medical information that provides the focal point for such decisions. To make such a direct intellectual move from a factual base or premise (the "is") to an evaluative conclusion (the "ought") is to commit a logical fallacy. Simply because a life-threatening medical condition can be effectively treated does not automatically mean that it ought to be so treated in every case.

More important than this logical point is that the relative objectivity of medical data does not, and cannot, lead to the same "objective" decisions being made by all persons who are informed about the data. Similar medical conditions in critically ill patients can lead physicians subscribing to the "technological imperative" to try "everything possible" to forestall death for as long as possible, whereas other physicians less enamored with the "technological imperative" may focus more on effective pain management and symptom control with their patients. Likewise, the same diagnostic results, treatment options, and pessimistic prognoses can lead some patients with advanced cancer to consent to every possible life-sustaining treatment (and perhaps to try illegal therapeutic options as well) in the long-shot hope of living longer, whereas other patients with the same kind of cancer at the same stage of development may decide to "make every day count" as patients in hospice programs once treatment options prove ineffective.

Among the reasons for these different decisions following the gathering and communicating of similar medical information is an indisputable fact: people often disagree about what counts as a "beneficial" consequence of a decision or action. In the context of physician–patient relationships, virtually everyone agrees that physicians have a moral obligation to provide the type of care for their patients that will result in more "benefits" on balance than "burdens" to the patients. Yet the exact meaning of "benefits," the determination of when and how such benefits occur in medicine, and the relationship between the medical prolongation of life and the production of patient-centered benefits are all matters of considerable dispute. For example, physicians who believe that the principle of beneficence requires them, above all else, to "salvage" and preserve their patients' lives for as long as technologically possible can be rebutted in a number of ways, including by pointing out that such an idea is a distinctly modern notion not found in earlier periods of medical practice.[18]

The variability in meaning that attends the goal of promoting the well-being of patients is easily illustrated. When physicians and other health care professionals refer to the "benefits" of particular medical treatments, they can be making any one of six different claims:

1. The treatment in question is "beneficial" in the sense of making the *medical management* of the patient easier for the health care providers involved in the case.
2. The treatment is "beneficial" in the sense of providing *immediate, short-term relief* to the patient, without any clear evidence that the treatment will provide long-term benefit to the patient.
3. The treatment is "beneficial" in the sense of *corrective therapy,* by improving an injurious or disabling condition or by replacing a lost function without being curative.
4. The treatment is "beneficial" in the sense of *curing* a pathological condition "once and for all."
5. The treatment is "beneficial" in the sense of *maintaining the status quo condition* of the patient for an extended period of time, with any deterioration in the patient's condition being spread over a period of months or years.
6. The treatment is "beneficial" in the sense of *medical experimentation* masquerading as innovative therapy, with any actual benefits of the experimental procedure accruing to other patients in the future.[19]

In regard to treatments recommended as beneficial for critically ill patients, especially treatments that can sustain such patients' lives for prolonged periods, it is important to focus on (1) *which of these meanings* of "beneficial" is being used and (2) *whose benefit* or well-being is being promoted with the administration of the treatment. Does the administration of chemotherapy, mechanical ventilation, technological feeding, or some other form of life-sustaining treatment in a particular case actually provide the possibility of benefit in a corrective or curative sense, or is the provision of such treatment in some instances realistically "beneficial" only in the sense of maintaining the patient's status quo condition for as long as possible? If the modality of treatment being recommended or used provides only a remote possibility of cure, improved health, restored consciousness, or some other tangible benefit for the patient on the receiving end of the treatment, for whose benefit is the treatment given: the physicians in the case? the nurses? the patient's family? the patient's guardian? the institutional administrator?

In the cases of autonomous patients presented in earlier chapters, all of those patients judged that the treatments capable of sustaining their lives were no longer beneficial to them in any sense that mattered to them. Precisely for that reason, Dax Cowart, Abe Perlmutter, William Bartling, and the other autonomous patients tried to exercise their *moral and legal right* to refuse the life-sustaining treatments being given to them. Partially for the same reason, the surrogates of Brother Fox, Edna Marie Leach, Paul Brophy, and several other previously autonomous patients refused life-sustaining treatments on their behalf that were regarded as not being beneficial in any important way to the patient. Surrogates of other nonautonomous patients, making decisions on the behalf of patients who had never been autonomous or who had never expressed their preferences regarding life-sustaining treatments while autonomous, concluded that the treatments being administered to Shirley Dinnerstein, Earle Spring, Claire Conroy, and other such patients were not beneficial on balance to the patient.

In some of these cases we have discussed, the physicians in the cases agreed that life-sustaining treatment was no longer beneficial on balance to the patient— yet felt obligated to continue the treatment out of concern for the law. In most of the cases, however, the physicians maintained that the treatment was beneficial to the patient, if only in the very limited sense of prolonging the patient's status quo condition: continued biological existence, often without consciousness, with virtually no hope for improvement. Given that dismal state of affairs for the patient, whether autonomous or nonautonomous, one can hardly help speculating about whose well-being was actually being promoted in these cases.

Clearly, then, the principle of beneficence does not provide definitive answers for morally problematic treatment-abatement cases any more than it provides definitive answers for some of the other moral problems we face in life. Neither does the principle of respect for autonomy. As *ethical* principles, the principle of respect for autonomy and that of beneficence provide decision makers in clinical cases with general, morally important perspectives on both easy and difficult cases, contributing sufficient moral guidance so that the easy cases can be handled with confidence that the right decision has been made, but with no guaranteed, "cookbook" answers for all of the difficult cases. As *prima facie* ethical principles, these two principles have the same status as other ethical principles that provide guidance for moral living: namely, each of them presents us with obligations that are to be carried out unless and until they come into conflict with competing obligations connected with other ethical principles. In this sense, the principles of respect for autonomy and of beneficence are equally important as ethical principles, with neither having an elevated status on the basis of which it can automatically "trump" the other. Precisely for that reason, both of these ethical principles are crucial for morally responsible action in clinical settings, each has to be weighed against the other in deciding the right course of action in particular cases, and the weight of each principle varies according to the different features of different cases.

Fortunately, these two ethical principles are compatible in determining the right course of action in most clinical cases, just as they generally are in providing guidance for decision making outside clinical settings. However, clinical cases involving decisions about the initiation, continuation, or abatement of treatment can, as we have seen throughout this book, sometimes limit the applicability of one or the other principle and occasionally place the two principles in conflict with each other. When such conflict occurs between these principles, the determination of a patient's best interests in a particular case obviously becomes more difficult.

Several kinds of situations that occasionally arise in cases involving the possibility of abating treatment reveal the limitations of both principles. Because the principle of respect for autonomy is neither absolute nor the only ethical principle applicable to such cases, it is problematic as an action-guide whenever (1) autonomous patients push autonomy to the limit by calling for the abatement of life-sustaining treatment that is regarded as clearly beneficial by most physicians and other knowledgeable persons, (2) the refusal of life-sustaining treatment by an autonomous patient seems to be part of a personally planned medical crisis (e.g., by a prisoner, or by a physically disabled person) involving deception of health care providers, (3) the autonomy of certain patients is questionable because of their advanced age, young age, or uncertain mental status, (4) previously autonomous patients indicated preferences for the abatement of life-sustaining treatment that now seems, in the view of objective observers, clearly to be in their best interests, (5) now-nonautonomous patients never provided a clue to their relatives or friends before losing autonomy regarding their views on the use of life-sustaining treatments, or (6) nonautonomous patients are alone in the world, with no relatives or friends available even to try to figure out what the patient would prefer in regard to the continuation or abatement of certain life-sustaining treatments.

Equally serious difficulties arise with the principle of beneficence. Because this principle also is neither absolute nor the only ethical principle applicable to such cases, it is problematic as an action-guide whenever (1) emergency, short-term treatment that would undoubtedly save a patient from a premature death is clearly not wanted by a clearly autonomous patient, (2) long-term treatment that would probably prolong a patient's life for years is clearly not wanted by a clearly autonomous patient, (3) the treatment that sustains a nonautonomous patient's life is incapable of improving the patient's health or restoring the patient's consciousness, (4) the treatment that sustains a patient's life also increases the patient's suffering, or (5) the treatment that can prolong a nonautonomous patient's life is so invasive and debilitating that it seems to the patient's surrogates to represent a form of technological abuse.

For these reasons, the principles of justice and nonmaleficence are necessary not only as independent ethical principles applicable to decisions about medical treatment, but also as helpful guides in defining the moral limits of decisions based on either of the other two principles. In this way the principles of justice and nonmaleficence help to establish the general moral context for determining when available medical treatment is and is not in an individual patient's best interests.

The principle of justice, which formally calls for the equitable handling of similar (nonmedical) cases, applies to decisions about medical treatment in two different ways: as a guide for handling individual medical cases, and as a guide for establishing policies that pertain to multiple cases belonging to the same medical and moral categories. In terms of individual cases, the principle of justice *reinforces the principle of respect for autonomy* (and the principle of beneficence) by requiring that all gravely ill, critically ill, or terminally ill patients be given equal access to the level of available, potentially beneficial health care they need and desire. In this sense, the principle of justice demands that a moral "bottom floor" be established so that autonomous patients who want potentially beneficial medical care—as well as previously autonomous patients with similar preferences—can be given care appropriate to their medical conditions. This requirement does not mean, especially in an age of technological medicine characterized by terribly expensive, exotic treatments *and* by limited private and governmental resources to pay for such treatments, that all critically ill patients should be given multiple forms of life-sustaining treatment merely because they desire such treatments. Rather, the obligations imposed by the principle of justice mean that no individual patients who need and want potentially beneficial life-sustaining treatment or potentially helpful palliative care should be singled out, and contrary to their wishes, be denied such care for the wrong reasons: discrimination based on race, religion, handicap, or socioeconomic status; false claims or self-serving reasons put forth by uncaring relatives; defeatist or uncaring attitudes on the part of physicians; or utilitarian judgments about the patient's minimal social worth. Moreover, when patients who need and want such care instead receive undertreatment because of their limited financial resources—as now increasingly happens with limited governmental funding for catastrophic medical conditions, geriatric care, and hospice care—the principle of justice demands that health care professionals become more politically active in support of increased funding for their Medicaid patients, Medicare patients (especially those in nursing homes and hospice programs), and other patients in serious financial need.

The principle of justice, or equity, also *supplements the principle of respect for autonomy* by requiring that other nonautonomous patients be given equal access (through their guardians or surrogates) to similarly beneficial medical care, unless the available treatment is regarded by objective observers as being contrary to an individual patient's best interests. Especially for patients who have never been autonomous because of serious-to-profound mental retardation (the Joseph Saikewiczes and John Storars of the world), the principle of justice calls for the administration of medical care appropriate to their medical conditions and the unusual features of their lives. Life-sustaining treatment may justifiably be abated in some of these cases, but not merely because the patient in need of the treatment is mentally retarded.

In addition, both in regard to the handling of individual cases and the establishment of health care policies, the principle of justice *tempers the principle of respect for autonomy* and sometimes provides the philosophical and legal basis for overriding the choices of autonomous patients. In individual cases involving public health concerns, the principle of justice limits the *negative right* of autonomous patients to refuse particular forms of life-sustaining treatment (e.g., antibiotics and other life-sustaining medications for patients with tuberculosis), lest the general public be placed at risk of contagion.[20] In other, more common cases of individual patients, the principle of justice places limits on the *positive right* of any autonomous patient to request a particular modality of treatment, even if the treatment is generally capable of sustaining patients' lives and the patient is financially able to pay for it. If the treatment requested or demanded by the patient would be medically useless in sustaining that patient's life, or if the desired treatment is sufficiently scarce that compliance with the patient's request would unfairly deprive other patients of equitable access to the same level of treatment, or if a patient's offer of payment for an expensive treatment (an offer possibly several times the going ''market'' rate) is an attempt to buy a privileged position on the waiting list for that scarce medical resource (e.g., a heart transplant), the physician(s) in the case are under no moral obligation to provide the treatment.[21] In this manner, considerations of justice impinge on the PBI standard and sometimes require, out of concern for the best interests of all similarly situated patients, that the request for a particular form of life-sustaining treatment by an autonomous patient be denied lest other patients also in need of the treatment be unfairly disadvantaged.

In terms of health care policies, the principle of justice tempers the principle of respect for autonomy at the institutional level and beyond. Some hospitals and nursing homes, as we have discussed in earlier chapters, have already established institutional policies whereby all critically or terminally ill patients are subject to the same written limited-treatment protocols. Fundamental to such policies is the idea that considerations of justice (along with beneficence and nonmaleficence) mandate that (1) patients who "are overmastered by their diseases" (to quote the famous statement in the Hippocratic literature) and/or (2) patients requiring excessively expensive life-sustaining treatment are subject to institutional decisions to abate treatment in cases belonging to certain categories, even when the patients are autonomous, so that the limited human and technological resources of the institution can be more equitably distributed among all of the patients in the institution. In this way, a moral "top floor" or "ceiling" is established so that autonomous patients whose cases fit the institutional categories for abating treatment will not receive overtreatment even if they request it.

With the escalating number of critically ill patients who can be kept alive technologically, and with the rapidly escalating costs of many forms of life-sustaining treatment, similar decisions to limit the treatment options of patients as a matter of policy are facing policy makers at the state and federal levels. A frequently cited example of the problem is the federally funded End-Stage Renal Dialysis Program, initiated in 1972 at a projected annual cost of $250 million and now costing $2.4 billion a year to provide life-sustaining treatment for 50,000 patients (these patients constitute less than 0.2 percent of Medicare-eligible patients).[22] A less well-known example of the problem, involving a previously autonomous patient, is the case of a permanently unconscious patient who was kept alive technologically for 18 years at an estimated cost of $6 million![23] Given these costs of sustaining a relatively few patients, the President's Commission correctly argued that "society is not obligated to provide every intervention that the patient or provider believe might be beneficial."[24] Going a step further, the participants in the Hastings Center project called for the development of policies regarding "costworthy care," meaning that the potential benefit of medical treatments for patients would be weighed against "the sacrifice that such treatments entail by requiring us to give up other forms of health care, or other legitimate individual and societal goods."[25] Should such justice-driven policies be established, the results in terms of the care physicians provide critically ill patients would be twofold: building the notion of costworthy care into the decisions of whether some life-sustaining treatments are in the best interests of some critically ill patients, and deciding to "refrain from providing some treatments and tests that might benefit the immediate patient for the good of other patients with whom they [the physicians] have no connection."[26]

The last of the four ethical principles, that of nomaleficence, provides the philosophical basis for claims made about the patient-centered "burdens" that sometimes accompany the technological prolongation of life. Long associated with the maxim *primum non nocere* ("above all, do no harm"), the principle of nonmaleficence functions on the opposite end of a continuum with the principle of beneficence. In this manner the principle of nonmaleficence provides an important limiting factor according to which decisions and actions based on the principle of beneficence—or at least those claimed to be based on the beneficence principle—can be tested to see if the actions are, on balance, actually proving to be beneficial or are actually harming the recipient of the actions in some important way.

The principle of nonmaleficence requires that moral agents avoid intentionally or negligently harming other persons. This principle is more stringent than the principle of beneficence, given the combination of three factors: (1) the relative ease of harming others, compared with helping them, (2) the almost limitless ways of harming others, ranging from actions bordering on the trivial to actions of such unrestrained cruelty that they are placed in that boundless moral category known as "man's inhumanity to man," and (3) the extraordinary capacity we have to engage in self-delusion, thereby sometimes convincing ourselves that we are helping others when we may be doing just the opposite.

In the context of medicine, the principle of nonmaleficence serves as a reminder to physicians and other health care professionals of the inherent risks involved in many medical procedures, and of the temptation to minimize the harm done to patients in the pursuit of promoting their well-being. The linkage of the principle of nonmaleficence with the principle of beneficence is therefore present from the beginnings of medical practice. As expressed in the Hippocratic Oath, the principles are placed alongside each other in the same sentence: "I will use treatment to help the sick according to my ability and judgment, but never with a view to injury and wrong-doing."[27]

Consequently, the principle of nonmaleficence has traditionally been used to catalogue and rank harmful actions that were not to be a part of the physician–patient relationship, because they offered patients an imbalance of burdens to benefits. In this sense, the principle of nonmaleficence has played the important role of helping to determine when and how actions performed by physicians were counter to the best interests of their patients. Chief among such actions, historically, has been any act done with the intention of causing a patient's death, as illustrated by the portion of the Hippocratic Oath in which a physician pledges neither to "give a deadly drug to anybody if asked for it" nor to "make a suggestion to this effect."[28]

Indicative of this traditional understanding of *death as the ultimate harm* to befall a patient are two rules of medical practice that have been derived from the principle of nonmaleficence: "do not kill" and "do not assist another person's death." Given the weight of these rules in medical practice, a physician has limited options in trying to show that a particular patient's death was justified on moral gounds:

1. Claim that the patient was not innocent but rather an "unjust aggressor" whose continuing life was not protected by the principle of nonmaleficence (e.g., a fetus in an ectopic pregnancy).
2. Establish that the patient's death was due to unpreventable natural causes.
3. Argue that the patient's death was unintended but foreseen as a possible secondary effect of the pain medication given the patient, and that such a "double-effect" death would not be prohibited by the duty of nonmaleficence.
4. Contend that the terminally ill patient was merely allowed to die, not killed, when life-sustaining medical treatments were withheld or withdrawn because they were judged to be medically useless for this patient.
5. Claim that the individual now dead was not yet a person (e.g., a fetus) or was no longer a person (e.g., an adult with PVS).
6. Contend that death was in the best interests of the patient in that it represented a lesser harm than sustaining a life of prolonged and unpreventable suffering.
7. Establish that the patient was intentionally killed only after he or she made a voluntary, informed decision that death was preferable to a continuing existence of intractable pain, and that the death-causing action was motivated by compassion.[29]

It is against the background provided by this historical understanding of the principle of nonmaleficence, and its applicability—above all else—to the deaths of patients, that the current debate about the morality of abating treatment takes place. It is also against this background that the current debate about the legality of certain forms of treatment abatement takes place, especially in terms of the debatable differences that exist between the abatement of life-sustaining treatment and the termination of patients' lives through acts of assisted suicide or euthanasia. When life-sustaining treatment is withdrawn from a critically ill patient, and especially when a patient dies subsequently to the abatement of life-sustaining treatment, the actions of the physician who stopped the treatment have to be explained in a morally and legally acceptable manner. For most pro-life advocates, the range of morally and legally acceptable explanations is limited to options 1–4 in the list just given. For most right-to-die advocates, the range of morally and legally acceptable explanations is expanded to include options 1–6. For some right-to-die advocates, as we have previously discussed, the range of morally and legally acceptable explanations includes all of the options listed.

Among the reasons for this disagreement about alternative ways of justifying patients' deaths is a fundamentally different understanding of the applicability of the principle of nonmaleficence to cases of critically and terminally ill patients. Among pro-life advocates, especially the more extreme ones, the principle of nonmaleficence is applicable to such cases primarily in terms of the traditional-interpretation of death as the ultimate harm that can happen to a patient. According to this view, all other aspects of a patient's case pale in contrast to the prevention of this ultimate harm. Physicians are therefore understood to have an obligation not only to refrain from killing their patients and from helping their patients commit suicide, but also to use whatever technological means they can to forestall their patients' deaths for as long as possible. Especially when patients are not dying and can be sustained for long periods of time with mechanical ventilation and/or technological feeding, the promotion of their best interests seems unquestionably from this perspective to call for the technological prolongation of their lives so that they will not be harmed by what the apostle Paul (in I Corinthians 15:26) once termed "the last enemy."

In sharp contrast, right-to-die advocates are convinced that the principle of nonmaleficence has broader applicability than merely focusing attention on the harm represented by patients' deaths. Although right-to-die advocates disagree about the moral and legal acceptability of euthanasia, they are universally agreed that the principle of nonmaleficence has applicability to the technological means used to sustain the lives of gravely impaired, critically ill, and terminally ill patients. According to this view, *the means used to forestall death* as the end of patients' lives *can themselves seriously harm the patients being kept alive.* The very nature of the medical technology capable of sustaining patients' lives therefore calls for a revision and expansion of the traditional understanding of medically produced harm.

Such a revision of the traditional understanding of harm is hardly new. As we discussed in Chapter 6, the ordinary/extraordinary distinction originated in the sixteenth century precisely because of moral concern over the medically produced harm attendant to the torturous surgical procedures used to prolong patients' lives. Now, of course, moral concern focuses on multiple medical, surgical, and technological ways of prolonging patients' lives, and the ordinary/extraordinary distinction seems to have outlived its usefulness. But the truth to which the distinction pointed four centuries ago still exists: in some instances, the harm caused to patients in the process of trying to prolong their lives outweighs the benefits of keeping them alive.

Discussions about the medical care that is appropriate in particular cases of critical or terminal illness therefore often focus on the possibly harmful aspects of certain life-sustaining treatments. Too frequently, however, such discussions—whether in clinical rounds, case conferences, journal articles, or other settings—stay at a fairly vague level. General references to "suffering," "extraordinary" means, "cruel and unusual punishment," and the "burdens" of treatment abound, with insufficient effort being given to a more precise interpretation of how patients can be harmed while being given life-sustaining treatment—and when such harm is sufficient for patients and other decision makers to conclude that life-sustaining treatment is contrary to the best interests of the patients involved.

There are multiple definitions of harm in the literature, ranging from very broad definitions that include injuries to one's important interests to more narrow definitions that focus on injuries to one's physical well-being. Instead of opting for any one of these definitions, it is more helpful to interpret the several dimensions of the concept of harm as a way of seeing how and when the principle of nonmaleficence applies to cases of critical and terminal illness.

The first dimension of harm is the broadest one and involves *the interference with or the invasion of one's interests.* Commonly used as an interpretation of harm in the legal literature, this dimension of harm pertains to "the violation of one of a person's interests, an injury to something in which he has a genuine stake."[30] To harm another person (or oneself) in this manner can involve any number of interests violated: health, property, reputation, domestic relations, privacy, or life itself. Within this broad range of interests, some interests are clearly more important than others. For most persons, a ranking of these interests in terms of importance normally ends up with life at the top, with health following as a close second. However, as illustrated by the Abe Perlmutter, William Bartling, and Elizabeth Bouvia cases, some autonomous, critically ill patients regard the interest in privacy as sufficiently important to use it as one of the moral and legal reasons for refusing life-sustaining treatment and thereby waiving the interest in life itself.

The second dimension of harm pertains to *the impairment of one's mental and psychological welfare.* Having its roots in the Old English term "hearm," this dimension of harm includes any psychologically defined experience that causes a person mental anguish, emotional disruption, or psychological trauma.[31] To harm another person (or oneself) in this sense is to do something that causes a normal mental and psychological condition to deteriorate. Actions that are harmful under this dimension are deception, harassment, intimidation, "brainwashing," verbal abuse, and any physical affront or invasion of one's "person" resulting in severe anxiety, emotional distress, or depression. The importance of this dimension of harm is evident to anyone familiar with the psychological factors behind many suicides: at least some persons feel sufficiently harmed by life that they regard death preferable to continued living. In a similar manner some autonomous, critically ill patients in ICUs and nursing homes feel sufficiently harmed by life as they currently experience it that they regard death preferable to continued living—especially when that continued living is characterized by mechanical ventilation and/or technological feeding administered against their will, and restraints on their wrists so that they cannot remove the technological apparatus that is sustaining their lives.

The third, and most narrowly focused, dimension of harm includes only *physical injury and the physiological effects of such injury.* To harm another person (or oneself) in this way requires actual physical damage and the pain and suffering that accompany it. In this sense, harm-causing actions include bruising the skin, rupturing the flesh, breaking a bone, subjecting the body to invasive techniques it cannot tolerate (e.g., through the use of chemicals, electricity, or radiation), or invading the body with a foreign object (e.g., a needle, a knife, a bullet) that impairs or paralyzes the normal functioning of one or more organs. The ultimate injury, when harm is interpreted in this manner, is any action that completely disables the heart and/or brain so that death ensues. Short of this ultimate injury, many critically ill patients—including advanced-cancer patients, burn patients, surgical patients, and patients brought back to life with CPR— experience this kind of harm in clinical settings. The key question in such cases is whether there is sufficient benefit in the treatment administered to compensate for the harm caused to the patient by the treatment itself.

A fourth dimension of harm has particular relevance to cases involving nonautonomous patients, although it can be applicable to the medical care provided to other critically ill patients as well. Many nonautonomous patients, depending on the reason for their lack of autonomy, can surely be harmed through physical injury and psychological damage; moreover, at least some of them have important interests that can be violated. Beyond these dimensions of harm, however, is a dimension of harm that applies even to those nonautonomous patients who, because they have a permanent loss of consciousness diagnosed as PVS, cannot be harmed in these other ways because they no longer have important interests to be violated, cannot experience psychological damage, and cannot respond to physicial injury except through reflex actions. However, even these PVS patients (like other nonautonomous patients) can be harmed *through aimless cruelty*. In my view, to use medical technology only to perpetuate minimal biological functions for years in a body that no longer possesses consciousness, no longer has any of the features characteristic of persons, no longer can articulate and defend values formerly held to be important, and no longer has any likelihood of ever regaining consciousness is to engage in an abuse of technology at the expense of a human body unable to defend itself. For such cases, as well as for some cases involving nonautonomous patients who are conscious, an "anticruelty policy" would be a helpful decision-making mechanism.[32] If enacted by IECs and other policy-making bodies, an anticruelty policy would serve to protect PVS patients and other nonautonomous, hopelessly ill/injured patients from being kept alive technologically whenever the prospects of benefit from the treatment administered are outweighed by the futility of the treatments in restoring the kind of life formerly valued by the patient.

Applying the patient's-best-interests standard

As the third stage of the debate over abating treatment continues to develop, the basic conceptual framework for decisions to abate treatment is becoming increasingly clear. Although all parties in the debate do not agree about the conceptual framework, most of those who have seriously wrestled with the issue of abating treatment are in agreement that the PBI standard is the best way of making such decisions—particularly in cases involving nonautonomous patients who have never been autonomous.

I agree. I have tried to show in the preceding pages that (1) the PBI standard is increasingly accepted in medical practice, especially when the medical care available to critically and terminally ill patients is understood as a continuum of treatment options reflecting several of the goals of medicine; (2) the PBI standard is central to biomedical ethics, especially when the standard is understood to represent the focal point for the four dominant ethical principles applicable to medical practice; and (3) the PBI standard is of fundamental importance in recent case law, especially in the number of cases involving nonautonomous patients in the post-*Quinlan* and post-*Conroy* eras. In making these points, I have built on the work already done by three deliberative bodies that deserve credit for having greatly increased our understanding of the PBI standard from the combined perspectives of medicine, ethics, and law: the President's Commission, the New Jersey Supreme Court (in *Conroy*), and the Hastings Center group.[33]

Nevertheless, problems persist in the use of the PBI standard, even though this standard is more objective than the sanctity-of-life standard, the substituted-judgment standard, or the quality-of-life standard. In medicine, the inherent vagueness of the PBI standard causes difficulties in precisely those cases for which the standard is most needed: cases involving patients who have never been autonomous. In law, the pluralistic views of what counts as "best interests" and how such interests can be assessed cause as many problems in treatment-abatement cases with nonautonomous patients as they do in guardianship cases with children, whether the latter cases involve standard issues of parental rights and the welfare of children or newer surrogacy issues arising out of third-party pregnancy contracts. In ethics, the combination of an inherently vague standard and the undeniable pluralism in values that influences how the standard is interpreted leads to different proposals concerning the use of the standard. For example, John Arras, in applying the standard to neonatal cases, suggests that the standard be interpreted narrowly in terms of the pain and physical suffering that severely handicapped infants sometimes have to endure.[34] Richard McCormick argues that the PBI standard is indistinguishable from the quality-of-life standard, and that the latter standard is preferable.[35] Ezekiel Emanuel thinks that the PBI standard is so vacuous that it should be replaced by "community-based standards" that would vary from one community to another.[36]

In my view, the PBI standard remains the best standard available to us, in spite of its vagueness and the differences that often arise in attempting to apply it to particular cases. I think that the PBI standard can be interpreted in a broader manner than Arras suggests, that it is both distinguishable from and preferable to straightforward quality-of-life judgments in many cases, and that it should remain as the operative ethical and legal standard—particularly for cases with nonautonomous patients—in clinical settings in diverse communities. In fact, I have already tried to show how the PBI standard can be helpful in making decisions to abate treatment in cases involving one class of nonautonomous, critically ill patients: namely, neonates for whom decisions must be made about life-sustaining treatment whenever they are extremely premature and/or severely disabled.[37]

Yet McCormick's claim about the relationship of quality-of-life judgments and the best-interests standard is important. If quality-of-life judgments are made as McCormick thinks they should be, with exclusive attention being placed on the patient's good (he emphasizes the "child's good, this alone" when discussing neonatal cases), the relationship between the two standards is indeed close. As a matter of fact, in some cases a serious consideration of the patient's projected quality of life and the patient's best interests would be duplicative.

However, many persons making quality-of-life projections in individual cases of critically ill patients seem not to follow McCormick in restricting quality-of-life considerations to the patient's good. Neither do they, as McCormick does, also emphasize the sanctity of individual patient's lives. Instead, as illustrated by the views of Joseph Fletcher, James Rachels, Jonathan Glover, Peter Singer, and Helga Kuhse (see Chapter 6), the use of the quality-of-life standard can, depending on how it is applied, move beyond emphasizing the patient's good to two errors: an emphasis on the interests of other parties to a case, and/or considerations of an individual patient's social worth.

Let me try to be clear about two possible misinterpretations of the position I am putting forward. First, I do not think, as many pro-life advocates claim, that quality-of-life judgments are necessarily bad. In fact, I think they are an essential feature of determining the patient's best interests in many cases. However, I do not limit the patient's best interests to quality-of-life considerations. Moreover, I think that use of the PBI standard enables us to avoid some of the errors that can occur when surrogate decisions about medical treatment are based exclusively on projections about an individual patient's quality of life in connection with that treatment. Specifically, I think that use of the PBI standard minimizes the possibility that surrogate decision makers in particular cases will make either of the errors mentioned earlier. By focusing on the patient's best interests, and these alone, decision makers can avoid the kind of "crass utilitarianism" (in Paris' words) that often attends use of the quality-of-life standard. The President's Commission agreed, arguing that use of the best-interests standard enables decision makers to concentrate on "the value of the patient's life for the patient."[38]

Second, I do not think that the PBI standard is exceptionless. Rather, I am convinced that in unusual cases, two exceptions exist to a straightforward use of the PBI standard. In some cases of autonomous patients, as we have seen in earlier chapters, the patient's perception of his or her best interests is at variance with what most objective observers of the case regard as the patient's best interests. In such instances, the patient's refusal of treatment means that he or she will *voluntarily* receive less treatment than would be called for through the use of the PBI standard by other participants in the case. In other cases involving autonomous or nonautonomous patients, an objective reading of the patient's best interests may, whenever the needed therapy is very scarce and/or excessively expensive, have to be overridden by policy decisions based on considerations of social justice. In these instances, the patient will, *either involuntarily or nonvoluntarily*, receive less treatment than would be called for through an application of the PBI standard to such cases in isolation from justice-driven policies.

What, then, is meant by the "patient's best interests," and how can the standard be applied to treatment-abatement decisions in individual cases? As used by the courts, the best-interests standard is usually regarded as a reasonably objective standard, contrasted with the substituted-judgment standard, and interpreted as a test of what "reasonable persons" would choose if placed in a particular nonautonomous patient's circumstances. However, the New Jersey Supreme Court, in *Conroy,* moved beyond this dualism of standards to include a third standard that consists of both subjective and objective factors. In the opinion of the court, written by Justice Schreiber, the "limited-objective" test is a compromise standard that contains, to some degree, elements of both the "subjective" test and the "pure-objective" test.[39]

The New Jersey court points us in the right direction. However, the court has not gone far enough in that direction even in its decisions subsequent to *Conroy.* Consequently, I have a suggestion that will take us beyond *Conroy* and, I think, provide decision makers in clinical cases (and in court cases) with an alternative approach that is preferable to the one put forward by the court. My suggestion is fourfold: that we use the PBI standard as *the only ethical standard* necessary and sufficient for making decisions to abate treatment, that we interpret the standard as having a combination of subjective and objective factors, that we apply the standard to individual cases in terms of the subjective and/or objective factors relevant to each case, and that the courts also use the PBI standard as *the only legal standard* relevant to treatment-abatement cases that end up in court. In this way we will move beyond the interminable sanctity-of-life/quality-of-life debate in ethics, get away from the impossible intellectual contortions occasionally required in law when the substituted-judgment test is used (such as ascribing autonomy to a patient who has never been and will never be autonomous), and have available to decision makers in clinical cases a single standard that can be applied to all cases requiring decisions about withholding, decelerating, or withdrawing treatment in the care of critically ill or terminally ill patients.

As a single ethical and legal standard, the PBI standard consists of eight identifiable variables, the first four of which are objective, or at least as objective as the scientific and mathematical foundation of medicine enables practitioners of medicine to be. The other four variables are subjective elements reflecting the fact that decisions about administering or abating treatment inescapably involve human values and moral choice. Put another way, the first four variables require the kind of medical judgments physicians are trained to make, whereas the last four involve value judgments on the part of patients, physicians, relatives of patients, and any other participants in the decision-making process.

These eight variables are listed numerically here, but the numerical order is not intended to suggest greater or lesser importance. Rather, the variables' relative importance depends on the particular facts of an individual clinical case. For any such case, at least some, if not all, of the following considerations must be taken into account in determining whether abating treatment is in the patient's best interests, particularly when the abatement of treatment will predictably result in the patient's death.

1. *The severity of the patient's medical condition.* Accurate diagnosis is the sine qua non of responsible care of patients having serious medical problems. Fortunately, physicians now have access to an array of diagnostic procedures not even imaginable in earlier generations: radiology, ultrasonography, CT scans, MRI scans, EEGs, ECGs, blood gas studies, biopsy techniques, and so on. In addition, physicians in various medical specialties have access to increasingly objective ways of determining the severity of an individual patient's condition compared with other patients having the same kind of disease or injury. Thus intensivists can use TISS or APACHE II to compare the conditions of ICU patients; cardiologists can determine the stage of a heart patient's condition according to the four-stage New York classification system; burn specialists can do empirical and statistical comparisons of patients in terms of the depth of a burn, the location of a burn, and the total body surface area burned; and oncologists and other physicians working with cancer patients can use a variety of procedures to determine the stage of the disease, the functional status of an individual patient (using the Karnofsky Performance Status Scale), and the pattern of metastatic spread of the disease.[40] Because of such objective tests and classification systems, physicians can often give patients or their surrogates a reasonably objective perspective on the severity of a life-threatening medical condition.

2. *The reversibility of the patient's life-threatening medical condition with treatment.* In contrast to the accuracy and precision that are often possible in clinical diagnosis, the related task of prognosis is characterized by subjective appraisals, uncertainty, educated guesses, and predictions that may or may not prove true. Moreover, a physician's forecast of the probable future of a diag-

nosed condition can be influenced by the physician's own inclination to be overly pessimistic (a prognostic strategy known as "hanging crepe") or overly optimistic ("hanging balloons"?) in regard to the course of a critically ill patient's disease or the trajectory of a terminally ill patient's dying. The difficulty of accurate prognosis is perhaps best illustrated by the problems that Medicare-certified hospice programs have whenever a patient predicted to have a 6-month life expectancy dies considerably "too soon" or lives "too long" (either way, the Medicare funding formula means the hospice loses money). Nevertheless, even though predictions regarding life expectancy are not as precise as physicians or patients could wish, the scientific and statistical data available on any individual patient's medical condition do enable the patient's physician(s) to make a much more reliable, and more important prediction regarding the likelihood of the patient's medical condition improving or deteriorating with treatment. This aspect of medical prognosis is crucial for decisions about medical treatment, because decisions to continue or discontinue certain treatments often hang on the medical judgment of a physician regarding the likelihood of a burn patient's returning to a functional life following burn treatment and rehabilitation therapy, a cancer patient's achieving remission following chemotherapy, an unconscious patient's regaining of consciousness, a ventilator patient's returning to spontaneous breathing, a technologically fed patient's resumption of oral feedings, and so forth.

3. *The achievability of important medical goals.* The goals of medicine are multiple and have been developed over the centuries in connection with the ethical principles of respect for autonomy, beneficence, justice, and nonmaleficence. Among the goals of medicine are the prevention of disease, the saving of lives, the effective relief of pain and other forms of suffering, the amelioration of disabling conditions, the effective management of disease-related symptoms, the avoidance of undue harm to patients in the course of treatment, the just allocation of scarce medical resources, and the prolongation of lives.[41] If we lived in a different world, all of these goals might be compatible with one another. Unfortunately, the world in which we live does not always allow such compatibility and in fact often forces decisions on us regarding the relative importance of these various goals. Such decisions occur regularly in the care of critically or terminally ill patients, especially when the goal of relieving the suffering of a patient and the goal of prolonging that patient's life conflict. A related, but different decision arises when the only achievable medical goal in a particular case of a nonautonomous patient is the prolongation of the patient's life, but at such a minimal level that the only "life" being prolonged is organic, not personal.[42]

4. *The presence of serious neurological impairments.* No patient should have life-sustaining treatment withheld, decelerated, or withdrawn merely because the patient is mildly or seriously demented, mentally retarded, or unconscious. How-

ever, the extent of dementia, the degree of retardation, and the predicted permanence of the unconsciousness in individual patients all have to be considered whenever the surrogates of such patients try to determine if a particular form of life-sustaining treatment is in the patient's best interests. If, for example, a profoundly retarded patient is unable to understand either the reasons for receiving a particular form of life-sustaining treatment or the side effects connected with the treatment, that inability to understand is surely one of the necessary considerations in the decision whether to administer the treatment. Especially in cases in which the treatment is not likely to reverse the patient's life-threatening condition but is likely to increase the patient's discomfort and suffering, the patient's inability to comprehend what is going on can be a decisive factor in deciding to abate treatment. Similarly, a severely demented patient's limited ability to understand much of anything connected with one or more kinds of treatment except an increased amount of discomfort, and the inability of a permanently unconscious patient even to experience pain and suffering (much less any of the joys of life) should surely enter into a determination of whether the form of life-sustaining treatment in question in a particular case is or is not in the patient's best interests. Equally important, but different sorts of questions concern what kinds of interests these various patients have, given their current medical conditions; whether the patient now demented, brain-damaged, or permanently unconscious is correctly understood as a former person who had identifiable interests and preferences; and what is to be done when a demented or permanently unconscious patient previously expressed autonomous choices that now seem to objective observers to be contrary to his or her current best interests. Fundamental to all of these questions is an accurate medical assessment of the extent of a given patient's neurological impairment by a psychiatrist or neurologist, depending on the nature of the case.

5. *The presence of unrelieved pain.* The perception of pain is, of course, a matter of subjective experience. Different critically ill patients having the same kind of medical condition and receiving the same kind of treatment experience the intensity of pain in different ways. Moreover, the same patient experiences pain as more or less intense at different times, depending on the numerous variables that influence the perception of pain. Because of the variability of pain perception, the differences in acute pain and chronic pain, the limited understanding of pain on the part of many physicians, and the experience of intense pain by one-half to two-thirds of all critically ill and terminally ill patients, the effective management of pain is a constant challenge to physicians working with such patients. Among the patients who experience the most severe pain—and who present the greatest challenges for medical management—are burn patients and patients with advanced cancer. For patients with third-degree burns over large portions of their bodies, the experience of pain results not only from the physiological, neurological, and emotional effects of the burn itself but also from

the various treatments given the patients. Topical antibacterial therapy, debridement, hydrotherapy, skin grafts, and exercise therapy are all painful experiences that can be countered only to a certain degree with narcotics, nonnarcotic analgesics, behavior-modification techniques, and stress-reduction techniques.[43] For many patients with advanced cancer (especially cancer of the bone, prostate, cervix, mouth, or stomach), the experience of pain is also a major problem. Even with the increasingly effective ways of administering morphine and other narcotics, some cancer specialists estimate that "25 per cent of all cancer patients die without relief from severe pain."[44] The estimated number of such patients (more than 100,000 in the United States, more than 30,000 in the United Kingdom) indicates the seriousness of the problem of unrelieved pain among some patients with advanced cancer. With severely burned patients and advanced-cancer patients, therefore, the presence of intractable pain is a necessary factor in determining whether the abatement of life-prolonging therapy is in the best interests of the patient enduring the pain.

6. *The presence of significant physical and psychological suffering.* Critically ill and terminally ill patients often suffer in ways other than the perception of a painful sensation. They sometimes have nausea, dyspnea, diarrhea, and other physical problems. They also experience anxiety, depression, feelings of separation and loneliness, denial, helplessness, humiliation, anger, and other emotional responses to their injury or disease. These multiple forms of psychological suffering may be triggered in autonomous patients by thoughts about the losses (of health, abilities, physical features, money, opportunities) already caused by the medical condition, or they may be triggered by thoughts related to present realities (physical dysfunction, pain, loss of privacy, insensitive physicians and nurses, multiple tubes and monitors, wrist restraints, the terrifying environment of an ICU), or they may be triggered by thoughts related to an uncertain future (mounting medical and hospital bills, lasting effects of the injury or disease, the prospect of death). Sometimes this psychological suffering can become overbearing, to the point that a patient feels "like a prisoner," "like a hostage to technology," or "like a caged animal." In nonautonomous patients, such psychological suffering is less focused, but no less real. In such instances, the presence of such psychological suffering can exacerbate the patient's pain, cause additional problems of medical management, considerably hamper the effectiveness of the medical treatment being administered, and raise questions about whether the continuation of the treatment is in the patient's best interests.

7. *The patient's perspective on an intolerable life.* The combination of one or more life-threatening medical conditions, unrelieved pain, other forms of physical suffering, and psychological suffering in some of its many forms can persuade some critically ill patients that life, as they personally and presently experience it, has become intolerable. This factor of intolerableness, like the factors of pain and psychological suffering, is obviously subjective. For some

patients, life becomes intolerable when the intense, prolonged pain they experience cannot effectively be relieved. For other patients, such as Dax Cowart, life becomes intolerable in connection with increasing impairment (see Chapter 1). Having endured pain so intense that he frequently lost consciousness, having suffered through burn treatments and rehabilitation therapy for months, and having returned to a reasonably happy, productive life even with blindness and fingerless hands, he says that life would become intolerable for him if he were to lose his hearing and thus not be able to listen to music or the voices of other people.[45] Numerous patients discussed in earlier chapters (Abe Perlmutter, William Bartling, Hector Rodas, and others) clearly demonstrate that life can and sometimes does become intolerable to the person living it. If such a person is unable to commit suicide, he or she may use the factor of intolerableness as a sufficient reason (at least for that person) for refusing additional life-sustaining treatment.

8. *The proportionality of treatment-related benefits and burdens to the patient.* The last factor pertaining to a determination of a patient's best interests is, in many respects, a summation of the previous factors. For the patient, the patient's proxy (possibly having durable power of attorney), a surrogate not chosen by patient, one or more physicians, a guardian, or whoever is responsible for making the decision(s) about abating treatment, a consideration of the benefits of the treatment to the patient as well as the burdens of the treatment to the patient is the "bottom line" for determining whether treatment abatement is in the patient's best interests. The importance of deciding whether the burdens connected with treatment are proportionate to the benefits derived by the patient from the treatment has been affirmed by numerous courts, deliberative bodies, religious authorities, and individuals addressing the issue of treatment abatement.[46] In making such an assessment, of course, the decision maker arrives at a subjective judgment that includes objective factors, but is not finally reducible to computer printouts, statistical data, or any other quantifiable information. In the end, a judgment regarding the proportionality of treatment-related benefits and burdens to the patient is a moral judgment. Moreover, this judgment can easily involve moral conflict, because in assessing the benefits and burdens of the treatment to the patient, one may conclude that a particular course of action is in the patient's best interests even though the interests of the patient's family (or other parties to the case) may cut the other way.

How should the PBI standard be applied to the various kinds of cases that arise?[47] In cases involving *autonomous patients,* as we have discussed at several points in earlier chapters, the patient is the ultimate decision maker. Any time a gravely impaired, critically ill, or terminally ill patient has the capacity to make decisions about his or her medical care, the PBI standard consists entirely of *the patient's perception of his or her best interests.* The patient's perception, hopefully, will be influenced by an accurate reading of the severity of the medical condition, the reversibility of the condition, and the achievability of important medical goals as these matters are communicated by physicians and other health care professionals involved in the case. But in the final analysis, the decision is the patient's decision, whether or not other parties to the case agree. If that decision is to abate treatment, the decision represents the patient's conclusion that the burdens prolonged by life-sustaining treatment (unrelieved pain, physical problems, serious psychological suffering, an intolerable existence) outweigh any benefits that might be gained by means of the treatment (such as improved functioning, lessening of pain, better medical management of debilitating symptoms, longer life). Such a decision should not be thwarted by physicians, nor should it elicit court action unless one or more minor children of the patient would clearly and seriously be harmed by the patient's death.

In terms of nonautonomous patients and patients whose status as autonomous decision makers is uncertain, the applicability of the PBI standard depends on the facts in the case. In cases involving *patients whose decision-making capacity is questionable*—because of shock, senility, mental illness, or youthfulness—the applicability of the PBI standard should be regarded in one of three ways. If the patient's current views or views clearly held earlier (e.g., as expressed in an advance directive, or as clearly expressed in some other manner to relatives and friends) are consistent with the interpretation of the patient's best interests by the physician(s) in the case and the person most likely to be designated as the patient's surrogate, treatment should be administered or abated in the manner all of these persons think is appropriate. If the views of the patient regarding his or her best interests are at variance with those of the physician(s) or likely surrogate, then any decision to abate life-sustaining treatment should be deferred until the patient is believed to have decision-making capacity, if such a delay is medically possible. If such a delay is not possible, the appropriate course of action is, regrettably, to consider the patient as a nonautonomous patient and then to have a surrogate decision maker assess the patient's best interests in the manner that best fits the circumstances of the case.[48]

In cases of patients who are *nonautonomous*—whether the cause is brain damage, profound mental retardation, permanent unconsciousness, or some other reason—the applicability of the PBI standard depends on (1) the availability of some trustworthy evidence of the patient's earlier views on treatment abatement when he or she was autonomous and (2) the particular facts about a case that provide the substantive content for a determination by the patient's surrogate of treatment-related benefits and burdens to the patient. Whenever a nonautonomous patient previously provided explicit treatment directives (written or oral) that were intended for the kind of medical situation that now exists, those earlier expressed preferences and directives should now be followed by health care professionals and the patient's surrogate as *a clear statement of the patient's perception of his or her best interests.* If the patient's earlier preferences fit the current situation, they should carry the same weight—decisive weight—as the decisions made by autonomous patients. In other words, such previously expressed directives that correctly anticipated later medical realities should not now be overridden or ignored by physicians, relatives, or anybody else.

Whenever a nonautonomous patient has not provided explicit written or oral directives regarding life-sustaining treatment, the weight of determining the patient's best interests falls on the patient's surrogate (or proxy, if previously selected by the patient). If the surrogate has personal knowledge of the patient's previous preferences and values (because of familial relationship, or personal relationship as a friend), he or she should try to *interpret the patient's best interests* in the current medical situation *as the patient would have interpreted them.* Likewise, if a "stranger surrogate" (to use Robert Veatch's terminology) has access to reliable sources of information regarding the patient's previous preferences and values, he or she should also try to interpret the patient's best interests in the current medical situation as the patient would have interpreted them. To do so does not require the language of "substituted judgment," nor the fictional practice that calls on a surrogate to "don the mental mantle of the incompetent." Rather, what is required of the surrogate is a careful, honest interpretation of the views previously held by the patient (as expressed in conversations, important decisions, religious beliefs, organizational memberships, life-style, expenditure of personal resources, etc.) and an assessment of the current treatment-related burdens and benefits to the patient in the light of those earlier views.

If the surrogate has no personal knowledge of the patient's "value history" (to use Edmund Pelligrino's language) and also has no access to trustworthy information about the patient's previous preferences and values (perhaps because the patient is profoundly retarded, or possibly because the patient is without relatives and friends), he or she should promote and protect the patient's best interests in as reasonable a manner as is possible. To do so requires an accurate assessment of the patient's medical condition, the prognosis for the patient, the likelihood of achieving important medical goals in addition to prolonging the patient's biological existence, the patient's neurological status, and the extent of pain and other suffering the patient seems to be experiencing. To do so also requires an objective assessment of the specific kinds of benefits that are possible for the patient—such as decreased pain, diminished discomfort, extended life, additional opportunities for pleasure and satisfaction, or the restoration of consciousness for a patient wrongly diagnosed as permanently unconscious—if given life-sustaining treatment in his or her medical circumstances. The same type of objective assessment is required concerning the kinds of burdens that life-sustaining treatment imposes or would impose on the patient, such as intractable pain, physical and psychological suffering, harmful side effects that the patient is incapable of understanding, or an endlessly nonpersonal and uncommunicative existence for a patient correctly diagnosed with PVS.

Making such a judgment about the patient's best interests on the behalf of a nonautonomous patient unknown by the surrogate requires, in some manner, an objective reading of what a reasonable person would decide about his or her own best interests if given the same medical situation, the same prognosis, and the same range of treatment options. Arriving at such a judgment is not, of course, easy. To maximize the possibility that such a judgment is as objective and reasonable as possible, we must have, at least in the more difficult cases, some sort of procedural mechanism that will provide a "check and balance" of the surrogate's decision, lest the patient be harmed by means of a precipitous treatment-abatement decision and a premature death. We will discuss procedural aspects of these decisions in the next chapter.

NOTES

1. The President's Commission, *Deciding to Forego Life-Sustaining Treatment* (Washington, D.C.: U.S. Government Printing Office, 1983), pp. 89–90.
2. The Hastings Center project, *Guidelines on the Termination of Life-Sustaining Treatment and the Care of the Dying* (Briarcliff Manor, N.Y.: The Hastings Center, 1987), p. 5.
3. Cynthia B. Cohen, ed., *Casebook on the Termination of Life-Sustaining Treatment and the Care of the Dying* (Bloomington, Ind.: Indiana University Press; and Briarcliff Manor, N.Y.: The Hastings Center, 1988).
4. For an example of deciding for treatment abatement out of ignorance, see Paul S. Appelbaum and Joel Klein, "Therefore Choose Death?" *Commentary* 81 (April 1986): 23–29. They describe a case in which a spouse refused surgery for her husband's lung tumor, mistakenly believing that exposing the tumor to air would cause it to spread.
5. See Robert M. Veatch, "Limits of Guardian Treatment Refusal: A Reasonableness Standard," *American Journal of Law and Medicine* 9 (1984): 427–68; and Judith Areen, "The Legal Status of Consent Obtained from Families of Adult Patients to Withhold or Withdraw Treatment," *Journal of the American Medical Association* 258 (July 10, 1987): 229–35.
6. Joan Rattner Heilman, "The Miraculous Story of a Coma Survivor," *Redbook,* July 1987, pp. 90–91, 131–32; Society for the Right to Die (SRD), "Newsletter," Spring 1987, pp. 1, 8; and Harry A. Cole, "Deciding on a Time to Die," *Second Opinion* 7 (March 1988): 11–25.
7. Gary v. State of California et al., Case No. 576123, Superior Court of California, San Diego, December 14, 1986; March 5, 1987; and April 15, 1987. For a helpful description of the case, see Concern for Dying (CFD), "Newsletter" 13 (Summer 1987): 3–4.
8. Kirk Johnson, "Hospital Backed in AIDS Right-to-Die Case," *New York Times,* July 28, 1987, p. 9; and *New York Law Journal,* July 28, 1987, p. 11.
9. This medical maxim is quoted by Robert G. Twycross and Sylvia A. Lack, *Symptom Control in Far-Advanced Cancer: Pain Relief* (London: Pitman Publishing,

1983), pp. 8–9; and by Albert R. Jonsen, Mark Siegler, and William J. Winslade, *Clinical Ethics* (New York: Macmillan, 1982), pp. 42 and 109.

10. See Twycross and Lack, *Symptom Control in Far-Advanced Cancer: Pain Relief,* p. 9. Some of the views of these two hospice physicians were presented earlier in Chapter 2.

11. Sidney H. Wanzer et al., "The Physician's Responsibility toward Hopelessly Ill Patients," *The New England Journal of Medicine* 310 (April 12, 1984): 955–59.

12. Ibid., p. 958.

13. Tom L. Beauchamp and Laurence B. McCullough, *Medical Ethics: The Moral Responsibilities of Physicians* (Englewood Cliffs, N.J.: Prentice-Hall, 1984), p. 44.

14. James F. Childress, *Who Should Decide?* (New York: Oxford University Press, 1982), pp. 64–66.

15. Willard Gaylin, "Still, A Person Owns Himself," *New York Times,* December 7, 1982. Reprinted in Annette T. Rottenberg, *Elements of Argument: A Text and Reader* (New York: St. Martin's Press, 1985), pp. 266–68. For the legal case, see In re Lydia E. Hall Hospital, 116 Misc.2d 477, 455 N.Y.S.2d 706 (Sup. Ct. 1982).

16. John Figgis Jewett, "Report from the Committee on Maternal Welfare: Total Exsanguination," *The New England Journal of Medicine* 305 (November 12, 1981): 1218. Quoted by Beauchamp and McCullough in their *Medical Ethics,* p. 35.

17. Harold Hanzlik, "Total Exsanguination after Refusal of Blood Transfusions" (Letter), *The New England Journal of Medicine* 306 (March 4, 1982): 544. Also quoted by Beauchamp and McCullough, *Medical Ethics,* p. 36.

18. See Darrel W. Amundsen, "The Physician's Obligation to Prolong Life: A Medical Duty without Classical Roots," *Hastings Center Report* 8 (August 1978): 23–30.

19. For a discussion of the benefits of medical treatment for neonates, see my "'Baby Doe' after Five Years: Ethical Perspectives," *Infant Mental Health Journal,* forthcoming.

20. Hastings Center project, *Guidelines,* p. 66.

21. For other case examples, see Allan S. Brett and Laurence B. McCullough, "When Patients Request Specific Interventions: Defining the Limits of the Physician's Obligation," *The New England Journal of Medicine* 315 (November 20, 1986): 1347–51.

22. Jonsen, Siegler, and Winslade, *Clinical Ethics,* pp. 156–57; and John C. Moskop, "The Moral Limits to Federal Funding for Kidney Disease," *Hastings Center Report* 17 (April 1987): 11–15.

23. Robert E. Field and Raymond J. Romanus, "A Decerebrate Patient: Eighteen Years of Care," *Connecticut Medicine* 45 (November 1981): 717–19. The cost estimate comes from an accompanying commentary on the case by John Paris, pp. 720–21.

24. President's Commission, *Deciding To Forego,* p. 97.

25. Hastings Center project, *Guidelines,* p. 121.

26. Ibid., p. 123.

27. Quoted in Stanley Joel Reiser, Arthur J. Dyck, and William J. Curran, eds., *Ethics in Medicine* (Cambridge, Mass.: MIT Press, 1977), p. 5.

28. Ibid., p. 5.

29. For a similar listing, see Tom L. Beauchamp and James F. Childress, *Principles of Biomedical Ethics,* 2nd ed. (New York: Oxford University Press, 1983), p. 112.

30. Joel Feinberg, *Social Philosophy* (Englewood Cliffs, N.J.: Prentice-Hall, 1973), p. 26.

31. John Kleining, "Crime and the Concept of Harm," *American Philosophical Quarterly* 15 (January 1978): 27.

32. For a proposal of such a policy, see Susan Braithwaite and David C. Thomasma, "New Guidelines on Foregoing Life-Sustaining Treatment in Incompetent Patients: An Anti-Cruelty Policy," *Annals of Internal Medicine* 104 (1986): 711–15.

33. See the President's Commission, *Deciding to Forego*, pp. 134–36, In re Conroy, 98 N.J. 321, 486 A.2d 1209 (1985); and the Hastings Center project, *Guidelines*, pp. 26–29.

34. John D. Arras, "Toward an Ethic of Ambiguity," *Hastings Center Report* 14 (April 1984): 25–33.

35. Richard A. McCormick, review of my *Selective Nontreatment of Handicapped Newborns*, in *Perspectives in Biology and Medicine* 29 (Winter 1986): 327–29.

36. Ezekiel J. Emanuel, "A Communal Vision of Care for Incompetent Patients," *Hastings Center Report* 17 (November 1987): 15–20.

37. See my *Selective Nontreatment of Handicapped Newborns*, pp. 234–43; and my " 'Baby Doe' After Five Years: Ethical Perspectives," *supra*, n. 19.

38. President's Commission, *Deciding to Forego*, p. 135, n. 43.

39. In re Conroy, *supra*, 486 A.2d 1209, 1232 (1985).

40. See Vincent Mor, Linda Laliberte, John Morris, and Michael Wiemann, "The Karnofsky Performance Status Scale: An Examination of Its Reliability and Validity in a Research Setting," *Cancer* 53 (1984): 2002–7.

41. For other lists of the goals of medicine, see Jonsen, Siegler, and Winslade, *Clinical Ethics*, pp. 13–14; and Beauchamp and McCullough, *Medical Ethics*, p. 37.

42. Jonsen, Siegler, and Winslade, *Clinical Ethics*, p. 149.

43. Janet A. Marvin and David M. Heimbach, "Pain Control during the Intensive Care Phase of Burn Care," in Thomas L. Wachtel, guest ed., *Critical Care Clinics: Burns* 1/1 (March 1985): 147–57.

44. Twycross and Lack, *Symptom Control in Far-Advanced Cancer: Pain Relief*, p. 8.

45. This point is made in the film "Dax's Case," produced by CFD in 1984.

46. See Barber v. Superior Court, 147 Cal. App.3d 1006, 195 Cal. Rptr. 484 (1983); In re Conroy, *supra*, 486 A.2d 1209 (1985); Brophy v. New England Sinai Hospital, Inc., 398 Mass. 417, 497 N.E.2d 626 (1986); President's Commission, *Deciding to Forego*, pp. 88–89; Hastings Center project, *Guidelines*; the Sacred Congregation for the Doctrine of the Faith, *Declaration on Euthanasia* (Vatican City, May 5, 1980); The Pope John XXIII Medical-Moral Research and Education Center, "When Should Catholic Facilities Permit Withdrawal of Life-Sustaining Procedures?" *Hospital Progress* (October 1983): 76–77; and articles previously cited in Chapter 6 by John Paris, Richard McCormick, Robert Veatch, and James Childress.

47. My views expressed here have been substantially influenced by the *Conroy* decision and by the Hastings Center *Guidelines*, pp. 26–29, but I choose to use somewhat different categories for patients.

48. Hastings Center project, *Guidelines*, p. 27.

9

An Agenda for the Future

For humane reasons, with informed consent, a physician may do what is medically necessary to alleviate severe pain, or cease or omit treatment to permit a terminally ill patient whose death is imminent to die. . . . Even if death is not imminent but a patient's coma is beyond doubt irreversible and there are adequate safeguards to confirm the accuracy of the diagnosis and with the concurrence of those who have responsibility for the care of the patient, it is not unethical to discontinue all means of life-prolonging treatment. . . . Life-prolonging medical treatment includes medication and artificially or technologically supplied respiration, nutrition or hydration.

The Council on Ethical and Judicial Affairs
of the American Medical Association[1]

As our story has become more widely known I have tried to determine how it fits into the right to life and death debate. I believe it fits at the point where I can adequately respond to the question most often asked of me: How could I, as a "man of God," decide to remove my wife [Jacqueline Cole] from her life-support systems while she was still legally, and medically, alive? . . . I simply wanted what was best for Jackie. I loved her and felt the need to make a fitting, yet heartbreaking, moral choice in response to the worst of all possible life and death situations. . . . I have always believed that the practice of medicine involves a moral obligation to try to cure an illness, even if it is predictably fatal. However, I also believe that the obligation to cure or even to support life in the face of an incurable illness ceases to exist when it can no longer contribute to a patient's ability or desire to live a purposeful life. . . . I regarded the court procedure as an unnecessary and unwelcome intrusion into a deeply personal matter. . . .

HARRY A. COLE, M.DIV.[2]

This chapter is the third part of my attempt to put forth a responsible position on the ethics of abating treatment. Ideally, it will be read in connection with the earlier chapters in the book, especially Chapters 7 and 8. In this respect, the chapter represents an effort on my part to expand on the themes, tie up the loose ends, answer some of the questions, and plug up some of the holes that have appeared in the earlier chapters. When read in this manner, the chapter is a summary and expansion of the earlier chapters.

In another respect, the chapter represents a beginning as well as an ending. The complexity of the issue of abating treatment—in terms of medicine, ethics, law, and public policy—means that a lot of serious-minded people have serious disagreements over certain aspects of the issue.[3] Moreover, the similarities between the issue of abating treatment and other end-of-life issues—especially euthanasia, as emphasized both by pro-life advocates and by utilitarian right-to-die advocates—means that the moral controversy over the appropriate way of making end-of-life decisions on the behalf of others is hardly likely to end with the publication of this book. Nevertheless, perhaps this chapter can help shape the agenda for the next phase of the debate.

To that end, this chapter will consist of questions and answers concerning some of the more difficult aspects of abating medical treatment, especially when a patient's death is the likely outcome. The responses to some of the questions will not be novel in that they will simply indicate my agreement with the "mainstream" views already put forth by various courts, the President's Commission, the members of the Hastings Center project on treatment termination, and numerous professionals in medicine, ethics, and law. The responses to other questions may be controversial for either of two reasons: (1) the questions being asked focus on aspects of abating treatment over which there is considerable disagreement, and/or (2) the positions I take are subject to criticism. Either way, my wrestling with some of the difficult aspects of abating treatment may be helpful to others.

Questions about substance, procedures, and policy

Considerable progress has been made during the second and third phases of the debate over the morality and legality of abating treatment with critically ill patients. Many of the earlier substantive and procedural questions regarding treatment abatement have been answered as we have worked out an ethical and legal consensus on many aspects of this complex issue. Consequently, few people would now deny that medical treatments can be administered only (outside of emergency situations) with the informed consent of autonomous patients, that patients with decision-making capacity have a moral and legal right to refuse any medical treatments they do not want, that the interests of nonautonomous patients can be represented by surrogates, and so on. Nevertheless, questions remain concerning some of the substantive aspects of abating treatment, other questions arise concerning the most appropriate procedural ways of handling cases with nonautonomous patients, and still other questions focus on treatment abatement as a matter of public and institutional policy.

What should be done when adult patients with questionable
decision-making capacity refuse life-sustaining treatment?

Treatment refusal by an adult patient often creates a crisis in a hospital or nursing home. The crisis may be due to the emergency situation in which the refusal takes place (as happened in a number of the early Jehovah's Witnesses cases), the high stakes involved in a patient's refusal of treatment needed to stay alive, mismanagement of a case by physicians or nurses, poor communication between a patient and the health care professionals responsible for the patient's care, the particular patient who refuses treatment, a physician's taking the refusal of recommended treatment as a personal affront, and/or anxiety about legal consequences on the part of the physician. An interesting example of the crisis environment that can result from a treatment refusal recently took place in the Elizabeth Bouvia case. One of Bouvia's nurses anxiously contacted the attending physician to report that the patient was "refusing to be turned," thus raising the spectre of a battle of wills, the increased likelihood of Bouvia's getting decubitus ulcers, and the possibility of additional legal problems. In fact, as it turned out when the physician arrived at the scene, Bouvia had refused to be turned in bed simply because she was watching a favorite television program and did not want to be turned until the program was over.[4]

Since Bouvia had been adjudicated as competent in two court hearings in the previous 5 years, none of the nurses caring for her should have doubted her capacity to understand something as simple as being turned in bed to minimize the possibility of bedsores. But if another patient with a similar medical condition had refused this simple form of nursing care—or something much more important—questions might have been legitimately raised regarding the patient's decision-making capacity. When patients with critical or terminal conditions refuse recommended medical treatment, the health care professionals caring for them often wonder about any of several possible factors that could be impeding an individual patient's capacity to make an informed, voluntary decision: the presence of significant anxiety or depression, significant drug use prior to admittance to the hospital, the presence of shock, vacillation in the patient's point of view, severe pain, drugs administered in the hospital or nursing home to combat pain or psychological problems, the possibility of mental illness, unusual influence on the patient's opinion by relatives, the presence of guilt, and so on. In such circumstances, physicians and nurses understandably wonder if a patient who refuses treatment actually understands the implications of the treatment refusal and has the capacity to make a sufficiently thoughtful refusal of the treatment.

Too frequently, physicians caring for patients with questionable decision-making capacity make either of two mistakes: they automatically reject the possible legitimacy of the patient's refusal of treatment because of the patient's physical or mental *status* (e.g., advanced age, a history of mental illness), or they reject the patient's refusal of treatment because the predicted *outcome* of the patient's decision makes the decision objectively "unreasonable" or "wrong" in the physician's view.[5] Believing that the patient's choice is poorly informed, inadequately reasoned, and/or contrary to the patient's well-being, such physicians proceed to adopt any of three strategies that may fit the situation: (1) refuse to accept the refusal, exhort the patient to change his or her mind, and use anger as a psychological tool to get a reversal of the patient's decision, (2) immediately try to circumvent the patient's decision by turning to the patient's family in the hope that they will counter the patient's choice by agreeing with the physician on the "right" decision, or (3) call for a psychiatric consultation.

All of these strategies can be misguided, for two fundamental reasons. First, by adopting any of these strategies, a physician may simply be *imposing his or her own agenda on a patient* rather than actually trying to determine whether that patient has the capacity to make a decision regarding the initiation, continuation, or abatement of treatment. For the purposes of saving time, being efficient, getting on with business, and other motivating reasons, a physician who is angered and frustrated by a patient's refusal of treatment may resort to deception and coercion to get a noncompliant patient to agree to treatment, as in the case of a senior attending physician in a teaching hospital who ordered a resident to go to the room of an older patient who had refused amputation and "get the damn consent."[6] Alternatively, a physician who disagrees with a patient's refusal of treatment may leap to the conclusion that the patient lacks decision-making capacity without taking the time and making the effort to assess the basis (or bases) for the treatment refusal.[7]

Psychiatric consultations provide the best example of the imposition of a medical (and sometimes legal) agenda on a patient whose decision-making capacity is questionable. Although psychiatrists are often used as consultants in clinical cases and as expert witnesses in legal cases concerning the competency of particular patients, the methodology employed by psychiatrists often seems ill-fitted to clinical cases involving treatment refusal. A standard approach is the use of one or more tests to determine a patient's "mental status." The most basic test is an attempt to determine whether a particular patient is "oriented times three" (oriented as to the correct date, correct place, and correct personal identity). Other mental status tests involve copying simple geometric figures, interpreting simple proverbs, and counting backward by sevens from 100 (the latter test being known as "serial sevens"). The problem with such tests in the context of a treatment-refusal case is that they constitute a standard psychiatric agenda that may indicate something about a patient's basic orientation to reality and something about that individual's simple skills in abstract and mathematical reasoning, yet not clearly indicate whether the patient understands and appreciates the seriousness of forgoing an amputation, kidney dialysis, technological feeding, or some other life-sustaining treatment.[8]

The second problem with the strategies just listed is that they tend to be based on *a narrow understanding of the patient's-best-interests (PBI) standard.* By trying to override or circumvent a refusal of treatment by a questionably autonomous patient, a physician is often simply acting out his or her own belief that the treatment in question is objectively in the patient's best interests. The objectivity of that judgment may be based on clinical tests, the patient's prognosis, the physician's ability to prolong the patient's life with medical technology, or an educated guess about what most people would decide to do in a medical situation similar to the patient's situation. While all of these are important aspects of the PBI standard, they do not address the question of the patient's decision-making capacity, nor do they automatically determine that the treatment being refused (either verbally or nonverbally) is actually in the best interests of the patient doing the refusing. If the patient lacks decision-making capacity, and has not previously indicated personal preferences regarding life-sustaining treatment, these objective factors can be definitive in determining that the refused treatment should be administered over the patient's objections. However, if the patient refusing treatment actually understands and appreciates the implications of forgoing treatment that can sustain his or her life, the refusal of life-sustaining treatment is more than likely based on one or more of the subjective aspects of the PBI standard discussed in the previous chapter: unrelieved pain, significant physical and psychological suffering, the patient's perspective on an intolerable life, and/or the patient's perspective on the proportionality of treatment-related benefits and burdens.

When the treatment being refused is capable of sustaining the patient's life, the stakes involved in trying to assess the patient's decision-making capacity are obviously very high. It is for precisely this reason that any attempt to assess the patient's autonomous capacity specific to a decision to abate treatment should be made in the moral context established by the PBI standard. It is clearly not in the best interests of a *nonautonomous* patient to die prematurely because he or she was denied medical treatment that would have, on balance, been beneficial to the patient and would have been chosen by most autonomous patients with the same kind of disease or injury. Equally important, it is not in the best interests of an *autonomous* patient to be forced to receive life-sustaining treatment that prolongs an intolerable existence for the patient and that, were the patient physically able to do so, would be physically rejected by the patient.

Given the high stakes, any refusal of life-sustaining treatment by an adult patient with questionable decision-making capacity should be handled with great care. As a beginning point, any adult patient should be presumed to be autonomous (and legally competent) unless demonstrated otherwise. The presumption of an adult patient's autonomous status means that physicians, nurses, and other health care professionals should interpret a patient's consent to recommended treatment or refusal of recommended treatment as being voluntary and deliberative on the patient's part, and consistent with the patient's value system, unless something the patient says or does creates doubt regarding the patient's capacity to make such a decision. As long as the patient consents to recommended treatment, doubt concerning the patient's decision-making capacity is not likely to be engendered among members of the health care team. However, a refusal to accept medically recommended treatment, especially life-sustaining treatment, almost always and understandably serves as the "trigger" for such doubt.

When doubt arises regarding an adult patient's decision-making capacity, it is important for physicians, other health care professionals, and members of the patient's family to try to assess the reasons behind the disagreement over the recommended treatment. Where does the locus of the problem lie: with the patient who has refused the treatment, the physician who has recommended the treatment, or possibly with members of the patient's family? Sometimes the problem lies not in a patient's inability to make an informed, deliberative refusal of treatment but in the attending physician's inability to accept (or a family member's inability to accept) the patient's refusal of treatment as a reasonable decision in the circumstances brought on by a life-threatening illness. In such circumstances, as we have seen in cases presented earlier, the attending physician (or relatives of the patient) may question the patient's decision-making capacity as part of a strategy believed necessary to prevent the patient's premature death.

There are, however, numerous cases in which the problem does lie with the patient, and has to do with genuine doubt on the part of health care professionals (and, in some cases, the patient's family) regarding the patient's capacity to make an autonomous decision specific to the realities of a life-threatening illness, one or more treatment options that may prove beneficial to the patient's condition, and the predictable outcome of death apart from the life-sustaining treatment. In other words, there are many cases in which the patient's decision-making capacity is questioned for reasons other than (1) the patient's physical or mental status (as a defining category), (2) the unacceptability of the patient's refusal of treatment, (3) the personal beliefs, interests, and values of the physician(s) in the case, or (4) the beliefs, interests, and values of the patient's relatives.

If the patient in such a case is not clearly lacking in decision-making capacity (e.g., unable to make a decision at all), if the patient's medical condition does not present an emergency situation, and if the patient's questionable decision-making capacity does not seem to be medically reversible (e.g., by a change in the drugs being administered), the attending physician bears the primary responsibility of assessing whether, in fact, the patient is capable of making an informed refusal of treatment that in all likelihood will result in the patient's death. To make this assessment, the physician (preferably in consultation with nurses and responsible members of the patient's family) should use *an interactional approach* with the patient, according to which he or she determines that the patient does or does not have the *functional ability* to make an adequately informed, sufficiently deliberative, and personally authentic decision specific to the recommended life-sustaining treatment.[9]

Given the seriousness of the decision to refuse life-sustaining treatment, the physician(s) interacting with the patient should err in the direction of having a more stringent standard for assessing decision-making capacity than would be necessary in cases of treatment refusal when forgoing treatment is less risky to the patient and/or the probable benefits of the recommended treatment are less certain to the physician. Several proposals for variable standards for assessing decision-making capacity have been put forward.[10] The most complete proposal, developed by James Drane, consists of a "sliding scale" for assessing the decision-making capacity of patients. According to this proposal, the least stringent standard (applicable to refusals of ineffective treatments) requires only the patient's *awareness* of the general situation and *assent* to recommendations of easy, effective treatments. A more stringent standard (applicable to refusals of possibly effective, but burdensome treatments) requires the patient to *understand* the risks and outcomes of alternative treatment options and be able to *choose* one of these somewhat uncertain treatments. Finally, the most stringent standard (applicable to refusals of life-sustaining treatment) requires the patient to have the capacity to *appreciate* the personal significance of the treatment refusal and be able to *give reasons* for the decision.[11]

In terms of clinical practice, an interactional approach aimed at assessing a patient's capacity to refuse life-sustaining treatment should usually take the form of one or more conversations (preferably more, over a period of several days) between the attending physician (or physicians) and the patient. On these occasions the physician(s) should, in attempting both to respect the level of autonomy possessed by the patient and to promote the patient's well-being, focus on why the patient regards the recommended treatment as being contrary to his or her best interests (as the patient perceives these interests), and the reasons the patient may put forward for that moral judgment.

In such interactions with the patient, the physician should try to determine whether the patient has the *general* autonomy necessary to understand, deliberate about, and freely decide against the administration of recommended life-sustaining treatment. In addition, the physician should try to determine whether the patient who refuses one or more forms of life-sustaining treatment has the *specific* autonomy necessary to make a decision to abate treatment that is consistent with his or her value system, to communicate that decision verbally or nonverbally, and to appreciate the personal implications of that decision in terms of his or her continued life. In making such a determination of the patient's decision-making capacity, the physician should have exchanges with the patient that cover the basic cognitive and decisional components of autonomy that were discussed in Chapter 3 (see Table 9.1).[12]

If the attending physician concludes after using this interactional approach that the patient understands and appreciates the risks entailed in the treatment refusal, no attempt should be made to override or circumvent that decision. By contrast,

TABLE 9.1   Questions for physicians to ask in assessing patient autonomy and decision-making capacity

Cognitive and decisional component of autonomy	Possible questions to the patient
Understanding	How would you describe your present physical condition?
	What is the treatment that is medically necessary for your condition?
	How will this treatment help you if you start it/stay with it?
	What problems could you have if you accept the treatment/ continue the treatment?
	What is likely to happen to you without the treatment?
Deliberation	Can you explain to me why you do not want to start/continue the treatment that can prolong your life?
	Do you think the pain you are experiencing is not going to get better?
	Is it possible that the treatment will make you feel better?
	Do you think the treatment is only going to prolong your physical and emotional suffering?
	Do you think you would rather not live than to continue living this way?
Voluntariness (focusing on internal and external constraints that could control decision making)	Have you been a patient in a hospital/nursing home before?
	What bothers you about this place?
	If you could change something about your situation, what would you like to change?
	What concerns you most about your future and your family's future?
	Are you aware that I am willing to accept your refusal of treatment, even though I do not agree with your decision?
	What do your relatives think should be done?
Authenticity	Have you always tended to be independent?
	Do you prefer to make your own decisions about important matters?
	Have you thought previously about the possibility of having this kind of illness/injury?
	Have you discussed the possibility of this kind of illness/injury with your relatives or friends?
	Have you communicated your present views to them?
Communication (regarding verbal comments or nonverbal communication)	Am I understanding you correctly?
	Am I right in thinking you do not want to start/continue the treatment I have recommended?
	Am I correct in believing that you think the recommended treatment is not worth having?
Appreciation	Do you realize that the treatment I want you to start/continue is the only way of prolonging your life?
	Do you realize that without the treatment, you will almost surely die within a fairly short period of time?

if the physician concludes that the patient lacks the capacity to make a decision specifically in regard to the recommended treatment, he or she should consider the patient to be nonautonomous and proceed to arrange for a surrogate to make a decision regarding the recommended treatment in terms of the patient's best interests (as discussed in Chapter 8). Neither conclusion should require a psychiatric consultation in most cases, unless there is evidence of a psychiatric illness requiring expert assessment. Moreover, neither conclusion about the patient's decision-making capacity requires the agreement of the patient's family, although they (and the patient) should be able to challenge through institutional channels a determination that the patient lacks decision-making capacity. Finally, neither conclusion about the patient's decision-making capacity requires the involvement of the courts, except as a last resort in very unusual cases.

When should a minor be permitted to refuse life-sustaining treatment?

As illustrated by the cases of Scott Rose (see Chapter 1) and Pamela Hamilton (Case 4.11), critically ill adolescents present their parents, physicians, nurses, and the rest of us with questions about decision-making capacity and the right of autonomous patients to refuse life-sustaining treatment. Traditionally, case and statutory law has functioned with an arbitrary age of majority (now 18 for most actions, in most jurisdictions), has presumed all individuals not having reached the established age of majority to be incompetent in regard to decisions of legal significance, and has therefore required that decisions involving consent to medical treatment or the refusal of medical treatment be made on the behalf of minors by their parents or legal guardians. Physicians, usually conservative about matters of health law, have generally subscribed to this legal presumption of minors' incompetence, and have therefore sought the consent of adolescents' parents (outside of emergency situations) before administering medical treatment to teenage patients—and surely before abating medical treatment that is capable of sustaining patients' lives.

The reasons behind this traditional approach in law and medicine are both paternalistic and practical. In terms of paternalism, adults have been interested in protecting adolescents from making ill-advised decisions and thereby harming themselves psychologically, physically, or financially (through contracts). To carry out this interest in protecting young patients in clinical settings, adults have erred in the direction of promoting the well-being of adolescent patients at the cost of ignoring or minimizing the preferences and choices often communicated by the patients themselves. Moreover, this paternalistic approach has blended with some of the practical realities of the value choices made by teenagers. Compared with adults, adolescents frequently differ in terms of their decisions about music, clothing, hairstyles, food, cars, management of money, management of time, and—sometimes!—virtually everything else. In regard to decisions about medical treatment, adolescents often place much more importance on body image, "quick fixes," physical attractiveness, and ambulation following treatment than do adult patients faced with similar treatment choices.

Nevertheless, in recent years a discernible trend has developed that correctly reflects two of the facts of individual human development: decision-making capacity differs in degree from one individual to another, and "maturity" is not limited to (or always evidenced by) individuals who have reached the age of 18. In part, this trend is evident in the United States in the continually expanding case and statutory law "exceptions" to the traditional presumption regarding the incompetence of minors: "emancipated" minors (on the basis of marriage, military service, consent of parents, or judicial order), "mature" minors (on the basis of their ability to understand the nature and purposes of recommended medical treatments), and minors empowered by specialized consent statutes to obtain medical treatment for specific diseases or conditions (usually sexually transmitted diseases or drug abuse) apart from parental approval.[13] In part, this trend is evident in the jurisprudence of other countries. For example, minors in the United Kingdom who are 16 or older have been able to give legally valid consent to medical treatment since 1969, and a combination of case law and statutory law in the provinces of Ontario and Quebec has granted some minors in Canada considerable freedom in making their own decisions about health care (minors aged 14 or older in Quebec can give valid consent to recommended medical treatment).[14] An additional part of the trend has to do with medical and socioscientific studies that now tend to support the claim of Justice William O. Douglas, in his 1972 dissenting opinion in *Wisconsin v. Yoder,* that "the moral and intellectual maturity of the 14-year-old approaches that of the adult."[15]

In my view, this trend toward greater acceptance of the health care decisions by teenagers is long overdue and has obvious implications for the decisions critically ill teenagers make in regard to life-sustaining treatment. I have no doubt that many critically ill, adolescent patients (like Scott Rose) are capable of understanding the options of continuing treatment or abating treatment, deliberating about the ramifications of those alternatives, freely choosing the alternative that is most consistent with their value systems, and appreciating the personal implications of their decisions. At the same time, as a parent of two teenagers and as a university professor, I am also aware of the inherent limitations in some teenagers' reasoning skills and the ease with which teenage peers and authority figures can sometimes influence the thinking of adolescents. The Pamela Hamilton case provides an example. Not only was she, at the age of 12, significantly younger (particularly in a developmental sense) than Scott Rose; she was also controlled in important ways, according to the press reports at the time, by the fundamentalist religious environment in which she had been reared and the strong antimedical views held by her father and other members of the religious sect.

To affirm the decisions to abate treatment made by adolescent patients such as Scott Rose and to protect the Pamela Hamiltons of the world from premature deaths, physicians caring for critically ill, adolescent patients should use some version of the interactional approach described in Table 9.1 to determine which of their patients are, in fact, capable of making autonomous decisions about the treatment options presented to them. To promote the self-determination of adolescent patients and to promote their individual well-being, particularly in situations of critical or terminal illness, physicians need regularly to interact with their patients in an attempt to ascertain which patients have the functional capacity to make decisions that could, if carried out, result in their own deaths. Adolescent patients who have this decision-making capacity can be regarded as autonomous patients, in both the general and specific senses of autonomy discussed earlier.

In working with such patients, physicians and other health care professionals should be alert to (1) the functional capacity, rather than only the biological age of the patient, (2) the patient's perception of whether, and how, the recommended treatment is in his or her best interests, or is contrary to those interests, (3) the views of the patient's parent(s) regarding the administration or abatement of the life-sustaining treatment available to the patient, and (4) the interactions between the patient and his or her parent(s). Along the way physicians also need to be alert to any evidence suggesting significant internal or external constraints (such as parental pressure) on the voluntariness of the patient's decision.

Given the differences in the autonomous status of adolescent patients, as well as the legal requirements imposed on physicians caring for adolescent patients, physicians should follow two general guidelines in connection with the possibility of abating life-sustaining treatment in individual cases. First, adolescent patients aged *14 and older should be presumed to be autonomous* patients for the purpose of consenting to or refusing medical treatment, except when individual patients demonstrate that they do not have the necessary decision-making capacity. Abating life-sustaining treatment with any autonomous, adolescent patient should also involve the consent of the patient's parent(s) or guardian. Serious differences of opinion about treatment abatement between such a patient and his or her parent(s) or guardian may be resolvable at the institutional level, but will probably require a judicial hearing. Second, adolescent patients aged 11 to 13 should be *presumed to be nonautonomous* in regard to making decisions about treatment abatement, except when, in rare cases, individual patients demonstrate a decision-making capacity advanced beyond their chronological years. Stated another way, the burden of proof is on a patient in this early, transitional period of adolescence to show that he or she can understand the treatment options, deliberate about the alternatives available, voluntarily decide to forgo treatment, and appreciate the personal implications of that decision. In the great majority of cases, such autonomous decision making will not be possible for such young patients. Instead, abating life-sustaining treatment with these early adolescents—as unusual as this decision is—should involve the *consent* of the patient's parent(s) or guardian and the patient's *assent* to that decision.

Should a patient's advanced age be regarded as an important
consideration in abating life-sustaining treatment?

The advanced age of a large segment of the population is an undeniable feature of life in the United States and the United Kingdom in the latter part of the twentieth century—as is, unfortunately, the prejudice and discrimination that is directed against the older members of society. The pervasiveness of the "age issue" is illustrated by a sign in a West Virginia cafe: "Don't criticize the coffee. You may be old and weak yourself someday."[16]

In terms of the issue of abating treatment, the consideration of advanced age in many critically and/or terminally ill patients confronts health care professionals and the rest of us with two problems that are not going to disappear. The first of the problems has to do with the relationship between advanced age and the autonomous status of individual elderly patients as they are asked to make decisions about their own medical care. The second problem has to do with the justifiability of using advanced age as a specific category in institutional or governmental policies of limiting medical treatment to certain classes of patients with critical or terminal conditions.

Regarding the first problem, the consideration of advanced age in individual patients is significant for a number of reasons discussed in Chapter 2. For older patients and for the relatives and health care professionals who care for them, the multiple effects of the aging process on individuals influence the medical problems common to older persons, the treatment options presented to older patients, the decisions made in relation to those options, and the locations in which medical and nonmedical care is given to older patients. Of central importance to our discussion, the consideration of advanced age also influences whether individual patients, their physicians and nurses, and their relatives regard particular life-sustaining technologies to be in the best interests of a given patient or contrary to the patient's best interests at least in part because of the patient's advanced age. Moreover, when a patient in the advanced years of life refuses a form of life-sustaining treatment that is regarded as medically necessary by the physician(s) in the case and/or by the patient's relatives, questions are frequently raised about whether the patient actually understands the life-and-death implications of the choice he or she has made.

In my view, cases involving the possibility of abating life-sustaining treatment in the care of individual geriatric patients are best approached in the following manner. First, all persons involved in such cases should *distinguish between age and functional ability.*[17] The fact of a patient's advanced age—whether it is 75, 80, 85, or older—does not mean that mechanical ventilation, feeding tubes, antibiotics, and other forms of life-sustaining intervention are contrary to his or her best interests. In some cases, *all* modalities of life-sustaining treatment are contrary to a geriatric patient's best interests because of the severity of the patient's medical condition, the physician's inability to reverse the downward course of the patient's life-threatening condition, and the patient's ongoing problems with pain, difficulty in breathing, and other forms of suffering. In other cases, the opposite is true. Because of differences in genetics, physiology, diet, exercise habits, life-style, environment, and other relevant factors, it is possible for some geriatric patients to respond better to treatment and have a better prognosis than some significantly younger patients with the same kind of life-threatening condition. The essential point has to do with variability in functional ability regardless of age, not the fact of advanced age itself.

Second, geriatric patients regardless of chronological age should be *presumed to be autonomous* patients for the purpose of consenting to or refusing medical treatment, except when individual patients demonstrate that they do not have the necessary decision-making capacity. Simply because a patient is in the advanced phase of life, is in a hospital or long-term care facility, and refuses a form of life-sustaining treatment that the patient's physician(s) and relatives regard as potentially beneficial does not mean that the patient is demented or delirious. Rather, the patient may simply have decided, on the basis of his or her own perception of unrelieved pain, ongoing psychological suffering, and/or an intolerable personal existence, that the burdens connected with living with the treatment outweigh the possible benefits provided by the treatment. Before acceding to the patient's refusal of treatment, however, a responsible physician should (1) interact with the patient along the lines suggested earlier to determine if the patient possesses the general and specific aspects of autonomy necessary for a justifiable refusal of life-sustaining treatment and (2) discuss with the patient his or her medical condition and the projected benefits of the recommended treatment at greater length, to ensure the patient's refusal of treatment is sufficiently informed.

Third, the *factor of advanced age alone* may justifiably be used by an autonomous patient in personally refusing life-sustaining treatment, but should *not* be used by the surrogates of geriatric patients who are asked to make decisions about the initiation, continuation, or abatement of life-sustaining treatment on the behalf of individuals unable to make such decisions themselves. The point is a fundamental one. Geriatric patients (and other patients) who are capable of understanding and appreciating the personal implications of their decisions to forgo one or more forms of life-sustaining treatment have a latitude or degree of moral freedom in making that decision that no one has or should have when carrying out the role of life-and-death decision maker on the behalf of someone else. If a geriatric patient voluntarily chooses to consider his or her own advanced age as a factor in deciding to refuse life-sustaining treatment, and if the personal consideration of age seems consistent with the value system he or she has had over the years, the patient's physician(s) and relatives should be willing to abide by the decision. By contrast, no surrogate of a nonautonomous geriatric patient should use the patient's age as a separate factor in determining whether the administration or abatement of life-sustaining treatment is in the patient's best interests. Simply because a demented, or severely retarded, or permanently unconscious patient is 84 or 92 (pick any number over 80), does not give someone else the right to declare that the patient has lived "long enough" or "too long." There may be justifiable reasons for deciding that the available life-sustaining treatment is contrary to the best interests of such a patient, but the patient's age alone is not one of them.

Now we turn to the second age-related problem mentioned earlier. Several thoughtful persons have wrestled with the question of whether advanced age can justifiably be used as a criterion in policy decisions to limit the allocation of life-sustaining technologies.[18] The same question has been addressed by members of the Hastings Center project on treatment-termination guidelines and by the staff and advisory panel of the Office of Technology Assessment (OTA) in their study of life-sustaining technologies used in the care of older persons.[19] Both of these deliberative groups urge policy makers to exercise caution in restricting health care on the basis of advanced age, but conclude that carefully formulated allocation policies based on age may be justifiable. In the words of the Hastings Center group, "there may be reasons for using age as a yardstick in making policy choices and allocation decisions."[20] The principles put forth by the OTA advisory panel emphasize that decision making in individual cases should not use a patient's chronological age as the decisive factor in abating treatment, but also state that "age may be a legitimate modifier regarding appropriate utilization of life-sustaining medical technologies."[21]

I agree, with some reluctance. I have already argued that in individual cases of critically or terminally ill patients, decisions regarding the abatement of life-sustaining treatment should be based on the PBI standard. That standard, as discussed in the previous chapter, encompasses several aspects of individual cases and applies to all cases involving critically or terminally ill patients— regardless of the patient's age. No geriatric patient, in trying to survive a life-threatening condition or injury, should have to worry about the physician(s) in the case possibly abating life-sustaining treatment on the basis of the patient's advanced age, whereas another geriatric patient with the same age and similar medical condition but under the care of other physicians (in the same hospital or a different hospital) receives the needed life-sustaining technology. Given the ongoing problems of prejudice and discrimination against older adults, no geriatric patients—especially those lacking decision-making capacity—should die merely because their physicians or relatives conclude that they are too old, no longer productive, or of insufficient social worth to keep alive.

Nevertheless, there are several indications that we as a society are on the verge of having to allocate life-sustaining technologies in some fashion. Given the continually expansive category of medical "need," the ongoing development of more sophisticated and more expensive life-sustaining technologies, the seductive attractiveness of what some persons regard as the technological imperative in medicine, the increasing percentage of the gross national product (GNP) devoted to health care expenditures (10.9 percent in 1986, compared to 9.1 percent in 1980), the total amount of expenditures for health care ($458 billion in 1986, compared to $248 billion in 1980), the rising per capita costs of health care ($1,837 in 1986), the increasing national costs of intensive care (in all of its forms), the cost-containment measures already federally mandated, and the disinclination of the government substantially to increase federal or state funding for health care, we are rapidly getting to the point of being unable to pay for some of the technological advances in medicine that our citizens want and often need.[22]

Particularly problematic are the economic facts related to health care expenditures by and for older adults. As mentioned in Chapter 1, older adults require more health services than do younger persons, older adults tend to have particularly expensive medical conditions, and per capita health care expenses for older adults are now 3.5 times greater than for persons under 65 years of age. Medicare expenditures for 31.7 million enrollees totaled $76 billion in 1986, compared to a total of $35.7 billion in 1980.[23]

Indicative of increasing public concern over rising health care costs and unmet health care needs is a grass-roots movement in several states focusing on the ethics and economics of health care. The first of several nonprofit citizens groups began in Oregon in 1983. Known as Oregon Health Decisions, the group has served as a model for similar groups in other states: Colorado Speaks Out on Health, The Carolinas Program on Medicine and Society, No Easy Choices (in Idaho), Taking Steps—Ethical Decisions for Living and Dying (in Vermont), and so on. Organized in an attempt to involve the public in health care policy making, these various groups are finding several widely held beliefs among citizens: the right to refuse life-sustaining treatment, the importance of advance directives, and the value of spending more public resources on prenatal and other preventive care than on expensive life-sustaining procedures at the end of life.[24]

We are thus facing growing pressure in our society to make difficult choices about the allocation of scarce medical resources, including life-sustaining technologies, and the advanced age of an increasing number of patients in hospitals and nursing homes is one possible criterion according to which such allocation decisions could be made. But would we be justified in using advanced age as a reason for making policy decisions in regard to abating life-sustaining treatment in the care of an entire class of patients? Does the advanced age of some patients have moral relevance in making macroallocation decisions when the gender, race, level of intelligence, or religious beliefs of patients do not and should never have moral relevance in making such policy decisions?

I think so, and suggest that the makers of health policy in the United States consider the following points in constructing a public policy of selective treatment abatement for the "oldest old" members of society (persons who are 80 or older).

1. In times of resource scarcity, *advanced age is a morally relevant way* of selectively limiting the use of life-sustaining technologies at the public policy level. The gender, race, ethnic background, intelligence level, and religious beliefs of patients are all morally irrelevant to decisions regarding the use of scarce medical resources at either the microallocation or macroallocation level. These identifying features of patients are morally irrelevant precisely because they have no bearing on the kinds of medical conditions (with the obvious exception of medical conditions specific to females or males) or injuries that produce life-threatening situations, nor on the likely benefits that will accompany the use of life-sustaining medications and procedures.

By contrast, the advanced age of patients is morally relevant because of the general decline in physiological function as individuals age, the age-related limitations on some therapeutic options, and the specific medical conditions statistically more common to persons in the later years of life. Moreover, the advanced age of patients is at least an indirect measure of likely medical benefit from certain life-sustaining technologies, as suggested by the practice of using the age of patients as an exclusion factor in several of the nation's heart transplant programs.

2. In times of resource scarcity, *advanced age is a fair way* of selectively limiting the use of life-sustaining technologies at the public policy level. The gender, race, ethnic background, intelligence level, and religious beliefs of patients are not and should not be used in policy decisions regarding the imposed abatement of life-sustaining treatment. Such comparative judgments related to critically ill patients are inherently unfair because they isolate features in patients that are not common to all members of the human community. Consequently, makers of health policy could, by choosing any of these features, exclude some critically ill patients from being given life-sustaining treatment on grounds that would automatically make the policy makers themselves eligible for the same life-sustaining treatment should they ever have the same kind of life-threatening medical condition or injury.

By contrast, basing a policy of selective treatment abatement on the factor of advanced age is a way of placing everyone at the same potential risk over time. All of us—if we avoid fatal accidents, do not contract fatal illnesses at relatively young ages, and do not commit suicide—can reasonably expect to live close to eight decades. Some of us, but we cannot know which of us in advance, will live longer than that. By basing a policy on the factor of advanced age, policy makers would therefore be selectively limiting life-sustaining technologies on moral grounds that potentially include us all, with the policy makers themselves no exception.

3. Advanced age should be used as *a category for a class of critically ill patients,* not as a way of drawing distinctions between individual patients. As previously mentioned, the problem of ageism is serious enough that geriatric patients who are critically ill should not have their health and continued living depend on judgments made about their advanced age by their physicians or relatives. Advanced age alone is not a sufficient reason for abating life-sustaining treatment in individual cases.

However, a public policy instituted in times of resource scarcity and economic limitations can justifiably use the advanced age of some patients as a reason for abating life-sustaining treatment—as long as the age criterion is applied fairly to all patients in the designated age category. If, for instance, a policy of selectively limiting the use of life-sustaining technology were instituted for all critically ill and terminally ill patients who are 80 or older, that policy should apply (with a few exceptions to be noted later) to all patients in the "oldest old" category regardless of their gender, race, professional background, socioeconomic status, or political power. Of course some geriatric patients having economic or political clout would probably try to beat such an allocation system (and some of them would undoubtedly succeed), but a justice-driven allocation system based on the advanced age of patients should at least attempt to keep such power plays to a minimum.

4. A national policy of using advanced age as a basis for the distribution of expensive life-sustaining technologies should *adopt an "over-the-lifetime" perspective on aging and individual well-being,* not a "slice-of-time" perspective on these personal and intergenerational matters. Several persons have discussed the differences between a synchronic (a "slice-of-time") perspective and a diachronic perspective: the former views individuals and events in terms of a specific, limited period of time, whereas the latter views individuals and events over a much longer period of time.[25] As Norman Daniels has pointed out, the differences between these two perspectives are especially significant when anyone considers using advanced age as a criterion for limiting the use of life-sustaining technologies. If one adopts a "slice-of-time" perspective on rationing life-sustaining technologies according to age, the inevitable result is intergenerational conflict and, in particular, conflict between critically ill patients whose ages mean that only one of them is eligible for the technological intervention necessary to sustain life for an indefinite period. If, instead, one adopts an "over-the-lifetime" perspective on the same rationing system, the advanced-age criterion is understood to represent consistent differential treatment by age over time.[26]

The main advantage in adopting an "over-the-lifetime" perspective on the allocation of scarce medical resources is that of prudence on the part of rational deliberators. If, as increasingly seems to be the case, we are simply unable as a society to meet all of the medical needs (and wants) of all our citizens, we should be encouraged as thoughtful individuals, family members, and citizens to consider how we would prefer to distribute the "goods" of technological medicine over our lifetimes (and our parents' lifetimes, and our children's lifetimes). As Daniels puts it, working with a Rawlsian conceptual framework, we should join together in developing a "Prudential Lifespan Account" according to which we allocate health resources on the basis of different stages of our lives.[27] In this manner we can come to see that "transfers [of health resources] *between* age groups are really transfers *within* lives."[28] By considering what is prudent over a life span, we are likely to opt for better public funding of prenatal care, neonatal care, preventive medicine, and care of chronic illnesses to increase our chances of reaching a normal life span, rather than for more funding of life-sustaining technologies aimed at enabling us to have a longer-than-normal life span.

5. To increase public acceptance, a public policy using advanced age as an exclusionary factor for life-sustaining treatment should *select a cutoff point slightly beyond the current natural life span*. My suggestion for an appropriate and justifiable cutoff point for the use of expensive life-sustaining technologies is the age of 80. Current data on life expectancy in the United States indicates that a normal life span for all persons is below 80, with females continuing to have substantially longer life expectancy than males (white females born in 1985 have a life expectancy of 78.7 years and black females 73.5 years; white males born in 1985 have a life expectancy of 71.9 years and black males 65.3 years).[29]

Daniel Callahan correctly interprets an age-based system of rationing health care in the context of expectations regarding a natural life span. In fact, he thinks that a public policy using advanced age as a criterion for limiting treatment would have as its main goal the assurance to everyone of "a chance to live out a natural life span."[30] The policy would be intended to save some of the nation's resources now spent in a disproportionate manner on high-technology "elder-care," but for individuals such a policy would be intended to improve their health and increase their enjoyment of the years in their natural life span. In Callahan's words:

Our ideal of old age should be achieving a life span that enables each of us to accomplish the ordinary scope of possibilities that life affords. . . . On the basis of that ideal, the aged would need only those resources which would allow them a solid chance to live that long and, once they had passed that stage, to finish out their years free of pain and avoidable suffering.[31]

6. Based on accurate cost figures, an age-based policy should *make expensive life-sustaining technologies unavailable to individuals aged 80 or older*. Tech-

nological medicine is expensive, regardless of the age of the patient receiving such care. Any patient receiving life-sustaining treatment in an acute care hospital—whether a severely premature or seriously impaired neonate, a teenage accident victim, a middle-aged stroke victim, or an elderly patient with multiple organ problems—creates substantial costs usually running into five or even six figures. Some of these costs, in some cases, are partially paid by the federal government through its Medicare and Medicaid programs. Other costs, such as those involved in sustaining the lives of impaired neonates in NICUs, are virtually ignored by the federal and state governments.

If we as a society decide that we simply cannot pay for high-tech medical care for everyone needing it, and if we decide to allocate expensive life-sustaining treatment to younger patients rather than older patients, such a policy of restricting expensive medical care on the basis of advanced age needs to correlate the age-based cutoff point for high-tech care with accurate information on the cost savings to be derived through such a public policy. At the present time, such information is sketchy. The best data are available in the OTA report on life-sustaining technologies. However, even that report gives only a range of costs for individuals receiving dialysis ($20,000–$30,000 per patient per year), tube feeding ($1,450–$28,200 for enteral nutrition per patient per year in a hospital setting; $9,125–$182,500 for parenteral nutrition for a hospital patient; $50,000–$100,000 for parenteral nutrition for a patient in a community setting), mechanical ventilation ($300,760 as an average charge per hospital patient per year as of 1985), and IV antibiotics ($30–$200 per patient per day).[32] Accurate data regarding costs for other life-sustaining technologies either could not be secured or were not reported by the OTA.

It is important that we secure more comprehensive, more specific, and more accurate data on cost figures before initiating an age-based allocation policy, for two reasons. First, if we as a society decide to limit life-sustaining technologies on the basis of advanced age, we need to be persuaded that the financial cost savings are actually worth the enormous other psychological "costs" of such a policy to at least some older patients who would regard the policy as being unfair to them. Second, to gain public approval for a policy denying life-sustaining technologies to persons 80 or older, and to help ease the resentment of at least some persons denied life-sustaining treatment on this basis, the makers and enforcers of the policy would have to show that the same amount (or more) of the federal (and state) health costs being saved through such an allocation program were being used to *fund other health programs* in prenatal care, preventive medicine, and so on.

7. A policy of selective treatment abatement for the "oldest old" members of society should *address the numerous practical problems connected with such a policy.* I will mention only three of the problems that would need attention. The first problem has to do with the "start-up" time for such a policy and the

immediate impact the policy would have on persons already over the age of 80 or close to that age. It is one thing to think about the possible personal implications of a policy that would ration life-sustaining technologies beginning at the age of 80 when most of us will not reach that age for several decades. It is a very different thing to think about the implications of such a policy when one is already somewhat rapidly approaching the target age. For younger persons, thinking about such a policy from an "over-the-lifetime" perspective may have a certain intellectual appeal. For persons in the "youngest old" category (ages 65–79), the same perspective may also work—or not, depending on an individual's value system and health condition. To allay the anxiety of persons already in the older phase of life, policy makers would need to consider two possibilities: a transitional "break-in" period for the policy during which persons reaching the age of 80 would still be eligible for some (but not the more expensive) life-sustaining technologies, or some version of a "grandfather clause" whereby persons already past a certain age (75? 70?) would be exempt from the policy.

The second problem has to do with the heterogeneity of older adults, including the "oldest old" members of society. As we have already discussed, it is important to distinguish functional ability from chronological age. Consequently, the makers of a policy rationing the use of life-sustaining technologies at the age of 80 should also include some provisions for exceptions to the policy. In particular, such a policy should provide for some discretion on the part of geriatricians (and possibly other physicians) when they are providing care for an 80-year-old patient (or older) who is unquestionably autonomous, in comparatively good health, and for whom the use of a particular life-sustaining technology *for a short period of time* would seem to provide substantial benefit and be costworthy. In such instances, the collective burden of proof would be on the patient, the patient's physician, and the patient's relatives to convince a disinterested third party (possibly an IEC) that the initiation or continuation of a short-term life-sustaining treatment is in the patient's best interests. To handle such cases, the policy might permit the use of at least some life-sustaining technologies for a defined period of time (measured in days or weeks). The point in using the technologies would be to enhance the patient's life during the last phase of life, not to forestall the patient's death.

The third problem has to do with older patients, their physicians, and their families who would try to circumvent the policy for reasons other than the patient's short-term best interests. It is not difficult to imagine, for example, some patients at or approaching the age of 80 in declining health, with multiple chronic and/or acute medical problems, whose severe medical conditions are not reversible with treatment, but who nevertheless would desperately cling to the biological existence remaining to them if given technological assistance. Likewise, it is not difficult to imagine some of these patients (and families) being financially able to pay for the needed life-sustaining treatment after Medicare funding and all other external reimbursement was stopped. To address this kind of situation, policy makers would be pressed to educate the general public regarding the necessity and merits of the allocation program, and to encourage through various channels as much support for the allocation program among physicians as it is possible to secure.[33]

8. To gain and keep widespread support, the policy would have to *specify the other health programs that would be funded with the resources saved* by means of the allocation program. The programs listed would need to be clearly in the long-term best interests of all persons in the society willing to adopt an "over-the-lifetime" perspective on health care and individual well-being. One way of encouraging such a perspective would be to group the areas of additional funding in an approximately chronological fashion, with some of the additional resources going to meet the health needs of children, other funding going to meet the health needs of adults in their middle years, and other funding being specifically targeted at the health needs of older adults. An alternative way of encouraging support for the allocation program would be that of restricting the saved resources for the specific purpose of providing life-sustaining and life-enhancing programs (better long-term care facilities, more day care centers, expanded home-based health care programs, expanded hospice programs, etc.) for older adults both before and after the age of 80.

What should be done when an individual's previous preferences regarding treatment abatement seem to conflict with that now-nonautonomous patient's best interests?

One of the features of finitude that all of us share is a seriously limited ability to anticipate or predict the future accurately. Most of us have had the experience of making some important decision (choosing a vocation, marrying, buying a car or house, relocating to a different city to take a new position) after having done a lot of thought and "homework" in relation to the decision, only to find out later that circumstances and events we had not anticipated at all have drastically changed the outcome we had planned and hoped to realize. Because of differences between the circumstances we anticipated and the circumstances that actually came to exist, many of us have sometimes come to realize that we took the wrong job, married the wrong person, bought a "lemon," purchased the wrong stock, and so forth.

The same limitations and problems confront those of us who try to plan for the circumstances that are most likely to exist should we ever become critically or terminally ill because of a life-threatening injury or illness. If we remain autonomous during our critical or terminal illness, and if we have a cooperative physician who is truthful with us about the existing medical condition and treatment possibilities, we will be able to adapt any written treatment plan and/or change our previously stated views regarding treatment abatement as our changing medical condition warrants. However, if we should become critically or terminally ill subsequent to the onset of severe dementia, or if we should become critically ill in connection with an accident that leaves us in a PVS, the possibility of changing our earlier views regarding treatment abatement does not and will not exist. In such a situation, the physician(s) caring for us and the surrogate(s) called on to make decisions on our behalf may be confronted with a task that is often quite difficult: determining whether the PBI standard calls for abating treatment in accordance with our previously expressed preferences, or whether the PBI standard calls for refusing to abide by those earlier preferences in order to promote our physical well-being as defined in a more objective fashion.

For physicians, this kind of decision in cases of nonautonomous patients is complicated by the important differences among such patients. Nonautonomous, critically ill patients obviously present a variety of life-threatening conditions to the physicians and health care professionals caring for them. In addition, nonautonomous patients who previously were autonomous vary significantly in terms of their earlier planning for the possibility of critical illness and the decisions about administering or abating life-sustaining treatment that would likely be necessitated by one or more life-threatening conditions. In this regard, critically ill patients who no longer possess the requisite decision-making capacity span the gamut from individuals who earlier gave considerable thought to the decisions that might become necessary in the personal event of a life-threatening injury or illness, to individuals who seem never to have entertained the thought that they might someday become critically or terminally ill.

For physicians and the surrogates of now-nonautonomous patients, the fact that a particular patient previously communicated preferences concerning treatment and treatment abatement does not necessarily answer the question currently being addressed. In fact, unless the attending physician chooses simply to disregard the earlier views of the patient, the presence of some evidence regarding the patient's earlier preferences may either simplify or further complicate the decision facing the physician(s) and the surrogate of the patient. To the extent that the patient while previously autonomous correctly anticipated the medical circumstances that now exist, the earlier expression of preferences can be helpful to the physician(s) and surrogate of the patient as they decide to initiate, continue, or abate life-sustaining treatment. To the extent that the patient's earlier views regarding treatment abatement now seem to be too vague, too laconic, too formal, or too easily interpreted in multiple ways, the earlier expression of preferences may serve only to add ambiguity to the decision-making process. Especially when the now-nonautonomous patient failed personally (1) to select a proxy, (2) to invest someone with the durable power of attorney, or (3) to give any future surrogate permission to adapt the patient's views to unanticipated medical circumstances, a vaguely worded written directive or very general comments to relatives or friends made prior to the loss of autonomy and the onset of critical illness may seriously complicate the application of the PBI standard to the case at hand. Furthermore, if the only evidence of the patient's earlier views is inferred from that individual's religious beliefs and/or pattern of conduct, such evidence may not be sufficiently "hard" or specific to provide much help to the decision makers in a particular case.

Lest I be misinterpreted, let me try to be very clear about the point I am making. I am not siding with those physicians (and other persons) who regard advance directives as "worthless pieces of paper." I have long believed that advance directives, especially when carefully formulated to reflect a particular person's value system, can be very helpful in aiding the physician(s) and surrogate of a nonautonomous patient in making difficult decisions on the behalf of that patient. Moreover, I think that even inferences about an individual's value system drawn from that person's earlier religious beliefs and pattern of conduct can, at least in some cases, provide important insights into how he or she would have decided about initiating, continuing, or abating life-sustaining treatment if able to do so. However, advance directives are not a panacea for all cases involving the possibility of abating treatment on the behalf of now-nonautonomous patients. Life—and clinical cases of critical illness—are much too complicated for such a simplistic view.

How, then, should we handle clinical cases involving an apparent conflict between a now-nonautonomous patient's earlier preferences and a current interpretation of the patient's best interests by the patient's surrogate and/or physician? The important point in deciding about treatment in such cases is to determine *the extent to which the patient's earlier views now fit the clinical situation* that exists. In wrestling with the question of "fit," physicians and surrogates should not err in having too high a standard for fitness by requiring that a patient's earlier views pass "tests" for using medical terminology correctly, diagnosing a medical condition correctly, or anticipating virtually every aspect of medical reality that now characterizes the case. Clearly it would be possible for physicians already suspicious of advance directives to set up "tests" for fitness that no person lacking medical education could ever reasonably be expected to pass.

Instead, the appropriate tests regarding the fitness of the patient's earlier views to current medical reality are (1) whether the now-nonautonomous patient correctly anticipated (in a general sense) the medical situation that currently exists, (2) whether his or her earlier stated preferences were clearly intended for this kind of situation, and (3) whether the forms of life-sustaining treatment that he or she earlier rejected in a hypothetical sense are actually the forms of treatment that are now applicable to the case. If so, the preferences communicated earlier (in language that could have been disease-oriented, organ-oriented, sense-oriented, function-oriented, or time-oriented, as well as treatment-oriented) should now be taken by other parties to the case as being *the patient's decisive interpretation of his or her best interests* in the case at hand. By contrast, if the patient's earlier preferences do not fit the current medical realities, the patient's surrogate should place less weight on the earlier views held by the patient. In such a situation, the surrogate is obligated to assess the patient's *current* best interests in as accurate and reasonable a manner as is possible, and then either to consent to life-sustaining treatment or refuse such treatment on the patient's behalf.

How are the best interests of a critically ill patient to be interpreted when that patient comes to have an acute, treatable condition in addition to the original medical condition?

The traditional version of this question dealt with autonomous patients who were terminally ill. For example, years ago Paul Ramsey articulated the traditional version of the question when he asked: Is a terminal cancer patient who suddenly develops diabetes obligated to begin insulin treatment and continue to die painfully of cancer, or "may the patient choose rather to pass into diabetic coma and an earlier death?" He continued by asking, "What of the conscious patient suffering from [a] painful incurable disease who suddenly gets pneumonia?"[34] For Ramsey, a "medical indications policy" would call for interpreting the use of insulin in the first case and antibiotic therapy in the second case as "extraordinary means" of prolonging life, and thus as optional courses of action for the patients and their physicians.

Recent developments in critical care medicine and in case law combine to call for an expansion of the traditional question in three ways. First, intensivists and other physicians are becoming increasingly aware of the multiple-organ failure syndrome in many critically ill patients. In addition, the growing knowledge base about AIDS indicates even to the general public that this progressive, degenerative disease manifests itself in multiple ways, some of which are chronic in nature (e.g., Kaposi's sarcoma) and others that are acute conditions (e.g., *Pneumocystis carinii* pneumonia). Consequently, the occurrence of a combination of acute conditions in the same patient, or of one or more acute conditions in addition to an underlying chronic condition in a patient is now known to be much more common than suggested by the traditional formulation of the foregoing question.

Second, the traditional formulation of the question regarding acute-on-chronic medical conditions did not address the plight of decision makers in cases of nonautonomous patients. Nevertheless, given the recent advances in mechanical ventilation, technological feeding, and other life-sustaining technologies, an increasing number of nonautonomous patients are having their lives sustained technologically for long periods of time. Some of these patients, of course, come to have acute medical conditions that are treatable, in addition to whatever chronic conditions the patients have that are not subject to curative treatment. For the surrogates and physicians of these patients, the combination of acute-on-chronic conditions means that a determination of the best interests of these patients requires an assessment of short-term, beneficial treatment in the longer-term context provided by the underlying chronic condition, the inability of physicians to reverse that underlying condition with medical treatment, and the long-term burdens to the patient that the short-term treatment extends.

Third, the traditional version of the question did not ask about critically ill patients who are not terminally ill, or whose medical conditions at the very least do not fit conventional medical definitions of terminal illness. Rather, the traditional question assumed a fairly straightforward distinction between nondying patients and dying patients, and further assumed that the ordinary/extraordinary distinction was applicable to cases of dying patients in a way it was not in cases of patients who were very sick but not known to be dying. However, as we have discussed in earlier chapters, the dying/nondying distinction is not always easy to make, and the ordinary/extraordinary distinction has become an obsolete way of approaching decisions about abating treatment. Instead, patients with ALS, or Alzheimer's disease, or PVS, or severe burns, or AIDS, or AIDS-related complex (ARC), or any number of other serious medical conditions force us to think seriously about what their best interests are in regard to life-sustaining treatment when they contract pneumonia or some other acute medical condition that is normally subject to curative treatment.

The Thomas Wirth case (Case 8.3) is an example of the problem. In an AIDS ward at Bellevue Hospital in 1987, Wirth had ARC and some of the symptoms associated with this form of infection by HIV. In particular, he was stuporous and had multiple brain lesions of unknown cause, although his physicians believed that the lesions were attributable to the parasitic infection known as toxoplasmosis. Having months earlier signed an advance directive calling for treatment abatement whenever "there is no reasonable expectation of recovering or regaining a meaningful quality of life," he nevertheless was given a series of antimicrobials for 2 weeks prior to a court hearing initiated by his friend and guardian, John Evans. Evans, who had been given "medical-power-of-attorney" authority by Wirth, sought a court order stopping all medical treatments. The trial court judge ruled otherwise, siding with the physicians and hospital in declaring the wording of the advance directive ambiguous, rejecting Evans' claim to be Wirth's chosen proxy, and emphasizing the importance of providing medical treatment whenever an acute medical condition can possibly be reversed.[35] The case was not appealed, because Wirth's condition later deteriorated and life-support measures were abated.

How are the best interests of patients in such cases to be determined? If a patient has a long-term medical condition that brings about critical illness, if survival with the condition is unlikely even though death is not expected soon, and if the patient is afflicted further with an acute, generally treatable condition in addition to the underlying long-term condition, does use of the PBI standard require treating the acute condition? The answer is negative, depending on the facts in particular cases. In cases involving autonomous patients, the patients have a moral and legal right to refuse any and all life-sustaining treatments they choose to refuse. Hopefully such treatment refusals will be made only after adequate consultation and communication with the physician(s) in the cases and a determination by the patients that *even effective treatment* of their acute conditions is contrary to their best interests, given their underlying medical conditions that will not be improved by the short-term treatment.

Cases involving nonautonomous patients should be handled in either of two ways. If a patient's earlier views regarding treatment and treatment abatement are applicable to the situation of acute-on-chronic conditions that now exists, the patient's surrogate should regard those views as determinative of the patient's best interests and make a decision on the patient's behalf that is consistent with the patient's earlier perception of his or her own best interests. Of course, the closer the now-nonautonomous patient's earlier views fit the clinical situation that exists, the better for the surrogate and any other parties to the case (including a judge, should a disputed case end up in court).

If a nonautonomous patient's earlier views on treatment and treatment abatement are unknown, or if the patient's earlier views (written or verbal) are too ambiguous to provide guidance for the surrogate and physicians in the case, the surrogate should make a reasonable assessment of the patient's best interests in regard both to the acute condition and the underlying, long-term condition threatening the patient's life. To do so requires that the surrogate determine the short-term benefits to the patient if the acute condition is successfully treated. In addition, the surrogate should assess the continuing severity of the patient's underlying condition, the inability of physicians to reverse the underlying condition, the difficulty of achieving important medical goals other than the prolongation of the patient's life, and the patient's ongoing pain and psychological suffering because of the long-term condition. An assessment of the benefits and burdens of treatment directed at the patient's acute condition should always be made in the broader context of the patient's long-term condition, since that condition will remain unaffected even if the acute condition is effectively reversed.

Do a patient's best interests in regard to treatment and treatment abatement always outweigh the interests of the patient's family?

Some cases involving the possibility of abating treatment have serious conflicts of interests among the parties to the cases, especially when in any given case the abatement of life-sustaining treatment will likely result in the patient's death.

Several persons involved in a case—the patient, the physicians, nurses, other health care professionals, relatives of the patient, and close friends of the patient—can end up seriously disagreeing as to whether abating treatment is in the best interests of the patient because they bring different "agendas" to that decision.

A conflict of interests between a critically ill patient and the patient's family can be particularly problematic. In any case involving an autonomous patient, the patient's family may seek to influence the patient's thinking about life-sustaining treatment and the abatement of such treatment in either of two ways. On the one hand, they may for any number of reasons try to convince the patient that they cannot bear the prospect of the patient's death, and thus try to persuade the patient that his or her consenting to life-sustaining treatment is in their joint best interests. On the other hand, they may (either subtly or with no attempt at subtlety) try to persuade the patient to forgo further life-sustaining treatment in order to put an end to the family's psychological stress, mounting financial debt, loss of time at work, and other problems connected with a lingering critical or terminal illness. In such cases, the significant if not undue pressure from the patient's relatives may raise questions regarding the voluntariness of the patient's consent to or refusal of treatment—and the patient's interpretation of his or her best interests in the light of that familial pressure.

In cases involving either kind of familial pressure, it is important for physicians and other health care professionals to try to determine if the patient is maintaining his or her status as an autonomous person. If so, the patient's perception of whether consenting to or refusing life-sustaining treatment is in his or her best interests should prevail, no matter how vociferously the patient's relatives may protest to the contrary. By contrast, if the patient's interpretation of his or her best interests seems influenced by familial pressure to the point of lacking deliberation and voluntariness, steps should be taken by the physician to obtain a surrogate for the patient who can give a reasonably objective interpretation of the patient's best interests and make a decision on the patient's behalf in the light of that interpretation. If necessary, the patient's physician should appeal to an IEC or, as a last resort, initiate court action to protect the best interests of the patient in such a case.

The problem of a conflict of interests between a patient and the patient's family is even more serious when the critically ill patient receiving life-sustaining treatment is unquestionably nonautonomous. In cases of critically ill patients who are severely demented, severely retarded, or permanently unconscious, the psychological stress and financial pressure on the patient's family can be enormous. In some instances, as in the Joseph Saikewicz case, the relatives of the patient simply opt out of the case and leave the decision making to other persons. In other cases, the relatives of demented, retarded, permanently unconscious, or otherwise nonautonomous patients try to cope with an exceedingly difficult situation, wrestle with the limited options they have, question the relevance of laws and institutional policies to the case at hand, and hope that God or "nature" or somebody will finally bring their suffering to an end.

Fortunately, the application of the PBI standard in many of these cases results in a morally responsible decision that the continuation of life-sustaining treatment is contrary to the patient's best interests. But what about cases in which physicians and other parties to a case (possibly including the patient's relatives) believe that the continuation of life-sustaining treatment is *in the patient's best interests,* even though the mounting expenses connected with the treatment are clearly and disastrously *contrary to the financial well-being of the patient's family?*

Several comments are in order. First, it is understandable and justifiable for an *autonomous* patient to include the future financial well-being of the family in an assessment of whether life-sustaining treatment is in his or her best interests. Although the financial aspects of life-sustaining treatment do not represent a separate component in the PBI standard (see the previous chapter), surely the prospects of a long-term financial burden on one's family would have a considerable influence on the psychological suffering of most critically ill patients. At least for some of these patients—depending on their relationship with other family members, the cost of their care, the availability of insurance or Medicare coverage, and the financial abilities and limitations of the family—the likelihood that the cost of the technological prolongation of their lives would overwhelm their families financially would, in itself, make the treatment contrary to their best interests as they interpret those interests.

Second, we have already discussed the enormous cost of several life-sustaining technologies and indicated that some justice-driven policies are justifiable in allocating medical resources that are very expensive and simply not available to all persons who need them. Consequently, some patients, whether autonomous or nonautonomous, may for policy reasons be denied life-sustaining treatment that would be in their individual best interests. I suspect that an increasing number of cases will have to be handled in this manner, quite apart from the financial capabilities of individual families.

Third, our society finally seems to be trying to deal with the growing problem of health care costs. Although progress is slow and government resources are still not adequately targeted at the enormous costs of technological medicine on some individual patients and their families, at least some movement is being made in the right direction. If we can expand the availability of home health care, increase the funding for hospice care, expand Medicare coverage for hospital and nursing home expenses, and join other industrialized nations in having a comprehensive national health insurance program, the individual cases of forced choice between the best interests of uninsured, nonautonomous patients and the financial interests of their families may (I hope) disappear.

However, that time may never come, or at least it will not come soon. In the meantime, how should such individual cases be handled? In my view, *no nonautonomous patient should be denied life-sustaining treatment,* except through necessary allocation policies, *that is clearly in his or her best interests* merely because such treatment is contrary to his or her family's financial interests. In saying this, I do not intend to minimize the problem that sometimes exists in individual cases, ignore the reality of health economics, or pretend that some critically ill patients are not already being denied life-sustaining care for financial reasons in decisions made by health care providers and by the families of some of the patients. My point is simply that treatment decisions in such cases should be based on the patient's best interests, and that health care providers (and the rest of us, to a lesser degree) have a moral obligation to see that nonautonomous, critically ill patients do not die prematurely for the wrong reasons.[36]

When are physicians justified in overriding a patient's refusal of life-sustaining treatment?

As indicated in the previous chapter, the principle of respect for autonomy and the principle of beneficence are the two most important ethical principles in establishing the ethical context for the PBI standard. Both principles are correctly understood as *prima facie* principles, neither is more important than the other, and each is useful in helping to define the applicability of the other principle. In determining the patient's best interests in any given case, the principle of respect for autonomy is helpful in emphasizing the patient's perspective on treatment or treatment abatement, and the principle of beneficence helps to establish the importance of promoting the patient's well-being from the standpoint of the physician responsible for the patient's medical care.

Sometimes, as we have seen in numerous cases throughout this book, the principles come into conflict as patients refuse life-sustaining treatments that their physicians think are clearly in the best interests of those patients. Of course, this kind of conflict does not arise in the same way in cases of unquestionably nonautonomous patients (1) who never provided a clue to their relatives or friends regarding their preferences on treatment abatement, or (2) who are alone in the world, with no relatives or friends to step in as surrogates. In such cases, an attending physician may come into conflict with a patient's surrogate or court-appointed guardian regarding the patient's best interests, but such conflicts have to do more with differing judgments on whether life-sustaining treatment is beneficial to the patient in question than on a physician's desire to provide treatment that a patient has refused.

The thrust of the question under consideration concerns other patients, patients who refuse physician-recommended, life-sustaining treatment. In these cases, when is it morally permissible for a physician to intervene to prolong a patient's life in a way the patient has indicated that he or she does not want? Stated another way, the question is when, if ever, may a physician seek to promote a critically ill patient's best interests by overriding the patient's differing perception of what those best interests are?

These questions bring forth some of the major concepts and arguments that have been developed in recent years in the conflict between advocates of patient autonomy and defenders of medical paternalism. The first question suggests the core content of paternalism in clinical settings, namely the overriding of a patient's preferences, communicated choices, and actions for that individual's own good by a physician and/or other health care professional.[37] Differing types of paternalism depend on the reasons for the paternalistic action. Two types of paternalism have to do with *judgments about the patient's autonomous status.* *Limited* (or "weak") paternalism involves overriding a patient's preferences, decisions, and actions because of doubt regarding that patient's present decision-making capacity. Alternatively, limited paternalism can involve overriding a now-nonautonomous patient's earlier preferences either because they are too vague and do not adequately fit the clinical situation that exists, or because they are insufficiently clear when communicated by the patient's relatives and friends. By contrast, *extended* (or "strong") paternalism involves overriding a patient's preferences, decisions, and actions even when that patient's decision-making capacity is not in question. A physician exercising extended paternalism chooses to promote a patient's well-being unilaterally by either (1) overriding the decision of an autonomous patient, or (2) simply rejecting the earlier preferences and choices of a previously autonomous patient who (though now lacking decision-making capacity) correctly and intentionally anticipated the clinical situation that now exists and communicated those choices through an advance directive.[38]

Two other types of paternalism that have bearing on our discussion provide other reasons for a physician to refuse to accede to a patient's decision about treatment or treatment abatement. These forms of paternalism do not involve judgments about the level or specificity of a patient's autonomy as much as they involve *differing views about the values that should inform a decision* about initiating, continuing, or abating life-sustaining treatment. *Consistent-value* (or "soft") paternalism is an attempt by a physician or other health care professional (or relative of the patient) to help a patient make a decision about treatment or abating treatment that reflects the patient's own value system. Thus, for example, a physician might hesitate to carry out a patient's decision to refuse treatment because he or she thinks the decision is at variance with the patient's long-held views or dominant value system. By contrast, *imposed-value* (or "hard") paternalism is an attempt by a physician or other party to a case to thwart a patient's decision about treatment or—far more common—abating treatment by subjecting the patient to a value system he or she does not personally accept. Thus a physician functioning with a vitalistic philosophy or adhering wrongly to the "technological imperative" might try to impose a technological prolongation of life on a patient to whom such value perspectives are alien.[39]

A discussion of these four types of paternalism highlights two of the central features of conflicts over decisions to abate treatment, namely (1) questions related to the autonomy of the patient who refuses treatment and (2) questions related to whether abating life-sustaining treatment is in the best interests of a critically ill patient or is contrary to those interests. Distinguishing among these types of paternalism in clinical settings helps to accentuate the question of *how much* a physician is obligated to respect a patient's autonomy, especially when the physician is convinced that the patient's decision to abate life-sustaining treatment is misguided, myopic, and wrong. Moreover, sorting out these types of paternalistic intervention helps focus our attention on when and what forms of paternalism are justifiable in trying to promote a critically ill patient's well-being.

When is paternalistic intervention justified in treatment-abatement cases? Certainly (1) when a patient is nonautonomous and never previously expressed preferences on the subject of abating treatment, (2) when medical intervention will predictably prevent substantial physiological harm to that patient (including a premature death), and (3) when the projected benefits outweigh, on balance, whatever burdens the life-sustaining treatment may bring to that patient.[40] In cases involving nonautonomous patients, therefore, a physician should assess, as objectively as possible, the specific kinds of benefits and burdens that life-sustaining treatment will likely provide the patient. Then, working with a surrogate for the patient, the physician is justified in intervening medically to promote the patient's best interests, including the patient's interests in extended life and improved health.

When patients with questionable decision-making capacity refuse life-sustaining treatment, the attending physician should use the interactional approach discussed earlier to determine if the patient actually has substantially reduced autonomy. If the physician concludes that the patient lacks the level of autonomy necessary to decide about the recommended treatment, and if the physician does not leap to that conclusion prematurely merely to provide an excuse for imposing his or her own values on the patient, then the physician is justified in intervening medically as long as such intervention offers a realistic prospect of promoting the patient's well-being. Assuming no emergency situation exists, the initiation or continuation of such an intervention should have the consent of a surrogate capable of making a decision on the patient's behalf.

The crunch comes, of course, with the perceived need to intervene medically to sustain an autonomous patient's life. If a critically ill patient demonstrates the general and specific features of autonomy (i.e., understanding, deliberation, voluntariness, authenticity, appreciation, and the ability to communicate in some fashion), the patient's perception of what his or her best interests are in relation to life-sustaining treatment and treatment abatement outweighs the views of the physician(s) and other parties to the case. When such a patient refuses life-sustaining treatment, that refusal should virtually never be overridden or circumvented by the physician responsible for the patient's medical care. Two exceptions (and only two) exist to this moral prohibition of extended paternalism in treatment-abatement cases: (1) when the refusal of life-sustaining treatment clearly seems to be part of a premeditated medical crisis (e.g., by a disabled individual such as Elizabeth Bouvia, or by an inmate in a prison) possibly involving deception of physicians and nurses in an institution, and (2) when the impending death of the patient in the absence of life-sustaining treatment would almost certainly cause substantial psychological if not physiological harm to a specific, identifiable minor child (but not a fetus) left without a parent or other adult relative willing and able to take on the role of parent.

Who should be the surrogate in cases of nonautonomous patients, and how should that person make a decision on behalf of the patient?

The first part of this question reflects a serious problem that occurs with some frequency in clinical cases. When a decision has to be made about initating, continuing, or abating life-sustaining treatment, and when the critically ill patient in the case is unable to make the decision, what procedure should be followed in identifying the most appropriate surrogate to represent the patient's interests?

One procedural alternative is to have the physician in the case make the decision unilaterally, but this alternative is unacceptable (except in emergency situations) because the decision about life-sustaining treatment in regard to a nonautonomous patient should both reflect the patient's value system (if that is known by the decision maker) and be subject to review by other persons. Another procedural alternative is to require a court-appointed guardian for the patient to make the decision, but this alternative is also unacceptable in most cases because it is time-consuming, cumbersome, and relatively expensive.

A preferable way of identifying the appropriate surrogate is to follow a serial or lexical ordering of decision makers that is most likely both to respect the autonomy previously possessed by the patient and to promote the patient's well-being. As we discussed in Chapter 4, an increasing number of courts are moving in this direction, with the Arizona Court of Appeals (in *Rasmussen*) being the most specific by putting forth a priority list of authorized decision makers: a judicially appointed guardian (if necessary), a person previously designated by the patient in writing, the patient's spouse, an adult child (or "a majority of the adult children who are reasonably available for consultation"), the parents of the patient, or the nearest living relative of the patient.[41] An increasing number of natural death acts also have priority lists of surrogates, although there are significant differences in the lists from state to state. The result is that both case and statutory law are coming to accept a new legal standard whereby individuals (especially family members) other than court-appointed guardians are being recognized as having legal authority to make decisions to abate treatment on the behalf of nonautonomous patients.[42]

In my view, the ordering of appropriate surrogates should also serve to protect nonautonomous patients (and their physicians) from (1) surrogates who may make a decision out of ignorance or deliberately contrary to the patient's best interests and (2) disputes among family members that may slow down the decision-making process and require judicial resolution. Consequently, my recommendation regarding this procedural question is that hospitals and nursing homes establish written policies regarding a serial ordering of surrogates for such cases. Furthermore, my suggestion is that such a policy indicate that in cases of nonautonomous patients the physician (or nurse, in some nursing homes) responsible for the patient's care will identify an appropriate surrogate in this order:

1. A proxy to whom the patient previously granted durable power of attorney to make health care decisions.
2. A proxy lacking durable-power-of-attorney authorization but previously designated by the patient in writing as the patient's representative.
3. A court-appointed guardian (an unnecessary step in most cases).
4. The patient's spouse.
5. An identifiable, long-term homosexual lover of the patient.
6. The most obvious other adult involved in the patient's case and concerned about the patient's well-being (an adult child, a sibling of the patient, a parent of the patient, or a concerned friend).[43]

One additional suggestion concerns the role of an IEC in this procedural process. Among the important activities for an IEC, an interdisciplinary group of professionals functioning in this capacity should meet in regard to a decision about abating life-sustaining treatment in any case involving a nonautonomous patient whenever any of three sets of circumstances exists: (1) evidence or strong suspicion of a surrogate's acting contrary to the patient's best interests, (2) an ongoing disagreement among family members regarding the course of action that is in the patient's best interests, or (3) a patient who does not have any adult relative or concerned friend available and willing to act as a surrogate.

Regarding the second part of the question, we have already discussed the centrality of the PBI standard. This standard should be used by all surrogates in all cases of nonautonomous patients. The exact interpretation of how the PBI standard applies to particular cases will depend, given the variable facts of individual cases, on whether the patient previously provided explicit treatment directives, the extent to which the surrogate has trustworthy knowledge of the patient's previous preferences and values, or a surrogate's ability in the absence of such knowledge about the patient to make an objective assessment of what the patient's best interests are in the given clinical situation.

Is there any morally significant or legally significant difference between withholding and withdrawing life-sustaining treatment?

By using the term "abatement" in reference to not starting life-sustaining treatment, decelerating such treatment, and stopping such treatment after it has been started, I have tried to reflect a widespread consensus among philosophers, religious ethicists, legal scholars, judges, and many physicians. That consensus, as it has been articulated numerous times, is that there is *no morally significant or legally significant difference* between withholding and withdrawing life-sustaining treatment.

A decision by a physician not to attempt to sustain a critically ill patient's life can be (but need not be) morally blameworthy and punishable by law; likewise, a decision by a physician to stop trying to sustain a critically ill patient's life can be (but need not be) morally blameworthy and punishable by law. The morality of either decision that results in a patient's death, as well as the legal liability connected with the patient's death, depends on the facts of a particular case. The patient's medical condition, the patient's wishes, the decision by the patient or surrogate as to whether the initiation or continuation of life-sustaining treatment is in the patient's best interests (especially if the patient is nonautonomous), and other facts all have bearing on the morality and legality of withholding *or* withdrawing life-sustaining treatment from a critically ill patient.

In spite of this moral equivalence, a number of physicians, nurses, and other health care professionals continue to think that withdrawing life-sustaining treatment is morally more significant and certainly more legally serious than withholding treatment. There seem to be a number of contributory reasons for this view. First, there are psychological reasons. Physicians know that initiating treatment—any treatment—with a patient creates expectations in the minds of the patient and the patient's relatives that the treatment will work, and that the patient will be better off for having had the treatment. When the treatment does not work as expected or hoped, and especially when the treatment offered the hope of extended life and improved health, a decision to stop the treatment can contribute to feelings of guilt and failure on the part of the physician. Moreover, when a patient dies subsequent to the withdrawal of treatment, some physicians feel that they somehow had a role in bringing about the death (through a faulty diagnosis, delayed intervention, the inability to manage the patient's symptoms, or whatever), in a way they would not feel in regard to a patient's death when no life-sustaining treatment was initiated because of the severity of the patient's condition. In addition, by refusing to withdraw all life-sustaining treatments as warranted, some physicians gain a sense of control over at least part of a bad situation. Frustrated by an underlying illness that defies medical intervention, they may persist in using antibiotics or technological feeding when such measures are actually contrary to a patient's best interests.[44]

A second set of reasons are philosophical. Physicians and other health care professionals are trained to treat diseases and cure patients of their medical problems. Given this "bias to treat," some physicians adhere to what they regard as the technological imperative and become convinced that anything less than "going all out" to prolong patients' lives is tantamount to "giving up" or abandoning patients at the time technological medicine should be able to meet their needs.[45] In addition, many physicians are convinced that the distinction between actions and omissions has particular relevance to clinical cases involving the deaths of patients. For them, withholding life-sustaining treatment is less serious morally because a physician merely omits to do something that may lead to a patient's death, rather than actually engaging in an action that may lead to a patient's death.

Third, there are practical matters. Some physicians who conclude that the life-sustaining treatment(s) being administered to a patient are contrary to the patient's best interests may still be reluctant to go through the hassle of actually withdrawing the treatment(s). Depending on the institution in which a physician works, he or she will at least have to discuss the decision with the patient or surrogate, issue a formal order to discontinue treatment, and formally document the decision in the patient's record. Occasionally, such a decision will also involve consultation with an IEC and/or the institution's legal counsel—and, rarely, the time and expense of involvement in a court hearing.[46] Another practical factor that consumes an inordinate amount of many physicians' "worry time" is concern about the legal ramifications of withdrawing dialysis, mechanical ventilation, burn therapy, or any other life-sustaining treatment. Given the current social and political climate, such physicians are especially concerned about legal liability when they consider withdrawing technological nutrition and hydration from critically or terminally ill patients.

In my view, the appropriate response to these several problem areas is as follows. The psychological aspects of withdrawing life-sustaining treatment are not to be minimized, because they are very real to many physicians. At the same time, no critically ill patient should have his or her life extended indefinitely merely to satisfy the psychological needs of the physician(s) in the case. If the prolongation of mechanical ventilation, technological nutrition, or some other life-sustaining technology is contrary to a patient's best interests, and if the physician responsible for the medical care of the patient cannot psychologically bring himself or herself to withdraw that treatment and end the patient's suffering, then the physician should transfer the care of the patient to another physician who is able to carry out the morally responsible decision.

The philosophical and practical problems connected with withdrawing treatment are more difficult to deal with. Physicians who subscribe to what they view as a technological imperative need to be persuaded to adopt another philosophical frame of reference, and that task is not easy. Nevertheless, the PBI standard provides a preferable frame of reference and can surely be used to show that doing "everything possible" to prolong a critically ill patient's life sometimes makes no medical or philosophical sense. The same basic point applies to physicians who simplistically and wrongly apply the omission/action distinction to treatment-abatement cases. Not only is the distinction itself sometimes ambiguous, but its applicability to clinical cases is often questionable as well. Certain events in a patient's treatment program (e.g., discontinuing a form of tubal feeding) can be described either as "acts" or "omissions," and certainly a physician can wrongly cause a patient's death through the omission of medically necessary treatment.[47] As to physicians who continually raise the spectre of the law, they and their patients would benefit by knowing more about recent case law. No court of final decision in any treatment-abatement case has placed importance on the withhold/withdraw distinction; indeed the *Conroy* court, as we have seen, rejected the applicability of the distinction to clinical cases, saying that the distinction "is more psychologically compelling than logically sound."[48]

In an important sense, the concern some physicians have about withdrawing life-sustaining treatment from their patients leads to morally irresponsible care of some critically ill patients. Whether for psychological, philosophical, or ostensible legal reasons, some physicians who think they cannot withdraw life-sustaining treatment once they have started it simply decide not to start it. Rather than intervening with a medical treatment that might or might not work, they prematurely decide not to try a treatment lest they subsequently be faced with the dilemma of either leaving a patient "stuck on machines" or having to withdraw the treatment once it proves futile or contrary to the patient's best interests.

A preferable alternative, for physicians and their patients, is the use of time-limited trials. By initiating a form of life-sustaining treatment for a specific time period (e.g., mechanical ventilation for 1 week, dialysis for 4 months), several benefits can be accomplished for all persons involved in a case. The physician can establish whether the treatment is beneficial in the case at hand, the nurses can observe improvement or the lack of same in a patient, an autonomous patient can decide if the treatment is wanted, and the patient's family can have a temporal milestone that will herald either improvement of the patient's condition or ineffectiveness of the recommended treatment. Even if the decision is to withdraw the treatment and thereby possibly hasten the patient's death, the withdrawal of a life-sustaining treatment that proves contrary to a patient's best interests is morally preferable to not having tried the treatment at all.[49]

How do the ethics of treatment abatement apply to PVS patients?

To answer this question requires several points. First, it is necessary to get the medical facts straight about the condition known as the persistent vegetative state, given the multiplicity of serious neurological impairments and the widespread conceptual and terminological confusion about the various conditions. As we have already discussed, some persons confuse the issue of treatment abatement with the determination of brain death because they fail to distinguish adequately between patients who are permanently unconscious and former patients who are now unburied corpses. Other persons indiscriminately refer to "comatose patients," "patients with PVS," "patients in irreversible coma," patients with "locked-in syndrome," and so forth, and then confuse the issue of treatment abatement by being unclear as to how, and whether, treatment should be abated from some or all of these patients.

Although there continues to be controversy about the clinical diagnosis of the PVS—until the PET scan or some better diagnostic technology becomes definitive—this condition of severe neurological impairment can at least be helpfully distinguished from other conditions with which it is often confused. Ronald Cranford has been particularly helpful in this regard. He makes the following suggestions: that the terms "irreversible coma" and "chronically and irreversibly comatose" not be used by physicians or anyone else trying to be careful in the use of language; that "brain death" and "neocortical death" be carefully distinguished from one another; that "permanent unconsciousness" be used as a broad-category term in reference to all patients with complete and permanent loss of consciousness, with such patients being subdivided into patients with eyes-closed unconsciousness (permanently comatose patients) and patients with eyes-open unconsciousness (persistently vegetative patients and anencephalic patients); and that the condition of persistent vegetative state be distinguished from coma, dementia, and the locked-in syndrome. For Cranford, PVS is distinguishable from these other conditions in the following ways:

Patients with the *locked-in syndrome* have such severe paralysis, especially of facial and head movements, that they sometimes seem on superficial examination to have diminished consciousness when in fact they have a fairly normal level and content of consciousness.

Patients with *dementia* have a progressive loss of cerebral cortical functions that results in abnormalities of the content of consciousness, with the increasing severeity of the neurological impairment occurring over a period of years (as with Alzheimer's disease).

Patients with *permanent coma* have an eyes-closed unarousability brought about by extensive damage to the brain stem, with some loss of reflex function (the cough, gag, and swallowing reflexes), frequent respiratory infections that are often fatal, and a life expectancy of 6 months to a year.

Patients with *persistent vegetative state* differ from these other patients in that they have a relatively intact brain stem but neurological destruction of the cerebral hemispheres, with the complete loss of cerebral cortical functions occurring over a period of 4–6 minutes because of the lack of blood flow (ischemia) or oxygen (hypoxia) to the brain, and leaving these patients (1) amented (not simply demented), (2) in a transient coma for a few days or weeks, (3) with a transient need for mechanical ventilation for a few days or weeks, (4) then in a prolonged eyes-open unconsciousness that can last for years, (5) with normal gag and cough reflexes and periods of wakefulness and sleep, (6) usually unable to take oral feedings, (7) with no experience of pain and suffering, (8) completely unaware of themselves or the external environment.[50]

A second type of conceptual and terminological confusion also needs to be addressed, namely the philosophical question whether PVS patients count as persons. As we discussed in Chapter 3, the issue of abating treatment occasionally calls on us to think not only about the autonomous status of many critically ill patients but their status as persons as well. It is possible, as we noted earlier, for a patient to have the properties of personhood, yet lack sufficient autonomy to make decisions about his or her health care. By contrast, it is not possible for a patient (or anyone else) to be autonomous, yet lack the properties of personhood.

Several philosophers have addressed the question of personhood in regard to permanently unconscious patients.[51] Yet this philosophical discussion has tended to focus more on the question whether permanently unconscious patients continue to possess interests and/or rights than on the conceptual question regarding whether permanently unconscious patients can reasonably be said not to be persons in a way that does not include human beings who undoubtedly are persons even though, for example, they are asleep. Likewise, insufficient analysis has been given to distinctions among human beings (and other beings) in terms of their possession of the properties of personhood, the likelihood of their future possession of such properties, or their irretrievable loss of such properties.

The philosophers who have discussed the properties of personhood do not entirely agree on what all of these properties are, as we observed in our earlier discussion. Nevertheless, there is a general consensus regarding the core properties or traits of personhood: consciousness, self-awareness, and a capacity for at least minimum rationality. Working with these core concepts, I suggest the following distinctions among human beings (and other beings) in terms of their possession of these properties:

1. *Persons* are beings who possess the necessary and jointly sufficient properties of personhood (consciousness, self-awareness, and at least minimum ratio-

nality) and thereby have the rights and obligations normally held by such beings (e.g., most adult humans).

2. *Potential persons* are nonpersonal beings who will become persons in the normal course of their development (e.g., most human fetuses and neonates).

3. *Possible persons* are entities that can become potential persons only as a consequence of some causal event or constitutive structural change (e.g., a human sperm or ovum).

4. *Pilgrim persons* are beings who possess the necessary properties of person-hood and will continue to have the capacities of consciousness, self-aware-ness, and at least minimal rationality even though they temporarily do not exercise some or all of these capacities (e.g., adult humans in a transient coma).

5. *Previous persons* are beings that earlier possessed the properties of person-hood and now seem, based on medical evidence, irretrievably to have lost these properties (e.g., adult humans in permanent coma or the persistent vegetative state).[52]

On the basis of the core concept of personhood and its applicability to human beings, the indisputable claim in regard to PVS patients is that they are no longer persons. They have been persons, and may have had interests as persons that should now affect decisions about their medical care. However, they are cor-rectly understood as previous persons only, whose physical bodies deserve re-spectful care because they are the bodies of previous persons, but who them-selves have only the most remote statistical chance of ever regaining consciousness and the other properties of personhood. The recognition of this fact is increasingly widespread. For example, the American College of Physi-cians Ad Hoc Committee on Medical Ethics states that "the 'person' no longer exists in any significant sense of the term" whenever a patient has had irrevers-ible loss of human cognition and awareness of self.[53] In Daniel Callahan's words, a PVS patient is a being that has "lost all capacities for personhood, though clinical death has not occurred."[54]

Against the background of these medical and philosophical realities, the re-maining points have direct bearing on the ethics of treatment abatement with PVS patients. We will turn first to the question of what kind of interests, if any, PVS patients have. When we consider that a correctly diagnosed PVS patient is no longer a person and is extremely unlikely ever again to be a person, such a patient can hardly be said to have *current* interests. As Joel Feinberg convinc-ingly argues, cognitive awareness is a necessary condition for the having of interests: "Interests are compounded out of *desires* and *aims*, both of which presuppose something like *belief*, or cognitive awareness . . . mindless creatures have no interests of their own."[55] Joseph and Clorinda Margolis essentially agree by pointing out that one can refer to the "interests" of a permanently unconscious patient only by "an extraordinary stretch of the imagination."[56]

Nevertheless, the *previous* interests of PVS patients can be relevant to the medical and nonmedical care they receive while in a permanently unconscious state. After all, the previous interests of individuals now dead can occasionally continue to place legal obligations on and block the desires of persons who survive them.[57] In somewhat the same way, the previous interests of PVS patients can and do impose moral obligations on the health care professionals and family members who care for such patients, at least when these parties in a PVS case know the patient's previous interests. If the previous interests of the patient are communicated in an advance directive, and especially if the previous preferences and aims correctly anticipated the possibility of the situation of permanent unconsciousness that now exists, the expression of those previous, forward-looking interests should have decisive weight in decisions regarding the continuation or abatement of life-sustaining treatment. If, unfortunately, such a case should end up in court, the patient's previously expressed interests should also have decisive legal weight.

Let us suppose, for the sake of argument, that PVS patients do have current interests as well as previous interests, as some pro-life advocates seem to want to maintain. How would the PBI standard apply to such cases? In terms of the severity of the patient's medical condition, the diagnostic technologies now available to neurological specialists are increasingly reliable and provide accurate data regarding one of the more severe conditions that can beset any human being. For many reflective persons, the prospect of being permanently unconscious for years is a prospect of a fate worse than death. In terms of the reversibility of the condition with medical treatment, no such scenario is a realistic possibility. One may believe in miracles, but the evidence is that only two patients in the United States accurately diagnosed with PVS have ever regained consciousness (Jacqueline Cole seems not to have been a PVS patient), and those two patients were left with extreme paralysis of all extremities and the locked-in syndrome.[58] In terms of the achievability of important medical goals, the only such goal that is realistically possible is the indefinite prolongation of a nonpersonal, biological existence. As to the presence of serious neurological impairments, the condition of PVS is arguably *the* most serious neurological impairment currently known that is compatible with life. It is sufficiently serious that Daniel Wikler, among others, suggests expanding the definition of death to include permanent loss of sentience as a way of handling such cases.[59]

The more subjective aspects of the PBI standard are more problematic, given the necessarily hypothetical manner we have to use in guessing what it would be like to be a PVS patient. With that proviso, it is clear that no PVS patient experiences pain and suffering. The American Academy of Neurology stated unequivocally in its *amicus curiae* brief in the Brophy case that "no conscious experience of pain and suffering is possible without the integrated functioning of the brainstem and cerebral cortex. . . . Noxious stimuli may activate peripherally located nerves, but only a brain with the capacity for consciousness can translate that neural activity into an experience."[60] Of course it is also true that no PVS patient experiences joy, satisfaction, challenge, excitement, love, or happiness. As to psychological suffering and an intolerable living situation, surely most if not all PVS patients (if they had current interests) would be enormously bothered by their mental and physical dysfunction, the prospect of being unconscious for 10 or 20 years, the emotional stress on their relatives, the financial costs of $2,000–$10,000 *per month,* and the virtual impossibility of any improvement in this unfortunate situation as long as life-sustaining treatment is continued.[61] Surely, also, most if not all thoughtful persons who consider the future possibility of such a permanently unconscious, nonpersonal existence for themselves subsequent to a serious head injury or cardiac or respiratory arrest would communicate an undeniably clear preference to their relatives, friends, and physician *not ever to be kept alive in such a condition.* As to the proportionality of treatment-related benefits and burdens to the patient, the only possible benefit is the extremely unlikely chance—bordering on zero—that the diagnosis of PVS was wrong and that a relatively normal recovery from unconsciousness will occur.

The upshot of this analysis is that life-sustaining treatment is contrary to the best interests of *all* PVS patients, once two requirements are satisfied. First, the clinical diagnosis of PVS must have been made with extreme care by a neurological specialist using the best diagnostic technologies available. Second, sufficient time must have been allowed to pass to rule out other severe neurological conditions (such as transient coma) that might have been misdiagnosed as PVS. My suggestion, obviously subject to revision by specialists in neurology, is a waiting period of 3 months (Jacqueline Cole regained consciousness after 47 days).

When these procedural safeguards are accomplished, the patient's surrogate and the health care professionals in a particular PVS case should conclude that the patient's best interests call for the abatement of *all* life-sustaining treatment. Technological feeding and hydration—and any other life-sustaining technologies that may be used in individual cases—are at that point contrary both to the current interests (if such exist) and previous interests of such a patient. Using life-sustaining technologies and medications to prolong a correctly diagnosed PVS patient's existence for years is contrary to the current interests of such a patient, because the burdens of the treatment (even excluding the factors of pain and physical suffering) clearly outweigh the remote chance of benefit the treatment provides. Moreover, using life-sustaining technologies and medications to keep a PVS patient biologically alive for years is contrary to the previous interests of any such patient who earlier gave even a passing thought to the possibility of being persistently vegetative for years.

Having said this much, I do not want to be misinterpreted as having suggested that "nothing more can be done" or should be done for PVS patients once life-sustaining treatment is abated. That is not the case. Throughout this book I have been discussing the *abatement* of *life-sustaining* treatment, not the *termination* of *all* treatment. Patients in PVS are examples of the importance of this distinction. If such a patient is unable to swallow feedings (a few can), and if technological nutrition and hydration is removed from the patient, the patient predictably will die "within one to thirty days."[62] Pro-life advocates often offer gruesomely vivid accounts of such patients having parched lips, dry mouths, swollen or cracked tongues, scaly skin, nosebleeds, convulsions, and numerous other physical problems. The patient's dying does not have to be that way. Instead, much can be done through medical care (e.g., anticonvulsants) and nursing care (e.g., oral hygiene, skin care) to show respect for the body of this previous person and to alleviate the emotional stress on the patient's relatives and the professional staff as the patient goes through the process of dying.[63]

When is the abatement of technological nutrition and hydration morally justified?

The continuing controversy over the abatement of technological nutrition and hydration is the most distinctive feature of the third phase of the debate about abating life-sustaining treatment. Fundamental disagreements over the morality of abating this form of life-sustaining treatment have brought forth an unusual number of policy statements by medical associations and other professional organizations, seriously divided Catholic moral theologians and other ethicists roughly along liberal/conservative lines, led to numerous court cases in the post-*Conroy* era, significantly influenced the wording and features of natural death acts in numerous states, brought about a proposed legislative statute in several states that would severely limit the authorized abatement of technological nutrition and hydration in cases of nonautonomous patients, and led to increased political activism by pro-life groups and right-to-die groups in courtrooms and legislative chambers throughout the United States.

The mainstream position that has emerged in this controversy regards technological nutrition and hydration as a form of life-sustaining treatment that is morally equivalent to mechanical ventilation and other life-sustaining technologies. The reasons for this judgment are several: "artificial" feeding and hydration initially requires skilled medical and nursing care, involves some medical risks and complications for patients, necessitates surgical intervention in some cases, requires sedation in some cases, is used to combat or cope with a disease process that inhibits a patient's normal ability to swallow, is not (in contrast to ordinary eating and drinking) universally needed by all persons, and is primarily intended to supplement nutritional intake or support nutritional and fluid needs for a limited period of time until a patient's underlying pathological condition improves. Although the provision of technological nutrition and hydration is beneficial on balance for the great majority of patients who receive this medical treatment, the circumstances in a minority of cases are such that this medical treatment is contrary to the best interests of the patients. To abate the technological provision of nutrition and fluids in these cases—many of them involving permanently unconscious patients—does not necessarily involve an intention to kill, nor does it necessarily represent the primary cause of death for these patients any more than would the abatement of mechanical ventilation in cases when that life-sustaining technology is judged to be contrary to the best interests of critically ill patients with whom it is being used.

Support for this mainstream position is diverse and widespread. Deliberative bodies that have formally accepted the abatement of technological nutrition and hydration when the circumstances of individual cases warrant include the President's Commission, the Committee for Pro-Life Activities of the National Conference of Catholic Bishops, members of the Hastings Center project on termination-of-treatment guidelines, the advisory panel of the OTA study on life-sustaining technologies and the elderly, members of the New York State Task Force on Life and the Law, and members of the Stanford University Medical Center Committee on Ethics.[64] Medical and health care groups supporting the position include the Council on Ethical and Judicial Affairs of the A.M.A. (as indicated by the quotation at the beginning of the chapter), the American Nurses' Association Committee on Ethics, and the American Dietetic Association.[65] Courts of final decision in 18 jurisdictions have ruled that autonomous and nonautonomous patients have a legal right to have technologically supplied nutrition and hydration abated, just as they have a legal right to have any other life-sustaining treatment abated that is contrary to their best interests. The National Conference of Commissioners on Uniform State Laws (in their "Uniform Rights of the Terminally Ill Act") and the natural death acts in three states (Alaska, Idaho, and Illinois) explicitly permit citizens to reject artificial feeding and hydration.[66] Furthermore, a number of influential physicians, attorneys, and ethicists have produced articles in support of this mainstream ethical and legal position.[67]

Opposition to the mainstream position is intense and well organized. A number of individual physicians, attorneys, and ethicists have criticized the courts and other deliberative bodies supporting the mainstream position, with some of the writers designating their own views as being "against the stream."[68] Pro-life organizations on the national and state levels have mobilized in the post-*Conroy* era in opposition to the abatement of technological nutrition and hydration, both by trying without much success to influence the opinions of justices in individual court cases (usually involving PVS patients) and by trying with great success to block the passage of natural death acts in various states unless the language of the statutes suggests that tube feeding is a part of ordinary nursing care.[69] Some disability rights groups have also joined in opposing the mainstream position, with formal statements being produced by the Association for Retarded Citizens of the United States (ARC) and by The Association for Persons with Severe Handicaps (TASH).[70]

Two events in 1987 illustrate some of the reasoning behind this opposing view, as well as some of the strategy used by advocates of this pro-life position. Early that year *Issues in Law and Medicine,* a publication of the National Legal Center for the Medically Dependent and Disabled, published a formal statement on technological feeding and hydration. Written by 10 professionals in medicine, ethics, and law (including Germain Grisez and Gilbert Meilaender) and signed by 95 others (including Paul Ramsey and Arthur Dyck), the statement was prepared for the Pope John XXIII Center in St. Louis.

Entitled "Feeding and Hydrating the Permanently Unconscious and Other Vulnerable Persons," this formal statement of opposition begins with a series of 10 "presuppositions and principles." Among other claims, these statements declare "human bodily life" to be "personal" rather than "subpersonal," the abatement of life-sustaining nutrition and hydration to be "an act of killing by omission" or "the deliberate killing of the innocent" indistinguishable from acts of euthanasia, and human life to be "inherently a good of the person . . . no matter how burdened it may be." Consequently, "remaining alive is never rightly regarded as a burden. . . ."[71]

The text of this formal document describes the mainstream position as justifying the abatement of life-sustaining nutrition and hydration from "noncompetent, nonterminal persons simply because their lives are thought by others to be valueless or excessively burdensome." Abating "food and fluids *on this rationale* is morally wrong because it is euthanasia by omission." Acknowledging that the abatement of nutrition and fluids is justifiable when a patient is "imminently dying," the writers reject any similar abatement of nutrition and fluids with "severely debilitated but nondying individuals." For them, the provision of nutrition and hydration can be regarded as neither "*really useless or excessively burdensome*" because it brings to these patients "a great benefit, namely, the preservation of their lives and the prevention of their deaths through malnutrition and dehydration." Additionally, it "benefits the nondying patient" by preserving "human life itself," which "remains good in itself no matter how burdened it may become due to the patient's poor condition." The writers conclude that "it is not morally right, nor ought it to be legally permissible, to withhold or withdraw nutrition and hydration provided by artificial means to the permanently unconscious or other categories of seriously debilitated but nonterminal persons."[72]

The second event of importance occurred later in 1987 in Oklahoma. Frustrated by the trends in recent case law, some of the leaders of two national pro-life groups decided to circumvent the courts by getting new legislation passed at the state level to protect nonatuonomous patients. The Oklahoma legislature was one of several legislatures to consider a bill drafted by these national pro-life leaders and was the first (and, thus far, the only) state legislative body to pass the bill on to the governor. The "Hydration and Nutrition for Incompetent Patients Act," having been given no publicity as a legislative bill by the state media, was signed by the governor and became state law on the first day of November.

The Oklahoma law presumes "that every incompetent patient has directed his health care providers to provide him with hydration and nutrition to a degree that is sufficient to sustain life." The only exceptions to legally mandated nutrition and hydration are the following: (1) if the attending physician "of the incompetent patient knows by clear and convincing evidence that the patient, when competent and with a specific illness or injury," gave informed refusal to such life-sustaining treatment, or (2) if the attending physician and a consulting physician agree that artificial nutrition and hydration will "cause severe, intractable, and long-lasting pain to the patient" or is "not medically possible," or (3) if the attending physician and a consulting physician agree that "(a) the incompetent patient is chronically and irreversibly incompetent, (b) . . . is in the final stage of a terminal illness or injury, and (c) the death of the incompetent patient is imminent." The final provision of the law states that, unless one of these three exceptional sets of circumstances applies, *"no guardian, public or private agency, court, or any other person* shall have the authority to make a decision on behalf of an incompetent patient" regarding artifically administered nutrition and hydration.[73] The upshot of the law is that no legal case similar to the nutrition and hydration cases that have been handled by the courts in 18 other states could take place in Oklahoma, unless the statute is declared unconstitutional.

Given the intensity of this ongoing controversy over technological nutrition and hydration, how should we approach this particular aspect of the issue of treatment abatement? Four points should suffice. First, we should be clear about the medical facts. Although pro-life advocates get considerable mileage out of framing the issue in terms of "food and water," "ordinary care," and "starvation and dehydration," such emotive language does not accurately reflect the reality of supplying nutrition and fluids to patients who are unable or unwilling to take oral feedings. A more accurate description focuses on enteral (by tube, not by mouth) and parenteral forms of administering nutrition and fluids as *technological procedures,* in the dual sense of delivery systems and the substances being delivered. The particular form of providing nutrition and hydration to a patient can be (1) into a functioning GI tract by means of a nasogastric tube, a nasoenteral tube, a pharyngostomy tube, or a gastrostomy tube, or (2) external to the GI tract by means of a peripheral IV line, a central (subclavian) venous line capable of providing total parenteral nutrition (TPN), or a jejunostomy tube directly entering the small intestine.[74] Regardless of the entry point into a patient's body, the invasive use of tubes as a delivery system for nutrition and fluids (often requiring surgical implacement) is surely more accurately described as a form of medical technology than as ordinary oral feeding by spoon. Moreover, the nutrients and fluids being delivered through the tubes are not usually comparable to ordinary food prepared in the kitchen of a hospital or nursing home. Although blenderized table food can sometimes be used, patients are more commonly given premixed chemical formulas tailored to specific metabolic disorders and a mixture of fluids containing water, electrolytes, and various medications. Nancy Dickey, M.D., who chaired the A.M.A. judicial council, says, "We're not talking about taking away Granny's water pitcher."[75] Ruth Macklin observes: "When we think literally of what this stuff is, we realize we're not talking here about poached salmon and *crème fraîche*. We're talking about chemically prepared, processed nutrients that are poured down a tube into someone's stomach. The resemblance to food is marginal."[76]

Second, we need to be clear about the central element in the controversy over technological nutrition and hydration, namely the occasional equation of this form of treatment abatement with euthanasia. The mainstream position always rejects such a moral equation, as mentioned earlier. By contrast, more extreme right-to-die advocates tend to interpret this form of abating treatment (and all other forms of abating treatment) as being morally indistinguishable from euthanasia, and virtually all self-proclaimed pro-life advocates seem to be convinced that this form of treatment abatement unquestionably represents "euthanasia by omission." Even some ethicists (Daniel Callahan and Robert Veatch, for example) who are generally very supportive of abating treatment and clearly against euthanasia think that abating life-sustaining nutrition and hydration is morally suspect in some cases.

Why is this the case? Numerous reasons are given by persons concerned about this particular form of abating treatment, but clearly the core concern is the belief or suspicion that the abatement of life-sustaining nutrition and hydration is merely a backdoor way of *intentionally causing the deaths* of (as Callahan puts it) "biologically tenacious patients." To address this concern requires that we separate its component parts, namely agent intentionality and the causation of death. As I argued in Chapter 7, these two features *usually* serve to distinguish acts of treatment abatement from acts of euthanasia.

In regard to the abatement of life-sustaining nutrition and hydration, one of these features (causation) continues to be helpful in distinguishing acts of cooperative treatment abatement from acts of voluntary or nonvoluntary euthanasia. When a physician decides to withdraw technological nutrition and hydration at the request of an autonomous patient, or when a nonautonomous patient's surrogate and physician agree that technological nutrition and hydration are no longer in the best interests of the patient, the act of stopping this form of life-sustaining treatment is no more "the cause" of the patient's death than the abatement of life-sustaining mechanical ventilation or life-sustaining antibiotics would be in other morally similar cases. There is little doubt that the physician's action is *a* causative factor in the patient's death, or that the physician's action does "causally affect" the timing of the patient's death.[77] However, the primary cause of the patient's death is the neurological injury or pathological condition (e.g., various cancers of the mouth, throat, or stomach) that brought about the need for technological nutrition and hydration in the first place.

The other distinguishing feature (agent intentionality) discussed earlier is more problematic, especially in cases involving PVS patients. When life-sustaining nutrition and hydration are abated in cases of autonomous patients and in many cases of nonautonomous patients (including severely demented patients and severely retarded patients), one can rightly argue, depending on the facts of particular cases, that the physician's intention is to act in the patient's best interests by relieving the patient's otherwise continuing pain and suffering. However, as we discussed in the previous section, PVS patients do not have any current interests, including interests in pain relief and the relief of psychological suffering, and do not have relevant previous interests unless those earlier interests are known by persons now involved in particular PVS cases. Consequently, when physicians abate life-sustaining nutrition and hydration in at least *some* PVS cases, one cannot, I think, argue that their intention is anything other than the termination of the patient's life.

In this one respect, the writers of the pro-life document discussed earlier are correct and some defenders of the mainstream position are wrong: at least in some correctly diagnosed PVS cases, the abatement of life-sustaining nutrition and hydration does seem to involve an aim to kill. However, these pro-life advocates are wrong in failing to distinguish PVS cases from other cases of severe debilitation, claiming that all nonautonomous patients retain personhood (many do, but PVS patients do not), failing to distinguish agent intention from the causation of death, maintaining that human life is an absolute good, claiming that "remaining alive" (no matter in what condition) can never rightly be regarded as a burden, and arguing that all instances of abating technological nutrition and hydration are morally equivalent to euthanasia.

Greater conceptual clarity and significant moral progress can be made, in my judgment, by (1) continuing to distinguish between most acts of abating life-sustaining nutrition and hydration and acts of euthanasia, and (2) admitting that in some PVS cases the act of abating technological nutrition and hydration necessarily involves the intention to kill the patient. In these cases, however, the intention to kill can be justified, reluctantly, in any of several ways: by acknowledging that PVS patients are no longer persons and will never again be persons, by concluding through an objective use of the PBI standard that a persistent vegetative existence of indefinite duration cannot reasonably be said to be preferable to death, and by admitting (as Paul Ramsey once did, also reluctantly) that intentional killing is morally justifiable in some exceptional clinical cases involving patients who are "irretrievably inaccessible to human care."[78]

The third point has to do with the appropriate ethical context for the abatement of technological nutrition and hydration. That context is the same as for treatment abatement with other life-sustaining technologies, namely the context provided by an honest assessment of the patient's best interests in the light of the patient's medical condition(s) and the proportionality of treatment-related burdens and benefits. For autonomous patients, the PBI standard means that they are morally justified in consenting to the use of tehcnological nutrition and hydration or refusing such treatment depending on whether they regard the technological prolongation of their lives in this manner as being in their own best interests. For nonautonomous patients who are conscious, self-aware, and minimally rational (most nonautonomous patients should be regarded in this manner), the PBI standard calls for an honest assessment by the patient's surrogate of the benefits and burdens being produced for the patient by the technological administration of nutrition and fluids. In such cases particular attention should be placed on any significant pain or psychological suffering the patient seems to be experiencing in relation to the technological prolongation of his or her life by means of tube feeding. For nonautonomous patients who are permanently unconscious (especially those correctly diagnosed as PVS patients), the assessment of whether the continuation or abatement of tube feeding is in the patient's best interests depends not on the patient's pain and suffering (they do not exist) but on the more fundamental philosophical and theological question of whether the technological prolongation of a minimally alive, nonpersonal, irretrievably unconscious existence can correctly be regarded as so overwhelmingly burdensome that it would be considered by any such patient (if able, for a few moments, to assess his or her situation) as a fate worse than death. My answer to that question is affirmative.

The fourth point has to do with the law. As mentioned before, some of the national pro-life leaders and state-based pro-life advocates (at least in Oklahoma) are so concerned about the abatement of technological nutrition and hydration that they are willing to *take away the moral and legal right* of treatment refusal from any number of citizens who might subsequently choose to exercise that right under conditions of nonautonomy. Even if a thoughtful individual were correctly to anticipate the possibility of subsequently needing technological nutrition and hydration in a life-threatening situation, and communicated a preference not to have such treatment to likely parties to such a future case (spouse, children, physician, friends), the current law in Oklahoma would probably not permit the abatement of technological nutrition and hydration in the event the case actually occurred. I am an example. As I write these words, I am a citizen of the state of Oklahoma with plans to move to Iowa. Should I be severely brain-damaged (assuming I am not that way already) in a car accident on the way home today, become permanently unconscious, and be provided technological nutrition and hydration for an indefinite period of time, all of my thinking and planning in relation to that unwanted situation would go for naught as far as the law is concerned. If some pro-life advocates succeed in their plans, your state may soon have a similar law—and your autonomous decision making may be similarly threatened.

What about the morality and legality of euthanasia?

The position I have taken in this book is subject to criticism from both the right and the left. To my right, pro-life advocates and at least some defenders of the mainstream position will be convinced that I have gone too far in developing a position on the ethics of treatment abatement. They will be concerned that I, especially in the views put forward on PVS patients and technological nutrition, have gone too far down the "slippery slope" in arguing for the abatement of all life-sustaining treatment in carefully diagnosed PVS cases.

To my left, the right-to-die advocates who are utilitarians or libertarians in philosophical orientation will be convinced that I have not gone far enough. For many of these persons, the position I have put forward is too traditional and places too much emphasis on at least some of the ethical distinctions developed largely by Catholic moral theologians. Rather than seeming radical or dangerous, the views I have defended in regard to PVS patients and technological nutrition will probably be dismissed by persons identified with position 6 (see Chapter 6) as being "much ado about nothing." To them, I should have ceased trying to distinguish between acts of cooperative treatment abatement and acts of euthanasia, and simply affirmed the merits of intentional killing as a moral alternative and argued for the legalization of euthanasia in a fairly wide range of cases involving critically ill and terminally ill patients.

I cannot agree with pro-life advocates for a number of reasons, including their claim that "remaining alive" is always beneficial for a patient (regardless of the patient's medical condition) and their limited sensitivity to the intractable pain and profound suffering that advanced-cancer patients, severely burned patients, and numbers of other critically ill and terminally ill patients often have to endure in hospitals around the world. Likewise, I cannot agree with utilitarian and libertarian proponents of legalized euthanasia. The predictable abuses by some physicians and others who would intentionally kill patients for questionable reasons (as illustrated by the "Debbie" case mentioned earlier), the temptation to kill patients who are nonautonomous for various reasons (not merely PVS patients), and the fundamental threat that a legalized practice of euthanasia would represent to the fiduciary relationship between physicians and their patients are sound reasons for pulling back from the legalization of intentional killing in medical contexts. Moreover, in spite of the resolution recently passed by the World Federation of Right-to-Die Societies claiming that patients have the "right to painless dying," no one has a *positive moral right to be killed* even if being killed is the only way in some cases to avoid a painful dying process.[79]

Having said this, however, I am convinced that *individual acts* of *voluntary* euthanasia are on very rare occasions justifiable on moral grounds. To make this move is not easy, because of the importance I place on the wrongness of killing another person for any reason. In my view, killing another person is *prima facie* wrong. However, in rare situations, the intentional killing of an autonomous patient who is gravely impaired, or critically ill, or terminally ill is morally justifiable, given the following conditions: (1) the patient's unrelieved pain and/or severe psychological suffering has made continued living intolerable for that individual, (2) the patient is physically unable to commit suicide, (3) no medical treatment is available that will reverse, correct, or cure the patient's underlying medical condition, (4) no life-sustaining treatment is being used that could be abated at the patient's request, and (5) the patient clearly, upon deliberation, and repeatedly requests (in front of witnesses, or in writing) to be killed. In such a situation, the patient's physician (or a relative, a close friend, or a nurse involved in the case) would be morally justified in intentionally killing the patient out of mercy. To do so, in these limited circumstances, would not only be merciful, but would also be respectful of the patient's autonomy, beneficent, and not contrary to the requirements of nonmaleficence or justice.

When such cases occur, the person who does the killing has obviously broken the criminal law. If the individual is reported to the legal authorities and arrested for the unlawful killing, how should the legal case be handled? At this point I think that James Childress is right and James Rachels is wrong. Rather than changing the criminal law so that "mercy killing" is a legally acceptable defense against the charge of homicide, the legal system should have to deal with the legal defense of conscientious objection to the law against killing suffering individuals at their request. To take this route is not, of course, without its legal risks or philosophical problems. However, it is one way of continuing to emphasize the *prima facie* wrongness of killing, discouraging physicians and others in medical contexts from intentionally killing persons who are their patients, and still excusing at least some of these acts of killing when they occur.

I hope to see the day when acts of intentional killing in medical settings are neither a moral problem nor a legal problem. Given recent advances in pain control, greater sensitivity to the medical and nonmedical needs of patients (particularly on the part of nurses), and the substantial developments in the ethics and legality of treatment abatement that have occurred in the post-*Conroy* era, we are beginning to move in the direction of more humane medical management of patients who are suffering. If geriatricians, hospice physicians, and nurses who work in geriatric units or hospice programs can become models of humane medical care to be emulated by other physicians and nurses responsible for the care of critically ill and terminally ill patients, those patients will be far less likely to request to be killed than they are now. In particular, as the medical care of critically ill and terminally ill patients increasingly focuses on more effective pain control, improved management of disease-related symptoms, and better palliative care, the need for individual acts of euthanasia will diminish. If and when that time comes, the intensity of the debate over the morality and legality of abating treatment may also subside.

Notes

1. The Council on Ethical and Judicial Affairs of the A.M.A., "Withholding or Withdrawing of Life-Prolonging Medical Treatment," adopted March 15, 1986.
2. Harry A. Cole, "Deciding on a Time to Die," *Second Opinion* 7 (March 1988): 19, 21–23.
3. One example of such disagreements among bright, responsible, and knowledgeable persons is the Hastings Center project on termination-of-treatment guidelines. When the guidelines were published, two persons (Leslie Rothenberg and Robert Veatch) among the group of 20 publicly dissented from selected portions of the report. See the Hastings Center project, *Guidelines on the Termination of Life-Sustaining Treatment and the Care of the Dying* (Briarcliff Manor, N.Y.: The Hastings Center, 1987), pp. 158–59. Similar disagreements occurred in the preparation of the New York State Task Force on Life and the Law report on life-sustaining treatment. See the task force's report, *Life-Sustaining Treatment: Making Decisions and Appointing a Health Care Agent* (New York: The New York State Task Force on Life and the Law, 1987), pp. 51–69 and 141–48. *Two* of the dissenting reports to this group report were by David Bleich, giving further evidence of the extremity of some of his views on treatment abatement.
4. Communicated by Alexander Capron in a conference on health care technology, ethics, and the law, held at the University of Oklahoma Health Sciences Center, March 31, 1988.
5. See the President's Commission, *Making Health Care Decisions: Report* (Washington, D.C.: U.S. Government Printing Office, 1982), p. 170; and the Hastings Center project, *Guidelines,* pp. 132–33.
6. Arthur Caplan, review of Ruth Faden and Tom Beauchamp's *A History and Theory of Informed Consent,* in the *Journal of the American Medical Association* 257 (January 16, 1987): 386.
7. Paul S. Appelbaum, Charles W. Lidz, and Alan Meisel, *Informed Consent: Legal Theory and Clinical Practice* (New York: Oxford University Press, 1987), pp. 194–201. Also see Paul S. Appelbaum and Loren H. Roth, "Patients Who Refuse Treatment in Medical Hospitals," *Journal of the American Medical Asscoiation* 250 (September 9, 1983): 1296–1301.

8. Ruth Macklin, *Mortal Choices* (New York: Pantheon Books, 1987), pp. 85–86. Also see Allen Buchanan and Dan W. Brock, "Deciding for Others," *Milbank Memorial Fund Quarterly* 64 (Suppl. 2, 1986): 41–43.

9. See the President's Commission, *Making Health Care Decisions,* pp. 169–71; idem, *Deciding to Forego Life-Sustaining Treatment* (Washington, D.C.: U.S. Government Printing Office, 1983), pp. 121–24; George J. Annas and Leonard H. Glantz, "The Right of Elderly Patients to Refuse Life-Sustaining Treatment," *Milbank Memorial Fund Quarterly* 64 (Suppl. 2, 1986): 114–15; and the Hastings Center project, *Guidelines,* pp. 23, 131–33.

10. See Loren H. Roth, Alan Meisel, and Charles W. Lidz, "Tests of Competency to Consent to Treatment," *American Journal of Psychiatry* 134 (March 1977): 279–84; Bruce L. Miller, "Autonomy and Refusing Lifesaving Treatment," *Hastings Center Report* 11 (August 1981): 22–28; and Buchanan and Brock, "Deciding for Others," pp. 32–37.

11. James F. Drane, "Competency to Give an Informed Consent," *Journal of the American Medical Association* 252 (August 17, 1984): 925–27; and idem, "The Many Faces of Competency," *Hastings Center Report* 15 (April 1985): 17–21.

12. For other suggestions along these lines, see George J. Annas and Joan E. Densberger, "Competence to Refuse Medical Treatment: Autonomy vs. Paternalism," *Toledo Law Review* 15 (Winter 1984): 577–80; and Appelbaum, Lidz, and Meisel, *Informed Consent,* pp. 194–202.

13. Alexander Morgan Capron, "The Competence of Children as Self-Deciders in Biomedical Interventions," in Willard Gaylin and Ruth Macklin, eds., *Who Speaks for the Child?* (New York: Plenum Press, 1982), pp. 65–76; and the President's Commission, *Making Health Care Decisions,* pp. 170–71.

14. Capron, "Competence of Children," pp. 82–85.

15. Quoted by Lois A. Weithorn and Susan B. Campbell, "The Competency of Children and Adolescents to Make Informed Treatment Decisions," *Child Development* 53 (1982): 1589–98. Also see Willard Gaylin, "The Competence of Children: No Longer All or None," *Hastings Center Report* 12 (1982): 33–38; and Sanford L. Leikin, "Minors' Assent or Dissent to Medical Treatment," Appendix K of the President's Commission, *Making Health Care Decisions: Appendices* (Washington, D.C.: U.S. Government Printing Office, 1982), pp. 175–91, reprinted in the *Journal of Pediatrics* 102 (1983): 169–76.

16. Quoted in William Reichel, ed., *Clinical Aspects of Aging,* 2nd ed. (Baltimore: Williams & Wilkins, 1983), p. xxiv.

17. Hastings Center project, *Guidelines,* p. 136.

18. Harry R. Moody, "Is It Right to Allocate Health Care Resources on Grounds of Age?" in Elsie L. Bandman and Bertram Bandman, eds., *Bioethics and Human Rights* (Boston: Little, Brown, 1978), pp. 197–201; Norman Daniels, "Justice between Age Groups: Am I My Parents' Keeper?" *Milbank Memorial Fund Quarterly* 61 (1983): 489–522; Mark Siegler, "Should Age Be a Criterion in Health Care?" *Hasting Center Report* 14 (October 1984): 24–27; James F. Childress, "Ensuring Care, Respect, and Fairness for the Elderly," *Hastings Center Report* 14 (October 1984): 27–31; Margaret P. Battin, "Age Rationing and the Just Distribution of Health Care: Is There a Duty to Die?" *Ethics* 97 (1987): 317–40; Timothy M. Smeeding, ed., *Should Medical Care Be Rationed by Age?* (Totowa, N.J.: Rowman & Littlefield, 1987); and Robert M. Veatch, "Distributive Justice and the Allocation of Technological Resources to the Elderly," a contract report prepared for the Office of

Technology Assessment in 1985 and partially used in the OTA report on *Life-Sustaining Technologies and the Elderly* (Washington, D.C.: U.S. Government Printing Office, 1987), pp. 151–61.

19. Hastings Center project, *Guidelines,* pp. 135–37; and the OTA report, *Life-Sustaining Technologies,* pp. 19–23, 76–80, 151–61.
20. Hastings Center project, *Guidelines,* p. 137.
21. OTA report, *Life-Sustaining Technologies,* p. 23.
22. The figures related to health care expenditures are taken from the National Center for Health Statistics, *Health, United States, 1987* (Washington, D.C.: U.S. Government Printing Office, 1988), p. 149.
23. Ibid., p. 171.
24. Alan L. Otten, "Local Groups Attempt to Shape Policy on Ethics and Economics of Health Issues," *Wall Street Journal,* May 25, 1988, p. 25.
25. See Daniels, "Justice between Age Groups"; Childress, "Ensuring Care, Respect, and Fairness for the Elderly"; and Veatch, "Distributive Justice and the Allocation of Technological Resources to the Elderly."
26. Norman Daniels, *Am I My Parents' Keeper?* (New York and Oxford: Oxford University Press, 1988), pp. 40–65.
27. See John Rawls, *A Theory of Justice* (Cambridge, Mass.: Harvard University Press, 1971), pp. 136–42.
28. Daniels, *Am I My Parents' Keeper?,* p. 63.
29. National Center for Health Statistics, *Health, United States, 1987,* p. 8.
30. Daniel Callahan, *Setting Limits: Medical Goals in an Aging Society* (New York: Simon & Schuster, 1987), p. 156.
31. Ibid., p. 135.
32. OTA report, *Life-Sustaining Technologies,* p. 13.
33. See Callahan, *Setting Limits,* pp. 197–200, for his discussion of this problem.
34. Paul Ramsey, *The Patient as Person* (New Haven, Conn.: Yale University Press, 1970), p. 115.
35. Evans v. Bellevue Hospital, No. 16536/87 (N.Y. Sup. Ct. N.Y. County, July 28, 1987); N.Y.L.J. July 28, 1987, at 11.
36. See Tom L. Beauchamp and James F. Childress, *Principles of Biomedical Ethics,* 2nd ed. (New York and Oxford: Oxford University Press, 1983), p. 135; and Albert R. Jonsen, Mark Siegler, and William J. Winslade, *Clinical Ethics* (New York: Macmillan, 1982), p. 156.
37. The best study of paternalism in health care is found in James F. Childress, *Who Should Decide?* (New York and Oxford: Oxford University Press, 1982). An excellent analysis of the concept of paternalism in general is done by Donald VanDeVeer, *Paternalistic Intervention* (Princeton, N.J.: Princeton University Press, 1986).
38. The distinction between weak and strong paternalism originated with Joel Feinberg. See his "Legal Paternalism," *Canadian Journal of Philosophy* 1 (1974): 113–16; and idem, *Social Philosophy* (Englewood Cliffs, N.J.: Prentice-Hall, 1973). The terminology of limited and extended paternalism, which I prefer, is used by James Childress in *Who Should Decide?*
39. The distinction between soft and hard paternalism originated with Rosemary Carter. See her "Justifying Paternalism," *Canadian Journal of Philosophy* 7 (1977): 133–45. I have used different labels, partially because I think they are more descriptive and also because the combined language of strong/weak and hard/soft paternalism easily becomes confusing.

40. See Childress, *Who Should Decide?*, pp. 102–13.
41. Rasmussen v. Fleming, No. 2 CA-CIV 5622 (Ariz. Ct. App. 2 Div. June 25, 1986), *petition for review filed* (Ariz. July 10, 1986).
42. Judith Areen, "The Legal Status of Consent Obtained from Families of Adult Patients to Withhold or Withdraw Treatment," *Journal of the American Medical Association* 258 (July 10, 1987): 229–35.
43. See the Hastings Center project, *Guidelines*, p. 24, for a slightly different ordering of surrogates.
44. John E. Ruark et al., "Initiating and Withdrawing Life Support: Principles and Practice in Adult Medicine," *The New England Journal of Medicine* 318 (January 7, 1988): 28.
45. OTA report, *Life-Sustaining Technologies*, p. 17.
46. Ibid., p. 17.
47. President's Commission, *Deciding to Forego*, pp. 60–68.
48. In re Conroy, 98 N.J. 321, 486 A.2d 1209, 1234 (1985).
49. Hastings Center project, *Guidelines*, pp. 30, 60–61, 130; OTA report, *Life-Sustaining Technologies*, p. 17; and Ruark et al., "Initiating and Withdrawing Life Support," p. 29.
50. Ronald E. Cranford, "The Persistent Vegetative State: The Medical Reality (Getting the Facts Straight)," *Hastings Center Report* 18 (February–March 1988): 27–32. Also see Ronald E. Cranford and Harmon L. Smith, "Some Critical Distinctions between Brain Death and the Persistent Vegetative State," *Ethics in Science and Medicine* 6 (1979): 199–209; Ronald E. Cranford, "Termination of Treatment in the Persistent Vegetative State," *Seminars in Neurology* 4 (March 1984): 36–44; and idem, "Patients with Permanent Loss of Consciousness," in Joanne Lynn, ed., *By No Extraordinary Means* (Bloomington, Ind.: Indiana University Press, 1986), pp. 186–94.
51. See Michael Tooley, "Decisions to Terminate Life and the Concept of Person," in John Ladd, ed., *Ethical Issues Relating to Life and Death* (New York: Oxford Univesity Press, 1979), pp. 62–93; Ellen Kappy Suckiel, "Death and Benefit in the Permanently Unconscious Patient: A Justification of Euthanasia," *The Journal of Medicine and Philosophy* 3 (March 1978): 38–52; Carson Strong, "Positive Killing and the Irreversibly Unconscious Patient," *Bioethics Quarterly* 3 (Fall–Winter 1981): 190–205; and Holmes Rolston III, "The Irreversibly Comatose: Respect for the Subhuman in Human Life," *The Journal of Medicine and Philosophy* 7 (1982): 337–54.
52. Edward Langerak influenced my thinking along these lines. See his "Abortion: Listening to the Middle," *Hastings Center Report* 9 (October 1979): 24–28. Readers who do not like the "pilgrim person" terminology might check into the notion of a "postliminous person" who, according to Roman law, was a person taken captive in war and then, upon returning to his own country, was restored to his original status and vested with all rights and obligations accruing for or against him during his absence.
53. American College of Physicians Ad Hoc Committee on Medical Ethics, "American College of Physicians Ethics Manual, Part II," *Annals of Internal Medicine* 101 (1984): 265.
54. Callahan, *Setting Limits*, p. 182.
55. Quoted by Strong in his article, "Positive Killing." The original statement is in Joel Feinberg, "The Rights of Animals and Unborn Generations," in William Black-

stone, ed., *Philosophy and Environmental Crisis* (Athens, Ga.: University of Georgia Press, 1974), pp. 52–53.

56. Quoted by Suckiel in her article, "Death and Benefit." The original statement is in Joseph Margolis and Clorinda Margolis, "On Being Allowed to Die," *Humanist* 36 (1976): 17.

57. Strong, "Positive Killing," p. 193.

58. Cranford, "Persistent Vegetative State," pp. 29–30. Also see the President's Commission, *Deciding to Forego*, pp. 179–80.

59. Daniel Wikler, "Not Dead, Not Dying? Ethical Categories and Persistent Vegetative State," *Hastings Center Report* 18 (February–March 1988): 41–47.

60. Quoted by Cranford, "Persistent Vegetative State," p. 31.

61. Ibid., p. 31.

62. Ibid.

63. See Bernard Lo and Laurie Dornbrand, "Guiding the Hand that Feeds: Caring for the Demented Elderly," *The New England Journal of Medicine* 311 (August 9, 1984): 402–4; Hastings Center project, *Guidelines*, pp. 59–62; and Robert Steinbrook and Bernard Lo, "Artificial Feeding—Solid Ground, Not a Slippery Slope," *The New England Journal of Medicine* 318 (February 4, 1988): 286–90.

64. President's Commission, *Deciding to Forego*, p. 90; Committee for Pro-Life Activities of the National Conference of Catholic Bishops, "Statement on Uniform Rights of the Terminally Ill," June 1986; Hastings Center project, *Guidelines*, pp. 59–62; OTA report, *Life-Sustaining Technologies*, pp. 26, 275–321; New York State Task Force, *Life-Sustaining Treatment*, pp. 36–40; and Ruark et al., "Initiating and Withdrawing Life Support," pp. 27–30.

65. Council on Ethical and Judicial Affairs of the A.M.A., "Withholding or Withdrawing of Life-Prolonging Medical Treatment," March 15, 1986; Committee on Ethics of the American Nurses' Association, "Guidelines on Withdrawing or Withholding Food and Fluid," January 1988; and the American Dietetic Association, "Position of the American Dietetic Association: Issues in Feeding the Terminally Ill Adult," *Journal of the American Dietetic Association* 87 (January 1987): 78–85.

66. Uniform Rights of Terminally Ill Act, §1–18, 9A U.L.A. 456 (Suppl. 1986); Alaska Rights of Terminally Ill Act, Alaska Stat. § 18.12.010 to 18.12.100 (Suppl. 1986); Idaho Natural Death Act, Idaho Code § 39-4501 to 39-4508 (1985 and Suppl. 1986); and Illinois Living Will Act, Ill. Ann. Stat. Ch. 110 1/2 § 701–710 (Smith-Hurd Suppl. 1986).

67. See Joanne Lynn and James F. Childress, "Must Patients Always Be Given Food and Water?" *Hastings Center Report* 13 (October 1983): 17–21; Joanne Lynn, "Those Who Provide Medical Care," in Lynn, *By No Extraordinary Means*, pp. 216–23; Lo and Dornbrand, "Guiding the Hand that Feeds," pp. 402–4; Steinbrook and Lo, "Artificial Feeding," pp. 286–90; Sidney H. Wanzer et al., "The Physician's Responsibility toward Hopelessly Ill Patients," *The New England Journal of Medicine* 310 (April 12, 1984): 955–59; David T. Watts and Christine K. Cassel, "Extraordinary Nutritional Support," *Journal of the American Geriatrics Society* 32 (March 1984): 237–42; Kenneth C. Micetich, Patricia H. Steinecker, and David C. Thomasma, "Are Intravenous Fluids Morally Required for a Dying Patient?" *Archives of Internal Medicine* 143 (May 1983): 975–78; George J. Annas, "Fashion and Freedom: When Artificial Feeding Should Be Withdrawn," *American Journal of Public Health* 75 (June 1985): 685–88; Rebecca Dresser, "Discontinuing Nutrition Support: A Review of the Case Law," *Journal of the American Dietetic Association*

85 (October 1985): 1289–92; Alexander M. Capron, "Ironies and Tensions in Feeding the Dying," *Hastings Center Report* 14 (October 1984): 32–35; James F. Childress, "When Is It Morally Justifiable to Discontinue Medical Nutrition and Hydration?" in Lynn, *By No Extraordinary Means,* pp. 67–83; Richard A. McCormick, "Caring or Starving? The Case of Claire Conroy," *America* 152 (April 6, 1985): 269–73; and John Paris, "When Burdens of Feeding Outweigh Benefits," *Hastings Center Report* 16 (February 1986): 30–32.

68. Gilbert Meilaender, "On Removing Food and Water: Against the Stream," *Hastings Center Report* 14 (December 1984): 11–13; and Mark Siegler and Alan Weisbard, "Against the Emerging Stream: Should Fluids and Nutritional Support Be Discontinued?" *Archives of Internal Medicine* 145 (January 1985): 129–31. Also see Robert Barry, "The Ethics of Providing Life-Sustaining Nutrition and Fluids to Incompetent Patients," *Journal of Family and Culture* 1 (Summer 1985): 23–37; Dennis Horan and Edward R. Grant, "The Legal Aspects of Withdrawing Nourishment," *Journal of Legal Medicine* 5 (December 1984): 595–632; Patrick G. Derr, "Why Food and Fluids Can Never Be Denied," *Hastings Center Report* 16 (February 1986): 28–30; and Alan J. Weisbard and Mark Siegler, "On Killing Patients with Kindness: An Appeal for Caution," in Lynn, *By No Extraordinary Means,* pp. 108–16.

69. See the Society for the Right to Die (SRD) chart on natural death acts in the Appendix.

70. The resolutions by the Association for Retarded Citizens of the United States and by The Association for Persons with Severe Handicaps were published in *Issues in Law and Medicine* 3 (Winter 1987): 313 and 315.

71. William E. May et al., "Feeding and Hydrating the Permanently Unconscious and Other Vulnerable Persons," *Issues in Law and Medicine* 3 (Winter 1987): 204–5.

72. Ibid., pp. 209–211. The italicized portions of these quotations are emphasized in the original.

73. Hydration and Nutrition for Incompetent Patients Act. 63 Okla. Statutes Sec. 3080.1–3080.5 (Suppl. 1987). My emphasis.

74. David Major, "The Medical Procedures for Providing Food and Water: Indications and Effects," in Lynn, *By No Extraordinary Means,* pp. 21–28; and the OTA report, *Life-Sustaining Technologies,* pp. 280–82.

75. Quoted by Claudia Wallis, "To Feed or Not to Feed?" *Time,* March 31, 1986, p. 60.

76. Ruth Macklin, "Medicine: The Tough New Questions," *Vogue,* April 1987, p. 393.

77. Dan W. Brock, "Forgoing Life-Sustaining Food and Water: Is It Killing?" in Lynn, *By No Extraordinary Means,* p. 127.

78. Ramsey, *The Patient as Person,* p. 161.

79. The Seventh Biennial Conference of the World Federation of Right-to-Die Societies, "Dying with Dignity: A Statement to the United Nations Human Rights Commission," April 10, 1988.

Appendix

My Living Will
To My Family, My Physician, My Lawyer and All Others Whom It May Concern

Death is as much a reality as birth, growth, maturity and old age—it is the one certainty of life. If the time comes when I can no longer take part in decisions for my own future, let this statement stand as an expression of my wishes and directions, while I am still of sound mind.

If at such a time the situation should arise in which there is no reasonable expectation of my recovery from extreme physical or mental disability, I direct that I be allowed to die and not be kept alive by medications, artificial means or "heroic measures". I do, however, ask that medication be mercifully administered to me to alleviate suffering even though this may shorten my remaining life.

This statement is made after careful consideration and is in accordance with my strong convictions and beliefs. I want the wishes and directions here expressed carried out to the extent permitted by law. Insofar as they are not legally enforceable, I hope that those to whom this Will is addressed will regard themselves as morally bound by these provisions.

(Optional specific provisions to be made in this space — see other side)

DURABLE POWER OF ATTORNEY (optional)

I hereby designate _____ to serve as my attorney-in-fact for the purpose of making medical treatment decisions. This power of attorney shall remain effective in the event that I become incompetent or otherwise unable to make such decisions for myself.

Optional Notarization: Signed_____

"Sworn and subscribed to   Date _____

before me this _____ day   Witness _____

of _____. 19_____."

                                            Address

_____   Witness _____

        Notary Public

          (seal)   Address

Copies of this request have been given to _____

_____   _____

(Optional) My Living Will is registered with Concern for Dying (No. _____)

Distributed by Concern for Dying, 250 West 57th Street, New York, NY 10107 (212) 246-6962

Concern for Dying, the "Living Will" and recommendations for its use. Reproduced by permission of CFD.

TO MAKE BEST USE OF YOUR LIVING WILL

You may wish to add specific statements to the Living Will *in the space provided for that purpose above your signature*. Possible additional provisions are:

1. "Measures of artificial life-support in the face of impending death that I specifically refuse are:
   a) Electrical or mechanical resuscitation of my heart when it has stopped beating.
   b) Nasogastric tube feeding when I am paralyzed or unable to take nourishment by mouth.
   c) Mechanical respiration when I am no longer able to sustain my own breathing.
   d) _____ ..

2. "I would like to live out my last days at home rather than in a hospital if it does not jeopardize the chance of my recovery to a meaningful and sentient life or does not impose an undue burden on my family."

3. "If any of my tissues are sound and would be of value as transplants to other people, I freely give my permission for such donation."

The optional Durable Power of Attorney feature allows you to name someone else to serve as your proxy in case you are unable to communicate your wishes. Should you choose to fill in this portion of the document, you must have your signature notarized.

If you choose more than one proxy for decision-making on your behalf, please give order of priority (1, 2, 3, etc.)

Space is provided at the bottom of the Living Will for notarization should you choose to have your Living Will witnessed by a Notary Public.

REMEMBER...

- Sign and date your Living Will. Your two witnesses, who should not be blood relatives or beneficiaries of your property will, should also sign in the spaces provided.

- Discuss your Living Will with your doctors; if they agree with you, give them copies of your signed Living Will document for them to add to your medical file.

- Give copies of your signed Living Will to anyone who may be making decisions for you if you are unable to make them yourself.

- Look over your Living Will once a year, redate it and initial the new date to make it clear that your wishes have not changed.

**Society for the
Right to Die**

250 West 57th Street/New York, NY 10107

Living Will Declaration

INSTRUCTIONS
*Consult this column for help and
guidance.*

T₀ My Family, Doctors, and All Those Concerned with My Care

---

*This declaration sets forth your
directions regarding medical
treatment.*

I, _____, being of sound mind,
make this statement as a directive to be followed if I become unable to
participate in decisions regarding my medical care.

If I should be in an incurable or irreversible mental or physical condition
with no reasonable expectation of recovery, I direct my attending physician
to withhold or withdraw treatment that merely prolongs my dying. I further
direct that treatment be limited to measures to keep me comfortable and to
relieve pain.

---

*You have the right to refuse
treatment you do not want, and
you may request the care you
do want.*

These directions express my legal right to refuse treatment. Therefore I
expect my family, doctors, and everyone concerned with my care to regard
themselves as legally and morally bound to act in accord with my wishes,
and in so doing to be free of any legal liability for having followed my
directions.

---

*You may list specific treatment
you do not want. For example:*

   **Cardiac resuscitation
   Mechanical respiration
   Artificial feeding/fluids by tubes**

*Otherwise, your general
statement, top right, will stand
for your wishes.*

I especially do not want: _____
_____
_____
_____
_____
_____

---

*You may want to add
instructions for care you do
want—for example, pain
medication; or that you prefer
to die at home if possible.*

Other instructions/comments: _____
_____
_____
_____

---

*If you want, you can name
someone to see that your wishes
are carried out, but you do not
have to do this.*

Proxy Designation Clause: Should I become unable to communicate my instructions as stated above, I designate the following person to act in my behalf:

Name _____
Address _____

If the person I have named above is unable to act in my behalf, I authorize the
following person to do so:

Name _____
Address _____

---

*Sign and date here in the
presence of two adult witnesses,
who should also sign.*

Signed: _____ Date: _____
Witness: _____ Witness: _____

**Keep the signed original with your personal papers at home.
Give signed copies to your doctors, family, and to your proxy.**

Christian Affirmation of Life

A STATEMENT ON TERMINAL ILLNESS

Christians believe that through death life is merely changed, not taken away and that death need not be resisted with every possible means. Dying is a natural part of life that should be made as comfortable as possible for the patient and should not be unnecessarily prolonged. Not unduly prolonging the dying process affirms belief in eternal life.

Patients have a legal and moral right to choose what will be done to care for them. It is their right to decide to what extent, if at all, physicians may treat their diseases. In order that patients be able to exercise this right, they should be fully advised of the diagnosis, the prognosis, the proposed treatment, other therapeutic options, and the risks and benefits of each course of action.

When a patient is unable to make decisions regarding treatment, others, usually the next of kin, must do so, and they must make these judgments in accordance with the patient's legitimate wishes, if they are known. The "Christian Affirmation of Life" is provided as a means of indicating one's desires regarding treatment for terminal illness. It is not a legal document but one of moral persuasion. In states where law gives binding effect to such declarations if a particular format is used, the state form can also be used.

To my family, friends, clergyman, physician, and lawyer:

Because of my Christian belief in the dignity of the human person and my eternal destiny in God, I ask that if I become terminally ill I be fully informed of the fact so that I can prepare myself emotionally and spiritually to die.

I have a right to make my own decisions concerning treatment that might unduly prolong the dying process. If I become unable to make these decisions and have no reasonable expectation of recovery, then I request that no ethically extraordinary means be used to prolong my life but that my pain be alleviated if it becomes unbearable. ("Ethically extraordinary means" signifies treatment that does not offer a reasonable hope of benefit to me or that cannot be accomplished without excessive expense, pain, or other grave burden.) No means should be used with the intention of shortening my life, however.

I request that my family, my friends, and the Christian community join me in prayer and sacrifice as I prepare for death. I request that after my death others continue to pray for me, that I will, with God's grace, enjoy eternal life.

Signed: _____

Date: _____

Catholic Health Association, the "Christian Affirmation of Life." Reproduced by permission of the CHA.

A PERSONAL STATEMENT OF FAITH

I believe that every person is created by God as an individual of value and dignity. My basic worth and value as a person is inherent in the relationship of love that God has for me and not in my usefulness in society.

I believe that God has endowed me as His creature with the responsibility and privilege of sharing with God in the dominion over my earthly existence. I believe in the sanctity of human life which is to be celebrated in the spirit of creative living because it does have worth, meaning, and purpose. Therefore, I am responsible to use all ordinary means to preserve my life.

I further believe, however, that every human life is given dignity in dying, as well as in living. Therefore, I am free to refuse artificial and heroic measures to prolong my dying. I affirm my human right which allows me to die my own death within the limits of social, legal and spiritual factors.

I believe I have the right to die with dignity - respected, cared for, loved and inspired by hope. I consider as unjust the continuation of artificial and mechanical life support systems through expensive medical and technological means when there is no reasonable expectation for my recovery of meaningful personal life.

In order to avoid the useless prolongation of my dying and the suffering of my loved ones, I am signing a document making known my will regarding my medical treatment in the case of my terminal illness.

INSTRUCTIONS FOR MY CARE IN THE EVENT OF TERMINAL ILLNESS

My faith affirms that life is a gift of God and that physical death is a part of life and is the completed stage of a person's development. My faith assures me that even in death there is hope and the sustaining grace and love of God. Because of my belief, I wish this statement to stand as the testament of my wishes.

I, _____ , request that I be fully informed as my death approaches. If possible, I want to participate in decisions regarding my medical treatment and the procedures which may be used to prolong my life. If there is no reasonable expectation of my recovery from physical or mental disability, I direct my physician and all medical personnel not to prolong my life by artificial or mechanical means. I direct that I receive pain and symptom control. However, this decision is not a request that direct intervention be taken to shorten my life.

This decision is made after careful consideration and reflection. I direct that all legal means be taken to support my choice. In the carrying out of my will as stated, I release all physicians and other health personnel, all institutions and their employees and members of my family from legal culpability and responsibility.

Signed _____

Date _____

Witnessed By:

_____

_____

American Protestant Health Association, the religious version of ''Instructions for My Care in the Event of Terminal Illness.'' Reproduced by permission of the APHA.

INTRODUCTORY STATEMENT

I believe that death is a natural event in the course of human life. Every person has the right to live and die with dignity. I affirm my human right of autonomy which allows me to die my own death within the limits of legal, social and personal factors. I have the right to die with dignity - respected, cared for and loved.

Death consists of more than biological factors. The personal and human processes of life are to be considered along with the biological. I desire that life support systems be used so long as they can aid the continuation of the quality of my personal and biological life.

I consider as unjust the continuation of artificial and mechanical life support systems through expensive medical and technological means when there is no reasonable expectation for my recovery of meaningful personal life. Therefore I am free to refuse such medical treatment which only prolongs my dying.

In order to avoid the useless prolongation of my dying and the suffering of my loved ones, I am signing a document making known my will regarding my medical treatment in the case of my terminal illness.

INSTRUCTIONS FOR MY CARE IN THE EVENT OF TERMINAL ILLNESS

I,_____ , request that I be fully informed as my death approaches. If possible, I want to participate in decisions regarding my medical treatment and the procedures which may be used to prolong my life. If there is no reasonable expectation of my recovery from physical or mental disability, I direct my physician and all medical personnel not to prolong my life by artificial or mechanical means. I direct that I receive pain and symptom control. However, this decision is not a request that direct intervention be taken to shorten my life.

This decision is made after careful consideration and reflection. I direct that all legal means be taken to support my choice. In the carrying out of my will as stated, I release all physicians and other health personnel, all institutions and their employees and members of my family from legal culpability and responsibility.

Signed _____

Date _____

Witnessed By:

_____

_____

American Protestant Health Association, the secular version of "Instructions for My Care in the Event of Terminal Illness." Reproduced by permission of the APHA.

CHECKLIST CHART OF LIVING WILL LAWS

The 39 living will laws enacted between 1976 and 1987 recognize the individual's right to die with dignity. They authorize an adult to execute an advance declaration instructing that, in the event of a terminal condition, life-sustaining procedures shall be withheld or withdrawn.

This chart shows the principal similarities and differences among the several statutes (variously known as "natural death acts," "death with dignity acts," "medical treatment decision acts," etc.). Also included are the provisions of the "Uniform Rights of the Terminally Ill Act," draft legislation recommended for adoption in all states by the National Conference of Commissioners on Uniform State Laws.

The Checklist Chart is intended to serve as a quick reference source for many of the most significant provisions of the laws. For complete information, the full statutes should be consulted.

Society for the Right to Die
250 West 57th Street, New York, NY 10107 (212) 246-6973

Society for the Right to Die, the "Checklist Chart of Living Will Laws," explanatory notes, and statutory citations. Reproduced by permission of the SRD.

CHECKLIST CHART

	AL	AK	AZ	AR	CA	CO	CT	DE	DC	FL	GA	HI	ID	IL	IN	IA	KS	KY	LA	ME	MD	MA
1. Advance declaration may include personalized instructions.	x	x	x	x[N]		x	x	x[N]	x	x	x	x		x	x	x	x		x	x	x	
2. Statute specifically authorizes proxy appointment.				x		x[N]	x		x		x[N]	x[N]		x[N]	x[N]				x			
3. Declaration may be signed by another at the direction of the declarant.	x	x		x		x[N]	x	x	x		x			x	x	x				x	x	
4. Statute authorizes oral declaration.									x[N]										x[N]			
5. Statute provides decisionmaking procedures for patients with no declaration.				x[N]			x[N]			x						x			x			
6. Physician notified of patient's declaration shall make it part of patient's medical record.	x	x	x	x	x	x		x	x	x	x	x		x	x		x		x[N]	x	x	
7. Statute provides immunity from liability to health professionals complying with declaration.	x	x	x	x	x	x	x[N]	x	x	x	x	x	x	x	x	x	x		x	x	x	
8. Before declaration is implemented, patient's terminal condition must be medically certified.	x	x	x	x[N]	x[S]	x[S]	x	x	x[N]	x	x[S]	x[N]	x	x	x	x	x		x	x	x	
9. Physician must implement qualified patient's declaration or make reasonable effort to transfer patient to another physician.	x[N]	x[N]	x[N]	x	x[S]	x[S]			x	x	x[N]	x[N]		x	x[S]	x[S]	x[S]		x	x[S]		
10. Statute specifies penalty for physician's failure to comply with this provision.		x		x	x	x					x			x			x			x	x	
11. Declaration must be signed in presence of two qualified witnesses.	x	x[S]	x	x[N]	x	x	x[S]	x	x	x	x[N]	x	x	x	x	x	x		x	x	x	
12. Special witnessing is required for nursing home patients.				x			x	x			x[S]				x							
13. Other formalities for execution are required.									x[S]		x[S]	x[S]	x[S]	x[S]								
14. The statute: (a) permits withholding or withdrawing of artificial feeding and hydration;	x	x[S]	x	x				x	x								x		x			
(b) could be interpreted to permit withholding or withdrawing of artificial feeding and hydration;				x								x		x	x	x					x	
(c) specifically prohibits withholding or withdrawing artificial feeding and hydration.					x[S]	x			x[S]	x		x							x			
15. Statute recognizes validity of out-of-state declarations.				x[S]		x[S]					x[S]										x[S]	x[S]
16. Statute does not impair or restrict other rights.	x	x	x		x			x	x		x	x	x	x	x				x	x	x	
17. Statute includes other provisions worth noting.				x[S]		x[S]	x[S]				x[S]	x[S]		x[S]					x[S]			x[S]

OF LIVING WILL LAWS

MI	MN	MS	MO	MT	NE	NV	NH	NJ	NM	NY	NC	ND	OH	OK	OR	PA	RI	SC	SD	TN	TX	UT	VT	VA	WA	WV	WI	WY	Uniform Act*
		x	x	x		x	x		x^N		x			x				x		x	x	x	x	x	x	x	x^N	x	x
																					x	x^N		x			x		
		x	x	x																	x	x			x	x	x	x	
																							x^N						
									x		x			x							x	x		x					
			x^N	x		x	x^N							x	x						x	x^N	x		x^N	x	x	x	x
		x	x	x		x	x		x		x			x	x			x		x	x	x	x	x	x	x	x	x	x
		x	x	x			x		x^N		x			x^N	x			x		x	x^N	x		x	x^N	x^N	x	x	x
		x^N	x^N	x^N		x^N	x		x^N					x^N	x^N			x		x^N	x	x^N	x^N	x	x^N	x^N	x^N	x	x
			x^N	x										x	x			x		x		x					x		x
		x	x^N	x		x	x		x^N		x			x	x			x^N		x	x	x	x	x	x	x	x	x	x^N
							x^N							x				x											
			x^N			x^N	x^N		x^N		x^N			x^N				x^N			x^N		x^N			x^N			
		x		x		x			x		x				x						x	x		x	x^N	x			x
							x							x				x					x			x		x	
			x																							x			
				x^N																									x^N
			x	x		x	x		x		x				x						x	x	x		x		x	x	x
		x^N	x^N						x^N												x^N	x^N	x^N	x^N	x^N			x^N		

*Uniform Rights of the Terminally Ill Act, adopted August 1985 by the National Conference of Commissioners on Uniform State Laws, which seeks to promote uniformity in state laws where appropriate.

Common Provisions Not Noted on Chart

- *Recognition of advance declaration* executed voluntarily by an adult of "sound mind," to express treatment choices in event of terminal condition and inability to participate in decisionmaking.

- *Definitions of terms*—some examples:

  "Qualified patient" typically refers to declarant in "terminal condition" with no prospect of recovery. (May also explicitly, as noted on chart, include patients in persistent vegetative state as "qualified," although absence of this explicit provision does not necessarily exclude PVS patients.)

  "Terminal condition" may be a condition that will cause death "imminently" or "within a short time" if life-sustaining procedures are not employed; or a condition where death will occur "with or without life-sustaining procedures."

  "Life-sustaining procedures" that can be withheld or withdrawn are defined as mechanisms that only prolong dying; may specifically include or exclude artificial nutrition and hydration; may not specifically mention, and may therefore permit, withdrawal of this form of treatment—see line 14(a); or may be unclear about withdrawing if not needed for patient's comfort—see line 14(b).

- *Revocation procedures*, usually simple.

- *Recognition that qualified patient's expressed wishes take precedence* over prior declaration.

- *Exclusion as witnesses to a declaration* those whose disinterest might be in question: e.g., persons related by blood or marriage to declarant; entitled to any portion of declarant's estate; professionally or financially responsible for declarant's medical care. (Note that the Uniform Act has no witnessing restrictions.) Statutes that require special witness for declaration of nursing home patients usually, but not always, specify state-appointed ombudsman or patient advocate.

- *Severability of statutory provisions*, i.e., invalidity of one does not affect validity of others.

- *Declaration's lack of effect on patient's life insurance or medical benefits.*

- *Penalties for concealing, forging or intentionally destroying* declaration or its revocation. (Physician penalty for noncompliance and nontransfer—see line 10—is most frequently "unprofessional conduct.")

- *Presumption that declaration is valid*; no presumption in absence of declaration.

- Stipulation that *statute does not condone suicide, aided suicide, euthanasia, or homicide*.

  N.B. Many of the laws also contain a *clause restricting the right of a pregnant woman in terminal condition* to forgo life-sustaining treatment. This provision has been challenged on grounds of unconstitutionality.

Notes

Notes to the chart, identified by "N" superscripts, are keyed to the numbered entries on the left.

ALABAMA

9. States only that physician "shall permit" transfer.

ALASKA

9. Applies also to health care facility in which declarant is a patient. Withdrawal of physician is effective only when another's services have been obtained.
11. Or can be "acknowledged by a person qualified to take acknowledgements under A.S. 09.63.010."
14(a). Declaration form specifically provides for choosing to accept or reject artificial feeding.
15. Declaration executed in another state which complies with that state's law is valid in Alaska.
17. No one may charge a fee for preparing a declaration.

ARIZONA

9. Or physician must not "hinder" transfer.

ARKANSAS

1. Statute contains suggested declaration forms for use in the event of either permanent unconsciousness or terminal condition.
5. And for patients who have not appointed a proxy.
8. Declaration becomes effective when patient has terminal condition or is in a "permanently unconscious state."
11. No witnessing restrictions.
15. Declaration validly executed in another state satisfies Arkansas execution requirements.
17. Declaration may be executed on behalf of minor.

CALIFORNIA

8. Physician must determine that directive fulfills statutory requirement, and, if patient competent, that directive is in accord with patient's wishes.
9. Directive is binding only if executed 14+ days after terminal diagnosis. Physician must honor directive or must transfer patient, not merely make "reasonable effort" to transfer. (Directive executed earlier than 14 days after diagnosis is not binding but may be "given weight.")
17. Directive, which must follow form in statute, is effective for five years only.

COLORADO

2. See note 8 below.
3. Signer on declarant's behalf may not be anyone whom the statute excludes as witness to its execution, with the exception of co-patient in declarant's health care facility.
8. Physician must also make "reasonable effort" to notify family members or patient's attorney-in-fact (proxy) of certification of terminal condition, and allow 48 hours before implementation of declaration for possible court challenge of its validity.
9. Physician who does not comply must actually transfer, not merely make "reasonable effort."
14(c). In 1987, a Colorado court in *In re Rodas* stated that this provision could not restrict a person's constitutional right to refuse artificial feeding.

CONNECTICUT

5. Permits physician to consider expression of incompetent patient's wishes through prior declaration or next of kin or guardian.
7. Immunity from liability dependent on physician obtaining informed consent of next of kin, if known, or guardian, if any, of incompetent patient.
11. Suggested document provides space for two witnesses' signatures, but no other reference to witnesses appears.

DELAWARE

1. No suggested declaration form provided.
13. Witnesses must attest that they are not prohibited by any of the disqualifications specified in statute.

DISTRICT OF COLUMBIA

8. If qualified patient is competent, physician must notify patient of terminal condition.

FLORIDA

4. If given orally, one of the two witnesses may sign declaration in the presence and at the direction of the declarant. Provides for oral declaration made only *after* diagnosis of terminal condition.
14(c). Florida appeals court ruled in *Corbett v. D'Alessandro* (1986) that state statute cannot restrict constitutional right to refuse artificial feeding.

GEORGIA

8. Attending physician must also make "reasonable effort" to determine that living will is executed in accordance with statute.
9. Physician who refuses to comply with directive must try to advise patient's next of kin or legal guardian of noncompliance and, if so ordered, (1) make "good faith" effort to transfer to complying physician, or (2) permit next of kin or guardian to obtain complying physician.
11. Declaration executed in hospital or nursing home requires as *third* witness chief of medical staff or medical director.
12. See note 11.
13. Witnesses must state in writing that they are not prohibited by statutory witnessing disqualifications.
17. No health care facility may provide living will forms except at patient's request.

HAWAII

2. Statute recognizes alternative authority of durable power of attorney (proxy).
8. Act contains suggested physicians' certification form. Specifies that medical care facility must develop system to visibly identify qualified patient's chart containing declaration.
9. Physician must without delay transfer, or make "good faith" effort to transfer, to complying physician.
13. All signatures on declaration must be notarized at same time.
15. Out-of-state document must substantially comply with Hawaii Act's requirements.
17. Physician participating in decision to withhold life support may not participate in organ transplant from patient.

IDAHO

2. Recognizes proxy appointment in form of durable power of attorney; statutory form, however, fails to provide space to name proxy.
13. Witnesses must certify that they are not prohibited by statute's witnessing disqualifications. Document prescribed by the Act includes notarization, a requirement not otherwise specified.

ILLINOIS

13. Declaration must be executed with same formalities as will of property.

INDIANA

2. Does not directly address proxy appointment; but by providing for consultation between physician and patient's representative under specified circumstances, statute implies proxy authority.
9. If physician doubts declaration's validity and patient is unable to verify, physician may consult any of several specified persons presumed to know patient's intentions. Physician must record consultations. Patient's declaration does not "obligate" physician but must be given "great weight" if patient incompetent.
17. Statute also contains suggested form for declarant to request all means to prolong life; physician "obligated" to comply.

IOWA

2. Provides, in absence of declaration, for treatment consultation between physician and patient's attorney-in-fact.
9. Applies also to patient's health care facility.

KANSAS

9. Physician must comply or transfer—not merely make "reasonable effort" to transfer.

LOUISIANA

4. May be made before two witnesses by competent patient diagnosed as being in terminal condition.
6. If declaration is oral or nonverbal, physician must record it in medical record and note why patient could not make written declaration.
17. Provides for execution of declaration on behalf of minor.

MAINE

9. Applies also to health care facility in which declarant is patient.
15. Declaration executed in another state in compliance with its or Maine's laws is held to be validly executed and, without actual notice to the contrary, is presumed to comply with Maine's statute.

MARYLAND

15. Out-of-state declaration may be given effect if it complies with Maryland statute.
17. Also provides, though contains no suggested form, for execution of document requesting "the initiation or continuation of life-sustaining procedures in accordance with standard medical practice."

MISSISSIPPI

9. Before implementing patient's declaration, physician must obtain certified copy of declaration, and certification that it has not been revoked—from Bureau of Vital Statistics, State Board of Health. Physician or medical facility not honoring declaration has "duty [to] cooperate" in transfer to another health care provider.
13. Declaration, and revocation if any, must be filed with Bureau of Vital Statistics, State Board of Health.
17. Law contains suggested revocation form. Written revocation, if declarant is capable of making it, must be signed in presence of two witnesses; if incapable, a clear expression, oral or otherwise, is sufficient. No physician participating in decision to withdraw life-sustaining mechanisms from declarant may participate in transplant of declarant's vital organs.

MISSOURI

6. Must do so at patient's request.
9. Applies also to declarant's health care facility.
10. Penalty is incurred unless physician has "serious reason" consistent with patient's "best interest" for not honoring declaration.
11. Execution of wholly handwritten declaration need not be witnessed.
17. Suggested declaration form contains revocation section.

MONTANA

9. Applies also to patient's health care facility.
15. Recognizes out-of-state declaration that complies with law of that state if executed in manner "substantially similar" to Montana's execution requirements.

NEVADA

9. Physician must "give weight" to declaration of qualified patient, but "may also consider other factors in determining whether [to follow] directions."
13. Must be executed with same formalities as a will of property.

NEW HAMPSHIRE

6. Must do so at patient's request.
12. Declaration executed in hospital must be witnessed by chief of medical staff; in skilled nursing facility, by medical director.
13. Witnesses' affidavit must be made before notary public or justice of the peace or other official authorized to administer oaths. Execution must meet requirements of state laws concerned with execution of documents.

NEW MEXICO

1. Statute contains no declaration form.
8. Provides throughout for patient who is either in terminal condition or in "irreversible coma," which as defined in statute includes permanent vegetative state.
9. Noncomplying physician must take "appropriate steps" to transfer.
11. Statute does not specify witnessing requirements but states that declaration must be executed with same formalities as will of property.
13. See note 11.
17. Provides also for execution of declaration on behalf of minor.

NORTH CAROLINA

13. Declaration must be certified or proved by clerk or assistant clerk of superior court, or notary public.

OKLAHOMA

8. If qualified patient is mentally competent, physician must verify that declaration expresses patient's wishes and must inform patient of steps to be accordingly taken.
9. If patient became qualified before executing directive, noncomplying physician must "make the necessary arrangements" (not merely make "reasonable effort") to transfer patient to physician who will comply. If not executed after terminal diagnosis, attending physician may "give weight" to directive, and may consider other factors in determining whether or not to comply.
13. Notarization required for declarant's signature and witnesses.

OREGON

9. Also applies to patient's health care facility.

SOUTH CAROLINA

11. Requires *three* witnesses.
13. Must be notarized. Declaration must contain witnesses' affidavits verifying that they are not disqualified.
17. Declaration must include in bold-face type revocation instructions.

TENNESSEE

9. Physician who cannot comply with declaration must inform declarant or, if incompetent, next of kin or legal guardian, at whose option physician must make "good faith reasonable efforts" to transfer patient to complying physician.
13. Witnesses must sign affidavit declaring they are not disqualified as witnesses. Declaration form includes notarization.
17. Specifically permits inclusion of declarant's desires regarding organ donation and body disposal.

TEXAS

6. Physician must also make witnessed nonwritten directive part of the medical record, with entry signed by the two witnesses.
8. Before implementing directive, physician must determine that all steps proposed comply with statute and desires of patient.
17. Includes procedures for executing directive on behalf of minor.

UTAH

2. Statute contains power of attorney form, to be substantially followed, which must be executed before notary public.
9. Noncomplying physician must actually transfer, not merely make "reasonable effort." Also applies to patient's health care facility.
13. Statutory declaration form (which must be substantially complied with) provides for witnesses to affirm that they are not disqualified by the statute's provisions.
17. Declaration made after occurrence of injury, disease, or illness must contain physician's diagnosis and directions for administering or withholding treatment. Directive executed by patient's appointed attorney-in-fact takes precedence over all earlier directives.

VERMONT

9. Noncomplying physician must inform patient of noncompliance and/or "actively assist" in transfer.
17. Suggested document includes naming persons who have been given copy.

VIRGINIA

4. After diagnosis of terminal condition, oral declaration may be made in presence of two witnesses and physician.
6. If declaration is oral, physician must make its existence part of medical record.
14(a). In *Hazelton v. Powhatan Nursing Home* (1986), a Virginia court held that artificial feeding was a "life-prolonging procedure" within the terms of the Virginia Natural Death Act and could be withdrawn under the Act.

WASHINGTON

8. Physician must also make "reasonable effort" to determine that declaration complies with statute, and, if patient is competent, that all steps to be taken comply with patient's desires.
9. Noncomplying physician must make "good faith" effort to transfer to complying physician.

WEST VIRGINIA

8. Statute also requires that health care facility visibly identify qualified patient's chart which includes declaration; and that physician inform patient, if competent, of terminal condition and make record of this communication.
9. Noncomplying physician must actually transfer (not merely make "reasonable effort" to transfer) to complying physician.
13. Witnesses must attest that they are not disqualified by any provision of statute; signatures and attestations must be notarized.

WISCONSIN

1. Form distributed by state's department of health and social services must follow form contained in statute. Fee may be charged for providing it.
9. Noncomplying physician must make "good faith" attempt to transfer patient to complying physician.
17. Only original declaration is valid instrument.

UNIFORM ACT

(Uniform Rights of Terminally Ill Act, adopted by National Conference of Commissioners on Uniform State Laws and endorsed by American Bar Association):
11. There are no special witnesses' qualifications or requirements.
15. Declaration executed in another state in compliance with law of that state is validly executed for purposes of this Act.

Statutory Citations

Alabama Natural Death Act [1981], Ala. Code §§ 22-8A-1 to -10 (1984).

Alaska Rights of Terminally Ill Act [1986], Alaska Stat. §§ 18.12.010 to -.100 (Supp. 1986).

Arizona Medical Treatment Decision Act [1985], Ariz. Rev. Stat. Ann. §§ 36-3201 to -3210 (1986).

Arkansas Rights of the Terminally Ill or Permanently Unconscious Act [1987], 1987 Ark. Acts 713. [Replaces Arkansas Act of 1977.]

California Natural Death Act [1976], Cal. Health & Safety Code §§ 7185-7195 (Supp. 1987).

Colorado Medical Treatment Decision Act [1985], Colo. Rev. Stat. §§ 15-18-101 to -113 (Supp. 1986).

Connecticut Removal of Life Support Systems Act [1985], Conn. Gen. Stat. §§ 19a-570 to -575 (1987).

Delaware Death with Dignity Act [1982], Del. Code Ann. tit. 16, §§ 2501-2509 (1983).

District of Columbia Natural Death Act of 1981 [1982], D.C. Code Ann. §§ 6-2421 to -2430 (Supp. 1986).

Florida Life-Prolonging Procedure Act [1984], Fla. Stat. Ann. §§ 765.01 to -.15 (1986).

Georgia Living Wills Act [1984, 1986, 1987], Ga. Code Ann. §§ 31-32-1 to -12 (1985 & Supp. 1986), amended 1987 Ga. Laws 488.

Hawaii Medical Treatment Decisions Act [1986], Hawaii Rev. Stat. §§ 327D-1 to -27 (Supp. 1986).

Idaho Natural Death Act [1977, 1986], Idaho Code §§ 39-4501 to -4508 (1985 & Supp. 1986).

Illinois Living Will Act [1984], Ill. Ann. Stat. ch. 110 1/2 §§ 701-710 (Smith-Hurd Supp. 1986).

Indiana Living Wills and Life-Prolonging Procedures Act [1985], Ind. Code Ann. §§ 16-8-11-1 to -17 (Burns Supp. 1986).

Iowa Life-Sustaining Procedures Act [1985, 1987], Iowa Code Ann. §§ 144A.1 to -.11 (West Supp. 1986), amended H.F. 360, 1987 session, 72nd Iowa General Assembly.

Kansas Natural Death Act [1979], Kan. Stat. Ann. §§ 65-28,101 to -28,109 (1985).

Louisiana Life-Sustaining Procedures Act [1984, 1985], La. Rev. Stat. Ann. §§ 40:1299.58.1 to -.10 (West Supp. 1987).

Maine Living Wills Act [1985], Me. Rev. Stat. Ann. tit. 22, §§ 2921-2931 (Supp. 1986).

Maryland Life-Sustaining Procedures Act [1985, 1986], Md. Health-General Code Ann. §§ 5-601 to -614 (Supp. 1986).

Mississippi Withdrawal of Life-Saving Mechanisms Act [1984], Miss. Code Ann. §§ 41-41-101 to -121 (Supp. 1986).

Missouri Life Support Declarations Act [1985], Mo. Ann. Stat. §§ 459.010 to -.055 (Vernon Supp. 1987).

Montana Living Will Act [1985], Mont. Code Ann. §§ 50-9-101 to -104, -111, -201 to -206 (1985).

Nevada Withholding or Withdrawal of Life-Sustaining Procedures Act [1977], Nev. Rev. Stat. §§ 449.540 to -.690 (1986).

New Hampshire Terminal Care Document Act [1985], N.H. Rev. Stat. Ann. §§ 137-H:1 to -H:16 (Supp. 1986).

New Mexico Right to Die Act [1977, 1984], N.M. Stat. Ann. §§ 24-7-1 to -11 (1986).

North Carolina Right to Natural Death Act [1977, 1979, 1981, 1983], N.C. Gen. Stat. Ann. §§ 90-320 to -322 (1985).

Oklahoma Natural Death Act [1985], Okla. Stat. Ann. tit. 63, §§ 3101-3111 (West Supp. 1987).

Oregon Rights with Respect to Terminal Illness Act [1977, 1983], Or. Rev. Stat. §§ 97.050 to -.090 (1985).

South Carolina Death with Dignity Act [1986], S.C. Code Ann. §§ 44-77-10 to -160 (Law. Co-op Supp. 1986).

Tennessee Right to Natural Death Act [1985], Tenn. Code Ann. §§ 32-11-101 to -110 (Supp. 1986).

Texas Natural Death Act [1977, 1979, 1983, 1985], Tex. Rev. Civ. Stat. Ann. art. 4590h (Vernon Supp. 1987).

Utah Personal Choice and Living Will Act [1985], Utah Code Ann. §§ 75-2-1101 to -1118 (Supp. 1986).

Vermont Terminal Care Document Act [1982], Vt. Stat. Ann. tit. 18, §§ 5251-5262 and tit. 13, § 1801 (Supp. 1985).

Virginia Natural Death Act [1983], Va. Code §§ 54-325.8:1 to -:13 (Supp. 1986).

Washington Natural Death Act [1979], Wash. Rev. Code Ann. §§ 70.122.010 to -.905 (Supp. 1987).

West Virginia Natural Death Act [1984], W. Va. Code §§ 16-30-1 to -10 (1985).

Wisconsin Natural Death Act [1984, 1986], Wisc. Stat. Ann. §§ 154.01 to -.15 (West Supp. 1986).

Wyoming Act [1984], Wyo. Stat. §§ 33-26-144 to -152 (Supp. 1986).

See also Uniform Rights of Terminally Ill Act, §§ 1-18, 9A U.L.A. 456 (Supp. 1986).

Index